WRITING/RIGHTING HISTORY

Twenty-Five Years of
Recovering the US Hispanic
Literary Heritage

Edited by Antonia Castañeda
and Clara Lomas

WRITING/RIGHTING HISTORY

Twenty-Five Years of Recovering the US Hispanic Literary Heritage

Edited by Antonia Castañeda and Clara Lomas

Arte Público Press
Houston, Texas

This volume is made possible by grants from the University of Houston and the Center for Regional Studies at the University of New Mexico. We are grateful for their support.

Recovering the past, creating the future

Arte Público Press
University of Houston
4902 Gulf Fwy, Bldg 19, Rm 100
Houston, Texas 77204-2004

Cover design by Adelaida Mendoza

The Library of Congress has catalogued Volume I of
Recovering the US Hispanic Literary Heritage as follows:

Cataloging-in-Publication (CIP) Data is available.

ISBN: 978-1-55885-139-9 (Volume II)
ISBN: 978-1-55885-251-8 (Volume III)
ISBN: 978-1-55885-361-4 (Volume IV)
ISBN: 978-1-55885-371-3 (Volume V)
ISBN: 978-1-55885-478-9 (Volume VI)
ISBN: 978-1-55885-526-7 (Volume VII)
ISBN: 978-1-55885-604-2 (Volume VIII)

19 20 21 22   5 4 3 2 1

Contents

This commemorative 25th Anniversary Volume is dedicated to Nicolás Kanellos and Tomás Ybarra-Frausto, who boldly envisioned and made possible the recovery of our literary heritage, and to the future generations of scholars who will continue the work of recovering, preserving, publishing and transforming the literary landscapes of the Americas.

Preface

A. GABRIEL MELÉNDEZ

University of New Mexico

As Director of the Center for Regional Studies at the University of New Mexico, I am pleased to lend CRS support to the publication of this 25th anniversary volume celebrating the brilliant work of the Recovering the US Hispanic Literary Heritage Program. Over the last two decades the Recovery Program's work has been to unearth early Latino/a writings and to critically reassemble these writings as the foundational epistemology documenting the experience of generations of Latinos living in the United States and to give proof of the many ways in which each generation has determined and shaped the political and cultural life of the nation. More has been achieved than could have been imagined in 1992 when a group of leading scholars, librarians and archivists from the United States, Mexico, Puerto Rico and Spain, set about "to research, locate, preserve and make accessible all literary-historical documents produced by Hispanics living in the United States from the Colonial Period to 1960." The 25th anniversary volume is an apt testimony to Dr. Nicolás Kanellos's foresight and his unrivaled ability to bring together a remarkable constellation of people to take on Recovery's ambitious mission. The Recovery Program's biannual conference and grant awards programs has stimulated the work of an impressive group of Recovery scholars whose work is reflected here and in prior Recovery proceedings, anthologies and literary histories over the last twenty-five years, so too Recovery's supremely talented in-house team of researchers and editors over the years: Carolina Villaroel, Gabriela Baeza Ventura, Alejandra Balestra, Helvetia Martell and others have through their work, dedication and intelligence secured the future of the Recovery Program. As a member of the Recovery Board, I celebrate the milestone that is the 25th anniversary volume, confident in the knowledge that the celebratory moment is truly deserved and sober in our mutual resolve to continue the unfinished work of fully recovering the *US Hispanic Literary Heritage.*

Introduction

ANTONIA CASTAÑEDA
Independent Scholar

CLARA LOMAS
Colorado College Professor Emerita

Writing was and continues to be an act of creation, and the archive connected creations from the past with creators in the present. . . . Social and political demands of the present call for a "full" accounting of the past, one that reflects fragmented, contentious and transnational identities across time.

—Raúl A. Ramos

Writing/Righting History: Recovering the US Hispanic Literary Heritage 25th Anniversary Volume commemorates the founding of the Recovery Program that empowered a new world of literary scholarship and gave rise to new ways of thinking, reading, theorizing and understanding American literature, from the colonial era to the present. This commemorative volume also represents Volume X of select, peer-reviewed papers from the Fourteenth Recovery conference, held at the University of Houston on February 10-12, 2017. The Appendices closing this commemorative volume reveal the depth and breadth of the transformative scholarship of the Recovery Program.

Appropriately, in keeping with memorializing the first quarter century of the Program, the volume opens with Considering Recovery's First 25 Years: Reflections y Testimonios. Here, the Recovery Program's Administrators and Board of Directors, some of whom have been with the Program since 1990, reflect upon a quarter century of recovering and writing/righting the US Hispanic Literary Heritage in the latter third of one millennium and the beginning of another. In both celebratory and sober modes, because there is both much to celebrate and much to give us pause in the current cultural and political climate of renewed anti-Hispanic doctrines, the multi-generational board of literary scholars, historians, archivists and librarians, engage the range of literary, historical, cultural, political and other issues rooted in the contentious encounter of Spanish and English literatures in the North American landscape and, in the due course of time, ingrained in the institutional fabric of the United States. In their reflections and *testimonios,* Board members signal the broad spectrum of critical, analytic and interpretative issues with which the Recovery Program has contended from its inception, and reflect too, on themes and topics not as present in the discourse of the time when Recovery was created. Among salient overarching issues are those of linguistic and cultural translation, of identity, of the Spanish, English, and bilingual archive, of transnationalism, of forging space within contentious intellectual environments and structured institutional inequalities, of teaching and pedagogy and of attendant resistance to canonical challenges that Recovery Program scholarship poses.

This section is comprised of two parts. In the first, the Director, Executive Editor and Director of Research, recount the challenges and accomplishments of a quarter century of recovering the written legacy of Latinas/os/x in the United States. In the second, organized into four thematic categories, members of the Board of Directors reflect upon, offer testimony and reveal the challenges and power of rethinking and righting the American literary canon.

Section II visually documents Recovery conferences and meetings, archival preservation and project events, through a collection of historical photographs.

The nineteen essays in Section III comprise Volume X of the Fourteenth Recovery Program conference. In keeping with publication of select works of Recovery conferences, this collection of essays builds upon, broadens and deepens the scholarship of writers, thinkers and scholars working with the Recovery Program's archives, periodicals and related primary sources. Divided into four parts, these essays explore themes and topics pertaining to historical and more contemporary processes of colonialisms; the presence and literary production of historical populations of Californios and Neo-Mexicanos; the literature of exile, immigration and the migration of Latina/o/x peoples across national and transnational spaces; and the analysis and theorization of the power of critical translation and a transnational narrative focused on one writer. The essays in Volume X explore and open new avenues to thinking, writing/righting historical and literary studies in the United States.

Part 1. Of Coloniality, Colonialism and Settler Colonialisms: Languages, Politics, Religion

The recovery and inclusion of Spanish-language colonial texts in the corpus of US literary history and canon, challenged historic paradigms of American literature. Spanish-language literary texts produced in the regions originally part of Spain's colonies in the North American continent (later part of the Republic of Mexico), and annexed to the United States at the end of the US Mexican War in the mid-nineteenth century Recovery scholars argued, are as much a part of the US literary legacy as the literature deriving from the original English colonies. In its movement to right the historical record and challenge US national literary historiography, Recovery has shaped the contours of an inclusive American identity and provided the power of the transnational narrative within the nation.

Charting colonialist eras and multiple, often overlapping colonialities, from the sixteenth to the twentieth centuries, Section I begins with "The Long Colonizing Process: From Cortés to Portolá," José Antonio Gurpegui's examination of Gaspar de Portolá, Junipero Serra, and José de Gálvez, key figures in the colonization of Alta California, a pivotal region long in the sights of Spain's imperial project. Mining archival records and correspondence of the era of reconsideration and reconsolidation of empire that the Bourbon Reforms represented, Gurpegui argues the centrality of internal conflicts and contentious interplay within and between military and religious institutions and the individuals, whose personalities, actions and inactions most directly affected the timing and scope of Spain's last military political colonialist project in North America. The essay contributes to the newer scholarship that is rethinking Transatlantic Studies, moving beyond singular focus on the North Atlantic to include Spain and Portugal, among the most active economic hubs in the early modern world, of this broader revisioning.

Writing and righting the historical narrative of Spanish colonialism, the following two essays plumb colonial archives to recover the languages, voices and identities, albeit in translation, of the diverse Indigenous peoples in the area of the eighteenth-century entradas between the Ríos Bravo and San Antonio in the region of Coahuila-Tejas, whom colonial authorities collectively named by the non-indigenous term, Coahuiltecos.

In "Un grupo documental para la evangelización de los coahuiltecos," Blanca López de Mariscal studies three bilingual texts translated from Spanish to Coahuilteco, the language the Franciscan missionaries determined most of the region's diverse indigenous peoples spoke or understood, to examine the linguistic challenges presented historically in the evangelization and Westernization of this colonial province. López de Mariscal's examination offers significant possibilities for new knowledge about the languages and ethnohistory of the native peoples of the Tejas-Coahuila region, while also exposing the complexities and contradictions of the bilingual texts the religious arm of the colonial state produced for the spiritual and material conquest of indigenous populations.

Similarly grappling with paradoxes of colonial archives, Paloma Vargas Montes' "La voz de las respuestas silentes: análisis etnohistórico de un texto religioso en lengua coahuilteca," employs ethnohistoric methods in recovery of Coahuiltecan identities and cultures. Combining analysis of Fray Bartolomé García's religious text, with other archival materials, Vargas Montes identifies the various Indigenous groups according to the number of times they appear in the written records, compares the questions addressed to the individuals in the confessional and analyzes queries and responses as a process of linguistic and cultural mediation. In concert with the developing field of critical archival studies, these essays reveal the ways in which records and archives serve as tools for both oppression and liberation.

Moving from the eighteenth-century colonial state to the nation states of the nineteenth and twentieth centuries, the following two articles frame changing but persistent forms of colonialism in North America, with legacies of both Spanish and English coloniality, and in the Caribbean Island of Puerto Rico, which became a US colony in the form of an unincorporated territory, at the end of the war with Spain in 1898.

In *"El México Perdido y Anhelado:* The Prose of Settler Colonialism Amidst the Diaspora," José Angel Hernández analyzes the prose in a cache of previously little known correspondence and petitions from diasporic Mexican and Mexican Americans, appealing to Mexican bureaucrats for land grants and permission to relocate to the homeland in the post Mexico/US War of the nineteenth century, as well as before and after the Mexican Revolution of 1910-1920. The petitioners, seeking land primarily in three Northern Mexican states, avail themselves of four major tropes and ideological constructions to argue the "value" to the Mexican nation of their repatriation. In his incisive critique of the petitioner's prose and the strategy of Mexican officials the documents reveal, Hernández identifies pivotal tropes of settler colonialism, which seek to eliminate and replace the indigenous population with an invasive settler society.

Articulating nation and coloniality in Puerto Rico, Bruno Ríos and Juan Carlos Rozo Gálvez examine the categories and concepts of nation, as well as migrations, nostalgia, and identity, in relation to the neocolonial condition of Puerto Rico in the twentieth century. These studies contribute to our understanding of the connections between historical events caused by coloniality and their continued resonance within the nation in the present. In "La nación intervenida: el concepto de la nación puertorriqueña en las crónicas de Jesús Colón," Bruno Ríos revisits Jesús Colón's satirical chronicles from 1927 to 1946, to chart the conceptual evolution of Puerto Rican nationhood in Colón's essays published in *Gráfico* and *Pueblos Hispánicos* and *Liberación.* Colón situates the nation, Ríos argues, not in a fixed territory in the islands of Puerto Rico and Manhattan but in the imaginary, hybrid, bilingual transnational community in constant movement between the two, a space where he envisions a communist nation. Whereas Ríos examines previously recovered texts, Juan Carlos Rozo Gálvez, in "La nostalgia de la patria/la patria nostálgica: una aproximación a la vida y obra de César G. Torres," brings to light the work of an understudied poet of the Puerto Rican diaspora to advocate for his place in Puerto Rican and US Latino anthologies. Through biographical information, thematic exposition of three *poemarios* (1949-1989) and significant scholarship to support his claim, Rozo charts Torres's articulation of nation, transmigrations and nostalgia, as he voices dissent regarding US imperial policy in Puerto Rico.

Part 2: Of Historical Populations and Literary Histories: Californios and Neo-Mexicanos

Recovery of mid nineteenth- and early twentieth-centuries US Latina/o literature places us squarely in the wake of the end of the US Mexican War (1848), the consequent political, economic, cultural, linguistic and literary hegemonic developments of a new colonial state in previous Spanish-Mexican territories, and the advent of wave upon wave of primarily English-speaking settler colonists. Californios, Neo-Mexicanos and Tejanos, Spanish-speaking mestizo descendants of Spain's imperialism, citizens of the Republic of Mexico until 1848, and now ostensibly US citizens by dint of war, composed, wrote, narrated and published, the complex, multi-layered reality of loss, displacement and disparagement of their history, language and culture under the new regime. Writing in Spanish, in English, as well as bilingually, drawing on oral and written literary traditions, and in all genres, their literary works both affirmed their language, culture and intellectual traditions, and refused, rejected and resisted their disparagement in the English-language press and publications. Recovering and reading the literary archive of Californios and Neo-Mexicanos also reveals the paradox of narratives that both counter US Western hegemonic historiography and sustain ancestral linguistic and cultural hegemony enforced against native peoples in Spain's former colonies.

Plumbing this complex post-war universe in "Mariano Guadalupe Vallejo: Recovering a Californio Voice from Mexican California," Rose Marie Beebe and Robert M. Senkewicz reclaim Vallejo's unpublished testimonial written in an era of dislocation and dispossession of the Californios to safeguard their identity, memory and history from the defamation and obliteration that American domination portended. This essay initiates Beebe and Senkewicz's larger recovery project, the translation and publication of Vallejo's extensive manuscript, offering new knowledge and understanding of historical complexities and paradoxes, related by a Californio who was born as a subject of Spain, served as an officer in the Republic of Mexico and had a pivotal role in shaping the transition of Alta California from a Mexican province to a US State.

Turning from a Californio's historical narrative to a Nuevo Mexicana's creative literary work, Leigh Johnson's "Imagined Alternatives to Conquest in Aurora Lucero-White Lea's "'Kearny Takes Las Vegas,'" presents a female gendered vision of the conquest of New Mexico in a short radio-play. Bringing much needed attention to an understudied early twentieth-century Neo-Mexicana feminist writer, Johnson's essay signals the convergence of modernity, the media platform that Lucero-White chose for her play in 1936 and the genre of historical romance within which the alternative "taking" of Las Vegas is set.

In "A Certifiable Past and the Possible Future of a Borderlands Literary and Cultural Episteme," A. Gabriel Meléndez examines intellectual developments among Neo-Mexicanos during the second half of the nineteenth century, a period of transition and deep uncertainty. Taking issue with the long-held notion that Latino literary criticism is rooted in twentieth-century analysis, Meléndez argues for self-reflective writing, including texts discussing "the status of the literary" much earlier. In the writing of editor and essayist José Escobar, Meléndez locates an example of literary criticism, and the means by which to assess the production of self-sustaining cultural knowledge, among early Mexican-American writers.

Two succeeding essays probe historical and intellectual legacies of the prodigious Neo-Mexicano Chacón family to deepen methodologic and analytic approaches in the recovery of American literary traditions forged on linguistic, cultural and politically contested ground. Francisco A. Lomelí, in "Literary Detective Work Reclaims Eusebio Chacón From the *Telarañas* of History: Exhuming a Forgotten Generation," charts the process of recovering and reclaiming nineteenth-century attorney, novelist and public intellectual Eusebio Chacón's critical importance to a generation of writers whose literary production, published mostly in Spanish-language periodicals, is here analyzed and interpreted as a Neo-Mexicano Renaissance. In the life and work of Eusebio Chacón, and his influence on a generation of Hispano intellectuals, Lomelí finds components of the first ethnic renaissance, suggesting that it predated the Harlem Renaissance by three decades.

Anna M. Nogar, in "Navigating a Fine Bilingual Line in Early Twentieth-Century New Mexico: *El cantor neomexicano*, Felipe M. Chacón," further recovers and delves into the archive of the extended Chacón family to offer a deep linguistic and cultural analysis of the literary production of this early twentieth-century writer and editor. F. M. Chacón, an integral member of the cadre of Neo-Mexicano intellectuals who expressed a resistive positionality carefully couched in nationalist self-identification, skillfully deployed language, writing in Spanish, English and bilingually, to subtly and subversively critique English monolingualism and its hegemonic propositions.

Manuel M. Martín Rodríguez's, "Of Modern Troubadours and Tricksters: The Upside-Down World of José Inés García," recovers the work of this little known New Mexican writer whose poetics align with the aesthetics of the minor genres, particularly satire, in vernacular Spanish. García, who called himself "El trovador moderno," reveals interesting paradoxes which, while presumably alluding to the tension between the traditional (oral culture/Spanish language) and the modern (English language print culture), disclose the reality of simultaneously being both.

Part 3. Of Exile to Immigration: Nationalism, Migrations and Transnationalism

As we broaden our understanding of the experiences of exile, immigrant and transnational migrants and their communities, both in the receiving and sending nations, our notions of nation, national identity and cultural citizenship have shifted significantly. We trace transitions of exiles aspiring to return to their countries of origin, to immigrants negotiating their sense of national belonging and, at times, to transnational subjects who conceive of their cultural citizenship as a multilocal process. One of the principal components of Recovery, the identification and recovery of primary sources, has made available valuable documents on the transnational flow of people, ideas, culture, merchandise, labor and capital through complex networks extending beyond nation-state boundaries. Each part of a larger project, the essays in this section, which cover the period from the late eighteenth to mid-twentieth centuries, invite further investigations of published and unpublished sources: chronicles, essays, play scripts and personal journals. They further reinforce our understanding of exile, immigrant, and migrant subjects and communities and their bidirectional movement between the US and Caribbean and European regions.

In her essay, "Del exilio a la inmigración: *Cosas de los Estados Unidos* de Simón Camacho," Catalina T. Castillón traces the evolution of a Venezuelan exile who, upon arriving to New York in the late nineteenth century, writes scathing satirical chronicles and essays looking critically at the United States, initially from the gaze of an upper middle-class man, to that of an immigrant writer concerned with the Hispanic community's adaptation and sense of belonging. The essay highlights Camacho's social commentary on cultural resistance, language, national and international conflicts, focusing his 1864 collection of chronicles and his critique of the role of women in society. Particularly insightful is Castillón's reading of the dynamics of literary writing/reading circuits in transnational communities, in which a Venezuelan writer's literary production in New York was a commodity meant to be consumed in Cuba by a predominantly female audience.

The following two essays reveal extensive primary research, archival investigation, and recovery work of understudied Cuban newspapers and heretofore unknown theatrical scripts produced by Cuban writers revealing the presence of Cuban creativity and politics before the twentieth century in Florida. Gerald E. Poyo's "Recovering Forgotten Voices: Cuban Newspapers in Florida, 1870-1895" provides a survey of newspapers that can potentially be mined for further documentation on the centrality of nationalism in Florida communities, anarchist labor organizing and American politics as addressed by Cuban diasporic editors during and after the Cuban Ten Years War. Moving into the twentieth century, Kenya C. Dworkin y Méndez' "Before Exile: Unearthing the 'Golden Age' of Cuban Theater in Tampa" opens with a bibliographical report of a corpus of unpublished theatrical works from 1920 to 1960 before focusing on an analysis of two samples of Cuban satirical *teatro bufo* of the 1920s. The essay foregrounds the transnational character of the Tampa communities by examining political, economic and anti(neo)imperial attitudes of Cubans on both sides of the Florida Straits in theatrical pieces that include blackface characters in its satire alluding to the colonialist legacy in Cuba as well as the United States.

Ana Varela-Lugo's "In Their Own Words: Recovering the History of Spanish Immigrant Experience in the United States Through Immigrants' Writing" convincingly argues for the significant role of journals in documenting transnational migrations with greater immediacy and intimacy than other discursive practices. The essay renders an incisive analysis of José González's three personal notebooks that illuminate Spanish migratory networks of early twentieth century and reveal both affective consequences of migrations on sending and receiving communities and complex transmigrant identities in global movements.

Part 4. Jorge Ainslie Writes Immigration: Methodologic and Analytic Approaches to Literary and Periodical Representation

Generating new critical assessments of early twentieth-century texts, the three essays in the last part of this section call attention to the significance of Jorge Ainslie, a Mexican national and immigrant to the United States, whose work deserves critical focus, assert the authors, for its exposure of post-Revolution travails of Mexican life in the Southwest as well as its promotion of voluntary repatriation in times of xenophobic expulsions by the US government. Considered a major voice for "el México de afuera," Ainslie writes immigration/exile through literary genres (novels, short stories, memoirs), fictionalizing historical events to different degrees, and uses Ignacio E. Lozano family presses as his publication outlets. These essays begin to generate assessments through analytic lenses of various critical methodologies to initiate national and transnational critical dialogues that complicate the narrative of the transnational exile community and Mexican repatriation in the 1930s. In "Critical Translation: The Politics of and Writings of Jorge Ainslie," José F. Aranda argues for the importance of translation not only as a methodology pertaining to language, but also a theory by which to apprehend the act of translating US cultures to Spanish-language readers. Drawing on Walter Mignolo's concepts of "conflict of literacies" and "colonial difference," Anibal Quijano's "coloniality of power" and definitions of translation by other theoreticians and critics, Aranda examines the "translational possibilities" of Ainslie's works and deepens our understanding of the power of the Spanish-language press—as an institutional site—to stage "critical translation" for its readers at the time of publication, as well as in the present.

In her article, "*Sintiendo vergüenza*: Intersections of Class, Race, Gender and Colonial Affect-Culture in Jorge Ainslie's *Los Repatriados* (1935)," Lorena Gauthereau similarly draws upon Quijano's notion of coloniality of power and applies it to Rosemary Hennessy's definition and theory of "affect-culture." She posits that reading for colonial affect-culture in this serialized novel can further demonstrate the ways people of Mexican descent in the United States, in particular women, experience the "materiality of gendered and racialized labor."

While Aranda and Guthereau study Ainslie's serialized novelistic production, Donna Kabalen de Bichara's essay, "Recovering the Memory of Revolutionary Activity in the Texas Periodical *La Prensa*: Jorge Ainslie's 'Mis andanzas en la Revolución Escobarista,'" offers a close reading of a serialized recollection of a journey into a counterrevolution authored by Ainslie, in which she correlates existing historical scholarship with textual literary representation. Jacques Derrida's notion of "differénce" and Hayden White's concept of historicity serve as theoretical approaches to probe hidden historical "truth" within the art form of the text in which autobiography, history and fiction intertwine.

The authors of these essays bring into focus serialized fiction in the Spanish-language press that merit further research and investigation. Of particular import is how these studies acknowledge the resonance of the past within the present cross-border movements, xenophobia, deportations and repatriations, and transnational subjectivities, inviting not only comparative studies but deliberations on epistemological and political ways of affecting the future.

CONSIDERING RECOVERY'S FIRST 25 YEARS: REFLECTIONS AND *TESTIMONIOS*

Recovering Our Written Legacy: Recounting the Challenge

GABRIELA BAEZA VENTURA, NICOLÁS KANELLOS AND
CAROLINA VILLARRROEL
University of Houston

A Background of Racialization, Discrimination and Neglect

Since the nineteenth-century expansion of the American Republic into regions previously populated by Hispanic-origin peoples, from East and West Florida to the California coast, such ideologies as Manifest Destiny and the Spanish Black Legend often cast Hispanic citizens of the United States, today known as Latinos, and immigrants from Spanish-speaking lands as the enemy, the primitive and inferior denizens of conquered lands, and a prime example of racial "mongrelization," to use a term coined by Texas Congressman John C. Box as late as 1930. Throughout the nineteenth century and most of the twentieth, if Mexican Americans, Puerto Ricans and other Hispanics of the United States were not seen as foreigners, they most often were treated as the "other." During nearly two centuries of anti-Hispanic propaganda and the creation of stereotypes and negative images in popular culture, it is no wonder that so much has been lost of our cultural history in the United States. That is, the official institutions of the society often did not collect and preserve the Hispanic community's intellectual and cultural documents, from hundreds of newspapers and thousands of books published as well as unpublished manuscripts, memoirs, letters, photographs and other documents that could have become part of the nation's official cultural heritage, popular culture and potentially integrated into the curriculum, at least in today's public schools in the most populous states where Latino students are already a majority.

3

Most Americans are unaware of the incredible tapestry of American literature and history that Hispanics have produced over the decades, especially in the Spanish language, prior to World War II and increasingly in English afterward. In addition to US expansion into and incorporation of previous Hispanic lands, since the early nineteenth century the United States has been the primary destination for political exiles and immigrants from Spain and Spanish America. All of them have contributed to American culture, although quite a bit of the documentary legacy that could sustain this statement has been lost or is subject to recovery. The National Endowment for the Humanities' Common Good program, launched in 2016, has recognized the need to acknowledge and recover and discuss such legacies when it asks, "How can the humanities assist the country in addressing the challenges and opportunities created by the changing demographics in many American communities?" An important part of that answer is to find that legacy wherever it resides, preserve it and make it accessible.

The Birth of Recovering the US Hispanic Literary Heritage

Recovering the US Hispanic Literary Heritage (Recovery) was created specifically to fulfill this mission: to research, preserve and make accessible the written culture produced by Latinos in the United States, from the sixteenth-century explorations and settlements to the 1960s civil rights movements. In 2017, Recovery celebrated its twenty-fifth anniversary. Since its founding, Recovery has become somewhat of a sub-discipline for faculty, researchers and graduate students in Spanish, English, History and Ethnic Studies departments and programs throughout the United States. At many academic institutions, the program has been integrated in one form or another into the curriculum and into the research deemed as a legitimate area of research, to be respected for faculty evaluation and advancement. The program has become the focal point for scholars around the country and abroad interested in reconstituting the cultural and documentary history of Latinos, and for librarians and archivists eager to expand their collections to include the written legacy of Latinos, who now make up the largest minority group in the country.

To even dream of establishing a project to find, preserve and make accessible the written culture of US Latinos was extremely difficult before the founding of Recovery in 1992. The first large generation of Latinos entering university teaching in the 1970s was largely decimated by departments that refused to recognize the roles foisted on Latino junior faculty of also serving as counselors, recruiters and activists in addition to teaching and publishing. A large part of this first generation was denied tenure, often for the very reason that the tenure system was developed: to protect the speech and intellectual activity of faculty. Senior scholars and department committees often scoffed at their Latino junior colleagues' attempts to research a Latino legacy that for the majority simply did not or never existed. It was not until the mid 1980s that a core group of scholars interested in reconstituting this legacy finally achieved tenure and was thus free to research themes from their heritage that had previously fallen outside academic canons.

In addition to the emergence of tenured researchers interested in these legacy themes, two other ingredients were needed to facilitate wide-ranging and deep investigation and recovery of the legacy: money and technology. Fortunately, these scholarly efforts developed at the same time that philanthropic foundations had once again "discovered the sleeping giant," as they had during the civil rights movements of the 1960s and 1970s. And, by the early 1990s, the Internet was blossoming and accessible to academic researchers.

With early backing from the Rockefeller Foundation, whose Humanities division was represented by the respected Chicano scholar Tomás Ybarra-Frausto and the director of the division Alberta Arthurs, a scholar-publisher who had researched the field since graduate school, Nicolás Kanellos, was funded to bring scholars, librarians and archivists from around the nation to discuss the possibility of recovering this legacy and feasibility of launching a project. The list of professionals recruited included scholars and librarian/archivists who at that point were leaders in finding, preserving and writing about previously lost or unknown texts and historical events: Edna Acosta-Belén, Antonia Castañeda, Rodolfo Cortina, José Fernández, Roberta Fernández, Juan Flores, Erlinda González-Berry, Ramón Gutiérrez, Virginia Sánchez-Korrol, Luis Leal, Clara Lomas, Francisco Lomelí, Genaro Padilla, Raymond Paredes, Nélida Pérez, María Herrera Sobek and Roberto Trujillo. Kanellos prepared a document synthesizing the findings of these scholars' research to serve as a point of departure for the meeting, which took place at the National Humanities Center in Research Triangle Park on November 17 and 18, 1990. The specific goal of this first conference was to engage in discussions that not only would identify the US Hispanic documentary legacy that could be recovered, but also to design approaches and methods for locating, making accessible and studying the works. Professor Henry Louis Gates, Jr., who had been instrumental in creating and administering such methods and approaches for African American literature, gave the keynote address at the conference and otherwise advised the conferees on the project.

This initial assemblage of scholars became the first board of what would be titled Recovering the US Hispanic Literary Heritage, despite the project's ambition of recovering all written culture, not just the literary. It was decided at the conference that the center to carry out the work of researching, recovering, preserving, making accessible and integrating into the curriculum at all levels this written legacy would be located at the University of Houston, under the direction of Professor Kanellos, who was also the director of Arte Público Press, the nation's largest Hispanic press, which could make many of the documents and books available to academia as well as the general public.

Recovery Becomes Institutionalized

Based on the work of the first conference and the plan developed for the Recovery Program, the Rockefeller Foundation and other funding entities began underwriting the effort in 1991. Rockefeller, in the lead, made a ten-year funding commitment, at the end of which period it also awarded a one-time continuation/stabilization fund. Over the course of twenty-five years numerous supporters have stepped forward, including the National Endowment for the Humanities, HumanitiesTexas, the Brown, Belo, Ford, AT&T, Meadows, Andrew W. Mellon and other foundations. In 2000, the Save America's Treasures program of the Interior Department awarded Recovery a substantial grant to microfilm for preservation and make electronically accessible some 300 books at risk of loss through acid burn. This was the first time that preservation dollars were dedicated to books rather than buildings and art of historic significance. Recovery ended up digitizing more than 500 such rare books suffering from acid burn.

Along the way, board members and numerous scholars have presented Recovery papers at such associations as Council on Library and Information Resources, Latin American Studies Association, Modern Language Association, American Historical Association, American Association of Teachers of Spanish and Portuguese, The Society for the History of Authorship, Reading and Publishing, HISPAUSA Asociación de estudios sobre la población de origen hispano en EEUU, Latino Studies Association, Texas Historical Association, Western Literature Association, Society of American Archivists and too many other conferences to name. University press books and scholarly editions of recovered texts have been published by the California, Cambridge, Florida, Harvard, New Mexico, Oxford, Texas, Texas A&M, Texas Christian, Princeton and other universities presses. The first comprehensive historical anthology of Hispanic literature (*Herencia: The Anthology of Hispanic Literature of the United States*, ed. Kanellos et al, 2002) was published by Oxford University Press; the accompanying anthology of Spanish-language original texts was published (*En otra voz: literatura hispana de los Estados Unidos*, ed. Kanellos et al, 2002) by Arte Público Press of the University of Houston.

Over the years, the program has funded scholars to conduct research (see Addenda 2. "List of Grants-In-Aid Awarded, this volume); created a comprehensive project database of some 500,000 documents (from one-page broadsides to entire books); microfilmed for preservation and digitized for online distribution some 2000 books; compiled and published the first comprehensive bibliography of Hispanic periodicals, *Hispanic Periodicals in the United States: A Brief History and Comprehensive Bibliography* by Nicolás Kanellos with Helvetia Martell; published with Greenwood Press the four-volume *Greenwood Encyclopedia of Latino Literature*; indexed and digitally scanned some 350,000 literary and historical articles from hundreds of newspapers for production of the electronic edition of periodical materials (in full text for distribution by EBSCO Pub. and Readex); held fourteen bi-annual national conferences to date; published in print some forty recovered volumes, plus nine volumes of the selected conference papers; published the two comprehensive anthologies mentioned above and various other documents and books; and underwrote the microfilming of various Hispanic collections from New York to Los Angeles. Since its founding, more than one hundred university press books have been published using Recovery materials or based on Recovery resources and/or research funding (see the Addenda 1. "Books Relating to Recovery Research; this volume).

Today, Recovery has the largest collection of Spanish-language periodicals published in the United States before 1960, some 1,400 titles, and continues to add to its collection through research and accession and microfilming. Recovery has made available through its distributors fully searchable, downloadable, e-mailable, etc., some 800 of these digitized periodicals through Readex (440 titles: "Hispanic American Newspapers 1808-1980" http://www.readex.com/content/hispanic-american-newspapers-1808-1980) and EBSCO (360+ titles: "The Latino-Hispanic American Experience, Arte Público Series 1 & 2," http://www.library.unt.edu/news/collection-development/trial-ebscohosts-arte-publico-1-2); thus far they have been made available to more than 100 university libraries in the United States, Germany, Mexico and Spain by subscription.

The Recovery program has reached out to small and midsize institutions since its founding, awarding grants and otherwise assisting in organizing, microfilming, digitizing and/or making materials accessible. Among the institutions that received this support were: American Sephardi Federation/Sephardic House Library; Archivo Histórico del Instituto de las Hermanas Catequistas Guadalupanas, Saltillo, Mexico; Biblioteca Nacional José Martí, Havana, Cuba; Casa Bautista de Publicaciones, El Paso; Centro de Estudios Martianos, Havana, Cuba; El Paso Public Library; Episcopal Theological Seminary of the Southwest Library; the Brownsville Historical Society; the Gilcrease Museum in Tulsa; Instituto de Historia Cubana, Havana, Cuba; Instituto Nacional de Antropología e Historia, Mexico City; Instituto Tecnológico de Monterrey, Mexico; Texas A&M-Corpus Christi Special Collections; Laredo Public Library; Natural History Museum of Los Angeles County; New Mexico State University Library; University of South Florida Special Collections; Center for Puerto Rican Studies Archives, Hunter College; San Juan Bautista Mission library, California; Western

Reserve Historical Society. Recovery has become a leader in Latino Digital Humanities and has conducted workshops and presentations at the following universities: Arizona State, Stanford, Texas A&M, University of Kansas, University of Pennsylvania, University of Virginia, University of Victoria, Canada, New York University. In addition, Recovery has conducted digital humanities workshops and made presentations in Brazil, Canada, Croatia, Cuba, France, Germany, Hungary, Italy, Mexico, Puerto Rico, Spain, United Kingdom.

Three Examples of Recovery Breaking Ground in US Latino Studies

Religious Documentation

The role of religion, in all of its diversity and historical evolution, in building Hispanic culture in this country can now be understood within a broader framework and in depth through the archival materials accessioned, microfilmed, published and/or digitized by Recovery, which has located a large body of religious thought written by US Latinos during the nineteenth and early twentieth centuries. In that treasure trove of manuscripts and printed material are hundreds of religious periodicals, previously unknown to scholars, that circulated in Hispanic communities during this time span: Baptist, Presbyterian and Methodist newspapers for wide circulation, weekly newspapers by church-related groups which served as a major source of information for the ethnic enclaves, and Catholic magazines for a general readership, Sephardic newspapers from New York and California, written in Ladino, an archaic form of Spanish, but printed in Hebrew characters. The varieties of language expression—monolingual, bilingual, at times trilingual—reveal further diversity of the reading habits and abilities of the congregations over time. Recovered, translated, digitized and published for the first time are memoirs of the religious, such as the extremely important autobiography of US civil war soldier and later protestant preacher Santiago Tafolla. Equally unknown, and now unearthed for the first time, are the hundreds of Spanish-language books published by and for Hispanic faithful from such religious centers as El Paso, San Antonio, Kansas City and Chicago that the Recovery Program has discovered. They run the gamut from Bibles, Catechisms and books of sermons in Spanish to autobiographies of converts and ministers, to memoirs of political exiles in the United States, to books detailing the role of religion in social and political life. In addition, Recovery has brought into its archives thousands of manuscript sermons, correspondence, book manuscripts, photographs, reports, studies, etc., that soon will become the raw material for scholarly examination and commentary. Of particular interest are the papers and memoirs of exiled Catholic bishops and archbishops during the

Mexican Revolution, as well as the hand-printed and bound "books of martyrs" produced by Cristeros in the Southwest.

Recovery was able to organize a conference in 2004 on Hispanic religiosity and its documentation and publish the papers in *Recovering Hispanic Religious Thought and Practice in the United States* (Cambridge Scholars Press, 2007). In addition, a large body of this religious legacy is included in the Recovery's Series 2 distributed through EBSCO Inc.

US Latina Activism and Writing

Challenging the misconception that Hispanic/Latina women lagged in their development of a feminist consciousness are the letters of María Amparo Ruiz de Burton in the nineteenth century; the essays of anarchists Luisa Capetillo and Blanca de Moncaleano in the early twentieth century; the writings of women for the New Mexico WPA during the Depression; the newspaper columns of Clotilde Betances de Yaeger and many others from the 1940s on. Loreta Janeta Velásquez's controversial memoir of disguising herself as Colonel Harry Buford during the Civil War in order to spy for the Confederacy demonstrates the willingness of Latinas to break boundaries and enter into a "man's" world. While we acknowledge Velasquez's resolve, we reject the cause of the slave-holding South she served. The entire archive of Leonor Villegas de Magnón, who worked with (or was involved with) the Mexican Liberal Party that brought on the revolution, includes all of her documents in organizing a nursing corps for the Venustiano Carranza army; her correspondence with presidents, generals and other officers; the manuscripts of the English- and the Spanish-language versions of her memoir of the revolution; her extensive collection of photos and other artifacts.

Many are the examples of early feminist thought and writing recovered, including the magazine, *Feminismo Internacional* (1923), published by Elena Arizmendi, an exiled Mexican intellectual and novelist. The complete archive of María Cristina Mena not only includes her manuscripts, but also correspondence and photos that document her relationship with D. H. Lawrence. Cross-border feminism is represented in the novels and newspaper columns of Mexican María Luisa Garza (Loreley), who resisted patriarchy while writing in newspapers owned and dominated by men but later rebelled and self-published her own novels. The extensive Pura Belpré collection includes original manuscripts in various stages of composition, correspondence and a partial memoir, among many other items. The EBSCO series 2 collection includes representatives from the nineteenth century to the present, but for the first time makes available Arte Público Press archives of the leading Latina novelists, playwrights and poets: Ana Castillo, Denise Chávez, Sandra Cisneros, Judith Ortiz Cofer, Alicia Gaspar de Alba, Carolina Hospital, Graciela Limón,

Nicholasa Mohr, Pat Mora, Dolores Prida, Beatriz Rivera, Evangelina Vigil, Helena María Viramontes and many others. Included is the very extensive archive of unpublished works, art, music lyrics, letters and other materials of the late poet and artist Angela de Hoyos. The authors' collections all include correspondence, reviews, interviews, original manuscripts, photos, broadsides and other artifacts.

Civil Rights History

It is generally unknown that Hispanic/Latino struggles for civil rights began as soon as lands formerly belonging to Mexico and Spain were incorporated into the United States in the nineteenth century. On those lands, the inhabitants now found themselves as citizens of a new and expanding empire, whose laws, religion and racial concepts and practices conflicted with those of their former nations. Many writers, intellectuals, religious, politicians and community activists led the way in helping the inhabitants acclimate to the new legal and government culture while defending the rights of Hispanics as citizens, landholders and workers of racial and cultural make-ups different from those imposed by the "pioneers" who moved south and west. Novels and correspondence by María Amparo Ruiz de Burton explore precisely the conflicting concepts of race and entitlements prior to, during and after the American civil war. The hand-written memoir of the leader of a Texas rebellion against the interlopers from the North, Catarino Garza, demonstrates the motives behind numerous movements to preserve legal and cultural rights among the native population in what the newly dominant culture termed as "banditry" but the natives vouchsafed as resistance and rebellion. The testimonial writing and letters of early Californians and Texans document their growing disenfranchisement and loss of their lands. New Mexicans, reacting to the racist ideology of Manifest Destiny, set out to create an ideology of prior civilization that their ancestors brought from Europe. On the other hand, the civil rights story is also represented in the struggle of labor to organize from the nineteenth century on. As well as the material mentioned above, recovered and made accessible are the complete archives of the five Spanish/Cuban mutual aid societies of Tampa, Florida, during the heyday of the cigar industry and its associated union periodicals. Some seventy anarchist and labor periodicals published in New York, Tampa and the Southwest provide a story never before examined, given that this is the only digitized collection of these newspapers. In these pages are essays and editorials by Mexican revolutionaries such as the Flores Magón brothers; anarchist feminists, such as Luisa Capetillo and Blanca de Moncaleano; and scores of exile figures from the Spanish Civil War. The archives of Jesús Colón, the manuscripts of Joaquín Colón, Puerto Rican activist brothers in New York; the Concerned

Latins Organization in Northwest Indiana; archives of Texas' Committee of One Hundred Loyal Citizens and the early years of the League of United Latin American Citizens are included in this historical collection, as well as the entire, extensive archive of one of the greatest Latino civil rights leaders of all time: Alonso S. Perales. Some of the documents of civil rights leaders of the 1960s and 1970s are have been digitized and are accessible, including those of José Angel Gutiérrez, Reies López Tijerina and Rodolfo "Corky" Gonzales, as well as interviews of other major leaders and participants in the Chicano civil rights movement, which were transcribed in preparation for Arturo Rosales' groundbreaking book, *Chicano! History of the Mexican American Civil Rights Movement* and for the famous four-part PBS series by the same title.

Recovery Today and Tomorrow

Ongoing is Recovery's accession of important collections of documents as they become available from families and regional archives or are shared by larger institutions collaborating with the effort to reconstitute the US Latino documentary legacy. The papers and writings of community historians such as Houston's Emilio Sarabia are discoveries offering formerly unknown sources and perspectives. The living legacies of such individuals as Candy Torres, the first Latina engineer at NASA not only preserve current Latino contributions but also open doors to the early twentieth century when her forebears settled in New York City from Puerto Rico.

The indexing and digitization of newspapers continues as the laborious work of processing some 600 periodicals ensues, so that the texts and metadata can be added to the databases for universal distribution. And the hunt for periodicals from the nineteenth and twentieth centuries that have disappeared continues with unfortunately slow progress due to the devastation caused by the flimsiness and acid-processed newsprint, as well as disregard and ignorance. Only rarely has Recovery found troves of numerous papers in an archive, such as the seventy Spanish-language anarchist periodicals accessioned as a group or the fortuitous preservation in Spain of copies of nineteenth-century Key West and Tampa newspapers that were included in consular reports to the Crown. Now, we are content to find a newspaper or two every six months or so. Part of the problem is that, if the periodicals have been saved, they may lay uncatalogued in a regional archive or historical society. To that end, Recovery is conducting surveys of small and medium-sized historical societies to identify their holdings and assist in their preservation, digitization and accessibility.

As more archives, periodicals, books and documents are identified, accessioned or borrowed, Recovery continues to preserve them, microfilm and/or digitize them and make them accessible. This is a daily exercise, and unending task, if you will, as the tools for finding materials become more and more effective in assisting our mission.

The Recovery board, as well, continues its work, which includes this volume celebrating our twenty-fifth anniversary. Beyond that, the board is currently planning to launch an online newsletter that will appear twice a year, and within two years, will also launch an online journal to publish articles related to the recovered legacy and to the methodologies of Recovery. The biennial conferences will also continue into the future as exposition and support for scholars, as well as introduction to Recovery work for graduate students. For all of these services and more, the board has decided to become a membership organization that charges a fee in order to sustain the work of Recovery in general, but most directly the conferences.

Digital Humanities in the Recovery Future

Although the written legacy of Latinos has been documented by the Recovery program and other institutions, there is almost no digital humanities work being developed in Latino studies, in great part because the primary sources were produced mainly in Spanish, and digital humanities expertise has not been systematically extended to Latino scholars, librarians and activists. For these and other reasons, Recovering the US Hispanic Literary Heritage is in the process of establishing the first center for Latina/o Digital Humanities in order to offer facilities and expertise on the technologies and methodologies needed for scientific interpretation of the documentary history of Latinos as well as its digital publication. The University of Houston was awarded an Andrew W. Mellon Foundation award to begin the center in 2019. Spearheaded by Drs. Gabriela Baeza Ventura and Carolina Villarroel, the role of the center is to provide the space, resources and technology for Latino studies programs and scholars to enter the conversation on digital humanities with Latino-focused materials in either English or Spanish. The center serves as a venue with a postcolonial emphasis for projects on the US Latino written legacy that has been lost, absent, repressed or underrepresented in colonial structures of power, as has been the case with much of the material digitized by Recovery. It is to be a place where scholars and students from throughout the United States (and Latin America) can receive support and training to access and participate in digital humanities in Latino Studies. There are opportunities and facilities for digital publication of Latino-based projects and scholarship, including data curation, visualization, spatial analysis, metadata creation, digitization, workshops and classes in order to further opportunities for digital scholarship and publication in the humanities in general.

Despite this dearth of digital humanities research in Latino Studies prior to the creation of this space, the Recovery Program has been working internally and externally to foster DH projects. The following are just a few examples:

- "Are We Good Neighbors?" This project maps cases of discrimination against people of Mexican descent in Texas during the 1940s as documented by affidavits collected by Alonso S. Perales.
- "A Corpus Methods for Linguistic Analysis of Recovered Texts." Linguists and Recovery research fellows compiled and prepared corpora in Spanish, based on Recovery's nineteenth- and early twentieth-century periodicals for in-depth linguistic analysis. Research fellows scanned the newspapers using OCR and converted them to a machine-readable (plain text) format that the linguists are able to annotate.
- "Cartografía de Periódicos Fronterizos de 1800 a 1960." Former graduate students, Sylvia Fernández and Maira Alvarez, created an online map of more than 100 Spanish-language newspapers published along the US-Mexico border in three different time periods to reflect the political and social circumstances and themes as represented in the pages of the newspapers. The initial phase of the project was to conduct a survey of the newspapers both from experts as well as from the repository of digitized periodicals at Recovery.
- "Delis Negrón Digital Archive." This digital archive highlights the life and work of Delis Negrón, a Puerto Rican writer who was also a director, editor, English professor and activist in south Texas and Mexico City.
- "Emilio Sarabia and the Latino History of Houston." This project highlights historic spaces important to the Houston Latino community. Recovery research fellows digitized all of the documents and photos and are in the process of creating metadata. The ultimate goal is to create an online map that offers information on historical sites for buildings, people and events in the Houston area.
- "Recovery Digital Storytelling Project." Recovery partnered with the Houston Community College's Digital Storytelling Initiative and started the first series of interviews with the founders of the Recovery program. Their interviews were recorded during the 25th anniversary conference and serve as a living archive of the legacy of Recovery scholars.
- "Recovering the US Hispanic Literary Heritage Blog." The blog is dedicated to highlighting archival documents, digital humanities projects, resources, workshops, events and news that also includes bilingual (Spanish and English) posts on archival materials, digital exhibitions of selected collections, collaborations across disciplines and institutions, and more.

- "Recovering the US Hispanic Literary Heritage Digital Archives." This digital archive contains a sampling of some of Recovery's collections, such as that of Alonso S. Perales and Angela de Hoyos. The digital collections include photographs, correspondence and other documents.
- "Survey of Small Historical Societies, Libraries and Museums for Hispanic Materials and Their Management (Museum Survey)." In 2017-2018, Recovering the US Hispanic Literary Heritage conducted a survey of small historical societies, libraries and museums in the Southwest that might hold Hispanic archival materials and to assess how they were preserved and made accessible. The results were digitally mapped as part of this survey to serve as a guide to Hispanic materials at small institutions.
- Twitter Bots: @Alonso S. Perales tweets out quotations from Alonso S. Perales' writings, information regarding Perales, and news regarding his collection. @Fillingthe_gaps Unveils Latino authors' written legacy recovered in newspapers published in the United States from 1808 to 1960. The bot asks people to contribute by responding with any additional information they've come across in their research.

Forthcoming

- "Alonso S. Perales Correspondence." Using a sampling of the correspondence in the Alonso S. Perales collection, this map visualizes the extent of the civil rights activist and LULAC Co-founder's reach.
- "Network of Women in Hispanic Periodicals." This project visualizes the vast network between women writing in the early Hispanic press in the United States.
- "Printed Pathways in US Latino Periodicals." This is a comprehensive authority list that contains robust bibliographic information about US Latina/o authors and poets who published in US Latino periodicals.
- "Visual Bibliography of Hispanic Periodicals in the US." The purpose of this visualization is to reveal the written legacy of US Latinos in serial publication form and create awareness of the historical extent to which the Latino community has made their presence in the United States. The information is based on the book *Hispanic Periodicals in the United States: Origins to 1960 A Brief History and Comprehensive Bibliography* by Nicolás Kanellos and Helvetia Martell.

External

- "Invisible Hands: Print Culture, Class and US Latino Modernism." Recovery digital resources and support underpins the current research project conducted by Dr. John Alba Cutler at Northwestern University. The project is aimed at creating several ways of visualizing not only the size and distribution of Recovery's periodical archive, but also networks of affiliation and the trajectories of individual texts. Currently, Cutler is utilizing such open-source tools as Palladio and Python to do topic modeling and data mining of our digitized periodicals.

- "Chicana por Mi Raza." We are currently collaborating with the University of Michigan's American Studies/Women's Studies Professor María E. Cotera in establishing a digital hub for Latino projects, which will involve research on capacity building, protocols, logistics, etc. in providing a singular platform for projects currently being developed by scholars and small cultural organizations.
- "Latino Digital Humanities Caucus." Recovery has spearheaded the formation of a caucus of humanists, librarians, archivists and linguists interested in DH. Our goal is to collaborate on projects, meet at scholarly conferences, such as at MLA, AHA, AATSP, Latino Studies, LASA, etc. and give papers and presentations on our research. We plan to establish communications via a dedicated section of the Recovery web page, to share knowledge and perspectives, as well as upcoming opportunities for funding and collaboration. One of the results of this initiative has been the creation of #usLdh as an effort to create a community of digital humanist in Latino Studies as well as a means to tag DH projects in this area of studies.
- Hashtags #usLdh and #southwesterndh. Through the use of #usLdh and #southwesterndh, the digital humanities program has established a significant presence and, using social media, Twitter, Facebook and Instagram; it has identified a network of allies across the US and abroad who are working on US Latina/o and US southwestern projects digital humanities projects. All of these projects are being documented in order to keep a record of their existence.

The goal of this program for digital humanitites is to build a bridge between the past and the present that will allow us to think of a future where US Latinas/os can enjoy the privilege of living as full subjects in and outside the country. A future where their history (official or not) will be reflected, studied and included in their communities, institutions and official records. We hope that our DH center (#usLdh), Recovery and Arte Público Press continue making use of all the tools available to help US Latinas/os/xs occupy spaces from which they can speak and act with the certainty that their heritage, history, language, ethnic identity take center stage within all hegemonic discourses.

RECOVERY BOARD OF DIRECTORS: REFLECTING AND RETHINKING AMERICA'S LITERARY HERITAGE

Origins

Abriendo Brecha: The Rockefeller Foundation and the Origin of the Recovery Program

TOMÁS YBARRA-FRAUSTO
Independent Scholar

During the turbulent upheavals of the 1970s and 80s American society was being transformed by national and institutional grass-roots movements for social justice and cultural equity. I was a young Assistant Professor of Chicano, Mexican and Latin American Literatures in the Department of Spanish and Portuguese at Stanford University. When I was awarded tenure, I was destined for a long-standing academic career in an elite and renowned university.

As luck would have it, soon after I received tenure at Stanford, I was summoned by the Rockefeller Foundation to be interviewed for a position in its division of the Arts and Humanities. The lure and mythic dimensions of Manhattan, a crossroads of world cultures, was very tempting, and I felt that working in the foundation would enhance and expand my intellectual horizons, allowing me to be involved with cutting-edge humanities scholars and their projects throughout the United States and abroad.

My vetting process included interviews with Peter Goldmark, the foundation president at the time, also conversations with Director of the Arts and Humanities Division Alberta Arthurs and other senior officers. I was duly impressed by the cordial reception and intellectually stimulating discussion with everyone I met and felt that the ambiance at the foundation was that of a learning community where knowledge was at the service of the Rockefeller's lofty motto: "For the well-being of human kind throughout the world."

I flew back to Stanford feeling comfortable that I could fit in with the objectives and scholarly goals of an institution invested in helping to solve major world problems by funding scholars and their projects at the cutting edge of their disciplines.

After a short interval, I received a letter inviting me to come East and join the Arts and Humanities Division as an Associate Director. I finished the academic year at Stanford and started a new career path in philanthropy.

I joined the Rockefeller Foundation in the fall of 1989, a turbulent time when the traditional humanities were experiencing a paradigm shift focused on the study of difference, defined by the emerging fields of ethnic studies, women's studies and gay and lesbian studies. Discreet boundaries and separation of fields were becoming more flexible and porous with a thrust towards inter- connections between disciplines, what Clifford Geertz called, "the blurring of genres," that promoted interdisciplinary formulations and new ways of working across traditional humanities and social sciences, including history, anthropology, literature and sociology. This turn towards the interdisciplinary joined new ways of working with creative and fresh intersections between fields of study. These two modalities, the study of difference and the "blurring of genres," defined the intellectual frameworks for different funding streams to expand pioneering scholarship in the humanities.

In site visits to promising centers of innovation, Lynn Swaja and I visited Nicolás Kanellos and learned about his project to collect and publish Hispanic literary works by Latino authors across a long historical continuum from the period of Spanish exploration and colonization up to the twentieth century.

Lynn Swaja and I were the two Rockefeller Arts and Humanities officers that oversaw due diligence and made a case for the Recovery Program as intellectually relevant in relation to the funding priorities of the Foundation. Both of us agreed that the Recovery Program was a significant, interdisciplinary multi-faceted program that pushed the boundaries of literary history by uniting the study of difference and the "blurring of genres," from such diverse humanities fields as linguistics, folklore, anthropology and history. The transnational hemispheric framework was also appealing since we were beginning to fund projects in Latin America and especially in Mexico, where the Rockefeller Foundation had a presence dating back to the 1950s, when it had promoted projects in the agricultural and cultural spheres. We also recognized that the Latino Civil Rights Movement of the 1970s and 80s had created a Cultural Reclamation Project to collect and restore tangible and intangible Latino heritage in all the arts from a base in community cultural centers throughout the country. The Recovery Program was a sophisticated and complex extension of this continuing process of maintaining a literary legacy.

Prior to inviting a proposal for the Recovery Program at the University of Houston, the foundation made a grant allowing Nicolás to gather a group of scholars from throughout the country who were researching and publishing academic papers on the different genres of Latino literature within a socio-historical context. The meeting was held at Research Triangle Park in Raleigh-Durham, North Carolina in 1991.[1] This convocation held before submission of a formal proposal was very useful for honing the scope, infrastructure, funding needs and content of the planned proposal. After the founding conference, Nicolás was invited to submit a project proposal.

On July 15, 1991, Nicolás Kanellos, head of Arts Público Press, submitted a proposal entitled "Recovering the Hispanic Literary Heritage of The United States" to the Arts and Humanities Division of the Rockefeller Foundation. The Proposal requested seed money totaling $270,000 for developing the first year of the project. The initial request was "to establish administrative and fundraising structures, plus putting in place various initiatives of high priority in three aspects of the project: recovery, research and publications." These three core objectives of the project would insert Latino literature as a constituent component of American literature and push forward the notion of a multicultural polyglot United States.

While other foundations supported the Recovery Program in its evolution, it was the Rockefeller Foundation that seeded and nourished it from 1991 to 2000 and made grants totaling $3,820,000 to sustain it.

Early in the project, the Foundation sponsored a meeting inviting several philanthropic foundations and agencies, such as the Ford Foundation, The Andrew W. Mellon Foundation and representatives from the National Endowment for the Humanities, the National Historic Publication and Records Commission and others to help continue the valuable, intellectual, cultural and social dimensions of the Recovery Program.

In 2002, Oxford University Press published *Herencia: The Anthology of Hispanic Literature in the United States*, the first historical compendium of Latino Literature from Spanish exploration to contemporary times, including examples of native literature, the literature of immigration and exile and multiple literary expressions from diverse regional Latino groups in the United States. One core theme of the "Overview" was a focus on resistance and affirmation within a long historical continuum and a transnational context. The essays gathered in the anthology were the result of years of research by scholars who recovered literary texts in multiple genres from private and public academic archives, personal collections, and newspapers and periodicals found in national and international repositories. The *Herencia* anthology was critically acclaimed, and the foundation invited Nicolás to come to New York and present the story of his quest to enhance American literature by expanding its historical, linguistic and cultural contours. Nicolás did a PowerPoint presentation to the entire Rockefeller Board. His training in Latino theatre served him well as he recounted the powerful narrative of the Recover Program and its scholarly accomplishments. Each board member was presented with a copy of *Herencia* with kudos allaround. The Kanellos presentation convinced the Rockefeller board that it had funded a singular and transformative project.

Looking back, I venture to say that among the thousands of humanities projects funded during my tenure at the Rockefeller Foundation from 1989 to 2005, the Recovery Program remains as a capstone endeavor. It has advanced research, teaching and publication of Latino literature. Simultaneously, it has nurtured many younger scholars and expanded diverse genres of oral and print culture.

Reclaiming the literary heritage of Latinos in the United States continues to be a formidable task. The stellar achievements of the Recovery Program, including its conferences, publications and research grants continue to create new knowledge about the literary and cultural achievements of US Latinos, now the largest ethnic group in the country. The recovered texts tell an alternative story of who we are, and our continual contributions to the intellectual commons of the nation. The compendium of books published by Arte Público Press is an enduring legacy that expands the quest to re-imagine the United States as a more diverse, equitable and compassionate society.[2]

Endnotes

[1]Participating in the National Humanities Center conference in Raleigh Durham N. Carolina in 1991 were: Edna Acosta-Belén, Antonia Castañeda, Rodolfo Cortina, José Fernández, Juan Flores, Erlinda González Berry, Ramón Gutiérrez, Laura Gutiérrez-Witt, Virginia Sánchez Korrol, Luis Leal, Clara Lomas, Genaro Padilla, Raymond Paredes, Nélida Pérez, Gerald Poyo, María Herrera Sobek and Roberto Trujillo.

[2]Thanks to Nicolás Kanellos for his reminiscences of the role that the Rockefeller Foundation and the officers in the Arts and Humanities Division played in the genesis of the Recovery Program.

Reminiscences

José B. Fernández

University of Central Florida

In November 1990, the most important event regarding the Hispanic Literary heritage of the United States took place at the National Humanities Center in Research Triangle Park, North Carolina, when distinguished Hispanic scholar Nicolás Kanellos brought together twenty noted scholars in the field to join in the project "Recovering the US Hispanic Literary Heritage."

At this conference, "Nick"—as he is known by us—informed the members of this "expeditionary" group, of the need to locate, rescue from perishing, evaluate, disseminate and publish collections of primary literary sources written by Hispanics in the geographic area that is now the United States from the colonial period to 1960.

In addressing us, he stated: "This ten-year project financed by the Rockefeller Foundation is the largest of its kind undertaken in the history of scholarly efforts to study the Hispanic culture of the United States. Its importance lies in filling the gap that exists in American literature: the Hispanic contribution."

Additionally, he reminded us that the broad scope of the project was to include recovery of all conventional literary genres as well as such forms as letters, diaries, oral lore and popular culture of Hispanics in the United States throughout the centuries.

At the two-day conference, the *expedicionarios* presented papers and discussed issues such as canonization, social class, gender and identity. After deliberations, the following six-point program was selected: the creation of an on-line data base, the building of a periodical literature recovery project, the establishment of an archival consortium, the launching of a grant-in-aid component, the establishment of a publishing consortium and the building of a communication and conference network.

After I left the conference, I must confess that I had my doubts about the project's scope. Its sheer magnitude appeared to be overwhelming. However, after reflecting for a while, I said to myself: "It's not impossible. We have a great leader in Nick, we have the backing of the Rockefeller Foundation, we have a unique group of scholars who are committed to the cause, and whatever we propose to do, we will accomplish it. We will rescue our literature, a rich literature that has been neglected, marginalized and outright excluded. *Así que pa'lante y pa'lante.*"

Within a year after the launching of the project other scholars from the United States, Mexico, Spain and Puerto Rico joined. These colleagues brought with them their energy, expertise, dedication, commitment and, above all, their sense of mission.

Initially, my work on the project was that of co-chairing the Grants-in-Aid Committee with Antonia Castañeda, which procured and distributed the necessary funds to support the work of established scholars and those starting their academic careers in searching for, collecting, indexing, editing and publishing materials. These *veteranos* and *pinos nuevos* turned out some of the finest works in the project.

One of my finest and fondest memories of participating on the project was that of being one of the co-editors of *Herencia: An Anthology of Hispanic Literature in the United States* published by Oxford University Press in 2002. For this endeavor, a team of five co-editors, guided by General Editor Nicolás Kanellos was assembled. It was composed of two Puerto Ricans, Kanellos and Agnes Lugo Ortiz; two Chicanos, Charles "Chuck" Tatum and Erlinda González Berry; and two Cuban-Americans, Kenya Dworkin y Méndez and myself.

Before beginning to access hundreds of texts, study and select them for inclusion, "Chuck" Tatum's article, previously published in the first volume of Recovering the US Hispanic Literary Heritage came to our minds, in which he stated:

> Those of us involved in recovering the literary heritage of US Hispanic literature would do well to remind ourselves that, despite our good will and best intentions, we, too, are capable of letting biases and baggage creep into our noble project. . . . We should take extreme care not to superimpose upon literature preconceived ideas of either what elements constitute valid literary forms or of how to arrange such forms into seemingly neat but useless categories. (Tatum 207)

We also reminded ourselves of the words of one of the *expedicionarios*, Francisco Lomelí, when he wrote "Reconstructive literary history can be understood as a method by which to fill in gaps; reformulate nuances, and recharacterize literary perspectives from the point of view of the people who created literature" (Lomelí 231).

From the start, we reminded ourselves that we were merely compilers, not literary pontiffs. We also checked our egos at the door and were guided by consensus rather than by our own opinions and biases.

In selecting the material, we obviously wanted to include the works of poets, novelists, short story writers, essayists and playwrights. We also wanted to include the works of journalists, political leaders, labor figures and common folk with their lore and testimony. Why did we decide to be so inclusive? Because we believed, as Nick stated in the anthology's introduction, that

> The literature of a people transcends not only class and educational boundaries, but also the limits of the literary. Indeed, a people's culture and identity are generated and expressed at every level of society in a wide spectrum of genres and for various audiences, including the self in society. (Kanellos 32)

We also wanted our anthology to incorporate "the voices of the conqueror and the conquered, the revolutionary and the reactionary, the native and the uprooted or landless" (Kanellos 1). In other words, we wanted our anthology to be the voice of the people, and for the people.

In order to make the material accessible to English readers, we translated a large portion of it. However, we also compiled another anthology, *En otra voz*, solely in Spanish, published by Arte Público Press for Spanish readers in 2002. Both anthologies represented the first attempt at interpreting and understanding the rich literary heritage of Hispanics in the United States.

Those of us involved in the two anthologies received little remuneration. Ours was a labor of dedication and love, and we are very grateful to Lynn Szwaja and our beloved Don Tomás Ybarra-Frausto of the Rockefeller Foundation. They believed in us, and we believed in them.

As to the Recovery Project, it is no longer a project; it is a reality and a fact of life. What started as a ten-year project is now in its more than a quarter century of existence. Our work, however, continues, for as Nick has pointed out:

> Historically, the diverse ethnic groups that we conveniently lump together as "Hispanics" or "Latinos" created a literature in North America even before the founding of the United States. The sheer volume of their writings over 400 years is so overwhelming that it would

take thousands of scholars researching for many years to fully recover, analyze and make accessible all that is worthy of study and memorializing. (Kanellos 1)

Nevertheless, we are confident that other generations will follow the footsteps of the *expedicionarios* and will continue to preserve and make accessible our literary heritage in the United States. Our heritage is not only for Hispanics, but for all of humanity.

Works Cited

Kanellos, Nicolás. "An Overview of Hispanic Literature of the United States." *Herencia: The Anthology of Hispanic Literature of the United States.* Eds. Nicolás Kanellos et al. Oxford: Oxford University Press, 2001

Lomelí, Francisco A. "Po(l)etics of Reconstructing and/or Appropriating a Literary Past: The Regional Case Model." *Recovering the U.S. Hispanic Literary Heritage.* Eds. Ramón A. Gutiérrez and Genaro Padilla. Vol. 1. Houston: Arte Público Press, 1993. 221-239.

Tatum, Charles. "Some Considerations on Genres and Chronology for Nineteenth-Century Hispanic Literature." *Recovering the U.S. Hispanic Literary Heritage.* Eds. Ramón A. Gutiérrez and Genaro Padilla. Vol. 1. Houston: Arte Público Press, 1993. 199-208.

Comments on the Recovery Program

ROSAURA SÁNCHEZ

University of California, San Diego

On the 25th anniversary of the Recovery Program, Arte Público Press is to be congratulated for its role in enriching the fields of Latino/a-Chicano/a Studies and American Studies by making available a number of Latino/a texts previously unknown, neglected, forgotten, published or unpublished, all texts that form a crucial part of our cultural history. While much has been made about the central role of oral tradition among particular ethnic groups, the existence of a written tradition has often been ignored, dismissed or outright denied. The Recovery Program is corrective of this erasure and has made abundantly clear to all that our history includes fiction, poetry, historiography and critical essays dating back to the nineteenth century, and beyond, as well.

Prior to the publications by the Recovery Program, it was difficult to find earlier publications by Chicanos/as in the Southwest, an area of special importance to me. Arno Press under the editorship of Carlos E. Cortés published a volume on the *New Mexican Hispano* in 1974 that included the work of Cleofas M. Jaramillo and Fabiola Cabeza de Baca. Two years later (1976), the Cortés anthology *Mexican California* appeared and included texts by José Bandini. The University of New Mexico Press did publish some works by Miguel Antonio Otero, but not until the more recent past has there been an effort of that university press to publish a good number of *testimonios*/memoires and volumes of prose and poetry by *nuevomexicanos*. In his "Visual History of Chicano/a Literature," Martín-Rodríguez provides images of book covers dating back to 1939 (see: faculty.ucmerced.edu/mmartin-rodriguez/index_files/OOVH.htm) as well as the book cover of Gaspar Pérez de Villagrá's *La Nueva Mexico* from 1610. The latter was published in translation in Los Angeles by The Quivera Society in 1933. A number of Martín-Rodríguez's cover images attest to publications by Chicanos/as before the 1990s, but before the Recovery Program, there was no concerted or sustained effort by a university press to recover texts published before the 1970s. Quinto Sol did publish a number of works by Chicanos/as including Tomás Rivera, Rolando Hinojosa, Rudolfo Anaya, Sergio Elizondo and Sabine R. Ulibarrí, but these were post-1970s works, although some were written at an earlier time. The finding and subsequent publication of Américo Paredes' novel *George Washington Gómez* was a landmark recuperation for Arte Público Press, even if not part of the Recovery Program.

Beatrice Pita and I were of course very happy to participate in the recovery of María Amparo Ruiz de Burton's two nineteenth century novels (*Who Would Have Thought It?* and *The Squatter and the Don*), fiction that has generated a good deal of critical analysis and debate and that has led to our subsequent research into her life and letters that appeared in the Recovery Program's *Conflicts of Interest: The Letters of María Amparo Ruiz de Burton.* The more recent publication of a good number of other late nineteenth- or early twentieth-century texts will no doubt also continue to generate critical assessments and reassessments within the fields of Chicano/a- Latino/a history and literature. The Recovery Program has fomented, nurtured and made possible this critical dialogue, enabling a good many young faculty members to stake out flourishing academic careers based on their critical scholarship dealing with the authors republished by the Recovery Program.

The Recovery Program has thus not only made lost or forgotten published texts available but also been crucial in the marked renewed interest in archival research as scholars have taken to the dusty and often forgotten archives to seek information and mine these archives for other writings by nineteenth- or twentieth-century writers; in the process a number of unpublished texts and/or historical or personal accounts have been unearthed. The Recovery Program has not only generated healthy polemics, critical analyses and vibrant debate in the field but also served to create a Latino/a-Chicano/a canon of sorts.

En resumidas cuentas: the Recovery Program has not only enriched the field of Chicano/a-Latino/a literary and cultural studies by making known and available a number of lost or forgotten texts, but it has also served as a catalyst for scholarship. In making a place or space for creative and critical works, it has also served as a crucible for debate, enabling intellectual exchange. It has most importantly served as a corrective for the literary/cultural vacuum that existed prior to its establishment. Our heartfelt thanks to Nicolás Kanellos and the Recovery Program team for initiating and sustaining this most important project.

Recovering the US Hispanic Literary Heritage—A Personal Reflection

VIRGINIA SÁNCHEZ-KORROL[1]

Add my voice to the chorus singing the praises of Recovery. Dr. Nicolás Kanellos and the entire team of the Recovering the US Hispanic Literary Heritage (Recovery) deserve countless kudos for the project's excellent achievements over the past twenty-five years.

Today, the Recovery Program counts on the participation of a broad base of scholars and institutions. A new generation of academics has come of age since its founding schooled in the digital advances of their generation and diverse cultural interactions. Many of them have grown up in majority Latino communities that have taken great strides to honor and celebrate heritage.

Twenty-five years ago, we faced a different reality. I remember a time when neither the technology nor the documentation about Latina/o history in the United States existed. Before Recovering the US Hispanic Literary Heritage opened its doors, a small group of Latina/o academics was locked in the Culture Wars. Whose America and whose history was at the core of the intellectual debates? The very definition of the American experience, the literary canon, was at stake. A dearth of texts and materials on the US Latino/Hispanic experience didn't help the situation, and fewer still were the professors who could guide our work in the ideological directions we wanted to go. But a commitment to erase the invisibility of our communities led the first sizable generation of Latina/o PhDs to research and write our history.

During the pre-Recovery period, as I recall, our research projects hovered in sluggish cyberspace. The absence of texts and primary sources meant educators, particularly the earliest bilingual teachers, had to create their own materials if they wanted to infuse classroom instruction with the very experience their stu-

31

dents brought to class. Many of us lacked the time and mimeograph equipment to do so. Internet access was nowhere near what it is today. Its use on many college campuses was relegated to retrieving electronic mail.

Against national trends and the gatekeepers of the academy, Latino/a activists took to the streets. Raising loud, angry voices, they clamored for historical validation. In barrios across the country, our young people had searched without success for their place in the national narrative. Robbed of a historical record, they were also denied knowledge of the role their ancestors played in the making of the United States. Any semblance of a Latino legacy was obscured, deemed inaccessible and inconsequential.

These lessons from the past are well known. Still, while we all know the story, it is worth remembering in light of Recovery's mission and productivity. Led by Drs. Nicolás Kanellos and Tomás Ybarra-Frausto, the Recovering the US Hispanic Literary Heritage Program sought to find or develop materials to document the US Latino/Hispanic experience utilizing a multi-layered agenda. A cadre of committed scholars, librarians and archivists joined Recovery, bringing their expertise and the methods to find obscure secondary or primary sources. Their efforts, and those of the project's institutional partners, kindled the assault on the cultural boundaries of the American experience.

I was then the newly elected chairperson of the Department of Puerto Rican Studies at Brooklyn College. I sat on a contentious curriculum framework commission for the New York State Department of Education and was embroiled in the vanguard of forming the Puerto Rican Studies Association.

Still, the scope of the Recovery Program carried an aura of excitement I hadn't expected and, frankly, could not resist. We, pioneers in Latina/o or Puerto Rican Studies, had long championed curricula that centered our lost history and culture. I was inspired by the insightful analysis of the extant literature and recommendations for future research outlined in what would be the first Recovery volume. Now, Recovery was proposing to uncover *thousands* of written sources, news-papers, novels, poetry, interviews and memoirs, from the earliest chronicles of exploration to the creative explosion of artistic expression embedded in the Civil Rights era communities. Such results, I thought, would be akin to finding buried treasure—the intellectual justification for our inclusion in the academy and the tools for complicating the "canon." Needless to say, when Dr. Kanellos called, I came to Houston.

Finding hidden sources, indexing, digitizing, translating, presenting papers on the new material and ultimately producing an array of bilingual texts brought together a multi-disciplinary community of scholars and learners. The scope of my own scholarship broadened as I had the opportunity to co-edit a collection of Jesús Colón's essays with Dr. Edna Acosta-Belén,[2] I became co-editor with

Dr. María Herrera Sobek of the third volume of conference research essays.[3] My historical novel, *Feminist and Abolitionist: The Story of Emilia Casanova,* based on primary sources, appeared in 2012 under the banner of the Recovery Program.[4] The number of books for and about women exceeded my expectations, and several formed basic texts in my courses. Moreover, the women writers of recovered literary texts were included in *Latinas in the United States,* the three-volume encyclopedia I co-edited with Dr. Vicki Ruiz.[5]

Recovery provided the venue to exchange ideas and to work together beyond the confines of the project. Indeed, we seemed to bring Recovery everywhere, to our students, colleagues, our professional organizations and onto the national boards on which we served. We learned from one another and, in my perspective, understood that together we were at the forefront of radically shifting the nation's narrative.

Thank you, Recovery, for shaping the contours of an inclusive American identity and being at the forefront of a movement to right the historical record. Thank you for unprecedented inroads in transforming the dominant narrative rendering a more complete, multi-faceted literary history that fills in the missing pieces. The undisputable recovered written record, and the vast array of primary sources uncovered over twenty-five years, not only lay to rest long held misconceptions about the continental Hispanic experience and its transnational connections, but also tell us who we are as a nation. For present and future generations of American Latinos, this is a remarkably empowering legacy.

Endnotes

[1]Dr. Virginia Sánchez Korrol is Professor Emerita in the Department of Puerto Rican and Latino Studies at Brooklyn College, City University of New York.

[2]Colón, Jesús. *The Way It Was and Other Writings.* Editors and Introduction, Edna Acosta Belén and Virginia Sánchez Korrol. Arte Público Press. University of Houston. Houston, Texas, 1993.

[3]*Recovering the U.S. Hispanic Literary Heritage, Volume III.* Editors and Introduction, María Herrera-Sobek and Virginia Sánchez-Korrol. Arte Público Press. University of Houston. Houston, Texas, 2000.

[4]Sánchez-Korrol, Virginia. *Feminist and Abolitionist: The Story of Emilia Casanova.* Arte Público Press. University of Houston. Houston, Texas, 2012.

[5]Vicki L. Ruiz and Virginia Sánchez Korrol, editors. *Latinas in the United States: A Historical Encyclopedia.* University of Indiana Press, Bloomington, Indiana, 2006.

Identities—Hispanic, Latina/o/x, Ladino

Archives and Identity: Recovery's Impact on Latino Identity Formation

RAÚL A. RAMOS

University of Houston

As a historian of the nineteenth-century US-Mexico borderlands and the Mexican-American people, the Recovery Program has provided me a treasure trove of primary sources to write, or better yet, rewrite, the history of the border. When the Recovery Board set out to gather, catalog and index the entirety of Spanish-language writing printed before 1960, the effort was initiated by literary scholars with an historical approach. While historians served on the board and edited early volumes of the conference proceedings, the focus on the printed word dominated the project's conferences and fueled the expansion of American and Latin American literatures. Since literature departments use a sense of canon to drive undergraduate teaching, this research in Spanish-language literature became critical to American literature. While the field of American history does not have a similar canon, it does have field survey textbooks and extensive primary source collections that have equally overlooked Spanish-language sources. This has rendered Spanish-speaking people, to use an outdated term, narratively invisible and likewise has distorted American history.

The commemoration of the 25th anniversary of the Recovery Program allows self-reflection and thoughtfulness to the subject of archiving and collecting, especially to how they can impact history, memory and identity. Thinking about the Recovery Program as an example of both historical preservation and historical construction led me to think about the future of the project by first looking at its past. In doing so, I answer the question by turning to the past in order to intentionally engage the future.

The last 25 years of the Recovery Program has opened new ways of conceiving of Latino identity for me. It stands to reason that recovering the literature of a people would provide evidence of and a connection to a past articulation of that identity. As a history professor at a public institution, I'm fully aware of the interests of the State in presenting official history and an official literature. Nation-states use historical narratives and literary canons to create a national culture and a sense of nationhood. Students in Texas public schools and public higher education are required to take American history and Texas history courses. When the state legislature mandated these requirements in the 1955, the goal was to create a bond among students to encourage civic belonging and participation.[1] Debates in the State Board of Education over the standards for these classes have become increasingly political.[2]

Just as they can for dominant society, these historical narratives and bodies of literary work also define and build ethnic identity. The inverse is true as well in that absences in history and literature function to erase and devalue ethnic sub-groups within dominant society. It is that silence that the Recovery Program confronted by undertaking the radical goal of compiling and making available a wide range of the literary production for a group of people. This is not to say that this was not already underway in other forms prior to 1990. Within my field of Chicano/a Studies, scholars and writers had been crafting narratives of resistance and accommodation to situate Latinos/as in an American context.[3] Like the political movement that accompanied these developments, their narratives were rooted in local and regional constructions of identity and at times struggled to imagine a larger ethnic group.

In another sense, though, the cultural production of Latin American nation-states temporarily stand in as an extension of "people-hood projects" for Latinos/as. The works of José Martí and José Vasconcelos blur the line of where and how these constructions would take place. Latino/a identity is rooted in the national identity constructions of these nations. Yet the transnational movement of these cultural projects ran into limitations on the American side. Whether they were silenced by dominant American culture, or denigrated by Latin American intellectuals, as was the case with Octavio Paz, they failed to reflect the range of experiences specific to Latinos/as. Recovered works provide evidence of generations struggling with this tension, finding space to create a new narrative.

This is where the Recovery Program steps in to build an institutional vehicle for developing the cultural apparatus for Latino/a identity. While Latin American national identities continue to build their own narratives, the literal and figurative imperial narrative of the United States ruptures any connections for Latino/a identity, leaving an empty space. Archives fill that space in multiple ways. In something of a dual move, the work of the Recovery Program both uncovered evidence of cultural production by Latinos/as, narrating their own place and developing a language for that experience, while accomplishing a similar goal in the present with the archive itself. They present the tools to make a Latino/a narrative. More importantly, knowing about the presence of a larger whole, even when using a small selection, gives a historical heft and weight to memory that feeds into identity. Raúl Coronado has referred to the narrative "fullness" of a complete narrative available in Mexico. He writes of his, " . . . search for the past, this desire to string events into a historical narrative that has closure and offers analysis or a 'moralizing' conclusion. . . . "[4] In a sense, being Latino/a in the United States has meant depravation from that complete history as the price of American expansion.

Historians working with Spanish-language documents and in archives that span our current national borders necessarily reframe American history. The documents themselves drive a different narrative trajectory of the region and people. Archives provide remnants and artifacts to make claims to belonging in the past. Some of the documents exist as a by-product of imperial expansion, as is the case with Spanish land titles. After Texas secession from Mexico in 1836, Anglo Americans needed to preserve their existing land titles. To this day, the General Land Office in Austin holds one of the best preserved archives of the Spanish era. Yet, the scars of imperial wars extend to the absence of archives. A Mexican historian notes ambivalence towards the loss of Texas that hinders collection of documents from that period. Furthermore, the existing neocolonial relationship between American academic institutions and Latin American universities resulted in an asymmetrical regime of preservation that has favored English-language, American period holdings. Those holdings drive the history that can possibly be written.

By centering Spanish-language archives, the Recovery Program drives the production of new historical narratives. Its focus on the location of the author and printer of the document throw into question the dominant narrative supporting the nation. This move preceded the recent moves to decenter American history through transnational methods. The recovery of Spanish-language archives ironically provided the power of a transnational narrative within the nation. Collecting the production of these authors revealed distinct conduits of national thought and influence. As Gabriela Ventura and Clara Lomas wrote in the introduction to volume eight of the Recovery conference proceedings,

> The conflation of both topics called for a revision and analysis of how the "contact zones" that were initiated and dominated by European travelers, merchants and conquistadors produced a multiplicity of diverse cultural clashes and/or syntheses. This is evident in many print-

ed works, which exist precisely because many Latino authors had the newspaper as a venue to print their works and share them with the newspaper's readership. These early publications were the means through which many Latino authors were able to preserve views and to, above all, contest and respond to a hegemony that was imposing and limiting. The contact zones that were generated via the newspaper formulated a decolonized "third space" that is now evident to U.S. Latino scholars.[5]

The preservation and access to these written works brought whole generations back to life, as it were. Historians could now look beyond an entry in a census record, marriage certificate or police report to conjure the social and emotional Latina/o world. Writing was and continues to be an act of creation, and the archive connected creations from the past with creators in the present.

Out of this archive, then, a new articulation of a Latino identity and past has come to life. Whether through novels, poetry, memoir or reporting, the Recovery Program harnessed these works to imagine a people. More often than not, though, that articulation has been more heterogeneous, certainly, than the one-dimensional portrayals of Latinos/as. As a historian, I look for these communities in places that extend beyond fictional accounts.

Along with language, the Recovery Program also prioritized geography by defining the current borders of the United States for inclusion in the archive. While the overarching goal might have been to identify the historical presence of American *Hispanoparlantes*, it has the ability to affect American history broadly. The need to recover Spanish-language texts reveals the historical binding of the English language with American nationalism. The meaning of that link between language and nation takes on greater meaning with American imperial expansion into the Mexican nation and across the Caribbean. Agnes Lugo-Ortiz explored these links in her article, "La antología y el archivo: Reflexiones en torno a *Herencia, En otra voz* y los límites de un saber" from the fifth Recovery volume. She began,

En la Hispanoamérica del sur del Río Bravo o Río Grande (según se lo vea), un paradigma duro de nación, que establece una sinonimia entre territorio, identidad y lengua, así como los paradigmas del discurso latinoamericanista tradicional —que entre otras cosas proyecta estas categorías a escala continental— no han admitido dentro de su campo de saber otro tipo de territorialidades culturales, ni permitido pensar otras zonas de contacto pertinentes a la comprensión de las dinámicas culturales de las Américas hispanas. Y sin embargo, el mundo hispánico también está en otra parte; y al presente siente, piensa, vive y escribe en inglés, o en Spanglish, o en un español que ya no sólo se mueve a las cadencias del quechua (como en los Andes) o del italiano (como en ciertas regiones del Cono Sur), o de las lenguas africanas (como en el Caribe), sino también al ritmo de la babel que se habla en New York, y que puede tener el color de los desiertos de Arizona. El mestizaje cultural de la América hispánica en el siglo XX y en las primicias del XXI tiene también como crisol el encuentro con los complejos conglomerados culturales (tanto hegemónicos como marginales) de los Estados Unidos. Y allí también se ha articulado la carencia del archivo, o el archivo como carencia. Los mestizos hispanos, tanto al sur como al norte del Río Bravo, han compartido los avatares de una experiencia colonial y subalterna y han participado desigualmente en los aparatos e instituciones propias del saber moderno.[6]

The use of "cultural territoriality" by Lugo-Ortiz here drives home the obstacles historians of Latinos/as face confronting the imposition of American national narratives over Latin American ones. The archival absences appear as artifacts of that colonial legacy. The remains of what can be collected then appear as "colonial avatars," or testaments to imperialism and the resulting structural and institutional inequality that entails.

The archival power of the Recovery Program over the previous quarter century begs the question of how it can and will evolve. Keeping in mind what Recovery has achieved in the sense of defining peoplehood, then similar foresight should be anticipated when expanding the scope of the project. That project turns initially to expand which people are covered under peoplehood. The historian in me would answer by saying the documents would tell us the audience. Reading publics create and define their community. The steps the Recovery Program takes moving forward can reflect new formations of identity, beyond the nation-state or region, along with new ways of thinking. Identity formations engage the social and political realms of their times, including queer identities, multiple localities and conflicting citizenships, and take distinct forms depending on available discourses.

The impact of Recovery then extends beyond discovering articulations of Latino/a identity at various points in time. It challenges entrenched lines of authority and analysis in scholarship. It requires a new imagination of the past that makes room for the politics of the present. The need to have the archive reflect these diverse Latinx identities has increased political significance. Social and political demands of the present call for a "full" accounting of the past, one that reflects fragmented, contentious and transnational identities across time.

Endnotes

[1]Texas Education Code 51.302 (first adopted by the Texas Legislature in 1955). http://www.statutes. legis.state.tx.us/Docs/ED/htm/ED.51.htm#51.302. The code also includes authorization for an "American Way" course for foreign-born students to gain, "familiarity and understanding of United States government and civic life and their sources, development, and character." Texas Education Code 501.301 (d).

[2]Tanenhaus, Sam, "In Texas Curriculum Fight, Identity Politics Leans Right," *The New York Times,* March 20, 2010.

[3]Ramos, Raúl A., "Chicano/a Challenges to Nineteenth-Century History," *Pacific Historical Review* 82:4 (November 2013): 566-580.

[4]Raúl Coronado, "Communing with the Past," *PMLA* 131.3 (May 2016): 765-773.

[5]Ventura, Gabriela Baeza and Clara Lomas (Editors). *Recovering the US Hispanic Literary Heritage,* vol. 8. Houston, TX: Arte Público Press, 2011. p vii.

[6]Méndez, Kenya Dworkin (Editor); Lugo-Ortiz, Agnes (Editor). Recovering the U.S. Hispanic Literary Heritage, vol. 5. Houston, TX, USA: Arte Público Press, 2006. p 143.

Inscribing a Maligned People: A Journey with the Recovery Program

GERALD E. POYO

St. Mary's University

Around 1993 I received an invitation to join the Recovering the US Hispanic Literary Heritage Program. What was it, I asked? An organization dedicated to the identification, recovery, preservation and publication of US Hispanic literary production from their origin to 1960. At my first meeting and in subsequent years, I came into contact with a multidisciplinary world of literary critics, historians, linguists, archivists, librarians and more. For the first time I was among like- minded scholars not frightened with the idea of Hispanic history writ large, which did not surprise given my background in Latin America. Recovery challenged scholars to employ archives to the task of uncovering particular micro histories but also connecting them across nationality, race, class, gender and other categories of analysis to incarnate the idea of Hispanic or Latino. As my personal and professional relationships grew with Mexican Americans, Puerto Ricans, Dominicans and others in the United States, especially in the Recovery Program, the affinities and shared experiences became clearer.

An extraordinary thirty-year boom in Latino scholarship during 1970s to the 1990s laid the foundations for the Recovery Program. That research pointed to intricate textures and layers of the political, socioeconomic and cultural intersections among the various nationalities. The specific methodological challenge for historians, I thought, was to identify themes and processes in the histories of the various national groups that might provide frameworks for understanding diverse human experiences within a coherent whole. If shared themes were eventually to be identified, they would emerge from the comparative study of

43

local communities, which, of course, rested on the discrete histories of the various national experiences. Historians and spent little time thinking about Latino history at the conceptual level, but they did produce necessary narrative histories of Mexicans, Cubans and Puerto Ricans that helped others articulate the Latino idea. I felt certain that the specific histories, diversities and complexities of the various national groups could ultimately reveal universal experiences they shared distinct from European-Americans, African-Americans and Asian-Americans.

The emerging Latino scholarship in a variety of fields offered clues about shared experiences, and it was concretely highlighted in a landmark Arte Público Press publication, *Handbook of Hispanic Cultures*, published in 1994. These volumes and the overall scholarship of the era confirmed that Latin Americans in the United States had developed as ethnic communities within shared historical contexts. Life in the United States forced them to adopt a posture that was defensive and affirmative at the same time. Latinos in the United States shared a sense of exclusion caused by the racist assumptions of the dominant society, but they also shared experiences steeped in the practices of maintaining cultural heritage and adapting old and new ways in order to coexist and conform to the United States life and customs.

On the first point, racism, unflattering stereotypes and unfavorable labor market structures, and their related socioeconomic consequences and realities, created experiences of exclusion among Latinos. They faced the full reality of discrimination as they were incorporated into the United States in the first half of the nineteenth century, which institutionalized economic disadvantage. Hispanic communities in San Agustín and Pensacola disappeared for all practical purposes. The inhabitants either left Florida altogether or were simply absorbed. In Louisiana, Hispanic communities remained isolated but began a slow process of absorption by the dominant society. Further to the west, the more numerous Hispanic communities did not face cultural annihilation but were marginalized and subordinated to second-class citizenship.

The racialization of Mexicans in the early nineteenth century created a precedent-setting development eventually imposed on most Latinos. The derisive stereotypes and prejudicial attitudes held by the dominant society led to historically debilitating and isolating discriminatory practices that resulted in severe implications for daily life. In the 1920s, Texas' economic and segregationist regime maintained Mexican Americans at the bottom of the social system. Dynamics differed from region to region, but Mexicans from Texas to California found it very difficult to move out of the traditional laboring classes. Mexican American elites, of whiter skin tones usually, survived disassociating themselves from their traditional communities and accommodating to the Euro

American system. Puerto Ricans and Cubans found similar realities as they established communities and entered employment markets in the United States. Twentieth-century pioneering memoirs of Puerto Ricans like Bernardo Vega, Jesús Colón and Piri Thomas depicted the harsh conditions of the Puerto Rican barrios and the racism to which their people were subjected.

Cuban and Spanish workers entering Florida cigar labor markets in the late nineteenth and early twentieth centuries also confronted harsh attitudes that on more than one occasion led to deportations and even lynching. Even the later Dominican and other Latin American immigrants felt rejected and subjected to discrimination and second-class citizenship. Historically, Latinos may not have rallied together as a group against this reality, and sometimes even engaged in racism against each other, but they did share a sense of rejection from Anglo American society. Many Latinos recognized this long tradition of anti-Latino feelings based on language, culture and civilization, which provided an intangible bond and a measure of mutual understanding.

Turning to the second point, the story's affirmative side is even more important. Specific cultural traditions and practices played a part in bringing Latinos together. Identification with the Spanish language was in the first instance perhaps the most powerful affinity. Historically, Chicanos, Puerto Ricans and Cubans used language to defend culture and identity. The Spanish language played an important role in connecting me to other Latinos, especially since I don't have stereotypical Latino skin tone or features. "Where did you learn to speak Spanish like that?' I heard often. "You don't look Cuban," people said in amazement. "What does a Cuban look like?" I would often answer. The language gave me a way to overcome those initial stereotypes that for some people justified keeping me at a distance. Language created solidarity.

Recovery research revealed that this was not new. Latinos in New York during the final quarter of the nineteenth and first half of the twentieth centuries were inextricably wedded to the use of Spanish in daily communication. They read Spanish language newspapers, saw films from Mexico and Argentina, listened to Spanish radio, formed associations to promote Spanish, and danced and listened to Latin music. Cubans in Key West and Tampa and Mexicans in San Antonio and Los Angeles did the same. Language maintained connections to national cultures of origin and, in many cases, with each other.

Newspapers proliferated in Hispanic communities beginning very early on. From the earliest *El Misisipí* (New Orleans, 1808) and *El Habanero* (Philadelphia, 1828) to the myriad newspapers even to this day, including *La Opinión* (Los Angeles), *El Nuevo Herald* (Miami) and *El Diario-La Prensa* (New York), their presses preserved language and culture. My own experiences identifying and recovering Key West's *El Yara* newspaper was exhilarating. Owned and edited by my great-great grandfather for twenty years, this publication was the longest-lived Cuban newspaper published in the United States during the nineteenth century. Not having grown up in the United States, this newspaper gave me a sense of historical belonging in this country that I never imagined possible. All these newspapers reflected the basic identity of the communities they served, in the Southwest, Florida, Louisiana, New York and many other places, but they also revealed a more cosmopolitan vision, reflecting awareness of Spanish and Latin American origins and connections.

The sense of community promoted in the press was amplified in other cultural activities. As Nicolás Kanellos revealed, theater had been part of Hispanic communities since the colonial days, not only for the sake of entertainment, but to ensure the continuation of traditions familiar to them. Mexicans in San Antonio, Cubans in Tampa and Puerto Ricans in New York had distinct theatrical traditions, mostly rooted in Spanish tradition and language. Theater served a common function in the diverse communities and, since the style, content and genres of the Latino stage were almost completely dominated by the Spanish tradition, cross-group collaboration was frequent, and a sense of Hispanicity infused their aesthetics.

Literature was similar and highlighted in another landmark Recovery publication in 2002. *Herencia: The Anthology of Hispanic Literature of the United States* speaks to a shared literary traditions. A literature of exploration and colonization including chronicles, diaries and testimonials, administrative, civil, military and ecclesiastical records, as well as oral traditions, chronicle multifaceted life in colonial settlements, from the sixteenth to the early nineteenth centuries from Florida to California. A Hispanic native literature by Mexicans, Cubans, Puerto Ricans and many others included English, Spanish and bilingual texts with themes reflecting the experiences of Latin American descent people as citizens. An immigration literature frequently explored racism and ethnic or national identity, conflict, pride in culture of origin, and appealed to justice. It was about adapting and reaching out to the broader society from an existing cultural tradition. An exile literature spoke to forced departures, yearning for the homeland and seeking balance between new and old places.

This kind of research inspired my own inquiry to consider the history of Latino Catholics in a similar holistic way. My book *Presente! Latino Catholics from Colonial Times to the Present. A Documentary History* (with Timothy Matovina) documents the Judeo-Christian traditions that mixed with African and Indigenous religiosity in Latino history and culture. Popular religious practice are evident in narratives of Mexican-American, Puerto Rican and Cuban Catholic communities. Starting in the 1970s, Latino Catholics sharing experiences as immigrants and exiles also came together in national *encuentros* where they struggled for ethnic and civil rights. For my part, Recovery Program scholarship provided clues on how to embark on this broad overview of Latino Catholics.

The US Latino scholars of the 1980s and 1990s in the fields of history, politics, theology, philosophy and literature and arts, among many others, provided the scholarly foundation for perceiving the emergence of Latino community expressions and aesthetics that while developing in particular settings were in many ways related and connected by heritage and experience. These were Hispanic historical traditions that spoke to cultural affinities and linkages across the various Latin American national groups in the United States. During almost twenty-five years as an advisory board member and as an historian for even longer, I have seen the dialogue between the particular and the universal grow through the practical work of placing archives in conversations with larger themes deeply rooted in US Latino history. Recovery scholars have conceptualized and highlighted the idea of Latino history, but much more research is needed. Another generation of archival research into the specific histories of the various groups is well on its way and is necessary before a credible, well integrated, and universal vision of Latino history is possible. In this, a new generation of Recovery Program scholars is in the vanguard.

"Not Your Conventional Gringos: Recovering the Sephardic/Latino Matrix"

AVIVA BEN-UR[1]
University of Massachusetts Amherst

The album: *Amor*. The ballad: "Piel Canela." The year: 1964. The artists: Eydie Gormé and Trío Los Panchos. The delicate chords of the Requinto guitar ushered in this *bolero*, or slow-tempo Latino dance song, written by Puerto Rican singer and songwriter Bobby Capó. "Cinnamon Skin" became an instant hit and lifted Gormé's backup band, which had enjoyed widespread renown the previous decade as Mexico's most popular *bolero* artists, out of a professional slump.[2] In a mellifluous Spanish, Gormé set the dusky eyes and cinnamon-colored skin of a lover against the backdrop of a brilliant sky and shining sea:

Que se quede el infinito sin estrellas,
O que pierda el ancho mar su inmensidad,
Pero el negro de tus ojos que no muera,
Y el canela de tu piel se quede igual.

Let the infinite skies lose all of their starlight,
And the vast oceans their immensity,
But that gleam in your black eyes, may it never lose its luster,
And the cinnamon in your skin, may it never relinquish its glow.[3]

The flip side of the album opened with yet another classic, "Sabor a Mí," once described as the collection's "cornerstone tune."[3] Lore would have it that a copy of the LP could be found in every Chicano and Mexican household of the era.[4] But how was it that this "gringa" could sing so beautifully in Spanish, with such "soul and spirit?" Unless, of course, we consider that she was not really a "gringa" at all, at least not in the conventional sense of the word.[5]

While Gormé did not share the Mexican and Puerto Rican origins of her band-mates, Spanish fit her like a second skin. Born in New York in 1928 to a tailor from Sicily and homemaker from the Ottoman Empire, the songstress, born Esther (Etty) Gormezano, grew up speaking Ladino, the language developed by Jews in the Eastern Mediterranean after their expulsion from Spain in 1492 by King Fernando and Queen Isabel.[6] Ladino was a fusion language, based on early modern Castilian, but made uniquely Jewish with its admixture of Hebrew, Aramaic, Arabic, Turkish, Greek, and Italian. It was spoken by the roughly 100,000 Jewish immigrants from the former Ottoman Empire who settled in the United States between 1860 and 1924. They called themselves "Sefaradím" or, in English, "Sephardim," a word derived from *Sefarad*, the Hebrew word for "Spain." From 1492 until the rise of the Latin American independence movements of the nineteenth century, the presence of Jews and the practice of Judaism within Spain and its overseas empire were categorically outlawed.[7] While it succeeded in removing Jews from Spain, the expulsion decree failed to remove Spain from within the Jews.

As for many other Ottoman Jewish immigrants and their US-born children, Eydie Gormé's linguistic heritage facilitated her mastery of the Spanish spoken in New York and Latin America.[8] After graduating high school in 1946, Gormé worked as a Spanish interpreter in the Theatrical Supply Export company and in the United Nations. By the following decade, she was hosting her own Hispanophone radio program called "Cita Con Eydie" ("A Date with Eydie"), which aired on the Voice of America.[9] But music was her true calling. Her training started while still in high school, when she sang weekends in the band of Ken Greenglass, who eventually became her manager. By the 1950s, she had launched a solo recording career, which led to frequent bookings on both radio and television. Her prominence culminated in 1963 with the peppy "Blame it on the Bossa Nova," which sold over one million copies and won her a gold disc. Her Spanish rendition of the song, "Cúlpale la Bossa Nova," an ode to the latest Brazilian music and dance craze, became a sensation in Mexico and other Spanish-speaking countries. This tune, along with her partnership with Trío Los Panchos, forged in 1964, secured her international popularity. With this band, Gormé produced three consecutive albums of *boleros*, the last in 1966.[10] Her partnership with husband, singer-songwriter Steven Lawrence, transformed Gormé into a national celebrity who could now add acting to her list of accomplishments. And yet, it was her contribution to Latino music that secured Gormé's international fame. Her Spanish songs in Latin America consistently outsold her Anglophone recordings.[11]

How many listeners back then understood that Gormé, a Jew singing and speaking in fluent, flawless Spanish, was a bonafide daughter of the Iberian diaspora and hence, a cultural "insider"? Probably more than today. Musicologist George Torres, for example, places Gormé within the context of "American" singers who interpreted Latino songs, often badly, and comments that "Gorme's Spanish is good."[12] Music critic Ernesto Lechner refers to her as the "charmingly accented Eydie Gorme,"[13] while an Argentine obituary refers to her "light foreign accent."[14] Caribbean studies scholar Roberto Strongman offers this devastating analysis: Gormé "did not speak Spanish" and her performances of *boleros* constitute "a parody of authentic identities," an "impersonation of ethnicity," and a "masquerade" concealing "a very clever act."[15] Today, being a Hispanic Jew may appear incongruous and Jews the least likely agents of cultural bridge-building between the Hispano- and Anglophone worlds. No wonder that a historical survey of United States Hispanics from 1986 concluded, "Sephardim in no way seem to have communicated with other Spanish-speaking groups in this country."[15]

But Eydie Gormé was not unique among Ottoman-origin Jews in her ability to straddle both worlds. Her success as a crossover artist caught the attention of RCA Argentina, which in the 1960s enlisted Gormé's distant cousin Neil Sedaka to record a number of songs in Spanish. The result was the album "Nuestro Amigo Neil Sedaka Canta en Español," released in 1963. Although less fluent in Ladino and Spanish than his older cousin, Sedaka's Spanish repertoire long remained a part of his performance career, particularly in Latin America, where he occasionally toured over the years. To this day, Sedaka regards this linguistic heritage as an integral component of US national identity. "Everyone in America should speak Spanish," he recently commented.[16]

Gormé and Sedaka are in fact late manifestations of a camaraderie between Ladino- and Spanish-speakers in New York that dates back to the 1920s and '30s. The familiarity facilitated by shared language led to friendships, romantic liaisons and intellectual collaboration between the two groups in Manhattan and Harlem (and later in Brooklyn and the Bronx,) where most Ottoman Jews in the United States established themselves. During those two decades, the Ladino press, headquartered on the Lower East Side, periodically reported on both casual sexual encounters and intermarriage between Sephardim and the largely Catholic Puerto Rican population of East Harlem.[17] Newly arrived Sephardic Jews were startled to discover that their intimate conversations on the streets of the *barrio* were understood by eavesdropping Puerto Rican neighbors. In the 1930s, one woman from Spanish Harlem discovered that she could understand the Hebrew-scripted articles in New York's Ladino weekly *La Vara*, when her Ottoman Jewish friend read them aloud to her. At Columbia University during the same decades, cultural and intellectual collaboration between Spanish- and Ladino-speakers flourished. In the late 1920s, Spanish exile Federico de Onís (1885-1966), who had founded the Instituto de las Españas in 1920, launched a "Sección Sefardí," whose mission was to advance the study of "Spanish-Jewish culture," through both academic investigation and the participation of the local

Ladino-speaking community. These Ottoman-born immigrants and their locally born children crowded the university's lecture halls and auditorium as students, and audience members, presenters and performers of Ladino ballads and Spanish Golden Age dramas.[18] The institute's programming combined general intellectual interest in Sephardic Jews with post-imperial fantasies of recapturing Spain's geopolitical influence after the loss in 1898 of the country's last remaining hemispheric American territories.[19]

The cessation of Jewish emigration from the former Ottoman Empire, post-World War II intramarriage with Ashkenazic Jews and acculturation to Anglo-American society eroded the linguistic and cultural distinctiveness of Ladino-speaking Jews, and hence their multi-pronged relationship with local Spanish and Latin American populations. By the second half of the twentieth-century, Spanish-speaking Jews were virtually unheard of and Hispanic Jews, so organic to Onís's pluralistic conception of "las Españas," became an ontological absurdity.[20] Performers like Eydie Gormé were considered outsiders crossing over rather than as cultural heirs to a distant branch of the Iberian diaspora.

The "Recovering the US Hispanic Literary Heritage," founded five hundred years after the expulsion of the Jews from Spain and the onset of Spanish imperial rule, has always been sharply attuned to the unexpected possibilities of Iberia's easternmost dispersions. The Recovery's commitment to a pluralistic vision of what constitutes "Hispanic" became clear to me in 2003, when I received an invitation from Nicolás Kanellos to contribute a conference paper and book chapter on US Sephardim.[21] Previously, I had co-taught a university course at Queens College on Sephardic literature with a specialist of Puerto Rican literature, and a few years later had cross-listed a similar course with my home institution's Program in Spanish and Portuguese. But the "Recovery" invitation was the first time anyone had ever asked me to contribute my *research* to a Hispanic Studies publication. On every other occasion, my studies on the intersection between the two groups had found a home solely in Jewish Studies venues. In 2003, at the first "Recovery" conference I attended, the slippage between the two categories, "Sephardic" and "Hispanic" crept in through the subtitle of my talk, misprinted in the program as "Encounters between Catholic Puerto Ricans and *Latino*-Speaking Jews in the Early Twentieth Century" (italics added).

Heretofore, most of my evidence of interactions between the two groups came from sources created by members of the Jewish community, a serious limitation informed by the asymmetrical proportion of Sephardim to the rest of the country's Spanish-speaking population. Ottoman Jews by the 1920s and '30s constituted a population of 100,000 individuals, vastly outnumbered by the several million Spanish speakers who traced their origins to Puerto Rico, Mexico, the former Mexican territories of the United States, the insular Caribbean and South America. The Recovery Program helped to remedy the source imbalance that marred my work. Did I know, Professor Kanellos asked, handing me the memoir of Bernardo Vega, that this Puerto Rican activist in New York mentioned Ottoman Jews in some detail? Sure enough, Vega recalls there that soon after his arrival in New York in 1916, he dined in "La Luz," a restaurant in Harlem whose proprietor, he anticipated, would be Puerto Rican. As the eatery's name seemed to promise, Vega immediately experienced an epiphany: the owner was not a fellow islander, but rather a Sephardic Jew. Seated alongside his companions, Vega found his senses both confounded and delighted. Conversations in "ancient Spanish or Portuguese" swirled around them and the cuisine he sampled was at once familiar and foreign. The seasoning was decidedly alien, but the sauces seemed to be of Spanish origin. "The restaurant impressed me because it was so hard to believe that it was located in the United States," he reminisced in the late forties. "The atmosphere was exotic. The furnishings and décor gave it the appearance of a café in Spain or Portugal. Even the people who gathered there, their gestures and speech mannerisms, identified them as from Galicia, Andalusia, Aragon, or some other Iberian region. I began to understand what New York really was: a modern Babylon, the meeting point for peoples from all over the world."[22]

Alas, Vega does not describe the menu, and it is thus difficult to determine whether the fare offered was indeed Iberian or, rather, replicated the Ottoman dishes common to the dozens of other eateries launched by Sephardic immigrants in Manhattan and the Upper East Side. The Izmir-born writer José M. Estrugo (1888-1962), who spent his last years in Cuba, argued in 1958 that the dishes prepared by Ottoman Sephardic Jews were identical to the cuisine of the Iberian metropole. Sephardim of Near Eastern heritage, he wrote, "remained hooked on the authentic dishes they brought with them from old Spain."[23] On the other hand, Ottoman Sephardic diners on the Lower East Side and Harlem typically served Middle Eastern options, including Turkish coffee, "delicious cheese and ricotta, pasta like in Turkey," *kaibapes* (shish kababs) and Turkish *halvah*.[24] An eatery serving a predominantly Caribbean clientele would have diverged from both the Iberian Spanish and Ottoman models, with a selection of foods rooted in the Puerto Rican staples of rice, bananas and coconut. By the late 1920s, about a decade after Vega's arrival, more than 125 Puerto Rican-owned restaurants were in operation in New York City, concentrated in the Upper West Side of Manhattan and in East Harlem.[25]

How suggestive, then, that Sephardic cuisine, despite its possibly Ottoman trappings, could have evoked in Vega, a *tabaquero* from Puerto Rico, a Proustian moment about Spain. Such paradoxes, similar to the Hispanophone recordings of Eydie Gormé and Neil Sedaka, are at the heart of Iberia's easternmost dispersions. Centuries of imperial expansion, sustained intolerance of a Jewish presence and trans-national migration have refracted Spain through many different lenses. Just as there was no single "Spain" for Federico de Onís and his collaborators to celebrate and study, there is also no single US Hispanic heritage that has awaited recovery. The Recovery Program's recognition of this fact has provided a framework in which Jews are decidedly not an instrument of Spain's post-imperial attempts to recover its geographical and political reach. Rather for the Recovery Program, Sephardic Jews constitute a legitimate component of Hispanic heritage, a heritage multifariously expressed most notably through literature, but no less through the flavors of cuisine and the cadences of music.

Endnotes

[1]I thank Luis Marentes for his reflections on Eydie Gormé's reception in Mexico; Felipe Salles for his thoughts on writing about modern music; the late Celia Hakim and Dinah Hakim for their memories of participating in the Spanish émigré community of New York; Joyce Rosenthal (née Joya Levy) for her memories of Eydie Gormé; and the "Recovery" Program's Antonia Castañeda, Kenya C. Dworkin y Méndez, Nicolás Kanellos, Clara Lomas, Gabriela Baeza Ventura and Carolina A. Villarroel. The inspiration for this chapter comes from Neil Sedaka, who granted a telephone interview conducted by me on November 29, 2017. I thank him and his manager Robert Cotto, who arranged that interview.

[2]The *bolero* originated in Spain during the eighteenth century and acquired distinctive Latin American forms in the 1800s, particularly in Cuba and Mexico. For an overview see George Torres, "The Bolero Romántico: From Cuban Dance to International Popular Song," in Walter Aaron Clark, ed., *From Tejano to Tango: Latin American Popular Music* (New York: Routledge, 2002): 151-71, 168.

[3]All translations in this chapter are mine. For an alternative translation of "Piel Canela" see Torres, "The Bolero Romántico," 161-62.

[4]Luis R. Torres, "Eydie Gormé—The Good Story Never Told," Latinopia.com, March 23, 2016 (http://latinopia.com/blogs/tales-of-torres-3-27-16-eydie-gorme-the-good-story-never-told/), last accessed April 28, 2019.

[5]*Ibid.;* Luis Marentes to Aviva Ben-Ur, December 7, 2017.

[6]Torres, "Eydie Gormé."

[7]Esther was Gormé's Hebrew name; her nickname was Etty. She assumed the name "Eydie" once she became a professional singer. Joyce Rosenthal (née Joya Levy), Hollywood, Florida, to Aviva Ben-Ur, telephone interview, December 15, 2017.

[8]Haim Avni, *Spain, the Jews, and Franco* (Philadelphia: Jewish Publication Society of America, 1982) and Judith Laikin Elkin, *The Jews of Latin America* (Boulder, Colorado: Lynne Rienner Publishers, 2014).

[9]Celia Hakim and Dinah Hakim to Aviva Ben-Ur, recorded interview, New York, New York, June 11, 2000; Aviva Ben-Ur, "A Bridge of Communication: Spaniards and Ottoman Sephardic Jews in the City of New York (1880-1950)," in Nicolás Kanellos, ed., *Recovering Hispanic Religious Thought of the United States* (Newcastle: Cambridge Scholars Press, 2007), 25-56 and "Embracing the Hispanic: Jews, Puerto Ricans, and Spaniards in Immigrant New York (1880-1950)," in Lanin Gyurko and Mary G. Berg, eds., *Studies in Honor of Denah Lida* (Potomac, Maryland: Scripta Humanistica, 2005), 403-413.

[10]Colin Larkin, ed., "Gorme, Eydie," *The Guinness Encyclopedia of Popular Music* 3 (Enfield, UK: Guinness, 1992), 1706-1707, 1706.

[11]"Blame it on the Bossa Nova" was co-written by Cynthia Weil, whose mother, Dorothy Mendez, was born in Brooklyn's Sephardic community. Scott R. Benarde, *Stars of David: Rock'n'roll's Jewish Stories* (Hanover, N.H.: Brandeis University Press, 2003), 49.

[12]Associated Press, "Singer Eydie Gorme Dies at 84: Entertainer had hit with 'Blame it on the Bossa Nova,'" *Variety* (August 10, 2013), http://variety.com/2013/music/news/singer-eydie-gorme-dies-at-84-1200576773/ (last accessed November 6, 2017).

[13]Torres, "The Bolero Romántico," 168 (the accent mark in "Gormé" is missing in the original). His Lafayette College faculty page identifies him as Jorge Torres. See https://music.lafayette.edu/jorge-torres/ (last accessed November 5, 2017).

[14]Ernesto Lechner, "Adventures in Multimedia," *Saludos Hispanos* (1997): 103-104, 104.

[15]N.a., "Eydie Gormé: Una voz que brilló con el Trío Los Panchos," *Clarín* (August 12, 2013, last accessed February 18, 2019).

[16]Roberto Strongman, "The Latin American Queer Aesthetics of El Bolero," *Canadian Journal of Latin America and Caribbean Studies / Revue canadienne des études latino-américaines et caraïbes* 32:64 (2007): 39-78, 53-54.

[17]L. H. Gann and Peter J. Duignan, *The Hispanics in the United States: A History* (Boulder: Westview Press/Hoover Institution on War, Revolution and Peace, 1986), 28.

[18]Neil Sedaka to Aviva Ben-Ur, recorded telephone interview, November 29, 2017. Sedaka also released "Neil Sedaka en Español" and "Neil Sedaka: Italian," both in 1964 with RCA. Rich Podolsky, *Neil Sedaka: Rock'n'Roll Survivor: The Inside Story of His Incredible Comeback* (London: Jawbone Press, 2013), 249.

[19]These relationships are mentioned in the following sources: Congregation Shearith Israel Sisterhood Archives, Alice David Menken, "Report on Conference of Members from Board of Directors of Sisterhood;" American Jewish Historical Society, Alice D. Menken Papers, Henry Pereira Mendes to Alice Davis Menken, December 17, 1933, 3; Bula Satula [pseudonym of Moïse Soulam],

"Postemas de Mujer," *La Vara* (July 26, 1929): 10; Ham Moshón [pseudonym of Moïse Soulam], "Postemas de Ham Moshón," *La Vara* (April 20, 1934): 8.

[20]Aviva Ben-Ur, *Sephardic Jews in America: A Diasporic History* (New York: New York University Press, 2009), 150-87; Joyce Rosenthal to Aviva Ben-Ur, telephone interview, December 15, 2017.

[21]For an analysis of Spain's incorporation of Jews into its post-imperial projects see Aviva Ben-Ur, "The 'Spanish Jewish Project:' Reciprocity in an Age of Westernization," in Joshua Miller and Anita Norich, eds., *The Languages of Modern Jewish Cultures: Comparative Perspectives* (Ann Arbor: University of Michigan Press, 2016), 174-203 and the bibliography therein.

[22]For the term "ontological absurdity" see Ella Shohat, in Loolwa Khazzoom, ed., *The Flying Camel: Essays on Identity by Women of North African and Middle Eastern Jewish Heritage* (New York: Seal Press, 2003), 115-21, 117.

[23]The invitation came following the suggestion of Board Member Kenya C. Dworkin y Méndez to Nicolás Kanellos that Ladino-speaking Jews be included in the scope of the Recovery Program. My paper, "A Walk Through Spanish Harlem/Little Jerusalem: Encounters between Catholic Puerto Ricans and Ladino-Speaking Jews in the Early Twentieth Century," was presented at the Recovering Hispanic Religious Thought in the Nineteenth and Early Twentieth Centuries Conference at the University of Houston in May 2003.

[24]Bernardo Vega, *Memorias de Bernardo Vega: contribución a la historia de la comunidad puertorriqueña en Nueva York* (Río Piedras, P.R.: Ediciones Huracán, 1977), 46-47.

[25]José María Estrugo (born José Meir Estrugo Hazan), *Los Sefardíes* (Seville: Renacimiento, 2002 [Havana: Editorial Lex, 1958]), 77.

[26]Advertisement for the "Shlomit and Company" restaurant at 24 Rivington Street, *La America* (February 5, 1915); *La Vara* (December 7, 1923); Benardete, *Hispanic Character and Culture of the Sephardic Jews* (New York: Hispanic Institute in the United States, 1953), 118. Two historians, without attribution, identify the owner of "La Luz" as a Sephardic Jew from Puerto Rico and his establishment as the "first Latino restaurant in East Harlem." Jonathan Gill, *Harlem: The Four Hundred Year History from Dutch Village to Capital of Black America* (New York: Grove Press, 2011), 218, citing Jeffrey S. Gurock, *The Jews of Harlem: The Rise, Decline, and Revival of a Jewish Community* (New York: New York University Press, 2016). Neither of these authors could provide me with a source; thus, the owner's alleged Puerto Rican nationality is likely a scholarly error.

[27]Henry Kamen, *The Disinherited: Exile and the Making of Spanish Culture, 1492-1975* (New York: HarperCollins, 2007), 401.

The Politics of Recovery

LAURA LOMAS

Rutgers University-Newark

For twenty-five years, the Recovering the US Hispanic Literary Program has been articulating an archive, a literary history and a more inclusive definition of American, Caribbean and Latin American literatures. Like the recovery of texts by women and African-Americans that redefined the literary canon in the 1970s and 1980s, the Program has dramatically changed American and related academic study; indeed, it has helped to define a broad multilingual archive spanning centuries through which we can now imagine Latina/o and Chicana/o culture and history in United States. Giving the lie to claims that we were reading a white male canon because "no one else has written anything worth reading," this archive foregrounds the antecedence, creative genius and interpretive power of the Spanish- and Latin American- descended US-residents within earshot, yet often invisible or incomprehensible to Anglos or non-Hispanic whites. Publishing in, but not necessarily identified with or assimilated to the United States mainstream, Latina/o writers have been prolific not just before and after the Civil Rights movements of the 1960s, but even before the United States came into existence. Indeed, this tradition draws upon civilizations that extend to a time before and beyond Spain.[1] In this brief reflection, I respond to a criticism of my argument that a major Cuban and Latin American writer of the nineteenth century, José Martí, can be read as part of this Latina/o literary history.[2] I want to acknowledge my debts to the Recovery Program, despite an ongoing quibble with its key organizing term "Hispanic," and reflect on the significance of related ethno-racial labels for this emerging field. Finally, I suggest some new directions for the Recovery Program's ongoing excavations in the next quarter century.

The Limits of a US Hispanic Frame

In my book on New York-resident Cuban poet and revolutionary José Martí as a cultural translator of the United States, I explored the writing of Cuba's founding father as that of an economic migrant within the scope of the Recovery Program, but not reducible to the category "US Hispanic." Among other things, *Translating Empire: José Martí, Migrant Latino Subjects and American Modernities* (Duke 2008) meant to challenge the notion that migrants from Latin America and the Caribbean to the United States necessarily *do*, or *ought to* identify with the United States and its dominant culture or leading writers. To circumscribe the aims of Recovery to territorial borders of the US nation-state obscures how borders have shifted over time, and may yet shift; it truncates the lines of flight across porous borders—even when they are fortified and policed—and invisibilizes the contact zones inside and outside the nation where transculturation occurs. Merely adding US Hispanic writers to spice up a white-bread national canon or demanding equality within a multicultural empire fails to interrogate the history of violence that has constituted it. The expansion of US borders and influence into places that previously were part of Spain, Mexico and beyond has contributed to the displacement of migrants from their places of origin. Recovery plays a key role in mapping the literary imagination of those who fear US annexation or occupation-as did Cuban migrant José Martí.

In fact, the omnivorous reading, writing and translation by Latin American and Caribbean migrants, exiles, the annexed and their descendants counter the myth of Anglo-Saxon and Puritan origins of the United States. The Recovery Program archive dismantles a discourse that locates the causes of annexed or weak Latin American and Caribbean states in hybrid languages, racial impurity, an imputed "effeminacy" or pathologized performance of gender/sex, or in the lingering effects of corruption (as if it were) unique to Spanish colonial legacies. Such groundless and hypocritical arguments, which tend to justify the replacement of the colonial power with a neoliberal empire, would be risible if these views did not continue to define the generalized misprision with which the United States' leaders-on the whole-consider the states south of the Rio Bravo and their migrants.

The United States' future as a majority minority country in which more of its inhabitants trace their origins to Latin American than to Europe by mid-century, foregrounds the question of how to define US culture: in terms of a powerful minority or its imminent majority of people of color (contingent, of course, on whether the 50 million-person Hispanic/Latina/o group refuses to identify with or as white non-Hispanic).[3] In 2003, we learned that a Hispanic minority had "nosed past blacks," in an article that sets ethno-racial fields of Black and

Hispanic Studies in competition, while presumptively "white" administrators of academic budgets figure as the bettors, punters and bookies.[4] As non-Hispanic whites face their future status as a minority in our time, the archive produced by Recovery usefully complements narratives that reveal the origins of the United States in violent settler colonialism. The question is whether the future non-white majority will refuse to identify as "exotic creoles" (Martí's term) who emphasize their European origin and identify with Eurocentric, white suprema-cist, cultural and political agendas.[5] Historically, as Martí pointed out in 1894, leaders of Latin American and Caribbean states often accept the position of "petted lapdog" to a foreign owner, privileging European or US ideas and styles, and disdaining the local (as Martí notes in "The Truth about the United States," 332). Built on corruption, this model inevitably comes to crisis; but it has a long and enduring history.

The imminent and promising demographic demotion of non-Hispanic, sep-aration and detention of thousands of child-migrants in coolers and cages, whites to minority status has characterized every class of brilliant, mostly work-ing-class, first- and second-generation immigrants and students-of-color at the only Hispanic-Serving campus of Rutgers University, where I teach.[6] Newark is a city that in the wake of the black and Puerto Rican rebellions of 1967 and 1974, respectively, is slowly coming to grips with its heterogeneous and mixed Caribbean, Central and South American Latina/o denizens, now over forty per-cent of the city. Living and teaching in Newark, I came to read Martí's conjuring of a not-yet-existing country—both Cuba and "the night"- as a reflection of the Latino migrant's unspeakable desire for something else besides the imposing imperial modernity of the United States.

In the post-Obama moment, the white settler colonial (future) minority is certainly strengthening its grip, perhaps especially in the face of demographic projections. The twenty-fifth anniversary of the Recovering the US Literary Heritage Program coincides with the largest transfer of wealth from the diverse working majority to an obscenely wealthy minority in the history of the United States; the dismantling of public institutions and resources such as schools, water and parks; the largest number of deportations of Latina/o migrants and threats to force Mexico to pay for an even longer wall between the United States and Mexico; the ongoing unpunished killings and detaining of unarmed people of color, including children; the exposé of rampant sexual abuse—of boys (especially by Catholic priests), of girls and of women; the unparalleled encroachment of government and corporate surveillance and increasing efforts to privatize access to information via the internet. Ten years after the publication of *Translating Empire*, these imperial United States more than ever "[parade] behind a mask of democracy" (*Translating Empire* xv). I joined the Recovery

Program Board in 2010, and it has become an invaluable intellectual community in which we ask questions that may shake the narrative foundations of this version of the United States.

Recovery Program scholars have spent years in the archives investigating emergent writers of a Latin American and Caribbean diaspora, of places that once were Mexican or Spanish and subsequently were annexed into an expanding United States empire. Since 1989, I have been dwelling between Spanish and English and learning to imagine the United States from the perspective of those who live here due to displacement by military interventions designed to neutralize anti-colonial movements or to facilitate corporate extraction of material resources. Many of the displaced migrants who have fled North find themselves denied claims to asylum and are often condemned to live as invisible or second-class citizens or detainees, likely victims of police abuse and/or threatened with deportation, all of which suggests commonalities to African Americans and Asian Americans, who have historically faced abuses, killings and detention by state-sanctioned actors. At home and in the archive, fighting to create opportunities for my bicultural children to continue to speak and think in both Spanish and English and to learn about the varied, largely untaught histories and literatures of Latina/o America, it has become urgent to work for recognition not only of the cultural traditions, but also the histories of resistance that developed in America's first European language, which is the second most commonly spoken in what is now the United States.

By situating a major Cuban and Latin American writer in his US context, I brought into focus the messy reality of bi- or multilingualism and racism, meted out by imperial subjects, as central to defining *Latinidad*. On entering the United States as an adult, after completing his education in law, philosophy and literature in Zaragoza (1873-1874), José Martí spoke accented F.O.B. English, with a confessed anguish, as he became increasingly critical of state-sanctioned white racism and anti-immigrant attitudes. While he may have imagined a future US-based readership that would take inspiration from him as a "Patrick Henry of Cuba," he did not become a US citizen and very rarely lectured or wrote in English.[7] In fact, Martí's translations—by which I mean literal renderings of US writers in Spanish and constant interpretation of North American culture, politics and literature—explicitly countered US-derived misconceptions of Latin America and of Latina/o America as necessarily derivative of or identified with an Anglo-American tradition that traces its cultural foundations to Puritan New England. Martí feared and denounced a "yankeemania" or Eurocentric bias in favor of "all that is fair-skinned as if that were natural and proper" ("The Truth about the United States," 332).

At the same time, Martí's late essays deconstruct the racializing binary Latin/Saxon in terms that look forward to the claims of African diaspora theorists such as James Baldwin or Frantz Fanon: "anything that divides men from each other, that separates them, singles them out or hems them in, is a sin against humanity" ("My Race," 318). He thus decries the racial procedure whereby *The Philadelphia Manufacturer* attributes to all Cubans (and by extension, all Latin Americans, its migrants and their descendants) essential characteristics of a so-called deviant lesser race: "a distaste for exertion" and "defective morals," a stereotype which in Trump's twenty-first century, has come to include the labels of "criminal," "drug-trafficker" and "rapist."[8] In response, Martí points out that Spanish-speakers need to know what the United States is saying about them and turns the accusation back on the United States, which has within it "all the violence, discords, immoralities and disorders of which the Hispanoamerican peoples are accused" (333).

I posit a definition of migrant Latina/o writing that includes the work of the major Cuban poet-statesman-revolutionary José Martí precisely because the group of multiracial Latina/o readers, translators and writers in which he travelled exceeded any single nation, color or a single language, even as his New York, Florida, New Orleans, Philadelphia and New Jersey supporters were in the thick of anti-colonial projects related to national liberation movements. This paradox has deeply troubled a few Martí scholars and some Latin Americanists who take issue with the application of the "discriminatory" ethnic label "Latino" to a light-skinned Cuban *letrado* son of Spanish migrants.[9] Martí, through close observation of racist violence toward natives, Chinese, blacks and Latinas/os, and through his own experience of being disdained, came to articulate a critique of race hierarchies and formed alliances with black anti-racists (as long as they did not serve the agenda of empire). Even more infuriating to a few critics was my suggestion that Martí had to unlearn his white privilege from his Afro-Latina/o collaborators.[10] But here is precisely the point: the great teacher and apostle, the child of a Canary-islander mother and Valenciano father, experienced discrimination and xenophobia, but he observed its most acute effects on his darker-skinned contemporaries and he needed to unlearn his white privilege. Martí formed alliances, however imperfect, with African-descended activists in opposition to the *ethos* of whitening, segregation and European-identification.[11] He would not have experienced this sense of himself as "minor," as part of a Spanish-speaking subculture in the United States, if he had not left his island, and if he had not chosen to write for *gente latina*.

I diverge from the Recovery Program's term "Hispanic" because of how it tends to paper over historic tensions between Spain and its former colonies in the Americas, an imperial legacy that informs the relations between the United

States, the Caribbean and Latin America and their diasporas. As Gloria Anzaldúa eloquently notes, to accept "the fiction that we are Hispanic" only accommodates "the dominant culture and its abhorrence of Indians."[12] Similarly, to claim or value European ancestors only, belongs to the procedure whereby greys—such as mestizo or *criollo* Hispanic immigrants—often stake a claim to whiteness, on the backs of blacks or *indios*.[13] In claiming "España," the term "Hispanic" tends to elide other languages and ancestors—especially the non-European-whose languages and cultures have shaped Latin America and its diaspora.

Despite Martí's anti-racism, Latina/o culture has frequently reproduced forms of anti- black *and* anti-indigenous racism. Its light-skinned scions, the *criollos,* have frequently benefited from and procured the special wages of whiteness or *enblancamiento*.[14] Latina/o American culture has been complicit in defining itself through repression of non-European legacies, by refusing to recognize the millennial technologies, the anteriority and innovations of the original civilizations, which have built, fed and enchanted the world with corn, tomatoes, chocolate, agave, potatoes, cassava, tobacco and quinoa. From non-Europeans have come the only original American musics. Martí's cultural decolonization project hinges on a critique of white-identified *Latinidad*. While this critique persuades me intellectually, it problematizes the already complicated relationship to the category "Latina/o" of any light-skinned person of Spanish descent (such as Martí, and in a more attenuated fashion, myself).

Claiming an Identity I was Taught to Despise

> Gradually, I came to recognize I was a black West Indian. Just like everybody else, I could relate to that, I could write from and out of that position. It has taken a very long time, really, to be able to write in that way, personally. . . .
>
> —Stuart Hall[15]

How does this process of disidentification from a dominant racial procedure take place? I find this quotation from Stuart Hall's autobiographical introspection instructive because it enacts the complex and anguished response to racial discourses that undergird the violence of colonization and whitening. Hall acknowledges the trauma behind how and why his ability to speak as a black occurs belatedly and haltingly. He spells out how he came to claim a "space" that he was taught to despise.[16] To rebel against this prescription was to risk the punishments faced by his lighter-skinned sister who fell in love with a dark-skinned Bajan and was committed to a mental health institution after her parents forbade the relationship.

The cultural studies tradition and its unique form, marked indelibly by the work of Stuart Hall, bears witness to the effects of such epistemic violence. The commas in the sentence I've quoted, and the interjection "really" acknowledge the difficulty and complexity of writing on behalf of a disdained, disenfranchised group, even if it is one to which we belong. Because Hall had various ancestries-African, East Indian, Portuguese, Jewish—he was the darker brother; his sister acknowledged him only as the "coolie" child in a striving, colonizer-identified, near-white Jamaican family, for to mention his blackness would be to acknowledge her own. Piri Thomas' great novel shows how such scenes of recognition can devolve into violence among siblings.

I inherited my surname from my father (i.e. not through marriage). I grew up in a family of people desperate to become white, who allowed the unconscious necessity of whitening to determine their life choices. I enjoy privileges of looking and sounding white and do not experience the violence meted out by the police to the visibly dark with astonishing lack of restraint. Nonetheless, like Hall, I am a darker sibling, a not quite/not white translator and political black sheep among strivers who settled (mostly) in New Jersey, Massachusetts and Maine, and our name reveals the abiding trace of an Hispanic background. My Lomas ancestors were penniless immigrants from England who ran a flower shop and sold whalebone corsets in Massachusetts, and my dad pursued medicine to escape his youthful poverty. From my mother's side of the family I inherited my *trigueña* skin that rarely burns, dark hair and eyes—the *dizque* Swiss or German wing of the family. My reflection in the mirror does not connote Scottish, Swiss, German or Anglo-Saxon-ness to me or to others.

My appearance raises doubts. People interrogate me about my background. Behind the public labeling is the assumption that one must look a certain way to do certain kinds of work. As a student at in Kingston, Jamaica, and in Brazil, I was hailed as "browning" and faced whispered questions about whether I had "the touch of the tar brush." When I say, I live in New York, my questioner inevitably counters, "but where are you really from?" When Latino poet Carlos Andrés Gómez encounters this question, he raps in reply: "You are not ready for the answers to the questions you ask, not ready for the worlds these words might shake free."[17]

Outside the anonymity of a mottled urban metropole at the center of empire, the story I'd learned of my family's default identification with whiteness became a question.

My family sealed the expedient bid for whiteness by forgetting the non-European ancestors, the dark women, who remain unnamed yet still shake me out of my sleep and demand that I remember them. I thanked my mother in my acknowledgements for answering the insistent questions I posed as a child by defining us as "mongrels." My DNA test reveals that not all my ancestors came from Europe. I have come to relish my Spanish-surname, my light brown skin and dark eyes. As someone who is not all white, who is of Hispanic Origin, and who has spoken Spanish at home with my partner and our two kids everyday for the past two decades. I have learned to call myself "Hispanic." I agree with Juan Flores that identities can change.

Rather than narrate the American dream, I research writers' whose critical translations articulate an escape route from the nightmare of empire. I aim to dig up a past that may open another future.[18] My work similarly complicates the definition of American (which for many problematically still refers to the United States). My Latin Americanist and African-Americanist teachers predicted that fields would change, and they have.[19] The work of Recovery makes it possible for us to imagine ourselves differently.

Multilingual Recovery, Spanglish and Latina/o Social Movements

> I have long maintained that Spanish is a father tongue, that of the conquerors. Our true mother tongues are indigenous languages, many wiped out in the genocide.
> —Demetria Martínez, *Confessions of a Berlitz Tape Chicana*

I close by mentioning two proposals for the coming quarter century: 1) promote Latina/o Studies and recovery of the many languages of Latin America and its heterogeneous diasporas and original inhabitants, including Spanglish, and 2) cultivate institutional memory and development by honoring forerunners and learning from the past.

Ana Celia Zentella and José del Valle and those who signed their petition convinced the *Real Academia Española* to change its derogatory definition of Spanglish in 2014. But bilingualism continues to be treated as more of a handicap than an asset in many of the largest cities in the United States. English-language learners often assimilate to English in order to get ahead, which means that bilingual children lose skills they had when first entering the school system. While New York city announced in 2016 a new initiative for strengthening dual language programs throughout the city's boroughs, in Manhattan (which includes Loisaida's and El Barrio's historic Spanish-speaking migrant communities), the only immersion programs are in Mandarin and English; New York's schools are still more segregated than they were in 1954, the year of *Brown vs the Board of Education*. The Recovering the US Hispanic Literary Heritage might successfully develop a research and advocacy program around Spanish-English bilingualism and Spanglish, not only as an area of interest to linguists.

Moreover, we should not stop there. It behooves the Recovery Program to promote the cultivation and preservation of the many other languages—especially Amerindian, but also of African and Asian origin—spoken by migrants from Latin America and the Caribbean. The Recovery Program could promote scholarship in Latina/o Studies that reads non-European linguistic contributions and help halt ongoing repression toward Amerindian, Arabic, African people, civilizations and languages, from Aymara to Zapotec, from Haitian Kreyol to Quechua, from Mayan Kakchiquel to Garifuna, from Arabic to Yoruba.

Recovery should acknowledge and build on community-based movements that created space for its academic institutionalization. During my participation on the board of the Recovery Program since 2009, we extended the period for Recovery from the colonial period through 1960 by two decades, up until 1980, to preserve evidence and literature of the Civil Rights and decolonial struggles. This archive urgently needs preservation due to the 2010 legislative bans in Arizona of books related to Chicana/o and Latina/o social movements. This move preserves the history of counterhegemonic efforts from below against the threat of oblivion.

This loss of memory affects even public universities bent on serving the diverse communities in which they are situated. For example, I co-authored and helped direct—with support from a new administration—a Latina/o Studies Working Group, which sought to recuperate institutional memory, to foster community collaborations, and to theorize Latina/o culture with an eye to paving the way for Latina/o Studies on our campus. Presentations from retired faculty, such as the Puerto Rican historian Olga Jiménez de Waggenheim, from alumni such as the award-winning Puerto Rican documentarian and activist William Q. Sánchez and Colombian journalist Gloria Montealegre, revealed a forgotten history of sacrifices, faculty-meeting takeovers and organizing that the institution only haltingly recognized and supported recently: Puerto Rican Studies struggled to function as an academic minor between the mid-1970s and 2003, and was effectively swept under the rug when its founder retired. With a large and growing Latina/o student body, our campus was first recognized in 2016 as an Hispanic-Serving Institution, yet our campus has no Latina/o, Caribbean and Latin American Studies Program, major, department, center or institute. Any efforts to build this curriculum and related programs should acknowledge the founders and vision of the first Puerto Rican Studies minor, even as we expand the scope of Latina/o and Latin American studies to reflect the heterogeneous Central and South American and diverse Caribbean migrant communities in our region and on campus. The Recovery Program teaches us to establish an archive to preserve historical memory of minor cultures threatened with oblivion and to acknowledge our debts to the forerunners who have made possible our present work.

Endnotes

[1]See John Morán González and Laura Lomas, eds. *The Cambridge History of Latina/o American Literature*, which addresses Latina/o literature from 1492 to 2017, especially chapters by Arturo Arias, Yolanda Martínez San Miguel and José Antonio Mazotti.

[2]For example, see chapters by Anne Fountain, Georg Schwarzmann, Jorge Camacho, Francisco Morán in *Syncing the Americas: José Martí and the Shaping of National Identity* (Bucknell University Press, 2018) and reviews of *Translating Empire: José Martí, Migrant Latino Subjects and American Modernities* (Duke, 2008) by Alberto López and Manuel Tellechea. For a variety of other responses to my first book, see reviews by John Morán González, Elizabeth Horan, Lázaro Lima, Leonora Simonovis, Amarilis Hidalgo de Jesus, Marissa López, Raúl Fernández, Caroline Levander, Richard Perez, Oscar Montero and Charles Hatfield.

[3]Zev Chafets, "The Post-Hispanic Hispanic Politician," *New York Times* (May 6, 2010), spells out a discourse that in Texas has interpolated Hispanic/Latinx people as white, and not black. This state-sanctioned pressure to identify with whiteness parallels a longstanding Latin American and Caribbean tradition that enforces or encourages white identification and eugenics: *enblancamiento*, or "whitening." Emerging Democratic Hispanic national leader, Julián Castro, according to Chafets, plans to mark himself as "other" in the next Census.

[4]Felicia R. Lee, "New Topic in Black Studies Debate: Latinos," *New York Times* (Feb. 1, 2003): A1.

[5]Martí, "Our America," *Selected Writings*, trans. ed. Esther Allen (Penguin, 2002): 288-296. All future citations to Martí are to this edition and cited parenthetically.

[6]*U.S. News and World Report* has ranked our campus the most diverse in the United States for the past eighteen years.

[7]See "The Patrick Henry of Cuba," *Equator Democrat*, November 24, 1892; rpt. Martí, *Obras completas,* vol. 28, p. 341.

[8]See Katie Reilly, "Here Are All the Times Donald Trump Insulted Mexico," *Time*, 31 August 2016. http://time.com/4473972/donald-trump-mexico-meeting-insult/. See also Samuel Huntington's claim that Mexican-American and Latino immigrants who form linguistic enclaves maliciously threaten to underminethe Anglo-Protestant foundation of the United States: "The Hispanic Challenge," Foreign Policy (March-April 2004): 30-45.

[9]See Andrea Pagni: "A una lectora fuera de ese contexto [estadounidense], le sorprende que sea necesario aclarar que el panamericanismo es una doctrina expansionista de los EE.UU., y que se lea a Martí como latino writer—fórmula que resuena, por lo menos a mis oídos, con un eco discriminatorio. . . . ," in *Revista Iberoamericana* XII.45 (2012): 235. I should note that many members of the Latin American and Caribbean diasporas reject the labels "Latina/o" or "Hispanic."

[10]See Lomas, "'El Negro es tan capaz como el blanco': José Martí, Pachín Marín, Lucy Parsons and the Politics of Late-Nineteenth Century Latinidad," in Rodrigo Lazo and Jesse Alemán, eds. *The Latino Nineteenth Century* (New York University Press, 2016): 301-322.

[11]James Baldwin singles out Leandro Pérez, isleño or Canary-islander white supremacist, as an example of how racism deforms white people. Pérez's violent promotion of race segregation—and Perez was Martí's mother's surname—represents a position that Martí openly criticized. And like Baldwin, Martí saw that the refusal to face the effects of racism would result in the demise of the United States.

[12]Anzaldúa, Gloria, *Borderlands/La Frontera: The New Mestiza*, notes 11 and 13. To this anti-indigenous stance, we might add the complicity with US negrophobia and anti-Asian racism.

[13]See Toni Morrison, "On the Backs of Blacks," *Arguing Immigration: The Controversy and Crisis over the Future of Immigration in America*, ed. Nicolaus Mills (Simon and Schuster,1994), 97-100.

[14]José Martí's son sat at the banquet celebrating the massacre of thousands of black Cuban men, women and children in the 1912 Race War; Gustavo Pérez Firmat even goes so far as to brag about "the Confederate flag on [his] desk" (*Next Year in Cuba: A Cubano's Coming-of-Age in America*, 209). As Silvio Torres-Saillant has argued, Latina/o racism begins at home and continues to burn throughout the hemisphere, making necessary the creation of new categories that acknowledge the peculiar inequality, violence and illegibility faced by the Latina/o person of African descent, and the same may apply for those who claim indigenous or Asian ancestry. See Silvio Torres- Saillant, "Afro-Latinidad: Phoenix Rising from a Hemisphere's Racist Flames," *Cambridge History of Latina/o American Literature* (Cambridge University Press, 2018).

[15]"The formation of a diasporic intellectual: An interview with Stuart Hall by Kuan-Hsing Chen," in *Stuart Hall: Critical Dialogues in Cultural Studies*, eds. Kuan-Hsing Chen and David Morley (London: Routledge, 2006), 491.

[16]Michelle Cliff, *Claiming an Identity They Taught Me to Despise* (Watertown: Persephone Press, 1980).

[17]See Carlos Andrés Gómez, "What does Hispanic look like?" available at https://www.youtube.com/watch?v=g8O4z7NfnTU.

[18]This construction of archives as means to remake the past follows in a tradition established by Arturo Alfonso Schomburg, the Afro-Puerto Rican bibliographer and historian, namesake of the Schomburg Center for Research in Black Culture in Harlem, New York City.

[19]Undergraduates occupied Hamilton Hall to demand Ethnic Studies on the 30th anniversary of the 1968 takeover of the same building, which led to the hiring of African- and Asian-Americanists, and eventually Latina/o Studies faculty, after I'd left campus.

Archival Research

On the Road to Recovery, or What It Means to (Finally) Join the Recovery Program

MANUEL M. MARTÍN-RODRÍGUEZ
University of California, Merced

As the newest (or one of the newest) members of its Advisory Board, one might wonder what could I possibly have to say about the Recovering the US Hispanic Literary Heritage Program. As an insider, very little, but as a scholar whose career has dovetailed with the Program and almost coincides in time with it, my perspective is somewhat richer. Moreover, my long and winding road to *the* Recovery is not without some interesting and fruitful moments, which I will address first (heeding our director's invitation to share personal anecdotes), saving some reflections on the significance of this effort for last.

In truth, my first contacts with recovery efforts started in the late 1980s, when I was still a graduate student and was fortunate to attend panels at a couple of conferences, most notably "Hispanic/Chicano Literature of the Southwest," convened by María Herrera-Sobek at the University of California, Irvine, on February 24, 1989. My own learning and research were focused at the time on twentieth-century literature, but these efforts struck me as a fascinating turn in the discipline.

My first encounter with the Recovery Program, however, happened in 1994, in the context of its first biannual conference open to outside scholars. Earlier, at the 1992 annual convention of the MLA (Modern Language Association of America), I had presented a paper at one of three panels entitled "Reclaiming the Americas." My paper, "Reclaiming California: Land and Labor in Early Chicano Literature," was focused on an analysis of María Amparo Ruiz de Burton's *The Squatter and the Don* (then yet to be recovered) and of Daniel Venegas'

Las aventuras de don Chipote, recovered in 1984 by Nicolás Kanellos, who had been my professor and M.A. thesis advisor at the University of Houston (1985-1987). Encouraged by the response received at that MLA panel, I decided to submit a longer version of my paper to *PMLA*. As most of my readers probably know, submitting to *PMLA* is the closest academic experience to Dante's ordeal through the nine circles of hell, and it seldom results in a vision of paradise. All in all, my paper did fairly well, clearing most of the levels of review, and being sent back down to hell only at the top circle, the dreaded executive committee. If memory serves, *PMLA* had published only one article on Chicana/o literature at the time, perhaps none.

Back to the point: though submissions to *PMLA* are rigorously anonymous, peer reviewers have the choice of identifying themselves when they submit their evaluations. For that reason, I knew that Kanellos had been one of the reviewers for my submission. His review was very favorable, but he pointed out that Arte Público Press was coming up with a new edition of *The Squatter and the Don* (published in 1993), and he recommended resubmission so that I (the anonymous author) could cite that edition and, more importantly, engage with the excellent long introduction by Rosaura Sánchez and Beatrice Pita that we are all familiar with now. Still very much alive in Dante's/*PMLA* inferno at that time, I decided to heed Kanellos' editorial advice. I did a full rewrite of the article, which added one layer of analysis, as I now discussed not only the texts themselves but the process by which they had been recovered and presented to their late-twentieth-century new audiences. I could not help being somewhat critical of that process, since I believed (and do so to this date) that both Kanellos and the Sánchez and Pita critical team had traced a too direct line between the older texts they recovered and contemporary Chicana/o literature, perhaps exaggerating some linkages while downplaying some major differences.[1]

When at the end of the lengthy review process I received the dreaded *thanks but no thanks* note from *PMLA*, I thought that my interaction with them was done, at least for the time being.[2] To my surprise, a second package from their office arrived shortly afterwards, forwarding a letter from Kanellos inviting the anonymous author (me) to present the paper at the Recovery Program 1994 conference. I was thrilled to read these news, of course, and wrote back revealing my identity and accepting the kind invitation. What came next was one the biggest scares of my early academic life. When the conference program was disseminated, I learned that I would present (alongside two then budding, now highly accomplished critics, Anne Goldmann and John Morán González) in the plenary session with not one but a battery of respondents: Nicolás Kanellos, Rosaura Sánchez and Beatriz Pita, that is, all the people whose work I took somewhat to task in my paper, and (I believe) at least someone else whose name escapes me now. To a young Assistant Professor like me, that did not look like the customary session respondent arrangement; it looked more like a firing squad! I put aside my fears, nonetheless, and decided to show up and do my best in front of an audience that included many of my former professors and some very senior colleagues. I think I did fairly well, discussing the works, their reception and some of the thinly veiled resonances of manifest destiny (or as I called it in Spanish, *desatino manifiesto*) present in *The Squatter and the Don* under the guise of medical cures and other health benefits associated with California. I even held my ground with the respondents, though Sánchez and Pita could not make it and were substituted by Antonia I. Castañeda.

A second noteworthy moment of interaction with the Recovery (at least as far as my family is concerned), came when I received a grant from the project to work on Fray Angélico Chávez's early poetry, much of which was then unpublished in book form and, in many cases, buried in obscure magazines and other venues. I had approached Chávez's work first through his mind-blowing *The Virgin of Port Lligat* and because of my own interest in allegory, and I had then moved on to do some research on his publications in periodicals, anthologies and the like. After completing my preliminary work on the subject, I presented the paper "Las almas y las letras: Fray Angélico Chávez's Religious Poetry" at the Recovery's 2003 "Religious Thought in the Nineteenth and Early Twentieth Centuries" conference. The day after presenting, I could hardly believe my eyes when I saw my name printed on the Religion page of the *Houston Chronicle*. I hastened to send the clip back home to finally dispel any family fears about the kind of life I had led as a graduate student in Houston a couple of decades earlier. As for Chávez's works, I soon learned that Dr. Ellen McCracken was also working on a recovery of his work, and I decided to move on to other projects of mine.

On and off, I remained in touch with the Recovery Program over the years, mostly as a participant in the 2002, 2004 and 2008 conferences. But, my work with lost or forgotten texts from the past was done independently. The most significant of those efforts has been my research on Gaspar de Villagrá and his 1610 poem *Historia de la nveva Mexico*. More than a decade of intense labor in archives and special collections all over the world allowed me to locate and recover multiple unknown documents on the poet (including his student records at the Universidad de Salamanca from 1571 to 1576, and—more recently—evidence of another history he penned before departing for the new Mexico). I was able to reconstruct Villagrá's biography, to prepare a critical edition and extensive reading of his poem, as well as to study the historical reception of the text in its more than four centuries of existence.

In the intervening time, I became a member of the advisory board of the "Pasó por aquí" series at the University of New Mexico Press, and my book *Cantas a Marte y das batalla a Apolo: Cinco estudios sobre Gaspar de Villagrá* (2014) inaugurated the Colección Plural Espejo, a series with which the Academia Norteamericana de la Lengua Española joined the task of recovering the US Hispanic cultural heritage. I also embarked on additional *rescates*, for example, digging up, publishing and analyzing Rolando Hinojosa's high school writings, which had been preserved at the Mercedes High School in Mercedes, Texas.

Going back to that place (Mercedes, TX) and that time (Hinojosa's youth), reminded me of the figure of P. Galindo, a south Texas journalist (and Hinojosa's next door neighbor at one point) whose influence Hinojosa has acknowledged a few times, but whose writings remained lost or inaccessible. Bringing them back to life became my next recovery project. After several years of archival work with more than eighteen thousand newspaper issues, I was able to recover almost six hundred writings by P. Galindo (including poetry, prose works, newspaper chronicles and miscellaneous items) and I prepared a critical edition of that work, which I submitted to Arte Público Press. The book was accepted (and published in 2016), and that led to an invitation to join the board of the Recovery Program.

As an "insider" now, I hope to continue my contributions to the recovery of US Hispanic literature from the past, and I hope to be able to publish in the near future a critical edition of the poetry of José Inés García, "El Trovador Moderno," a fascinating figure of early twentieth-century Colorado and New Mexico. García was not only a poet, but also a translator, a newspaper editor, a bookstore and print shop owner, and an important figure in the cultural hub of Trinidad, Colorado. The interested reader will find in this same volume a scholarly article of mine in which I analyze García's significance in more detail, as well as some of his works.

From my dual location as a longtime outsider who has recently joined its board, evaluating the importance of the Recovery Program is an easy, yet monumental task. In a nutshell, the Recovery has transformed forever our understanding of what US Latina/o literary and cultural history was like. As I have stated elsewhere, thanks (largely) to the Recovery Program, Chicana/o and Latina/o literatures currently grow as much toward the past as they do toward the future. This somewhat paradoxical, yet exhilarating situation, is a direct result of the digitization of thousands upon thousands of periodicals, of the regular publication of recovered books, of the release of searchable databases and, in sum, of the transformative work that the Recovery Program has carried out and sponsored.

Another aspect of the Program that I have learned to appreciate over the years is the way in which it promotes a broad dialogue and participation by scholars, regardless of whether or not they officially belong to the ranks. The Recovery, in that sense, is much, much bigger than its board and its staff, and therein lies a significant part of its success. In the two decades in which I was not officially affiliated with the project, I still felt I was a part of it, as I am sure did many (if not all) of those who presented at its conferences or interacted one way or another with its publications and activities.

For me, then, the Recovery Program has been an integral and constant part of my academic career: I have used the recovered texts in my classes, I have participated in its conferences and debates, I have received occasional funding, I use its databases on a regular basis, and I am responsible for one of its published volumes. Like me, an entire generation of scholars has seen the transformative, paradigm-shifting role that the Recovery Program has played, and it is safe to say that future generations will keep benefitting from the results as well.

Endnotes

[1]For full details on my concerns, please see "Textual and Land Reclamations: The Critical Reception of Early Chicano/a Literature," in *Recovering the U.S. Hispanic Literary Heritage,* vol. 2, Charles Tatum and Erlinda Gonzales-Berry, eds. Houston, TX: Arte Público, 1996. 40-58.

[2]Subsequently, *PMLA* published another article of mine in 2005, entitled "Recovering Chicano Literary Histories: Historiography beyond Borders," *PMLA* 120.3 (2005): 796-805.

Recovering the US Hispanic Literary Heritage: 25 Years into It

A. GABRIEL MELÉNDEZ
University of New Mexico

I attended my first Recovering the US Hispanic Literary Heritage Conference in December 1994. The theme of the meeting was forward looking: "The Legacies of a Literature: Impact and Implications of the US Hispanic Contribution." I was privileged to have shared a panel on Printing and Periodical Literature in the Southwest with *don* Luis Leal, already a legend, and with Laura Guitiérrez-Witt, who would become the second director of the Benson Latin American Collection at UT Austin. Our session was moderated by Julián Olivares, best known to me for his work as the editor of *Américas Review.* In addition, the 1994 conference included a host of colleagues with whom I would collaborate over the next 25 years. Among them were researchers for whom I have the greatest respect: Nicolás Kanellos, Michael Olivas, Antonia Castañeda, Francisco Lomelí, José "Pepe" Fernández, Richard Flores, Genaro Padilla, John Morán González, Erlinda Gonzales-Berry, Manuel Martín Rodríguez, Clara Lomas, Kenya Dworkin y Méndez, Emilio Zamora and José Aranda. In retrospect, I see that conference organizers understood how the contemporary explosion of Latino writing in the United States was deeply connected to the work of recovery scholarship, and they made sure the *noche de cultura* would be memorable. The event featured the playwright and novelist Lionel García and poets Lorna Dee Cervantes and Evangelina Vigil-Piñón. My conference paper had the ambitious title, "Spanish-language Journalism in the Southwest"; now I see that the title was my not-so- subtle attempt to signal that I was working on a book on this subject.

77

Two pivotal developments would raise the significance of this third meeting of the Recovery Program. First was the milestone publication of volume one of the essays presented at the founding meeting at Research Triangle Park in 1990 and of the second Recovery meeting in 1991. Volume editors, Ramón Gutiérrez and Genaro Padilla, formidable researchers that had been with the Recovery group from the beginning, affirmed that here was "the first of many volumes that will be published" (1993, 17) by Recovery. A second equally key event was the debut of the first fully realized recovery of a single authored book and the republication by Arte Público Press of María Amparo Ruiz de Burton's *The Squatter and the Don,* a work I dare say unknown to most of us attending the Recovery conference for the first time. My sense is that up to this point the work of recovery had been largely exploratory, and recovery researchers in the words of Gutiérrez and Padilla, were running on a mixture of "enthusiasm and provocations generated by the first conference" (1993, 17). My particular training paired with my research of the Spanish-language press in the Southwest had sharpened my focus on questions of literary history and textual genealogy. The work brought forth by Beatrice Pita and Rosaura Sánchez and their re-introduction of Ruiz de Burton's novel went beyond provocation. In regard to Ruiz de Burton's work they remark that "While inveighing against corruption, the novel, in keeping with a reformist stance that has no basic quarrel with capitalism in and of itself—nor with patriarchy for that matter—argues for full enforcement of existing laws guaranteeing the righting of wrongs and a more principled capitalism" (992, 31-32). I admit that at the time I was inordinately surprised by what I saw as a redirection of recovery's initial conference call "to assess the known and, as yet, unknown aspects of this literary past" (17). So surprised in fact that this second development caused me to go back to the seminal work of *don* Luis Leal, the first researcher to have ever mentioned Ruiz de Burton in regard to early Californiano writings, to ascertain how he could have missed mentioning such a key and formidable work like *Squatter.*

The matter was not eased by Sánchez and Pita's claim that "C. L. or C. Loyal" [*ciudadano leal*] was the author *of Squatter* and that the initials could stand for María Amparo Ruiz de Burton. Nor was it all that easy to understand how Recovery scholars could recast a piece of "hacienda literature" into a precursor of Chicana literature. Irrespective of my initial qualms, *The Squatter and the Don* remains the largest selling Recovery title and is the single most cited and discussed work recovered by the Program.

This then was the context of my introduction to a group of like-minded scholars all of whom in their separate ways embraced the mission set before us. Over the course of the last two decades, the Recovery Program has expanded exponentially and has registered milestone after milestone in identifying early

Latino writings and reintroducing them to an ever-growing group of students and researchers. More has been achieved than could have been imagined in 1992 when a group of leading scholars, librarians and archivists from the United States, Mexico, Puerto Rico and Spain set about "to research, locate, preserve and make accessible all literary- historical documents produced by Hispanics living in the United States from the Colonial Period to 1960" (Gutiérrez and Padilla, 1993, 13). Precisely now, considering the large corpus of materials that Recovery has made available to students and emerging scholars, is a time to reconsider the means (the methodologies) with which the significance of these writings can be critically assessed.

For some time now a war has raged in the humanities and social sciences over, on the one hand, what are to be the accepted means of knowledge apprehension and, on the other, over the utility of the methodologies by which to verify knowledge claims and research assumptions. Armed camps inhabit the halls of academe, and Arts and Letters disciplines once placid enclaves of inquiry are riddled by the claims and counterclaims emerging from postmodern vs. poststructuralist theorists, defenders and adversaries of canonical vs. non-canonical typologies, and theoreticians vs. historians of the archive. Of course, it was never assumed that the Recovery Program in its mission to rebuild or reconstruct the US Latino literary legacy would be spared these convulsions. In his 1993 essay, Francisco Lomelí had flagged the fault line running beneath recovery scholarship by asking, "In the process of erecting demarcations and parameters, one pivotal concern has emerged: how to grapple with the politics and poetics of reconstructing and or/appropriating a literary past?" (1993, 226). Even as Lomelí asserted that "the literature's legitimacy is no longer much in question," he cautioned recovery scholars to prepare for push- back by the scholarly community of "be[ing] accused of fabricating a past for the sake of having one, or that we are randomly taking authors and works out of a hat or out of context" (228). Uppermost in Lomelí's thinking was the question of how Chicano critics should establish "an adequate historical framework for early Chicano literature" in view of the claim he and others held (myself included) that Chicano/US Latino literature had "its beginnings at the point of initial contact between Europeans and Native Americans in what was the outer fringes of the northern frontier of New Spain" (227). Still, Lomelí was voicing a complex set of assumptions, matters that I am not fully able to address here. I will only say that it appears to me that Lomelí was focused on how first-wave recovery scholars (those represented in volume one and those convened by the first two Recovery conferences) might unwittingly "be subsuming or claiming something as are own" and "declaring that it is rightfully ours" (227). Aside from the deep irony residing in the idea that Chicanos, the subjected peoples of imperial Spain, might be appropriating the colonial texts of their conquerors to legitimate a presence within the present- day boundaries of the United States. I think it also telling that Lomelí was focused on appropriations as might be exercised over a past literary legacy. The double irony here being that second or third wave Recovery scholars might be in the process of becoming "clever fabricators" using the materials of their literary ancestors to redound onto concerns evident in present-day cultural studies discourses. Here too appears another massive and complicated matter, which I will not attempt to ferret out, rather only seek to share the sense of satisfaction and purpose that I have experienced in doing Recovery work.

As I was finishing up the writing of *So All is Not Lost,* I was able to contact Herminia Chacón and made arrangement to interview her in in November of 1995. I met her at the door of her tidy apartment at the Jewish Housing Federation Complex in El Paso, Texas. I have never felt more honored in doing recovery work than during the time I spent in conversation with Herminia. Over the years I have come to more fully recognize how truly remarkable and how priveledged I was not just to speak to her about the activities of her father, Felipe Maximiliano, but to find out that she too was a writer who had participated in the closing phase the cultural movement José Escobar so avidly encouraged in his 1896 essay. On the twenty-fifth anniversary of the Recovering the US Hispanic Literary Heritage Program, I think it immensely valueable to consider this period of borderlands writing as a catenuated and dynamic cultural moment. It is time, I urge, to re-evaluate how the activities of several generations of Mexican American writers, at least in this one corner of the borderlands, started out as and were meant to be arranged like a chain binding the desire and struggle of one generation to others that follow.

Some time after the publication of *So All is Not Lost* a good friend and a very capable researcher, Anselmo Arellano, clipped an item from *The Santa Fe New Mexican* that he thought would be of special interest to me. It was a short article published in May 1919 that reported on the closing exercises for the eighth-grade graduation at the public school in Mora, New Mexico a school then run by the Sisters of Loreto. The report gave an account of how, Felipe Maximiliano Chacón, the editor of the Spanish weekly, *El Eco del Norte,* had given a rousing talk exhorting the graduates to continue their education. There among the twelve graduating eighth graders sat my father, Manuel Santos Meléndez. The article relays how the children listened to Mr. Chacón deliver a talk in eloquent and formal English in which he exhorted this now bilingual classroom of children to improve themselves through education. I can imagine Felipe Maximiliano wanting to fire them up in Spanish with ringing exhortations. Perhaps he thought to read them a poem from his about-to-be published

Prosa y poesía, but already by 1919, the signs were clear that even in the most rural Mexican American hamlets, English had become the formal language of instruction and so one link in the chain of inter-generational promise was being hacksawed in two as Felipe Maximiliano spoke. His speech, reported *El Eco del Norte* (in Spanish), was loaded with moralizing zest, surging in its zealous condemnation of sloth, the kind of thing one would expect to hear at just such ceremonies across the United States in 1919. And while the message was coming from a solid member of the Nuevomexicano community, whose accomplishments could serve to uplift an audience of students, parents and teachers-residents of one of the poorest, rural communities in the nation—in all likelihood the whole matter of how men and women of his generation had dared to dream of writing works of literature in the effort to stave away ignorance and defamation was not mentioned at all. Thus, a second link in the transmission of José Escobar's "Progreso literario," as I make mention elsewhere in this volume, was also frayed.

When the matter of collaborating with her father at *La Bandera Americana* comes up, Herminia resists the idea of being a writer in her own right. To help her see her accomplishments, I brought copies of a number of short stories and news items that she placed in the paper. "Well, I would just go to the paper just to help him, so that he wouldn't be left by himself." But isn't it true that you also wrote? I ask. "Well," she answers, "from time to time some things occurred to me." I ask a recovery question because I am also interested in her reaction to the dimishing of Spanish-language publication. On the issue of the dissolution of the papers she and her father issued, she suggests it came about " . . . because people, the New Mexicans, have forgotten Spanish, they've forgotten the language and *we were encouraged to forget it"* (215). When I ask if the language shift made it difficult for her father to keep publishing, she remarks, "I don't think he noticed. Nobody did at the time. He thought it was a pity afterwards. Because I think it was by 1930 that people were speaking more English and they used to tell us they weren't going to teach their children Spanish."

Herminia's memories of the shift in language use speaks to the requirements for linguistic conformity that characterized whole epochs in the Southwest.lvi Linguistic intimidation proved corrosive to the extent that F. M. Chacon's *Prosa y poesía* was tossed aside and, so too, Herminia's short stories and other writings. In the moments before completing my interview with Herminia, she motions toward her bookshelf and asks me, "Do you have a copy of my father's book?" Before I can answer she continues, "Well you can have that copy. I still have some left. It was 1995, *doña* Herminia was 92 years old. The book she handed me had been published 71 years earlier on the presses of *La Bandera Americana* in the Barelas neighborhood just south of downtown Albu-

querque. Herminia, it appeared to me, was still occupied in the work of disseminating the work of Mexican American print culture, albeit, individually, personally in the realm of her private life. Still, in one sense she was a precursor to the
work of recovering Mexican American literary texts. Her knowledge and
instinct were at work and sufficiently intact to know that something of value
resided in the lofty pursuit of education and literacy her forebearers had undertaken. She wrote to me after *So All is Not Lost* was published, and her words
stay with me: "Dr. Meléndez—Just a note to congratulate you on *So All is Not
Lost*. I was somewhat overwhelmed that you put me in the epilogue. You do me
too much credit. By the way, do you read, *La Herencia del Norte*? The December issue has a story written by me." Who indeed overwhelms whom? Recovery
scholars, *¡Adelante!*

Institutional Politics and Pedagogy

Tirando del hilo se construye la historia

ROSE MARIE BEEBE

Santa Clara University

Abuela, cuéntame la historia de la explosión del barco Maine.

Abuela, cuéntame cómo mi bisabuelo obtenía quinina para los cubanos sin que los americanos supieran lo que estaba haciendo. Abuela, anoche me picó un mosquito. ¿Crees que necesito quinina?

Abuela, ¿por qué tuvieron que irse de Cuba?

Abuela, ¿por qué nunca aprendiste a hablar inglés? ¿Por qué dicen que tu inglés está "roto"?

I was first made aware of the importance of recovery and preservation by a wonderful woman. She was Inés Mantilla de Sunyer, wife of Manuel Mallafré Sunyer (stonemason), mother of five daughters, Cuban immigrant, seamstress, cannery worker and "*mi abuela.*" This strong, courageous and feisty woman was fiercely proud of her humble Cuban roots and her resilience when faced with any obstacle put in front of her. She never tired of describing what life was like for her and the Cuban people from the time she was born (1898) to the late 1930s. Her presentation of those experiences had a profound impact on me. Her eyewitness accounts and vignettes about historical and political figures, as well as economic and social challenges, provided her listeners with vivid images of class struggle, discrimination, poverty, the impact of a United States "presence" and more. The desire to share these episodes with others was my grandmother's way of preserving her country's history, as well as her own, and enabling others to recover that important, and too often hidden, heritage.

My grandparents had to flee Cuba in the 1930s for political reasons and they relocated to the United States. My grandmother experienced a particular set of challenges when she arrived as an immigrant to this country. Her biggest challenge was the English language. It did not come easily to her, no matter how hard she tried. Her communication skills in English were limited, and there were times when I overheard people laugh at her. They would say she spoke "broken English." As a child, I didn't understand what was meant by that term. My grandmother wasn't "broken!" I knew it bothered her to be viewed as an outsider, as the "other" in the neighborhood, but in her "lived wisdom" she intuitively knew how to turn these crass and hurtful comments into what today we would call a "teachable moment." No matter how much the insult stung, she always taught me to be proud of the fact that, because of her, I could speak TWO languages.

As I look back and reflect on my almost forty-year career as a university professor of Spanish language and literature, I cannot help but acknowledge the pivotal role my grandmother played in guiding me toward a teaching career. She would be proud to know that our shared love of language and history has informed my teaching, research trajectory and publications in very significant ways. Primary source documents written in Spanish, such as historical accounts, reports, diaries, letters and memoirs from the eighteenth and nineteenth centuries, have formed the subject of my academic work. The recovery, preservation, translation and dissemination of these voices from the past are my passion. And that passion began to become focused when I was alerted back in October 1992 to a conference in Houston that focused on "Recovering the US Hispanic Literary Heritage." Not only my career, but my life in general would have taken a very different turn if I had not attended that conference and met scholars who were engaged in the type of work that I was interested in.

From 1978 to 1990, my position at Santa Clara University was that of lecturer in Spanish language. In 1990, I had the opportunity to advance to a tenure-track position and accepted the challenge, knowing that in addition to maintaining a good track record in teaching, I would be expected to contribute significantly to my field in the areas of research and publication in order to be granted tenure. But where to begin? A normal tact for a newly minted Ph. D. who has a tenure-track position is to mine the dissertation for articles and such. I did not want to go down that path, even though it seemed like the normal thing to do. My grandmother had been gone for over fourteen years, so I could not seek her out for some good advice. A wise friend, Santa Clara University archivist Julia O'Keefe, helped me articulate the solution to my research/publication dilemma. What had motivated me to pursue degrees in Spanish and teach at the university level? What aspects of my studies had truly energized me? The answers to these questions were easy: my love for the Spanish language and oral histories in that language. Julia told me that several years prior, the university had acquired a handwritten Spanish manuscript from 1851 entitled *La historia de Alta California*. She thought that I might be interested in looking at it because I was so fascinated by historical recollections and memoir. The manuscript was written by Antonio María Osio in the form of a letter to Fr. José María Suárez del Real at Mission Santa Clara. In a cover letter, Osio told Suárez del Real that what the priest had asked him to do, "write about the history of California," was beyond his ability. Instead, Osio said that he would write a letter, or *relación,* of events since 1815, detailing especially "what I have experienced and observed since the year 1825." This 220-page manuscript had never before been transcribed or translated. I was intrigued by this *relación*. At first glance, the nineteenth-century handwriting was not difficult to decipher; I had seen this careful and flowery script before, in notes and cards that my grandmother had written. Perhaps I could translate this man's historical account and share it by publishing it. Perhaps this could be my research project.

Some of my departmental colleagues objected. They did not deem this translation project to be an example of "scholarship." They warned me that it would not carry great weight in my tenure application. I listened, but decided to heed my grandmother's words ("Que el estudio sea siempre el faro que ilumine tu vida."), take a huge risk and dive headfirst into this project. I soon realized that I needed to collaborate with a historian in order to delve deeply into the manuscript, especially its people and events. I needed to discover why Osio's voice and his account of California's early history should be taken down from an archival shelf and "recovered." I asked Professor Robert M. Senkewicz of Santa Clara University's history department if he might be interested in collaborating with me, and he agreed. I spent the months of June and July 1990 maneuvering through the Spanish transcript of Osio's work. Professor Senkewicz and I were equal partners in this project; his skills in Spanish were sharpened and polished, and I was able to deepen my knowledge of California history. We spent countless hours at The Bancroft Library consulting primary source accounts that were contemporaneous with Osio's manuscript. These sources were recollections or *testimonios* by Californio women and men who had been interviewed by Hubert Howe Bancroft's scribes as part of Bancroft's efforts to collect as much primary source material possible for his history project. The language employed by these nineteenth-century women and men was similar to the Spanish spoken by my grandmother. These Californios were "speaking" to me from those dusty manuscript pages. I began to think that I could be a kind of steward for them, that I could recover their voices and share their stories. Julia O'Keefe was correct when she suggested that my research path had been clearly defined for me long ago. I just hadn't realized it. The passion for oral history that my grandmother had instilled in me did indeed have a direct and strong correlation with the Osio research project and my hopes for its publication. Why, then, did many of my colleagues not consider this to be "legitimate scholarship?"

All sorts of information crosses the desk of a department chair. Fortunately for me, my department chair paid attention to an announcement regarding the 1992 Recovering the US Hispanic Literary Heritage conference and brought it to my attention. This chairperson happened to be from a different academic discipline and did not hold the same negative opinion of my research, as did my other colleagues. She felt that the conference might be a venue for me to connect with scholars who were engaged in work similar to mine and they might be able to provide me with guidance. I quickly bought my airplane ticket, paid the registration fee and headed off to Houston. The conference presentations were relevant to my interests in recovering texts and voices from the past. After years of relative neglect by historians, first-person accounts such as the Osio manuscript were being rediscovered as valuable sources by respected Recovery Program scholars such as Genaro Padilla and Rosaura Sánchez.[1] Listening at the conference to scholars engaged in this recovery work was a form of validation and confirmed for me that I was on the right research path. So many scholars were generous with their time and did not act put upon when I asked for a few minutes of their time to speak about my project. One scholar in particular, Dr. Antonia Castañeda, would become my inspiration and she continues to be my role model. Dr. Castañeda's groundbreaking work, "Presidiarias y Pobladores: Spanish-Mexican Women in Frontier Monterey, Alta California, 1770-1821," was a key volume that I consulted while working on the Osio manuscript.[2] Her other pioneering works continued to be instrumental in shaping and focusing the trajectory of my research. I also was grateful to Dr. Castañeda and other scholars at the conference for encouraging me to submit a paper proposal about the Osio manuscript for presentation at a future conference. The 1992 Recovering the US Hispanic Literary Heritage conference made me feel that I had found my research "home."

In December 1994, Robert Senkewicz and I presented a paper entitled "The Recovery of the First History of Alta California: Antonio María Osio's *La historia de Alta California*" at the third Recovery conference. Seated in the audience was Dr. Luis Leal. At the end of the session, he came up to us and strongly emphasized the importance of recovering and publishing texts such as the Osio manuscript. Two years later, the annotated translation of *The History of Alta California: A Memoir of Mexican California by Antonio María Osio* was published. We had succeeded in recovering, preserving and sharing Osio's voice. And the Osio book helped me obtain tenure![3]

During the years I worked on the Osio translation, I frequently would share with my students the manner in which Osio depicted Californio society. These vignettes sparked lively conversation among the students, especially those students who were from Spanish-speaking families. They started to make comparisons between Osio's depictions and the experiences of their own family members, especially their grandparents. Several students asked me if I would be willing to teach them how to "recover" their past by learning how to read and translate "old documents." I shared this idea with Robert Senkewicz, and we proposed offering a translation course based on historical documents written in Spanish. We had used documents from the Pueblo Papers collection housed at History San José when working on the Osio project and knew that this collection was an amazing untapped resource. I approached my department chair (a different one) about offering this course and he said, "No." So, recalling my grandmother's wise words ("Que el estudio sea siempre el faro que ilumine tu vida."), I said, "Fine. I shall teach the course as an unpaid overload," and that is exactly what I did. Robert Senkewicz and I selected a set of documents from 1809 that the students would transcribe, translate and annotate under our direction. The student work resulted in a bilingual publication: *A Year in the Life of a Spanish Colonial Pueblo, San José de Guadalupe in 1809, Official Correspondence,*[4] which can be found in many university libraries, historical societies, and even the Archivo General de la Nación!

Word spread quickly among the upper division Spanish students about the historical translation course, and we were able to offer it as a regular course many more times. The students were fascinated by the language and the content of the documents. The documents were filled with topics and themes that were often not found in the official mission documents and high-level government reports that formed the backbone of the traditional presentation of the history of California and the Southwest borderlands before 1848. Students read about boundary disputes, the types of punishment meted out to various transgressors, the number of *fanegas* of crops harvested, cases of sexual assault and other matters. Over the years, students presented their findings and translations at professional conferences in California. On one occasion, several students accompanied us to a conference in La Paz, Baja California where they were able to share their work with Dr. Miguel León-Portilla. And over the past twenty years, we have seen students from the translation courses pursue careers as official court translators, lawyers for Spanish-speaking clients, advocates for children of Spanish-speaking parents and social workers. One of our translation students used her translation skills in her job as an award-winning journalist for *Sports*

Illustrated and was able to uncover evidence about an overage baseball player from the Dominican Republic. We recently re-connected with four students from translation courses in the early 2000s. All four told us they still have their binders of translations of those voices from the past!

After the Osio book, Robert Senkewicz and I have continued to collaborate on the recovery, translation, annotation and publication of primary source material in Spanish. With the encouragement of pioneering California publisher Malcolm Margolin of Heyday Books, we undertook a documentary history of pre-US Alta California. We decided to include only voices from people who lived in the area during that time period and not to include the diaries and correspondence of North American travelers that had been the staple of many conventional accounts. Among the sixty-nine entries we included in the volume were sixteen original translations from Spanish documents that we were privileged to recover and share.[5]

In the same vein, a few years later, we translated and published in one volume the *testimonios* of the thirteen women interviewed by Hubert Howe Bancroft's staff for Bancroft's seven-volume *History of California*. This project confirmed for us the invaluable contributions the recovery enterprise can make to historical understanding. When Apolinaria Lorenzana or Eulalia Pérez described their roles at Missions San Diego and San Gabriel, they painted a picture of daily life at the missions that had largely been absent from mission historiography. These women turned out to have been the glue that held these missions together, and their *testimonios* offered a view of Spanish and Mexican California that could not be found in the sacramental registers, official reports or travelers' diaries.[6]

We are now engaged in our largest recovery effort, a translation of Mariano Guadalupe Vallejo's five-volume "Recuerdos históricos y personales tocante a la Alta California: historia política del país, 1769-1849; costumbres de los californios; apuntes biográficos de personas notables."[7] Vallejo (1808–1890) was born in Spanish California and came of age at the beginning of the Mexican era. A member of the elite, he rose to a high position as a member of the military and became an extensive landowner who conscripted hundreds of indigenous Californians as laborers on his estates. After the US conquest, he served as a member of the California Constitutional Convention and in the first legislature. He composed his *testimonio* for Bancroft in 1874–1875. While his perspective, like all perspectives, was limited by his class position, he provided a unique account of life in California before the gold rush. His account also provides impressive testimony to the resentment many Californios felt as they were losing their lands and position to Americans who thought the Californios and their culture were irredeemably inferior. This recovered perspective will, we hope, provide an important complement to California and southwestern history.

Abuela, espero que estés orgullosa de mí. A través de mi vida y mi carrera he tratado de incorporar y compartir las lecciones que me enseñaste. Esa pasión por nuestros antepasados y sus historias me acompaña en todo lo que hago. Sigo investigando la historia de los californios y lo hago con mi esposo y colaborador, Roberto. Pero eso ya lo sabías, ¿verdad?

¿Te acuerdas de cuánto te "fastidiaba" yo con mis preguntas acerca del pasado? Pero ahora me doy cuenta de que no era un fastidio. Te encantaba contestar mis preguntas, no con meros datos sino con tus recuerdos. Siempre me decías que era importante preservar, apreciar y compartir estos recuerdos con otros para que se dieran cuenta de que no hay solamente una manera de ver las cosas sino una variedad de perspectivas. Como me decías, 'Tenemos que examinar la historia por medio de muchos lentes.'

Pues, he intentado fomentar en mis alumnos esa pasión por encontrar, estudiar, y preservar las voces del pasado como tú hiciste conmigo. ¡Ahora me toca a mí contestar las preguntas!

—Profesora, cuéntenos cómo es posible que Apolinaria Lorenzana, una mujer, pudiera tener tanta influencia en el manejo de la Misión de San Diego que supuestamente era el dominio de los misioneros.

—Profesora, sabemos que Eulalia Pérez era la llavera de la Misión de San Gabriel pero no entendemos por qué tuvo que encerrar a las indígenas en ese lugar que llamaban monjerío. No eran monjas. ¿Nos pudiera explicar la razón por ese tipo de encerramiento o quizás se pudiera llamar encarcelamiento?

Pero lo que más me alegra es cuando me dicen, -Profesora, quiero saber más de mi cultura, de mi historia. Yo quiero escuchar las voces de mis propios antepasados. ¿Me pudiera ayudar a identificar esas voces para buscarlas en algún archivo?

Es cierto, Abuela. El estudio sigue siendo el faro que ilumina vidas.

Endnotes

[1]See, for example, Padilla, Genaro M. "The Recovery of Chicano Nineteenth-Century Autobiography." *American Quarterly* 40. 3 (1988): 286-306; Sánchez, Rosaura. "Nineteenth-Century Californio Narratives: The Hubert H. Bancroft Collection." in *Recovering the U.S. Hispanic Literary Heritage* Vol. I. eds. Gutiérrez, Ramón A. and Genaro Padilla (Houston: Arte Público Press, 1993), 279-292.

[2]Castañeda, Antonia I., "Presidiarias y Pobladores: Spanish-Mexican Women in Frontier Monterey, Alta California, 1770-1821" Ph.D. dissertation, Stanford University, 1990.

[3]Beebe, Rose Marie and Robert M. Senkewicz,, "The Recovery of the First History of Alta California: Antonio María Osio's 'La historia de Alta California,'" in *Recovering the US Hispanic Literary Heritage* Vol. 2, eds. Gonzales-Berry, Erlinda and Chuck Tatum (Houston: Arte Público Press,1996): 168-184; Beebe, Rose Marie and Robert M. Senkewicz, eds. and trans., *The History of Alta California: A Memoir of Mexican California* (Madison: University of Wisconsin Press, 1996).

[4]Lambert, Diane, Naomi Reinhart, Ludivina Russell, Gregory von Herzen, with Rose Marie Beebe and Robert M. Senkewicz. *A Year in the Life of a Spanish Colonial Pueblo, San José de Guadalupe in 1809, Official Correspondence.* Research Manuscript Series on the Cultural and Natural History of Santa Clara, No. 9, Santa Clara University, Santa Clara, CA. 1998.

[5]Beebe, Rose Marie and Robert M. Senkewicz, eds. and trans. *Lands of Promise and Despair: Chronicles of Early California,* 1535-1846 (Berkeley: Heyday Books, 2001).

[6]Beebe, Rose Marie, and Robert M. Senkewicz, eds. and trans. Testimonios: *Early California through the Eyes of Women,* 1815-1848 (Berkeley: Heyday Books and The Bancroft Library, 2006).

[7]Vallejo, Mariano Guadalupe, "Recuerdos históricos y personales tocante a la Alta California: historia política del país, 1769-1849; costumbres de los californios; apuntes biográficos de personas notables," mss., The Bancroft Library, C-D 17-21.

The Lean Years: Coming Up Short and Then Finding Someone Else's (Unused) Pay Dirt

KENYA C. DWORKIN Y MÉNDEZ

Carnegie Mellon University

At my home institution, when I realized that despite my growing laissez-faire attitude towards how my work was being perceived, I understood it was incumbent upon me to create a narrative with which to explain, to the totally uninitiated, what the connection was between my prior research on Cuban literature and identity and my Tampa-based work. Coming up for another review gave me that opportunity. By this time, I was a scholar whose activism was born out of the frustration I felt when I realized what the prevailing attitude was of my Anglo, male, academic seniors. Despite the discomfort of some, I successfully explained that it was ultimately about identity and the many different circumstances under which a national identity can be shaped and reshaped by immigration, exile and contact with a host society. That seemed to placate them, although it helped that by this time I was writing about an American chapter of the Tampa Latin theater story—the Spanish-language Federal Theatre project of 1936-37. Managing to publish a lengthy, well-researched and well-received article in English on the subject bought me some time: time to keep searching for a stash of plays that I soon found out were practically within reach, except for one very big problem.

Many years after first starting my search for scripts, I was confronted with an ugly lesson in academic dishonesty. The person who became the institution's new president, a historian at a local university, gained access to whatever material that was available in the building—even in an old-fashioned safe—and took it all home under the pretext he was going to research and write *the* definitive book about Tampa Cubans.

When I found out the materials had been recovered, and assuming they would go to Special Collections at the University of South Florida, where they'd be properly processed, catalogued and made available, but had ended up in boxes at his home, I contacted him. Upon having to uncomfortably ask him if he knew if he had theatrical materials and, if so, would it be possible for me to see them, he stipulated that he would agree to allow me access, but only for a very limited time, and only if I agreed not to share any information with another local scholar (and good friend of mine) at his own institution who was studying anti-black racism among Tampa Cuban cigar makers. I made a brief visit to his home and told him the situation was untenable and that I would wait until these valuable historical documents were where they should be: in the archive. Since then, I have been expecting a new publication on the history of Tampa Cubans. Our unnamed scholar went on to bigger and better things: high-level university administration. This denouement brings to mind a saying in Spanish—*Dios le da barba al que no tiene quijada*—which loosely translates into something like "God gives bread to those with no teeth."

Fast Forward Ten Years, to Now (2017-2018): Out of Chaos Comes Clarity

Ten years later, when I got word that the collection had finally gone to its rightful home, I felt ready to go. Except, I wasn't. An unforeseen, serious health issue spoiled my plan to head straight down there the very next summer, an issue that continued (and continues) to plague me now. Therefore, I had to wait until after the second summer, and with persistence was able to accomplish what I should have been able to do nearly twenty years earlier. I organized all the scanned play materials, put them on a separate drive and personally handed them to Nicolás Kanellos at our next Recovery board meeting, at the upcoming conference in February 2017. I wrapped the drive in a small jewelry box and ceremoniously handed it to him explaining—in front of everyone—that it was one small way for me to give back. The Recovery Program, the foremost rescuer and archivist of Latino print materials, now possessed a substantial stash of plays from Tampa—more than 55—for current and future generations of scholars and academics to enjoy. I now felt like I was really a contributor, because among the group were others who had done just this sort of salvage work.

After getting back to the "Burgh," the reading marathon began! Cursory readings allowed me to document the corpus as best I could, whenever possible: by author, date, title, place of origin, performance dates and thematic content. This allowed me to finally devise a way to understand Tampa Latin theater's evolution, from its Peninsular roots, to its Cuban adaptation, to its Tampa transplantation, its incipient ethnic Americanization, and beyond. Interestingly enough, I realized that the lessons I had learned from working on the Recovery anthologies greatly served me when deciding how to classify the works, create categories for them that remained porous enough to represent the truly translational nature of this theater, and allowed me to describe how the plays responded to different local, national and international events and people for audiences on both sides of the Florida Straits.

Something I had so long suspected finally became clear to me: the Golden Age of Cuban theater in Tampa (theater written in Cuba but presented there) was the 1920s. It was during this raucous decade that folks (and governments) on both sides of the straits enjoyed both the rise and endured the fall of ten years that perhaps should be described as an economic, social, moral and cultural roller coaster. Cuba's "*vacas gordas*" and the US's "Roaring Twenties" were a great inspiration for the fertile imaginations of Cuban playwrights who had seen the debacle of the US-mitigated "independence" from Spain and its economic and social aftermath on the island. Back then, their eyes were trained on the uncomfortable pattern of American interference and influence that was developing in Cuba; that, and the equally distressing impact that a series of bad governments and ever-expanding US investments were having on Cuba's complete sovereignty. Couple all that with the rise of fascism on the world scene and the economic disaster that abruptly burst the world's economic bubble, and a small but important group of Cuban playwrights knew it was crucial to bring all this to a popular audience's consideration—through easily accessible theater. To be able to authoritatively declare the twenties to be this pivotal period in Tampa's working-class, popular theater, and that this decade's plays inspired local, cigar maker-playwrights to continue this practice in coming decades, was a gift I had sorely needed and finally received.

The fruits of this gift very quickly manifested themselves. In 2017, a presentation at the "Reading Cuba" conference at Florida International University and a separate invitation from Jesse Alemán (another member of my Recovery family), after our most recent Recovery conference in February, allowed me to focus on the Cuban and Tampa 1920s, theater and playmaking. Before year's end, I was fortunate enough to have two articles, one in Spanish, one in English, representing my first serious attempt to discuss this important decade with Cuban and English-language readers—a small contribution to spreading my and our Recovery work to new audiences.

Now, in early 2018, as I complete this reflection, the biggest question is: "What is left for me to do?" Well, the obvious answer is to *finally* complete *the* book on Tampa Latin theater, whose current working title is *Before Latino: Performing Cuba in Tampa, 1886-1960*. Twenty-four years after I unwittingly stumbled across the phenomenon of Latin theater in Tampa, while at the last minute filling in for someone at a symposium, after painfully slowly and falteringly finding a path forward from discovery to recovery, I am in a position to finally do this subject justice. There is still a lot of work for me to do, other decades and topics to examine and reexamine, now that so much more primary materials have given me much better perspective. Moreover, what may be my final hurdle will be to see if I can devise a way to create an approach that allows me to integrate both a chronological and thematic analysis—although issues of race, class, gender and national identity permeate the entire corpus. What I do know is that the next month or so I will have to craft my plan of action for the next calendar year, at the end of which I hope to have a complete manuscript. Were I to bend to institutional pressure, I'd be planning to submit it to a "reputable university press," but after all this time and experience, I strongly believe it belongs with the folks at the Recovery Program in Houston, if they will have it. Nowhere else would be a more natural home, I think, than in the place and with the people who first believed in me and supported me along the way. However, finishing this book project will not mark the end of something, but rather the beginning of something else, which, no doubt, will bear the unmistakable stamp of Recovery, whether it is about Tampa writer José Yglesias, or an analysis of Spanish-language journalism in Tampa through critical Spanish and Cuban political periods between 1922 and the 1960s, or even Sephardic-Puerto Rican relations in New York City—all projects entirely within the Recovery Program's purview, and all of immense interest to me.

Approaches for Teaching Early Twentieth-Century Mexican-American Literature in Undergraduate Classrooms

Yolanda Padilla
University of Washington, Bothell

The Recovering the US Hispanic Literary Heritage Program has been enormously successful in its goals of researching, recovering and reprinting Latinx writings from the colonial era to the 1960s. It is an inspiration to anyone drawn to the project of textual recovery, that process of locating and situating texts that have been excluded from the purview of traditional history, literary and otherwise, both by the cultural assumptions governing the creation of archives and by the discourses of history. However, despite the Recovery Program's herculean efforts to create comprehensive and searchable databases, release volumes of recovered texts with thorough and meticulously researched introductions, and host conferences for scholars to share their work, the field of US literary studies has shown a marked lack of interest in engaging these newly available materials. Numerous scholars have criticized—and rightly so—this indifference.[1] Jesse Alemán points out that a large part of the problem is the field's lack of facility with Spanish (viii).

If language is a problem for researchers, the issue is compounded in the classroom where, depending on the department in which one teaches, it is unrealistic and even counter-productive to require students to know Spanish. Yet I think that enough recovery texts are available in English—whether because that is the original language in which they were written or because they have been translated by the Recovery Program and other entities—that we can and should add a focus on field transformation through the incorporation of these texts into classrooms alongside a focus on scholarship. It would be beneficial for those of us who already use Recovery texts in the classroom to help facilitate their use more widely in US literature classes and beyond by sharing our syllabi and basic information about how we use these texts.[2] I have in mind something akin to the "Instructor's Guides" provided as a supplement to the *Heath Anthology of American Literature*. These guides facilitate teaching by providing information on themes and historical perspectives, significant form, style and artistic conventions, and connections among clusters of texts. In that spirit, I will share some of the ways that I use Recovery texts in my classes. I begin with a brief discussion of some of my key learning objectives in teaching these materials, followed by a discussion of two texts I have used often in a variety of classes: Jovita González's 1929 master's thesis, published in 2006 with the title *Life along the Border*, and Leonor Villegas de Magnón's memoir of the Mexican Revolution, *The Rebel,* which she wrote in the 1920s and was published for the first time in 1994.[3]

"'Communal Longings' and Disjunctions"

Numerous difficulties arise when incorporating recovery texts in the classroom, especially if one is teaching in a US or Anglophone-centered department (English departments are a prime example). While instructors often provide necessary historical and cultural context in most classes, the topics that students will encounter when studying recovery materials will likely be much less familiar to them. In a class that incorporated early twentieth-century literature by ethnic Mexicans, for example, students might need to learn about topics such as social patterns on Mexico's northern frontier, ranching practices in the Rio Grande Valley or the Mexican Revolution. These would have to be studied alongside subjects that might seem more familiar, but which students also struggle with, such as US notions of race and ethnicity or debates over the meanings of citizenship. The nomenclature can also be confusing, and one will need to spend a few minutes providing working definitions for terms such as "Mexican American" and "Tejano." Relatedly, the writers' differing subject positions (immigrants, migrants, exiles, etc.) reflect the fluidity of identities on the border during this period and require care in the generalizations one makes.[4]

Yet, precisely because of such difficulties, these readings provide rich opportunities to expand and complicate student thinking in a number of areas. They enable a denaturalizing of some of the most commonly held understandings of issues such as immigrant and national identity. They require a consideration of how other national contexts shape US social formations, literary traditions and intellectual currents, and thus challenge notions of American exceptionalism. And they introduce students to critical concepts such as "transnationalism," "transnational persons" and "immigrant nationalism," to name only a few possibilities. Moreover, and increasingly, there are resources to help instructors situate these readings, such as the recently published volume *The Latino Nineteenth Century* and the forthcoming *Cambridge History of Latina/o American Literature.*

I've used recovery materials in a variety of classes: "Race, Ethnicity, and Immigration," "US Literature Survey," "The Mexican Revolution in the Greater Mexican Imagination," "Latina/o Literature and Culture," "Politics and Culture on the US-Mexico Borderlands" and others. While my objectives in assigning Latinx texts written prior to the 1960s vary depending on the class, I find myself emphasizing a few regardless of the specific course. My first objective is the most obvious one to pursue when using such texts—to impress upon students the long history of Latinxs in what is now the United States. While this history might seem evident, Kirsten Silva Gruesz has characterized the ways in which Latinxs are dehistoricized by media rhetoric that refers to them primarily through a language of emergence and visibility that "registers only the contemporaneity of Latinas/os with respect to immigration, as if Spanish- speakers and their descendants had not lived within the boundaries of the United States since the seventeenth century, as if Latinos were not subjects of national history— 'subjects' in the sense of actors with agency, as well as oppressed subjects" (56). One of the educators in the documentary *Precious Knowledge* puts this point more bluntly, and just as powerfully: "They try to tell us that we don't belong here, that we're brand new. Well, it's not true, we've been here for 7000 years."[5]

While emphasizing the historical place of Latinx peoples in the US is important for all students, I want to point to a second objective by briefly touching on its benefits for Latinx students specifically. I must begin this discussion by pointing out that I will be making broad generalizations in how I talk about Latinx students. This is not because I am unaware of the impossibility of speaking of them as one unified block, but because despite the risks that come with such generalization, it allows me to express something about my approach to classroom dynamics that might be useful to instructors teaching Recovery materials. They should keep in mind that they can take nothing for granted with respect to the array of subject positions, experiences and perspectives represented by such students.

As *Precious Knowledge* shows so well, primary and secondary school curricula historically have either erased Latinx peoples from US history and culture or denigrated their presence, and this has had a negative effect on Latinx students, among others. The importance of challenging Eurocentric curricula has long been established by research in numerous fields—starting with ethnic studies—and many educators have transformed their classes in response.[6] Yet I find that many of the students in my classes still arrive without having had the opportunity in their primary or secondary school educations to study texts created by Latinxs—or, for that matter, by other people of color—and that they unsurprisingly continue to crave more inclusive subject matter. As I discuss below, my impulse when teaching recovery texts—and any text, really—is to hone in on points of contradiction, tension and uncertainty. In that, I am no different from any instructor teaching students critical reading skills.

However, over time I have responded to the deficiencies in the education students have experienced and their eagerness for material that they can identify with on a personal level by slowing down and making space for that kind of identification to happen, instead of immediately problematizing such inclinations. I know that many instructors already do this, but the approaches to reading that I had developed in graduate school left me uncomfortable with such identification to a degree that I was unaware of for the first few years of my teaching. I now give myself permission to allow and in selective ways encourage such connections because of the positive impact this process has had for many of my students.[7] In his introduction to *The Latino Nineteenth Century*, Rodrigo Lazo rightly emphasizes the disjunctions among Latinos, explaining, "the documents of a Latino past point as much to multiplicity and flight as they do to something we might call heritage" (12). Yet he also talks about what he calls the "communal longings" embedded in the term "Latino/a," longings that one discerns whether studying writings from the nineteenth century or talking to students in the present moment. In fact, he suggests that using "Latino/a" when discussing earlier centuries is not anachronistic precisely because of such longings, which are manifested through the cultural and linguistic connections Spanish-speaking peoples established in these periods (3).

My classes are always very diverse, so it's not possible for me to create assignments with only Latinx students in mind. However, I have tried to implement approaches that benefit all students while keeping in mind the points about identification that I outline above. For example, when Latinx students express knowledge about the texts based on their personal experiences or on cultural similarities, I try to validate and cultivate their reactions rather than problematize them too quickly. Along with the important knowledge that they contribute, this enables them to earn a sense of authority in the classroom that they might not feel otherwise, and which benefits all students. I also encourage all students to engage in a process of reflection with respect to the materials we engage at least to some extent, and to do so in the context of our discussions of power and culture. Discussing the very real connections between the early Latinx writers we study and Latinx communities of today can give more meaning to the idea that Latinxs have always been part of the national—and transnational—fabrics of what is now the United States, and provides a focus that many students appreciate. Of course, such connections are easier to make with some texts than others. For example, Daniel Venegas's *The Adventures of Don Chipote*, published in Los Angeles in 1928, is written from a working-class perspective that can be interpreted in terms of a proto Mexican American or proto Chicano identity.[8] Other texts that are not so easily legible in the context of current culture and politics can be discussed through more involved engagements with ideas of modernity or historiography.[9]

I make space for these kinds of discussions at the same time that I follow my impulse to examine how the writings also elucidate deep fractures among Latinxs along political, regional, gender, class and other lines. In fact, the students are often the ones who bring up these tensions, as they are quick to notice the differences between a working-class writer such as Luis Pérez and a more privileged writer such as Maria Cristina Mena, as well as the differences between those writers and themselves. Of course, and as I note above, the profound heterogeneity of Latinx peoples one finds in these earlier periods is a quality that is just as true in the present moment. Students benefit from seeing this connection before moving to a consideration of how those differences manifest themselves in the Recovery literature. One easy index for the differences in identity is the multiplicity of names ethnic Mexicans in the United States used to identify themselves. These include Tejano and Nuevo Mexicano, *fronterizo*, *mexicano*, *mexicano- americano*, *hispano* and even Chicano, a term that appears in *The Adventures of Don Chipote*. Students understandably want clear explanations of these terms and whom they refer to. I provide such information, but also emphasize that the nomenclature is slippery for good reason. Identities were extremely fluid in the early twentieth century, in part because the border was not strictly policed. Thus, individual and community location with respect to the international line did not map on to notions of identity in ways that have come to seem natural to us today. And, of course, the rigor with which the boundary was policed changed over time. While the border was much more permeable in the 1950s than it is today, it marked a legal, political and cultural divide that had to be reckoned with at mid-century to an extent that was not true in, say, the 1920s. Consequently, categories of identity such as "migrant" and "immigrant," "citizen" and "non- citizen" not only had different valences in the early twentieth century than they do in our contemporary moment, but they also connoted significant differences *during* the early decades as well. Changes in the meanings of the international line, then, combined with differences in other key elements of identity formation, such as class, gender, race and ethnicity, resulted in the wide-range of subject positions occupied by ethnic Mexicans. These points pair well with Mary Pat Brady's arguments about understanding the border not as a site but as a process, one that can make and unmake subjectivities, and produce and sustain structures of inequality.

Teaching González's *Life along the Border* and *Magnón's The Rebel*

I have assigned the acclaimed Tejana folklorist Jovita González's master's thesis in a number of classes. Her thesis constitutes what María Cotera calls a "counterhistory," a narrative that "offers a Mexican perspective on the history of Texas and contests negative representations of Mexicano culture and people" (17). She begins her thesis defiantly, arguing that those Anglo Americans who view border Mexicans as "interlopers, undesirable aliens, and a menace to the community" should consider, first, that

> the majority of these so-called undesirable aliens have been in the state long before Texas was Texas; second, that these people were here long before these new Americans crowded the deck of the immigrant ship; third, that a great number of the Mexican people in the border did not come as immigrants, but are descendants of the agraciados who held grants from the Spanish crown.

I often use this passage as an anticipatory set early in my class on immigration,[10] asking students to identify ideas and themes relevant to the study of immigration in the United States. Without fail they are struck by the characterization of border Mexicans as "undesirable aliens" and as a "menace to the community," remarking on the similarity to how Mexicans and other immigrants of color are described today. As one might guess from my involvement with the Recovery Program, my classes always have a strong historical perspective, and the idea that much of the alarmist and denigrating rhetoric used with respect to immigrants today has a long history is one that we consider throughout the term. While the cyclical patterns of such attacks is all too familiar to those well versed in immigration history, I find that for students this and the shifting nature of "whiteness" with respect to immigration and citizenship are among their biggest takeaways from the class.

Students are also struck by the way that González challenges the notion that all Mexicans are immigrants, and her assertion that, in fact, Anglos were the "new Americans." This provides the opportunity to discuss the fact that ethnic Mexicans in the United States encompassed (and continue to encompass) an array of backgrounds as migrants, immigrants, exiles and longtime residents who traced their family lines back to when the US Southwest was still the Mexican north. Such a discussion would remind students that what is today the US

Southwest is formerly Mexican land, and that the Mexicans who lived in that region were not immigrants; rather, they were a conquered people suddenly subjected to the rule of their conquerors (the famous slogan from the Chicano Movement—"We didn't cross the border, the border crossed us"—works very well to emphasize this point). Moreover, I always make space to discuss resistance on the part of those subjugated, and González's thesis is an excellent example of such resistance. This returns us to the idea of her thesis as a "counterhistory," one that challenges American exceptionalism's mythification of the nation's Anglo-Protestant essence by centering Tejano history and culture.

Of course, many of these issues would also be relevant in a class on the US-Mexico borderlands (among others). In addition, when I teach González in a borderlands class, I do so in the context of Mary Louise Pratt's concept of "contact zones." I find this concept extremely useful to try to get students to move beyond dualistic thinking and "us vs. them" mentalities. Pratt uses the term "contact zone" to refer to "social spaces where cultures meet, clash and grapple with each other, often in contexts of highly asymmetrical relations of power" (1991, 34). One of the benefits of a contact framework is that it enables a "decentering of community to look at how signification works across and through lines of difference and hierarchy" (1993, 88-89). As the opening to *Life along the Border* indicates, González devotes significant attention to conflict and violence between Anglos and Tejanos. However, these are not the only dynamics of "difference and hierarchy" to which she attends. For example, she also describes at length contact and violence between Mexicans and Indians, and the profound tensions between border Mexicans and the Mexican government (50-54). Moreover, she details class fractures among border Mexicans, especially the power dynamics underpinning the relationship among landlords, *vaqueros* (cowboys) and *peones*, whom she describes as "Indian immigrants from Mexico" (76). This latter point shows that ethnic Mexicans were a diverse group, encompassing wealthy elites who traced their ancestry to the original Spanish conquest of the region, modest ranchers, laborers, deeply rooted residents and more recent arrivals from Mexico.

Another Recovery text I have used in various classes is Leonor Villegas de Magnón's memoir *The Rebel*. Magnón was born in 1876 into an affluent and cultured family that was part of the Mexican frontier's "rural aristocracy." While she spent the first years of her childhood in Nuevo Laredo, Tamaulipas—just across the border from Laredo, Texas—she was educated in the United States and lived in south Texas for most of her life. Yet, as was typical in an era when the border was extremely permeable, there is no indication that she considered herself an immigrant, a Mexican American or even a *Tejana*. Rather, she defiantly identified herself as a Mexican, but one whose primary allegiance was to the borderlands, a region constituted through its transgression of the international boundary. In fact, a desire to validate that borderlands identity motivates her remarkable memoir of the Revolution, as she uses her narrative to push back against a Mexican center that by turns ignores and disparages the peoples—especially the women—and cultures of the border:

> History has assumed responsibility for documenting the facts, but it has forgotten the important role played by the communities of Laredo, Texas, and Nuevo Laredo, Tamaulipas and other border cities which united themselves in a fraternal agreement. (Qtd in Lomas 1994, xxxix)[11]

Like González, Magnón shows a strong sense of *fronterizos* as historical agents in the terrain of politics and culture, and she very explicitly challenges nation-based historiographies that ignore them. One can relate this passage to Magnón's engagement with "official" Mexican history and impress upon students that in many ways Mexicans north of the border had a relationship with the Mexican nation that could be just as conflicted as the one they had with the United States. This raises an important theme of much Mexican American literature, that of the simultaneous "insider/outsider" status that ethnic Mexicans often feel in relation both to the United States and to Mexico. Numerous Mexican American writers have thematized the feelings of placelessness and alienation that arise from such a status. One can also talk about how such feelings of alienation played a part in the rise of the vibrant border culture that scholars describe as a mix of US and Mexican cultural practices that remained fairly autonomous from both national centers, albeit in a violent field of relations. Drawing from work in postcolonial studies, historian David Gutiérrez provides a valuable analysis of this borderlands culture through the concept of the "third space." He devotes a section of his article to the early twentieth century and the Mexican Revolution, which connects very well with Magnón.

Students are often puzzled by the commitment to Mexico and Mexican affairs Magnón expresses here and throughout her memoir. After all, while she was born in Mexico, she settled on the US side of the border from a fairly young age. Their confusion stems from their understanding of the identities of Mexicans in the United States through traditional immigration models. Such models view migration as a one-way process in which immigrants assimilate the cultural values and political allegiances of their new homelands. Mexicans in the United States—like a number of ethnic groups—do not comfortably fit this model. Magnón's memoir, like González's work, provides an opportunity to complicate notions of immigration and citizenship. Informed by Jessica Enoch's work on Magnón and writings by other border women, I discuss *The Rebel* in the context of "cultural citizenship," which conceptualizes how members of a subordinated culture construct a kind of citizenship based in practices, beliefs and understandings that are central to how they live their lives. Cultural citizenship "centers on the right of its members to maintain their culture even when certain cultural claims run counter to the broader requirements and expectations of national citizenship" (122).[12] For the border writers that were part of Magnón's circle, this meant participating in key Mexican political and social events, and certainly included their participation in an event of the magnitude of the Mexican Revolution. It also meant preserving Mexican cultural traditions and the Spanish language while being active participants in US civil society. More generally, it meant choosing not to choose one national identity over the other, as they embraced aspects of both for as long as they could.

One can also discuss these issues on a more conceptual level, using the readings as an opportunity to denaturalize notions of nation and national belonging through the concept of the "transnational." This would entail contrasting older models of migration that emphasize one-way movement and permanent settlement with newer models that develop the idea of the "transnational subject," emphasizing two-way movements across relatively fluid national borders. Such back and forth movement as an aspect of everyday life was certainly Villegas de Magnón's experience. But the concept of the "transnational" is also relevant for those ethnic Mexicans long-settled and anchored to particular locales north of the border. To elaborate on this idea, one can turn to Moya and Saldívar's essay. They develop the concept of "transnational persons," meaning individuals "whose lives form an experiential region within which singularly delineated notions of political, social and cultural identity do not suffice" (2). With this, Moya and Saldívar provide a more expansive understanding of the "transnational subject," one that refers to those whose subjectivities are shaped by phenomena that exceed national boundaries and that include cultural mores, political commitments, intellectual currents, etc. This notion of the transnational subject applies to long-settled Mexicans in the United States, like Magnón, who engaged the Mexican events such as the Mexican Revolution and were shaped by and attempted in turn to influence Mexican history, politics, and culture.[13]

Introducing students to the concept of transnationalism, then, can provide them with a framework that challenges them to re-think rigid conceptualizations of national identity. But it is important to convey that transnationalism does not supersede or make irrelevant the nation. Rather, in Moya and Saldívar's words, it helps us to understand "competing nationalisms" alive within the nation (4), or as Shukla and Tinsman put it, it elucidates "social formations of migrants and other racialized groups across multiple nation-states" (11). One implication of such thinking is that it allows students to consider not only how Mexicans north of the border were excluded from the United States, but also how they operated as dynamic parts of multiple nations.

Works Cited

Alemán, Jesse. "Preface." *The Latino Nineteenth Century.* Eds. Rodrigo Lazo and Jesse Alemán. New York: New York University Press, 2016. vii-ix.

Brady, Mary Pat. *Extinct Lands, Temporal Geographies: Chicana Literature and the Urgency of Space.* Durham: Duke University Press, 2002.

Cotera, María Eugenia. "A Woman of the Borderlands: 'Social Life in Cameron, Starr, and Zapata Counties' and the Origins of Borderlands Discourse." Introduction to *Life along the Border: A Landmark Tejana Thesis.* Ed. María Cotera. College Station: Texas A&M Press, 2006. 3-33.

Enoch, Jessica. *Refiguring Rhetorical Education: Women Teaching African American, Native American, and Chicano/a Students,* 1865-1911. Carbondale: Southern Illinois University Press, 2008.

Flores, William V. and Rina Benamayor. "Constructing Cultural Citizenship." *Latino Cultural Citizenship: Claiming Identity, Space, and Rights.* Eds. William V. Flores and Rina Benamayor. Boston: Beacon, 1997. 1-23.

González, Jennifer. "Know Your Terms: Anticipatory Set." *Cult of Pedagogy,* 6 September 2014, www.cultofpedagogy.com/anticipatory-set/. Accessed 1 October 2017.

González, Jovita. *Life along the Border: A Landmark Tejana Thesis.* Ed. María Cotera. College Station: Texas A&M Press, 2006.

Gruesz, Kirsten Silva. "Utopia Latina: The Ordinary Seaman in Extraordinary Times." *Modern Fiction Studies* 49.1 (Spring 2003): 54-83.

Gutiérrez, David G. "Migration, Emergent Ethnicity, and the 'Third Space': *The Shifting Politics of Nationalism in Greater Mexico." The Journal of American History* 86. 2 (Sept 1999): 481-517.

Kanellos, Nicolás. Introduction to *The Adventures of Don Chipote, or, When Parrots Breast Feed* by Daniel Venegas. Houston: Arte Público Press, 2000. 1-17.

Lamas, Carmen E. "Raimundo Cabrera, the Latin American Archive, and the Latina/o Continuum." *The Latino Nineteenth Century.* Eds. Rodrigo Lazo and Jesse Alemán. New York: New York University Press, 2016. 210-229.

Lazo, Rodrigo. "Historical Latinidades and Archival Encounters." *The Latino Nineteenth Century.* Eds. Rodrigo Lazo and Jesse Alemán. New York: New York University Press, 2016. 1-17.

Lomas, Clara. Introduction to *The Rebel* by Leonor Villegas de Magnón. Houston: Arte Público Press, 1994: xi-lvi.

___ "Transborder Discourse: The Articulation of Gender on the Borderlands in the Early Twentieth Century." *Frontiers* 24, nos. 2-3 (2003): 51-74.

López, Marissa. *Chicano Nations: The Hemispheric Origins of Mexican American Literature.* New York: New York University Press, 2011.

Luis-Brown, David. "The Transnational Imaginaries of Chicano/a Studies and Hemispheric Studies: Polycentric and Centrifugal Methodologies." *Borders, Bridges, and Breaks: History, Narrative, and Nation in Twenty-First-*

Century Chicana/o Literary Criticism. Eds. William Orchard and Yolanda Padilla. Pittsburgh: University of Pittsburgh Press, 2016. 40-62.

Moya, Paula and Ramón Saldívar. "Fictions of the Trans-American Imaginary." *Modern Fiction Studies* 49.1 (2003): 1-18.

Padilla, Yolanda. "Literary Revolutions in the Borderlands: Transnational Dimensions of the Mexican Revolution and its Diaspora in the United States." *The Cambridge History of Latina/o Literature.* Ed. John M. González and Laura Lomas, 2018.

___"Mexican Americans and the Novel of the Mexican Revolution." *Open Borders to a Revolution: Culture, Politics, and Migration.* Eds. Jaime Marroquín Arredondo, Adela Pineda, and Magdalena Mieri. Washington, D.C.: Smithsonian Institute Scholarly Press, 2013: 133-152.

___"The 'Other' Novel of the Mexican Revolution." *Bridges, Borders and Breaks: History, Narrative, and Nation in Twenty-First-Century Chicana/o Literary Criticism.* Eds. William Orchard and Yolanda Padilla. Pittsburgh: University of Pittsburgh Press, 2016: 63-79.

Palos, Ari. (Director). *Precious Knowledge.* Documentary. United States: Dos Vatos Productions, 2011.

Pratt, Mary Louise. "Arts of the Contact Zone." *Profession* (1991): 33-40.

___"Criticism in the Contact Zone: Decentering Community and Nation." *Critical Theory, Cultural Politics, and Latin American Narrative.* Eds. Steven M. Bell, Albert H. Le May, and Leonard Orr. Notre Dame and London: University of Notre Dame Press, 1993: 83-102.

Shukla, Sandhya Rajendra and Heidi Tinsman. Introduction to *Imagining Our Americas: Toward a Transnational Frame.* Eds. Sandhya Rajendra Shukla and Heidi Tinsman. Durham: Duke University Press, 2007. 1-33.

Sleeter, Christine. *The Academic and Social Value of Ethnic Studies: A Research Review.* Washington, DC: National Education Association, 2011.

Ventura, Gabriela Baeza. *La imagen de la mujer en la crónica del "México de afuera."* Ciudad Juárez, Chih., México: Universidad Autónoma de Ciudad Juárez, 2006.

Villegas de Magnón, Leonor. *The Rebel.* Houston: Arte Público Press, 1994.

___*La rebelde.* Houston: Arte Público Press, 2004.

Endnotes

[1]The volume *The Latino Nineteenth Century* was conceived in part as a response to this issue.

[2]While I believe that taking steps to facilitate the use of Recovery materials in the classroom is important, I make this suggestion with some misgivings, knowing that this kind of labor is seldom recognized at an institutional level.

[3]The original Spanish-language version was published in 2004 with the title *La rebelde.*

[4]Lamas's conceptualization of the "Latino continuum" provides a suggestive way to understand Latinx identities that are informed both by Latin America and the United States. She writes that such identities are not "merely transnational, which is ultimately tied to the geographic/spatial; rather, it is a sort of identity that simultaneously occupies multiples spatialities while inhabiting and crossing diverse temporal moments" (212). She further asserts that such identities from the nineteenth century continue to shape Latinidad into the present day.

[5]*Precious Knowledge* tells the story of the banning of the Mexican American Studies (MAS) program in Arizona's Tucson Unified School District. MAS was an extremely effective program developed to address negative outcomes for Chicanx students.

[6]See Sleeter for more on the role of ethnic studies in transforming curricula and the benefits of such work for students of all races, including white students.

[7]remember clearly my soaring feelings of recognition and pride when I read literature by Chicanx writers for the first time—something that didn't happen until I was an undergraduate at UC Davis. The class was called simply "The Chicano Novel." I was very lucky to take that class with Professor Angie Chabram Dernersesian. The first texts we read were Sandra Cisneros's *The House on Mango Street* and Tomás Rivera's . . . *y no se lo tragó la tierra*.

[8]For more on *Don Chipote*, see Kanellos's introduction.

[9]For examples, see my work on Mexican American literary engagements with the Mexican Revolution, and Marissa López's comparative analysis of *Las Aventuras de Don Chipote* and the short stories of María Cristina Mena.

[10]A brief set piece used at the beginning of a lesson to get students' attention and prepare them for the issues and materials they will engage in the rest of the class. See Jennifer González, "Cult of Pedagogy."

[11]Lomas provides a thorough introduction to Magnón's life and the significance of her work in her introduction to *The Rebel*. For more on the role of women in borderlands print culture during the Revolution, see Lomas's essay "Transborder Discourse."

[12]Enoch takes the concept of "cultural citizenship" from Flores and Benmayor

[13]Luis-Brown frames this very usefully as a "centrifugal" approach to transnationalism.

A Librarian and Archivist Reflection about the Recovery Program

Marisol Ramos

I was invited to join the Recovering the US Hispanic Literary Heritage Program Advisory Board in 2010, and I have been a witness of the great efforts of this Program to document and make accessible the documentary history of Hispanic Americans across time and space. Nicolás Kanellos and his team of dedicated archivists, scholars, and students have recovered, cataloged and digitized, through the help of EBSCO, a rich archives of images, magazines, newspapers and archival collections from the nineteenth century to the 1960s and there are plans to expand this range to include the rest of the twentieth century and beyond.

As a librarian and archivist for Latin American, Caribbean and Latina/os Studies, having access to the several projects led by the Recovery Program such as the Readex database, *Hispanic American Newspapers 1808-1980* and the two EBSCO collections, Arte Público Hispanic Historical Collection: Series 1 and 2, facilitate my teaching of primary sources to our Latino students population and allow our faculty to incorporate this rich corpus into their teaching. It is always a pleasure to introduce these resources to students during my library instruction's presentations and see their eyes light up when I showcased the many images, newspapers articles, poetry available to them. At the library, it is always our hope that giving access to these collections will allow new research discoveries and insights about the many groups that composed the complex historical, cultural and economic tapestry that is the Hispanic Americans people in the United States.

Members of the first Recovery board and staff: (back row, left to right) Helvetia Martell, Nélida Pérez, Gerald E. Poyo, Luis Leal, Roberto Trujillo, Ramón Gutiérrez, Raymond Paredes, Virginia Sánchez-Korrol, (front row) Juan Flores, Clara Lomas, Genaro Padilla, María Herrera-Sobek, Rodolfo Cortina, José B. Fernández, Erlinda Gonzales-Berry, Tomás Ybarra-Frausto, Nicolás Kanellos, Elsie Herdman Dodge and Antonia Castañeda (Edna Acosta-Belén missing).

Tomás Ybarra-Frausto y Nicolás Kanellos Recovery Conference 2008

The first coordinator of the periodicals Recovery Program, Helvetia Martell, works with a graduate research assistant.

Recovery Board members at Arte Público Press, 2017. (Back row, left to right) Gabriela Baeza Ventura, Manuel M. Martín Rodríguez, Francisco Lomelí. (Front rows, left to right) José B. Fernández, Genaro Padilla, Clara Lomas, Alejandra Balestra, Emilio Zamora, Antonio Saborit, Blanca López de Morales, Gerald E. Poyo, Monica Perales, A. Gabriel Meléndez, John Alba Cutler, Helvetia Martell, Kirsten Silva Gruez, Carmen Lamas, José F. Aranda, Yolanda Padilla, John Moran González, María E. Cotera, Raúl Coronado, Carolina Villarroel and Nicolás Kanellos.

Antonio Saborit, Nicolás Kanellos and Antonia Castañeda give a workshop on Recovery at the Instituto Nacional de Historia y Antropología, Mexico City.

A roundtable discussion on the progress of Recovery at a Recovery conference in Houston. Left to right: Francisco Lomelí, Antonio Saborit, Gerald E. Poyo, Nicolás Kanellos, A. Gabriel Meléndez, Kenya C. Dworkin y Méndez and Clara Lomas.

Board members Kelley Kreitz, Gerald E. Poyo and Emilio Zamora at a Recovery Conference.

Recovery dinner attendees listen to speaker Michael Olivas in 2017. Seen at tables are board members John Moran González, Raúl Coronado, Emilio Zamora, Antonio Saborit, Yolanda Padilla, Carmen Lamas and Donna Kabalen de Bichara.

Silvio Torres-Saillant welcomes the Recovery conference to Syracuse University in 2014.

Recovery board members during the closing ceremonies of the 2017 conference. Left to right: José F. Aranda, Gerald E. Poyo, Gabriela Baeza Ventura, Manuel M. Martín-Rodríguez, Antonio Saborit, Francisco Lomelí, Nicolás Kanellos, Clara Lomas, Kenya Dworkin y Méndez, Blanca López de Mariscal, A. Gabriel Meléndez, Alejandra Balestra, Carolina Villarroel, María E. Cotera and Donna Kabalen de Bichara.

Mariana Alegría, graduate research fellow, scanning just one of thousands of books.

Former graduate research fellow, Montse Feu López, indexing scanned items.

The 2017 board meeting at Arte Público Press headquarters.

Roberto Calderón and José F. Aranda.

Panel attendance at the conference on "Recovering Religious Thought."

Gabriela Baeza Ventura gives a presentation at a Recovery conference.

RECOVERING THE US HISPANIC LITERARY HERITAGE VOLUME X

Of Coloniality, Colonialisms and Settler Colonialisms: Languages, Politics, Religion

Like me, an entire generation of scholars has seen the transformative, paradigm-shifting role that the Recovery Program has played, and it is safe to say that future generations will keep benefitting from the results as well.

—Manuel Martín-Rodríguez

The undisputable recovered written record, and the vast array of primary sources uncovered over twenty-five years, not only lay to rest long held misconceptions about the continental Hispanic experience and its transnational connections, but also tells us who we are as a nation.

—Virginia Sánchez-Korrol

The recovery of Spanish-language archives ironically provided the power of a transnational narrative within the nation.

—Raúl A. Ramos

The Long Colonizing Process of California: From Cortés to Portolá

JOSÉ ANTONIO GURPEGUI
Instituto Franklin-UAH

1. Introduction.

Ion de la Riva, Spanish Ambassador on Special Mission for the Asia-Pacific Plan -2004 / 2007-, recalled that in his "Introduction" to *El lago Español*, O.H.K. Spate stated that "it was Spain that 'discovered' the Pacific for the West and circumnavigated the orb with Juan Sebastián Elcano by opening a new maritime "Silk Road" between Europe, the New World, and Asia." (11). The nickname of "Spanish lake", as the Pacific Ocean was known four centuries ago, is a reflection of the historical reality from those years. Hernán Cortés was the first to show interest in navigating the new open sea. He chose the name of *New Spain* for the territories he was conquering for the crown because of "the similarity that all this land [has] with Spain"[1], and from the first moment reaching the islands of Asian shores became an obsession for Cortés. Demonstrating the clear vision of a strategist, Cortés understood that it was imperative to build a link of communication between the two coasts and opened the route between Coatzacoalcos in the Gulf of Mexico, and Tehauntepec in the Pacific[2]. The outward journey was simple, to arrive to the territories of the Philippines, China, and Cipango . . . was quite easy; but the return, the *"tornaviaje,"* seemed impossible until the cartographer Andrés de Urdaneta, member of the expedition commanded by Miguel López de Legazpi, achieved it in 1565[3].

From that year, a very important trade route between east and west (and vice versa) was established. It started in Manila, and after passing through Acapulco, Mexico, and Veracruz, arrived in Seville / Cádiz, to finish in Madrid. The most compromising part of that journey of thousands of miles was the trip between Manila and Acapulco, because the ships had to take a northern drift to later descend more than 2000 nautical miles along the coast to reach port. Therefore, after crossing the Pacific, it was necessary for the crew to rest, replenish provisions, and repair the ships, which meant finding a secure location at the first point of arrival to the American shores.

In 1602, the Viceroy Gaspar de Zúñiga, Count of Monterrey, ordered Sebastián Vizcaíno to search for a safe harbor for the Manila Galleon. In that expedition, the Carmelite, Antonio de la Ascensión, traveled as a cosmographer and he precisely defined the coast from Acapulco to Cape Mendocino (north of the current state of California) which had been described as early as 1543 by Bartolomé Ferrero[4]. The bay of Monterey, a site where the galleon could dock with great security, and the possibility of proposing a permanent establishment in that location, was taken as a priority. However, it took more than a century and a half before that settlement could become a reality. The reasons ranged from the complexity of the trip and the hostility of the indigenous people, to the scarcity of funds, and the poor results reported by the colonization of Baja California.

The new overseas policy driven by the Bourbons and a series of historical coincidences, such as the expulsion of the Jesuits and Russian and British expansionism, motivated the Spanish crown to promote the creation of settlements, *presidios*, and missions in those distant territories just as the century before had done with the settlement of Los Adaes in Texas[5] to prevent the French advance. The expedition of Portolá / Serra in 1769 was the result of the colonization process of the Alta California that had been already planned by Hernán Cortés, had arisen in the Cabrillo expedition, was programmed with Vizcaíno, and was finally executed with Portolá . . .

This essay examines the importance of Alta/Vieja California to the Spanish Crown from the very start of the colonial period to the end of the "Empire." The essay draws on selected texts to support this affirmation, beginning with Cortés' letters to King Carlos I, informing him of the vital importance of these lands to the crown's initiatives in the Americas. Later writings, including those of Urdaneta, abound on the topic. We also located numerous legal and religious texts. However, we found that the true impulse of the colonization of Alta California was in the writings of Visitador (Inspector General) Gálvez. In these, we can appreciate and examine how the original interest in colonizing those territories is united to the implementation of the Bourbon social model based on Enlightenment principles. Our interest in examining the intricacies, internal conflicts, and contentious nature of the process of Spanish colonization and maintenance of empire, most specifically how these factors played out in the

1769 Portolá/Serra Expedition to Alta California, is to contribute to the Recovery Program's expanding scholarship and engagement with other ways of thinking "Transatlantic Studies."

2) The Bourbon transformations.

After more than four hundred years (1492-1898), the Spanish presence in the American territories is traditionally seen as something monolithic, homogeneous, and even today, in its purest form as reductionism, this whole period is called "the conquest". The truth is that the "conquest" itself was developed in the first fifty years. In 1550, there was already full awareness of the vastness of the territory between Tierra del Fuego and the icy waters of Alaska, and the relations with the indigenous—*encomiendas, mitas*, Christianization, conquest . . .—had already been established.

The most important turning point during the aforementioned four centuries of Spanish presence in America occurred with the change from the Habsburg dynasty to the Bourbon dynasty. Unlike the Habsburgs (Felipe I, Carlos I, Felipe II, Felipe III, Felipe IV, Carlos II), the first Bourbons (Felipe V, Luis I, Fernando VI, Carlos III), saw the American territories as "colonies" which the metropolis did not obtain the benefits and profitability that it potentially had. One of the most visible measures to implement the greatest control of the metropolitan government in the overseas territories was to increase the number of peninsular officials to occupy key positions in the administrations of those territories. The later Bourbons (Carlos IV, Fernando VII, Isabel II, Alfonso XII, Alfonso XIII) attended the dismemberment and total disappearance of one of the most powerful empires in the history of mankind[6]. During the Habsburg period, the American territory was seen as a mining operation from which to extract precious metals. The Bourbons, without disregarding gold and silver, knew how to see the economic potential represented by raw materials such as cotton, tobacco, or sugar. They also saw the economic benefit that trading could provide, especially the trade of products that could arrive from the East on the route of Manila. They also saw that there was a market and need for manufactured materials in the new territories. Felipe V initiated a series of political-administrative reforms, which would be implemented and extended by his descendants, with the primary purpose of having economically profitable trade with "the Indies." The existing viceroyalties were reorganized and the governorships were replaced by intendancies—the two viceroyalties and the 12 existing governorates in the days of the Habsburgs became four viceroyalties and 14 "audiencias" with the Bourbons. An American army was established; the "Casa de Contratación" ("House of Hiring") changed its location from Seville to Cadiz; commercial companies were created; and in general, trade was liberalized by replacing the fleet system with a registration system, eliminating cumbersome and useless bureaucratic procedures, finally full freedom of trade was achieved between Spanish and American ports.

It is precisely the process of colonization of Alta California that most clearly represents the profound change that the Bourbons sought to develop in the American continent, especially during the reign of Carlos III. It is certain that "chance" had a particular role. That is, had it not been reported that the Russians had disembarked on the American[7] coast in 1767 had not the Jesuits not also been expelled that same year, the method that substantiated those historical events would have been completely different. Originally, neither the viceroy de Croix, the Visitor General Gálvez, the military officer Portolá, nor the Friar Serra, had intentions to initiate any type of expedition to the northern territories. Gálvez's original mission was to inspect the courts, to implement a tax reform that would invigorate the Royal Treasury increasing the collections, and in a singular way establish the tobacco industry that was increasingly demanded in Europe. Subsequently in Mexico, he set the goal of pacifying the territories of the already inhabited North, establishing secure borders, in a campaign of pacification known as "The expedition to Sonora" (1765-1771)[8]. He also aimed to appease the mood of the population by expelling the Jesuits who had the support of the natives and part of the population of Spanish origin. Finally, he went down in history as having impelled the Santa Expedición ("Holy Expedition") in order to establish the first settlements in the current state of California.

While this historical milestone would mark the future of present day California, it is no less true that the interest in colonizing the coasts in the northern territories went back to the very origins of the Spanish presence in the North American territory. But in the second half of the eighteenth century, it became absolutely necessary or urgent in any case, to no longer delay the purpose of the crown that had been in play for more than two centuries. The Spanish expansion to the north of New Spain followed three main routes: 1) the route that led to the territory of Texas; 2) the route that led to the territory of New Mexico; 3) the route that led to Sonora and the Californias. The third route was the last one to be developed, but from the first moments, and especially since the *tornaviaje* was opened to the Galleon of Manila, was understood as a way to colonize and populate the territory. The fundamental problem for the delay was the shortage of available means and human resources; but in the colonial imaginary, the clerical apostolate, and the governmental plans, as much as in the metropolis in Mexico, the establishment of populations, missions, and presidios was a "reality" that should be effected sooner rather than later. Undoubtedly, it was Carlos III who systematically developed a reformist process, according to the principles of Enlightened Despotism, which sought to transform Spanish and Indian societies. Kuethe establishes three phases of the reformist plan that the governments of Carlos III designed for America. The first dates from 1762 when Spain lost Havana to the English to the Motín de Esquilache (Esquilache Mutiny); the second centers on the expulsion of the Jesuits and the government of Floridablanca, and the third in the last decade of his reign until 1788. According to Navarro García,

> La idea clave de todo el plan es bien simple: es necesario reforzar la defensa militar de las Indias, aportándole hombres, navíos, fortificaciones y elementos de combate, y por lo tanto es necesario procurar el incremento de las rentas reales de aquellos reinos y provincias, para lo cual convendrá inspeccionar toda su administración, con especial atención a la de la Hacienda. (2)[9]

Be that as it may, the monarchy's intent was to modernize. During this process, it was fundamental to transform the relationship that the metropolis maintained with the overseas territories that, in that moment, was endeavoring to convert into colonies. As stated by Salvador Bernabeu (2017),

> La Nueva España se convirtió en el siglo XVIII en la posesión ultramarina más rica de los Borbones, dictándose numerosas medidas para convertirla en una auténtica "colonia" al servicio de la península durante los reinados de Carlos III y Carlos IV, cuyos ministros quisieron gobernarla según las máximas del despotismo ilustrado y convertirla en una permanente fuente de riqueza para pagar las necesidades financieras de la Corona, que se habían incrementado en todos los rubros: marina, ejército, gastos de la corte y la familia real, defensa de las fronteras, etc. (15)[10]

The colonizing process was initiated between 1765-1771 with the trip of José de Gálvez y Gallardo, a native of Micharavialla (January 7, 1720), who in 1765[11] was appointed to the position of General Visitor of the Viceroyalty of New Spain. Omar Guerrero states: "the General Visit created the public administration necessary to make the Hispanic State assume all the attributes of power in New Spain" (7). Gálvez was one of the most convinced Bourbon reformers and empathized with Viceroy, Carlos Francisco de Croix, who participated the renovating approaches[12]. In addition to the coincidence between, Gálvez and de Croix, two other figures who, although having different vocations, shared similar ethical-moral principles. These two characters were the military officer Gaspar de Portolá and the Franciscan Junípero Serra. The conjunction of these four figures, with four different personalities, gathering at the same time and place, resulted in and decided the success of the mission.

Gálvez disembarked in the port of Veracruz in July 1765; he was the substitute for Francisco de Armona, secretary to the minister Marqués de Esquilache, who was appointed against his will as visiting general for New Spain, and who had died in circumstances never clarified during his trip to Mexico. Gálvez's first mission was to organize the cultivation of tobacco and the tobacco business[13]. Even then, his efforts and his resolute and determined spirit awarded him success [14] . The confrontations with Viceroy Cruilles[15] and with Jacinto Diaz Espinosa, commissioner of Carlos III, for the monopoly of tobacco and favorable to the free commerce of the tobacco industry, arose from the first moments. Solving his relationship with local authorities after the appointment of the Marquis de Croix[16], Gálvez focused his efforts on the expedition to Sonora. And therein to his plans, he received news of the expulsion of the Jesuits decreed by Carlos III on the 25th of June of 1767. Once again, history sided with Gálvez because Francisco de Lorenzana, archbishop of Mexico, who applauded and encouraged the Sonora expedition, was a regalist and reformist who approved the expulsion of the Jesuits[17].

Once again, the coincidence of events played in favor for Gálvez, because in the same year that the Jesuits were expelled, Gálvez was entrusted with the mission of occupying the territories of Alta California and establishing a stable colony in Monterrey. Gálvez's actions in implementing the tobacco monopoly had been highly effective. However, the reforms undertaken in the reorganization of the administration and the Royal Treasury had not been so successful as expected. Nor had the Sonora mission been incontestably successful after failures such as those of October 23, 1768, when Spanish troops commanded by Domingo Elizondo confused friendly Indians with the enemy; and in the following year in Cerro Prieto, where the Seri Indians had concentrated[18]. Gálvez decided to personally move in order to lead the military campaign, and on May 8th, 1769, he published an edict proposing a kind of amnesty for those who ceased their hostilities.

Declaro à todos los habitantes de estas provincias de Sinaloa, y Sonora, al desembarcarme en su distrito, que por ser el principal objeto entre las que me traen a ellas proveer à su tranquilidad, y bien público, que han perturbado, y destruido los enemigos Seris y Pimas cometiendo las mayores crueldades y excesos . . . que para dar las más evidente y última prueba de la soberana piedad con que Ambas Majestades oyen y admiten el arrepentimiento verdadero, aún de los mayores delincuentes, señalo y concedo el término perentorio de cuarenta días . . . a fin de que se me presenten todos los sublevados o los cabecillas de ellos, en el Real de los Álamos, y que rindiéndose a su discreción como deben al rey nuestro señor, imploren el perdón bajo las condiciones que en su real nombre yo les impusiere [19]

The edict implies a recognition of vulnerability, or weakness if one prefers, in the face of the complex reality of those territories, with Indian tribes who had resisted any integrating pretension on the part of the Spaniards since the 16th century. Gálvez's interest in pacifying the territory by offering an amnesty had more *"entente cordiale"* than generosity after the victory, because neither Seris nor Pimas had been completely defeated. Proof of this is that Gálvez extended the period of forty days and after the new term of the pardon was completed, Captain Juan Bautista de Anza left with a detachment of forty *dragones* and *soldados de cuera* to pursue the rebellious Indians[20]. In addition, the campaign had been paid with private contributions and the donors requested a quick and definitive victory.

Whatever it may be, José de Gálvez contracted a strange illness, malaria according to the official version. However, this incident has been the subject of debate, Navarro accepts the official version, but many others question this as the real reason Gálvez left the expedition. In his doctoral thesis, Gonzalo Quintero advances the theory of Mario Hernández Sánchez Barba, who raised the question " . . . whether his madness was true or feigned, because it could be that the Visitor had simulated his illness `to be removed from the expedition, without suffering or undermining his own honor, committed to that company so personally his'". Quintero also mentions the theories of Héctor Cuauhtémoc Hernández who relates the disease "with an obscure operation to hide from the Crown the reality of the northern frontier of New Spain, carried out between José de Gálvez himself and Viceroy Croix". A related analysis is that of Salvador Bernabéu Albert and Ignacio del Río, who "insist on the idea of analyzing the episode from the perspective of the tensions generated by the Bourbon reforms in New Spain."[21]

The possibility of establishing colonies in San Diego and Monterrey gave him an unexpected opportunity to establish himself as a political-military strategist, and at the same time gave him the opportunity to substantiate the new modernizing reformist reality. He had the necessary armed forces that moved to Baja California and the missionaries - whether Franciscans or Dominicans - eager to expand their area of influence. The instructions Gálvez to Portolá in *"Cabo de San Lucas and the twentieth of February of 1679-Dn. Joseph de Gálvez"*[22] are conclusive about his motives and intentions. Thus, the first instruction states that " . . . the main purpose of this expedition is to extend the Religion among the

Gentiles who inhabit the North of this Peninsula by the peaceful means of establishing missions that make the spiritual Conquest in said areas . . . " ; the second organizes the details of the trip to San Diego; in the third Gálvez orders "good treatment towards the Indians," ordering the punishment of those who "commit injury or violence towards their women be punished, because in addition to the offense of God, those who would commit such excesses could jeopardize the whole of the Expedition"; the following four instructions detail the expeditions to Monterrey; in the eighth instruction, once in Monterrey, one must "formalize the solemn act of Possession on behalf of his Majesty", the ninth indicates to precede with "sagacity and prudence" to attract the Indians "making them understand the benefit that will result from living in brotherhood with the Spaniards "; in the tenth instruction, he continues recommending "to treat the Indians with kindness and love", but for those who "obstinately oppose their passage, then force will be used . . . let them know the superiority of our weapons, without bloodshed despite the whatever action, . . . "; in the last two instructions, he continues to dispose aspects related to the established settlements showing their future intentions, as those who transit through the territory must "always examine the going and the return, the most opportune stops for the establishment of the new Missions."

Gálvez's intentions had been made explicit when in 1768 he sent the king his "Plan for the erection of the Government and General Command that includes the peninsula of California, and the provinces of Sonora, Sinaloa, and Nueva Vizcaya", in which he advocated establishing settlements in Alta California. Quoting the words of José A. Sanz, "He had to let them go for the future. But he did not forget about him. "(144). Paradoxically, the reasons he argued were exactly the same as those the monarch himself exposed months later. Proof that he had not forgotten the aforementioned plan; he sent a proposal in 1769 to Viceroy Croix for the creation of the new intendancies of Sonora and the Californias. In spite of the existing harmony between them, the proposal did not prosper. As the Spanish proverb says "when one door closes another opens" and the new opening was an ordinance to populate New California. He had the necessary tools to carry out his mission: the soldiers who had been assigned to Sonora and who, after fulfilling their mission of expelling the Jesuits, had no greater occupation; and the missionaries who were willing to sacrifice anything in order to expand their areas of influence. In addition, both military and clergy were led by two figures in whom he had full confidence. The service sheet of the Lleida- born Gaspar de Portolá was impeccable, having shown and demonstrated his warlike capacities, and his ability to command European campaigns -Italy and Portugal in the 7-year war- and command American campaigns. In addition, he had very satisfactorily fulfilled his mission of expelling the Jesuits from Baja California, avoiding any uprising and uproar as had happened in other territories[23]. The Mallorcan Serra had amply demonstrated his evangelizing and pacifying capacity in the mission of Sierra Gorda, where he had been appointed president of those missions in 1751.

Portolá had arrived in New Spain in 1764 as part of the contingent of the new colonial army. As early as 1767, he originally was going to participate with his Dragones company in the Sonora campaign, but being in Tipec about to embark, he was required to take over the California Governorship, and expel the Jesuits. Father Serra's reputation was also enviable. He left his native Petra in 1749, and quickly became involved in the mission of the Indians. His greatest achievement had been the Christianization of Indians in Sierra Gorda. His next destination was the dangerous mission of San Saba, in Texas, where Franciscan missionaries had already lost their lives. The expulsion of the Jesuits opened new possibilities for the Franciscans who had tried repeatedly to settle in California, but once and again, the authorities of New Spain had canceled their mission concessions. Originally, it had been considered and decided that the Dominicans would take charge of the missions abandoned by the expulsion of the Jesuits. Fray Junípero was in the mission of Ixmiquilpan, in the current state of Hidalgo. From the first moment, he was personally involved in obtaining the permits so that it would be the Franciscans, and not the Dominicans, who would occupy the now abandoned missions[24], requesting it repeatedly to the Viceroy and the Visitador Gálvez. Finally, the first Franciscans arrived in Loreto on April 1st, 1768.

In the middle of 1768, on the way to San Blas, the Visitor would receive the Royal Order commanding him to occupy the territories of Alta California, establishing settlements in San Diego and Monterrey. For the first time in more than two centuries, the combination of all the elements allowed for the task to be possibly successful: governmental will, logistical possibilities, geo- political needs, and, of course, human capacity and leadership. Fernando Boneu asks himself about Gálvez's intentions: "It is difficult to know exactly what the visitor's plans were for Alta California, when in 1767 he appointed Portolá as governor and chose Serra to take possession of the missions"(43). Undoubtedly, the pacification of the Indians was their most important objective, but it is not unreasonable to think that the expansion of the northern territories could have been an unconfessed intention. José Sanz, who ventures to guess Gálvez's plans, refers to the letter sent to Father Serra on May 16, 1768, stating that " . . . he had great projects for the improvement of the natives of Baja California . . . But in Gálvez's mind there was another, more ambitious project: the occupation and development of Alta California."[25] In any case, he got down to work from the moment he received the notification and prepared the expedition with special zeal and care.

The operation was planned in San Blas, from where he went to Baja California[26] to finalize his plans with Portolá and Serra. With Portolá, he addressed logistics. There would be two double expeditions; that is, one by land and another by sea, and that each of them had at the same time two sections with separate routes until reaching San Diego. The boats - the San Carlos and the San Antonio—would carry the supplies and everything necessary for the foundations that were expected to be carried out[27]. Also on board the ships, the Volunteers of Catalonia (Compañía Franca de Voluntarios de Cataluña), journeyed with Pedro Fages, who in San Diego would join those who had traveled by land. With Fray Junípero Serra, Gálvez planned the foundation of missions: from Santa María (the last one in Baja California) six more would be founded down to San Diego; from there, ten more were to be founded until Monterrey -even the name of each mission had been chosen-. For the provisioning of the expedition, Fernando de Rivera y Moncada–who commanded one of the two terrestrial expeditions—collected all the necessary materials in terms of transport and supply, and this depleted the resources of the missions, especially with regard to horses and mules, as well as cows and sheep. The total of Spanish expeditioners was 231[28], as far as the number of neophytes[29] it is difficult to establish, but it is calculated that their number was superior to the Spaniards. When they reached Monterrey, those who travelled by land had walked more than 2,000 kilometers.

The territory of California belonged to the Spanish crown until Mexican independence in 1821. Fifty years of Hispanic presence that had as much impact on the subsequent historical development as three centuries in other latitudes. To do so, a series of coincidences had to be combined, as it rarely happens, all of these coincidences galvanized in the figure of the Visitador José de Gálvez who, back in Spain, occupied the Ministry of the Indies between 1776-1787. His actions during those years were cardinal in the immediate historical development of the overseas territories, "reorganized forced marches of the administrative division of the Indies with the creation of new territorial entities, introduced the system of intendencias almost everywhere, promulgate two successive Ordinances, implemented "free trade", dispatched visitors, quelled riots, and generally left the principle of the omnipotence of the royal authority."[30]

3) Interest of the religious orders.

The presence of religious orders in New Spain was a reality since the arrival of Cortés. He was accompanied by the Franciscans, Diego Altamirano and Pedro Melgarejo, and in 1524 Cortés himself asked Carlos I to allow religious orders to go and evangelize Mexico. Moreover, Cortés proposed the eradication of traditional ecclesiastical structures that were ineffective and expensive, to be replaced by members of religious orders, and to which even bishops should belong [31]. Although Cortés' request did not take full effect, the Spanish king obtained from his old teacher, Pope Adriano IV[32], the Papal Bull *Exponi Nobis Nuper Fecistis -Exponi Nobis-* popularly known as *Bula Omnímoda*[33] (1522). It recognized the mendicant orders as authorities in areas where there were no bishops. It also established that the king send Franciscan missionaries to America - "Godly and God-fearing men, well-educated, literate and experienced, to doctrine the faith to the natives and impose good manners"- leaving the superiors of the order subordinated to royal authority. Francisco de Quiñónes, Vicar General of the Franciscans at that time, favored and supported the arrangement. Its predecessor is found in Papal Bull of Pope Leo X *Alias felicis recordationis* (1521) in which "the privileges of the mendicants are confirmed and particularly those that the Franciscans of the Observance family possessed since the Middle Ages."[34] The first Franciscan expedition that applied the new norm was headed by Fray Martín de Valencia, who arrived in New Spain in 1524 along with 11 other Franciscan brothers[35]. It is worth noting, continuing with Garcia and Garcia, that the superiors of the orders were to be chosen by those who made up the missionary expedition, which was established in the Papal Bull, in fact it was the general of the Franciscans who appointed them.

The brief *Exponi Nobis* indelibly marked the general evangelization of America and of New Spain in particular; but it is no less true that it became a reference point for the conflicts between the secular clergy and the mendicant orders[36]. Beyond the figure of the king, the question of who was the religious authority in America, was an issue that various Popes had to arbitrate. A benchmark in this conflict is the Papal Bull promulgated by Gregory XV in 1622 *Inscrutabili Divinae*, which regulated the ecclesiastical affairs in the Indies. The document satisfied the bishops, and it was these precepts upon which the Franciscans founded their colleges of *"Propaganda Fide"* that same year, fundamental in their mission in New Spain.

It has already been mentioned that the driving force of the expedition of Gaspar de Portolá, together with the Franciscan Junípero Serra, in Alta California was to stop the Russian and English advance that had been descending along the Pacific coast. The missionary process of colonization in Baja California also had a similar purpose. The origin is found in the interest shown by European piracy, mostly English, who wandered through those waters since Drake discovered the strait that crossed the Pacific and mapped those coasts. The Manila route had been established not long ago, and the crown considered it essential to establish settlements in order to facilitate and consolidate navigation in the Pacific. By the attributions granted in the brief *Exponi Nobis* the settlements were going to be administrated by the religious orders; not only they were pre-ferred by the crown, but there was also a shortage of secular religious priests.

As it would happen decades later in Alta California, the Spanish crown understood that the establishment of stable colonies was imperative, and that the missionaries, with their model of evangelizing the natives, were the vehicle to achieve it. The establishments that emerged as a result of the evangelizing mis-sionary work would serve as a refuge, and supply for the Spanish ships, at the same time, would pose an added danger that would make corsairs and pirates desist from their intentions. The Spanish crown knowing of the presence of pirates on the shores of Baja, promoted settlement expeditions. The most impor-tant expedition was that of Isidoro de Atondo in 1683, but as it happened with previous expeditions, it was not successful. At the end of the seventeenth centu-ry, coinciding with the sighting of the corsair ships of Charles Swan, the Spanish government offered the Society of Jesus, present in New Spain since 1572, an aid of 40,000 pesos and full powers to settle in the peninsula of Baja California. The company rejected it, arguing that the inhospitality of that land and the hos-tility of the natives made the establishment of missions impossible.

In 1671, Alonso Fernandez de la Torre decreed in his will the donation of more than 200,000 pesos to the Jesuits in order to establish churches in the mis-sions of Sinaloa and Sonora, and to begin the missionary process in California. The first mission, *Nuestra Señora de Guadalupe,* had an ephemeral life of only four months between April and July of 1683, the same year it had been founded. Just a few months later, in October, the legendary Jesuit Father Kino founded the mission of San Bruno, also in Baja California. In 1685, it closed due to a prolonged drought. In 1686, the viceroy Portocarrero asked the king to delegate the missions to the Jesuits. It was granted in 1696, although without budgetary allocation from the Royal Treasury[37], and Father Juan Maria Salvatierra assumed the call to Christianize the Californias. In 1697, the legendary Jesuit established the mission of Loreto Concho, which would in time become a pio-neer in the process of Christianization of the Californias. The religious vocation of the orders, like the Jesuits, Franciscans, or Dominicans, has traditionally been praised because of their evangelizing work in a region as inhospitable as the Californias. But it is also true that the crown promoted the process of coloniza-tion with the intention of preserving its territories. Although the Jesuit missions originally had to be self- sufficient, there is evidence of a donation of 6,000 pesos from the Royal Treasury to the Pious Fund of California in 1698.

At the beginning of the XVIII century, in 1708, a royal decree was issued urging the viceroy to take the necessary measures "to foster the spiritual con-quest of California, which also reminded him of the metropolitan interest in the exploration of the Pacific coasts, and the establishment of colonies and presidios on those northwestern coasts." (Hilton, 63). The Viceroy Valero agreed to endow, with 18,000 pesos a year, the maintenance of the missions, as well as assign 25 soldiers and two ships with their crews for the defense of that territory. The decade of 1720 was especially calamitous, because locusts destroyed the harvests causing a famine unknown until then. In the year 1730, the indigenous uprisings took place, and the presidio of San Lucas was established. The regulations of this establishment are especially significant, since the relationship between soldiers and clerics undergoes an important transformation because they lost their authority over these areas. The captains of the presidios had to report only and directly to the viceroy. The viceregal decree of the 13th of July of 1740 is exhaustive:

> advertido dicho gobernador [del presidio], capitanes y demás cabos de los citados presidios el estar sujetos a dichos religiosos como sus párrocos, deben respetarlos en sus personas, por su estado y ministerio, como sus feligreses; y de los citados padres [estarán] en inteligencia de que deben atender a los cabos militares como ministros de su majestad, portándose los unos y los otros con recíproca y buena correspondencia, sin mezclarse los religiosos en el gobierno político, sino por vía de dirección, ni los capitanes y cabos en lo espiritual y que conduzca a la educación de los indios.[38]

The Jesuit leadership understood such a deposition, cutting off its attributions as an affront, and maneuvered the Madrid court to repeal that provision. They achieved their objective and on November 13th, 1744, a royal decree was issued, taking up the old system of government, and the friars even obtained new privileges, since it was they who received the soldiers salary and had the authority to not deliver it to those who did not behave as the ordinances required.

Just a decade before, in 1734, the political organization of New Spain was restructured creating a new governmental unit with the name of Sinaloa-Sonora which was formed by three provinces of Nueva Vizcaya (Sinaloa, Ostimury, and Sonora) and two of Guadalajara (Rosario and Culiacán). Manuel de Huidobro was appointed governor, "a man who was going to rally against the system of missions" (Hilton, 42). Five years before, in 1729, the Viceroy Marqués de Casafuerte had promulgated the *Regulation for the Presidios of the Internal Provinces,* in which officers were ordered to promote peaceful relations with the natives, and resorting to violence or war only in extreme situations, after exhausting all possibilities of peaceful agreement and understanding. It was singled out by the Border Captain, who by obligation, was to visit the tribes regularly trying to win their friendship and collaboration. Felipe V had shown a clear interest in maintaining the Jesuit missions, and the mission system was largely established in these territories. Missionaries like Juan de Ugarte, Juan Basaldúa, Julián Mugazábal, Pedro de Ugarte, Jaime Bravo, Julián Mayorga, Francisco Peralta . . . had begun their missionary activity in the northern territories between 1700 and 1710. The crown was in a way responsible for the expansion, because one of the first measures implemented by Felipe V after his ascension to the throne in 1700 was to promote the evangelizing work by approving the payment of 6,000 pesos per year as aid; an amount that increased progressively until reaching the 30,000 annual pesos destined to the missions of California[39]. The Christian intentions of the religious clashed with the customs of some tribes such as the Yaquis and Mayos, who were beginning to rebel against a social system radically different from their own.

The Mexican missionary Miguel de Venegas, one of the first historians of California - although he was never there- as well as being the author of *Noticias de California*, called the missionaries "spiritual conquerors"[40] and equated the role of Juan María de Salvatierra, the founder of the Jesuit Californian missions, with that of Hernán Cortés. In the dissemination of the work of Venegas, the edition the Jesuit, Andrés Marcos Burriel published in Spain[41], was fundamental. Father Kino himself had shown his desire to evangelize the northern territories, but it was Burriel who most vehemently defended the need to establish settlements and ports in Northern California, arguing and pointing out in a special way its strategic location.

> Desde el cabo de corrientes, y aún desde el mismo puerto de Acapulco hacia el Norte, no pueden tener seguridad las costas americanas sobre el mar del Sur, mientras no estuviere sujeta a Dios y el Rey Católico, la California.[42]

The new California, along with the territories of the Paraguayan Chaco, had become the space where the Jesuits could develop their socio-religious project in a territory where the natives had continuously resisted evangelization. The crown did not turn a deaf ear to the opinions of the influential and prestigious Burriel, and the Jesuits seemed predestined to continue their mission in the northern territories. But all their plans to create a society that "flourished on the border between earthly and heavenly life" vanished on May 30th, 1767 when a letter arrived in New Spain with the enigmatic and well-known inscription: "Penalty of Life. Do not open this sealed document until June 24th at the end of the afternoon." La Pragmática Sanción ("The Pragmatic Sanctio")[43] by Carlos III dictating the expulsion of the Jesuits following what happened in Portugal (1759) and France (1762) put an end to 70 years of Jesuit presence in the Californias where they founded 18 missions (15 in Baja California) to Christianize the natives of an area greater than two million square kilometers.

Contrary to the foreseeable, there were no public disorders in Baja California. The military officer, Gaspar de Portolá, quickly empathized with the missionaries. It did not take him long to verify that the mythical treasure of the Jesuits was another lie of the thousands that were around during that time. Contravening the orders he allowed the priest to enjoy some freedom of movement while waiting for their transfer to the port of San Blas. According to Father Ducrue, a Jesuit chronicler, "[Portolá] saw the reality of California and the falsity of these slurs . . . And if he could never cancel these orders, he made it clear the inconvenience they caused him. For this reason, we should be grateful to this Catholic Knight and discreet judge, who with his compassion lightened our sufferings."[44]

Most of the missions were given to the Franciscans, and in other cases, secularization was chosen[45]. Not in vain, the missionary project always had an estimated timeline of about 10 years for mendicant orders, later they had to be secularized[46]. It was the Franciscans who took charge of the Jesuit missions after the chaotic months in which they were in the hands of civil officials and the military. Originally, the Dominicans were to occupy the missions, and only the tenacity and the resolve of Father Serra, as mentioned, changed the provisions in favor of the Franciscans. In exchange, the Franciscans had to leave the territory of Baja California in favor of the Dominicans. The turnover was carried out in 1773, but at that time, there was not an established border between the Old and New California. The crown ordered the two religious orders to settle the border litigation fraternally. Father Serra's biographer, another Majorcan Francisco Palou, solved it in a wise way with the well-known "Mojonera de Palou": he nailed a wooden cross on the ground at Punta El Descanso, about 25 kilometers south of the current border between Mexico and the United States; what was to the south of the cross would correspond to the Order of the Dominicans[47], and whatever lay to the north was for the Franciscans[48].

The clashes between missionaries and the military were constant during the first years of colonization. It was nothing new; the confrontation with the farmers for the occupation of missional lands was an everyday issue. There were also repercussion due to the confrontation that the Franciscans had with Velez Cachupín, governor of New Mexico. But even within the order itself there were certain tensions when the fernandinos[49] heard that the Viceroy, in a last-minute change, had arranged for them to go to Sonora and that it would be the Franciscans of the Queretaro College who would be missionaries in the Californias. Urgently, Father Serra sent his fernandino brothers, Francisco Palou and Miguel de la Campa, to meet with Gálvez so that he could revoke the order of Croix, and reassign it to them. The success that this group had in the christianization of Sierra Gorda, and the confidence that it had in the good work of Father Serra, motivated Gálvez to accede to the request. The Visitor understood, as a well-educated reformer, that the church, be it diocesan or mendicant, was a state institution and as such its actions should be aimed at the benefit of the state. But at the same time, he was tremendously pragmatic and knew how to see things clearly and understood that it was missionary potential what could lead to the success of his campaign. The success of Serra and his companions in Sierra Gorda was not exclusively that of the Christianization of hostile Indians, but it went beyond that, because he had managed to create a space of peace where natives, missionaries, and colonists coexisted.

That was Gálvez's purpose for the new territories. He knew that nothing would be achieved without indigenous participation in the project; he knew of the traditional tensions between friars and military, and the tensions between the friars and settlers; he knew of the abuses that the military and colonists exercised against the natives. If the model of Sierra Gorda could be reproduced in Alta California, success was practically certain. The five missions[50] built between 1750 and 1760 had profoundly transformed indigenous social structures. The natives, especially the Pames, came to assimilate Spanish cultural principles, in the broadest sense of the term, to the point of occupying positions of responsibility in the new societal model.

The Franciscan missionaries had vast experience in the acculturation of the Indians. They knew the saying that "honey" was more beneficial than "bile." First, indigenous people were allowed freedom of movement in the mission; they were provided with basic necessities, such as provisions and clothes with the intention of attracting them recurrently to the missions while at the same time providing them with security. Once accepted, the missionaries urged the Indians to abandon their harvesting traditions and dedicate themselves to agriculture; pressured them to abandon ancestral principles and customs, including polygamy, in favor of Christian principles derived from baptism and communion, the Franciscan then integrated the Indians, now newly Christianized, into the community. That was the model intended to be implanted in Alta California. Indigenous participation was fundamental, and Galvez placed special care on highlighting the exemplary treatment that should be given to the Indians in the aforementioned provision that was delivered to Portolá.

Fray Junípero Serra did not say goodbye to his parents when he left his native Majorca in the direction of the American apostolate; he did not want to see them or make them suffer. Waiting in Cádiz to embark to New Spain, he wrote an emotional farewell letter to his parents, in which he seems to advocate what history had prepared for him.

Si yo, con la ayuda de la gracia de Dios, llegase a ser un buen religioso, serían más eficaces mis oraciones y no serían ellos poco interesados en esta ganancia; y lo mismo digo de mi querida hermana en Cristo, Juana, y Miguel mi cuñado: que no piensen en mí por ahora sino para encomendarme a Dios para que yo sea un buen sacerdote y un buen ministro de Dios; que en esto estamos todos muy interesados, y esto es lo que importa. Recuerdo que mi padre, cuando tuvo aquella enfermedad, tan grave que lo extremaunciaron, y yo, que ya era religioso, lo asistía, pensando que ya se moría, estando él y yo a solas, me dijo: «Hijo mío, lo que te encargo es que seas un buen religioso del Padre S. Francisco». Pues, padre mío, sabed que tengo aquellas palabras tan presentes como si en este mismo instante las oyera de vuestra boca. Y sabed también que para procurar ser un buen religioso emprendí este camino.[51]

Conclusion

Since it was first discovered, the coast of California held a special place of interest for the Spanish crown. Hernán Cortés was the first to see the economic and military potential offered by the Mar del Sur, and in 1523 Carlos I commissioned him to explore those shores. Once Ferdinand Magellan's expedition reached the Philippines in 1521, the need to find a return route, the "tornaviaje", became a priority. The disaster of the expedition of Loaysa (1527) made it clear that the maritime expeditions to the "islas de la especierías" needed to sail from the coasts of California. The crown was extremely interested in finding a way back, which led to the promotion of different expeditions. Finally, when Urdaneta managed to discover the route of the "tornaviaje" (1565), the coast of Alta / Nueva California acquired a special interest. The territories around Cape Mendozino were the first lands to be seen by those who had crossed the 2000 miles of the Pacific in an easterly direction. The different monarchs of the Habsburg dynasty saw the need to build a safe harbor in those lands. It was not only due to its geostrategic value, since it was the first land they saw on the continent; there were business interests related to the pearl trade and geopolitical interests that tried to evade the incursions of English, French, and Dutch pirates also at play. But for many different reasons this pursuit could never be carried out. The ascension of the Bourbon dynasty marked a clear turning point in the relationship between the overseas territories and the metropolis. The colonization of the northern region of New Spain once again became a primary goal of the crown. During the reign of Carlos III, the foreign powers of Russia and Great Britain began to descend from the Pacific coast. The historic purpose of establishing a colony on the northwest border was no longer an option but a necessity to prevent the advances of enemy nations. The Creole bourgeoisie lost its power in favor of the Spanish-born "peninsulares" who were sent to New Spain to put an end to the chaos and corruption in the finances and the government. José de Gálvez forced the dismissal of Viceroy Cruilles, who was replaced in the Viceroyalty by the Marquis de Croix. Both propitiated the expedition of Portolá / Serra to establish a settlement in Monterey Bay—described by Vizcaíno in 1602—and at the same time erect different missions and presidios.

In 1769 a series of historical circumstances made real an expedition that the Spanish crown had long projected: The crown wanted to stop rival Russians and British imperial interests descending from Alaska; finally, the religious orders, particularly the Franciscans, saw in Alta California the "last frontier" where they could carry out their evangelizing work.

Works Cited

Beck, Lauren. "Claiming California: From Terra Incognita to Miguel de Venegas." *Terrae Incognitae*, vol. 45 n°. 1, April 2013, (2–18).

Bernabéu Albert, Salvador. "La frontera califórnica: de las expediciones cortesianas a la presencia convulsiva de Gálvez (1534-1767)." Estudios (nuevos y viejos) sobre la frontera. Francisco de Solano y Salvador Bernabeu, Coordinadores. Madrid: Consejo Superior de Investigaciones Científicas. 1991.

___. "Por tierra nada conocida." El diario inédito de José de Cañizares a la Alta California (1769). *Anuario de Estudios Americanos*. vol 60. nº 1. 2003. (235-276).

___. "Don Gaspar de Portolá en la Nueva España: de la defensa fronteriza a los retos de su gobierno en California" / "Don Gaspar de Portolà a la Nova Espanya: de la denfensa fronterera als reptes del seu govern a Califòrnia," en Josep Lluís Ribes Foguet (ed.), *El món de Gaspar de Portolà*, Lleida, Institut d'Estudis Ilerdencs de la Diputació de Lleida. (15-50). 2017.

Boneu Companys, Fernando. *Gaspar de Portolá: descubridor y primer gobernador de California*. Lleida: Diputació de Lleida. 1986.

Cano Sánchez, Ángela; Neus Escandell Tur; Elena Mampel González. *Gaspar de Portolá: Crónicas del descubrimiento de la Alta California*. Ediciones de la Universidad de Barcelona. Barcelona. 1984.

Díaz de Ovando, Clementina. "Baja California en el mito." *Historia Mexicana*; El colegio de México. vol II, nº1. (5) julio-septiembre 1952. (23-45).

García y García, Antonio. "Los privilegios de los religiosos en la evangelización de América;" *Mar Océana*, nº 11-12. 2002 (45-63).

Guerrero Orozco, Omar. *Las raíces borbónicas del estado Mexicano*. México. UNAM. 1994. Gutiérrez López, Edgar Omar. "José de Gálvez y sus aliados políticos en el financiamiento de la expedición militar a Sonora 1765-1771." Transatlantic Studies Network. Nº 2. Julio–diciembre 2016. (45-50)

Hilton, Sylvia. *La Alta California Española*. Madrid: Editorial Mapfre. 1992.

Kuethe, Allan J. "Towards a Periodization of the Reforms of Charles III," *Bibliotheca Americana*. vol 1; nº3. 1984. (143-167).

León Portilla, Miguel. "El ingenioso don Francisco de Ortega sus viajes y noticias Californianas 1632-1636." *Estudios de Historia Novohispana*. Año 34, Vol 56. Enero-Junio 2017. (1-43).

___. *Cartografía y Crónicas de la Antigua California*. México. Universidad Autónoma de México. 2001.

Mathes, W. Michael. "Datos biográficos sobre el almirante de las Californias, Isidro de Atondo y Antillón." *Calafia*. vol. 8. nº 8. Dic. 1998. (7-10).

Navarro García, Luis. "La crisis del reformismo borbónico bajo Carlos IV." *Temas Americanistas*. nº 13. 1997. (1-22).

Quintero Saravia, Gonzálo M. *Bernardo de Gálvez y América a finales del siglo XVIII* (Tesis doctoral no publicada. Sylvia Hilton, directora) UCM. 2015.

Río, Ignacio del. *A la diestra mano de las Indias*. Méjico D. C.: Universidad Autónoma de Méjico. 1990.

Sanz, José A. *Cruces y flechas: Junípero Serra y los gentiles*. México: Palibrio. 2015.

Sheridan, Thomas E. *Empire of Sand: The Seri Indians and the Struggle of the Spanish Sonora, 1645-1803*. Tucson: The University of Arizona Press. 1999.

Riva, Ion de la. Presentación (11-12) en O.H.K. Spate, Edición en español de *El lago español* (2006; trad. Clara Usón.) Madrid: Casa Asia. 2006.

Torres Campos, Rafael. *España en California*. Madrid: Establecimiento tipográfico "Sucesores de Rivadeneyra." 1892.

Endnotes

[1]"From what I have seen and understood about the similarity that this whole land has to Spain, as in (?) its fertility is the greatness and coldness that it has, and in many other things that equate to it, it seemed to me that the most convenient name for this said land was to be called the New Spain of Mar Oceáno; and thus, in your majesty's name, this name was dedicated to you. I humbly implore your Highness to have it for the good and the order that it be named like this" Letter of Relationship of Hernán Cortés to Carlos I (30 / X / 1520).

[2]This route would be completed by Sebastián Vizcaíno, then mayor of Tehuantepec, at the beginning of the seventeenth century (circa 1604/5).

[3]Prior to Urdaneta, there were up to five attempts to find the return route from the Philippines to New Spain: 1) Gonzalo Gómez de Espinosa, participant of the Magallanes / El Cano expedition with the ship *Trinidad* in 1522; 2) Álvaro de Saavedra in 1528 with the ship *Florida*; 3) New attempt of Saavedra, that would die, with the same ship in 1529; 4) Bernardo de la Torre - by mandate of Ruy López de Villalobos—in 1544 on board the ship *San Juan*; 5) Iñigo Ortiz de Revetes, also with the ship *San Juan*, in 1545.

[4]He assumed command of the fleet commanded by Juan Rodriguez Cabrillo, after his death, in 1543. It was named Cape Mendocino in honor of the first Viceroy of New Spain, Antonio de Mendoza.

[5]Currently in Louisiana state. The Adaes became the capital of the province of Texas between 1729-1770.

[6]See the essay by Luis Navarro García "La crisis del reformismo borbónico bajo Carlos IV" in which he states: " . . . in the reign of Carlos IV seems to exhaust the renewal of Indian policy, leading to what I have called the 'crisis of reformism.'" (1).

[7]It was Álvaro de Navia Osorio, an extraordinary ambassador in the Swedish court who at the end of 1767 informed the Spanish court of the intentions of Russian expansionist. Some information points to the Count of Lacy as the informer of the Russian intentions, but his appointment as an ambassador dates back to 1772.

[8]See Edgar Omar Gutiérrez López, " José de Gálvez y sus aliados políticos en el financiamiento de la expedición militar a Sonora, 1765-1771". TSN, no. 2. July-December 2016. (45-50).

[9]The key idea of the whole plan is simple: it is necessary to strengthen the military defense of the Indies, providing men, ships, fortifications and combat elements, and therefore it is necessary to seek the increase of Royal (?) income of those kingdoms and provinces, for thus it will be convenient to inspect all its administration, with special attention to that of the Treasury."

[10]New Spain became the richest maritime possession of the Bourbons in the eighteenth century, and many measures were taken to convert it into an authentic "colony" at the service of the peninsula during the reigns of Carlos III and Carlos IV, whose ministers wanted to govern it according to the maxims of enlightened despotism and turn it into a permanent source of wealth to pay for the financial needs of the Crown, which had increased in all areas: navy, army, expenses of the court and the royal family, defense of borders, etc.

[11]In the same year, he was also named honary member of the Council of the Indies.

[12]The good relations with Croix contrast with the problems he had with his predecessor, Viceroy Cruilles. He had very challenging confrontations with him,

to the point of forcing his dismissal, and return to Spain where he was tried for fraud by the Royal Treasury.

[13]Tobacco was the second most exported product, only behind silver. On the importance of Gálvez's reforms regarding tobacco, see Susan Deans-Smith *Bureaucrats, Planters and Workers: The Making of the Tobacco Monopoly in Bourbon Mexico.* University of Texas Press. 1992.

[14]" . . . in this way, and in a short time, the General Visitor [Gálvez] established a business which had cost so many years of work" (118) Eduardo Arcila. *Reformas económicas del S. XVIII en Nueva España.* Mexico: Ministry of Public Education. 1974. The actions of Gálvez boosted the General Directorate of Tobacco and the income derived from this product became the largest income for the Royal Treasury. Due to this, the prohibition of 1766 declared that the manufacturing of cigarettes and cigars was decisive, thus the establishment of the Factory of Cigarettes and Cigars in 1769 (May 12).

[15]Esquilache already had information about Viceroy Cruillas' handling and asked Gálvez—formerly of Armona - to find out "if it is true that he [Cruillas] sells the jobs; holds prohibited games in his house for the interest that they produce for him; disperses many favors benefiting all of them; stops the royal decrees of provisions of governments or other jobs until they do some service . . . " (463, in Jesus Varela Marcos.) "Los prolegómenos de la visita de José de Gálvez a la Nueva España (1766). Don Francisco de Armona y la instrucción secreta del Marqués de Esquilache" *Revista de Indias*, v. XLVI, No. 178 (1986), pp. 453-470.

[16]In his doctoral thesis *Bernardo de Gálvez y América a finales del siglo XVIII* (UCM, 2015. Sylvia Hilton dir.), Gonzalo M. Quintero Saravia mentions the possibility that José de Gálvez himself influenced the appointment of Croix to the viceroy position. p. 180.

[17]Paradoxically, Lorenzana had studied at the Jesuit College of León. Although he was archbishop of Mexico, he despised that nation and those who populated it. Despite fraternizing with Gálvez, he also complained to the Minister of the Indies, Julián de Arriaga, about some of his actions in New Spain in an attempt to hide the bankruptcy, according to Lorenzana, into which the de Croix government had fallen into.

[18]" . . . the Sonora Expedition, despite its manpower and expense, did not change the basic patterns of Seri society nor the ways in which Seris and Spaniards related to one another." Sheridan, p. 403.

[19]Quoted in Sheridan, p. 373. I declare to all the inhabitants of these provinces of Sinaloa, and Sonora, when I disembark in their district, for that being the main object among those that bring me to provide tranquility, and to the good public, that have disturbed, and destroyed the enemies Seris and Pimas by

committing the greatest cruelties and excesses . . . than to give the most evident and ultimate proof of the sovereign piety with which both Majesties hear and admit true repentance, even from the greatest delinquents, I point out and grant the peremptory term of forty days . . . . . . so that all the insurgents and their leaders may appear to me, in the *Real de los Alamos*, and that surrendering at their discretion, as they should to the king our lord, implore forgiveness under the conditions that in the royal name I impose on them . . .

[20]See Sheridan pp. 375-378.

[21]Quoted in Gonzalo M. Quintero p. 193.

[22]See all the instruction transcribed in Boneu Company pp. 63-67. The following quotes are taken from said reproduction of the document.

[23]As a result of the disturbances caused by this measure, between 70 and 80 insurgents were executed.

[24]After the departure of the Jesuits, civil and military personnel were appointed to take care of the establishments. According to Boneu Companys "This administration that only lasted, fortunately few months, was so calamitous that in a short time the most scandalous plundering, cattle slaughter and looting were committed, to the extreme that the visitor personally dismissed the administrators appointed by the governor and returned the administration of the missions to the missionaries" (43).

[25]In Sanz p. 97.

[26]He disembarked on July 6, 1768.

[27]Fernando Boneu (pp. 52-56) offers the official list of all the accoutrements and supplies—civil, religious or military—that were taken on the expedition.

[28]In reference collected by Fernando Boneu p. 52.

[29]Natives that were already Christianized.

[30]In Navarro García p. 4.

[31]For information on this topic see Antonio Garcia and Garcia "Los privilegios de los religiosos en la evangelización de América; *Mar Océana*, nº 11 (45-63).

[32]Adriano IV was already familiar with the affairs of the Indies, because before being appointed Pope, he had an active part in the plan Cisneros-Las Casas for the reformation of the Indies.

[33]"The brothers who were guided by the spirit, voluntarily and spontaneously wanted to go to the Indies to convert and instruct the faith to the Indians . . . They can go freely and lawfully; upon this we carry the conscience of the superiors who are to send them; and no one, of whatever degree, can prevent them from going, under penalty of excommunication . . . "

[34]In García y García p. 49.

[35]The Dominicans arrived in 1526; the Augustinians in 1533; the Jesuits in 1572; and finally the Carmelites in 1585.

[36]Significant conflicts in the Far East, especially in Japan and China. See García y García, p. 62.

[37]To cope with the expenses, the Pious of Californias Fund was created. At the time of the expulsion of the Jesuits, this fund was worth $126,000. In Omar Guerrero, p. 208.

[38]*Despacho del excelentísimo e ilustrísimo señor Vizarrón*. México 13 de julio de 1740. AGNM. California 80 f. 162v. Quoted in Ignacio del Río; *El régimen jesuítico de la Antigua California.* said governor [of the presidio], captains and other corporals of the aforementioned presidios, are subject to the orders of the religious, such as their parish priests, must respect them, by their state and ministry, as their parishioners; and of the aforementioned fathers [will be] with the intelligence attend to the military corporals as ministers of his majesty, treating one another with reciprocal and good correspondence, without mixing the religious figures in the political government, but by way of direction, nor in the spirituality of the captains nor the corporals and that lead to the education of the Indians.

[39]In Hilton, p. 62.

[40]The title of the work reflects this same principle: *Noticia de la California, y de su conquista temporal, y espiritual hasta el tiempo presente, sacada de la Historia manuscrita, formada en México [en el] año de 1739, por el padre Miguel Venegas, de la Compañía de Jesús*. The decree by Viceroy Valero in 1708 aims to "encourage spiritual conquest." Also in his instructions to Portolá, Gálvez speaks of "the spiritual Conquest being made."

[41]Nor was Burriel ever in California, nor even travelled to America. Although he made a vow to travel to California, his appointment by Fernando VI to head the Archives Commission kept him in Spain for the rest his life.

[42]In León Portilla (2001, p. 144). From the end of streams, and even from the same port of Acapulco to the North, the American coasts towards the southern seas cannot be safe, as long as it is not subject to God and the Catholic King, California.

[43]It established " . . . to miss of all my domains of Spain, the Indies, the Philippine Islands, and others adjacent to the regulars of the Society [of Jesus], priests as coadjutors or laymen who made the first profession and novices who wanted to follow them; and that all the temporalities of the Company be occupied in my domains."

[44]Quoted in Boneu Companys p. 42.

[45]Benedict XIV, with the promulgation of *Cum Nuper Charissimus* in 1751 secularized the parishes of the religious in the Indies.

[46]Sylvia Hilton mentions as a key event in the process of secularization of the missions was the conflict that arose in 1717 between the farmer José de Subi-

ate and the missionary Daniel Januske. The latter argued that the farmer had 7,000 head of cattle -not the 1,500 allowed - and that the cattle grazed on mission lands. The missionary won the court hearing "but this incited the farmers and certain local authorities to propose secularization to eliminate the root of the missionary resistance to their economic activities (40).

[47]The transcendence of the Franciscan missionary has overshadowed to a large extent the exploits of the Dominicans in an area even more dangerous than that assigned to the Franciscans. The Dominicans founded the missions of Rosario -1774-, Santo Domingo -1775-, San Vicente Ferrer -1780-, San Miguel Arcángel -1787-, Santa Catalina -1797- . . . . All of them served as a link between Baja and Alta California.

[48]Its exact location continues to be the subject of debate. In any case, it was in the municipality of Las Playas de Rosarito.

[49]The so called Fernandinos were those who had been trained in the school of Propaganda Fide of San Fernando, as was the case of Fray Junípero Serra and who accompanied him first in Sierra Gorda, and later in Baja and Alta California.

[50]Santiago de Jalpan; Santa María de la Purísima Concepción; San Francisco de Asis; Nuestra Señora de la Luz; San Miguel de Concá.

[51]If I, with the help of God's grace, became a good religious man, my prayers would be more effective and they would not be interested in this gain; and I say the same of my beloved sister in Christ, Juana, and Miguel my brother- in- law: that they do not think of me for now, but to entrust me to God so that I may be a good priest and a good minister of God; in this we are all very interested, and this is what matters. I remember that my father, when he had that illness, so severe that they exacted it, and I, who was already a religious man, attended to him thinking that he was dying. While he and I were alone, he said: "My son, what I bestow upon you the responsibility to be a good religious man of Father S. Francisco ». Well, my father, know that I have those words so present as if I heard them from your mouth right now. And you also know that in order to be a good religious man, I must start on this path.

Un grupo documental para la evangelización de los coahuiltecos

BLANCA LÓPEZ DE MARISCAL

Tecnológico de Monterrey

Durante el virreinato de la Nueva España, como parte de los esfuerzos de la evangelización cristiana, se crearon textos religiosos en lenguas indígenas que son testimonios de primer orden para el estudio de las lenguas y las culturas de los pueblos originarios. Manuales, confesionarios y doctrinas bilingües son fuentes primarias para los estudios etnohistóricos y de lingüística histórica de México. Son textos que guardan información sobre el proceso de aculturación que vivieron los grupos indígenas ante la conversión al cristianismo, elemento fundamental de occidentalización. Este ensayo se propone realizar una exploración sobre el proceso de evangelización que se llevó a cabo en el Septentrión del Virreinato de la Nueva España, que comprende los territorios hoy en día ocupados por, Tamaulipas, Nuevo León, Coahuila y el sur de Texas.

Se revisarán algunos de los esfuerzos que los misioneros franciscanos utilizaron para conseguir la cristianización de una serie de grupos indígenas cuyas prácticas y organización social presentaba particularidades que las órdenes mendicantes no habían encontrado en los espacios del centro y del sur de lo que hoy conocemos como Mesoamérica: grupos nómadas, extremadamente combativos y hablantes de múltiples realizaciones dialectales. Todos estos factores presentaron retos muy importantes, especialmente de orden lingüístico, para la imposición de la nueva religión y la aculturación de la gente nativa. Si bien los documentos bilingües para la evangelización, escritos en las lenguas del centro y sur del país como el náhuatl, el zapoteco o el otomí, han sido estudiados con gran profundidad, los documentos religiosos bilingües de la región noreste de

México y el extremo suroriente de Texas, como los aquí presentados, requieren en la actualidad de una especial atención de parte de los editores críticos. Es necesario estudiar el grupo documental desde la filología para fijar dichos documentos con rigor crítico textual. Este ensayo es parte de un trabajo filológico de largo aliento en el que se está elaborando por primera vez una edición comprensiva y total que presentará en un solo corpus textual tres documentos a partir de la metodología de la crítica textual.

El trabajo se divide en dos partes. En la primera, a manera de introducción y para lograr entender los retos a los que los misioneros se enfrentaban, se presenta una somera revisión histórica de las primeras incursiones de los misioneros españoles en los territorios comprendidos entre el río Bravo y el río San Antonio; zona en donde posteriormente se establecieron las misiones centro de nuestro interés. En la segunda parte se aborda el trabajo desarrollado por los misioneros para lograr la pacificación y evangelización de los naturales así como los esfuerzos realizados para lograr establecer un diálogo con los habitantes de la zona, a través de la elaboración de documentos bilingües, escritos en castellano y en lengua texana o coahuilteca[1], realizados para favorecer el proceso de evangelización. Se trata de tres documentos: un Manual para la administración de los sacramentos, un Confesionario y un Cuadernillo, hoy en día resguardados en la Biblioteca Cervantina del Tecnológico de Monterrey que nos brindan un camino de aproximación para, a través de las estrategias de la conquista espiritual y la conquista lingüística de los misioneros españoles, entender una cultura hoy extinta.

Las primeras incursiones

La exploración y pacificación de los territorios hoy día ocupados por Coahuila, Nuevo México y el sur de Texas, se llevó a cabo en las últimas dos décadas del siglo XVI, a iniciativa del virreinato de la Nueva España. Para ello, se realizaron una serie de expediciones[2], de las cuales la más conocida es la de 1590 de Castaño de Sosa[3], quien comandó un viaje de exploración desde el Nuevo Almadén, hoy Monclova, y que recorrió los territorios del Río Bravo o Grande, del Río Sabinas, el Río Salado o Conchos, el Río Pecos y el Río del Diablo.

Es muy interesante analizar los textos que nos dan noticia de estas primeras expediciones ya que describen a los pobladores de la zona como chichimecas, gentilicio que en la época era sinónimo de indios bárbaros o gentiles, grupos nómadas que no poseían una estructura social, pero sobre todo que vivían agrupados en bandas que hablan dialectos diferentes y que no eran capaces de entenderse entre sí. Los cronistas de esta primera época los caracterizan siempre como organizados en grupos pequeños, específicamente utilizan la expresión "pocos en número," e insisten en que se trata de hablantes de muy diversas lenguas o dialectos. Este hecho puede, de alguna manera, explicarnos por qué la evangelización de estos pueblos resulta una acción tan tardía de parte de los colonizadores españoles.

Los trabajos de los misioneros, en estos territorios, no iniciaron sino hasta 1670 a cargo de los frailes franciscanos procedentes de los colegios de la Santa Cruz de Querétaro y de Nuestra Señora de Guadalupe de Zacatecas. En esos primeros tiempos las misiones se fundaban aun cuando no existiera un poblado español cercano. Esto dejaba a los predicadores que las habitaban, que en ocasiones no eran más de un par, en situación muy precaria, por lo que no era de extrañar que murieran en manos de los pobladores hostiles, o que abandonaran la misión porque dejaban de llegar los recursos para continuar su labor evangelizadora[4].

En su *Chrónica apostólica y seráphica de todos los Colegios de Propaganda Fide de esta Nueva España de Misioneros Franciscanos Observantes* . . . Fray Isidro Félix de Espinosa[5], narra las penurias que estos primeros evangelizadores solían enfrentar. No era extraño que les faltara lo más indispensable para su propio sustento:

> Los años 17 y 18 fueron entre los indios muy escasas las cosechas de maíz, y frijol, por haber faltado a su tiempo las aguas: y como de su mano solíamos tener el socorro, faltándoles a ellos era preciso nos alcanzase a nosotros la suspensión y el entredicho temporal de esta calma [. . .] Muchos días amanecía sin tener cosa alguna a que apelar, y como la necesidad es industriosa, sugirió a un misionero, que no sería despreciable la carne de los cuervos, que son pequeños, como los grajos, y abundan en las mañanas en los árboles, y con una escopeta, había todos los días carne segura. (Félix de Espinosa, 444)

Incluso llegó a faltar hasta el pan y el vino para consagrar, por lo que no era posible celebrar la Eucaristía. Es así como se malograron los primeros intentos civilizatorios, como también sucedió con el grupo de cuatro misiones fundadas en los dos márgenes del Rio Grande en el distrito de Coahuila.

Debido a estas circunstancias, los primeros intentos de evangelización fracasaron y fueron necesarios grandes esfuerzos para concretar nuevamente la fundación de las misiones; es también el caso de las misiones establecidas en el territorio habitado por los texas. La ocupación permanente de la Provincia española de Texas se inició con la expedición del capitán Domingo Ramón en 1715[6]. La expedición acompañó a un grupo de misioneros de los colegios de Querétaro y de Zacatecas a los territorios de los indios texas o asinaís[7], en el este de lo que hoy es el estado de Texas, con el propósito de establecer una cadena de misiones. Tres de ellas, a cargo de los Frailes del Convento de la Santa Cruz de Querétaro con Fray Isidro Félix de Espinosa quien fungió como presidente de la misión y las tres restantes estarían a cargo de los misioneros del convento de Guadalupe en Zacatecas[8] a cargo de un superior, Fray Antonio Margil de Jesús[9].

Figura 1. Nuevo México y la Florida, de Nicolás Sanson, 1656.[10]

Como resultado de estos esfuerzos se establecieron cuatro Misiones y un presídium entre las que se encontraban la Misión de San Antonio de Valero y la de Nuestra señora de la Purísima Concepción de Acuña; en el verano de 1716, y en 1717, antes de que empezara la gran hambruna debida a las sequías, se fundaron las otras dos misiones. (Habig 119; Gómez de Orozco 142). Fray Isidro Félix de Espinosa en su *Chrónica Apostólica y Seráfica* . . . da también cuenta de las diversas refundaciones que los misioneros tuvieron que realizar, hasta llegar a su establecimiento definitivo en las márgenes del Río San Antonio con la fundación de la Misión de San Antonio de Valero:

En el año 21, juntas ocho compañías se fue marchando para Texas, y el río San Antonio se incorporaron todos los religiosos de los dos colegios; y a 28 de julio llegó toda la gente a dar vista a los Texas, donde salieron muchos indios e indias a recibir a los españoles; y el día cinco de agosto se celebró la restauración de la primera misión de N. P. S.

Francisco con fiesta muy solemne de misa cantada, con salva general de todas las compañías. El día 8 se restableció la misión de la Purísima Concepción, [. . .] en la misa, que cantó el V. P. fray Antonio Margil y predicó el P. Presidente del Colegio de la Santa Cruz a que concurrieron multitud innumerable de indios; y este día, el señor Marqués y Capitán general regaló al gobernador de los texas con un vestido de paño azul bordado y con chupa de tela, con lo correspondiente del vestido, y lo sentó a su mesa, [. . .] El día 13 se hizo la fundación de la misión del Señor S. José. (Félix de Espinosa 455)

Las misiones encontraron su lugar definitivo a orillas del río San Antonio, donde quedaron solemnemente fundadas el 4 de mayo de 1731, poco más de cuatro décadas después del primer intento (Habig; Gómez de Orozco). Los primeros encuentros con los naturales estaban teñidos de diversos matices, en ocasiones los misioneros parecen encontrar un terreno fértil para la evangelización:

. . . a rezar con el Padre las oraciones y mostraban afecto al santo bautismo, y prometían venirse a la misión que les fundasen, sin repugnancia alguna. Causóle al apostólico misionero mucho regocijo de haber encontrado mies tan copiosa, y causándole dolor el dejar tantas almas en aquellos campos sin ministros que se emplearon en su reducción, casi estuvo resuelto a quedarse con ellos; pero el cuidado de sus compañeros y el hacerse cargo de la mucha distancia para poner misión

Figura 2. La América Septentrional, de José Antonio de Alzate y Ramírez, 1768.[11]

y mantenerla le obligó a dar la vuelta, con la esperanza de congregar con el tiempo todas aquellas naciones, fundándose sus pueblos. (Félix de Espinosa 463)

Así, poco a poco va prosperando la construcción de las misiones que, como las de Nuestra Señora de la Purísima Concepción de Acuña, la de San José, la de San Francisco de la Espada y la de San Juan Capistrano, llegaron a tener no solo iglesia de cal y canto, sino también edificios de piedra dedicados al convento de los frailes, a las habitaciones de los indios e incluso almacenes. La vida de estos primeros misioneros transcurría entre temporadas en las que se podían dar a las tareas de evangelizar y bautizar al mismo tiempo que se dedicaban al cultivo de las tierras, al pastoreo, e incluso, en la misión de San Francisco, a la construcción de un acueducto que era parte de sistema de irrigación de la comunidad (Habig 233). Todos estos progresos no impedían, como contraste, que los habitantes de la misión vivieran en alerta de guerra, ya que las misiones se encontraban a menudo asediadas por grupos hostiles:

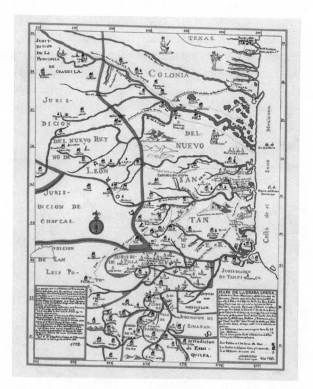

Figura 3. Mapa de la Sierra Gorda y Costa del Seno Mexicano, anónimo, 1792.[12]

. . . en especial de la bárbara Nación de los Apaches, que infestan aquellos parajes y territorios, porqué deberán estar siempre preparados para
la defensa, procurando tener por amigos a todos los Indios de las
Naciones circunvecinas, a sus gobernadores, y capitanes, para poderlos
resistir y ofender en las ocasione que se ofrecieren, y fueren acometi-
dos por su bárbara temeridad: con la cierta confianza de que todos sus
servicios serán atendidos, y gratificados por la Real Magnificencia de
su Majestad (que Dios guarde). (Félix de Espinosa 448)

Esto significa que no resultaba fácil en absoluto encontrar la estabilidad: en ocasiones las tribus del Este de Texas se rehusaron a acompañar a los misioneros,
por lo tanto fue necesario congregar algunas de las muchas naciones, nómadas,
que habitaban en las planicies entre el Río Bravo y el Río de San Antonio, tales
como los *pacaos, pitalaques y pajalates*.

Sin embargo, la evangelización presenta grados de dificultad que no solo
tienen que ver con la problemática de trasladar complejas cuestiones teológicas
de una cultura a otra, sino también y en primera instancia, problemas reales de
comunicación, que no se resuelven con la presencia de un intérprete ya que en el
catolicismo es especialmente delicado el proceso de impartir el sacramento de la
confesión o penitencia. Se trata de una práctica privada que implica el secreto de
confesión y por tanto requiere, por parte de los evangelizadores, del dominio de
la legua de los catecúmenos[10]. Antes de que se dieran los primeros intentos por
documentar la lengua de los pobladores de la región, la evangelización se realiz-
aba utilizando la lengua náhuatl o mexicana, como se le solía llamar. Fray Isidro
Félix de Espinosa narra la forma en que se impartió el sacramento de la extrema
unción a un indio que se encontraba agonizando a causa de la lepra:

. . . compadecido uno de los misioneros, se desnudó de los paños de la
honestidad para limpiarle de tan asquerosa lepra. Después, a la sombra
de un árbol se sentó a confesar al enfermo en lengua mexicana, que
entendía el ministro, y tardó hora y media en confesarlo, dándole el
Señor fortaleza y tanta claridad para explicarse, que dejó escrito de su
letra el mismo ministro que quedó sumamente consolado y alabando a
Dios por las extraordinarias misericordias que usa con sus redimidos.
Recibió dentro de cinco días el sacramento de la extrema unción y
murió con señales de mucha piedad; y se le dio entierro con las cere-
monias eclesiásticas en el lugar destinado para la iglesia. (Félix de
Espinosa 461)

Poco a poco los misioneros empezaron a manejar la lengua de los grupos indígenas a los que atendían y a través de estas primeras incursiones "los procura-

ban ir desengañando de sus errores y les persuadían de la suma importancia de recibir el Santo Bautismo confesando la verdad de un Dios Trino y Uno" (Félix de Espinosa 439). Pero la tarea no resultaba fácil, ya que al igual que en el altiplano y en el sur de lo que hoy es México la translación de conceptos como la Santísima Trinidad, la Concepción Inmaculada de María, o el mismísimo concepto del demonio es una tarea muy compleja. Lo mismo sucedía con conceptos como la salvación eterna, el infierno y, sobre todo, el tránsito de una religión politeísta al monoteísmo, o a una religión en la que la vida futura depende solamente de la forma de vida. Por lo que, según narra Fray Isidro de Espinosa, los misioneros intentaban por todos los medios hacerles ver las bondades de la "Buena Nueva", en otras palabras, de lo predicado en los *Evangelios*:

> . . . haciéndoles conocer la mucha ceguedad en que habían vivido, pero todo ello lo tomaban como cosa superficial; porque están tan creídos de lo que heredaron de sus mayores, que es menester todo el auxilio divino, para arrancarles del corazón aquellas vanas credulidades con que se criaron desde niños. (Félix de Espinosa 439)

Cuando finalmente se logró cierto grado de estabilidad, el presidente de las misiones, fray Gabriel de Vergara, se dio a la tarea de completar un texto bilingüe, para favorecer la comunicación con los grupos indígenas que se buscaba convertir, ya que resultaba indispensable elaborar herramientas lingüísticas para comunicarse con los naturales. Esta labor presentaba retos tremendos, ya que las tribus nómadas utilizaban realizaciones dialectales diversas, al grado de que, como se dijo antes, no se entendían entre sí. Por tanto, los franciscanos tuvieron que recurrir a una lengua franca con la cual pudieron comunicarse con los diferentes grupos, tal y como se había utilizado el náhuatl en el centro y el sur de la Nueva España. Esto propició que en el seno de las misiones de la Purísima Concepción y de San Francisco de la Espada, se elaboraran tres documentos, dos manuscritos y un impreso, de gran interés filológico, lingüístico y etnohistórico. Los tres pueden ser consultados actualmente en la Biblioteca Cervantina del Tecnológico de Monterrey:

- *Confesionario de indios en coahuilteco y español*, sin autor y sin fecha, atribuido a Bartolomé García, posiblemente elaborado en la primera mitad del siglo XVIII, Colección Robredo, 13.7 X 8 cm., 40 fojas.
- *Cuadernillo de la lengua de los indios pajalates, en pajalate y español*, 1732, atribuido fray Gabriel de Vergara. Colección Robredo, 14.5 X 8.5 cm., 13 fojas.

- *Manual para administrar los santos sacramentos de penitencia, eucharistia, extrema-uncion, y matrimonio: dar gracias despues de comulgar, y ayudar a bien morir a los indios de las naciones: pajalates, orejones, pacaos, pacóas, tilijayas, alasapas, pausanes, y otras muchas diferentes, que se hallan en las missiones del Rio de San Antonio y Rio Grande . . .*, de Fray Bartolomé García, Imprenta de los herederos de Doña María de Rivera, México, 1760[13].

De acuerdo con Eugenio del Hoyo[14], quien llevó a cabo la única edición parcial conocida de los dos manuscritos en 1965, los manuscritos fueron adquiridos por la Biblioteca del Tecnológico de manos del señor Don Felipe Montes Villaseñor. Es posible que ambos documentos hayan pasado de la Misión de la Purísima Concepción al Hospicio Franciscano de Boca de Leones, en Villaldama, Nuevo León, en 1794 cuando las misiones de Texas fueron secularizadas y de allí hayan sido vendidos y, posteriormente, comercializados. Las condiciones del hallazgo de estos textos son interesantes pues el manuscrito del Cuadernillo había sido doblado y utilizado para elaborar las tapas del volumen en que se encontraba el Confesionario: "[a]l tratar de restaurar las pastas del libro, tuvo la fortuna de descubrir que éstas estaban formadas por varias hojas de papel, manuscritas también en español y una lengua desconocida" (Del Hoyo 3). Ambos manuscritos formaban parte de un libro que cuenta con otras dos piezas: *Definiciones morales* en latín y *Caridad o amor del prójimo según su propiedad que pone San Pablo*.

La autoría del *Cuadernillo* atribuida a fray Gabriel de Vergara por Eugenio del Hoyo, la datación y el título son discutidos por Rudolph Troike en su artículo titulado "The date and authorship of the Pajalate (Coahuilteco) 'Cuadernillo'":

> it is not likely that Vergara could have been the author of the Cuadernillo/Cuaderno if it was composed after his departure, as the date would indicate. It is still possible, of course, that he was involved in its development in some way, such as initiating or authorizing its composition, before he left office. But unless we gain more information on the history of the San Antonio missions, we shall probably never know the answer.[15]

El *Confesionario* no ha sido publicado de manera íntegra, pues su editor Eugenio del Hoyo, determinó que se trataba de un texto que dio base al *Manual* impreso, por lo que publicó solo aquellas páginas en las que el *Confesionario* difiere en contenido del *Manual*, además hemos encontrado omisiones importantes, seguramente resultado de una práctica de censura, sobre todo en aquellos pasajes en los que el confesor pregunta al penitente sobre su observancia del sexto mandamiento.

El único impreso que forma parte del grupo documental es el que lleva por título *Manual para administrar los santos sacramentos de penitencia, eucaristía, extremaunción y matrimonio*. El autor del *Manual* es el fraile Bartolomé García,

Figura 4. Fray Bartolomé García, *Manual para administrar los santos sacramentos de penitencia, eucharistia, extrema-uncion, y matrimonio: dar gracias despues de comulgar, y ayudar a bien morir a los indios de las naciones: pajalates, orejones, pacaos, pacóas, tilijayas, alasapas, pausanes, y otras muchas diferentes, que se hallan en las missiones del Rio de San Antonio y Rio Grande . . .*, Imprenta de los herederos de Doña María de Rivera, México, 1760.

del Colegio de la Santísima Cruz de la Ciudad de Querétaro, fue misionero en la Provincia de Texas entre 1748 y 1760 (Portillo 127). A él se le atribuye una "sonora voz de su lengua cuando canta" (folio 3v). Su *Manual* fue realizado como guía para los evangelizadores de las Misiones del Río de San Antonio y Río Grande. Como ya se dijo fue publicado en la Imprenta de los herederos de Doña María Rivera en la calle San Bernardo en 1760. Contamos con la edición prínceps del *Manual* de 1760, y con una edición moderna realizada por Nicolás León en su *Bibliografía Mexicana del siglo XVIII* pp. 451-512.

Durante su estancia en San Francisco de la Espada Fray Bartolomé García se dio a la labor de conformar el *Manual para la administración de los sacramentos*. Debido a que las numerosas tribus que se encontraban representadas en las misiones del río San Antonio hablaban diferentes dialectos, los misioneros tuvieron que reducirlos a una sola lengua que poseía rasgos comunes. Ésta ha sido denominada como lengua texana o cohauilteca (Habig 212).

El libro cuenta con las aprobaciones de rigor, entre ellas una del fraile José Guadalupe Prado, capellán del Colegio de San Fernando de México, quien según sus palabras vivió 22 años discurriendo por las misiones de las provincias de Coahuila y Texas. Prado da fe de la calidad como intérprete de García, de quien dice "se ha señalado en aprender la lengua de nuestros indios, hasta predicarles en ella sermones cuaresmales, con aprobación de los intérpretes más limados y no menos edificación y aplauso de los otros. Y sobre la evidencia de estos antecedentes está la obra presente con tanta propiedad traducida, que de ella misma se infieren y constan los progresos de su autor en aquel idioma" (*Manual*, folio 2v).

Desde sus primeras páginas el texto señala que la lengua en que está escrito el *Manual* es "la lengua más común a todas las conversiones franciscanas que se plantaron desde la misión llamada la Candela hasta las que bordan las amenas márgenes del Río de San Antonio" (*Manual*, folio 3r). Extensión de más de cien leguas, agrega el mismo fraile, para continuar puntualizando que todas las misiones, desde la primera de la Señora de los Dolores hasta la última de San Juan Capistrano, excepto una, se fundaron con indios hablantes de la lengua del *Manual*. "Me atrevo a decir que este *Manual* no solo es general, sino generalísimo cuanto a dichas Misiones fundadas más que les adjuntan Indios, pues de esta que tratamos tenemos muy larga experiencia que la gente nueva a breve tiempo la entiende o habla y los muchachos, que son la porción de nuestra mayor esperanza, al año ya como dice, cortan el pelo con el dicho idioma" (*Manual*, folio 3v).

Todo esto nos permite conjeturar que el texano o coahuilteco funcionó como un tipo de lengua común a mediados del siglo XVIII en la zona del Río de San Antonio y que si no era la propia de los grupos indígenas sí era adquirida por los diferentes grupos como lengua franca, con el apoyo y promoción de los frailes franciscanos: "[t]he pajalates were a Coahuiltecan band found in the San Antonio area and incorporated into several missions. Their language, and that of closely related bands to which the name Coahuilteco is applied was apparently adopted by the Spanish as a lingua franca in the missions" (Troike 1978, 329).

El fraile Prado aborda la preocupación que causa a los misioneros las traducciones incorrectas que se hacían de la doctrina, pues había un grupo de intérpretes que auxiliaban a los frailes para impartirla:

> [a] este peligro tan probable y bien fundada sospecha de que la versión de los indios intérpretes corrompa el genuino sentido de nuestra Doctrina Cristiana muchas veces por falaces y negligentes . . . y no pocas por . . . ignorantes, se llega otro embarazo nada menos considerable y es aquella suma dificultad que trae consigo la materia de nuestra predicación. (*Manual*, folio 4r)

Por otra parte, subraya que la variedad de lenguas dificultaba la posibilidad de hacer un manual para cada una de ellas, por lo que hubo que elegir de todos los idiomas el más común, el "que sea entendido de los indios más principales, cual es este sin controversia, un duda en todas aquellas naciones" (*Manual*, folio 5r).

En la "Nota, *Consectario moral* y *Dedicatoria*" Bartolomé García da a entender que ha elaborado un Arte de la lengua, cuya ubicación actual es desconocida:

> [a]sí lo tengo anotado en el Arte de este lenguaje, apoyándolo con razones del doctísimo Abulense[14] y convenciéndolo con el ejemplo de nuestro propio castellano, que sin embargo de correr con mucha más variedad en su estilo y dialecto, aun con toda esa tan desigual diferencia, todos reputamos la lengua española por una misma. (*Manual*, folio 7r)

La creación del *Arte* fue considerada como una aliada del *Manual,* según las palabras de García:

> [d]eben los misioneros en cumplimiento de la suya, aplicarse con celo eficaz, al uso del presente Manual, y juntamente a las reglas del Arte, que se hizo por solo el fin de formarlo y entenderlo y supuesta ya la formación de uno y otro, nada más falta sino menos que la mitad del trabajo y ninguna excusa para con Dios. (*Manual*, folio 7v)

El *Manual*, como cualquiera de los editados en el centro del país para la evangelización, está compuesto por diversas secciones entre las que destacan Sacramento de la penitencia, Interrogatorio para confesar a los dichos indios, Modo de pedir materia para la absolución cuando no se halla en la presente confesión, Exhorto para después de la confesión, Catecismo de los principales misterios de nuestra santa fe, Modo de administrar el sagrado viático a los enfermos, Modo de administrar el Santo sacramento de la Extremaunción, Modo de ayudar a bien morir y Modo de administrar el santo sacramento del matrimonio. Es importante hacer notar aquí que tres de los sacramentos están ausentes del *Manual*: el bautismo, la confirmación y el orden sacerdotal, los dos últimos por razones obvias[15]. Pero llama la atención que el *Manual* no se ocupe del bautismo, debido a que bautizar a los infieles era sin lugar a duda la labor principal de los misioneros. El número de los bautizados es uno de los datos que año con año se consignan en los reportes de las misiones; por ejemplo, sabemos que en San Juan Capistrano "[e]n 1740 el número de los bautizados llegó a 278 y llegaron a tener hasta 216 individuos viviendo en la misión, algunos ya bautizados, otros en proceso de formación" (Heusinger 122-26).

Desde el siglo XIX diversos investigadores se han ocupado del estudio de la lengua coahuilteca a través del *Manual para administrar los sacramentos* de Fray Bartolomé García. Francisco Pimentel en el Tomo segundo de su *Tratado de filología mexicana,* publicado en 1862, da noticia del idioma tejano o coahuilteco del que informa que era el más usado en las provincias de Coahuila y Texas y que se hablaba desde "la Candela hasta el río de San Antonio". El autor asevera que se trata de una lengua que tiene diversas realizaciones dialectales "cuyas diferencias consisten en la pronunciación o en la forma de algunas palabras" (Pimentel 78).

Manuel Orozco y Berra en su *Geografía de las lenguas y Carta etnográfica de México,* de 1864, clasifica al coahuilteco como una lengua extinta (61) que se llegó a hablar en el territorio de Coahuila, Nuevo León y Tamaulipas (63). Asimismo, clasifica a los coahuiltecos como una tribu que habitaba en Coahuila y Nuevo León (68). Utiliza el *Manual* como fuente e identifica su lengua como coahuilteca:

> [l]os pajalates, orejones, pacoas, tilijayas, alasapas, pausanes, pacuaches, mescales, pampopas, tacames, chayopines, venados, pamaques, pihuiques, borrados, sanipaos y manos de perro, usaban la lengua, cuya gramática compuso el P. Fr. Bartolomé García: no dice el nombre de ella y para distinguirla la nombraremos coahuilteca. A esta familia deben referirse todas las tribus que se encontraban al este de las misiones de Parras y al norte de Saltillo, hasta tocar con el Río Grande; no olvidando que si todas hablaban coahuilteco, se notaban en muchas algunas diferencias. (Orozco y Berra 309)

En su *Linguistic material from Southern Texas*, Swanton presenta un vocabulario inglés- coahuilteco a partir de la traducción del *Manual* de Bartolomé García (10-55). Además, conjetura que la lengua coahuilteca tenía una gran diversidad de dialectos, hablados por distintos grupos, los cuales enumera en una lista de 212 entradas de nombras de tribus (134-36). John Swanton se dio a la tarea de analizar dos tipos de documentos. Un tipo estaba formado por documentos etnohistóricos: registros, censos de misiones, confesionarios y manuales hechos por frailes entre el siglo XVII y el XVIII. El segundo tipo eran estudios etnográficos realizados en el siglo XIX por Berlandier, Uhde y Gastchet, quienes lograron entrevistar a algunos de los últimos hablantes que subsistían en la zona. Como resultado de su investigación, Swanton reconoció la existencia de siete lenguas: coahuilteco, cotoname, maratino, solano, comecrudo, karankawa, tonkawa o aranama. Swanton construyó vocabularios y listas de elementos gramaticales como pronombres, artículos y numerales.

> Estas lenguas, según Swanton y posteriormente Edward Sapir, pueden ser incluidas dentro de una familia que denominaron "hokano-coahuilteca" y que además correspondería a la macro-familia hokana, la cual, de acuerdo con la tesis de Sapir, cubría la franja norte del territorio mexicano, hasta que en algún momento fue dividida al extenderse la macro-familia yutoazteca hacia el sur dejando dos grandes porciones hokanas, una en el Noreste de México y otra en el extremo norte de Baja California. (Reyes y Valadez 577)

El estudio de las lenguas de la zona fue continuado, ampliado y discutido por la labor de investigadores como Gabriel Saldívar, el ingeniero Roberto Weitlaner, el historiador Eugenio Del Hoyo, y los lingüistas Karl-Heinz Gursky, quien identificó la lengua quinigua de Nuevo León, Ives Goddard y Morris Swadesh. Resulta destacada la investigación Rudolph Troike que ha realizado sobre la lengua coahuilteca en la segunda mitad del siglo XX hasta la actualidad.

Utilizando como corpus el *Manual* y la edición de Eugenio del Hoyo del *Confesionario* y el *Cuadernillo*,Troike ha estudiado aspectos lingüísticos del coahuilteco como oraciones de relativo, concordancia de sujeto-objeto, lexicografía, préstamos del náhuatl, entre otros.

En conclusión:

Los textos religiosos en lenguas indígenas que se crearen como parte de los esfuerzos de la evangelización en la Nueva España, son testimonios de primer orden para el estudio de las lenguas y las culturas de los pueblos indígenas ya que se trata de textos que guardan información sobre el proceso de aculturación que vivieron estos grupos durante el transcurso de su conversión al cristianismo. Por otra parte los documentos religiosos bilingües de la región noreste de México y el extremo suroriente de Texas, como los aquí presentados, requieren en la actualidad de una especial atención en su recuperación, ya que su rescate mediante una publicación moderna será particularmente relevante y de gran utilidad para los estudiosos que forman parte del Recovery Program que tanto éxito ha tenido, bajo la dirección de su fundador Nicolás Kanellos, en sus primeros 25 años.

En el proyecto que estamos llevando a cabo propone que el grupo documental de textos bilingües en idioma texano o coahuilteco y español debe ser estudiado en conjunto, entre otras cosas, debido a que existe una filiación entre los tres documentos que requiere de un estudio crítico textual para determinar sus semejanzas y diferencias. Con esto se logrará una íntegra recuperación del valioso material contenido en ellos. Una edición de rescate de rigor filológico es necesaria para proporcionar a los investigadores un material de trabajo que les permita ampliar el conocimiento del texano o coahuilteco y sus hablantes.

Bibliografía

Boltin, Herbert Eugene. *Texas in the Middle Eighteenth Century: Studies in Spanish Colonial History and Administration*. Austin Texas: University of Texas, 1970.

Campbell, T.N. y T.J. Campbell. *Indian Groups Associated with Spanish Missions of The San Antonio Missions*. The University of Texas at San Antonio: National Historical Park, Center for Archeological Research, Special Report, N° 16, 1985.

Castañeda, Carlos E. "Biographical Introduction", en *History of Texas: 1673-1779. By Fray Juan Agustin Morfi, Missionary, Teacher, Historian*. Transl. with Biographical Introduction and Annotations by Carlos E. Castañeda. In two parts. Albuquerque [NewMexico]: The Quivira Society, 1935, retrs., ils., maps. (The Quivira Society, 6), p. 13.

De la Mota y Escobar, Alonso. *Descripción geográfica de los reinos de Nueva Galicia, Nueva Vizcaya y Nuevo León*. Editorial de la Universidad Juárez del Estado de Durango, 2009. De León, Alonso. "Relación y discurso del descubrimiento, población y pacificación de este Nuevo Reino de León." *Historia de Nuevo León con noticias sobre Coahuila, Tamaulipas, Texas y Nuevo México*. Fondo Editorial Nuevo León, 2005.

Heusinger, Edward W. *Early Explorations and Mission Establishments in Texas*. Naylor Co., 1936.

Espinosa, Fray Isidro Félix de. *Chronica apostólica y seráphica de todos los colegios de Propaganda fide de esta Nueva-España, de misioneros francis-*

canos observantes erigidos con autoridad pontificia, y regia, para la reformación de los fieles, y conversion de los gentiles. Consagrada a la milagrosa cruz de piedra, que como titular se venera en su primer Colegio de propaganda fide de la muy ilustre ciudad de San-Tiago de Querétaro sita en el arzobispado de México. Viuda de D. Joseph Bernardo Hogal, 1746.

García, Fray Bartolomé. *Manual para administrar los santos sacramentos de penitencia, eucharistia, extrema-uncion, y matrimonio: dar gracias despues de comulgar, y ayudar a bien morir a los indios de las naciones: pajalates, orejones, pacaos, pacóas, tilijayas, alasapas, pausanes, y otras muchas diferentes, que se hallan en las missiones del Rio de San Antonio y Rio Grande, pertenecientes à el Colegio de la santissima cruz de la ciudad de Queretaro, como son: los pacuaches, mescales, pampopas, tacames, chayopines, venados, pamaques, y toda la juventud de pihuiques, borrados, sanipaos, y manos de Perro.* Imprenta de los herederos de Doña María de Rivera, 1760.

García, Fray Bartolomé. *Manual para administrar los santos sacramentos de penitencia, eucharistia, extrema-uncion, y matrimonio: dar gracias despues de comulgar, y ayudar a bien morir a los indios de las naciones: pajalates, orejones, pacaos, pacóas, tilijayas, alasapas, pausanes, y otras muchas diferentes, que se hallan en las missiones del Rio de San Antonio y Rio Grande* . . . En Nicolás León, *Bibliografía Mexicana del siglo XVIII*, pp. 451-512.

Gómez de Orozco, Federico. *Crónicas de Michoacán.* Universidad Nacional Autónoma de México, 1940.

Habig, Marion Alphonse. *The Alamo Chain of Missions. A History of San Antonio's Five Old Missions.* Franciscan Herald Press, Publishers of Franciscan Literature, 1997.

Morfi, Juan Agustín. *Diario y derrotero: 1777-1781.* Ed. de Eugenio del Hoyo y Malcolm D.

McLean. Monterrey, [Nuevo León]: Instituto Tecnológico de Estudios Superiores de Monterrey, 1967, xx, 472 p., maps. (Serie Historia, 5. Noticias Geográficas e Históricas del Nores te de México, 2).

____. *History of Texas: 1673 -1779. By Fray Juan Agustin Morfi, Missionary, Teacher, Historian.* Transl. with biographical introduction and annotations by Carlos E. Castañeda. In two parts. Albuquerque [New Mexico]: The Quivira Society, 1935, retrs., ils., maps. (The Quivira Society, 6).

____. *Viaje de indios y Diario del Nuevo México.* Con una introducción biobibliográfica y acotaciones por Vito Alessio Robles. 2a ed. Con adiciones de la impresa por la Sociedad Bibliófilos Mexicanos. México: Antigua Librería Robredo de José Porrúa e Hijos, 1935 [9], 306 p., ils., maps.

Orozco y Berra, Manuel. *Geografía de las lenguas y carta etnográfica de México*. Imprenta de J.M. Andrade y F. Escalante, 1864.

Portillo Valadez, José Antonio. *Diccionario de clérigos y misioneros norestenses*. 2011.

Reyes Trigos, Claudia y Moisés Valadez Moreno, "Identificación geográfico-lingüística de los grupos indígenas del noreste de México (siglos XVI-XIX)." *Tercer Encuentro de Lingüística en el Noreste*. Eds. Zarina Estrada Fernández, Max Figueroa Esteva y Gerardo López Cruz. Editorial Unison, 1996.

Sapir, Edward. "The Hokan and Coahuiltecan Languages." *International Journal of American Linguistics*, vol. 1, no. 4, 1920, pp. 280-290.

Swanton, John Reed. *Linguistic material from the tribes of southern Texas and Northeastern Mexico,* U.S. Government, 1940.

Troike, Rudolph. "A contribution to Coahuilteco lexicography." *International Journal of American Linguistics*, vol. 29, no. 4, 1963, pp. 295-299.

____. "A descriptive phonology and morphology of Coahuilteco." Dis. University of Texas, 1959.

____. "A Nahuatl loan-word in Coahuilteco." *International Journal of American Linguistics,* vol. 27, no. 2, 1961, pp. 172-175.

____. "A Structural Comparison of Tonkawa and Coahuilteco." *Studies in Southwestern ethnolinguistics: meaning and history in the languages of the American Southwest*. Eds. Dell H. Hymes y William E. Bittle. Mouton, 1967.

____. "Center-Embedding relative clauses in Coahuilteco 1." *International Journal of American Linguistics,* vol. 81, no. 1, 2015, pp. 133-142.

____. "Coahuilteco, a language isolate of Texas." *Languages. Handbook of North American Indians. 11.* Ed. Ives Goddard. Smithsonian Institution, 1996, pp. 644-665.

____. "Notes on Coahuiltecan Ethnography." *Texas Archeological Society Bulletin,* vol. 32, 1961, pp. 57-63.

____. "Researches in Coahuiltecan Ethnography." *Texas Archeological Society Bulletin,* vol. 30, 1959, pp. 301-309.

____. "Subject-Object concord in Coahuilteco." *Linguistic Society of America,* vol. 57, no. 3, 1981, pp. 658-673.

____. "The date and authorship of the pajalate (Coahuilteco) 'Cuadernillo'." *International Journal of American Linguistics,* vol. 44, no. 4, 1978, pp. 329-330.

____. "The typology of relative clauses in Coahuilteco, an indian language of Texas." *Southwest Journal of Linguistics,* vol. 29, no. 1, 2010, p. 111.

Vergara, Gabriel de. *El cuadernillo de la lengua de los indios pajalates (1732)*. Ed. Eugenio del Hoyo. ITESM, 1965.

Notas

[1]Este es el nombre que el lingüista Orozco y Berra le da a la lengua de los habitantes de las provincias de Coahuila y Texas: "Llamo a este idioma tejano o coahuilteco, porque, según los misioneros era el más usado en las provincias de Coahuila y Texas, hablándose desde la Candela hasta el río San Antonio. Las tribus que usaban este idioma eran las conocidas con los nombres de pajalates, orejones, pacoas, tilijayos, alasapas, pausanes, pacuaches, mescales, pampoas, tacames, chayopines, venados, pamaques, pihuiques, borrados, sanipaos y manos de perro". Orozco y Berra, Manuel. *Geografía de las lenguas y carta etnográfica de México*. Imprenta de J.M. Andrade y F. Escalante, 1864, p. 77.

[2]Como las realizadas por los capitanes Alonso de León en 1689 y 1690, Domingo Terán de los Ríos entre 1691 y 1692, Domingo Ramón en 1716, Martín de Alarcón en 1720 y el marqués de San Miguel de Aguayo en 1721, así como los diarios y las crónicas de los frailes que formaron parte de esas expediciones como fray Damián de Mazanet y fray Isidro Félix de Espinosa.

[3]Gaspar Castaño de Sosa junto con Luis de Carvajal y de la Cueva fue uno de los primeros exploradores y colonizadores del Nuevo Reino de León, escribió *Memorias del descubrimiento que Gaspar Castaño de sosa hizo en el Nuevo México . . . 27 de julio de 1590*. Colección de documentos inéditos, relativos al descubrimiento de las antiguas posesiones españolas . . . Imprenta de J. M. Pérez: Madrid, 1871, t. XV, p. 191.

[4]Por ejemplo, las misiones de San Antonio de Valero y San José y San Miguel de Aguayo, se fundaron en tres ocasiones y cada vez en un sitio diferente. La misión de Nuestra Señora de la Purísima Concepción fue también, fundada, temporalmente abandonada y refundada en diferentes ocasiones. Cf. Habig, Marion Alphonse. The Alamo Chain of Missions. A History of San Antonio's Five Old Missions. Franciscan Herald Press, Publishers of Franciscan Literature, 1997.

[5]Fray Isidro Félix de Espinosa, franciscano, ingresó al Colegio de la Santa Cruz de Querétaro en 1696, del que fue nombrado Guardián y Cronista. Inició su actividad misionera en Texas, escribió, entre otras muchas obras su *Chronica apostólica y seraphica de todos los colegios de Propaganda Fide de esta Nueva España, de missioneros franciscanos observantes: erigidos con autoridad pontificia, y regia, para la reformación de los fieles y conversión de los gentiles. Consagrada a la milagrosa Cruz de piedra, que como titular se venera en su primer Colegio de Propaganda Fide de la muy ilustre ciudad de Santiago de Querétaro, sita en el arzobispado de México. Escrita por . . . , predicador, y missionero apostólico, hijo y ex-guardián de dicho Colegio, qualificador, y revisor del Santo Officio, chronista de la Santa Provincia de S. Pedro, y S. Pablo de Michoacán, y de todos los Colegios de missioneros apostólicos*

observantes de esta Nueva-España. Parte primera. Con licencia en México por la Viuda de D. Joseph Bernardo de Hogal, Impressora del Real, y Apostólico Tribunal de la Santa Cruzada en todo este Reyno, año de 1746, [100], 590, [24] p. Reimpresa bajo el título de *Crónica de los Colegios de Propaganda Fide de la Nueva España.* 2a. ed., nueva edición con notas e introd. de Lino Gómez Canedo, O. F. M. Washington, D. C.: Academy of American Franciscan History, 1964. 972 p., il., maps.

[6]El Capitan Domingo Ramón comandó una expedición cuya finalidad era restablecer la prescencia española en el este de Texas, la expedición contaba con un total de setenta y cinco personas entre las que se encontraban doce frailes franciscanos procedentes de los Colegios apostólicos de la santa Cruz de Querétaro y el de Nuestra señora de Guadalupe Zacatecas. La expedición, que tenía como finalidad establecer una serie de presidios y misiones, partió del río Grande o Bravo en abril 27, 1716. En Julio 5 la expedición estableció la misión de Nuestro Padre San Francisco de los Tejas, posteriormente se fundaron tres misiones adicionales Nuestra Señora de la Purísima Concepción, Nuestra Señora de Guadalupe y San José. (Habig 195-199).

[7]Estos son los nombres que le da Fray Isidro Félix de Espinosa en su *Crónica Apostólica y Seráfica* . . .

[8]Ambos colegios, el de Querétaro y el de Zacatecas funcionaron como punta de lanza para la evangelización de los territorios del septentrión de la Nueva España.

[9]Fray Antonio Margil de Jesús, llamado el apóstol de la Nueva España, fue misionero en Texas cerca de seis años, 1716-1722, en donde fundó la misión de San José y otras cuatro misiones. Fue nombrado presidente del grupo de franciscanos procedentes del Colegio de Propaganda Fide de nuestra Señora de Guadalupe de Zacatecas, del que también fungió como Guardián. Participó también en diferentes misiones de Centroamérica. Dentro de la orden francis-cana es considerado como santo, el Papa Gregorio XVI lo nombro venerable en 1836.

[10]La práctica privada de la penitencia exige una comunicación personal entre el penitente y el sacerdote, con lo cual la presencia de un intérprete resulta ina-ceptable. Desde el siglo VII en Europa continental se realiza la práctica "pri-vada" de la Penitencia: "El sacramento se realiza desde entonces de una man-era más secreta entre el penitente y el sacerdote [. . .] A grandes líneas, esta es la forma de penitencia que la Iglesia practica hasta nuestros días." *Catecis-mo de la Iglesia* . . . 1447-1456, http://www.vatican.va/archive/catechism_sp/p3s1c1a8_sp.html.

[11]Este último es el único texto que ha llegado a la imprenta del grupo, aparte de la Biblioteca Cervantina del Tecnológico de Monterrey encontramos ejem-plares del mismo en la John Carter Brown Library, en la Nettie Lee Benson

Latin American Collection, entre otras. Existen también ediciones digitales del mismo, se recomienda: http://pueblosoriginarios.com/textos/coahuilteco/coahuilteco.html

[12]Eugenio del Hoyo fue director de la Biblioteca Historiador. Catedrático del Instituto Tecnológico de Monterrey. Autor de: Jerez, el de López Velarde (1949); Descripción del Nuevo Reino de León (173S-174), 1962; Índice del ramo de causas criminales del Archivo Municipal de Monterrey (1963); Vocablos de la lengua quinigua de los indios horrados del Noreste de México (1960); Cuadernillo de la lengua de los indios pajalates (1965); Encomienda y esclavitud de indios en el Nuevo Reino de León (1965). Preparó una Historia del Nuevo Reino de León y El diario de bolsillo de fray Agustín de Morfi.

[13]"The date and authorship of the pajalate (Coahuilteco) 'Cuadernillo'." International Journal of American Linguistics, vol. 44, no. 4, 1978, pp. 329-330.

[14]Alonso Fernández de Madrigal, llamado el abulense, fue Gran Canciller de Castilla, y Arzobispo de Ávila.

[15]Debido a que la impartición de ambos sacramentos corresponde a los obispos. La confirmación junto con el Bautismo y la Eucaristía constituye el conjunto de los sacramentos de la iniciación cristiana. En el rito latino implica una unción en la frente de cada uno de los confirmados. Esta unción es signo de una consagración y es realizada siempre por el obispo. De la misma manera la impartición del sacramento del Orden, mediante el cual se ordena a sacerdotes y diáconos, corresponde a los obispos. Se trata de dos sacramentos que no se contemplaba que fueran impartidos por los frailes de misiones como las del Río San Antonio que se encontraban tan alejadas del centro de sus diócesis. *Catecismo de la Iglesia Católica,* 1285-1301 y 1536-1568, http://www.vatican.va/archive/catechism_sp/p3s1c1a8_sp.html.

La voz de las respuestas silentes: análisis etnohistórico de un texto religioso en lengua coahuilteca

PALOMA VARGAS MONTES

Tecnológico de Monterrey

En el siglo 18 se establecieron en los bordes del Río de San Antonio cinco misiones franciscanas que tenían como objetivo la reducción y evangelización de los grupos indígenas de la región. La dificultad para reconstruir la historia y la identidad particular de estas naciones presenta hoy en día grandes retos para el investigador. En el presente trabajo se mostrará cómo el estudio de un grupo de textos religiosos elaborados en las misiones texanas aporta conocimiento acerca de la etnohistoria de las naciones indígenas cuyo territorio de movilidad se encontraba en el sur de Texas y noreste de México.

Antecedentes

El *Manual para la administración de los sacramentos de penitencia, eucaristía, extremaunción, matrimonio, gracias después de comulgar y ayudar a bien morir* . . . está dirigido a los confesores de los indios reducidos a las Misiones del Río de San Antonio y Río Grande, las cuales pertenecían al Colegio de la Santísima Cruz de la Ciudad de Querétaro. El *Manual* dice haber sido compuesto por Bartolomé García, predicador apostólico y misionero franciscano de dicho Colegio. Fue impreso en 1760. Existen otros ejemplares de este libro en los acervos de bibliotecas de fondos antiguos, en la Nettie Lee Benson y en la John Carter Brown, por dar un ejemplo. Sin embargo, solo en la Biblioteca Cervantina del Tecnológico de Monterrey se localizan también dos documentos manuscritos asociados a este *Manual* impreso. Es posible que estos manuscritos sean borradores, o primeras versiones en las que se recogieron notas sobre la lengua coahuilteca y que luego le sirvieron a García para componer la obra que finalmente llegaría a la imprenta en la segunda mitad del siglo 18. Los textos asociados al *Manual* son: *Confesionario de indios en coahuilteco y español*, manuscrito, sin autor y sin fecha, atribuido a Bartolomé García, posiblemente elaborado en la primera mitad del siglo XVIII y el *Cuadernillo de la lengua de los indios pajalates, en pajalate y español*, manuscrito, 1732, atribuido a fray Gabriel de Vergara.

En el presente trabajo se tiene como objeto de estudio al *Manual para la administración de los sacramentos*. El análisis se divide en dos partes. La primera se centra en las denominaciones étnicas que enuncia el *Manual* como hablantes de la lengua coahuilteca, a partir del cotejo de la portada del libro con la información contenida en la base de datos de investigación de archivo sobre la evangelización del noreste publicada por Cecilia Sheridan en 2015. La segunda parte del trabajo consiste en un análisis comparativo del confesionario en coahuilteco contenido en el *Manual*, a partir del cotejo con otros textos religiosos de la misma naturaleza, elaborados a lo largo del período colonial novohispano. El objetivo es identificar particularidades y elementos comunes. En su conjunto, a partir de los resultados de estas dos clases de análisis, el trabajo proporciona información de carácter etnohistórico sobre los grupos indígenas hablantes del coahuilteco, como: lugares, años y causas con que se documenta su presencia, creencias y hábitos sociales.

La razón por la que fueron creados los textos religiosos antes mencionados era para servir de herramienta a los misioneros en la evangelización del noreste novohispano. Los primeros asentamientos españoles en el noreste de México comenzaron alrededor de 1590. Fue hasta 1718 cuando los europeos llegaron a San Antonio: 128 años después (Campbell 82). Hacia la mitad del siglo 18 el territorio se veía afectado por la masiva colonización española al norte de Tamaulipas y el movimiento de grupos Apaches de la Meseta de Edwards hacia la planicie costera del sur de Texas (Campbell 89). Los grupos autóctonos se desintegraron a causa de estos dos frentes de invasión. Esto produjo la llegada de indígenas a las misiones que se fundaron en las cercanías del Río de San Antonio. "The story of the San Antonio missions is, from an Indian point of view, the story of refugee groups who abandoned their former hunting-and-gathering way of life and were transformed into settled mission Indians who raised European livestock and practiced the Spanish style of irrigation agriculture" (Campbell 79).

De acuerdo con Campbell el número preciso de grupos indígenas representados en las misiones de San Antonio no se puede conocer con exactitud, sin embargo, con la información disponible, se calcula que la población de indígenas en cada misión oscilaba entre los 300 y 400 individuos, de denominaciones variadas (Campbell 82-83). El número de indígenas reducidos a misión oscilaba según las épocas: las epidemias, el estilo de vida de la misión, las costumbres de recolección de los indígenas, entre otros, afectaban a que los indios dejaran la misión en ciertos momentos y luego volvieran buscando la protección de los misioneros, al ser acosados por las invasiones apaches y españolas.

Si bien tradicionalmente se ha considerado como escasa la información existente sobre los grupos indígenas de la región, la aproximación de los estudios etnohistóricos ha arrojado nuevas posibilidades para interpretar documentos diversos y obtener de ellos datos que fundamenten valiosas hipótesis sobre la vida y costumbres de los grupos autóctonos. Es de esta manera que el estudio de crónicas y libros coloniales, textos religiosos y documentos de archivo permiten reconstruir aspectos de la vida cotidiana de los indígenas que habitaban la región y su interacción con los españoles[2].

Las denominaciones e identidades étnicas de los grupos indígenas que habitaron el sur de Texas y noreste de México es uno de los grandes problemas a los que se enfrenta el etnohistoriador de la región. En especial, la lengua coahuilteca y el grupo coahuilteco ha sido tema de discusión entre los expertos. En el siglo XIX Orozco y Berra (61-68, 309) y Pimentel (407-413) denominaron como coahuiltecos a ciertos grupos indígenas porque se creía que hablaban dialectos de un lenguaje que se había usado en Coahuila y Texas (Campbell 39).

Desde el siglo 19 el *Manual* que aquí estudiamos ha sido la fuente principal para el estudio lingüístico del coahuilteco. Sin duda esta obra ha tenido una influencia en los lingüistas y antropólogos para entender el coahuilteco no solo como una lengua sino como una cultura, pues relaciona un idioma con los nombres de 18 naciones indígenas. Sin embargo, es importante considerar que, si bien no hay duda de la existencia de una lengua común a los grupos de la región, la cual ha sido denominada coahuilteca, no podemos asegurar que todos los grupos se reconocieran a sí mismos como miembros de una sola cultura: la coahuilteca. De hecho, es muy posible que muchos grupos hayan adquirido el coahuilteco como una segunda lengua, al llegar a las misiones de San Antonio, pues como señala fray Bartolomé García, si bien no todos los indígenas de las misiones de San Antonio tenían como lengua materna el idioma en que está escrito el *Manual*, "la gente nueva a breve tiempo la entiende o habla y los muchachos, que son la porción de nuestra mayor esperanza, al año ya como dice, cortan el pelo con el dicho idioma" (García 3v).

Recopilación de datos sobre las denominaciones étnicas

Con el objetivo de responder a la pregunta: ¿quiénes eran los hablantes del coahuilteco? este trabajo propone una aproximación etnohistórica que combina

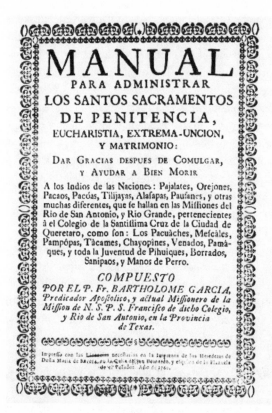

Figura 1. *Manual para la administración de los sacramentos de penitencia, eucaristía, extremaunción, matrimonio, gracias después de comulgar y ayudar a bien morir, Bartolomé García, 1760. Biblioteca Cervantina, Tecnológico de Monterrey.*

el estudio de un texto religioso, el *Manual para administrar los santos sacramentos* . . . de Bartolomé García, con la revisión de un amplio corpus de documentos de archivo y crónicas, publicado en *Fronterización del espacio hacia el norte de la Nueva España* (Sheridan 2015). El punto de intersección son los nombres de los grupos indígenas. En la portada del *Manual* se menciona una lista de los grupos hablantes de la lengua en la que está escrita la obra. Tomamos como base los nombres de estas naciones y buscamos sus recurrencias en el corpus de Sheridan. Dicho corpus de denominaciones está conformado por documentos etnohistóricos localizados en el Archivo Histórico de la Provincia Franciscana de Michoacán, el Archivo Franciscano del Fondo Reservado-UNAM, el Archivo Franciscano de Celaya, Colegio de la Santa Cruz, el Archivo General del Estado de Nuevo León, el Archivo Franciscano del Fondo Reservado-

UNAM, Archivo General de Indias y el Archivo General de la Nación, entre otros. El objetivo de esta aproximación es conocer la frecuencia de menciones de cada grupo, en qué regiones es documentada su presencia y los contextos de acciones en los que aparecen ligados, por ejemplo reducidos a misión, alzamiento o alianza interétnica, por mencionar solo algunos[3]. A continuación los resultados:

1. Pajalates. Mencionados 8[4] veces entre 1730 y 1766 con causas "reducido a misión" e "intento de reducción" en Misiones de Texas, Misiones de Coahuila, San Antonio de Valero Texas y Nuestra Señora de la Purísima Concepción Texas (Sheridan 273, 303).
2. Orejones. Mencionados 10 veces entre 1731 y 1762 con causas "reducido a misión", "mención en crónicas" y "localización de ranchería o campamento indio" en Misiones de Texas, San Juan Capistrano Texas (Sheridan 271, 302).
3. Pacaos. Mencionados 4 veces entre 1730 y 1762 con causa "reducidos a misión" e "intento de reducción" en San Antonio de Valero Texas, San Francisco de los Tejas o de La Espada y Misiones de Texas (Sheridan 271).
4. Pacoas. Mencionados 26 veces entre 1708 y 1804 con causa "reducidos a misión", "localización de ranchería o campamento indio", "revuelta, alzamiento o sublevación" en Dulce Nombre de Jesús-Peyotes, Río Grande, Misiones de Río Grande, San Bernardo (Río Grande), San Juan Bautista (Río Grande), El Carrizo (Coahuila), (Sheridan 271, 272).
5. Tilijayas. 16 menciones entre 1673 y 1804 con causas "reducidos a misión", "localización de ranchería o campamento indio", "mención en crónica", "mención de naciones", "indios piden misión", "visita eclesiástica" en San Juan Bautista (Río Grande), Río Nueces, Señor San Joaquín del Monte (Tamaulipas), San Bernardino de la Candela (Coahuila), Misiones de Coahuila, Misiones de Río Grande (Sheridan 286, 287).
6. Alasapas. 56 menciones entre 1605 y 1779 con causas "mención en crónica", "registro parroquial", "propiedad española", "localización de ranchería o campamento indio", "testigos en juicios civiles y criminales", "instrucciones de trato a indios / abusos", "indios piden misión", "homicidios de indios", "revuelta, alzamiento o sublevación", "alianza interétnica", "nación extinta que habitaba en las cercanías de . . . ", "cautivo o presas tomadas por españoles", "guerra", "mención de naciones", "recuento de males / hostilidades" en Texas, San Antonio Galindo de Moctezuma (Coahuila), Río Sabinas (Texas), Misiones de Coahuila, Sierra de Tamaulipa y paraje El Pilón (Nuevo León), Río de la Pesquería

Chica (Nuevo León), Valle de las Salinas (Nuevo León), Haciendas en la jurisdicción de Monterrey (Nuevo León), Río Grande (Coahuila), Señor San Joaquín del Monte (Tamaulipas), Valle del Pilón (Nuevo León). Aliados: Aguatas, Vaxares, Borrados (Sheridan 234, 235).

7. Pausanes. 13 menciones entre 1700 y 1804 con causas "reducido a misión", "indios gobernadores", "localización de ranchería o campamento indio", "solicitud de asiento, tierras o aguas" en Río Grande (Coahuila), San Juan Bautista (Río Grande), San Buenaventura (Coahuila), Río San Antonio (Texas), Misiones de Río Grande (Coahuila), Misiones de Coahuila, San Francisco Solano (Río Grande). Aliados: Tattepliegigo (Sheridan 276, 277).

8. Pacuaches. 9 menciones entre 1688 y 1804 con causa "reducido a misión", "mención en crónica" en San Francisco Solano (Río Grande, Coahuila), San Antonio de Valero Texas, San Bernardo (Río Grande, Coahuila), Misiones de Río Grande (Coahuila), Texas (Sheridan 272).

9. Mescales. 66 menciones entre 1670 y 1807 con causa "reducido a misión", "expedición / campaña española punitiva o de persecución", "indios piden misión", "cautivos o presas tomadas por españoles", "juicios a indios por adulterio, robo u homicidio", "intento de reducción", "ataque indio", "guerra interétnica", "acuerdo de paz", "mención en crónica", "alianza interétnica", "refugio indio", "recuento de males / hostilidades", "revuelta, alzamiento o sublevación", "guerra", "se niegan a tratado de paz", "informes sobre indios", "agregados a los españoles o reducidos en asentamientos", "localización de ranchería o campamento indio", "mención de naciones", "visita eclesiástica", "indios piden misión" en San Juan Bautista (Río Grande, Coahuila), San Antonio de Valero Texas, Misiones de Río Grande (Coahuila), Texas, Valle de Santa Rosa (Coahuila), Nueva Vizcaya, Sierra Rica (Nueva Vizcaya), San Antonio de Béjar (Texas), Nuestra Señora de la Purísima Concepción Texas, Bolsón de Mapimí (Nueva Vizcaya), Río Grande o San Juan Bautista (Coahuila), Río Sabinas (Coahuila), Presidio del Norte (Nueva Vizcaya), El Carrizo (Coahuila), Río Grande (Coahuila), Misiones de Coahuila, Señor San Joaquín del Monte (Tamaulipas). Filiación Salineros, Apaches. Rivales: Lipanes. Aliados: Faraones / llaneros / mimbreños / gileños; Ijiaba / Jumanes (Sheridan 266-268).

10. Pampopas. 61 menciones entre 1738 y 1804 con causa "reducidos a misión", "localización de ranchería o campamento indio", "mención en crónica", "aliados con españoles" en San Juan Bautista (Río Grande), San José de los Nazonis (Texas), San Miguel de Aguayo de los Adaes (Texas), Misiones de Río Grande, Misiones de Coahuila, Río Nueces

(Texas), San Antonio de Béjar, Texas, San Joaquín del Monte (Tamaulipas). Rivales: Apaches (Sheridan 274-275).

11. Tacames. 3 menciones entre 1745 y 1762 con causa "reducido a misión" y "mención en crónica" en Nuestra Señora de la Purísima Concepción (Texas) y Señor San Joaquín del Monte (Tamaulipas), (Sheridan 284, 306).

12. Chayopines. 2 menciones en 1745 con causa "reducido a misión" en Misiones de Texas (Sheridan 247, 298).

13. Venados. 3 menciones entre 1732 y 1752 con causa "informes sobre indios", "localización de ranchería o campamento indio", "mención en crónica" en Señor San Joaquín del Monte (Tamaulipas) (Sheridan 289, 290).

14. Pamaques. 17 menciones entre 1731 y 1762 con causa "reducidos a misión", "localización de ranchería o campamento indio", "intento de reducción", "mención en crónica", "nación extinta que habitaba en las cercanías de . . . " en San Juan Capistrano (Texas), San Francisco de Vizarrón (Coahuila), San Bernardo (Río Grande, Coahuila), Misiones de Texas, Señor San Joaquín del Monte (Tamaulipas), Río Nueces (Texas), Río San Antonio (Texas), (Sheridan 273, 303).

15. Pihuiques. 12 menciones entre 1745 y 1766 con causa "reducido a misión", "intento de reducción", "nación extinta que habitaba en las cercanías de . . . ", "localización de ranchería o campamento indio" en Misiones de Coahuila, San Juan Capistrano (Texas), Misiones de Texas, Río San Antonio (Texas), Costa de Texas, (Sheridan 278, 305).

16. Borrados. 105 menciones entre 1597 y 1772 con causa "reducido a misión", "propiedad española", "cautivos o presas tomadas por españoles", "mención de naciones", "indios huidos" (fugitivos), "testigos en jucios civiles y criminales", "juicios a indios por adulterio, robo u homicidio", "dotación de agua y/tierras", "expedición / campaña española punitiva o de persecución", "localización de ranchería o campamento indio", "intento de reducción", "alianza interétnica", "muerte por epidemia", "nación extinta que habitaba en la cercanías de . . . ", "acuerdo de paz", "ataque indio" en San Juan Bautista (Río Grande), Nuestra Señora de la Purísima Concepción Texas, San Francisco de los Tejas o de La Espada, San Xavier de Nájera, Misiones de Texas, Purísima Concepción del Valle del Maíz (San Luis Potosí), La Concepción, Río de los Comalucos (Nuevo León), Sierra de Tamaulipa y paraje El Pilón (Nuevo León), Río de la Pesquería Chica (Nuevo León), Valle de las Salinas (Nuevo León), Haciendas en la jurisdicción de Monterrey (Nuevo León), Cerro de Tamaolipa (Nuevo León), Misiones de Coahui-

la, Valle del Pilón (Nuevo León), Misiones de Río Grande (Coahuila), Nuevo Reino de León, Río San Antonio (Texas), San Pablo de Labradores (Nuevo León), San Antonio de los Llanos (Nuevo León), Valle del Guajuco (Nuevo León), Valle de Santa Catarina (Nuevo León). Aliados pelones / pamoranes, alasapas, (Sheridan 241, 242, 297, 313).

17. Sanipaos. 2 menciones de 1762, con causa "reducido a misión" en Nuestra Señora de la Purísima Concepción (Texas), (Sheridan 282, 306).

18. Manos de perro. 8 menciones entre 1745 y 1766 con causa "reducido a misión", "intento de reducción" en Misiones de Coahuila, Nuestra Señora de la Purísima Concepción Texas, Misiones de Texas, San Juan Capistrano (Texas), Río San Antonio (Texas), (Sheridan 264, 300).

Una primera interpretación de los datos arriba mencionados arroja las siguientes conclusiones preliminares. No hay ninguna denominación étnica mencionada por el *Manual* que no haya aparecido al menos una vez en el corpus de documentos etnohistóricos. Sin embargo, sí resaltan a la vista grandes diferencias en cuanto al número y diversidad de contextos en los que se les menciona. Los grupos que aparecen en mayor medida son los Alasapas, Mescales, Pampopas y Borrados, mientras que los menos mencionados son los Tacames, Chayopines y Sanipaos. La nación más activa son los Borrados, se documenta su presencia durante casi toda la época colonial, desde 1597 hasta 1772, y la diversidad de la naturaleza de los documentos en que aparecen nos muestran la complejidad del proceso cultural al que estuvieron sujetos: desde documentos que señalan dotación de aguas o tierras hasta reporte de ataques a los españoles. Por otra parte, no todos los grupos más mencionados aparecen en contextos beligerantes, los Pampopas por ejemplo son mencionados en causas que reflejan contextos más pacíficos como reducidos a misión y como aliados de los españoles, por ejemplo.

El corpus etnohistórico de Sheridan recoge las denominaciones o nombres con que los grupos indígenas fueron registrados en documentos oficiales y crónicas, a lo largo de un período que abarca desde el siglo XVI hasta el XIX, en la región hoy conformada por el noreste de México y sur de Texas. Se trata de una herramienta de trabajo que nos permite aproximarnos al rastreo de los patrones de movimiento de las naciones indígenas, influenciados tanto por la conquista europea, como por los rasgos culturales autóctonos de nomadismo y recolección.

Los datos arriba mencionados deben ser utilizados para crear mapas de movilidad que permitan visualizar la presencia geográfica de las naciones indígenas. En el estudio de la etnohistoria mesoamericana la dimensión del espacio

Mapa de movilidad hablantes de Coahuilteco

Figura 2. Mapa de movilidad de hablantes del coahuilteco.

en su relación con el grupo étnico está anclada a centros urbanos o ceremoniales alrededor de los cuales la cultura se desarrollaba. En Aridoamérica, en cambio, el etnohistoriador debe de partir de la premisa esencial de la movilidad como un rasgo cultural, no solo resultado de las prácticas de recolección para la subsistencia, sino como un aspecto cultural que sin duda determinaba la cosmovisión de los grupos indígenas de la región.

En el corpus se registran más de 4 mil entradas de nombres de naciones indígenas. En los datos arriba mencionados se indica el número de veces que cada grupo hablante de lengua coahuilteca apareció en dicho corpus. La recurrencia de la denominación étnica es importante para aproximarse a la continuidad del grupo en la dimensión de tiempo y espacio. Los Borrados, por ejemplo, son los más mencionados de las 18 naciones de habla coahuilteca. Esto implica que su denominación étnica fue la más recogida en el corpus de documentos y su existencia se detecta durante casi todo el período colonial. Es decir, hay una alta probabilidad de que mantuvieran una identidad étnica sólida en el tiempo y en el espacio y que no hayan sido absorbidos por otro grupo o extinguidos. En cambio, los Chayopines solo son mencionados 2 veces en ese corpus de más 4 mil entradas y su presencia se registra solo en 1745 en las misiones texanas. Estas características nos inducen a conjeturar que la identidad étnica de este grupo no trascendió en el tiempo y que pudieron haber sido absorbidos por otro grupo o extinguidos.

Con respecto a la variedad de lugares en que se documenta la presencia de los grupos, es de notar que en las misiones del Río San Antonio, en la segunda mitad del siglo XVIII, habitaban naciones diversas. Algunas de ellas concentraban sus movimientos migratorios en zonas cercanas, pero a otros los encontramos mucho más lejos, hacia el Bolsón de Mapimí. Los grupos indígenas cuya existencia solo se registra en Texas son los Orejones, Pacaos, Chayopines y Sanipaos. Los que migraban entre Coahuila y Texas eran los Pajalates, Pacoas, Pausanes, Pacuaches, Pihuiques y Manos de perro. Los grupos cuya movilización alcanzaba hasta Tamaulipas eran los Tilijayas, los Tacames, Pamaques, Venados y Pampopas. Los Borrados y los Alasapas se movían por toda la región, se documenta su presencia en Nuevo León, Tamaulipas, Coahuila y Texas, mientras que los Mescales, de filiación Apache, además de la región noreste, habitaron en la Nueva Vizcaya, hoy en día los estados de Durango y Chihuahua.

Es relevante señalar que en el corpus de Sheridan no se encuentra recogida la denominación coahuilteca. Encontramos, en cambio, las formas coahuilas en 1605, coahuileños en 1722 y 1725 y coahuiles en 1676 (248-249). Las tres acepciones reúnen 7 menciones en el corpus de más de 4 mil entradas, una cantidad similar a la que vemos con el grupo Manos de perro mencionado en la portada del *Manual para la administración de los sacramentos*. Esta evidencia del corpus se alinea con el hecho de que el término coahuilteco fue utilizado por los lingüistas del siglo XIX para dar nombre a la lengua, utilizada en Coahuila y Texas principalmente, en que está escrito el *Manual para la administración de los sacramentos*, fuente primaria principal para el estudio histórico de este idioma.

Sin embargo, es muy importante subrayar y no perder de vista que a pesar de las diferencias entre los grupos y las formas en que aparece documentada su vida en los documentos etnohistóricos, el *Manual para la administración de los sacramentos* los identifica a todos como hablantes de una misma lengua. No es posible determinar cuáles eran los grupos indígenas para quienes era idioma materno o bien, adquirido. Sin embargo, el compartir la lengua implica el compartir una cultura. Es por ello que desde el siglo XIX se ha acuñado y desarrollado la noción de la lengua coahuilteca enlazada con un grupo cultural y una denominación étnica.

Ahora bien, tras haber profundizado en la información disponible sobre los grupos indígenas mencionados en la portada del *Manual para la administración de los sacramentos*, es momento de abordar el análisis de las funciones y características del texto religioso, objeto de estudio de este trabajo. No debemos de perder de vista que el *Manual* está dirigido a los misioneros que llevan a cabo la evangelización. No se considera a los indígenas como lectores, pero sí como interlocutores potenciales de las preguntas registradas por escrito en una dimensión oral, en el sacramento de la confesión.

El texto religioso: de la evangelización a la etnografía

Los confesionarios bilingües son textos religiosos que fueron compuestos en español y lenguas indígenas en el México colonial. Ligados estrechamente con la evangelización de la Nueva España, son textos hechos con una finalidad muy específica: ayudar a los misioneros a administrar correctamente el sacramento de la reconciliación. Su función consistía en contener en los dos idiomas, el español para el sacerdote y la lengua indígena para el penitente, las preguntas necesarias para realizar una adecuada exploración de los pecados cometidos. Es por eso que en su gran mayoría están escritos a doble columna, izquierda para el español y derecha para la lengua indígena, o viceversa. Otra característica es que los bloques de preguntas están divididos por mandamientos. Es decir, cada mandamiento está asociado a una batería de preguntas, cuya respuesta indaga sobre los pecados con los cuales se violó dicho mandamiento. Es importante considerar que una correcta administración del sacramento implica la exploración, indagación de parte del sacerdote. No se trata de que el penitente llega a la confesión con la claridad total de los pecados que va a enunciar. Es labor del sacerdote hacer una limpieza a profundidad, ayudar a la reflexión a través de las preguntas, asegurarse de que el penitente ha dicho cada pecado asociado a cada mandamiento. La confesión es un sacramento de gran importancia, pues es a través de él que, según la doctrina cristiana, el hombre se arrepiente de sus pecados y obtiene el perdón de Dios.

Por otra parte, la confesión fue un acto de mediación lingüística y cultural, entre los indígenas y los misioneros durante la evangelización. En los confesionarios coloniales encontramos testimonio del proceso de traducción a un nivel literal, pero también podemos hallar evidencias del fenómeno de aculturación religiosa a través de las preguntas registradas. Si bien, todos los confesionarios comparten preguntas, temas y estructuras muy similares, no son idénticos. En sus diferencias y similitudes encontramos información vinculada a aspectos etnohistóricos de los grupos indígenas. En el afán de adentrarse en el pensamiento indígena para localizar los pecados, los misioneros registran en los confesionarios elementos que denotan la tensión religiosa y cultural entre los indígenas y los frailes, y echan luz sobre la cosmovisión de los nativos.

Para detectar los aspectos etnohistóricos de los grupos indígenas pertenecientes a la denominación coahuilteca se hizo un análisis comparativo de las preguntas contenidas en los siguientes textos: *Manual para la administración de los sacramentos* de Bartolomé García, *Confesionario mayor en la lengua mexicana y castellana* compuesto por el franciscano Alonso de Molina, en 1578, *Confesionario en Lengua Mixe*, de Agustín de Quintana, Orden de los Predicadores, Puebla, 1733 y *Arte de la lengua Névome* que se dice Pima, propia de

Sonora, con la doctrina cristiana y confesionario añadidos, San Agustín de la florida, 1862. Con esta selección de confesionarios tenemos una muestra representativa de cuatro regiones de la Nueva España: el centro con el confesionario de Alonso de Molina para el pueblo nahua, el sur con la lengua mixe de Oaxaca, el noroeste con la lengua pima en Sonora y el noreste con la lengua coahuilteca. Además, las fechas de composición de las cuatro obras son diversas y se distribuyen desde los inicios hasta la caída del virreinato.

Este análisis es interesante tanto porque si los frailes preguntaban por cosas que habían visto en otros grupos indígenas mesoamericanos y se los atribuían a los indígenas del norte, o bien, si las preguntas responden a una realidad de la conducta de los indígenas en la misión. Si es lo primero, esto implica que las preguntas del confesionario imprimían en la consciencia de los nativos un universo de lo prohibido, importado de otros grupos indígenas. Lo cual también resulta en un proceso de aculturación, o de culturas en contacto. Si es lo segundo, las preguntas nos indican hábitos culturales autóctonos de los indígenas de la región.

Las preguntas del primer mandamiento "Amarás a Dios sobre todas las cosas" se relacionan con la indagación de las creencias prehispánicas de los grupos indígenas. Es interesante notar que los cuatro confesionarios preguntan sobre los sueños, concretamente si el penitente cree que los sueños tienen un significado específico y son el agüero de algo. Preguntas como: ¿Has creído lo que sueñas? (¿Japasc'átzáujt'am tuchêm mamayáspámo jam é?) en coahuilteco (García 8), ¿crees los sueños? (Molina 22v) en náhuatl, ¿por ventura crees lo que sueñas? en pima (10) y ¿has creído en sueños? (210) en mixe aparecen en todos los textos como evidencia de la importancia que daban los misioneros a ese aspecto de la cosmovisión indígena.

Ahora bien, al continuar en la exploración de pecados relacionados con la idolatría, encontramos particularidades para cada confesionario. En el caso de los nahuas, Molina pregunta: "[. . .] o por ventura tuviste por agüeros a la lechuza, al búho, a la comadreja, al escarabajo pinauiztli y tlalacatl, al epatl que se meó en tu casa o a los vilos de las telarañas cuando algunas veces pasando por tus ojos o cuando te tiemblan los párpados de los ojos, cuando tienes hipo o estornudas? Tuviste también por agüero al fuego, cuando hace gran ruido la llama o la leña o sacaste fuego nuevo cuando entraste tu casa" (22v). Además de esto se pregunta sobre prácticas adivinatorias utilizando agua y cordeles (22r).

En el caso de los mixe de Oaxaca, el confesionario contiene cerca de 44 preguntas que indagan sobre la realización de sacrificios y prácticas idolátricas. Además, las preguntas son seguidas de la explicación detallada de cómo documentar y presentar denuncias sobre idolatrías. Incluso incluye una carta ejemplo. "Adviértase que cuando el penitente dice que sabe que otra persona es idó-latra, hechicera, bruja, etcétera, no se ha de absolver hasta que denuncie Extra Sacramentum" (214). En este texto aparecen referencias a la creencia en el Rayo y el Viento como deidades o fuerzas sobrenaturales con preguntas como: "¿Has creído que el Rayo o el Viento hacen dar el maíz o la grana u otras cosas?" (210), "¿Has hecho tortillas de Rayo y se las has ofrecido al Rayo?" Además, preguntas sobre prácticas como: "¿Has creído que cuando la gente muere enton-ces va a trabajar al otro mundo como dicen los idólatras?" (212), "¿Has hecho sacrificio por enfermedad o por la milpa?" (208), "¿Has tenido por agüero cuan-do grita algún animal?" (210), "¿Has matado gallos y derramado su sangre en tu casa o en tu milpa o en otra cualquier parte al modo de los antiguos?" (209).

En el confesionario en lengua pima encontramos en el octavo mandamiento alrededor de 15 preguntas para indagar sobre la práctica de hechicería, pero ade-más una larga amonestación (única de esta longitud en todo el confesionario) en la que se advierte sobre lo malo que es la práctica de la hechicería por ser de inspiración demoniaca. "Notense primero que el nombre general de hechicero es simacaigama, (los Tecoras dicen macaga) del verbo simacaiga hechizar, genérico, vel soplar, vel chupar, vel curar. El verbo en particular es enhechizar es hiboina, hacer el hechizo, echando o dando algo en la comida o ropa" (27). Describe a los hechiceros chupadores, que chupan la herida y sacan de ella obje-tos como palos y piedras. Los sopladores que se llamaban bustana y los curado-res, verbo doadida.

En el confesionario coahuilteco también aparecen varias preguntas relacio-nadas con prácticas hechiceras, incluso se le pide al penitente que entregue los objetos con los cuales hechiza (García 8). Además encontramos la pregunta:

¿Cuándo canta el tecolote u otro pájaro o cuando llora algún animal crees algo? (García 7)	¿Taclajpô mac aguayám pil'in apajlê tucuajâm mac pinguacâi pil' t'an apaguâyo tucuajám, pil' chem mamayáspámo yam é?

La pregunta sobre la creencia de algo ante el canto o llanto de un animal es recu-rrente en los demás confesionarios, pero la mención al tecolote merece que nos detengamos un momento. Tecolote es una castellanización del náhuatl tecolotl, un tipo de búho, ave rapaz. Ni el confesionario pima, ni el mixe mencionan a este animal, pero el nahua del siglo XVI sí lo hace. Es posible que el confesio-nario coahuilteco siga la pauta de los confesionarios del centro del país y pre-gunte sobre una creencia de los nahuas a los coahuiltecos. Sin embargo, también existe la posibilidad de que tanto entre los nahuas como entre los coahuiltecos el búho fuera un animal con poderes sobrenaturales. Esta es una veta de inves-tigación en la que es pertinente profundizar.

El quinto mandamiento "No matarás" proporciona preguntas interesantes sobre prácticas que implican ciertos grados de violencia contra uno mismo y contra los otros. En el confesionario pima aparece el toloache, una planta utilizada por los chamanes con fines curativos y espirituales. "Habiendo querido morir comiste el toloache" (16), "¿Habiendo de matar a uno le diste toloache u otra cosa?" (16) "Llámese también gugurh aagama" (16), "¿Habiendo querido alguno matarse, y habiéndote pedido toloache u otra cosa, se lo diste, o se lo trujiste?" (17). Ningún otro confesionario menciona a esta sustancia. En cambio, en el confesionario mixe se pregunta sobre el consumo de tierra o carbón: "¿Frecuentemente has comido tierra? ¿Cada rato has comido carbón?" (233) Por su parte, en el quinto mandamiento el confesionario coahuilteco pregunta sobre el consumo carne humana, peyote y frijolillo, además de mencionar la participación en mitotes, bailes rituales comunitarios. Prácticas que aparecen documentadas como características de los indígenas del noreste en la crónica de Alonso de León del siglo XVII.

¿Has comido carne de gente? (García 15)	¿Pîlam ahêuh (vel aháuh) t'an mamâihám am é?
¿Has comido el peyote? (García 15)	¿Pajé chem mamâihám am é?
¿Te emborrachaste? (García 15)	¿Mamáiyâman am é?
¿Has comido frijolillo? (García 15)	¿Samîn chem mamâihám am é?
¿Has bailado mitote? (García 15)	¿Tjé mamáijâ yam ê?

Dado que las prácticas sexuales de un grupo humano están relacionadas con su cultura y cosmovisión, no es de extrañar que las preguntas relacionadas con el mandamiento sexto, "no fornicarás" sean abundantes. En el confesionario pima se denota la práctica de que los jóvenes vivan juntos o tengan relaciones sexuales antes del matrimonio "¿No has mandado que tu hija, queriendo que se case, se acueste con algun muchacho?" (20), "¿Queriendo que tu hijo se case, le mandaste acostar con una muchacha?" (20). Es también significativa la importancia que se le da a la homosexualidad masculina, pues las preguntas sobre sodomía solo están escritas en latín/pima y son precedidas por esta explicación: "Notense que este nombre shubima significa un hombre que vive y anda como una mujer, sirviéndole de mujer a otro hombre. Esto lo usaban siendo gentiles. Ahora parece que ya no. (A el tal mal hombre le llamaban shubima) Este verbo vbicoarhta significa exercere actionem succumbendo. Verdad es que los que lo usan aun se avergüenzan del nombre; pero es fuerza hacerles las preguntas, ut sequitur" (24).

En el caso de los mixe resulta diferente pues las preguntas más bien indican la práctica de matrimonios arreglados sin el consentimiento de los contrayentes "¿Has impedido a tus hijos casarse con las mujeres que querían y a tus hijas casarse con los hombres que deseaban y les hicistes fuerza a que se casaran con otras diversas personas que no querían?" (227). El sexto mandamiento de este confesionario se caracteriza por presentar casi 15 preguntas sobre masturbación con la particularidad de que es un pasaje que incluye respuestas del penitente, quien admite masturbarse hasta varias veces al día (238-240).

En el confesionario coahuilteco la anotación del padre García nos indica el choque entre el concepto de promiscuidad desde la visión católica y el ejercicio de una sexualidad no monógama autóctona. "Los más de los indios no saben explicar el número de las personas, ni las veces, cuando son muchas, ni con cuántas casadas, etcétera. Y aunque el modo dicho de preguntar para esta gente es el seguro, pero algunas veces parece será muy pesado preguntar: con otra, con otra, con otra, etcétera, cuando hay tanta multitud de personas con quienes han pecado, que no lo pueden explicar" (16). Es también muy interesante que en este confesionario no se hacen preguntas sobre homosexualidad masculina, pero sí de la femenina. "¿Has pecado con otra mujer haciendo como que fornicabais? (¿Tâgu pil't'an mamaiájpîu guáj chic am ê?) (García 23). Finalmente, una amonestación sobre la costumbre de vivir varias parejas en una sola vivienda denota el enfrentamiento de la relación casa/ pareja monógama del paradigma occidental con la posible práctica autóctona casa/parejas múltiples.

Yo no te confieso ahora porque todavía no te has quitado de los pecados. Yo te mando que salgas de esa casa y vivirás en otra casa y no volverás otra vez a la casa donde está esa mujer (ese hombre) y no le hablarás a solas y no la visitarás. Si no haces así te engañará el demonio y volverás a pecar (García 18)	Páyam acuén tzin nacamâlcûita guacô yajám mijtó pâyam cuém sajpám pinapsá (vel pin apsac'áuj) tuchém cánac cuém jasá yajám inô tzin nac tánco juâi pita cué cuém joujpacô snô, co juâi pil'aimá máitjám cam; mat pil'inyô cuém juâi ta, tágu pitapó (vel jagû pitapô) apasá tucuém, mayátzâlam ajám cam co jánmo cuêm miyajlé guacó yajâm cam, co mayácámam ajâm cam: pûhum miahôi ajám aguajtá, tamój ta micashîpt'ám cam, co sajpám pinapsá (vel pin apsac'áuj) maihói tzaj in cám

Finalmente, es de relevancia que este análisis comparativo mostró que el uso de las lunas como unidad de contabilidad del tiempo era un rasgo común a los coahuiltecos y a los pima. Noroeste y noreste unidos en este aspecto lingüístico y cultural que denota la relación entre las naciones. Dice el confesionario en pima "Algunos declaran los amancebamientos por lunas o por años", también usan ¿cuántas aguas? (30). En la introducción al sacramento de la penitencia del confesionario en coahuilteco nos encontramos con la siguiente pregunta:

¿Cuántas lunas han pasado, después que te confesaste? (García 2)	¿T'âjat (vel jat) ánua apchîca mip'âqenmam é, guamalejtá japamâlcûita tucuajât?

Posteriormente, en el quinto mandamiento la fórmula vuelve a aparecer:

¿Cuántas lunas han pasado que ya no le hablas? (García 15)	¿T'âjat (vel jat) ánua apchîca mi p'áqenmam é nâmo japajlê guacó yajâm tucuaját?

En el Corpus diacrónico del español (CORDE)[5] encontramos registrado el uso de la frase "¿cuántas lunas?" solo en un caso —en la obra *Los Barateros* de Mariano José de Larra, publicada en 1836—. Esta asusencia del uso de la fórmula en la tradición textual hispana nos lleva a conjeturar que "¿cuántas lunas?" no es de origen castellano, sino una frase traducida del coahuilteco. De hecho en el sexto mandamiento tenemos una pregunta con las dos fórmulas: ¿cuántos años? Y entre paréntesis ¿cuántas lunas? Lo que nos indica una anotación de traducción del concepto.

¿Cuántos años (cuántas lunas) ha que pecas con esa mujer? (con ese hombre) (García 17)	¿T'ájat (vel jat) âjacó apchîca [t'ájat (vel jat) ánua apchîca] tágu pitapóyó (vel jagû pitapôyô) sajpâm pinapsá (vel pin apsac'âuj) mahôi salaté?

Conclusiones

A lo largo de este trabajo se ha presentado un análisis de carácter etnohistórico sobre el *Manual para la administración de los sacramentos* de Bartolomé García. La primera parte del trabajo indagó sobre las denominaciones étnicas. El valor de esta sección es el cruce entre la investigación de archivo realizada por Cecilia Sheridan y las naciones mencionadas por Bartolomé García como hablantes del coahuilteco. Esta comparación nos permitió ubicar a todas las naciones en los lugares y años donde se documentó su presencia. En cuanto a la segunda parte del ensayo, si bien el análisis comparativo de los confesionarios es de carácter preliminar y no es exhaustivo en absoluto, está formado por una muestra representativa en años y lugares diversos que nos permiten identificar de manera general las particularidades y los elementos comunes que comparten este tipo de textos religiosos. Si bien es cierto que el hecho de que las preguntas aparezcan en el confesionario no nos indica la frecuencia con que se realizaban las prácticas aludidas, su mención tiene un valor significativo para describir la cosmovisión tanto del indígena como del misionero que indagaba. La contribución de este trabajo consiste en la recopilación de la información derivada de fuentes primarias y aspira a ser de utilidad para otros investigadores en la tarea de la reconstrucción de la historia de los pueblos indígenas del noreste de México y sureste de Estados Unidos.

Referencias

Campbell, Thomas. *The Indians of southern Texas and Northeastern Mexico.* Austin, Texas Archeological Research Laboratory, 1988.

García, Fray Bartolomé. *Manual para administrar los santos sacramentos de penitencia, eucharistia, extrema-uncion, y matrimonio: dar gracias despues de comulgar, y ayudar a bien morir a los indios de las naciones: pajalates, orejones, pacaos, pacóas, tilijayas, alasapas, pausanes, y otras muchas diferentes, que se hallan en las missiones del Rio de San Antonio y Rio Grande . . .*, México, Imprenta de los herederos de Doña María de Rivera, 1760.

Grammar of the Pima or Névome, a language of Sonora, from a manuscript of the XVIII century, ed. Buckingham Smith, New York, Cramoisy Press, 1862.

Molina, Alonso. *Confesionario mayor en la lengua mexicana y castellana*, México, Casa de Pedro Balli, 1578.

Orozco y Berra, Manuel. *Geografía de las lenguas y carta etnográfica de México.* México, Imprenta de J.M. Andrade y F. Escalante, 1864

Pimentel, Francisco. *Cuadro descriptivo y comparativo de las lenguas indígenas de México: o Tratado de filología mexicana.* México, Tipografía de Isidoro Epstein, 1862-1865.

Quintana de Agustín, *Confesionario en Lengua Mixe*, Puebla, Viuda de Miguel de Ortega, 1733.

Sheridan, Cecilia. *Fronterización del espacio hacia el norte de la Nueva España.* México, CIESAS, Instituto Mora, 2015.

Troike, Rudolph. "The date and authorship of the pajalate (Coahuilteco) "Cuadernillo". *International Journal of American Linguistics*. 44. 4, 1978, pp. 329-330.

Vergara, Gabriel de. *El cuadernillo de la lengua de los indios pajalates.* Ed. Eugenio del Hoyo. Monterrey, ITESM, 1965.

Notas

[1]Una parte de este trabajo será publicada en el VI Recorrido por Archivos y Bibliotecas Privados de México, A. C. por ser representativo de la investigación realizada en el acervo de la Biblioteca Cervantina por el grupo Patrimonio Cultural de la Escuela de Humanidades y Educación del Tecnológico de Monterrey.

[2]Hay abundancia de documentos etnohistóricos de bajo rendimiento "low yield" sobre los indígenas que habitaron en el sur de Texas: "The effort has gone primarily into finding documents with high data yield, and I suspect that a substantial number of these may have been found. But I also believe that there has been general neglect of low-yield documents, whose number is phenomenal. Here, I think, lies the greatest opportunity. It is in these low-yield documents that one often finds critical information on population size, seasonal range of hunting-and-gathering groups, migrations, intergroup economic cooperation or conflict, earliest introduction of European trade goods, and non-linguistic evidence of linguistic affiliation", Campbell, 1988, p. 3.

[3]Utilizamos la nomenclatura de clasificación de causas de los documentos utilizada por Cecilia Sheridan, 2015.

[4]Los números de menciones remiten a un corpus integrado por más de 4 mil entradas de denominaciones indígenas.

[5]Disponible en línea http://corpus.rae.es/cordenet.html.

El México Perdido y Anhelado: The Prose of Settler Colonialism Amidst the Diaspora

JOSÉ ANGEL HERNÁNDEZ

The University of Houston

In the period following the end of the Mexican-American War, Mexican politicians and intellectuals came to the tragic realization that their northern neighbors where in equal competition in an imperial race to settle and colonize the vast expenses of what was perceived to be empty deserts.[1] In some ways, and as some historians have noted, this battle for supremacy of the continent began with the so-called discovery of the "Americas" and the continuation of those struggles was therefore inherited by the post Independent nations of the western hemisphere.[2] Neither of these two mighty hegemons—the US or Mexico—of the continent cared very much that a multiplicity of independent indigenous groups occupied those vast expenses that they coveted, and in fact actively sought to play them off one another throughout the entirety of the nineteenth century.[3] After the signing of the *Treaty of Guadalupe Hidalgo* in 1849, with the ink still coagulating from the bloody encounter with its neighbor once again, the Mexican State immediately sought to institutionalize a process to remedy what they blamed for the loss of their Northern Territory: the "failure" to colonize their northern territories with ideal and loyal settlers.[4] It is a well-known story that the invitation of North American colonists to Texas was in effect "too successful," and served as the spear point for the eventual occupation of Mexico's sparsely-populated Northern Territories.[5]

The role of independent indigenous groups in this process is central to this particular history, and their forced westward migration by American imperialism and its settler colonists, propelled them into Mexican territory and therefore towards a raiding modality *vis-à-vis* Mexican Settlers of the northern Frontier. These independent indigenous groups eventually came to find themselves betwixt and between these two competing and expanding imperial powers. In describing the "Indios Bárbaros" of the northern regions, José María de Lacunza of Ministry of Foreign Relations notes : "two events have been notable in our border states of this part of the Republic: the first is the peaceful immigration of some tribes: the second the hostile invasions of others."[6] This combination of structural factors, he believed, led in many cases to total devastation and to a depopulation of Mexico's northern states due in large measure to flimsy post-Independence colonization policies.[7]

As many of Mexico's settlers sought protection from these constant Indian raids, many began to migrate northward into now US territory, further irritating what was Mexico's primary problem, which was the depopulation of its sparsely settled northern Frontiers.[8] Due to constant Indian raiding and pillaging along the northern Frontiers, Mexicans not only migrated northward in large numbers, but eventually started to raise families and then generations in what eventually becomes the United States of America.[9] The Mexican Government immediately deciphered this process and therefore implemented a number of colonization policies attempting to entice these lost populations back to Mexico in order to assist the Mexican state in settling, colonizing, pacifying, and civilizing what was considered a "barbarous northern frontier."[10]

A multiplicity of laws were passed by the Mexican Government throughout the nineteenth Century attempting to entice and invite any Mexican American or Mexican migrant in the US to return to Mexico, culminating with the *1883 Land and Colonization Law*, which is notable for exclusively granting this dias-poric population with the most beneficial of all colonization propositions.[11] The belief of the time was that Mexicans in the US were somehow "more modern," more loyal, and therefore ideal colonists to settle and protect these northern frontiers against *norteamericanos* and indigenous groups that had refused to submit to either Mexican or US hegemony.[12] These laws, as they were written throughout the nineteenth Century, seeped into public discourse via newspapers, decrees, pronouncements, and advertisements throughout the Southwest.[13] The option to return to Mexico, therefore was also part of the Mexican-American imaginary, and this was not lost upon the local population, as their correspon-dence makes clear throughout the rest of this essay.[14] In stark contrast to other ethnic and so-called "minority groups" throughout the US during this period, Mexicans and Mexicans in the US always had the option to "return to Mexico," and so numerous consulates peppered Mexican-American communities throughout the US in order to encourage trade and thereby also archive how this population articulated why they would be an asset to the nation.[15]

Hence, although we have Mexican laws to point towards, and concrete examples as to how many Mexicans and Mexican-Americans may have returned to Mexico during the nineteenth century, what is often left out are the very voices of those Mexican migrants attempting to articulate, define, and justify why they merit such rewards.[16] In each of the colonization laws of course, the state awarded thousands of acres to potential settlers, if they could prove and provide certain requirements as dictated by the laws.[17] This social contract was made clear in the laws itself, which were published throughout the southwest, and debated by the Mexican diaspora as well.[18]

In a series of research trips to Mexico City over the past decade, I've come across numerous requests by Mexicans and Mexican Americans in the US requesting lands and tax exemptions in order to return to the motherland, and I've come to divide these into four categories.[19] The following categories—or tropes if you prefer—that can be read in each of these letters are not only requests to return to Mexico proper, but the justifications for asking to return are usually in the context of (A.) Technology transfer; (B.) Fears of Americanization and possibly more territorial losses; (C.) Anti-Americanism and Anti-assimilation; and finally, (D.) Benefits to the nation and therefore a capacity for Indian killing. This list is not exhaustive, and more research into these letters will most likely reveal other patterns, but for those letters that I've come across thus far, these are some preliminary results that I believe will complexify research in Chicano, Borderlands, the Tejano, Mexican history, and studies on Settler Colonialism.[20] Indeed, the notion that the country of Mexico could be considered as an example of "Settler Colonization" will come as a surprise to some, particularly those unaware of the nation's historic attempts to settle "La Gran Chichimeca" dating back to even before the Mexica-Aztec period, and continuing to a minor degree, even today under different governmental agencies like *La Secretaría de Desarrollo Agrario, Territorial y Urbano* (SEDATU).[21]

In the following essay, my hope is to amplify and complexify the ongoing debates within each of the aforementioned fields and disciplines by analyzing the correspondence and prose of potential settler colonists along the Mexican borderlands. The nation's most celebrated and noted intellectuals have all observed, written about, and highlighted these settler colonial impulses in their essays about colonizing the vast northern deserts, but they never categorized them in such terminology.[22] Instead, the vast majority of observers, especially historians in the United States, have elected to historiographically paint the entirety of that nations past as a victim in the struggle for continental suprema-cy.[23] In their ignorance of the Spanish language, many Latin@ historians have seemingly sought to characterize the totality of Mexican historiography as one of "failure" followed by "tragedy" instead of the brutally honest pragmatic and practical characteristics that usually accompany successful empires that expand to the detriment of local indigenes.[24] This pragmatism, however, was not only a top-down process, but a reciprocal modality that was characteristically oppor-tunistic—as most viruses and epidemics tend to be—and also fueled by poten-tial settler colonists willing to accept and abide by the social contract and legal provisions of a settler colonial state.[25]

Colonization Laws and the Mexican Diaspora: A Brief Overview

Following the postwar period of the Mexican American War (1846-1848) the administration of José Joaquin de Herrera issued a decree on August 19, 1848 addressing "those Mexican families that are found in the United States and want to emigrate to their *patria*." Issued shortly after the important July 5 "Proyectos de Colonización" of 1848, the decree was considered an extension of the Treaty of Guadalupe Hidalgo, signed on February 2. The decree formal-ized the creation of a *Federal Repatriate Commission* charged with the enor-mous task of repatriating and then colonizing the thousands that were to return after the end of hostilities.

To this end, the northern frontier was divided into three regions, and a com-mission was assigned to each. Because the New Mexico Territory was the most heavily populated, the commission for this region was considered the most important of the three. Consisting of two dozen articles, this comprehensive repatriation decree addressed a wide range of topics. These included the com-position of the commission , the states that would accommodate repatriates, the particulars of the repatriates' travel back to Mexico, responsibilities and pay-ments to repatriates, the salaries and duties of the commissioners, and agree-ments with state and federal officials concerning land. Although never a perfect process, these initial efforts eventually allowed the government to pacify the border region and economically develop a border region that now constitutes a number of very important border towns founded by these repatriates—Tijuana, Tecate, Mexicali, Ciudad Juárez, Laredo, Piedras Negras, and Reynosa.

The trials and tribulations of this first *Federal Repatriation Commission* set in motion a series of patterns that continue to this day, and the Mexican archives are filled with requests for repatriation and colonization for the remainder of the century. Various State laws and decrees were also passed and debated throughout the rest of the century, the vast majority of which underscored the benefits of having Mexicans from the US return to Mexico with all of their knowledge and labor skills. These debates and discussions about the constant flow of return migrants ultimately led the passage of the *1883 Land and Colonization Law* a generation later that stood in as official immigration policy, provided a preferential treatment to Mexicans and Mexican Americans because many officials believed that these repatriates "had acquired skills in a developing nation and their loyalty to Mexico could not be in doubt." Indeed, Article XVI states "Mexicans residing in a foreign country who are desirous of establishing themselves in the uninhabited frontiers of the Republic will have the right to a free land grant, up to an extension of 200 hectares (double that of foreign immigrants) and enjoy them for fifteen years. The maximum amount of land that a single colonist could request was 2,500 hectares, so Mexicans from the US qualified for an additional 200 more hectares. Furthermore, Section III of Article III "stipulated that the colonists receive title to the land grant after at least one-tenth of it has been cultivated for five consecutive years." Previous scholars have suggested that such legislation in nineteenth century Mexico constituted a kind of "awakening of a nationalistic consciousness that entailed seeing the northern frontier settled by repatriates." Of the several scholars that have actually examined this particular history, not one has considered that these repatriates could also be seen as "settler colonists," particularly from the perspective of various indigenous groups that had inhabited the northern deserts for centuries. Apparently, the fact that a Department of Colonization was charged with settling colonists along the states frontiers was not enough of an indicator of settler colonization.

The creation of a *Department of Colonization* and its subsequent incorporation into the *Departamento de Fomento* thereafter led to a number of notable statistics in terms of how many colonies were actually founded, and how many Mexican Americans returned to Mexico as settler colonists. By the end of that century, and up to the time of the Mexican Revolution in 1910, sixty colonies would be established: Sixteen by the administration of Porfirio Díaz and forty-four by private companies. Mexicans and Mexican Americans populated eight of the sixteen colonies established by the government, or 50%. In the colonies founded by private companies, Mexicans repatriated from the United States composed almost 25% of the settlements during this thirty-five- year period. Mexico therefore not only encouraged Mexicans in the US to return and help settle and colonize the nation, but Mexicans themselves sought ways to convince and articulate why they merited such considerations, and as such, appears in the archival record and in the correspondence.

The Letters from El México Perdido y Anhelado

Although reasons for repatriation vary from period to period, and region to region, these particular set of letters share four themes that are worth considering. Letters soliciting repatriation usually share the common tropes of requesting lands on which to settle, or simple pleas for assistance with funds for railroad or ferry passages, usually enunciated a variety of requests that appealed to particular nineteenth century nationalist sensibilities. As such, potential repatriates requesting lands in Mexico made mention of their impoverished condition, dispossession of lands in the southwest, fears of Americanization, rising rents and increased demands for taxation, and the continued attack of so-called "barbarous Indians" raiding along the US-Mexico border. In order to strengthen these appeals, repatriates also outlined potential benefits to the "nation" by sprinkling their letters with mention of their patriotic sentiments, their skills with modern agricultural and manufacturing technologies, their desire to continue "being Mexican," and their capacity to fight against "barbaros" and other "extranjeros." Vicente Ochoa's letter to the *Departamento de Fomento*, in this regard, offers us a lens from which to examine the process of repatriation through words, appeals and actions.

Of all the requests for lands on which to colonize and settle in Mexico proper, perhaps none is more representative than the solicitation presented by Vicente Ochoa of Southern New Mexico in 1878, only a year after Porfirio Diaz took the reins of power in Mexico City.[39] Representative in this particular context suggests that Ochoa's letter of appeal to repatriate over 160 Mexican-origin families together with two-dozen Tarahumara families is illustrative of the many letters that the Mexican government receives for repatriation throughout the nineteenth century, and hence an interesting window into the very *mentalités* of the settler colonists.[40]

Vicente Ochoa is definitely part of an educated elite whose family ties extended from Southern New Mexico to West Texas and Northern Chihuahua. The last name Ochoa is not only prominent throughout this region, but like Olguin, Chaves, Porras, and Chacon, it also shares a steady appearance in the indices of the *Archivo Histórico de Terrenos Nacionales*—a fantastic and now inaccessible set of documents under the charge of the *Secretaría de la Reforma Agraria* in Mexico City.[41] Ochoa begins his request for lands in Mexico by not only appealing to the sentiments of the nation, but also by placing himself as the representative of the colonists and therefore speaking on their behalf. After outlining some preferred location for colonization and, in at least two other requests for colonization that I located under his name, he points out how particular plots of lands in Chihuahua were abandoned or being used as *rancherías* by the Apache.[42] The petitioner proceeds to describe the number of families willing to return to the country if recourses are provided for their repatriation, hence proposing that New Mexican repatriates replace the Apache in a more practical form of "Indian removal." This proposed colonization project was not a speculative endeavor, but one intended to accomplish a variety of objectives, according to this petitioner. Ochoa notes, for instance, "that there are at least 150 Mexican families now reunited whom the *Treaty of La Mesilla* made Americans, and they can no longer suffer at their hands any longer." He continued, moreover, that "more than 25 poor Mexican families, that for a few months I've been helping, and who only await sign from the government for land and help in order to begin their work."[43] This brief paragraph, of course, has much information that is worth exploring at length. Aside from the mention of 175 Mexican families that are willing to return to Mexico, the separation of the first 150, who the *Treaty of la Mesilla* "made American," is made distinct by the mention of the other 25 poor Mexican families that Ochoa has been helping. These families, collectively, are simply awaiting word from "the government" so that they can begin their southward trek to the proposed colony of "Riva Palacio," named in honor of the then Secretario of *El Departamento de Fomento*. These twenty-five families were impoverished, and like recent migrants to the area, Ochoa makes a distinction between the first one hundred families of the total one hundred and seventy five, perhaps as leverage in order to get reimbursed later by the authorities.

Later on, Ochoa and others from the colony will mention another twenty five Tarahumara families that are also willing to relocate south to the location in question, seemingly emplotting a multicultural appeal under the guise of cooperative assimilation. Note here the inclusionary impulse of the letter, but as anthropologist Patrick Wolfe notes regarding the practices and policies of assimilation: "Thus assimilation should not be seen as an invariable concomitant of settler colonialism. Rather, assimilation is one of a range of strategies of elimination that become favoured in particular historical circumstances."[44] We don't know what became of these 25 Tarahumara families and more in depth local archival research would be required to come to some conclusions. We also do not know if these Tarahumara families that proposed to return were assimilated into the colony of "Riva Palacio" or if they joined other groups of Tarahumara in Chihuahua, the largest state in Mexico.

The twin discourses of nationalism and anti-Americanism are evident with the proposed name of the colony and by the mention of their status as "Americans," by virtue of the "Gadsden Purchase" of 1853. In this context, Ochoa points out that because the *Treaty of La Mesilla* has "made them American," these potential settlers "can no longer suffer at their hands any longer," thus alluding to their refusal to endure "the New Order of Things."[45] The proposed name, as well, is not merely an appeal to the current politician occupying the position of *Secretary of Development*, but one chosen consciously to appeal to the nation and quite typical of the numerous requests for colonization during this period. This element is made quite evident if we examine other colonization proposals where non-patriotic names are employed in order to appeal to particular sentiments of the period.

Thus, the proposed settlement of "Compañía de Colonos La Esperanza" or "La Colonia Cosmopolita" are named as such in order to invoke certain particularities or sentiments of the proposed colonization projects, such as the "The Hope: Company of Colonists" and their notion of late nineteenth century "modernity."[46] "La Colonia Cosmopolita," or translated literally as "The Cosmopolitan Colony," was intended to convey the idea of cosmopolitanism because of the varied ethnic make-up of the colony, which was disproportionately composed of European and Euro- American settlers.[47] By contrast, "Colonia La Esperanza" invokes the sentiment of hope, coupled with patriotism, with the proposed colony composed of European and South American immigrants from Upper California.[48] The use of a Spanish name, for sure, is a rhetorical device intended not only to convey a particular meaning, but also intended to direct the attention of the reader and thus frame the argument as such. "Esperanza" is a double, and perhaps even triple, entendre suggesting hope for the colonists, hope for the nation, and the hope to be rewarded for lands in the Republic of Mexico in exchange for protection against "the barbarous Apache."[49]

No doubt that that the use of the Spanish language served a particular political purpose; however, my point here is that the proposed colony of "Riva Palacio" shares a more discernible element of nationalism that is made all the more evident when the correspondence continues to reiterate that the treaty of Mesilla "made them Americans" and "they can no longer suffer at their hands any longer."[50] Although no evidence is sallied forth to provide an example of how these potential colonists suffer at the hands of the *norteamericanos*, there is corroborating evidence that could and would be able to substantiate these particular claims, especially if the petitioners themselves had been the victims of well-documented cases of land displacement in Southern New Mexico.[51]

Combined with these patriotic sentiments is also the mention of the many modern benefits that these repatriations will have if they are allowed to return to the country of Mexico, specifically with respect to agricultural technology and familiarity with killing machines.[52] Hence, these modern accouterments of modernity had much to do with the use of and knowledge of traditional practices learned as a result of frontier life, such as Indian killing. The killing of "barbarous Indians" is not only employed within the colonization contract celebrated between Ochoa and the *Departamento de Fomento*, but the justification for monies apportioned for each colonists is justified by this well- established practice of modernizing the frontiers by removing those vestiges of the past. *Mesilleros* from this region, as Mary Taylor and Nona Barrick have pointed out, had extensive experience when confronting the "Indios Barbaros" that refused to submit to both Mexican and American hegemony. Taylor and Barrick argue that the Mesilla Guard, for example, had been involved in the murder of various Native Americans through the entirety of the nineteenth century via their frontier defense force, including that of the infamous case of "Cuentas Azules."[53] If one were inclined to provide for an alternative example among *Tejanos* or *Chihuahenses*, for instance, the fighting of Indians was not only rewarded by the state via a social contract, but social prestige was also bestowed upon those that demonstrated their expertise in violence with killing machines.[54] Or as Anthropologist Ana Alonso describes the *Namiquipans* of northern Chihuahua as "experts in violence."[55]

The state of New Mexico, following the end of hostilities in 1848, became a militarily run government with the US Army managing much of the economy, particularly those economies around infrastructure and military forts. Historian Charles Montgomery calculates that between 1848 and 1860, "campaigns against Apache and Navajo bands cost the government some $3 million annually and provided both wealthy and poor Hispanos, who supplied soldiers with food, firewood, and ancillary labor, their major source of revenue."[56] This economy permeated all aspect of life, even the social contract negotiated between colonists and the State. The price paid for each colonist was also measured within the economy of Indian killing. Thence, "It is interesting to note the distribution of 150 pesos per family, for help and transportation, for tools and firearms, that today more than ever are indispensable, to make the neighbors respect us and because of the frequent invasions by the barbarians."[57] This contribution was subsequently passed on to the *Secretaría de Fomento* by José González Porras when he added that "Also, the establishment of this colony, because of its convenient situation, would powerfully influence the prevention of barbarian invasions like those of contraband."[58] One could certainly entertain a number of analytical positions from these pragmatic suggestions by Porras, but the practicality of repatriation was seen in light of other larger geopolitical factors during this postwar period. Here, it is clear that Porras is extending the benefits of the nation to even the problem of frontier contraband! Both countries sought to further fortify and settle their boundaries with the available resources, and the possibilities of repatriation were therefore imagined in similar terms. *Realpolitik* was the approach of the "colonizer and the colonized."

Keeping in mind the common trope of the border region between those indigenes considered "civilized" versus those that were supposedly "uncivilized," the groups under question were primarily the Apache, Comanche, and other indigenous groups that partook in particular modalities of raiding economies.[59] Raiding economies were counter to the usual trade and barter system, or the moneyed and bank note exchanges of the period, and therefore anathema to a civilized way of life, at least according to late nineteenth century Mexican sensibilities of Mexico City. Residual aspects of this culture seeped into the upper echelon of the borderlands, and the moneyed classes were quite nuanced in their understandings of which group of indigenes constituted a less threatening civilization.[60] In the letter in question, Gonzalez Porras added that on top of the families disposed to migrate southward, there were another 25 Tarahumara peoples whose presence would "powerfully influence the prevention of barbarian invasions like those of contraband."[61] This repatriation of "old Mexican families should benefit the nation."[62] Indeed, the benefits to the nation, at least in the context of Indian killing is nuanced by the inclusion of Tarahumara Indians willing to migrate southward and thus disposed to kill other Indians, namely Apache. Various indigenous groups, as Borderlands Historian, David Weber points out, were distinguished between those that were "civilized" and those considered "barbarous," and the shifting variables also shifted in accordance to the local and historical context.[63]

As demonstrated in Ochoa's request for lands nestled along the Rio Bravo, various themes emerge for this appeal for repatriation and these can be categorized in a number of different modalities that include questions of nationalism, defiance of assimilation, and an articulation regarding potential benefits to "the nation." However, as mentioned at the beginning of this essay, this particular appeal stands out merely because it encapsulates a number of varied themes that dozens of letters by repatriates and other potential migrants made mention of. As such, the letter is only unique in that it covers several themes that appear in the dozens of letters appealing for resettlement and repatriation, but representative of other appeals for colonization. The themes that are covered, and which I will illuminate in this section, make an effort to further diagram the handful of tropes related to nineteenth century repatriation letters requesting lands of which to colonize.

The Fear of Americanization

As Ochoa's letter has demonstrated, one of the pretexts for requesting lands in Chihuahua has to do with the fear of losing their national identity amidst US westward expansion that began as early the 1830s when a series of *Indian*

Removal Acts reached a fevered pitch. The period of the nineteenth century, as most of the historiography suggests, becomes a location where a once Mexican territory is transformed via mass internal and global migrations, in what we now describe as the American southwest. The centennial migrations of that era increased during the 1830s and pushed indigenous populations westward and onto the traditional homeland of other groups, setting off wars between various groups.[64] In Texas, for instance, the local Tejano population was overwhelmed by an influx of Euroamerican settlers within a few years, and hence indigenous groups came into conflict with one another and also Mexican settlers.[65] In California, particularly after the Gold Rush of 1849, that state would eventually outnumber the local Californios and Chumash Indians in a matter of months, especially in the region surround modern day San Francisco.[66] Only in the New Mexico territory did the Mexican-origin peoples maintain a majority of the populace, at least until the 1930s when the local Hispano population became a demographic minority.[67] But even so, Euro-American settlement in the territory slowly and surely began to exact a *dominance without hegemony* within the New Mexico territory.[68] Thus, although a numerical majority, the impact that came along with the new order of things impacted what eventually became the state of New Mexico, only this time as part of the US. This new order of things naturally gave way to a fear and resistance to the influences of "Americanization" that can be read in the requests for repatriation to Mexico during the nineteenth century.

In response to the *1875 Land and Colonization Law* passed under Mexico's liberal government, Maximo Zenon Fernández appealed to both patriotism and progress, and later to the problems of "Americanization."[69] This particular request from Fernández of Alta California, like all of the others, is requesting lands from the consulate office in San Francisco on behalf of himself and a number of other Mexican families in California. For him, his efforts to repatriate those Mexicans residing in California was not based on some selfish motivation or as a way to ingratiate himself to "the nation" but one undergirded by a sincere patriotic impulse. Fernández states "In my sense I only work for true patriotism, the progress of my mother country and the return of so many children to the glorious Mexican soil."[70] This language of patriotism also manifested itself in a species of anti-Americanism-cum-nationalism when Fernández alluded to the timeliness of this repatriation that threatened to forcibly assimilate those Mexicans in Castroville, California.

For Fernández, his requests for repatriation are also undergirded by his fears of *norteamericano* assimilation. He notes, for instance, that there were an "infinity of families almost destitute, with more or less capability, but they lack protection, and if our government does not provide for their return to their native country, not only will the country lack these heads of family, and its subjects, but so many more that if they make their return, today they carry with them (as with their children) those who with more time in this country will take on the character of 'Americans' instead of Mexicans, as is desired."[71] This last sentence is worth going over here briefly, since it is this twin discourse of nationalism and its adjoining benefit to the nation that appears to come along with an anti-American sentiment shared by a number of other petitioners. This desire of Fernández, along with the government of Mexico, is that repatriation will also serve to re-acculturate those Mexicans who have resided in the US for extended periods of time or those that are slowly losing their culture and taking on, as Fernández points out earlier, "will take on the character of 'Americans' instead of Mexicans, as is desired." But to add just one more dimension to this observation is also the point that potential repatriates and government officials agree upon, and this is the idea that repatriates have not lost their *Mexicaness*, or in this case their citizenship. In this particular case, and there is much more that could be discussed, the government sends along a favorable response in the form of a certified letter allowing these colonists to enter the country duty free at the border.[72] As such, both the state and these particular set of settler colonists consider themselves *ideal* for pacifying and inhabiting the northern frontiers of the Republic.

These Mexican sentiments, perhaps described as patriotic nationalism in our day, are also present in earlier requests for repatriation, like an 1871 letter from the *Jefe Politico* of Baja California to the *Ministro de Estado y del Despacho de Gobernación* in Mexico City regarding the desire of many Californios to migrate to Mexico if only they had the resources to do so. According to his extensive observation of the territory of Baja California, he notes that "In Alta California there also exists Mexican families that have vehement desires to return to their native lands; but aside from lacking resources to verify this, they are afraid of not finding a home or work that will ensure their livelihood . . . I am mindful that I could procure good emigration towards the border, where there are lands and mines that can provide lucrative work to those unfortunate Mexicans who have the right to expect protection from their government, while now those lands and mines lay in ruinous speculations."[73] These examples of the state's concern for Mexican identity among migrants was interpreted as a sign of resisting "Americanization" under a US system of government, and these forms of resistance were therefore beneficial for the nation.

The maintenance of Mexican citizenship, for many Mexican migrants, was also seen as a sign of resisting "Americanization" in the new order of things, but also as demonstration of their loyalty to the Mexican nation. Note, for instance, another letter written by Juan Armendariz of Socorro, Texas who in 1882, one year prior to the passage of the *1883 Land and Colonization Law*, wrote to the

Mexican government inquiring about *terrenos baldios* in the neighboring state of Chihuahua. The 38-year-old Armendariz noted for the Departmento de Fomento that he was born in Socorro, Texas and that although he had lived in that location with his family all of his life, his sentiments continued to be "Mexican." For what reason he continues to feel this way, Armendariz does not say but the following sentence certainly reveals his perspective on the social conditions of the southwest during this particular point in time. Armendariz states in his letter that "for much time I have lived here in distaste because I suffer like all others of my race among the foreigners, the latter despise us, committing abuses against our race and in conclusion do not omit means of harming us in everything that concerns our well-being."[74] The immediate observation, no doubt, has to do with the question of abuses committed by "foreigners" against "our race" who look for any pretext to prejudice their well being. For sure, this particular observation could be substantiated by primary and secondary resources; however, what is especially interesting about this particular letter are a number of factors that have to do with appeals toward Mexican citizenship and the very nature of "homeland" as well. Note, for example, how Armendariz defines "the other" in his letter, a perspective that he shares as one being from Socorro, Texas—a bordertown with a long history of violence and conflict with the Euro-American settlers of the area. Although technically living in the US, Armendariz continues to describe Americans as "foreigners," arguing that "my sentiments are Mexican."[75]

The "suffering of the migrant" is perhaps another trope among this sort of correspondence, and one can also note his insistence that he suffers like the others of his "race." This may suggest that he is not given the respect he deserves because of his social position by also alluding to his own privileged position, especially in terms of income. His financial intentions are later revealed in the letter when he requests to be excused from paying certain fees, tariffs, or duties. Indeed, after pointing out the abuses he has suffered, without ever providing evidence of any such cases that he has personally witnessed or experienced, he goes on to request permission to return to Chihuahua without having to pay customs duties for $20,000 pesos of personal capital. A follow up letter written to the Administrator of the Customs House, Armendariz continues along the same narrative plot where he discusses his birth along the border and therefore his "Mexicaness." For the author, though, the newly established border and therefore Socorro, are not American but ultimately still part of Mexico. Armendáriz maintains that his current place of residence "still belonged to Mexico, and because I was young at that time, I could not have my own free will, and therefore subject to the dominion of my parents, I had to remain developing under the formula of the US Government that had managed to annex their nation, instead of my birthplace."[76] Blaming his parents and his young age, Armendáriz had no choice in the matter and therefore had to develop under an American "formula" that although it had managed to annex the country, it could not annex his birth, or birthright. In several ways, his argument regarding his age is quite reminiscent of the arguments that one hears today around so-called "Dreamers," or those impacted by DACA. These were children brought to the US by no fault of their own, and were therefore not responsible for the "criminal actions" of their parents whom illegally entered the US without proper documentation, or who overstayed their tourist visa when they found better employment. Armendariz makes an identical argument, only this time for justifying his "development under an American government formula," as a pretext for returning to Mexico—a country he has never really known.

The term "formula" interestingly enough, alludes to the new order of things that is the transition from a Mexican system of governance to one that under "the formula of the US Government." Not content with the new order of things, Armendariz then proceeds to point out that his own economic success under the "formula" has provoked the ire of his American competitors who desire to ruin him because it is "painful to see the betterment of all Mexicans." In other words, His wealth had invited the envy of his American competitors and is mentioned as a way to further demonize the concept of "Americanization" by embracing it with the stain of envy and inconsistency. This envy is mentioned as a negative when he states that it is painful for the Americans to see a successful Mexican, hence another reasoning for petitioning the government to return to Mexico. Besides, and according to his own words, his proper sentiments was not annexed to the US, only the physical territory.[77]

His initial mention of $20,000 has by this time, only four months later, increased to something between $80-$100,000 pesos in merchandise, monies, and other manufactured items. After some deliberation, however, neither his discourse of discrimination, nor his social status was enough to allow him entrance back to Mexico as a repatriate. Mexican officials rightly argued that allowing him into the country "duty free" would have a negative impact on the local merchants who were probably subject to some kind of tariff or taxes on US made goods and wares. Had Armendariz been alive today, he would most likely have been allowed to return to the country with his merchandise on a one time basis, depending on how he presented himself to the consulate at the border. But in the past, Mexican officials were still learning about the impacts of trade, contraband, and now repatriates returning from the US with an abundance of merchandise, monies, and other technological modalities. Indeed the "Jefe de la Seccion 1ª of Colonization" noted that

"The section informs that the provision related to the introduction of duty free merchandise by Mexicans residing in the United States who return to Mexico, is contracted only for the purpose of use, but in no way for purposes of commerce such as the one claimed by the petitioner, because in acceding to this concession, it would come to lay a disastrous precedent for the treasury system. In addition, the trade would be unbalanced with this supposed concession that the citizen Armendariz is introducing duty free merchandise, and could price them so low that they could not compete with those [local] merchants who introduce their wares upon payment."[78]

As it turns out, the law did not permit any repatriate this sort of advantage when importing so much merchandise that could easily be sold in northern Mexico, particularly since the absence of import duties would allow Armendariz to sell his wares at well below market value. Given the number of petitions that met with favorable outcomes, perhaps Armendariz should have highlighted his martial skills instead of simply just his finances . . .

This observation is accurate for a number of reasons and a topic of some discussion among borderland historians. The economy of *fayuca*, for instance, was lucrative and one where the economic impact of this "black market" cannot be underestimated. Historian Juan Mora-Torres's excellent historical analysis of the political economy of the Mexican American borderlands following the end of hostilities in 1848, especially their growing economic divergence is worth considering here. In an exchange between the two diplomats, Mexican Ambassador Extraordinaire and Minister Plenipotentiary, Matias Romero pointed out that "given the commercial differences between the two nations, goods on the Mexican side of the boundary costs two to four times more than on the US side, inciting 'the inhabitants of the Mexican towns to emigrate to those of the United States.' Others simply crossed the Río Bravo to purchase goods in Texas and then 'smuggle them over to the Mexican side.'"[79] Hence, the refusal to allow Armendariz entrance into the national territory should also serve as a warning for historians. Ultimately, the justification used to deny Armendariz request is valid and can be corroborated historically based on the secondary literature insofar as border officials and customs house administrators attempted to lessen the illegal and thus duty-free smuggling of *fayuca* and other contraband. Manuel Payno, Mexico's Minister of Economic Development, noted that "contraband goods emanating from the north had inundated Mexico City as early as 1850, causing a significant drop in legal commerce."[80] In this regard, repatriates were favored by the law around a variety of different issues like lower and larger tracts of land, exemption from military service, and the forgiveness of having to pay property taxes for several years; however, the free importation of industrial goods and machine made products was something that even today is a source of continued tension between the Mexican state and returning migrants, especially during the holidays.[81]

The Many Benefits to the Nation

Advantages to the nation and the preoccupation with "Americanization," however, was not exclusively the concern of potential repatriates, but also of politicians interested in the benefits of *realpolitik*. For instance, outnumbered and in direct competition with cheap labor, Mexicans in California began to repatriate on their own to the border towns nestled along the international boundary. The case of Quitovaquita, Sonora in the early 1880s offers us a case in point. The reasoning behind this repatriation, according to the border governor writing from the area, is directly tied to the current influx of Asian and European immigrant labor competition. Because Mexicans were undercut in their wages by this onslaught of cheap foreign labor, and due to their lack of the English language, now was the time to take advantage of this "favorable migration" that now sought recourse to return to Mexico. According to the governor of Sonora, now that "Our compatriots begin to find themselves in difficult circumstances in the cited state of California and in the territory of Arizona, where Asian and European immigration leaves them without a lucrative occupation."[85] Indeed the immigrants to California throughout the nineteenth century, as Historical Sociologist Tomas Almaguer points out in his own interpretation of California history, increased to a degree where the local Mexican population was outnumbered almost immediately following the finding of gold in the middle of the century.[86] This favorable migration, as well, was a different sort of migration that deserved even more attention exactly because of their Mexicaness and patriotism, an attribute that at that time could not be learned, but explained primarily through inheritance. As previously mentioned, this border governor noted that these repatriates were not just any kind of immigrants, but the kind that "have not wanted to lose their nationality as Mexicans." *Realpolitik* entered the equation when the governor noted the benefits to the nation while at the same time articulating his exasperation with Mexican emigration to the US when he noted that these repatriates-cum-settler colonists "could well become very important for our country, especially for our depopulated state" of Sonora.[87] In other words, because Sonorans were still suffering from depopulation due to northward migrations and also Indian raiding, and now that the US economy had started a downward spiral, it would be ideal to focus their misfortunes upon our national project pacifying the northern frontiers.

Mexican politicos, as such, agreed that this "favorable migration" should be encouraged, even if those migrants, now destitute and in need of assistance, were provided with the means to do so. Moreover, their patriotism could not be in doubt, even after extended years of residence in the United States. Several politicos who entertained repatriation requests in their offices noted their refusal to assimilate to US culture. For instance, the governor of Sonora pointed out that "the immigrants that I attend to, have the most important merit that despite their long residence abroad, they have not wanted to lose their nationality as Mexicans and justify it with certificates in all forms to the United States authorities." Furthermore, he added, "please allow me to draw your attention to this irrefutable proof of patriotism."[88] Here, inherited patriotism meets the era of Passports and documentation—an aspect of which was then used to demonstrate these petitioners' sense of "national identity," even if that identity is formulated in opposition to the country in which they currently reside. *Mexicaness* in this context therefore, it seems from our vantage point, is being formed and informed in another country and then seemingly repatriated along with these new settler colonists. The Mexican case, as it were, is not unique. It is commonplace even today to see that nationalists are often more nationalistic when abroad, than the very people whom actually reside within the national territories.[89]

In other examples, loyalty by way of Mexicaness was necessary if Mexico was to retain its territorial integrity. These "unimpeachable acts patriotism" were necessary if the country was to avoid other episodes of secession when it came time to settle the frontier with potential immigrants. Here, one more example is worth noting with the repatriation request of Quirino M. de la Garza and approximately two hundred families from Kinney, Texas requesting lands in Chihuahua in late 1882. Border officials articulated their sense of realpolitik along nationalist lines when the agency official outlined these positive aspects of Mexican repatriation. For him, "today as in another similar case, the section believes that the government should take advantage of all the opportunities presented to it, in order for Mexicans to enter the country who are located outside of it, both with the object of increasing the number of arms, to populate the frontiers that find themselves in disrepair and in which there should not be foreigners."[90] Several things about this particular letter stand out to the reader, but the first is that it is a year before the landmark 1883 Mexican legislation; and secondly, that the struggle for labor and settlement continues a full generation after the end of hostilities between the two nations.

Another observation regarding this exchange between the *colonizer* (Department of Development) and the Settler Colonists (Quirino M. de la Garza) is the practicality for both sides of this social contract. As Wolfe remarks about these sorts of arrangements in multiple examples throughout the globe, "frontier individuals' endless appeals for state protection not only presupposed a commonality between private and official realms."[91] But their interests are seemingly mutual, and dare I say, Pragmatic. From the perspective of State and Border Officials, the Mexican government should take advantage of the situation and encourage repatriation because the country needs more laborers, and their presence would discourage foreigners—who, besides, should not be there. From the standpoint of the settler colonists, they feel entitled to colonize on the lands of other indigenous groups, and as we have seen, this entitlement comes with a willingness to kill on behalf of the nation if necessary.

The repatriates themselves, as mentioned earlier, also articulated this observation by state officials, especially amongst those that appealed directly to state officials. Recall Ramon Castillo's letter that states unequivocally "I have never renounced my Mexican citizenship," or Juan Armendariz's earlier statement of having "Mexican sentiments," even though each of these individuals mentioned had resided in the US for 38 years each![92] Mexico's foremost anthropologist, Manuel Gamio, explained this exalted sense of nationalism in the US during the late 1920s as he observed how Mexican migrants and Mexican Americans formed fraternal and political organization and newspapers around Mexican nationalist themes. According to his extensive and excellent ethnography of Mexican communities during his time as Fellow with the *Social Science Research Council*, he states the following, which I will quote at length:

> "*Nationalism*: It has more than once been remarked that many inhabitants of rural districts in Mexico have little notion of their nationality of their country. They know their town and region in which it is situated, and this is a 'little country' for them. It is notable that people of this type, when they become immigrants in the United States, learn immediately what their mother country means, and they always think of it and speak of it with love. Indeed, it can be said that there is hardly an immigrant home in the United States where the Mexican flag is not found in a place of honor, as well as pictures of national Mexican heroes. Love of country sometimes goes so far that very often altars are made for saints and flag or hero, or both, giving patriotism thus and almost religious quality."[93]

The letters that we've examined thus far also reveal that much of this exalted sense of nationalism was in response to *norteamericano* aggressions, labor and land competition, and their seemingly nomadic existence in a country that they no longer considered their own. Contemporary day Sociologists describe this particular phenomenon as "reactive ethnicity" while others describes this process as more celebratory than conflictive. Sociologist Alejandro Portes and Ruben Rumbaut have described "reactive ethnicity" as a "Made in America Product" that is the result of a "confrontation with an adverse native mainstream and the rise of defensive identities and solidarities to counter it."[94] But this "reactive ethnicity," whether conflictive or celebratory, needs to be examined in light of the documentation, which is ultimately written in Spanish, appealing to Mexico, and articulating their subject position in defiance of assimilation and in resistance to the new order of things.

Sacrifice and the willingness to die on behalf of Mexico was also one of the many tropes that ran through the correspondence of these potential settler colonists, not to mentioned the aforementioned religious nature of the Mexican nation. For those familiar with the historiography of Nationalism, the centrality of "sacrifice" and so-called "imagined communities" are well known and have a rather long historiography. At the time that these letters were being exchanged between the colonizer and the colonized, the well-known French intellectual Ernest Renan penned his famous 1883 essay delivered at the Sorbonne in where he pointed out that "A nation is a spiritual principle resulting from the profound complexities of history—it is a spiritual family, not a group determined by the lay of the land."[95] Collectively these writings, have also become part of the theoretical debate about the variables that constitute national identity. A willingness to die on behalf of the nation can be seen in Quirino de la Garza's letter to the government as he requested lands in Chihuahua. Initially, one of his main pretexts was due to violence in Texas during this period, and his allegations and the evidence that he musters to corroborate his accusations, can probably be verified since he mentions the victims by name and date. However, note the very violent services that he in turn offers the Mexican government if his requests is accepted. If the Mexican President approves his requests, de la Garza urges, "We will be eternally grateful and we will be his most addicted servants, and in case of war against our nation we will be the first to defend the honor of Mexico, and our glory will be in spilling our blood in defense of the country, well chastised are those who suffer outside her."[96] If resettled on Mexican soil, and like many religious converts, the petitioner suggests to the government that they will be the most "addictive servants" that will spill blood in defense of the nation; moreover, and this is in the same sentence, the potential settler colonists posits himself as being outside of the nation state. In other words, his physical absence of not-being on Mexican soil generates a sacrificial discourse about the feelings of patriotism for those outside of its national borders.

Technology Transfer, Indian Killing & National Identity

Technological progress during the mid to late nineteenth century had a significant impact in those parts of the globe where the industrial revolution had its earliest impact: England, Germany, France, Japan, and the United States. Mexico's proximity to the US and its interconnection with global trade markets also had regions within the country that experienced similar national dilemmas to "overcome modernity," to use Historian Harry Harootonniuns's apt phrase.[97] And as in every locale, efforts and articulation to "overcome modernity" and the seeming onlslaught of new technologies also provided particularly acute conditions that molded the ways in which national identity was discussed, debated, and formulated. National identity was being discussed and debated in a period of intense global changes in technology that provided the canvas on which to debate the notion of Mexican identity during this period, and each nation impacted by these global changes responded and pondered the introduction of these new technologies in accordance with their own historical, sociological, political, and cultural modalities. The apt interconnections between modernity are stamped throughout the correspondence of repatriates during this period, and within the trinity of technology, Indian killing, and national identity. The three notions were interconnected and fit within the prevailing historiographical traditions of Mexican and borderlands historiographies, particularly as it relates to the introduction of Industrial Manufacturing, machine guns, and the subsequent decline of Apache cultures.

Ramon Castillo is a native of Monclova, Coahuila, Mexico who has resided in the US for the past 38 years and now wants to return to Mexico and settle under the *1883 Land and Colonization Law*. Simple subtraction from his age and the year of his letter (1886-38 years of age = 1848) tells us he migrated to the area during the Mexican War. Castillo states that for the past 28 of his 38 years in the US, he has been occupied with the raising of livestock and the cultivation of various crops. Castillo mentions that he worked "as a farmer [who] knows more about the cultivation of cotton, corn, and wheat in the style of the Americans." Thereafter, he continues by stating "that he has never revoked his Mexican citizenship."[98] Thus, no contradiction is seen when discussing these two competing ideologies when we consider that the state also argues for such a position: extolling Mexicaness while proclaiming the technological superiority of its northern neighbor. Neither the petitioner, nor the Mexican government ever articulates either the name of this technology al "American style," its advantages, or how it will ultimately be applied in Mexico once repatriated. Is the new technology hydrological; electrical; new irrigation technologies; new field/crop rotation techniques; or the introduction of revolutionary fertilization methods? Or is technology here being used as a proxy of mass agro-industrialization of the southwestern US and the Mexican north.

By way of a second example, let us return to the earlier correspondence of the words of Maximo Zenon Fernández as an example of how the idea of colonization is imbricated into the language of progress and modernization. Quite matter-of-factly, proclaims Fernández,

> "Lord knows the immense desires that your pleasing feelings have in elevating the aggrandizement of our mother country by promoting, with your wise intelligence, and no less elevated patriotism, arranging, and encouraging, to the effect with the initiative that the case requires of colonization, whose work is so beneficial for the development of such an advantageous *progress*, and that it elevates to a smiling future, and no less admirable to our country."[101]

This argument, although embedded with much meaning, not once tells us exactly which technological effects will be returned with this repatriation, but the discourse sounds practical, even when it emerges from government officials.

Government officials writing on behalf of potential repatriates used the same line of reasoning when describing the benefits of repatriation. P. Ornelas, the Mexican Consulate for the offices in San Antonio, Texas noted that "upon repatriation, they bring with them practical knowledge of cotton farming and cattle raising, two resources that constitute a notable part of the remarkable prosperity of the State of Texas."[102] These sentiments, one could argue, were not exclusively limited to places like Texas, which in fact did have a significant crop of cotton and livestock, but can be seen with other examples from other border states as well. A.K. Coney of the Mexican Consulate in San Francisco, California noted in his extensive report to the SRE that "I have intimate knowledge that it would be very useful for our country the return of Mexicans—who after having been for some years in the agricultural and manufacturing centers of this country—would bring a wealth of knowledge in different arts and then communicate it to our farmers and industries."[103] Although this is a constant trope, it is also important to point out that more research would be required to empirically ascertain the degree to which this sort of technological transfer occurred.[104]

Much like the rest of the correspondence that highlights these skills that repatriates will communicate to those that never left, this correspondence by government officials rarely provide examples or evidence for these claims, particularly in light of the fact that nineteenth century livestock technologies were "borrowed whole cloth" from Mexican rancheros and not the other way around. Indeed, even the very butchering technologies of the Mexicans, which became the medium that eventually gave rise to the assembly line process of this period, was seemingly acculturated as well.[105] As a final example, and after having pointed out examples from Texas and California, here might be an opportunity to insert a case from the border state of Sonora. For Carlos M. Ortiz:

> "The government in my charge, understanding of the great goods that will bring to the state the return of those emigrants who will be so useful, at the moment that said movement that is developing in the country, and how necessary the arms are for industry and agriculture, and on the other hand, for reasons of patriotism and humanity, it is proposed to make as many efforts as possible in order to arbitrate resources to help all those of our compatriots who wish to return to their country."[106]

Contextualizing this letter a bit may help to examine the real fears behind this discourse of modernity that becomes entangled with that of repatriation and colonization. The US is seen as progressing while Mexico is thought of as underdeveloped, dangerous, and infested with "barbarous Indians" that do not allow for peace and therefore development. As a result, laborers migrate northward thereby leaving the border regions depopulated and bereft of a cheap labor pool necessary to progress. In the midst of growing wave of emigration, border officials became the first victims, observers and therefore critics of Mexican migration to the US. But at the same time, it is not only "American technologies" that are touted as benefits to the nation. Indian killing is also mentioned an encouraged by both repatriates and government officials. As we have seen with the case of the Mesilla Guard, Mexicans in the US shared long histories of frontier fighting and a tradition that was shared by dozens of communities throughout the southwest.

Conclusions

The history of colonization in Mexico is also a "*structure rather than an event*," and one where the "logic of elimination" could not eliminate what was essentially the majority indigenous populations following Independence. Unlike its neighbor to the North, Mexico embraced its indigenous past and Mestizo genealogies, but the "logic of elimination" via colonization policies marched toward the formation of a hegemonic Mexican consciousness that sought to pacify, incorporate, or destroy independent indigenous groups that refused to submit to central authority. In this struggle for continental supremacy, diasporic Mexicans now found on the US side of the International Boundary after the Mexican American War therefore become the ideal, modern, and loyal settler colonists to assist in this nationalist project. Like Wolfe's "frontier individuals," these diasporic Mexicans' "endless appeals for State protection not only presupposed a commonality between the private and official realms," it was codified within colonization law.[107]

It is in this regard that I approached the aforementioned set of documents, which constitute hand written letters penned by Mexicans and Mexican Americans in the US requesting lands in Mexico on which to colonize and settle. Much like the analysis and observations made by some post-colonial writers it is indeed among the colonies and therefore its colonists that we also find a kind of reciprocal discourse of violence, or justification for settler colonization. Indeed, one of the most common tropes that one reads in these letters are their capacity for Indian killing, an uncomfortable aspect which is often overlooked in numerous historiographies. One of the most often overlooked aspects of settler colonization, aside from its penchant of constantly examining the State, is that it often overlooks the very agency of voice of the colonists themselves, particularly their own personal and private interests. These varied interests may not always coincide with the State, but what is often included in their prose are justifications for being settler colonists—along with all the benefits of that state-sponsored modernity.

The incorporation and use of Mexicans in the United States as "ideal colonists" to pacify the northern frontiers, therefore, constitutes merely a different modality in the longer history of frontier colonization. In other words, and to employ the language of settler colonialism, the incorporation and employment of Mexican Americans and Mexican migrants is yet another series of events in the longer structural history of Mexican colonization laws and practices.

Endnotes

[1]"The war of invasion" according to the Minister of Interior and Foreign Relations historicizing the event, "did nothing more than remove the veil that covered the eyes of those that hoped the disordered public administration and the vicious organization of our Army, would not embarrass a defense made in accordance with the rules of the art (of War), neither would they inspire the discouragement of the good servants of the nation." Original: "La guerra de invasión no hizo más que descorrer el velo que cubría los ojos de los que esperaron que la desordenada administración pública y la viciosa organización de nuestro ejército, no embarazarían una defensa hecha conforme a las reglas del arte, ni inspirarían desaliento a los buenos servidores de la nación."See México, *Memoria del Ministro de Relaciones Interiores y Esteriores, D. Luis G. Cuevas, leída en la Cámara de Diputados el 5 y en la de Senadores el 8 de Enero de*

1849, (México: Imprentade Vicente García Torres, Ex-Convento del Espíritu Santo, 1849), 6.

[2]Felipe Fernández Armesto, *The World: A History,* 2nd Edition, (Pearson, 2009); Alfred W. Crosby, *Ecological Imperialism: The Biological Expansion of Europe, 900-1900,* (Cambridge: Cambridge University Press, 1986); also, Pope Alexander VI, *Inter Caetera: Division of the undiscovered world between Spain and Portugal,* 1493 at http://www.papalencyclicals.net/Alex06/alex 06inter.htm

[3]Jorge Chávez Chávez, *Los indios en la formación de la identidad nacional,* (Ciudad Juárez, Chih.: Universidad Autónoma de Ciudad Juárez, 2003); Fernando Jordán, *Crónica de un país bárbaro,* (México: Costa-Amic, 1967); Luis Aboites Aguilar, *Norte precario: poblamiento y colonización en México, 1760-1940,* (México: El Colegio de México, Centro de Estudios Históricos: Centro de Investigaciones y Estudios Superiores en Antropología Social, 1995); Ana María Alonso, *Thread of Blood: Colonialism, Revolution, and Gender on Mexico's Northern Frontier,* (Tucson: The University of Arizona Press, 1995); Brian DeLay, *War of a Thousand Deserts: Indian Raids and the US-Mexican War,* (Yale University Press, 2009).

[4]"Decreto de 19 de Agosto de 1848; para que familias mexicanas que se encuentren en los Estados Unidos puedan emigrar a su patria," en Francisco F. De la Maza, *Código de Colonización y Terrenos Baldíos de la República Mexicana, formado por Francisco F. De La Maza y Publicado Según el Acuerdo del Presidente de la República, Por Conducta de la Secretaría de Estado y del Despacho de Fomento, Años de 1451 a 1892,* (México: Oficina Tipográfica de la Secretaria de Fomento, 1893), 407-412.

[5]See Moisés González Navarro, *La colonización en México* (1960); also *Los extranjeros en México y los Mexicanos en el Extranjero, 1821-1970, 3 tomos,* (México: Centro de Estudios Históricos, COLMEX, 1994).

[6]México, *Memoria del Ministro de Relaciones Interiores y Esteriores Leída en las Cámaras en 1851,* (México: Imprenta de Vicente García Torres, 1851), 13; Original: "Dos acontecimientos han verificado notables en nuestros Estados fronterizos de esta parte de la Republica: en primero es la inmigración pacifica de algunos tribus: el segundo la invasiones hostiles de otras."

[7]Moisés González Navarro, *La política Colonizadora del Porfiriato,* (México: Separata de Estudios Históricos Americanos, 1953) and also *La colonización en México, 1877-1910,* (México: 1960); Ignacio González-Polo, "Ensayo de una bibliografía de la colonización en México durante el siglo XIX," *Boletín del Instituto de Investigaciones Bibliográficas 4,* (1960): 179-191; George Dieter Berninger, *Mexican Attitudes Towards Immigration, 1821-1857,* (PhD Dissertation, Department of History, University of Wisconsin, 1972) ; Igna-

cio González-Polo y Acosta, "Colonización e inmigración extranjera durante las primeras décadas del siglo xix," *Boletín bibliográfico de la Secretaria de Hacienda y Crédito 412*, (1973): 4-7; Dieter Berninger, "Immigration and Religious Toleration: A Mexican Dilemma, 1821-1860," *The Americas 32(4)*, (April 1976): 549-565; José B. Zilli Mánica, "Proyectos liberales de colonización en el siglo XIX." *La palabra y el hombre 52*, (Octubre-Diciembre 1984): 129-142; Jan de Vos, "Una legislación de graves consecuencias: el acarpamiento de tierras baldías en México con el pretexto de colonización, 1821-1910," *Historia Mexicana 34(1)*, (Julio-Septiembre 1984): 76-113; Moisés González Navarro, *Los extranjeros en México y los mexicanos en el extranjero, 1821-1970, 3 Vols.*, (México: Centro de Estudios Históricos, COLMEX, 1993); Fernando S. Alanís Enciso, "Los extranjeros en México, la inmigración y el gobierno: ¿tolerancia o intolerancia religiosa?, 1821-1830," *Historia Mexicana, XLV:3*, (1996): 539-566; Jürgen Buchenau, "Small Numbers, Great Impact: México and Its Immigrants, 1821-1973," *Journal of American Ethnic History*, (February 2001): 23-49; David K. Burden, *La idea salvadora: Immigration and Colonization Politics in México, 1821-1857*, (PhD Dissertation, Department of History, University of California-Santa Barbara, 2005).

[8]Carta de Gobernador de Sonora a Ministerio de Relaciones Exteriores, 3 Octubre 1849, AHSRE, 6-17-41; quoted in Ángela Moyano Pahissa, *Protección Consular a Mexicanos en los Estados Unidos, 1849-1900*, (México: Archivo Histórico Diplomático Mexicano, Secretaria de Relaciones Exteriores, 1898), 28-30. [Hereafter cited as *Protección Consular a Mexicanos*]; Original: "¿De qué servirá que el gobierno ofrezca ricas tierras en despoblado si no se puede disfrutar ni gozar sin seguridad? ¿Y que persona puede dedicarse a trabajar cultivo o descubrir, si el gobierno no les garantiza una fuerza que los libre de los acometimientos salvajes?"

[9]Mariano Paredes, *Proyectos de leyes sobre colonización y comercio en el estado de Sonora, presentados a la Cámara de Diputados por el representante de aquel estado, en la sesión de extraordinaria de día 16 de Agosto de 1850*, (México, DF: Ignacio Cumplido, 1850), 4-5; quoted in Patricia Herring, "A Plan for the Colonization of Sonora's Northern Frontier: The Paredes Proyectos of 1850," *Journal of Arizona History, vol. 10, Number 2*, (1969): 103-114.

[10]"Decreto de 19 de Agosto de 1848; para que familias mexicanas que se encuentren en los Estados Unidos puedan emigrar a su patria," en Francisco F. De la Maza, *Código de Colonización y Terrenos Baldíos de la República Mexicana, formado por Francisco F. De La Maza y Publicado Según el Acuerdo del Presidente de la República, Por Conducta de la Secretaría de Estado y del*

Despacho de Fomento, Años de 1451 a 1892, (México: Oficina Tipográfica de la Secretaria de Fomento, 1893), 407-412.

[11]Most of these laws can be located in the obligatory reference point for these questions: Francisco F. De la Maza, *Código de Colonización y Terrenos Baldíos de la República Mexicana, formado por Francisco F. De La Maza y Publicado Según el Acuerdo del Presidente de la República, Por Conducta de la Secretaría de Estado y del Despacho de Fomento, Años de 1451 a 1892*, (México: Oficina Tipográfica de la Secretaria de Fomento, 1893), passim.

[12]José Angel Hernández, "El México Perdido, El México Olvidado, y El México de Afuera: A History of Mexican American Colonization, 1836-1892, 2 Vols," (PhD Dissertation, Department of History, The University of Chicago, 2008). A reduced version of the study appeared as *Mexican American Colonization during the Nineteenth Century: A History of the US-Mexico Borderland*s, (Cambridge: Cambridge University Press, 2012); a more in depth analysis of the post independence period also appeared as *"Indios Bárbaros* and the Making of Mexican Colonization Policy after Independence: From Conquest to Colonization," Chapter in *Transnational Indians in the North American West*, "Connecting the Greater West Series," Andrae M. Marak & Clarissa Confer, Eds. (Texas A&M University Press, 2015): 89-117.

[13]Jesús Islas, *Situación de los habitantes Ispano-Americanos en el Estado de Alta California*, 26 Junio 1855, (Puerto de Mazatlán: Imprenta de Rafael Carreon, 1855).

[14]See for instance the case of Maximo Z. Fernández, whose names appears and reappears in the archival record, and which I will discuss at length later in this essay. "Máximo Fernández Pide A Nombre de Varios Mexicanos Residentes en el Condado de Monterrey, Estado de California, Que el Gobierno Les Proporcione Terrenos en el Estado de Chihuahua, 25 Junio 1888," in *Archivo Histórico de Terrenos Nacionales* [Hereafter AHTN] , 1.29 (06), Exp. 316.

[15]See Ángela Moyano Pahissa, *Antología: Protección Consular a Mexicanos en los Estados Unidos, 1849-1900*, (México: Archivo Histórico Diplomático Mexicano, 1989), passim; [hereafter cited as *Protección Consular a Mexicanos*].

[16]There are obviously debates about these numbers in the estimates for return migration, and they stand in stark contrast to the primary estimates. For instance, William Douglas Taylor, places the number at 3,000; however, he only cites the [Chihuahuan] study undertaken by Martín González de La Vara (1994), and then only this one case. Douglas states that "Aunque no se sabe con exactitud el número de mexicanos que eventualmente se hayan mudado a México, se calcula que alrededor de tres mil personas aceptaron la oferta y volvieron." See "La Repatriación de Mexicanos de 1848 a 1980 y su papel en

la colonización de la región fronteriza septentrional de México," *Relaciones 18*, no. 69. (1997), 198-212. However, aaccording to made by the First Repatriation Commission to New Mexico in early June 1848, Father Ramon Ortiz estimated that in addition to the 900 families that had already signed up to help found the colonies in Chihuahua, another 16,000 families totalling upwards of 53,000 souls could migrate south if monies were set aside for this endeavour. An additional $1,653,342 pesos would be necessary if all of the potential repatriates opted to leave, or about $1,628,342 pesos more than the original $25,000 that was initially extended. See Correspondencia of Ramón Ortiz, in *Three New México Chronicles*, 148-149; AHSRE, L-E-1975 (XXV), "Asunto: Ramón Ortiz—Nombramiento del citado para que pase a Nuevo México, comisionado para la traslación de familias a territorio de la República, 1848"; AHSRE, 2-13-2971, "Gobierno del Estado de Chihuahua. Escrito a mano: No. 68: El Gobernador de Chihuahua participa que se ha nombrado agente del Señor comisionado Ortiz al Licenciado Don Manuel Armendáriz para que informe al Supremo Gobierno sobre la inmigración a este Estado de las familias Nuevo Mexicanas, 1849."

González Navarro also provides for some conflicting numbers, but his study of only analyzing "official colonies" during the Porfiriato does provide for some appropriate samples, which this manuscript attempts to articulate for the mid nineteenth century. He states "During the long government of Porfirio Díaz there were established, with very unequal success, 16 official colonies and 44 private, 60 in total; eight of the official and 10 of the private (colonies) were formed by Mexicans; three of the first and two of the second with repatriates." In other words, ethnic Mexicans (native and repatriated) composed 69% of the official colonies (11/16) during the Porfiriato and they constituted over 27% of the private colonization projects, or 12/44. If we combine both the private and government sponsored colonies, ethnic Mexicans constitute 38.8% of the grand total. What the author does not take into account as he points out his examples of "foreign" and "American" colonies were the number of ethnic Mexicans that not only composed each of these colonies, but that were written into the colonization contracts for almost every single case. See *Los extranjeros en México II*, 133.

[17]See, for instance, the contract given to one settler colonist where it is mentioned that he could do as he pleased with the land "if and whenever as citizen of the frontier he is quick to defend the Country from the enemies that harass it and to track them in their persecution when the authority deemed it." Original: "siempre que como ciudadano de la frontera esté pronto a defender el País de los enemigos que lo hostilicen y a salir en su persecución cuando la autoridad lo disponga, para lo que cuidará de estar provisto de armas y caballo así

como también ha de residir con su familia en la nueva población al menos por espacio de cuatro años." In "Títulos de José Anaya, 28 Febrero y 8 Mayo de 1854," in *Don Juan Vigil, emigrado de Nuevo México como apoderado de los demás emigrados en la colonia de Guadalupe y San Ignacio en el Paso del Norte pide se concedan a dicha colonia varias tierras baldías. [El Agente remite 287 Títulos], 1849-1855."* AHTN, 1.29 (06), Exp. 239.

[18]"Decreto de 19 de Agosto de 1848; para que familias mexicanas que se encuentren en los Estados Unidos puedan emigrar a su patria," en Francisco F. De la Maza, *Código de Colonización y Terrenos Baldíos de la República Mexicana, formado por Francisco F. De La Maza y Publicado Según el Acuerdo del Presidente de la República, Por Conducta de la Secretaría de Estado y del Despacho de Fomento, Años de 1451 a 1892,* (México: Oficina Tipográfica de la Secretaria de Fomento, 1893), 407-412.

[19]I first made this division in the following presentation, "Letters from "El Mexico Perdido": Digitizing Correspondence from *El México de Afuera* to *La Madre Patria* during the Nineteenth Century," Paper Presented at the *25th Anniversary Recovering the US Hispanic Literary Heritage Conference*, The University of Houston, 10 February 2017.

[20]There are various definitions of what constitutes "settler colonialism," but here I will just share the two most known. "Settler colonialism is a form of colonialism which seeks to replace the original population of the colonized territory with a new society of settlers. As with all forms of colonialism, it is based on exogenous domination, typically organized or supported by an imperial authority. Settler colonialism is enacted by a variety of means ranging from violent depopulation of the previous inhabitants, to more subtle, legal means such as assimilation or recognition of indigenous identity within a colonial framework. Unlike other forms of colonialism, the imperial power does not always represent the same nationality as the settlers. However, the colonizing authority generally views the settlers as racially superior to the previous inhabitants, which may give settlers' social movements and political demands greater legitimacy than those of colonized peoples in the eyes of the home government. The land is the key resource in settler colonies, whereas natural and human resources are the main motivation behind other forms of colonialism. Normal colonialism typically ends eventually, whereas settler colonialism lasts indefinitely, except in the rare event of complete evacuation or settler decolonization." For a variation of this quote see Patrick Wolfe "Settler Colonialism and the Elimination of the Native." *Journal of Genocide Research 8.4,* (2006): 387–409.

Another definition is "Settler colonialism is a global and transnational phenomenon, and as much a thing of the past as a thing of the present. There is no such thing as neo-settler colonialism or post-settler colonialism because settler colonialism is a resilient formation that rarely ends. Not all migrants are settlers; as Patrick Wolfe has noted, settlers come to stay. They are founders of political orders who carry with them a distinct sovereign capacity. And settler colonialism is not colonialism: settlers want Indigenous people to vanish (but can make use of their labour before they are made to disappear). Sometimes settler colonial forms operate within colonial ones, sometimes they subvert them, sometimes they replace them. But even if colonialism and settler colonialism interpenetrate and overlap, they remain separate as they co-define each other." In Edward Cavanagh & Lorenzo Veracini, "Editors Statement," *Settler Colonial Studies vol. 3;1*, (2013).

[21]Jaime Mata-Míguez, Lisa Overholtzer, Enrique Rodríguez-Alegría, Brian M. Kemp, Deborah A. Bolnick, "The Genetic Impact of Aztec Imperialism: Ancient Mitochondrial DNA Evidence from Xaltocan, Mexico," *American Journal of Physical Anthropology, 149;4*, (December 2012): 504–516; also Enrique Florescano, *Memory, Myth, and Time in Mexico: From the Aztecs to Independence*, (Austin: University of Texas Press, 1994); for a comparative approach to Mesoamerican civilizations, see Friedrich Katz, *The Ancient American Civilizations*, [(New York: Praeger, 1975) First published in Germany in 1969 by Kindler Verlag under the title of *Vorkolumbische Kulturen*]; finally, for more modern examples, see Carlos Tello Díaz, "La colonización de la costa de Jalisco: 1953-1959," *Relaciones. Estudios de historia y sociedad, 35(140)*, (2014): 267-293.

[22]The examples are many, but some early writings are representative of ongoing debates throughout the rest of the century. See Juan N. Almonte, *Proyectos de Leyes Sobre Colonización*, (México: Ignacio Cumplido, 26 Enero 1852); translated in Odie B. Faulk, "Projected Mexican Colonies in the Borderlands, 1852," *The Journal of Arizona History 10*, (Summer 1969): 115-128; Mariano Paredes, *Proyectos de leyes sobre colonización y comercio en el estado de Sonora, presentados a la Cámara de Diputados por el representante de aquel estado, en la sesión de extraordinaria de día 16 de Agosto de 1850*, (México, DF: Ignacio Cumplido, 1850 in Patricia Herring, "A Plan for the Colonization of Sonora's Northern Frontier: The Paredes Proyectos of 1850," *Journal of Arizona History, vol. 10, Number 2*, (1969); José María Lacunza, "Circular de Agosto 31, 1850. Se nombra una comisión que levante planos de los terrenos de Sonora en que pueda establecerse la colonización," sección in Manuel Dublán y José María Lozano, *Legislación Mexicana o Colección Completa de las Disposiciones Legislativas Expedidas desde la Independencia de la Republica, Ordenada por los Licenciados Manuel Dublán y José María*

Lozano, Edición Oficial, (México: Imprenta de Comercio, a Carga de Dublán y Lozano, hijos, 1876), 734-735.

[23]One can obviously not categorize the entirety of a school of thought, but suffice it to say that even this particular interpretation has changed over time. My point is that in the American academy today, the notion of discussing Mexican history along the lines proposed by contemporary scholars of settler colonialism is absent. When discussing settler colonialism, it is usually the United States serving as Settler Colonists on Mexican soil, like the Mormons or some elements of "Manifest Destiny."

[24]John A. Ochoa, *The Uses of Failure in Mexican Literature and Identity,* (The University of Texas Press, 2004).

[25]See footnote 17.

[26]The Journal *Settler Colonial Studies,* for instance, had its first issue published in 2011.

[27]See E.J. Hobsbawm, *Primitive Rebels: Studies in Archaic Forms of Social Movement in the 19th and 20th Centuries,* (New York: WW Norton & Company, 1965).

[28]See Journal *Subaltern Studies* published between 1981 and 2005.

[29]Dipesh Chakrabarty, "A Small History of Subaltern Studies," in *Habitations of Modernity: Essays in the Wake of Subaltern Studies,* (Chicago: The University of Chicago Press, 2002), 3-19.

[30]*Ibid,* 9.

[31]Ranajit Guha, *Elementary Aspects of Peasant Insurgency in Colonial India,* (Oxford University Press, 1983).

[32]Patrick Wolfe, "Settler Colonialism and the Elimination of the Native," *Journal of Genocide Research 8;4,* (December 2006), 387-409. Here, it is important to point out that Mexican intellectuals of the past have covered similar ground (like the term "ethnocide" versus "genocide" and "homicide"), with the best example being that of Guillermo Bonfil Batalla's class monograph, *México Profundo: Una Civilización Negada,* (México: Grijalbo, 1987).

[33]*Ibid,* 390.

[34]*Ibid.*

[35]*Ibid,* 393-394.

[36]*Ibid,* 393-394.

[37]Friedrich Nietzsche, *Also Sprach Zarathustra. Ein Buch Für Alle und Keinen.* (Chemnitz, 1883).

[38]Wolfe, "Settler Colonialism," 402.

[39]AHTN 1.29 (06) Exp. 286—"Vicente Ochoa: Presupuesto Para Colonizar Los Terrenos Baldíos de Las Márgenes Del Bravo Con Familias Mexicanas." Diciembre 3, 1878.

[40]*Mentalités* is in obvious reference to the Annales School of France. In particular, Marc Bloch's notion that "For in the last analysis, it is human consciousness which is the subject matter of history. The interrelations, confusions, and infections of human consciousness are, for history, reality itself." The Historians Craft, (New York: Vintage Books, 1953), 151. Originally published in 1949 as *Apologie pour l'histoire ou Métier d'historien*, or translated literally as *Apology for History or Profession of Historian*.

[41]During my first extensive research trip to Mexico City in the Summer of 2003, I gained limited access to the materials and a handful of researchers were also working the dusty archives, but now my requests have been rejected after the publication of my monograph, *Mexican American Colonization during the Nineteenth Century: A History of the US- Mexico Borderlands*. Unprecedented access to the materials occurred the following summer when I received my first Fulbright Fellowship, and the materials revealed that this particular locale housed the land archives of the now defunct *Departamento de Fomento* that was charged with the responsibility of settling ALL immigrants to Mexico during the nineteenth century, which as it turns out, was composed primarily not of Europeans, but of ethnic Mexican migrants in the US and Mexican Americans.

[42]"Carta de Ochoa a José González Porras, 9 Septiembre 1878; AHTN, 1.29 (06), Exp. 286, Vicente Ochoa Colonizar Los Terrenos Baldíos de Las Márgenes Del Bravo Con Familias Mexicanas, 1878.

[43]"Carta de Ochoa a Porras, 9 Septiembre 1878; AHTN, 1.29 (06), Exp. 286, Vicente Ochoa Colonizar Los Terrenos Baldíos de Las Márgenes Del Bravo Con Familias Mexicanas, 1878. Original: "que están reunidos por lo menos ciento cincuenta familias de Mexicanos a quienes el Tratado de la Mesilla hizo Americanos, y que no pueden sufrir el tratamiento de estos, más veinte y cinco familias de Mexicanos pobres, que hace algunos meses estoy auxiliando, y que solo esperan el señalamiento de terreno y los auxilios del gobierno para comenzar sus trabajos."

[44]Wolfe, "Settler Colonialism," 401.

[45]"Carta de Ochoa a Porras," 9 Septiembre 1878; AHTN, 1.29 (06), Exp. 286.

[46]See "Pimentel, I.M.—Compañía de Colonos para el Estado de Sonora "La Esperanza" Propuesta," in AHTN 1.29 (22) Leg. 8, Exp. 290. 28 Diciembre 1878. For "Colonia Cosmopolita" see "Bon P.M.—Pide por sí y a nombre de varios mexicanos residentes en Santa Bárbara California, que el gobierno les proporcione los terrenos necesarios en el Rio Yaqui Sonora para establecer una colonia de Mexicanos repatriados." In AHTN 1.29 (22) Leg. 8, Exp. 297. 5 Febrero 1888.

[47]"Colonia Cosmopolita" see "Bon P.M.—Pide por sí y a nombre de varios mexicanos residentes en Santa Bárbara California, que el gobierno les proporcione los terrenos necesarios en el Rio Yaqui Sonora para establecer una colonia de Mexicanos repatriados." In AHTN 1.29 (22) Leg. 8, Exp. 297. 5 Febrero 1888.

[48]"Pimentel, I.M.—Compañía de Colonos para el Estado de Sonora "La Esperanza" Propuesta," in AHTN 1.29 (22) Leg. 8, Exp. 290. 28 Diciembre 1878.

[49]The Original Spanish states " . . . Yo y mi familia fuimos sufrimiento de vidas y intereses dos veses nos ataca el varbaro apache yevandonos nuestros intereses matándome los arrieros y yo salve la suerte . . . " see "Bon P.M.—Pide por si y a nombre de varios mexicanos residentes en Santa Bárbara California, que el gobierno les proporcione los terrenos necesarios en el Rio Yaqui Sonora para establecer una colonia de Mexicanos repatriados." In AHTN 1.29 (22) Leg. 8, Exp. 297. 5 Febrero 1888.

[50]Carta de Porras a Secretaria de Fomento, 15 Octubre 1878; AHTN, 1.29 (06), Exp. 286.

[51]David Correia, *Appendix: Land Grant Speculation in New Mexico during the Territorial Period*, 48 NAT. RESOURCES J. 857 (2008). Available at: http://digitalrepository. unm.edu/nrj/vol48/iss4/4

[52]The capacity to assist the Mexican state in pacifying the indigenes is an early frontier trope, but for an example coming directly from the diaspora, one need look any further than the popular broadside of the middle of the nineteenth century. Jesús Islas, *Situación de los habitantes Ispano-Americanos en el Estado de Alta California*, 26 Junio 1855, (Puerto de Mazatlán: Imprenta de Rafael Carreon, 1855).

[53]See "Asesinato del Jefe 'Cuentas Azules,' Cometido por Mexicanos que huyeron a La Mesilla. Lista do los Prisioneros en el fuerte Webster Nuevo México, 1853." In AHSRE, Exp. 30-16-58.

[54]See Jane-Dale Lloyd's, *Cinco ensayos sobre cultura material de rancheros y medieros del noroeste de Chihuahua, 1886-1910*, (México: Universidad Iberoamericana, 2001) also *El proceso de modernización capitalista en el noroeste de Chihuahua, 1880-1910*, (México: Universidad Iberoamericana, 1987); Friedrich Katz, *The Life and Times of Pancho Villa*, (Stanford: Stanford University Press, 1998); Ana María Alonso, *Thread of Blood: Colonialism, Revolution, and Gender on Mexico's Northern Frontier*, (Tucson: University of Arizona Press, 1995).

[55]Alonso, *Thread of Blood*, 30.

[56]Charles Montgomery, *The Spanish Redemption: Heritage, Power, and Loss on New Mexico's Upper Rio Grande*, (Berkeley: University of California Press, 2002), 42–43.

[57]Carta de Ochoa a José González Porras, 9 Septiembre 1878; AHTN, 1.29 (06), Exp. 286, Vicente Ochoa Colonizar Los Terrenos Baldíos de Las Márgenes Del Bravo Con Familias Mexicanas, 1878. Original: "es de todo punto interesante la entrega de ciento diez pesos por familia, para trasportes y auxilios, los útiles y las armas, que hoy más que nunca se hacen indispensables, para hacerse respetar por los vecinos y por las invasiones frecuentes de los barbaros."

[58]Carta de Jose González Porras a Secretaria de Fomento, 15 Octubre 1878; AHTN, 1.29 (06), Exp. 286. Vicente Ochoa Colonizar Los Terrenos Baldíos de Las Márgenes Del Bravo Con Familias Mexicanas, 1878. ORIGINAL: además el establecimiento de esta por su conveniente situación influiría poderosamente para impedir así las invasiones de los barbaros como el contrabando."

[59]Jorge Chávez Chávez, *Los indios en la formación de la identidad nacional*, (Ciudad Juárez, Chih.: Universidad Autónoma de Ciudad Juárez, 2003); Fernando Jordán, *Crónica de un país bárbaro*, (México: Costa-Amic, 1967); Luis Aboites Aguilar, *Norte precario: poblamiento y colonización en México, 1760-1940*, (México: El Colegio de México, Centro de Estudios Históricos: Centro de Investigaciones y Estudios Superiores en Antropología Social, 1995); Ana María Alonso, *Thread of Blood: Colonialism, Revolution, and Gender on Mexico's Northern Frontier*, (Tucson: The University of Arizona Press, 1995); Brian DeLay, *War of a Thousand Deserts: Indian Raids and the US-Mexican War*, (Yale University Press, 2009).

[60]David J. Weber, *Bárbaros: Spaniards and Their Savages in the Age of Enlightenment*, (New Have: Yale University Press, 2005).

[61]Carta de Porras a Secretaria de Fomento, 15 Octubre 1878; AHTN, 1.29 (06), Exp. 286.

[62]Carta de García Cubas a Ministro de Fomento, 17 Octubre 1878; AHTN, 1.29 (06), Exp. 286. Original: "Antiguas familias mexicanas, debe redundar en beneficio de la nación."

[63]David Weber, *Barbaros*, 19-51.

[64]Andrés Reséndez, *Changing National Identities at the Frontier: Texas and New Mexico, 1800-1850*, (Cambridge: Cambridge University Press, 2004), 45-55.

[65]The best source is perhaps the report written during that period in the late 1820s. See *Texas by Terán: The Diary Kept by General Manuel de Mier y Terán on His 1828 Inspection of Texas*, Edited by Jack Jackson, Translated by John Wheat. (Austin: University of Texas Press, 2000).

[66]Tomás Almaguer, *Racial Fault-Lines: The Historical Origins of White Supremacy in California*. (Berkeley: University of California Press, 1994).

[67]John M. Nieto-Phillips, *The Language of Blood: The Making of Spanish-American Identity in New Mexico, 1880s-1930s* (Albuquerque: University of New Mexico Press, 2004).

[68]The term "dominance without hegemony" is borrowed from Ranajit Guha, *Domination without Hegemony: History and Power in Colonial India*, (Cambridge: Harvard University Press, 1997).

[69]Fernández's case is distinct with respect to the many petitioners of colonization projects in that he appeals to a number of occasions and thru the course of the 1870-1880. See AHTN, 1.29 (06), Exp. 316 and AHTN 1.29 (22), Legajo 8, Exp. 292.

[70]"Carta de Fernández a Secretaria de Fomento," in "Cónsul de México en Tucson Sobre Inmigración de Familias Mexicanas a Sonora, 25 Agosto 1881. In AHTN, 1.29 (22), Legajo 8, Expediente 292. Original: "solo hobro en mis centidos el berdadero patriotismo, el progreso de mi madre patria y regreso de tantos hijos del glorioso suelo Mexicano."

[71]AHTN, 1.29 (06), Exp. 316, "Maximo Fernández Pide A Nombre de Varios Mexicanos Residentes en el Condado de Monterrey CA, 1888." Original: "Ynfinidad de familias hay casi en la indigencia con mas o menos capacidad pero les falta la protección y si nuestro gobierno, no se las imparte para hacer su regreso a su país natal, no solo carecerá de estas cabezas de familia, y súbditos sullos, sino de tantos más que si hacen su regreso, lleban hoy consigo (que con sus hijos) los que con más demora en este país tomarán el carácter de 'Americanos' en vez de Mexicanos, como se desea."

[72]AHTN, 1.29 (06), Exp. 316, "Maximo Fernández Pide A Nombre de Varios Mexicanos Residentes en el Condado de Monterrey CA, 1888." Original: "Ynfinidad de familias hay casi en la indigencia con mas o menos capacidad pero les falta la protección y si nuestro gobierno, no se las imparte para hacer su regreso a su país natal, no solo carecerá de estas cabezas de familia, y súbditos sullos, sino de tantos más que si hacen su regreso, lleban hoy consigo (que con sus hijos) los que con más demora en este país tomarán el carácter de 'Americanos' en vez de Mexicanos, como se desea."

[73]"Carta del Jefe Político de Baja California a Ministro de Estado y del Despacho de Gobernación," 4 Noviembre 1871, AGN, Ramo Gobernación; 871 (11) 17 (2), "Repatriación de familias Mexicanas de California, 1871." Original: "En la alta California también existen familias Mexicanas que tienen deseos vehementes de volver al suelo patrio; pero que a más de carecer de recursos para verificarlo abrigan temor de no encontrar hogar ni trabajo que les asegure el sustento…tengo la conciencia que procuraría buena emigración para la frontera, en donde hay terrenos y minas que pueden proporcionar trabajo lucrativa a esos desgraciados Mexicanos que tienen el derecho de esperar pro-

tección de su gobierno, mientras ahora son esos terrenos y minas de ruines especulaciones."

[74]Carta de Armendáriz a Presidente de México, 30 Enero 1882; AHTN, 1.29 (06), Exp. 288, "Juan Armendáriz Solicita Regresar a La Republica Para Radicarse en Chihuahua," 1882. Original: "hace mucho tiempo vivo aquí disgusto en rason a que sufro como todos los de mi raza entre los extranjeros, estos últimos nos desprecian, cometiendo abusos contra nuestra raza y en conclusión no omiten medio de perjudicarnos en todo aquello que concierne a nuestro bien estar . . . "

[75]Carta de Armendáriz a Presidente de México, 30 Enero 1882; AHTN, 1.29 (06), Exp. 288. Original: "mis sentimientos son Mexicanos."

[76]Carta de Armendáriz a Admo Manuel Dias de La Vega, 20 Mayo 1882; AHTN, 1.29 (06), Exp. 288. Original: "pertenecia aun a Mejico y como en aquel tiempo yo no podía disponer de mi voluntad por encontrarme muy joben, y por lo mismo sugeto al dominio de mis padres, tuve que permanecer desarollandome bajo la formula del Govierno de EU que havian conseguido anexar a su nasion en lugar de mi nasimiento."

[77]His Personal Sentiments.

[78]Carta del Jefe de la Sección a Secretaria de Fomento, 1 Marzo 1883; AHTN, 1.29 (06), Exp. 288. Original: "la sección informa que la disposición relativa a la introducción de efectos, libre de derechos, por Mexicanos residentes en los EEUU que regresan a México solo se contrae a los efectos de uso, pero de ninguna manera a efectos de comercio como la que pretende el peticionario, pues de accederse a esta concesión, vendría a sentar un precedente funesto para el sistema hacendario. Además el comercio se desnivelaría con esta concesión supuesta que el Ciudadano Armendáriz introduciendo sus efectos libres de derechos, podía realizarlos a precios tan bajos que no podrían competir con ellos los comerciantes que introducen los suyos previo pago."

[79]"Matias Romero to Bayard," Washington, DC, February 10, 1888, 2:1266-1267. Quoted in Juan Mora Torres, *The Making of the Mexican Border: The State, Capitalism, and Society in Nuevo Léon, 1848-1910.* (Austin: University of Texas Press, 2001), 31.

[80]*Ibid*, 35.

[81]There are literally thousands of stories on this Social Fact. See Max Aub, "Discriminados. Paisanos lamentan maltratos en EU . . . y en México," 10 Febrero 2018, En *El Universal*. The byline to this piece is worth citing here as well: "Deportados o de Visita, connacionales se quejan del calvario que pasan entre 'los suyos' y la forma como las autoridades intentan sacarles mordidas, sin importar situación." http://www.eluniversal.com.mx/mundo/discriminados-paisanos-lamentan-maltratos-en-eu-y-en- mexico#.Wpm9xdfrerU.twitter

[82]The amount of "Cargo" or merchandise that comes across the border is in the billions of dollars, just as are the monies that are sent to Mexico each year. Last year those monies numbered almost $30 Billion USD in Remittances to Mexico—even as the current US Administration threatens to deport millions of ethnic Mexicans. See "En 2017 subieron 6.6% remesas a México; alcanza monto histórico," Enero 2, 2018, NOTIMEX, http://www.excelsior.com.mx/nacional/2018/02/01/1217483

[83]Again, there are many pieces on this question, but the following by Erick Suarez, is illustrative: "Exentan del pago de impuestos a los migrantes repatriados," 13 Marzo 2017, *El Heraldo de Chiapas*. Note the description where it states "LOS COMPATRIOTAS podrán introducir su equipaje con todo lo que incluye, electrodomésticos usados que formen parte de su mudanza y las herramientas que usaban para trabajar en la Unión Americana con un valor máximo de 5 mil dólares." The article interesting, also points out the many benefits and tax exemptions for potential repatriates. "Por medio de un comunicado, el órgano recaudador dijo que los compatriotas podrán introducir su equipaje con todo lo que incluye, electrodomésticos usados que formen parte de su mudanza y las herramientas que usaban para trabajar en la Unión Americana con un valor máximo de 5 mil dólares, todo libre de cargas impositivas. . . . Aunado a ello, los conciudadanos podrán importar de manera definitiva vehículos de segunda mano mediante un desembolso y un proceso burocrático a desahogarse en la aduana. Por último, las mexicanas y los mexicanos también podrán ingresar más de 10 mil dólares en efectivo, cheques o cualquier otro documento por cobrar, aunque antes el interesado deberá declarar la cantidad en la aduana, detalló." https://www.elheraldochiapas.com.mx/local/exentan-del-pago-de-impuestos-a-los-migrantes-repatriados/

[84]Again, there are many pieces on this question, but the following by Erick Suarez, is illustrative: "Exentan del pago de impuestos a los migrantes repatriados," 13 Marzo 2017, *El Heraldo de Chiapas*. Note the description where it states "LOS COMPATRIOTAS podrán introducir su equipaje con todo lo que incluye, electrodomésticos usados que formen parte de su mudanza y las herramientas que usaban para trabajar en la Unión Americana con un valor máximo de 5 mil dólares." The article interesting, also points out the many benefits and tax exemptions for potential repatriates. "Por medio de un comunicado, el órgano recaudador dijo que los compatriotas podrán introducir su equipaje con todo lo que incluye, electrodomésticos usados que formen parte de su mudanza y las herramientas que usaban para trabajar en la Unión Americana con un valor máximo de 5 mil dólares, todo libre de cargas impositivas . . . Aunado a ello, los conciudadanos podrán importar de manera definitiva vehículos de

segunda mano mediante un desembolso y un proceso burocrático a desahogarse en la aduana. Por último, las mexicanas y los mexicanos también podrán ingresar más de 10 mil dólares en efectivo, cheques o cualquier otro documento por cobrar, aunque antes el interesado deberá declarar la cantidad en la aduana, detalló." https://www. elheraldodechiapas.com.mx/local/exentan-del-pago-de-impuestos-a-los-migrantes-repatriados/

[85]See "Inmigrantes de Los Angeles California que han regresado a la Republica en los meses de Diciembre y Enero, Marzo 26 de 1883." In AHTN, 1.29 (32), Exp. 171. Original: " nuestros compatriotas comienzan a encontrarse en difíciles circunstancias en el citado estado de California y en el territorio de Arizona, donde la inmigración asiática y europea los deja sin ocupación lucrativa."

[86]Almaguer, *Racial Fault-Lines*, passim.

[87]"Inmigrantes de Los Angeles California que han regresado a la Republica en los meses de Diciembre y Enero, Marzo 26 de 1883." In AHTN, 1.29 (32), Exp. 171. Original: "que puede llegar a ser muy importante para nuestro pais y muy especialmente para nuestro despoblado estado."

[88]Carta de Felizardo Torres a Secretaria de Fomento, 27 Febrero 1883; AHTN 1.29 (22) L. 8 Exp. 289—"V. Mariscal, Gobernador del Estado de Sonora Pide Que el Supremo Gobierno, Facilite los Medios de Trasporte a Los Mexicanos Que se Hallan en los Estados Unidos y Desean Volver a Su Patria." Julio 3, 1876. Original: "los inmigrantes de que me ocupo, tienen el mérito importantísimo de que a pesar de su larga residencia en el extranjero no han querido perder su nacionalidad como mexicanos y lo justifican con certificados en toda forma de las autoridades de los Estados Unidos. me permito llamar atención de usted sobre esta prueba irrecusable de patriotismo."

[89]The obvious reference point are the Works by Manuel Gamio, PhD. See *Mexican Immigration to the United States: A Study of Human Migration and Adjustment*, (Chicago: The University of Chicago Press, 1930) and also *The Mexican Immigrant: His Life Story*, (Chicago: The University of Chicago Press, 1931).

[90]"Carta de Sección 1a Sr. Ministro de Fomento, 3 Febrero 1884," in AHTN, 1.29 (32), Exp. 138, "Quirino de la Garza solicita a nombre de él y de varias familias repatriarse a esta Republica para lo cual pide unos terrenos para poder colonizarlos, 28 Noviembre 1882." Original: "hoy como otra vez en caso análogo, la sección opina que el gobierno debe aprovechar todas las ocasiones que se le presenten, para hacer ingresar al país los Mexicanos que se hallan radicados fuera de el, tanto el objeto de aumentar el número de brazos, cuanto para poblar las fronteras que se hallan deshabilitadas y en las cuales no debe haber extranjeros."

[91]Wolfe, "Settler Colonialism," 390.

[92]AHTN, 1.29 (32), Exp. 138, "Quirino de la Garza solicita a nombre de él y de varias familias repatriarse a esta Republica para lo cual pide unos terrenos para poder colonizarlos, 28 Noviembre 1882." Also Carta de Armendáriz a Presidente de México, 30 Enero 1882; AHTN, 1.29 (06), Exp. 288, "Juan Armendáriz Solicita Regresar a La Republica Para Radicarse en Chihuahua," 1882.

[93]Gamio, *Mexican Immigration to the United States*, Chapter 9, 128-139.

[94]Alejandro Portes and Ruben Rumbaut, *Legacies: The Story of the Immigrant Second Generation*, (Berkeley: University of California Press and the Russell Sage Foundation, 2001), 284.

[95]Ernest Renan, "What is Nation?" Text of a Conference delivered at the Sorbone on March 11, 1882, In *Qu'est- ce qu'une nation?* (Paris, Presses-Pocket 1992). (Translated by Ethan Rundell).

[96]Carta de Quirino de la Garza al Sr. Cónsul de México, 20 Octubre 1882, AHTN, 1.29 (32), Exp. 138, "Quirino de la Garza solicita a nombre de él y de varias familias repatriarse a esta Republica para lo cual pide unos terrenos para poder colonizarlos, 28 Noviembre 1882." Original: "le seremos eternamente agradecidos y seremos sus mas adictos servidores, y en caso de contienda contra nuestra nación seremos los primeros en defender el honor de México, y nuestra gloria será derramar nuestra sangre en defensa de la patria, pues bien escarmentados estamos los que sufre fuera de ella."

[97]Harry Harootunian, *Overcome by Modernity: History, Culture, and Community in Interwar Japan*, (Princeton University Press, 2002).

[98]AHTN, 1.29 (32), Exp. 338, Castillo, Ramón—Solicita repatriarse pidiendo terreno considerándolo como colono." Enero 12, 1886. Original: ""como labrador [que] conoce mas el cultivo de algodón, del maíz, y del trigo al estilo de los Americanos y que jamás ha renunciado de su ciudadanía de Mexicano."

[99]"¿Y cuando major época para Sonora que aprovechando las circunstancias se atraiga bajo leyes liberales y protectoras la única emigración que le conviene por su idioma, religión y costumbres? Ahora pues es el tiempo de poblar sus fronteras con una población útil, enérgica, amaestrada por el contacto de la raza sajona, única que puede contener los avances del bárbaro apache." "Situación de los Hispano-Americanos en California," *El Clamor Público*, 23 Octubre 1855, no. 19.

[100]"Cesará desde luego la emigración y los mexicanos que hoy viven en el extranjero impedidos por su patriotismo y propia conveniencia, volverán a su país natal para restituirle sus fuerzas, impulsar su movimiento y contribuir a su engrandecimiento y prosperidad." Carta de M. Escalante, Cónsul en Tucson, Arizona a Secretaría de Relaciones Exteriores, 2 Febrero 1879," *Archivo*

Histórico de La Secretaría de Relaciones Exteriores, Exp. 11-2-106. f. 29-41.
[hereafter cited as AHSRE]

[101]My italics on *progress*. See "Fernández a Fomento," 20 Febrero 1888; AHTN, 1.29 (06), Exp. 316. Original: "se sabe Señor los inmensos deseos que vuestros sentimientos gratos elevan al engrandecimiento de nuestra madre patria fomentando con vuestra sabia inteligencia, y no menos elevado patriotismo, disponiendo, y fomentando, para el efecto con la iniciativa que al caso requiere de la colonización, cuya obra es tan benéfica para el desarrollo de un progreso tan ventajoso, y que hace elevar a un porvenir risueño, y no menos admirable a nuestro país."

[102]"Carta de P. Ornelas a SRE, 3 Noviembre 1887; AHSRE, 3741-21, F. 17-18. Orginal: "al repatriarse, llevan consigo conocimientos practicos del cultivo del algodón y de la cría de Ganado, dos recursos que constituyen una buena parte de la notable prosperidad del Estado de Texas."

[103]Carta de E.K. Coney a SRE, 16 Octubre 1890; AHSRE, Exp. 3741-21. Orignal: "tengo el intimo conocimiento de que seria de grande utilidad para nuestro país el regreso de mexicanos que después de haber estado por alguno años en los centros agricultores y manufactureros de este país llevarían consigo un caudal de conocimientos en diferentes artes que comunicar a nuestros agricultores e industriales."

[104]Edward Beatty, *Technology and the Search for Progress in Modern Mexico.* (University of California Press), 2015.

[105]See especially Part II on the "Business of Cattle," in particular Chapter 8 on the "Industrialization of Meat." Laurie Winn Carlson, *Cattle: An Informal Social History*, (Ivan R. Dee, 2002).

[106]AHTN 1.29 (06), Exp. 293. Original, "El gobierno de mi cargo, comprendiendo de los grandes bienes que traerá al estado la vuelta de esos emigrados que tan útiles serán, en momento que el movimiento que se está desarrollando en el, y que tan necesario los brazos para la industria y agricultura, y por otra parte por razones de patriotismo y humanidad se propone hacer cuantos esfuerzos le sean posibles con el objeto de arbitrar recursos para auxiliar a todos aquellos de nuestros compatriotas que desean volver a su país."

[107]Wolfe, "Settler Colonialism," 393-394.

La nación intervenida: el concepto de la nación puertorriqueña en las crónicas de Jesús Colón

Bruno Ríos
University of Houston

1. Introducción

La situación sociopolítica de Puerto Rico es única en el mundo. Se diferencia principalmente de otras naciones latinoamericanas cuyo proceso de formación comienza durante las primeras dos décadas del siglo XIX, constituyéndose como estados independientes. El caso de Puerto Rico es único dado que fue, en primera instancia, el último territorio colonial que perdiera España en 1898, obligada en gran medida por la presión militar y política de Estados Unidos terminada la guerra Español-Americana bajo los preceptos del Tratado de París, y terminando con el imperio español que dominó la mayor parte del nuevo mundo por unos tres siglos. Por otra parte, la condición de Puerto Rico se volvió peculiar al momento de pasar de un estado colonial a otro, de la corona española al capitalismo estadounidense.

Ante su historia, la situación actual de la nación puertorriqueña, a nivel político y sociocultural, no ha cambiado demasiado. Puerto Rico sigue siendo un territorio no incorporado a la unión americana de manera formal, y su estatus político desde 1952 sigue siendo el de "Estado Libre Asociado", es decir, un territorio que hasta cierto punto tiene autonomía para decidir el rumbo de su vida política, pero que a su vez, no tiene representatividad a nivel macro en las decisiones del país al que, supuestamente, pertenece. A la luz de dicha situación, la nación puertorriqueña se ha extendido de manera constante, mediante oleadas migratorias y exilios durante toda su historia, hacia Nueva York principalmente, pero también hacia otras ciudades de la América continental. Hasta cierto punto, propongo, la colonia puertorriqueña se ha desplazado, aún como colonia, a la *otra* isla, una extensión territorial de la que ya hay numerosos estudios. Esto está directamente relacionado con el hecho de que los puertorriqueños son ciudadanos norteamericanos desde principios del siglo XX, a pesar de que tampoco tienen representatividad política activa dentro del territorio de la unión: son ciudadanos, pero no pueden votar.

Esta compleja situación me lleva a preguntarme, si no se formó la nación al momento de obtener la independencia, o mejor dicho, el proceso de formación de nación como concepto general e imaginado de unidad no comenzó al momento de independizarse, como sucedió en las demás naciones latinoamericanas por obvias razones, ¿dónde se encuentra y cómo sucede el proceso de formación, y por ende de escritura, de la nación puertorriqueña? Una manera de responder a esta pregunta es trasladarnos a ciertos escritores que dan clave de cómo, ante una nación desterritorializada, se ha construido un concepto de nación que unifica, de una u otra manera, ese grupo étnico, social y político.

En este ensayo, rastreo el proceso de construcción de la nación que presenta Jesús Colón (1901-1974), un intelectual autodidacta puertorriqueño que fue uno de los cronistas hispanos más productivos e influyentes en la comunidad puertorriqueña en Nueva York durante gran parte del siglo XX. Mi enfoque se basa en la recopilación de sus crónicas periodísticas desde 1927 hasta 1946, publicadas bajo el nombre *Lo que el pueblo me dice . . .* en 2001, gracias al esfuerzo de recuperación de su material por parte del Recovering the US Hispanic Literary Heritage Program. En esta colección de crónicas y textos intergenéricos, publicados originalmente en los periódicos hispanos más influyentes de la ciudad como lo fueron *Gráfico, Pueblos Hispanos* y *Liberación,* los últimos dos de corte marxista y obrero, en español, representan las primeras dos etapas de su escritura periodística, la cual desembocará posteriormente en un paso natural hacia el inglés como lengua de escritura minoritaria. Estos textos son relevantes en la medida en la que conservan la lengua española como vehículo de la escritura y están, sobre todo, dirigidas hacia la comunidad puertorriqueña y de habla hispana de su época.

Lo que propongo es que, durante la escritura de estos textos, el concepto de nación que Colón acuña para Puerto Rico va evolucionando paulatinamente, sobre todo ante la situación colonial del territorio nacional. Colón propone diversos puntos de vista de la nación, que van trasladándose desde arriba hacia abajo, desde el cronista subido en un pedestal, mirando hacia abajo, hasta la postura radical del comunismo y de la izquierda obrera, terminando por un traslado del territorio de la isla original hacia la isla adoptiva, es decir la de Manhattan. La manera en la que Colón definirá al final el concepto de nación, es precisamente como algo sin un territorio fijo, una nación que no se encuentra ya atada a la isla de Puerto Rico, sino que se mantiene solamente en el imaginario de la comunidad, en el aire. La nación se traslada entre islas en un gesto transnacional de constante movimiento. Lo que esto implica, y que Colón articula, es que Puerto Rico es una nación intervenida hasta el día de hoy, una nación que mantiene y a la vez resiste la precariedad de su situación colonial, sobre todo en la actualidad con la crisis humanitaria y política provocada por los desastres naturales de 2017. Ya desde finales de los 40, Colón construyó a través de la opinión pública el modelo ideológico y político que sostienen hasta ahora los movimientos independentistas puertorriqueños y que se mantienen vigentes para entender la compleja relación entre la diáspora y la población de la isla. Para poder acercarme a estos conceptos, reviso brevemente las propuestas ya clásicas de Anderson y Bhabha para contraponerlas con la muy reciente propuesta de Kojin Karatani en su libro *The Structure of World History,* la cual les da una dimensión política y económica más compleja y actual.

2. Algunas consideraciones sobre el concepto de nación

El concepto de nación ha sido algo que, desde mediados del siglo anterior, se ha estudiado de manera constante a través de la producción teórica. Pero es en la práctica de la nación, es decir, en las producciones culturales y artísticas, en donde el concepto de nación ha encontrado un nicho en donde anclarse y mostrarse. Como asevera Nicolás Kanellos, la literatura hispana de los Estados Unidos es, en términos generales, altamente nacionalista, sobre todo por un un sentido de constante amenaza en la situación en contacto en la que se encuentra. ("La literatura hispana en los EE.UU. y el género autobiográfico" 225). Esto no solamente se da en los estratos sociales obreros, sino que también sucede en la clase media alta, desde los empresarios culturales y los escritores de mayor capacidad adquisitiva y prestigio social. Esta actitud nacionalista se exacerba al momento de escribir la nación, ya que la amenaza que representa la cultura norteamericana, con sus valores antagónicos y su materialismo cultural —desde su punto de vista—, es inminente. El solo hecho de convivir de manera constante entre ambos conceptos, el propio y el ajeno, hace que la literatura de inmigración hispana se vuelque hacia modelos claramente construidos como medidas de conservación de un concepto nacional que desea preservarse, que es, por ende, deseable, y que representa a la vez un anclaje hacia el pasado original.

El concepto de nación desde la teoría crítica se ha definido como un concepto de identificación comunal de un grupo determinado, ya sea desde diferentes puntos de vista, por elección o no. Raymond Williams advierte que el concepto de nación es complejo, debido a que existe un sobreposicionamiento constante entre grupos que tratan de unificarse: "The persistent overlap between grouping and political formation has been important, since claims to be a nation, and to have national rights, often envisaged the formation of a nation in the political sense, even against the will of an existing political nation which included and claimed the loyalty of this grouping." (160). La nación es entonces, según Williams, una formación política que unifica, incluso a costa de la oposición de ciertos grupos dentro de esa comunidad, el total de personas que lo integran. Esta conformación política tiene, necesariamente, connotaciones étnicas, lingüísticas y raciales, y se encuentra en constante transformación.

Esto tiene relación directa con la ya sumamente citada teoría de nación de Benedict Anderson, de donde parten la gran mayoría de los estudios contemporáneos sobre el tema. El concepto de "comunidad imaginada" ha sido muy útil al momento de pensar la nación, ya no como un anclaje necesario a un territorio determinado, sino como, precisamente, una comunidad imaginada que sea independiente del territorio y del Estado. La comunidad es lo que, además, le da un sentido de permanencia al concepto de nación. No es algo dado y eterno a priori, sino una construcción sociopolítica que subsana las escisiones que genera el Estado nacional. Por otro lado, y siguiendo a Anderson, Homi Bhabha propuso que la nación es siempre, a su vez, una práctica. La nación es también una narración que está en constante lucha consigo misma, y que representa, una idea que unifica a la nación como una fuerza simbólica (1). El *Volk,* es decir, el pueblo, es el que asume la necesaria tarea de desambiguar la idea de la nación, de construirla, de narrarla.

Sin embargo, ¿cómo aplicamos todo esto ante la situación de Puerto Rico? ¿Cómo leemos la nación puertorriqueña si su condición nacional, de Estado y de comunidad, está irrevocablemente ligada a su condición política colonial? En otras palabras, ¿cómo entendemos el Estado Libre Asociado, o el territorio no incorporado, en términos de "nación"? Es en este sentido en el que la propuesta de Karatani es sumamente útil, la cual se alimenta de manera central en las propuestas antes descritas. Karatani explica de manera minuciosa y extensa que la nación solamente es posible tras la construcción de una entidad anterior: el estado-capital. Karatani piensa la estructura de la historia mundial en términos de modos de intercambio como base económica de los grupos humanos. El modo de intercambio que genera al estado-capital es precisamente el de las monarquías absolutas, lo que después genera el estado-nacional: "The nation-state is a coupling together of two elements with different natures: nation and state. The nation-state's emergence however, requires the previous appearance of capital-state—that is, a coupling of capital with state. This was achieved with the absolute monarchies" (209).

Con la conjunción del estado-capital, el estado-nación es posible, ya que el modo de intercambio de las monarquías implicaba una distribución económica piramidal: desde arriba hacia abajo. Sin embargo, lo que propone Karatani es que la transición de la monarquía absoluta al estado capitalista moderno implica la necesidad de construir a la nación como un elemento imaginario, y por ende simbólico, que unifique la comunidad en contra de su modo de organización opresivo. La manera en que la nación nace es esa manera en la que es posible formar una triada: estado-nación-capital. La sustitución del sistema absolutista por el capitalismo genera la destrucción de un sentido de comunidad anterior, una comunidad que se encontraba unida por la reciprocidad. Antes del sistema del estado-capital, las comunidades, explica Karatani, subsistían en un modo de intercambio parecido al trueque, que además, era a su vez una ecología: una técnica de conservación que se heredaba. La generación nueva se encargaba de la supervivencia recíproca de la comunidad. Pero, con la instauración del sistema del estado-capital, ese sentido de comunidad se pierde: "The destruction of community at the hands of capital-state had, as Anderson indicates, enormous significance: the disappearance of the community meant the disappearance of a generational sense of time that had previously underwritten a sense of permanence" (215). Es por ello que la nación implica, a su vez, un sentido de permanencia: la comunidad imaginada de la nación incluye a los miembros de dicha comunidad en el pasado, en el presente y en el futuro.

En suma, la propuesta de Karatani es que la nación es pura nostalgia, una nostalgia de una comunidad imaginada que ha sido destruida por el estado-capital, y en los estados modernos, por el capitalismo. Esto se añade a la idea de que la nación es ambigua: "At the same time, however, as the imagined resolution to contradictions generated by capital-state, the nation also shields capital-state from collapse" (220). La nación entonces, a la vez, es una resistencia y un soporte para el estado capitalista, subsana sus contradicciones pero también las resiste. La nación es una estética nostálgica que se construye desde una narración fundacional, desde la construcción de un pasado original que sostenga lo que "realmente" es la comunidad.

Pero entonces, ¿no es esta precisamente la situación específica de Puerto Rico? Si tenemos un territorio, que es a su vez, estado-capital, aunque no sea propio, ¿no es la nación precisamente una idea que resiste y que subsana los embates del sistema capitalista norteamericano? Me parece que esa es la forma en la que tenemos que leer y pensar la nación puertorriqueña, sobre todo en la manera en que se basa su estética y su narración. La figura del Jíbaro, ese campesino rural que precede al capitalismo y al imperialismo estadounidense es el modelo nostálgico de la construcción de la nación tradicional. El caso de Puerto Rico es el de una nación con una ambigüedad territorial, que imaginariamente y transnacional-mente, mantienen la unidad simbólica de la comunidad ante un estado-capital que no es el propio. La triada no se da en la isla: Puerto Rico es pura nación.

3. Jesús Colón y la crónica como testigo

Para poder comprender de manera acertada la manera en que Colón escribe sus crónicas desde la gran manzana, es necesario primero entender qué significa realmente para un inmigrante puertorriqueño, de raza negra, autodidacta y posteriormente comunista, escribir en los Estados Unidos. La reflexión principal, que hay que hacer un poco por obligación, como anota Patricia Ortiz-Owen en su muy importante artículo sobre el hermano de Jesús, Joaquín Colón (1896-1964), es la del "incumplimiento de la historia periodística y literaria estadounidense, las cuales han ignorado en sus cánones narrativos fundacionales" (41-42) a escritores como Joaquín y Jesús Colón, así como otros escritores minoritarios como afroamericanos u otros grupos de latinos en los Estados Unidos. El completo desdén desde la tradición norteamericana es sistemático, y lo que ha generado es lo que asevera Nicolás Kanellos en su introducción a la revista del Centro de Estudios Puertorriqueños, que editó en 2014: "Sus obras sólo existen en el archivo y no gozan de ediciones accesibles, tal vez porque casi nunca se editaron en la Isla, o por lo obvio: los textos no fueron escritos en inglés" (6). Los textos que Jesús Colón escribió en los periódicos hispanos de la ciudad de Nueva York durante buena parte del siglo XX sólo han sido posible recuperarlos, sobre todo aquellos que fueron escritos en español, a través de un proceso arduo de trabajo con el archivo. Sin ese archivo, sin ese trabajo, no los tendríamos a la mano y el trabajo crítico con su obra sería imposible. Sin embargo, no todo es negativo. Como lo ha dicho Edwin Padilla en su introducción a la edición de *Lo que el pueblo me dice . . .* , Nueva York fue quizás el único lugar posible para que esta práctica escritural se llevara a cabo, ya que su voz seguramente hubiera sido ignorada de haber permanecido en la isla de Puerto Rico (xix).

Las crónicas escritas en español por Jesús Colón desde 1927 hasta 1946, año en el que da el salto definitivo al inglés y deja por un lado su participación en el periódico *Liberación,* son textos que evolucionan conforme cambia también la postura del que escribe. Padilla las separa en dos periodos: el primero que va desde 1927 con la participación de Colón en el periódico *Gráfico* bajo los seudónimos "Miquis Tiquis" y "Pericles Espada", como cronista, y que concluye en 1935 ya firmando con su nombre en el periódico *El curioso;* y el segundo periodo que abarca desde 1943 con la entrada de Jesús Colón al periódico comunista *Pueblos Hispanos* y que concluye en 1946 con su salida de

Liberación, también de corte comunista y apegado a la ideología de la izquierda obrera hispana.

En la primera etapa, encontramos a un Colón que se apega al género híbrido de la crónica y que escribe desde arriba, desde un pedestal en el cual mira a la comunidad puertorriqueña en Nueva York y en la isla. En este primer periodo, Colón asume el papel tradicional de la crónica, que es la de, con un humor característico, fungir como testigo didáctico de los aciertos y las debilidades de la comunidad. Pero no solamente eso: Colón también tiene un pie en Puerto Rico.

Colón asume el rol de testigo, pero también el de juez ante las fallas y los errores tradicionales de la comunidad puertorriqueña. Lo vemos en su crónica, que firma como Miquis Tiquis, "La brosa puertorriqueña":

> Mas, para el que haya tenido oportunidad para observar por algún tiempo el público, que se reúne el día de las entradas de los barcos, le es muy fácil separar la persona seria del asiduo desocupado, que a falta de la quora pa el cine, se va al muelle a reírse de la manera en que desembarcan sus paisanos. Este residuo social se apiña conjuntamente de la misma manera que las moléculas de afines propiedades se juntan en la materia. (12)

Hay un claro juicio ante lo que Colón llama la "brosa" puertorriqueña, la merma. Tomando esta cita de ejemplo, la primera etapa de Colón sacrifica, hasta cierto punto, el contenido nacionalista más duro, es decir, no hay un esfuerzo real y explícito por definir la nación. Más bien, la escritura se centra en lo anecdótico o lo didáctico, centrándose en el contraste entre los educados y los ignorantes. Es una postura clásica del género que, además, se repite constantemente en otros cronistas hispanos como Martí, O'Farril o Jorge Ulica.[1] En este sentido, la nación puertorriqueña no está presente de manera directa, sino que está representada por aquellos inmigrantes de baja educación que no se han adecuado al cambio de siglo, a la modernidad, a la nueva manera de ver el mundo. Esta postura cambiará radicalmente en el último momento de su primer periodo como cronista y que, a mi parecer, le costará su participación en *Gráfico:* la publicación de la serie de textos titulada "Cartas inmorales a mi novia", firmados con el seudónimo "Pericles Espada".

No es casualidad que Colón asuma la figura de Pericles, el gran orador y político de la época dorada ateniense, para firmar sus textos. Es en esta serie de crónicas intergenéricas, asumiendo el género epistolar como forma tradicional costumbrista, el escritor puertorriqueño comienza a hacer la transición a finales de los años veinte hacia el cronista que veremos después, ya enteramente comprometido con la ideología marxista y afiliado al Partido Comunista de los Estados Unidos.

Pericles Espada, asumiendo su rol político y la carga semántica de su nombre, genera su artificio al momento de escribir esta serie de cinco cartas a una "novia" alegórica. La novia, destinatario de las cartas, es una alegoría de la nación, de la isla. Puerto Rico es, en estas cartas, esa novia tradicional y anquilosada que sigue reproduciendo los valores coloniales de los cuales no puede desprenderse. En la primera carta, vemos cómo Colón comienza a entrar en la dinámica del aquí y el allá sin decirlo. Obviamente la novia todavía en la isla, y la carta viene desde Nueva York. Colón comienza a entonces a construir un concepto de nación que sustituirá la figura tradicional que impera en el conservadurismo de la isla:

> Yo quiero que desaparezcan los múltiples convencionalismos que se basan en la tradición y la costumbre. Ellos serán reemplazados por conocimientos, quizás más nuevos; pero probados, no por inconsciente repetición, sino por los dictados de las realidades y necesidades modernas. Trataré de sustituir la frase: "Porque mis abuelos así lo hacían"; con la de: "Porque la razón y la ciencia así lo dictan." (38)

La manera en que Colón traza su concepto de la "nueva nación" moderna está en directa contraposición con el tradicionalismo. Las costumbres son reemplazadas por la ciencia, por el conocimiento. Sin embargo, el cronista sigue instalado en su posición de privilegio, en una postura desde la cual se permite juzgar al otro: en una posición de verdad. Lo que denuncia Colón a través de la condena hacia la tradición es un artificio meramente ideológico. La ideología imperante en la isla es la del conservadurismo católico, que a los ojos de Colón no le dejan al pueblo puertorriqueño "levantarse", salir adelante, educarse. Lo vemos en la segunda carta:

> Mi clase no cree que esta organización social que nos sujeta y esclaviza con sus leyes y sus reglas, sus tradiciones y sus costumbres, sea la forma más perfecta a que puede aspirar el género humano. Nacimos y este hecho de importancia sólo para nuestra familia es proclamado oficialmente mediante un certificado del estado que notifica al mundo en general el simple y nada nuevo accidente de haber nacido. (40)

Es de interés notar que Colón habla de "mi clase" sin definir cuál es. La idea de que el escritor pertenece a una clase distinta a sus lectores, que idealmente serían aquellos que se encuentran en la isla, pero que en realidad son con quienes comparte comunidad, lo pone en aprietos. La idea de nación de Colón es, a su vez, una idea ambigua de sustitución que no se ha definido todavía. Es por ello que considero esta serie de textos como un proceso de transición en donde Colón todavía no ha entrado de lleno a la ideología marxista que permeará toda su producción posterior. En las Cartas, vemos una postura que contiene el germen de la izquierda obrera, un germen que irá creciendo y evolucionando para tratar de definir la comunidad imaginada de Puerto Rico.

En las cartas posteriores, Colón se entromete en un tema delicado: la religión. Es aquí en donde es posible notar el germen de las izquierdas marxistas que parece retomar el famosísimo argumento de Marx: "la religión es el opio del pueblo". Para Colón, la religión católica en la isla, y por ende en la tradición moral de "la novia", es una institución regente que domina el curso moral de la nación, y que es heredada de su condición colonial:

> Querer imponer un código moral a todo el mundo sería imposible. Las nuevas instituciones, las nuevas relaciones de los sexos, al igual que las nuevas posiciones económicas, y el avance y evolución de todas las ideas hacia el futuro, lo impedirán siempre así. La moral no es cuestión de emanación divina sino de evolución humana; que no es una ley incambiable, uniforme y sacrosanta, sino una ley social, multiforme adaptada al siglo y al país, a la época y al modo de pensar de los millares de pueblos que habitan nuestra tierra. (45)

El concepto de sustitución, de la contraposición entre el aquí y el allá, pareciera favorecer la manera en la que la separación moral entre Estado e Iglesia funciona en los Estados Unidos, y en los demás países desarrollados. Después, conforme avance el proceso, veremos que esto realmente es una ilusión: el modelo a seguir no es la unión americana, sino la unión soviética. La moralidad, que Colón asume como propia, que se contrapone como codificación conductual a lo que sucede en la isla, es la de un relativismo adelantado a su tiempo. En pocas palabras, la moralidad institucionalizada es la que, de uno u otro modo estanca a la nación, la envuelve en un velo de analfabetismo y no le permite crecer. Colón termina en su quinta carta de esta manera:

> Recibí tu retrato. Eres en él lo que siempre has sido: simple, inocente, sublimemente bella. Recibí tu carta. Escribes como siempre has escrito: interrogando, aconsejando, mas para aconsejar es preciso haber estudiado y meditado sobre aquello que queremos aconsejar. (47)

El artificio de la respuesta, de un destinatario que participa en el diálogo, le da dinamismo y verosimilitud ante el lector. Hay una respuesta clara en Colón: la nación es lo que siempre ha sido, inmutable, anquilosada, antigua. Y su respuesta, la del cronista, es la del conocimiento: la educación es la única manera en la que la nación puede construirse en su nueva condición. Pareciera que Colón, al final, está abogando por el avance irremediable del conocimiento y de la educación como fundamento para construir esa nación que, a pesar de todo, no es independiente. El sujeto escritor, el que enuncia en estos textos, está escindido entre el Estado y la Nación. La única manera en la que Colón puede escribir es la de asumir que es necesario dejar atrás los valores coloniales. Sin embargo, esto se complica al momento de darse cuenta de que la nación no es posible en la isla, ya que el elemento colonial sigue ahí: la nación no se ha independizado, sólo ha cambiado de manos.

4. La nación intervenida

Es en este esquema en donde Colón da el salto hacia la construcción de la nación desde el materialismo histórico. Colón asume que la nación puertorriqueña está en la colonización. Es consciente, además, de que la isla es partícipe directa en el conflicto de la Segunda Guerra Mundial, y que su comunidad provee mano de obra indispensable ante la empresa bélica. Ante esto, el cronista escribe el texto "El racionamiento de los alimentos", en donde denuncia de manera directa la forma en que el gobierno de los Estados Unidos está haciendo uso de su poder sobre el territorio sin darle los beneficios de ser parte de la unión:

> No es sólo como puertorriqueños que demandamos que se envíe comida a Puerto Rico. Es como amantes de la justicia y de la democracia y porque sabemos la poderosa arma que se pone en manos de la reacción de Puerto Rico y Estados Unidos —una reacción que es el brazo derecho del Eje— que pedimos que se envíen barcos con comestibles en cantidades suficientes para satisfacer las necesidades del pueblo puertorriqueño. Una cosa es racionar, con lo que estamos todos de acuerdo y otra cosa es condenar a la muerte paulatina a tres cuartas partes de una nación como lo es Puerto Rico. (93)

Es en este momento en que comenzamos a ver la estética de la narrativa de la nación que construye Colón. Los valores en este texto son claros: no es solamente los valores de la nación puertorriqueñas lo que valen, sino los valores universales que construyen el concepto de Nación en general, el de la justicia y la democracia. El racionamiento de alimentos que se da en la isla es apremiante durante la guerra, por lo que Colón se pronuncia para que el colonizador, que está explotando al pueblo puertorriqueño se haga cargo del asunto. Cabe aclarar que el punto de vista de Colón en este momento específico se generaliza, se internacionaliza. La guerra, hasta cierto punto, hace *tabula rasa,* iguala al "mundo libre" a través de una causa común: el fascismo en Europa. La guerra hace que Jesús Colón escriba múltiples textos sobre la amenaza fascista, ensalzando a su vez, el proyecto de nación soviético como la potencia que era en aquella época.

Es al finalizar la guerra que Colón volcará los ojos sobre Puerto Rico nuevamente. La construcción de la nación sirve, sobre todo en este periodo, como la define Karatani: en un sentido ambivalente que permite denunciar la convivencia del estado capitalista con el concepto de la nación en el sentido nostálgico del término. Colón aboga por la construcción de la nación que precede al estado colonial capitalista. Lo vemos en el texto "Los otros Estados Unidos":

> También hay dos Puerto Ricos. El Puerto Rico de los vende patrias. El Puerto Rico del naciente capitalismo nativo que hace causa común con el capitalismo absentista del Norte, pagando salarios de indigencia al proletariado puertorriqueño; el Puerto Rico de los esbirros que ametrallan al pueblo que marcha en un domingo de ramos o que clama por un pedazo de pan más en una huelga. Hay también un Puerto Rico glorioso de la tradición revolucionaria: el Puerto Rico de Betances y Albizu Campos, el de Ruiz Belvis y Hostos; el Puerto Rico que un día ha de asombrar al mundo. (109)

La nación puertorriqueña en este caso está escindida, ahora, por dos discursos opuestos que se enfrentan para tener la hegemonía ideológica. Queda muy claro que la imposición del estado capitalista se ha enraizado en la ideología de la isla, y que ha generado lo que Colón llama "capitalismo nativo". Lo interesante es que la contraposición ante ese discurso de los "vende patrias" es el de los intelectuales nacionalistas que, eventualmente, se exilian en los Estados Unidos. El nexo es sutil pero evidente: la confusión entre nación y nacionalismo se subsana al momento de que Colón asocia la ideología nacionalista puertorriqueña con el comunismo. Esto se logra también con un proceso de desterritorialización. Colón comienza pronto a ocuparse de utilizar la crónica, sobre todo en los periódicos de su segundo periodo, como un modo de propaganda y de concientización de la opinión pública. Es imperativo para Colón generar una influencia política e ideológica en la comunidad puertorriqueña de Nueva York, ya que se encuentra convencido de que esa es la única manera de generar un cambio: desde afuera hacia adentro. En su crónica "Somos muy pequeños para ser libres", el cronista comienza de lleno a abogar por la independencia de Puerto Rico. Asume ya que la condición colonial imperialista en la que se encuentra es lo que tiene a la isla sumida en la miseria. Sin embargo, el proceso de independencia implica también un proceso de construcción de la nación a nivel político, económico y social. Colón dice:

los pueblos no se juzgan por la extensión física de sus tierras sino por la posición geográfica de la misma, los grandes hombres y las provechosas ideas que hombre nacidos en un país han aportado al pensamiento y a la acción universal, sobre todo, a la clase de pueblo con que cuenta la nación a la que nos referimos. (119)

La única manera que Colón encuentra para construir una justificación natural, compartida por otras naciones, que promueva en la opinión pública la idea de independencia, es la justificación ideológica. Lo que Colón hace en esta crónica, y lo hace de manera brillante, es desterritorializar la nación. Al momento de decir que un pueblo no puede ser juzgado por la extensión de su territorio, el cronista está fundamentando la nación en el terreno de las ideas, de la ideología, que conlleva a la vez a lo que dice Karatani: su permanencia. La única manera en la que Puerto Rico puede ser una nación es la de la validez y potencia de sus ideas. Pero esto no es todo, el territorio tiene un valor. En una franca utopía romántica y económica: "La futura república puertorriqueña, por su posición en este mapa, será un gran centro marítimo y aéreo cuya cultura propia será ampliada y enriquecida día a día por el pensar y el sentir del mundo que pasa por su cielo y por sus puertos" (119). La construcción política desterritorializada se ancla en una idea: la idea geográfica de un punto modular que, debido al tiempo en el que se encuentra, en plena posguerra y el inicio de la Guerra Fría, sería estratégico para la Unión Soviética.

No cabe duda de que Colón está pensando en la URSS como modelo nacional. Ya en el texto "Puerto Rico es también una nación", se asume de manera explícita:

Puerto Rico es también una nación; o sea, "una comunidad estable, históricamente formada, de idioma, de territorio, de vida económica y de psicología, que se traducen en una comunidad de cultura", segunda la moderna definición de este concepto. (141)

El concepto que Colón utiliza para definir a la nación puertorriqueña es una cita exacta de Joseph Stalin, una definición que se acuña como formato ideológico que a nivel macro abarca la totalidad del proyecto de la Unión Soviética. Irónicamente, la estética de la nación, está colonizada por la ideología comunista. Y por ende, el enemigo de la nación ya no es el fascismo, sino el imperialismo estadounidense: "Si algo tenemos los puertorriqueños, los VERDADEROS puertorriqueños, superior a los norteamericanos, es la completa ausencia de prejuicios raciales en nuestra personalidad como pueblo" (141-142). El comparativo no es gratuito: el imperialismo norteamericano es, en este caso, fascista. El hecho de asumir que la nación puertorriqueña no tiene prejuicios raciales no es solamente absurdo, es un gesto completamente ideológico. La superioridad racial de los gobiernos fascistas es ahora antepuesta con el prejuicio racial estadounidense. La nación puertorriqueña es entonces una nación con una historia compartida y un pasado original (pre-capitalista), con una lengua (el español), con un territorio (la isla), con una vida económica (no hay respuesta, la respuesta es la desterritorialización), y con vida psicológica (la nación verdadera, la nación comunista), y una cultura (la diáspora).

Es en esta definición en donde culmina la empresa de Colón que, sin embargo, se halla en problemas. El hecho de desterritorializar a la nación en el ámbito de las ideas implica incluir, de una u otra manera, a la comunidad puertorriqueña en Nueva York. Es ahí en donde la definición de Stalin falla para Puerto Rico: la comunidad homogénea no existe dentro de un territorio común, sino que existe solamente en el concepto de nación ante un territorio escindido. La nación puertorriqueña es, ante todo, una comunidad transnacional, una comunidad que se encuentra fundamentalmente dividida entre la isla y la comunidad "nuyorican". Colón lo expresa muy claramente en su texto "Hace falta una estatua":

> Nosotros también tenemos nuestro barrio puertorriqueño: nuestra "Pequeña Borinquen". Desde la calle novecientos hasta la ciento dieciséis y desde la avenida Lexington hasta la avenida Manhattan, está radicada la ciudad puertorriqueña de más habitantes en todo el mundo, incluyendo a Puerto Rico. Ciento cincuenta mil puertorriqueños viviendo en un radio de cien bloques cuadrados. (151)

Es en este punto en donde Colón comienza, ya al final de su segundo período, a hacer una transición que lo llevará a pensar más en la comunidad puertorriqueña de la diáspora que en la isla. Dicha transición culminará en 1961, casi 20 años después, con la publicación de su libro *A Puerto Rican in New York,* que presenta una recopilación de crónicas en inglés. Esto habla de que la desterritorialización de la nación puertorriqueña se completa. Ya no existe un anclaje a la isla para construir la nación, sino que la nación es solamente posible en su constante movimiento. La extensión territorial de la isla de Puerto Rico a Manhattan es la solución imaginada de la escisión entre Estado y Nación.

5. Conclusiones

La evolución que se presenta en las crónicas escritas por Jesús Colón desde 1927 hasta 1946 dejan en claro que la intencionalidad de construir una nación puertorriqueña anclada en la isla es infructuosa. Esto se debe precisamente a la idea central de que la situación sociopolítica de Puerto Rico es disímil a otros procesos nacionales latinoamericanos. La nación puertorriqueña es una nación ya no desterritorializada, sino que es una nación transnacional, una nación que se encuentra ubicada en el tránsito continuo entre comunidades. El tránsito es lo que unifica su cohesión cultural. A final, no es posible, como lo entiende bien Jesús Colón, pensar en la comunidad puertorriqueña sin pensar en la diáspora "nuyorican". La construcción de una narrativa que explique la nación desembocará en un discurso doble, un discurso que dialoga entre lenguas, entre el inglés y el español, y que finalmente se construirá a sí misma una identidad propia, híbrida, ni puertorriqueña ni estadounidense. Hasta los últimos días de su vida, como bien argumenta Juan Flores en su admirable libro *Divided Borders,* Colón mantuvo el espíritu doble de la lucha obrera y de la identidad puertorriqueña, o en sus palabras, "he identified himself as a Puerto Rican and as a worker: as a Puerto Rican standing for independence from colonialism, and as a worker in the United States fighting for economic and political change" (136). Las crónicas en español de Colón reiteran la convicción de pensar la condición colonial puertorriqueña desde tierras norteamericanas, con una empatía creciente por la clase trabajadora y los más desprotegidos.

Asimismo, los textos de Colón mantienen una vigencia sorprendente. Los controversiales plebiscitos de 2012 y de 2017, en los que la gran mayoría de los electores se pronunciaron a favor de la anexión de Puerto Rico como el estado número 51 de la unión —a pesar de que menos de un cuarto de posibles votantes participó en el último—, sólo reafirman la compleja situación económica, social, y política en la que se encuentra la nación puertorriqueña en el presente. Con una población empobrecida, una situación legal de nula representatividad política, así como la eterna pugna por definir un concepto de nación que es pura potencia, que aún representa algo que está por venir, Puerto Rico sigue siendo una nación intervenida que se sostiene de forma simbólica en la relación entre la diáspora y la isla. A la situación actual es necesario añadirle la hondísima crisis que provocaron los huracanes Irma y María en 2017, justo después del voto del plebiscito. En comparación con la respuesta que el gobierno federal norteamericano tuvo ante el desastroso Huracán Harvey en Texas, Puerto Rico sigue sufriendo el desdén político por ser un territorio colonizado más que considerarse una parte integral de la identidad nacional norteamericana. Esto se tradujo en una respuesta lenta y abismalmente menor que vino a agravar la ya precaria situación económica y social de la isla. Con esto en mente, creo que la respuesta de Jesús Colón ante la situación actual de la comunidad puertorriqueña sería la misma que tuvo durante la Segunda Guerra Mundial: manden comida a Puerto Rico, manden la ayuda necesaria, no las sobras; honren lo que los puertorriqueños le han dado a la nación americana desde siempre, su mano de obra, su sudor, su sufrimiento. Y es ante el desastre de la isla, ante la poquísima ayuda y el hambre, la falta de luz y de servicios básicos, que el concepto de nación híbrida y en tránsito al que llega

Colón cobra aún mayor relevancia. Hoy en día, los vínculos que anclan a la comunidad en una idea simbólica de la nación en tránsito son todavía más fuertes tras la destrucción de los desastres naturales de 2017. Son esos vínculos, incluso en su constante movimiento, lo que resiste y a la vez subsana la pobre respuesta del Estado-Capital para con la isla. En otras palabras, es la nación intervenida, alejada de su idealización nostálgica, la que se mantiene vigente frente a la precariedad de sus condiciones de posibilidad.

Obras citadas

Anderson, Benedict. *Imagined Communities*. Verso, 2006. Bhabha, Homi K. *Nation and Narration*. Routledge, 1990.

Colón, Jesús. *Lo que el pueblo me dice...* Arte Público Press, 2001.

Flores, Juan. *Divided Borders. Essays on Puerto Rican Identity*. Arte Público Press, 1993. Kanellos, Nicolás. "Introducción" *Centro Journal* XXVI.1, 2014, pp. 4-9.

___. "La literatura hispana en los EE.UU. y el género autobiográfico." *Hispanos en los Estados*

Unidos. Ed. Rodolfo J. Cortina, M y Alberto Moncada. Ediciones de Cultura Hispánica, 1988, pp. 220-230.

Karatani, Kojin. *The Structure of World History*. Verso, 2013.

Ortiz-Owens, Patricia. "Discurso de origen e identidad en la narrativa de Joaquín Colón López." *Centro Journal* XXVI.1, 2014, pp. 34-55.

Padilla Aponte, Edwin Karli. "Introducción." Colón, Jesús. *Lo que el pueblo me dice . . .* Arte Público Press, 2001, pp. xiii-xxxix.

Williams, Raymond. *Keywords*. Oxford University Press, 2014.

Notas

[1]José Martí (1853-1895), el gran cronista cubano del exilio, escribió sus crónicas para construir un modelo de nación cubana desde el contraste entre el aquí y el allá. Por otro lado, Alberto O'Farril (1899-?) que también escribió durante un largo periodo en *Gráfico* y que llegó a ser su director, publicó sus "Pegas suaves" satirizando la comunidad hispana. Finalmente, Jorge Ulica, seudónimo de Julio G. Arce (1870-1926), cronista mexicano, publicó sus *Crónicas diabólicas* en el diario La Crónica de San Francisco, en donde, asumiendo el rol de moralista, se burlaba de los inmigrantes mexicanos a través de su lenguaje y de su postura de clase alta.

La nostalgia de la patria / la patria nostálgica: una aproximación a la vida y obra de César G. Torres

Juan Carlos Rozo Gálvez
University of Houston

I. Introducción

Después de consultar una docena de antologías de literatura puertorriqueña y de literatura hispana en los Estados Unidos, y corroborar que el poeta César Gilberto Torres solo se encuentra en una de estas (*Papiros de Babel: antología de la poesía puertorriqueña en Nueva York*),[1] es evidente que el autor puertorriqueño hace parte de un conjunto de escritores relegados, por diversas razones, a los márgenes del denominado canon literario. No obstante, la estimable producción literaria del autor puertorriqueño —seis poemarios y numerosos textos publicados en periódicos hispanos de la ciudad de Nueva York—, la mención de su nombre se reduce a semblanzas breves y esporádicas en catálogos de autores puertorriqueños, sin ninguna mención o inclusión de fragmentos específicos de su obra. Es innegable que uno de los efectos colaterales del proceso antológico es la exclusión de algunas obras y/o autores, debido a numerosos factores como derechos de reproducción, costos de adquisición de dichos derechos, razones estéticas, temáticas y/o estilísticas, etcétera; sin embargo, debido a que cada antología da prioridad a uno u otro factor, podría pensarse que la poesía de César G. Torres podría tener cabida en, al menos, un par de tantas.

En este artículo me propongo indagar acerca de las razones por las que César G. Torres se encuentra semienterrado en el archivo y ausente en las antologías de poesía puertorriqueña. Asimismo, proveeré una semblanza biográfica en la que se resalten los hechos que influyeron en la obra de Torres y, finalmente, realizaré un análisis preliminar de su poética, con el fin de mostrar cómo

241

su producción dialoga con la producción literaria de otros autores puerto-rriqueños. A través del análisis de su poética, así como de su contextualización dentro del devenir histórico de la isla y de la colonia puertorriqueña en los Estados Unidos, se sustentará el argumento a favor de la recuperación, preservación y estudio de la obra de César G. Torres, así como su inclusión en futuras antologías de literatura puertorriqueña y/o de literatura hispana en los Estados Unidos.

II. Acerca de César G. Torres:

César Gilberto Torres Rodríguez, poeta, promotor cultural y activista políti-co, nació en San Sebastián del Pepino, Puerto Rico, el 31 de diciembre de 1912. Cabe mencionar que San Sebastián del Pepino, municipio al centro-occidente de la isla, fue una de las poblaciones que tuvo incidencia directa en el Grito de Lares de 1898, movimiento de insurrección en aras de la independencia de Puer-to Rico. La relación entre San Sebastián y el Grito de Lares, de acuerdo con el escritor y periodista Carlos López Dzur, ha hecho que los pepinianos —como se les conoce a los oriundos de San Sebastián— expresen una actitud patente de compromiso con la independencia de Puerto Rico ("El independentismo en San Sebastián"). En efecto, César Torres, como muchos pepinianos, manifestó a través de su obra una firme adhesión al proyecto independentista.

También es importante mencionar que la familia de César Torres era de clase media-baja. Su padre, Segismundo Torres Avilés, fue empleado público (inspector del departamento de salubridad) y su madre, Pilar Rodríguez Hernán-dez —quien murió cuando César tenía 12 años— fue ama de casa (Betanzos Palacios 5). La temprana muerte de su madre resultó en la interrupción de los estudios de César, quien únicamente llegó a cursar el octavo grado (López, "César Gilberto Torres"). Lo anterior pone de manifiesto el carácter autodidacta de su formación académica, intelectual y literaria, y el cual tendrá incidencia directa en la estética y el estilo del poeta. Por otra parte, el hecho de que sus primeros poemas hayan sido publicados en un folleto titulado "Flores entre lágrimas", en 1922 (Arana Soto 184),[2] da fe de que la vocación literaria se ma-nifestó en Torres a muy temprana edad.

Un último evento que repercutió en la etapa de formación de César G. To-rres antes de emigrar a Nueva York fue su afiliación al Partido Nacionalista de Puerto Rico, del cual fue miembro activo "desde los días en que el [político independentista] Dr. Pedro Albizu Campos reorganizara dicho movimiento patriótico hasta que el mismo fuera desarticulado en los primeros años de la década de los cincuenta" (López-Adorno 113). De la amistad que César Torres entabla con Albizu Campos, presidente del PNPR desde 1930, quedan como prueba algunos poemas que Torres le dedica, como "Albizu" en que encon-tramos los siguientes versos: "Todo el aire se aroma con tu bendito nombre/ y hasta en las cunas duermen soñando con Albizu/ los hombres del futuro que harán libre la patria . . . " (Torres "Pasión del alma" 24). Otro ejemplo es "El medallón", también titulado "El ladrón", en el que Torres se refiere a Albizu como "El maestro" o "la mano que cultiva flores" ("El ladrón"). Es evidente que la relación entre Torres y Albizu afianzó el compromiso del poeta pepiniano con el movimiento independentista. Compromiso que, adicionalmente, dio pie a que Torres ocupara puestos de liderazgo regional en la isla y también asegurara la continuidad de su actividad política en Nueva York.

En cuanto a la fecha en que César Torres emigró a Nueva York, no hay suficiente certeza. Según Pedro López-Adorno, Torres partió a Nueva York cuando tenía 18 años, es decir en 1930 (113). El periodista y escritor Mario López Ortiz, por otra parte, afirma que el año de partida fue 1935. Aunque no se pueda brindar una fecha exacta, es claro que César Torres emigró a Nueva York durante la primera mitad de los treinta. De acuerdo a la semblanza biográfica que provee Mario López Ortiz, además, se sabe que César Torres radicó inicialmente en el Barrio Latino, ubicado en la parte oriental de Harlem, y posteriormente se mudó a Brooklyn. Desde su llegada a Nueva York el poeta puertorriqueño se sostuvo económicamente como empleado en distintas fábricas ("César Gilberto Torres"). Lo anterior es fundamental en cuanto que su condición obrera y su experiencia directa de las circunstancias del proletariado inmigrante en la metrópoli norteamericana delinearon y configuraron gran parte de su discurso poético.

Aun cuando César Torres tuvo que subsistir como obrero —lo que implica que gran parte de su tiempo fue invertido en el trabajo de fábrica— su interés por la literatura y la cultura nunca pasó a un segundo orden. Prueba de dicho interés es la fundación del Círculo de Escritores y Poetas Iberoamericanos (CEPI), en la que también participaron los españoles Odón Betanzos Palacios y Federico Onís, además del también puertorriqueño Juan Avilés Medina (López Ortiz "César Gilberto Torres"). El CEPI, con base en Manhattan y todavía existente, fungió como punto de encuentro de literatos, escritores y periodistas, así como de promoción cultural (López- Adorno 113). Consta, como ejemplo de las actividades organizadas por el CEPI (presidida entonces por Torres), el homenaje al poeta puertorriqueño Felipe Arana, el cual se realizó en conjunto con la revista "Albor" ("Homenaje a Felipe Arana"). Asimismo, Torres fue fundador de otras dos instituciones culturales: Amantes de la Poesía y Casa de San Sebastián, puntos de encuentro cultural en Nueva York (Betanzos Palacios 5). Como muestra final de la participación activa de César G. Torres en el ámbito cultural neoyorquino está su asistencia a reuniones artísticas como la que organizaba el Club Cultural Hispano del Bronx, en las que se ofrecían recitales de poesía y pequeños conciertos. En una de estas reuniones, en honor a Puerto Rico, César G. Torres recitó "El ladrón" (dedicado a Albizu Campos), el cual fue recibido con "cálidos aplausos" ("Club Cultural Hispano del Bronx").

Aparte del cultural, César G. Torres también se destacó por su participación activa en el ámbito político y por su presencia constante en movimientos sociales puertorriqueños e hispanos en general; activismo que indudablemente nutrió la poética de Torres y el cual se enmarcó en una época sumamente convulsa tanto en Puerto Rico como en Nueva York, sobre todo durante las décadas de los treinta y cuarenta. La tensa relación política entre los Estados Unidos y Puerto Rico responde a numerosas razones que se remontan a 1898, cuando Puerto Rico pasó a ser, en sus términos más amplios, una colonia de los Estados Unidos. Aunque la exploración de dichas razones se desborda de los límites y propósitos de este ensayo, sí conviene profundizar en el movimiento nacionalista ya que este toca las fibras ideológicas de César G. Torres, además de tener incidencia directa en la problemática de las décadas mencionadas.

En "Imprisonment and Colonial Domination, 1898-1958", José Paralitici estudia la forma en que el gobierno de los Estados Unidos ha perseguido y oprimido, por medio de la encarcelación, cualquier manifestación nacionalista o conato independentista, sobre todo cuando se conformó el Partido Nacionalista de Puerto Rico como fuerza organizada (67-68). Sin embargo, esta persecución se intensificó una vez que Pedro Albizu Campos tomó las riendas del partido y, bajo su mando, "the Nationalist movement broke away from its traditional method of moderate opposition" (Paralitici 71). Como consecuencia, el gobierno estadounidense militarizó el gobierno puertorriqueño, reestructurándolo y asignando a oficiales de las fuerzas armadas estadounidenses a cargos en las tres ramas del poder público (71). De la misma manera, el gobierno estadounidense propició una ola significativa de arrestos: "The incarceration of Nationalists began in early 1936, after several confrontations and judicial cases. The first case was that of poet Juan Antonio Corretjer, at the time secretary general of the Nationalist Party and director of the Nationalist paper, *La Palabra* . . . " (Paralitici 71).

A esta ola de arrestos, que continuaría después de la Segunda Guerra Mundial, se sumaron otros hechos que recrudecieron la tensión entre el movimiento nacionalista y los Estados Undidos; uno de ellos fue la Masacre de Ponce, que ocurrió el 21 de marzo de 1937. Aquel día, domingo de ramos, una manifestación organizada por el PNPR protestaba en contra de la recurrente violación de los derechos civiles de los puertorriqueños por parte del gobierno y las fuerzas armadas estadounidenses; la respuesta de la policía resultó en 19 personas muertas y cientos de heridos (Paralitici 72). Este evento recobraría un carácter emblemático en la lucha independentista y en el imaginario puertorriqueño, y se tornaría en un referente capital para César Torres y, en general, para el movimiento nacionalista. Un ejemplo de ello es la reunión anual que la Junta Nacionalista Puertorriqueña de Nueva York organizó para conmemorar el aniversario de la masacre. El 9 de abril de 1949, en el periódico *Liberación*, se publicó una nota en la que el poeta apareció como uno de los concurrentes a la conmemoración, participando además como orador.

Ahora bien, el PNPR no fue el único movimiento en el que César Torres participó: para finales de los años 30 emergieron otros grupos como la Confederación de Sociedades Puertorriqueñas, de la cual también fue miembro el poeta puertorriqueño (Sánchez Korrol 217). Un año después de la Masacre de Ponce, Torres tuvo un primer desencuentro con la ley, ya que fue "condenado a año y medio de prisión, acusado por encabezar un atentado contra el Cuerpo de la Detective de [Brooklyn], en represalia por la invasión realizada por agentes del referido organismo al Cuartel Nacionalista. Para su suerte, la sentencia le fue suspendida" (López Ortiz "César . . . ").

Por último, durante la Segunda Guerra Mundial se produjo una segunda ola de arrestos a puertorriqueños por resistirse a prestar el servicio militar obligatorio. Si bien los puertorriqueños de la isla fueron los primeros implicados, los embates de esta nueva ola de arrestos terminaron por extenderse a los puertorriqueños que vivían en Nueva York. En palabras de Paralitici, "Nationalists residing in New York also resisted the draft. Four cases have been identified, three of them members of the Nationalist Party Board: Amaury Ruiz, Roberto Acevedo, and César G. Torres Rodríguez" (75-76). Torres, por su parte, fue condenado a cuatro años de prisión, "cumpliendo los primeros dos en una cárcel de Lewisburg, Pennsylvania (1943-1945) y, los dos restantes, en el penal de Danburry, Connecticut (1945-1947)" (López Ortiz "César . . . "). Después de esta etapa convulsa, César G. Torres retornó a sus labores en fábricas y a la poesía. Mientras residió en Nueva York, César G. Torres también participó en la prensa puertorriqueña y latina de la metrópoli estadounidense. Varios poemas y artículos de su autoría fueron publicados en diarios como *Eco Antillano* (semanario progresista, 1941-1942), *Pueblos Hispanos* (1943-1944, en el que concordó con Jesús Colón), y *Ecos de Nueva York* (1946-1957). Finalmente, regresó a su natal San Sebastián del Pepino en 1975, donde radicó por el resto de su vida. César Gilberto Torres falleció en 1994.

III. La obra de César G. Torres

Además de los poemas que publicó en periódicos, revistas literarias y folletos de poesía como "Flores entre lágrimas", "El Gorrión", "Palique", y "Maguey" (López Ortiz "César . . . "), César G. Torres fue autor de seis poemarios: *Flores entre páginas* (Imprenta Cardona, 1930-1932); *Abanico de fuego* (Editorial Puerto Rico Inc., 1945); *Aromas de limón* (Azteca Press, 1949); *Resolana* (antología poética), (Editorial Mensaje, 1972); *Guanín* (Imprenta Hostos, 1981) y *Pasión del alma* (Moca, 1989).[3] Aunque algunos de sus poemarios se publicaron en Puerto Rico, Torres escribió la mayoría de su obra en Nueva York, y dicha condición —la de un obrero inmigrante en la metrópoli— permeó su obra poética. Sin embargo, profundizaré en el análisis de este contexto de inmigración más adelante; es necesario, en primer lugar, rastrear la evolución estilística y temática del poeta pepiniano, y encontrar así los denominadores comunes que dejan al descubierto sus preocupaciones estéticas y poéticas. Asimismo, me enfoco en tres poemarios específicos: *Aromas de limón, Resolana* y *Pasión del alma*, ya que es en éstos en donde se hace evidente que, aparte de la cuestión política y la vida del obrero inmigrante —temas fundamentales para el autor— el amor, la patria, el jíbaro, entre otros, son tópicos alrededor de los que también gravita la poesía de Torres (Ríos Ríos 2-3).

Además de la diversidad temática, en la obra de Torres se hace patente la forma en que el poeta recurre a dispositivos estéticos y estilísticos de varios movimientos literarios. Por ejemplo, en *Aromas de limón,* publicado en 1949, se aprecia la apelación a una imaginería y recursos herederos del romanticismo latinoamericano. Uno de esos recursos tiene que ver con la insistencia en la exuberancia de la naturaleza como articulación de la excepcionalidad nacional, aunque dicha articulación se haya realizado por medio de lo que el crítico Haroldo de Campos denominó una "superación de los lenguajes exclusivos" (281-283). En otras palabras, en Torres se observa la apelación a la imaginería criolla y a la reconstrucción de la nación desde sus particularidades geográficas y naturales, y dicha reconstrucción se lleva a cabo desde un registro que, aunque lírico todavía, deja de ser exclusivo. Un ejemplo de ello se aprecia en "Ansias criollas":

Sólo quiero en el bosque una cabaña,
y amar en el crepúsculo violeta
la hermosa floración de la montaña.
¡Vestir de jíbaro! Herir con la piqueta
de la amorosa tierra las entrañas;
....
Jugarle la peseta al gallo pinto,
Y demostrar que soy dos veces hombre. (*Aromas de limón,* 33)

Por otra parte, en *Aromas de limón* se atisba también una temática de corte social y político que se hará más recurrente en publicaciones posteriores. De igual manera, el tema de la inmigración pasa a ocupar un lugar estimable en la obra en virtud de que para cuando se publica *Aromas de limón* Torres ha vivido en los Estados Unidos por casi veinte años. Hay, además, un claro sesgo patriótico en su poética y una comparación latente entre el aquí (que desde 1930 fue Nueva York), y el allá (su natal Puerto Rico). Por consiguiente, la obra de Torres puede enmarcarse dentro de lo que se entiende como literatura de inmigración; como el crítico Nicolás Kanellos ha demostrado, la literatura de inmigración se caracteriza por su relación estrecha con la clase obrera, por la promoción del nacionalismo, el rechazo de mitos como el "sueño americano" o el "crisol de razas", así como el recelo a la aculturación en pos de la preservación de la cultura y la lengua de la tierra natal, entre otros (xxxiii). Ciertamente, dichas características se reflejan en la poesía de César G. Torres, ya que "el amor, la patria y el proletariado puertorriqueño son las tres áreas temáticas más representativas de su obra" (López-Adorno 114); Lo anterior es evidente en el poema "Obrero", repleto de versos desesperanzados y críticos de la explotación a manos del "blanquito", es decir, el estadounidense: "Obrero: el señorito/ te pide la sangre;/ te pide la hija;/ te explota la carne." (*Aromas de limón* 34). Del mismo modo, en la poesía de César Torres se pone de manifiesto su preocupación por la problemática del idioma entre los hispanos que viven en los Estados Unidos. En el poema "Sátira", por ejemplo, Torres critica la rapidez con que, según el poeta, el inmigrante hispano olvida su lengua nativa:

> Muchos hispanos que vienen
> A la ciudad de Nueva York
> Se olvidan de nuestro idioma
> Por un lenguaje peor . . .
> Francisco se llama Frank
> Y a José le dicen Joe . . . (*Aromas de limón* 38)

Ahora bien, la referencia a los Estados Unidos en *Aromas de limón* no se restringe a los poemas de inmigración, sino que, además, entra en diálogo con cuestiones patrióticas y/o políticas. Por ejemplo, en "El patriota", Torres describe las virtudes de aquellos hombres que, haciendo caso omiso de la persecución institucional, luchan por sacar a su patria de la situación colonial: "Ante el imperialismo con su fobia/enamora a la patria como su novia/y por ella se entrega al sacrificio" (*Aromas de limón* 12). Finalmente, en "Odio del sur", se puede apreciar una clara crítica sociopolítica de parte de César Torres a la segregación racial, vigente todavía en el sur estadounidense:

> En Estados Unidos
> En ese sur de odios
> y de torpes blanquitos,
> un niño negro lleva
> a enterrar a su perrito
> en el cementerio
> de los canes blanquitos . . .
> —Aquí no hay perros negros
> Y el tuyo aunque sea rubio
> Siempre será negrito. (Torres *"Aromas de limón"* 65)

En cuanto a *Pasión del alma*, último poemario que publicaría César G. Torres, es importante señalar la notoria evolución temática de Torres, ya que, además de las cuestiones que exigen la atención del poeta en *Aromas de limón,* vemos en *Pasión del alma* la incorporación de otros temas como la nostalgia por amores pretéritos ("Remembranzas") y la melancolía de la vejez ("¡Setenta y cinco años!"); es innegable que estos tópicos están de manera latente en poemarios anteriores, pero en *Pasión del alma* pasan a un primer orden y cobran notoriedad. Otra constante de este último poemario tiene que ver con lo religioso; de hecho, por lo menos ocho de los poemas tienen referencias directas a Cristo, o contienen tropos e imaginería característicos de la doctrina católica. Pero, además de estos poemas religiosos, es importante hacer mención de un poema en *Pasión del alma* que, además de estar en consonancia con el carácter nostálgico y retrospectivo del poemario, hace referencia, una vez más, a los Estados Unidos y específicamente a uno de los momentos más convulsos de su vida; este se titula "Cárcel de Lewisburg" y es, a mi juicio, uno de sus poemas más íntimos y reflexivos:

> Aquí estoy tras los muros carcelarios
> y una puerta me cubre que se abre y se cierra
> como todas las puertas automáticas.
> Y todo es soledad ¡Ay, cuánto vale
> recibir desde lejos varias cartas!
> …………………………………..
> Regreso nuevamente al cautiverio.
> Miro tras el cristal de mi ventana
> los barrotes de acero que lo adornan
> y miro al cielo azul de Pensylvania:
> a un pájaro que vuela a lo infinito,
> y una nube pequeña, muy pequeña
> que me dibuja el mapa de mi patria. (*Pasión del alma* 44)

En estas dos estrofas, con las que inicia y termina el poema, Torres no solo rememora la desesperanza del confinamiento, sino que además recrea una nostalgia pretérita, la de la tierra natal a la cual pudo volver años después y desde donde escribe estos versos. "Cárcel de Lewisburg" es uno más de aquellos poemas en los que la tierra natal es un referente inexorable, configurado y recreado desde y a través de la nostalgia. Lo anterior resulta, por supuesto, del extenso período de tiempo que el poeta residió como inmigrante en los Estados Unidos.

Es innegable que la patria es un tema capital en la obra poética de César G. Torres. Ya sea que ella entre en diálogo con cuestiones migratorias, políticas, o nostálgicas, la isla y la identidad puertorriqueña son referentes insoslayables en su creación literaria. En palabras del crítico y poeta Odón Betanzos Palacios, "[e]xiste una llamada subterránea de tierra que le gana y lo eleva: esa patria pequeña en dimensión y grande en el corazón de su gente. Es la tierra-patria-pueblo su elemento virginal a la hora de la creación" (6). Aun así, hay diferencias en la forma en que Torres versa sobre la patria en *Aromas de limón* y *Pasión del alma*. Mientras que en el primero de los poemarios la patria es la isla allende, explotada por el colonialismo estadounidense, que debe ser salvada del imperialismo yanqui; en el último la patria, entendida como el locus de enunciación de Torres, es una constelación nemónica de lugares e imágenes que remite al poeta a los tiempos de sus padres, sus abuelos y a los recuerdos de su propia experiencia vital. La patria de *Pasión del alma* es una amalgama de recuerdos nostálgicos. Cito, por dar un ejemplo, algunos versos de "Campana de San Sebastián":

> ¡Vieja campana de la antigua torre
> de ese sagrado templo!
> Despidió de mi padre y de mi madre
> sus funerales restos.
> Tocó muy dulce la canción de bodas
> cuando aquí se casaron mis abuelos
> ....
> Despertó la mañana de mi infancia
> su melodioso acento . . . (*Pasión del alma* 18)

En *La poesía de Puerto Rico*, el autor Cesáreo Rosa-Nieves sostiene que: "Tres maneras distintas han tenido nuestros poetas al cantar el tema de la patria en Puerto Rico: político, filosófico y físico" (99); En el caso de Torres, se prevé una construcción poética que oscila entre lo político, lo filosófico y lo físico; incluso, podría decirse que la imaginería de Torres es una conjunción de las tres maneras mencionadas. En ese sentido, "Al presidente Roosevelt", "El Cordero de mi Patria" y "Campanas de San Sebastián" son paradigmáticos de las tres maneras en que César Torres le ha cantado a la patria.

En fin, tanto *Aromas de limón* como *Pasión del alma* dan fe de los ejes temáticos sobre los que gira la poética de César G. Torres, entre los que está el amor y el deseo, la memoria y exaltación de su patria, la lucha por defender y vindicar la clase obrera y, sin agotar las posibilidades, la crítica incesante de Torres contra la situación neocolonial a la que se enfrenta Puerto Rico (López-Adorno 114). Estas inquietudes temáticas, aunadas a una economía del lenguaje y un estilo despojado de excesos, se concretan en la antología poética *Resolana*, cuya división temática (Poemas patrióticos, poemas líricos, poemas jíbaros, poemas negros), manifiesta el desarrollo poético en Torres. Las reocupaciones perceptibles en *Resolana* se pueden extender a la cosmovisión literaria puertorriqueña, que oscila (a veces de manera tensa y a veces de manera conciliadora) entre la isla y la metrópolis, es decir, entre el aquí y el allá. En ese orden de ideas, *Resolana* es el poemario que más se ajusta a los procesos de cambio y las innovaciones que se pueden encontrar en otros poetas puertorriqueños, tanto en la isla como en Nueva York. Según el crítico Roberto Márquez, a partir de la Segunda Guerra Mundial, la poesía de Puerto Rico se ha caracterizado por la actitud crítica, la revuelta y la renovación. Una de las características principales de la poesía de esta época es, "[the] increasing recognition of figures—the urban servant, working or transnational (im)migrant clases, black, and homosexuals, among others—formerly marginalized, ignored, evaded, or generally proscribed" (xxxiv). En efecto, estas figuras marginalizadas son también las que encontramos en César G. Torres, sobre todo en *Resolana*, en la que los poemas jíbaros y negros ocupan gran parte del poemario. Asimismo, uno de los poemas más elocuentes de Torres, antologado en *Resolana* es "Al Presidente Roosevelt", el cual considero como referente fundamental de la obra del poeta pepiniano por conjugar en sus versos varias de sus preocupaciones: la situación colonial, la patria, la raza, la explotación, el activismo político, etc.:

> Voy a quitar la máscara que cubre
> tu sonriente faz en Casa Blanca
> en nombre de los héroes de Borinquén
> y en nombre de los mártires de Atlanta.
> Tú eres culpable, sí, culpable eres
> de lo que en Puerto Rico pasa,
> el cacique bebiendo en copas de oro
> y el patriota azotado en las espaldas
> porque mientras al aire tú pregonas
> el derecho de paz y democracia
> le diste mano libre a Blanton Winship
> para matar en tierra borincana . . . (*Resolana* 34)

Uno de los aspectos que más resalta del poema anterior el uso de contraposiciones para hacer hincapié en la brecha social y política entre Estados Unidos y Puerto Rico, así como la relación esquizoide que se ha establecido históricamente entre las dos naciones. Un claro ejemplo de lo anterior se encuentra en los últimos versos citados, en los que se desnudan los valores estadounidenses de paz y democracia con el nombramiento del general mayor Blanton Winship en la gobernación de Puerto Rico. Como lo han establecido numerosos estudios históricos,[4] el nombramiento de Winship tuvo como propósito principal la neutralización del Partido Nacionalista por medio del encarcelamiento de sus líderes y la militarización de la fuerza policial puertorriqueña con el fin de poder reprimir cualquier levantamiento de la población.

Del mismo modo, en "Al presidente Roosevelt" se observa la desarticulación que hace Torres de ciertos términos ligados estrechamente a los imaginarios de las dos naciones. Por ejemplo, palabras como "patriotismo" y "patriota" han sido fundamentales en la formación del excepcionalismo estadounidense; asimismo, y sobre todo desde la perspectiva occidental, palabras como "cacicazgo" o "cacique" se relacionan usualmente con sociedades colonizadas y verticales; no obstante, en el poema de Torres encontramos una inversión en el uso de los términos: "el cacique bebiendo en copas de oro", en referencia a Roosevelt, y "el patriota azotado en las espaldas", en referencia al pueblo puertorriqueño. El uso del término "patriota", además, enfatiza la noción de Puerto Rico en cuanto que *patria* y la reivindica, así, de su reducción nominal a estado o territorio. En ese orden de ideas, la inversión y desarticulación de términos que lleva a cabo Torres remite a una de las estrategias decoloniales que alguna vez expresó Frantz Fanon: "La violencia con la cual se ha afirmado la supremacía de los valores blancos . . . hace que, por una justa inversión de las cosas, el colonizado se burle cuando se evocan frente a él esos valores" (38).

En resumidas cuentas, es evidente que el concepto de patria es transversal en la obra de César G. Torres. Todos los demás temas son atravesados de una u otra manera por dicho concepto. Asimismo, y como quedó demostrado en los poemas citados, la obra de César G. Torres pone de manifiesto una evolución y (re)articulación del término "patria" según su situación inmediata y su lugar de enunciación. En tal virtud, en la obra de Torres se aprecia la construcción afectiva de la nación. Construcción que, como explicaré más adelante, inserta a Torres en una constelación de poetas contemporáneos quienes llevaron a cabo operaciones poéticas similares.

IV. César G. Torres, ausente en las antologías

Como mencioné en la introducción, llama la atención el hecho de que Torres, no obstante el haber publicado seis poemarios y varios textos en periódicos y semanarios (varios de ellos con muy buena recepción), solo esté presente en una de varias antologías consultadas. Es posible que la ausencia de Torres en las antologías de literatura puertorriqueña (tanto de la isla como de Nueva York), se deba principalmente a cuestiones estilísticas y estéticas. Hay, además, un agravante de carácter sociohistórico que tiene que ver con la forma en que la producción literaria de los puertorriqueños residentes en Nueva York ha sido recibida tanto en la metrópoli como en la isla. Como sostiene Efraín Barradas, "en el contexto estadounidense la obra de los puertorriqueños que allí residen se ve como piezas prescindibles, como curiosidad etnológica, como aullido mal articulado de otro *minority group* más" (11). Lo anterior revela la desigual recepción de la producción desde Nueva York en comparación con la producción proveniente de Puerto Rico. Sin embargo, y como pudo observarse en el apartado anterior, la obra de Torres dista de ser una mera "curiosidad etnológica". Por el contrario, esta dialoga de manera eficaz y productiva con la obra de otros puertorriqueños que escribieron y publicaron desde Nueva York. Por otro lado, el hecho de que la obra de los puertorriqueños en Nueva York pueda considerarse como producto de un grupo minoritario no la hace prescindible; al contrario, considero que la intervención de otros voces y discursos en el acervo literario estadounidense —como es el caso de la producción literaria puertorriqueña— es fundamental y necesaria para en un proyecto de diversificación de un canon demasiado constreñido por estéticas y discursos occidentales.

En cuanto a la cuestión estética y de ejecución —a mi juicio, la más subjetiva de las razones por las que Torres ha sido excluido—, esta se manifiesta en los "defectos" que varios críticos han encontrado en la poesía de Torres. En el prólogo de *Aromas de limón,* por ejemplo, el crítico Max Ríos Ríos arguye que:

... [las] fuerzas que inspiran y arrebatan a César Torres dan a su poesía espontaneidad muy suya, pero a la forma cierto descuido que parece entrar de lleno en las normas poéticas de hoy. Hay algunas rimas imperfectas, lo cual no es defecto, aunque puedan afirmar lo contrario los admiradores de la perfección escultórica en el verso. Acaso más tarde se decida por una escuela u otra este joven poeta que tiene muchos años para florecer . . . (v-vi)

Llama la atención aquello de que "acaso más tarde se decida por una escuela u otra". Aunque Ríos Ríos no clarifica a qué escuelas se refiere, parece ser que una es la de "la naturaleza", pastoril, bucólica, y la otra es la del amor, con rasgos modernistas y un estilo más contemporáneo. Aun así, el que Torres no se enmarque dentro de una poética o escuela específica no desdice de su producción literaria. De hecho, y como han manifestado algunos críticos,[5] la oscilación entre estilos discursivos y estéticos es patente en otros escritores y poetas puertorriqueños que habían emigrado a los Estados Unidos durante las décadas de los cuarenta y cincuenta del siglo XX, así como en aquellos escritores que fueron testigos de los cambios socioeconómicos y políticos que se dieron en la isla durante la década de los cuarenta, como lo fue la industrialización y los procesos de migración tanto interna como externa (Vásquez 167). Asimismo, la temática en la que se enfoca César Torres converge que las preocupaciones de otros poetas contemporáneos como Juan Antonio Corretjer, Francisco Matos Paoli o Clemente Soto Vélez, cuya obra gravita alrededor del imperativo nacionalista, así como la construcción poética de la nación puertorriqueña, a partir de una poesía que conciliara lo estético con lo político (Vásquez 168). No obstante, a diferencia de Corretjer or Matos Paoli, quienes escribieron acerca de Puerto Rico desde la isla, César Torres nos brinda una perspectiva emergente de la experiencia obrera de los puertorriqueños en los Estados Unidos. Dicha perspectiva emergente cobra una especial importancia debido a que diversifica la construcción espacio-afectiva de la nación puertorriqueña, proyecto que, como ha establecido el crítico Michael Dowdy —y como explicaré más adelante—, ha constelado a la mayoría de autores puertorriqueños tanto en la isla como en la diáspora (41-42).

Después de una lectura acuciosa de la obra es innegable que, aunque es posible detectar una evolución estilística en Torres, esta no sucedió de la misma manera que evolucionó la poesía puertorriqueña tanto en la isla como en los Estados Unidos. Por un lado, y como demostré en el apartado anterior, la poesía de Torres presenta gestos y recursos poéticos característicos del romanticismo. La mayor parte de sus poemas acerca de la naturaleza, por ejemplo, mantiene los rasgos de la poesía pastoril y bucólica del siglo XIX: "Oí cantar a una orquídea/porque en su torre de pétalos/un ruiseñor hizo un nido." (Torres *Aromas de limón* 11). Aunque la poesía, como movimiento cultural en Puerto Rico, tuvo inicialmente una evolución rezagada en comparación con la poesía de otras latitudes latinoamericanas (Rosa-Nieves 21-22), es claro que, a partir de la segunda década del XX, en Puerto Rico surgen movimientos propios que potencian la evolución de la poesía en la isla. De acuerdo a Roberto Márquez, antes de 1950 pudo observarse en Puerto Rico una eclosión de movimientos estéticos y estilísticos que superaron el modernismo, entre los que figuraron la poesía post-modernista, la vanguardista, la negrista, etc. (xxxiii). No obstante, no vemos la misma evolución en Torres, lo que posiblemente causó que se tomara al autor pepiniano como rezagado o anacrónico en términos de estilo y, en consecuencia, se le excluyera de las antologías de poesía puertorriqueña. No obstante, sí es posible observar otro tipo de evolución temática en su poética que se refleja en ciertos rasgos discursivos. Por ejemplo, a diferencia de *Aromas de limón*, de 1949, en *Pasión del alma*, de 1989 se aprecia el uso de una versificación más libre y, del mismo modo, se aprecia la incorporación de lo que la escritora Cristina Rivera Garza denominó una estética citacionista, es decir, de la desapropiación y reapropiación de citas para rearticular el discurso poético. Por ejemplo, en el poema "Johana Rosaly" encontramos versos como:

Johana Rosaly,
"lindo capullo de alelí"
fresca amapola,
miel de caña.
"Preciosa la llaman las olas
del mar que te baña." (*Pasión del alma*, 9)

Así pues, los versos entre comillas remiten a dos canciones del autor puertorriqueño Rafael Hernández Marín, "Capullito de alelí" y "Preciosa". Es necesario acotar que este dispositivo estético se observa de manera muy austera y todavía conservadora, pero pone de manifiesto ciertos gestos evolutivos en la obra de César G. Torres.

Por otra parte, la poesía puertorriqueña escrita en los Estados Unidos ha presentado una evolución que, a mi juicio, es incluso más radical y pronunciada que la de la isla. El estudio de la poesía puertorriqueña de los Estados Unidos pone de manifiesto "[a] more dramatic general refusal on the part of the poets of the diaspora . . . to conform to established, antiquely presumed, and expected insular (or more normative metropolitan) linguistic, literary, or patrician protocols and conventions in order to give voice to their uncommonly distinctive *puertorriqueñidad* . . . " (Márquez xxxv). Efectivamente, un común denominador de las antologías de poesía puertorriqueña de los Estados Unidos es la subversión de muchas de las convenciones estilísticas, estéticas y lingüísticas presentes en la poesía insular, y en la del resto de Latinoamérica. Entre los mecanismos de subversión se encuentra, por ejemplo, la inserción del inglés o de anglicismos, el cambio de código, la secularización y proletarización del registro poético y la incorporación de cuestiones obviadas —e incluso prescritas— por los insulares, como el sincretismo, la transnacionalización y transculturación, el tránsito constante entre la metrópoli y la isla y, finalmente, la consolidación del nuyorrican o, lo que algunos han llamado el "AmeRícan sancocho" (Márquez xxxv-xxxvi). En ese orden de ideas, un parangón entre la poesía puertorriqueña de los Estados Unidos y la obra de César G. Torres, demuestra que la poesía del poeta pepiniano es considerablemente más conservadora, se ajusta a las convenciones de la poesía canónica de la isla, y evita la incorporación de un estilo o una estética subversiva e innovadora. El estilo conservador de Torres se adscribe más al estilo de una generación anterior de poetas puertorriqueños en Nueva York, sobre todo durante la década de los 40. Acerca de dicha generación el crítico Juan Flores sostiene que: "What little is available of this material shows it to be largely conventional Spanish-language verse making little reference to the migration or to life in New York, much less anticipating . . . the complex bilingual situation of the generation to come" (63). El hecho de que la mayor parte de la obra de Torres se publique en una época donde una nueva generación de poetas está subvirtiendo normas y convenciones estilísticas y lingüísticas, puede explicar la ausencia de César G. Torres en las antologías de poesía puertorriqueña de los Estados Unidos o, en general, de poesía hispana de los Estados Unidos.

V. Cuatro poemas de César G. Torres para una antología

No obstante las razones de su exclusión y los "defectos" que la poesía de César G. Torres pueda tener, considero que hay un conjunto de poemas que tienen cabida en una antología de literatura hispana de los Estados Unidos o, específicamente, de poesía puertorriqueña en los Estados Unidos; máxime si se tiene en cuenta que muchas de las antologías de literatura hispana en los Estados Unidos parten de la premisa de que las convenciones esteticistas no pueden ser las únicas o las preponderantes al momento de llevar a cabo un proyecto antológico. Por el contrario, la importancia sociohistórica de una obra, su aporte al acervo literario, sus particularidades discursivas y temáticas, etc., son otros factores que se deben tener en cuenta junto con la cuestión estética. De hecho, es a la luz de estas consideraciones que la antología de poesía puertorriqueña en Nueva York, *Papiros de Babel*, incluye a poetas como César G. Torres (esta es la única, de las antologías consultadas, en incluirlo). En palabras del antólogo, Pedro López-Adorno, el rasgo principal de la poesía puertorriqueña en Nueva York es la polifonía, que se manifiesta en lo discursivo, lo temático, lo estético, etc. (2-3). Debido, entonces, a este carácter polifónico, sería necio restringir un proyecto antológico a aquellas obras que se ajusten a las convenciones estéticas impuestas, muchas veces, "por el 'amiguismo' y por los caprichos e interrelaciones del antólogo" (López-Adorno 3).

En tal virtud, considero que sería productivo incluir poemas como "Cárcel de Lewisburg", "Al Presidente Roosevelt", "Sátira" y, finalmente, "El ladrón" en una antología de la literatura hispana en los Estados Unidos. He incluido "El ladrón" porque este es uno de los poemas más conocidos del autor puertorriqueño, ya que ha sido publicado en varias ocasiones en periódicos hispanos neoyorquinos y, de acuerdo a algunos artículos, el poeta recitó "El ladrón" en varias reuniones culturales, en las que el poema tuvo muy buena recepción ("Club Cultural..."); así pues, parece haber un consenso en lo tocante a la calidad de "El ladrón". También, considero que "El ladrón" es una de las mejores representaciones de la poesía de Torres ya que en el poema se aprecia una alegoría sofisticada y eficaz de la casa como nación, y el ladrón como sujeto cuya consciencia despierta ante una imagen "divina", de la misma manera en que Torres esperaba que la consciencia de sus compatriotas despertara ante la imagen de Pedro Albizu Campos, materializada dentro del poema en el medallón que el ladrón encuentra. Además, con "El ladrón" se puede comenzar a trazar un esquema del pensamiento independentista de Torres, así como de la evolución en su producción poética de corte político.

Los poemas seleccionados no sólo dan fe de las preocupaciones de César G. Torres como poeta y, sobre todo, como inmigrante en la metrópoli estadounidense. Es cierto que, si se lee la obra de Torres con el rigor esteticista con que el que se leen los autores canónicos, la obra de Torres podría juzgarse de menor, abundante en versos "imperfectos" o medianamente logrados, y de una poética simple, por lo que su valor literario bien podría cuestionarse. Sin embargo, una aproximación al valor literario de la obra de Torres desde lo estético es, por decir lo menos, improductiva ya que, no obstante los "defectos" que puedan hallarse en su poesía, es innegable que los versos de Torres son eficaces a la hora de prefigurar un contexto sociopolítico, y representar la experiencia vital de un inmigrante obrero en los Estados Unidos. Poemas como "Cárcel de Lewisburg", "Muebles adentro" y "Odio al Sur", entre otros, articulan una voz de protesta contra el racismo y la discriminación, la represión social y política, la explotación y el abuso. Lo anterior es evidente en la exhortación que Torres hace a sus compatriotas para reconocer el tipo de trabajo que ofrece "el blanquito":

> Obrero: el blanquito
> anhela casarse
> y alquila tus manos
> para que le laves;
> para que le cosas,
> para que le cargues. (*Aromas de limón* 34)

Con los versos anteriores Torres critica la labor de servidumbre que muchos inmigrantes, como el mismo poeta, han ejercido en la metrópoli de manos del "blanquito".

Finalmente, —e insistiendo en lo comentado anteriormente—, es necesario tener presente que una de las premisas capitales de las antologías de literatura hispánica en los Estados Unidos es la aceptación de una polifonía evidente entre los autores antologados; es decir que, en vez de un grupo homogéneo de obras que se ajusten a las convenciones estéticas de la hegemonía cultural, la antología se compondría idealmente de obras disímiles, heterogéneas, que reflejen a una comunidad poliédrica y multicultural, como lo es la comunidad hispana en los Estados Unidos. La obra de Torres aporta a dicha polifonía a partir de aquello que el crítico Michael Dowdy denominó como la imaginación espacial afectiva de los poetas puertorriqueños. Así, mientras la atención de muchos de los poetas contemporáneos de Torres volcaban su atención hacia la ciudad y su fenomenología, o hacia la oscilación entre el aquí—Nueva York— y el allá—Puerto Rico (Dowdy 45), Torres construía su patria afectiva volcándose hacia la experiencia del jíbaro, hacia el campo y el pueblo natal. Por medio del énfasis en la construcción bucólica y nostálgica de la naturaleza y la tierra puertorriqueña, Torres nutre dicha imaginación espacial afectiva, entendida como la colectividad de conocimientos, emociones y experiencias con que los autores tanto de la isla como de la metrópoli configuraron la patria puertorriqueña (Dowdy 46). En otros términos, una imaginación poliédrica, polifónica, en la que se construye Puerto Rico en cuanto que patria, nación, estado soberano, colonia, el allá que se recrea en la memoria y el acá que se recrea desde la nostalgia. En muchas de aquellas construcciones participa César G. Torres y, de esa manera, contribuye al acervo cultural y literario puertorriqueño. En ese orden de ideas, es importante anotar que, más allá de la inclusión o no de la obra de Torres en proyectos antológicos futuros, es fundamental que su obra sea recuperada, preservada y estudiada. Ya sea como artefacto literario y cultural, o como documento de valor sociohistórico, la obra de César Gilberto Torres debe entenderse como patrimonio cultural de la comunidad hispana en los Estados Unidos y, como tal, merece ser desenterrada del archivo y accesible a la comunidad académica y al público en general.

Bibliografía

Arana Soto, Salvador. *Catálogo de poetas puertorriqueños*. Sociedad de Autores Puertorriqueños, 1968.

Barradas, Efraín y Rafael Rodríguez. *Herejes y mitificadores: muestra de poesía puertorriqueña en los Estados Unidos*. Ediciones Huracán, 1980.

Berríos Martínez, Rubén. "Puerto Rico's Decolonization". *Foreign Affairs*, vol. 76, no. 6, 1997, pp. 100-114.

Betances, Clotilde. " . . . Era el pensamiento de tres mil Larenos". *Pueblos Hispanos* [Nueva York] 17 Julio 1943, p. 9.

Betanzos Palacios, Odón. Prólogo. *Resolana (antología poética)*. Por César G. Torres. Editorial Mensaje, 1970.

"Club Cultural Hispano del Bronx". *Pueblos Hispanos* [Nueva York], 24 abril 1943.

Campos, Haroldo de. "Superación de los lenguajes exclusivos". *América Latina en su literatura*, coordinado por César Fernández Moreno, Siglo XXI, 2000, pp. 279-300.

Denis, Nelson A. *War Against All Puerto Ricans: Revolution and Terror in America's Colony*. Nation Books, 2015.

Dowdy, Michael. "A mountain / in my pocket": The Affective Spatial Imagination in Post-1952 Puerto Rican Poetry." *MELUS*, vol. 35, no. 2, 2010, pp. 41-67.

Fanon, Frantz. *Los condenados de la tierra*. Traducido por Julieta Campos. Fondo de Cultura Económica, 1963.

Flores, Juan. "Literatura puertorriqueña de EE.UU: segunda etapa: las décadas de 1950 y 60". *Enciclopedia de Puerto Rico*. https://enciclopediapr.org/encyclopedia/literatura-puertorriquena-en-ee-uu/#1464837989298-2f6260ee-41c4.

___. "Puerto Rican Literature in the United States: Stages and Perspectives". *Recovering the U.S. Hispanic Literary Heritage*. Editado por Ramón Gutiérrez y Genaro Padilla. Arte Público Press, 1993, pp. 53-68.

Godreau, Isar P. *Scripts of Blackness: Race, Cultural Nationalism, and U.S. Colonialism in Puerto Rico*. U of Illionis P, 2015.

"Homenaje a Felipe Arana". *Ecos de Nueva York* [Nueva York], 27 agosto 1950, p. 17.

Kanellos, Nicolás, editor. *En otra voz: antología de la literatura hispana de los Estados Unidos*. Arte Público Press, 2002.

"La Junta Nacionalista Puertorriqueña Conmemoró Aniversario de la Masacre de Ponce". *Liberación* [Nueva York], 9 abril 1949, p. 4.

Laguerre, Enrique A. y Esther M. Melón. *El jíbaro de Puerto Rico: símbolo y figura*. Troutman Press, 1968.

Lamadrid Navarro, Antonio G. de. *Testimonio: Los indómitos*. Editorial Edil, 1981.

López-Adorno, Pedro. *Papiros de Babel: antología de la poesía puertorriqueña en Nueva York*. Editorial de la Universidad de Puerto Rico, 1991.

López Ortiz, Miguel. "César Gilberto Torres". *KoolturActiva.com*. CREW, Dic. 2010. http://www.kooltouractiva.com/kooltouractiva/art/boricuas-para-la-historia/475-cesar-gilberto-torres.html. Accedido 25 julio 2017.

Malavet, Pedro A. *America's Colony: The Political and Cultural Conflict between the United States and Puerto Rico*. New York UP, 2004.

Márquez, Roberto. Introducción. *Puerto Rican Poetry: An Anthology from Aboriginal to Contemporary Times*. Por Márquez. U of Massachusetts Press, 2007.

Morales, Jorge L., editor. *Poesía antillana y negrista:* Puerto Rico, República Dominicana, Cuba. Editorial Universitaria, 1976.

Paralitici, José. "Imprisonment and Colonial Domination, 1898-1958". *Puerto Rico Under Colonial Rule: Political Persecution and the Quest for Human Rights*. Editado por Ramón Bosque-Pérez y José Javier Colón Morera. State University of New York Press, 2006, pp. 67-82.

___. *No quiero mi cuerpo pa' tambor: el servicio militar obligatorio en Puerto Rico*. Ediciones Puerto, 1998.

Rosa-Nieves, Cesáreo. *La poesía en Puerto Rico: historia de los temas poéticos en la literatura puertorriqueña*. Editorial Edil, Inc., 1969.

Ríos Ríos, Max. Prólogo. *Aromas de limón.* Por César G. Torres. Azteca Press, 1949.

Sánchez Korrol, Virginia. *From Colonia to Community: The History of Puerto Ricans in New York City.* Greenwood Press, 1983.

Torres, César G. *Aromas de limón.* Azteca Press, 1949.

___. "El ladrón". *Pueblos Hispanos* [Nueva York] 27 marzo 1943, p. 7.

___. "En defensa de mi libro". *Pueblos Hispanos* [Nueva York] 7 agosto, 1943, p. 8.

___. "La abolición de la esclavitud". *Eco Antillano* [Nueva York] 21 marzo, 1942, p. 8.

___. *Pasión del alma.* Moca, 1989.

___. *Resolana (antología poética).* Editorial Mensaje, 1970.

Vásquez, Carmen. "La poesía puertorriqueña del siglo XX". *Revista Nuestra América,* no. 8, 2010, pp. 161-179.

Vega, Bernardo. *Memoirs of Bernardo Vega: A Contribution to the History of the Puerto Rican Community in New York.* Traducido por Juan Flores, Monthly Review Press, 1984.

Ward, James H. "A Tentative Inventory of Young Puerto Rican Writers". *Hispania,* vol. 54, 1971, pp. 924-930.

Notas

[1]Ver López-Adorno, 1991.

[2]Según algunas fuentes, el primer poemario de César G. Torres se titula *Flores entre páginas,* y fue publicado en 1930 o 1932, dependiendo de la fuente. Por ende, a menos que haya una errata en la entrada de Arana Soto, *Flores entre páginas* no debe confundirse con el folleto "Flores entre lágrimas" (1922), en el que se publican los primeros poemas de Torres. Para más información, ver Arana-Soto 184, López-Adorno 113, y López Ortiz "César Gilberto Torres".

[3]No se pudo tener acceso a los siguientes poemarios: *Flores entre páginas* (1940), *Abanico de fuego* (1943), y *Guanín* (1981). No se encontró información alguna de los dos últimos más allá de las referencias que se hacen en las semblanzas biográficas del autor. En cuanto a *Flores entre páginas,* según la base de datos WorldCat, solo la biblioteca de la Universidad Interamericana de Puerto Rico tiene una copia de este libro.

[4]Ver Berríos Martínez 105; Denis 65-72; Paralitici 73-76, entre otros, para un análisis más profundo de las políticas represivas del gobernador Winship, resultantes en masacres como la de Ponce, el 21 de marzo de 1937.

[5]Ver, por ejemplo, Flores "Literatura puertorriqueña en EE.UU.: segunda etapa: las décadas de 1950 y 60"; Vásquez 167-168, para una descripción más detallada de las transiciones literarias perceptibles en la producción puertorriqueña de mediados del siglo XX.

Part 2: Of Historical Populations and Literary Histories: Californios and Neo-Mexicanos

[T]his archive foregrounds the antecedence, creative genius and interpretive power of the Spanish- and Latin American-descended US-residents within earshot, yet often invisible or incomprehensible to Anglos or non-Hispanic whites.

—Laura Lomas

We read the archive by resurrecting the archive.

—Anna M. Nogar

Mariano Guadalupe Vallejo: Recovering a Californio Voice from Mexican California

ROSE MARIE BEEBE AND ROBERT M. SENKEWICZ
Santa Clara University

One of the longest and most substantive documents produced by a nineteenth-century Mexican American in the United States was composed by Mariano Guadalupe Vallejo over a number of months in 1874 and 1875. The document, "Recuerdos históricos y personales tocante a la Alta California: historia política del país, 1769-1849; costumbres de los Californios; apuntes biográficos de personas notables" ["Historical and Personal Remembrances relating to Alta California: Political History of the Country, 1769-1849; Customs of the Californios; Biographical Sketches of Notable People"] was the first comprehensive history of California written before the Gold Rush. This document originated as one of the seventy-eight interviews of residents of Mexican California conducted by members of Hubert Howe Bancroft's staff in the 1870s as part of the research for Bancroft's eventual seven-volume *History of California.* Vallejo's five-volume manuscript has been at The Bancroft Library for almost a century and a half. But the document has remained largely inaccessible to many readers since its composition. Some important excerpts have been published in Spanish (Sánchez, Pita, and Reyes 138–43). Also, an eighty-year-old in-house English translation effort is available at The Bancroft Library. But neither a complete Spanish version nor a complete English translation has yet been published. We are currently in the final stages of a project to recover and publish this Californio voice.[1] In this essay, we introduce Vallejo and analyze some of the crucial themes Vallejo articulated in his writings. These themes offer an alternative history of the North American Southwest and the Pacific Coast before the US takeover. In doing so, they serve to make the origins and development of the varieties of cultural diversity that are woven into the contemporary "American" identity better known and appreciated.

The Californio narratives that Vallejo and the other residents of pre-Gold Rush California produced in the 1870s, have been most studied by literary scholars. In the 1990s Genaro Padilla and Rosaura Sánchez published extensive studies of these narratives. Padilla focused on the interviews of Vallejo and of eleven of the thirteen women to whom Bancroft's staff spoke and who had lived in Alta California before it became part of the United States (Padilla 77-152). Padilla's interest was in the role of these accounts in the formation of Mexican American autobiography. He termed Vallejo's document a "narrative of dispossession" that was set against the narrative of success that undergirds the classic American autobiography. He argued that, by infusing his own story with the social history of the Californio financial and cultural losses after the American conquest, Vallejo produced a "counterhegemonic discourse" (59, 88).

Rosaura Sánchez examined the Bancroft narratives within the context of the development of Chicano literature. In her extensive analysis she termed these documents *"testimonios,"* which she described as "mediated narratives by a subaltern person interviewed by an outsider" (Sánchez 7). Most scholars, including the present authors, have adopted Sánchez's terminology. She stated that the Bancroft testimonios were "historical and literary contestations of contemporary nineteenth century historiography, which often portrayed the Californios as lazy, cowardly, and incompetent" (6). She argued that the testimonios as a whole produced spaces of a collective identity that was neither Mexican nor American, but Californio (232, 296).

More recent literary analysis of the testimonios and of Vallejo has been undertaken by Marissa López. She argued that Vallejo did not consider himself marginalized in the mid-1870s and that his testimonio sought to offer a positive vision of California's potential. She stated that Vallejo focused on international relations and offered California as a model for "an open and prosperous engagement with the world." In her view, Vallejo's testimonio "suggests a new, expansive origin story" for Chicano literature (López 2007, 876, 895–96, 898).

Each of these literary approaches offers significant insight into Vallejo's work. Our own approach is, we hope, complementary to these authors' efforts. We begin by noting that Vallejo presented himself in his testimonio as a historian who was engaged in "the arduous and difficult task of writing the history of Alta California" (Vallejo Recuerdos 1: II).[2] Vallejo was very aware that history—the study of a particular past conducted by a person living in a particular present—inevitably has a dual temporal focus. He was aware that in some writers, present realities could warp the interpretation of the past and that, in other writers, romantic and unrealistic versions of the past could work their way into the present. For him, the remedy to both dangers was for the historian to try to be impartial. He stated, "my writings have no other objective than to serve as an impartial judge, which in civilized countries is consistently accorded to historians who write without deviating from the truth" (Vallejo Recuerdos 1: III). He insisted that his commitment to impartiality overrode any personal relationships with people whose actions were part of the history he was composing. When, for instance, he criticized some political actions of those who had been his boyhood companions, such as Juan Bautista Alvarado and José Castro, he stated that the burden resting on the historian was a heavy one:

> I cannot keep secret that I find it exceedingly distressing to find myself compelled to allude to that fact, because during my first years of public service I was a friend of Don José Castro. I shared glories and perils with him and Alvarado. And, I confess that it would give me great pleasure to shower him with deserved praise. However, the blistering impartiality of the historian forces me to be harsh, even with my most beloved friends. I trust that they will have the wisdom to interpret my criticism in the spirit in which it is given, that is, stripped of selfish intentions or personal aims. (Vallejo Recuerdos 5: 21)

A few months after he completed his work, he wrote to his son Platón that he had composed "the impartial truth, written to serve as a guide for posterity" (Vallejo, Letter to Platón Vallejo, 22 Aug. 1875).

At a number of points in his testimonio, Vallejo explicitly cited official documents, mission records, letters from friends, and documents collected by his father or himself. He sometimes volunteered additional source information, such as reporting that Pablo de la Guerra had given him a copy of the speech by Governor Mariano Chico that he had quoted (Vallejo Recuerdos 3: 108). In all of this, he stated somewhat grandiloquently, that he was merely following Cicero's dictum that history was "the illuminator of reality, the witness of the ages" (Vallejo Recuerdos 1: 45; translation Cicero 133).

Vallejo considered himself uniquely positioned to write the history of Alta California, for his family had been present in the region from almost the beginning of Spanish colonization.[3] His father, Ignacio, a low-ranking soldier serving in Jalisco, was recruited for service in Alta California by newly-appointed governor Fernando de Rivera y Moncada in 1773. Ignacio arrived in Alta California the following year. He served at a number of missions, presidios, and pueblos and was at San Diego during the Kumeyaay revolt of 1775. He married María

Antonia Isabela Lugo in 1790. They had thirteen children, of whom Mariano Guadalupe, born in 1808, was the eighth. When he was a child in the provincial capital of Monterey, Mariano Guadalupe, along with his nephew Juan Bautista Alvarado (1809-1882) and friend José Castro (1810-1860), was chosen for a personal and more liberal education by the last Spanish governor, Pablo Vicente de Solá.

Mariano Guadalupe followed his father into the military in 1824 and was promoted to *alférez* (second lieutenant) three years later. In 1829 he led an expedition against the indigenous leader Estanislao, who was refusing to return to Mission San José and was gathering forces in the interior of California. The military campaign was indecisive, although Vallejo's forces engaged in summary executions and a brutal massacre. In the end, Vallejo and the army simply declared victory and returned home. Vallejo served as commander of the San Francisco Presidio for three years in the 1830s and was also a delegate to the provincial legislature, the *diputación*. He married Francisca Benicia Carrillo in 1832 and the couple eventually had twelve children.

After a trip to the Russian settlement at Fort Ross in 1833, Vallejo was sent north to supervise the secularization of Mission San Francisco Solano and to prepare for the arrival of a colonization party being sent from Mexico that the new governor, José Figueroa, wished to settle in the Santa Rosa area. Vallejo also began to accumulate land for himself, as Figueroa in 1834 granted him some land in the area of Petaluma, north of San Francisco.

As an emerging upper-class Californio, he personally profited from secularization at the expense of both native Californians, ordinary soldiers, and lower-class Californios. While his education with former Governor Solá had given him a deep appreciation of Enlightenment principles, he nevertheless established himself as a quasi-feudal landed baron in Northern California. Vallejo formed an important alliance with a prominent native chief of the area, Sem-Yeto, better known by his Christian name of Solano. This pact enabled him to wage various campaigns against other native groups of the North, and to conscript many of them as laborers on his extensive *rancho* at Petaluma. He was formally appointed military commander of the North in 1838 when his nephew Alvarado was appointed governor. The relationship between the two quickly soured, as Alvarado believed that Vallejo was using his position to establish a military power center in Sonoma to compete with the governor in Monterey. Part of the reason Alvarado gave an extensive land grant on the Sacramento River to John Sutter in 1839 was so that Sutter could function as a counterweight to Vallejo.

Vallejo's term as commander ended in 1842, but he remained in the area. He was generally friendly to Americans who began to arrive in Alta California by way of an overland route that brought them into northern California. Along with many other Californio landholders, Vallejo resented the attempts of newly appointed Governor Manuel Micheltorena to assert the authority of the central government in Mexico City. Although he was not unfriendly to the notion of a US takeover of California, Vallejo was arrested by the Bear Flaggers in 1846 and held in prison at Sutter's Fort for a few months.

After his release Vallejo became a leading proponent of cooperation with the new authorities. He served in the Constitutional Convention in Monterey in 1849 and in the first State Senate, in which his report on the proposed names of the California counties was very influential. He also engaged in unsuccessful land speculation with some of the North American newcomers. Schemes that he and some Americans adopted to try to make the settlement he organized on the northern shores of San Francisco Bay, which he named after his wife Benicia, the capital of California, came to naught.

At some point in the late 1850s or early 1860s, Vallejo decided to write a history of California with emphasis on California before the Gold Rush. He was most likely led to this endeavor through experiencing negative attitudes that recently-arrived Americans had towards the Mexican residents of Alta California. His experiences in the Constitutional Convention (in which the permissibility or impermissibility of voting by darker-skinned Mexicans was the subject of animated discussion), in the first legislature (in which the discriminatory Foreign Miner's Tax was passed), and before the California Land Commission (in which the validity of land grants made during the Mexican regime was systematically attacked by squatters and their lawyers) made him realize first hand that both the Mexican era (1821–1848) in California and the Mexican population living in American California were regarded extremely negatively by the Anglo population of the state.

Vallejo was determined to write a history of California to correct the negative portrayal of the Mexican era, in the hopes that doing so would also enable Mexicans currently living in California to be regarded more favorably by the Anglo-Americans. As he told Anastasio Carrillo at the time, "My principal objective is for our successors, the Americans, to understand that not all Californios during those times were indigenous people or a herd of beasts. For when they took over this country, there was civilization and men who belonged to a race equal to, if not better than, theirs." He concluded, "If this work is not done, we will disappear and thus be disregarded by the entire world" (Vallejo, Letter to Anastasio Carrillo 19 Dec. 1866). As a resource for this he intended to use a good number of the documents his family had collected, which stretched back to the later eighteenth century. He began working on this project at his home (the "Casa Grande") on the Sonoma Plaza. However, his manuscript was destroyed when the Casa Grande burned to the ground in 1867. For the next few years he stayed close to Sonoma, attempting with little success to minimize his financial losses and stabilize his situation.

In March 1874 Vallejo received a letter from Enrique Cerruti, an Italian adventurer who had recently been hired by Hubert Howe Bancroft, a San Francisco bookseller and literary entrepreneur (Cerruti, Letter to Mariano Guadalupe Vallejo 22 Mar. 1874). Bancroft was finishing up production of a five-volume work entitled *Native Races of the Pacific States of North America* and had determined to bring out a multi-volume history of California (Bancroft 1874-75). As part of this project, Bancroft wanted to collect documents and reminiscences from people who had lived in California before its acquisition by the United States. To this end, Bancroft instructed Cerruti to try to establish a relationship with Vallejo. In the letter, without mentioning Bancroft, Cerruti said he would like to talk to Vallejo about the history of California. Vallejo agreed and Cerruti arrived at Sonoma by the end of that month.

As Cerruti's connection with Bancroft quickly became apparent, Vallejo decided to cooperate with Bancroft's proposed history of California by composing his reminiscences. Between April 1874 and November 1875 Vallejo worked with Cerruti to dictate his testimonio. They worked in Sonoma and also on the road, as Vallejo arranged interviews for Cerruti with other Californios in the Santa Clara Valley and the Monterey Bay area (Beebe and Senkewicz xix-xx, 17-24, 49-55, 69-76).

The final result of these efforts was a five-volume testimonio in which Vallejo traced the history of California from the beginning of Spanish occupation until the American takeover. Vallejo consistently read and reread the notes Cerruti took down of their conversations and made changes to them as the process developed. Bancroft related that at one point near the beginning of their relationship Cerruti was pushing Vallejo to move quickly on the composition of the testimonio, but Vallejo insisted on maintaining as much control over the process as he could. According to Bancroft, Vallejo replied, "I am willing to relate all I can remember, but I wish it clearly understood that it must be in my own way, and at my own time . . . I will not be hurried or dictated to. It is my history, and not yours, I propose to tell" (Bancroft 1890, 393). Whether Bancroft's recounting of this encounter was entirely accurate, it is indisputably true that Vallejo's five-volume testimonio was not composed in a hurried fashion. Besides revising it himself, Vallejo gave sections of it to his son, Platón, for critique. Indeed, some of Platón's comments and suggestions are included in the final version of the testimonio.

The content of the testimonio was not hurried either. Vallejo began with a chapter describing the customs and culture of native Californians, especially those of the Sonoma area. He then constructed his narrative in a chronological yet very leisurely fashion. His treatment of the 1769 Portolá expedition, for instance, included an extensive discussion of Visitor General José de Gálvez. Vallejo believed historians had underappreciated Gálvez's role in the settlement of California.

This approach marked Vallejo's treatment of virtually every event he described in his testimonio. The overall organization was chronological, and political developments, such as the tenures of successive California governors, determined the specific temporal divisions of the manuscript. Vallejo did not hesitate to include in his manuscript what he regarded as significant documentary material as well. As he was talking to Cerruti, Vallejo routinely consulted the rich collection of primary sources he had acquired over the years. For example, his treatment of Governor Figueroa's battle with the Híjar-Padrés colonization party sent from Mexico in 1834 contained the entire text of Figueroa's published defense of his actions, entitled *Manifiesto a la República Mejicana*. At one point, Vallejo included an 1875 letter that Juan Bautista Alvarado wrote to him in which Alvarado provided remembrances of events in Monterey in 1815. Vallejo also occasionally included letters that he himself had written, such as a letter to a missionary official in 1840.

In addition to these documentary inclusions, Vallejo tended to digress significantly as he told his story. For example, his treatment of the appointment of García Diego as Bishop of The Californias in 1839 contained an extensive section in which he recounts political developments in Mexico in the late 1830s. A request made by members of the Hudson's Bay Company to erect a Protestant church in the Sonoma area led Vallejo to compose a long section in which he detailed the type of education that the Californios received in Monterey in the 1810s.

The presence of such extensive documentary inclusions and the series of considerable digressions that interrupt the narrative give Vallejo's manuscript a character profoundly different from any of the other Californio testimonios Bancroft's staff collected. As Rosaura Sánchez has remarked, Vallejo hoped "to be able to reach out to a wider audience" (Sánchez 26). Indeed, the manuscript richly repays extensive reading, for it contains material not found in any other treatment of Spanish and Mexican California. The manuscript also served as one of the primary sources for the Spanish and Mexican sections of Bancroft's seven-volume *History of California* (Bancroft 1884-90).

This rich and dense manuscript was structured around four themes that Vallejo regarded as central to the history of California: (a) the role of the soldiers in the conquest and settlement of Alta California; (b) the role of culture and education in Californio society; (c) the competing world views of the missionaries and the Californios; and (d) the relationship between the indigenous peoples and the Californios. We shall consider each in order.

Vallejo's first theme was that the California that Americans inhabited in the 1870s had been created by Mexican soldiers, many of whose descendants were still living. Vallejo was very aware that by the time he was writing, popular opinion in California was beginning to accord missionaries the major role in the Spanish settlement and development of the state. An 1876 essay that Bancroft published in an attempt to spark interest in his own upcoming histories of California made this point. Entitled "The Manifest Destiny of California," Bancroft's essay divided California history into two phases, "missionary domination" and "the flush times following the gold discovery." Bancroft celebrated the mission era as a time of "brotherly kindness and charity." He termed the Spanish period as "a spiritual conquest on a grander scale than the world has ever seen." He concluded, "Other missionary enterprises there have been, but none so great, none so successful, none so lasting" (Bancroft 1876).

Vallejo vehemently disagreed. About a year after he finished composing his testimonio, he countered Bancroft in a speech celebrating the centennial of Mission Dolores. Deliberately choosing to give his address in Spanish, Vallejo said that whatever successes the missions might have enjoyed were due to the soldiers that protected them. Addressing an audience that included San Francisco Archbishop Joseph Alemany, Vallejo provocatively stated:

> It is essential to take into account that the Spanish flag was waving over California and that the Fathers did nothing more than comply with the king's orders while at the same time looking out for their own interests and that of the missions. Since the soldiers were always busy serving as escorts at the missions or engaged in continuous campaigns to keep the Indians under subjection, without them the Indians would have revolted continuously and all the *gente de razón* would have perished. (Vallejo 1876)

The manuscript Vallejo had recently completed emphasized the role soldiers played in establishing all of the institutions that characterized Spanish and Mexican Alta California– missions, presidios, pueblos, and ranchos. Vallejo included the exact wording of various regulations relating to the life of the soldiers, to their powers and privileges, their salaries, and their activities. Close to the beginning of the manuscript, he devoted an entire chapter to military matters. In this chapter he inserted large sections of the Royal Regulation of 1772 on the management of presidios (Vallejo Recuerdos 1: 17-22; Brinkerhoff and Faulk 11-67). At the very end of the manuscript, in the last chapter, he inserted another quote from this same Regulation (Vallejo Recuerdos 5: 235-37). By using this presidio-related document as a virtual frame for his entire testimonio,

Vallejo was clearly underscoring the importance he assigned to soldiers in Alta California's history. This emphasis upon the role of the soldiers continues to be an important corrective to popular treatments that accord a primary and almost exclusive role to missionaries and civilian settlers in the development of early California. As Vallejo succinctly put it, the survival of the missions was due to "the great vigilance on the part of the soldiers" (Vallejo Recuerdos 1: 25). Mission communities, far from being primary actors, existed only because of the protective boundary provided by the military.

The fact that the original soldiers were the founders of the Californio families that came to dominate the region in the 1820s through the 1840s led to Vallejo's second theme. This was that these Californio families had a tremendous desire for knowledge and a deep love of culture. Vallejo bristled most intensely in his manuscript when he described ways in which foreigners in Mexican California (mainly, but not exclusively, Anglo-Americans) looked down upon Californios as an uncivilized and semi-savage group of people. Some of his greatest scorn was directed at French visitor Eugène Duflot de Mofras. According to a well-known story within the Californio community, which Vallejo repeated, this Frenchman had a very low opinion of Mexican Californians. Yet he himself became hopelessly drunk when he lied his way into getting Teresa de la Guerra Hartnell to afford him hospitality at her rancho (Vallejo Recuerdos 4: 246-50). Vallejo also told a story about a young man in 1840s Monterey, Pedro Estrada, who demonstrated a surprising natural ability to play the piano. Governor Alvarado was so impressed that he proposed to the regional assembly that it provide funds to send Estrada to Mexico for more formal training. The proposal was shot down by American David Spence, who argued that it would be "an utter waste of money to pay teachers to teach music to young boys. It would be better if the boys learned a useful trade in order to get a job" (Vallejo Recuerdos 4: 333). In Vallejo's telling, the lesson is that the Californios were more interested in cultural refinement than the money-grubbing Americans. As Vallejo approvingly quoted Alvarado in another part of the testimonio, "The Yankees have money on the brain" (Vallejo Recuerdos 1: 127). At another point Vallejo quoted Alvarado's description of a festival that occurred in Monterey. In their judgment the dress of the participants, the caliber of the music and dancing, and the quality of the cuisine all demonstrated, that "the gringos who claim to be the most civilized of people are mistaken" (Vallejo Recuerdos 1: 126).

Vallejo insisted that a desire for education, for culture, and for intellectual advancement was an integral part of life in California during the Mexican era. Formal education, he wrote, was a very important priority for each governor of Spanish and Mexican California and for the local communities, especially Monterey, where he had lived. Vallejo used memories of the 1815 arrival of Governor

Pablo Vicente de Solá as an occasion to talk about the importance accorded to education in California as well as to highlight his own personal engagement in the issue. After the citizens of Monterey had thrown a party to honor the recently arrived governor, Solá immediately turned his attention to education and had the local schoolmaster bring all his pupils before him so he could determine the strong and weak points of the local schools. Solá personally founded two schools for boys and another school for girls. For the governor, education was "of prime importance and he was determined to address the issue as soon as possible." In addition, Solá took Vallejo, Juan Bautista Alvarado, and José Castro under his wing. He tutored them in private sessions and took them through a series of Enlightenment- related works that gave them a broad intellectual foundation. "After the governor explained to them how useful and important it was for them to apply themselves wholeheartedly to their studies, as well as the advantages to be gained in the future from what they learned by reading books, he gave them some copies of the *Gazeta del gobierno de México*, which was a daily newspaper published in Mexico City. He also gave them several copies of the Constitution of 1812, several decrees from the Spanish Cortes of 1813, and Cervantes's *Don Quixote de la Mancha*. He told them that for now they should study all of these materials. But very soon he would have even greater books to give to them" (Vallejo Recuerdos 1: 128-30). Vallejo also detailed the manner in which grammar schools were conducted in Mexican California and he insisted that Californios valued education, culture, and learning. To demonstrate that this foundation was solid, Vallejo included in his manuscript a number of poems that he and his contemporaries wrote in the 1810s and 1820s. In his view Californio culture deserved to be remembered and celebrated, not forgotten or disrespected. But he feared that was happening in 1870s California, and, on the next-to-last page of the final volume of his manuscript, he pleaded, "French and German are taught in the schools of San Francisco. Why are there no classes in Spanish?" (Vallejo Recuerdos 5: 240).

Vallejo's emphasis on Californio culture points to his third major theme. He insisted that there had been a major contrast between missionary backwardness and Californio desire for progress and improvement. He argued that missionaries were backward in two ways. First, their desire to accumulate wealth, prestige, and power symbolized their medieval and out-of-date world view. In many ways he regarded material wealth and power as the distinguishing characteristic of the California missions. He wrote, "There is no reason to be surprised that the missionaries had accumulated so much wealth because in terms of their relationship with the neophytes and catechumens, the missionaries were both civil governors and spiritual fathers. Without consulting any other law than that which suited them best, they established as they pleased an ever-growing number of *reducciones*, missions, and pueblos. But in all of them, up until 1821, they were the ones in charge" (Vallejo Recuerdos 2: 131).

Vallejo's favorable treatment of secularization flowed from that perspective. He regarded the missionaries hold on so much land as inimical to California's future economic growth and development. In pushing for secularization, the Mexican government and Governor José de Echeandía, who initiated the process, were seeking California's betterment. Vallejo characterized Echeandía's first moves in the direction of secularization as a "new era in Alta California which pleased the young people very much." On the other hand, Vallejo went on, "the Reverend missionaries and their followers were exceedingly troubled by this news since they would never be in favor of sanctioning changes that the Enlightenment and its laws would bring about" (Vallejo Recuerdos 2: 48). Vallejo said that he agreed with Echeandía's contention that it was unfair that "twenty-one mission establishments possess all of the fertile land . . . while more than one thousand gente de razón families possess no more than what the missionaries might be willing to give them" (Vallejo Recuerdos 2: 107). The missionaries simply desired to prevent the sons of the founding soldiers of the province from developing California's economic potential.

The second way in which missionaries were backward was manifested, Vallejo maintained, in their pre-enlightenment intellectual views. Vallejo claimed that the missionaries feared that, if Californios became familiar with the kinds of books Solá had given to him, Alvarado, and Castro in the 1810s, the missionary monopoly on learning would disappear. He believed that this outcome would be beneficial, and he did all he could to further it. In his testimonio he gleefully told the story of how he managed to smuggle forbidden books into the country and how he thwarted Fr. Narciso Durán's desire to excommunicate him for that offense (Vallejo Recuerdos 3: 109-17). It is true that some of the missionaries, such as Junípero Serra, received favorable treatment from Vallejo's pen. But it should be noted that Vallejo emphasized Serra's role as a pioneer more than his role as a priest (Vallejo Recuerdos 1: 79). Overall, Vallejo argued that the missionaries, for all their personally admirable qualities, sought to thwart California's economic and intellectual development. In his view the missionary mentality promised Alta California a sterile stability rooted in the past. Echeandía and Vallejo's generation, on the other hand, sought to disrupt that stability by moving into what they believed could be an enlightened and prosperous future. For that reason, he insisted that the missionaries' overall effect on California was negative.

At one point, Vallejo argued that the subordinate position of California Indians during the Mexican era was due to the fact that the missionaries had failed to educate them (Vallejo Recuerdos 2: 42). This observation points to the fourth major theme in his testimonio, the complicated relationship between the Californios and California's indigenous peoples. As his 1866 letter to Anastasio Carrillo, quoted earlier, indicated, Vallejo shared the view widely held by settler colonists throughout the Americas that indigenous cultures were significantly inferior to European cultures. So, he termed the native peoples "barbarous" and said that they were under the "bloody grasp of idolatry" (Vallejo Recuerdos 1: II). Vallejo reserved positive assessments of the indigenous people for those who allied with the Spanish and Mexicans and served, for instance, as scouts for the military. And he insisted that the Spanish mission/pueblo policy, offering native peoples a choice between accepting "the crucifix" or being attacked by "lances," offered a better model of European/indigenous relations than the North American policy of sustained Indian removal (Vallejo Recuerdos 1: 18).

Vallejo probably had more consistent and sustained contact with non-mission Indians than any other individual who lived in Spanish or Mexican California. Soon after he established himself in Sonoma in the mid-1830s, he began an extensive set of campaigns to bring the native peoples who lived in the areas north of Sonoma under his influence. He said that he was able to do this by using the "Roman policy of divide and conquer" (Vallejo Recuerdos 1: IV). Vallejo, along with John Sutter, was one of the most prominent northern California men who used various Indian groups as laborers on their extensive ranchos. In Vallejo's case, his alliance with the Suisun Indian leader Sem-Yeto/Solano enabled him to gather a large labor force for his Petaluma rancho. Vallejo supported Solano's endeavors against other Indians. At one point, Vallejo said that he undertook a campaign against an indigenous leader named Zampay because Solano "wanted to rid himself of that chief" (Vallejo Recuerdos 3: 235). In this instance Vallejo's interests coincided with Solano's, for Vallejo stated that Zampay's "complete and utter downfall was the only recourse I had left to guarantee the peaceful colonization of the Napa Valley" (Vallejo Recuerdos 3: 290).

Vallejo was also active in organizing and prosecuting campaigns against indigenous people farther north. In 1836 his brother Salvador attacked a group of Indians near Clear Lake and brought a number of them back to the Sonoma area as conscript laborers. Vallejo also fought battles against a number of other Indian groups of the northern California area. In his testimonio Vallejo consistently inflated the number of Indians against whom he battled. He also inflated the number of tribes that he successfully "subdued." In this he was consciously associating himself with the Americans and presenting himself as an "Indian fighter" in the tradition of the American military which, at the time Vallejo was composing his memoir, was prosecuting war against the Plains Indians. But he believed that the Spanish policy of offering some indigenous people a position —even though it was explicitly an inferior position—in their society through the mission system enabled the "divide and conquer" policy that he favored. That approach resulted, he believed, in more culturally and militarily effective forays against the native peoples than the North Americans were able to mount.

These contradictory attitudes and arguments, along with the complicated relationship between Vallejo and Solano (at one point he had Solano arrested for conscripting native children as laborers) illustrate the crosscurrents against which the indigenous people of California struggled both before and after the Gold Rush (Vallejo Recuerdos 3: 331-32). Vallejo's relationship with Solano did much to form Indian/Mexican relationships in northern California before the Gold Rush.

Vallejo's manuscript not only presents his experiences with the native peoples of his region but also acknowledges how various indigenous groups, even those whom Vallejo counted as his allies, resented his incursion into their land. At times the testimonio revealed that, for all his bravado, Vallejo could be uncertain of his own position. At one point he was describing the return to Yerba Buena of some people who had visited Sonoma. Vallejo had some of his Suisun allies row the visitors back. During the trip the Suisuns told the visitors that the Mexican government had no right to give any land grants to anyone in the area, for all of the land was actually theirs (Vallejo Recuerdos 4: 103).

Vallejo was quite aware that the themes around which he structured his history and the opinions that he expressed in his work were at tremendous variance with the opinions being expressed about California by other historians and writers. He was especially aware of what others were saying about secularization and he explicitly attacked some of these writers in his work (Vallejo Recuerdos 2: 111). These writers included Alfred Robinson, who had stated in *Life in California during a Residence of Several Years in That Territory* that secularization was simply a process by which the Californios "plundered" the missions (Robinson 178). Vallejo also had harsh words for Duflot de Mofras who had argued in *Exploration du territoire de l'Orégon, des Californies et de la mer Vermeille, exécutée pendant les années 1840, 1841 et 1842* that Vallejo and his brother José de Jesús had personally pillaged missions San Francisco Solano and San José (Duflot de Mofras 194, 254). And Vallejo had little patience with the views of Catholic historians William Gleeson and John Gilmary Shea, who argued that secularization had been an attack on the Church and that it had harmed the Indians (Gleeson 143; Shea 104-15). These examples demonstrated that Vallejo hoped that his views would be able to correct what he regarded as a distorted historical narrative concerning Alta California.

For this he relied on Bancroft. Vallejo believed that Bancroft, who had flattered him by among other things presenting him with a personally embossed copy of *Native Races*, would do justice to Vallejo's views about Mexican California. Indeed, in the first volume of his *History of California*, published in 1884, Bancroft wrote very favorably of Vallejo and his work. He called Vallejo "the most prominent and enlightened of Californians." He praised Vallejo for giving him a large number of valuable documents and said that, of all the testimonios he had acquired from Mexican Californians "General Vallejo's narrative, expanded into a formal Historia de California, is the most extensive and in some respects the most valuable of all" (Bancroft 1884-90, 1: 49, 55).

But Vallejo was deeply disappointed in the outcome. He faulted Bancroft for paying what he considered to be insufficient attention to the very testimonios and interviews he had personally solicited for Bancroft. He believed that the result was that Bancroft had presented too much of an Anglo-American and biased view of Alta California history. He expressed his feelings in marginal notes he made on his personal copies of *History of California*.[4] When Bancroft discussed in 1831 a criminal case in which Vallejo had played a role, Bancroft stated that Vallejo's personal grievance against Governor Manuel Victoria influenced Vallejo's behavior. Vallejo wrote in the margins, "How absurd!" (Bancroft 1884-90, 3: 193). And, when Bancroft criticized Echeandía, Vallejo wrote, "Well, if Bancroft does not believe what I and others say, Bancroft can just go to hell and write his history there. A historian must be truthful. Bancroft has no business doubting those who know more about the events than he does" (Bancroft 1884-90, 3: 201). Vallejo especially resented Bancroft's explicit doubts that Vallejo's story of being publicly and openly receptive to the possibility of an American takeover in the middle 1840s was actually true. Bancroft argued that the meeting at which Vallejo maintained he had made an impassioned speech to that effect had never happened. Regarding this, Bancroft simply stated, "I believe that all that has been said of this meeting, including the eloquent speeches so literally quoted, to be purely imaginary. . . . I am sure that General Vallejo's memory has been greatly aided by his imagination" (Bancroft 1884-90, 5: 62-63; Vallejo, Letter to W. F. Swasey 31 Aug. 1886).

While Vallejo remained publicly friendly with Bancroft, he had discovered, much to his regret, that he had given over much of his voice to someone else. In reading Bancroft's work, he looked in vain for themes that he believed told the true story of the Californios. He wanted to correct Bancroft's errors. By the mid-1880s he told his son that he wanted to write a book on the history of the missions "without the intervention of H. H. Bancroft" (Vallejo, Letter to Platón Vallejo 18 Apr. 1884, emphasis in original).

Like most human voices, Vallejo's was not univocal or entirely consistent. It was complicated, complex, and at times contradictory. It was a voice that spoke of community and boundary, of memory and erasure, of stability and disruption, of conquest and deceit. As such, it spoke not only of its own time but also of ours. The recovery and publication of Vallejo's manuscript will provide readers with a rich and relatively untapped source for a deeper understanding of the cultural diversity, social tensions, and multiple identities that feature prominently in the contemporary study of the "borderlands."

Works Cited

Bancroft, Hubert Howe. *History of California*. Bancroft Co., 1884-90, 7 vols.

___. *Literary Industries*. History Co., 1890.

___. "The Manifest Destiny of California." *Sacramento Daily Record; Sacramento Daily Union*, 1 Jan. 1876, p. 4.

___. *The Native Races of the Pacific States of North America*. D. Appleton and Company, 1874-75, 5 vols.

Beebe, Rose Marie, and Robert M. Senkewicz. *Testimonios: Early California Through the Eyes of Women, 1815-1848*. U of Oklahoma P, 2015.

Brinckerhoff, Sidney B., and Odie B. Faulk. *Lancers for the King: A Study of the Frontier Military System of Northern New Spain: With a Translation of the Royal Regulations of 1772*. Arizona Historical Foundation, 1965.

Brown, Madie D. "Gen. M. G. Vallejo and H. H. Bancroft." *California Historical Society Quarterly*, vol. 29, no. 2, 1950, pp. 149–59.

Cerruti, Enrique. Letter to Mariano Guadalupe Vallejo. 22 Mar. 1874. Vallejo Family Papers, C- B 441, box 3, folder 24, The Bancroft Library, Berkeley.

Cicero, Marcus Tullius, et al. *Cicero on the Ideal Orator (de Oratore)*. Oxford UP, 2001. Duflot de Mofras, Eugène. *Duflot De Mofras' Travels on the Pacific Coast*. Translated by Marguerite Knowlton Eyer Wilbur, Fine Arts Press, 1937.

Emparán, Madie Brown. *The Vallejos of California*. Gleeson Library Associates, University of San Francisco, 1968.

Gleeson, William. *History of the Catholic Church in California*. Printed for the author by A.L. Bancroft and Co., 1872.

López, Marissa K. *Chicano Nations: The Hemispheric Origins of Mexican American Literature*. New York UP, 2016.

___. "The Political Economy of Early Chicano Historiography: The Case of Hubert H. Bancroft and Mariano G. Vallejo." *American Literary History*, vol. 19, no. 4, 2007, pp. 874–904.

McKittrick, Myrtle Mason. *Vallejo, Son of California*. Binfords & Mort, 1944.

Padilla, Genaro M. *My History, Not Yours: The Formation of Mexican American Autobiography*. U of Wisconsin P, 1993.

Robinson, Alfred. *Life in California: Comprising a Description of the Country and the Missionary Establishments*. Wiley & Putnam, 1846.

Rosenus, Alan. *General M. G. Vallejo and the Advent of the Americans: A Biography.* U of New Mexico P, 1995.

Sánchez, Rosaura. *Telling Identities: The Californio Testimonios.* U of Minnesota P, 1995. Sánchez, Rosaura and Beatrice Pita. "The Literature of the Californios."

The Cambridge Companion to the Literature of Los Angeles. Edited by Kevin McNamara, Cambridge University Press, 2010, pp. 13–22.

Sánchez, Rosaura, Beatrice Pita, and Bárbara Reyes, editors. *Nineteenth Century Californio Testimonials.* UCSD Ethnic Studies/Third World Studies, 1994.

Shea, John Gilmary. *History of the Catholic Missions Among the Indian Tribes of the United States, 1529-1854.* Edward Dunigan & Bro., 1855.

Vallejo, Mariano Guadalupe. Discurso Histórico. 8 Oct. 1876. The Bancroft Library, C-E 64.

___. Letter to Anastasio Carrillo. 19 Dec. 1866. de la Guerra Family Papers/Vallejo, DLG Vallejo 54, letter 1, Santa Bárbara Mission Archive-Library, Santa Barbara.

___. Letter to Enrique Cerruti. 24 Mar. 1874. Vallejo Family Papers, C-B 441, box 1, folder 6, The Bancroft Library.

___. Letter to Platón Vallejo. 22 Aug. 1875. Vallejo Family Papers: Additions, BANC MSS 76/79c, box 1, The Bancroft Library.

___. Letter to Platón Vallejo. 15 Apr. 1884. Vallejo Family Papers, C-B 441, box 2, folder 1, The Bancroft Library.

___. Letter to W. F. Swasey. 31 Aug. 1886. Vallejo Family Papers, C-B 441, box 2, folder 2, The Bancroft Library.

___. Recuerdos Históricos y Personales Tocantes á La Alta California, 1769-1849: Historia Política del País, 1769-1848. Costumbres de los Californios. Apuntes Biográficos de Personas Notables. Obsequio de Autor á Hubert H. Bancroft. 1875. The Bancroft Library, C-D 17-21, 5 vols.

Endnotes

[1] We are presently finishing a project to publish an annotated English translation of the complete Vallejo "Recuerdos," along with a companion volume of interpretive essays. These volumes will be published by the University of Oklahoma Press. At the time of publication, The Bancroft Library will also place our typed and searchable transcript of the entire Spanish document on its website.

[2] All translations from the Spanish in this article were done by the authors. References to Vallejo's "Recuerdos" are indicated by the volume number before the colon and the page number in the hand written Spanish version at The Ban-

croft Library after the colon. Volume 1 contains a "Prologue" before the first chapter of the testimonio, and the pages of the Prologue are recorded in Roman numerals in the Spanish handwritten version.

[3]Information on Vallejo's life is taken from the volumes by McKittrick, Emparán, and Rosenus listed in the bibliography.

[4]Vallejo's personal copies are at his home, Lachryma Montis, located in the Sonoma State Historic Park. We thank Carole Dodge for allowing us access to Vallejo's personal library.

Imagined Alternatives to Conquest in Aurora Lucero-White Lea's "Kearny Takes Las Vegas"

LEIGH JOHNSON

Marymount University

To the group of scholars and students familiar with Recovering the US Hispanic Literary Heritage, names like María Amparo Ruiz de Burton, Fabiola Cabeza de Baca Gilbert, Leonor Villegas de Magnón, Adina de Zavala, María Cristina Mena, and Jovita González spring readily to mind when discussing women writers of the late nineteenth and early twentieth century. Even though she did not produce as much literary work as the above, Aurora Lucero-White Lea deserves a place in this lineage by virtue of her short play, "Kearny Takes Las Vegas" (1936), extensive folklore collections and curation, and oratorical essay "A Plea for the Spanish Language" (1911). Because she and her work are less familiar to readers, new biographical information will expose her life trajectory in relation to her literary production. A brief discussion of her award-winning oratory sets the historical context before turning to an extended analysis of the play. As a product of 1930s politics and social change, Lucero-White's play provides an imagined alternative conquest, in which New Mexicans write their own terms into the agreement with the United States military and government.

Born February 8, 1894, to Antonio and Julianita Lucero of Las Vegas, New Mexico, Aurora Lucero was the first of seven living children. Antonio Lucero was a professor, journalist, and associate editor of *La Voz del Pueblo*, as well as a Democratic candidate for Governor in 1920 (Meléndez 179; Whaley 95). In June 1919, Aurora married Garner White and moved to California (*Albuquerque Morning Journal*); according to the 1920 US Census, the rest of her family continued to live in northern New Mexico and found work in the publishing and teaching fields. She returned to New Mexico by 1924 to begin a long bilingual teaching and advocacy career, including a time as Superintendent of San Miguel County schools (1925-1927) (Meléndez 180; Nieto-Phillips 200). Women held positions of prominence in the educational systems of northern New Mexico, where Fabiola Cabeza de Baca, Nina Otero-Warren, and Cleofas Jaramillo all influenced curriculum and educational design. John Nieto-Phillips explains their remarkable prominence as a direct result of the 1912 law that granted women "the right to vote and serve on school boards of education" (200). Belonging to elite families, this cadre of women was well positioned to exercise their new authority. Lucero-White continued to collect folklore from New Mexico, and she was especially interested in religious and historical plays produced in small villages. She received her Master's in Romance Languages from New Mexico Normal University in 1932. While she was collecting folklore for the New Mexico Writer's Project, she wrote an original play, "Kearny Takes Las Vegas," dated in the WPA record as June 15, 1936. She published several volumes of folklore, including *The Folklore of New Mexico* (1941) and *Literary Folklore of the Southwest* (1953). According to the 1940 Census, she and her 18-year-old daughter Dolores lived in Santa Fe, and at some point, after 1942, Aurora married Preston King Lea. He had moved to New Mexico from Arkansas, probably to find work with the New Mexico Power Company, as noted on his 1942 draft card. She retired from teaching in 1954 but remained active in the folklore community; Aurora Lucero-White Lea put forward a paper to the New Mexico Folklore society in early 1963, but it was read by Anita Thomas, suggesting that she was unable to attend the meeting (*Western Folklore* 210). She lived in Santa Fe until her death in 1963; her life spanned a time of transition for the US Southwest, and New Mexico in particular.

Like many of the other women writers of the period, Lucero-White's early publication efforts were supported by powerful male relatives, her father in particular. However, she became well known upon publication of her award-winning oratory "A Plea for the Spanish Language" in 1911. To underscore her importance to northern New Mexican political and social life, Lucero was one of six Hispanas, along with her cousin Nina Otero-Warren, recruited by the Congressional Union to lead suffrage efforts in the 1910s (Whaley 84). In the 1930s, she turned her attention to folklore of the Southwest, collecting some for the WPA (Rebolledo xx), but largely collecting, compiling, and documenting for her own books. Her writings reflect her work and passions for educational and political success for *Nuevomexicanas*. For the purposes of discussing her work, I refer to her as "Lucero" when discussing her oratory and as "Lucero-White" when analyzing "Kearny Takes Las Vegas" since that is how she signed the play, even though her later collections are signed Aurora Lucero-White Lea.

In his mapping of the history of Latina/o literature, Louis Gerard Mendoza argues that "the formation of 'minority' identities is guided by a larger interest in the role of culture in retaining and refashioning identities in colonial and postcolonial contexts, particularly when it occurs at contested sites of struggle" (16). For women writers, especially the Nuevomexicanas such as Aurora Lucero-White, "sites of struggle" incorporate land, gender, language, and class.

Events throughout the later nineteenth century and the earlier twentieth century shaped Mexican American identity. Articles VIII and IX of the Treaty of Guadalupe Hidalgo declared that Mexicans living in the Southwest in 1848 could become citizens of the United States with all their civil rights and property intact. However, those who chose not to become US citizens and maintained Mexican citizenship were quickly disenfranchised; this resistance to US citizenship was more common among New Mexicans that the other Southwest territories. Despite the Treaty of Guadalupe Hidalgo's provisions, new residents of the United States found themselves having to defend properties they had always assumed were theirs (including spaces previously occupied by indigenous tribes of the Southwest). Instead of turning Nuevomexicanos into Americans, the treaty caused assert their identity as a community, with its own language, territory, and religion—part of and separate from the United States.

Mexican Americans (mostly men) published frequently in Spanish-language newspapers that served the populations of New Mexico, California, and Texas. While these writings might be construed as romanticizing the past due to their nostalgic tone, Gabriel Meléndez argues that these writings are resistant to US invasion. In a study of Spanish languages newspapers from 1834-1958, he remarks, "These editors saw their work in journalism as a way to inform but also to educate the masses of Spanish-speaking *nativos*. Here too was a means to contest the dehistoricizing tendencies of the 1848 Anglo-American conquest of their homeland" (63). Interestingly, Stephen Kearny, upon his conquest of New Mexico with the Army of the West, in 1846, "employed the Martínez press, the only one in Santa Fe, and ordered publication of the Kearny Code, the general's mandate installing military law over New Mexico" (Meléndez 20). Kearny's arrival then, marks a linguistic, territorial, and literary shift to New Mexicans identities. As Spanish-language newspapers served the Mexican American population of the Southwest, poetry, editorials, and short fiction offered a way for writers to engage their communities in dialogue resistant to Anglo American cultural assumptions about Mexican Americans. Furthermore, as women began publishing in the newspapers, concerns about gender and racial equality emerged simultaneously as questions of modernity around the turn of the century.

Women-authored editorials (such as those by *Tejanas* Jovita Idar and Emma Tenayuca in the 1920s and 1930s) called for an end to the exploitation of cheap Mexican labor, voiced an emergent *mestizaje*, and asserted language, educational, and political rights for Mexican Americans. Elements of the texts are sentimental, but again, the writers were not naïve, taking economic factors into account with their arguments. Congressional reluctance to New Mexico's statehood hinged on the language and cultural traditions of *Neuvomexicanos*. As John-Michael Rivera points out, "By denying statehood, New Mexico's racialized inhabitants remained politically, socially, and economically subordinated to a distant, ruling metropolitan center (Washington, D.C.) after that same center had, by force [. . .], conquered and incorporated the region into its growing empire" (118). The political climate at the turn of the century and the debates around statehood had a direct influence on continued Mexican American literary production. Articulating a unique identity was an urgent literary project in the face of Anglo celebrations of dominance throughout the 1930s Southwest.

Many of the women who wrote editorials about class and labor also wrote promoting women's rights, especially the right to vote and work. Furthermore, Meléndez argues that Aurora Lucero's "essay on language registers the participation of women in the struggle for cultural and civil rights [. . .] break[ing] from the anonymity of pseudonyms and see her work recognized for its own intellectual merits" (182). Not only does Lucero challenge the overt racism in depictions of New Mexicans but she also points out that New Mexico was a dynamic environment. New Mexicans did resist the racist depictions of themselves. Certainly, the Lucero family identified themselves as White on the 1900, 1910, and 1920 Census. Racial groups in New Mexico struggled to gain power through various avenues, but overwhelmingly, Nuevomexicanos did not docilely accept Anglo laws and discrimination as their lot as a conquered territory.

As debates swirled about statehood, and what it would mean for the Spanish-speaking population in the territory, Aurora Lucero entered into the conversation while a student at New Mexico Normal School. Her essay, "A Plea for the Spanish Language," is sentimental in its call for maintaining teaching in the language of the ancestors, but her central point is economic: that Spanish is useful for trade and financial advancement for New Mexico and the United States. To try to divorce their interests would be foolish, especially economically, and the key to more prosperity for everyone is better quality of life for Mexican Americans through education and political equality. Lucero's essay chastises Congress for hypocritically depriving New Mexicans of "the right of language in man [which] is a God-given right, and as such it is guaranteed and secured to him by the federal constitution when it declares that the natural rights of all men are inalienable" (137). Her insistence on language as equivalent with statehood, education, history, and economics, reflects the concerns that New Mexicans had as American citizens. Granted statehood in 1912, Nuevomexicanos continued to chafe under laws and regulations that rendered them second-class citizens.

Negative, racist, and nostalgically patronizing portrayals of New Mexico abounded in the popular media of the time. For instance, Lebaron Bradford Prince, a lawyer, politician, and judge, spent more than thirty years in New Mexico territorial government, but seemed to learn very little. While he claimed to champion New Mexico's progressive race relations, in his writings it is evident that he saw "Pueblo Indians and Mexican Americans as people trapped in their quaint past" (Gómez 65). He argued for New Mexican statehood, but his "progressive view of race" was problematic in that it subscribes to an assumption of white racial superiority; Prince's view held that "no person or group was responsible for social inequalities that increasingly matched racial lines, and thus no person could do anything to rectify a situation that was, after all the result of an inevitable clash between a dynamic culture wedded to progress and the native static cultures hampered by their allegiance to ancient, outmoded traditions" (66). "A Plea for the Spanish Language" counters the idea that Spanish and those who speak it are a primitive, static culture immune to American ingenuity and progress. Lucero emphasized that the need for learning in Spanish is due to the nobility of the language, the potential for commerce on a global stage, and the duty, which the United States owes to the Mexican American citizens because of the Treaty of Guadalupe Hidalgo. Instead of seeing Spanish as a relic of the "quaint past", she points out that Spanish is a language of the future, rooted in history. By claiming that Spanish lends the advantage to those who turn to South America as an "unlimited field for the investment of American energy and enterprise," Lucero argued that New Mexicans are uniquely positioned to be more dynamic and adaptable than Americans (138). Her early ideas about language and gender return in a playful, more creative way in "Kearny Takes Las Vegas."

By the 1930s, New Mexico had been a state for a generation, and New Mexicans felt they had proven their patriotism through their service in World War I; however, continued restrictions on political and social mobility aggravated the population, making it seem that nothing had changed for the better in almost 100 years. Aurora Lucero-White's short play "Kearny Takes Las Vegas" reimagines the agreement New Mexicans had struck with the United States via the Army of the West. Describing the moment of US acquisition of New Mexico territory, her writing reminds her audience that the history of conquest in New Mexico requires acknowledgement of women's participation as well as resistance to the historical amnesia of the unfulfilled promises the United States made to Nuevomexicanos in exchange for their peaceful cooperation. Meléndez describes New Mexican literature of the 1930s as squarely within a "trend to record the quaint and colorful aspects of a vanishing culture, a trend that reached a fevered pitch in anticipation of New Mexico's Coronado Cuatro Centennial celebration of 1940" (204), whereas John Morán González describes the lead up to the 1936 Texas Centennial as a crisis that "spurred Texas-Mexican writers to formulate literary responses that critiqued the link between racist representations and racial domination while envisioning a prominent and honored place for their community within the Lone Star State" (1). These contradictory impulses frame the tension inherent in Lucero-White's play, and her resolution to this conflict is an imagined alternative to conquest. New Mexico, via women's agency, asserts power over a dominant, masculine US invasion.

Written in 1936, "Kearny Takes Las Vegas" uses the backdrop of the United States Army of the West's invasion and conquest of New Mexico to tell the story of Dolores, a young woman on the verge of marriage to a man she does not love or respect. However, because her father is the mayor, she is bound to marry where he bids her. On the eve of their betrothal, the US Army invades, and she meets the charming Robert Kearny, nephew to the General. When her intended husband would rather return to Mexico than become an American, Dolores finds herself free to choose a husband for love. In a dramatic surrender to the US Army, Dolores's father relinquishes the rooftop platform to General Stephen Kearny who gives the longest speech of the play. Watching Kearny's speech, Dolores topples off a ladder into the waiting arms of Robert Kearny. He claims that this seals their love: "The conquest is complete" (13), but Dolores resists his overture, declaring the last line of the play herself: "No, New Mexico has taken the United States" (13).

The dramatic irony, humor, and stage awareness the play contains reveals Lucero-White's deep familiarity with dramatic productions from across northern New Mexico. Her folklore collections and interest in literary genres make this not only a historically interesting play but also a fascinating literary creation. The archival finding aid at the Center for Southwest Research calls it a radio play, but there is no evidence in newspaper articles or other ephemera that the play was produced for radio broadcast; on her resume for the WPA, there is a handwritten note next to the title (*NM Normal*), which perhaps means that the play was produced at the University, but this, too, is only conjecture. At the time the play was written, Lucero-White's daughter, also named Dolores, was 14 years old, and living with her mother in Santa Fe, while her father remained in California. Although it is unclear from the collection of materials, the play is in whether it was ever performed, but it is easy to imagine that, as a teacher, Lucero-White would have had ample opportunity student actors to stage the play in the community.

"Kearny Takes Las Vegas" engages the folklore of the Southwest to root it in the pre-Conquest narrative, while simultaneously implicating the Eastern United States in the lineage of the West. For instance, Dolores, is the daughter of the *alcalde* (mayor) of Las Vegas and his child-bride from Washington. Because Dolores's mother was so unhappy in the West ("she became bored with the life of the rancho"), her husband allowed her to return East, but kept Dolores with him (4). This seems like a strange resolution to the question of maternal unhappiness, but perhaps Dolores's mother recognized that her daughter would not have been considered "white" by Eastern standards. Like Lola Medina of María Amparo Ruiz de Burton's *Who Would Have Thought It?*, Dolores's body would be suspect in the East. At mid-century, "Although American attitudes were not homogeneous, a broad consensus existed among Euro-Americans that Mexicans were non-white because they were racially mixed" (Gómez 83). For Dolores, the possibility of a mixed marriage (or racial heritage) is unproblematic in New Mexico. Her status in Washington DC, though, would have not only rendered her in between white and non-white but also cast doubt on her mother's whiteness as a parent of a non-white child.

Before the US-Mexico war, the Nuevomexicano population already understood whiteness differently from Eastern elites. The territory was fraught with a history that included and excluded women, Natives, Nuevomexicanos, and Anglos, as their bodies signified the anxieties of historical contact zones. Suzanne Bost explains the phenomenon thusly, "Normative *mestizaje* was strange to Anglo-Americans who came from a region where miscegenation was illegal though frequent and where races were officially segregated" (648). For Aurora Lucero-White, normative *mestizaje* was always already the normative identity for New Mexicans. Her play envisions a "taking" that is an alternative to cultural betrayal, and instead functions as cultural protection and propagation. Marriages between Anglo men and Hispana women in New Mexico was common, with investment in whiteness as a central part of the exchange. Many of the Nuevomexicanas who participated as scholar-teachers in the WPA collections have Anglo additions to their last names. Pablo Mitchell adroitly shows how these marriages formulate a special instance in which the "Hispano elites played the trickster (or the *coyote*) to Anglo racialization projects" and prevented Anglos from staking the only claims to respectability (whiteness) in the territory (121). Even as they resisted Anglo dominance, though, there were undeniable similarities in how Hispanos and Anglos regarded the white body. Mitchell argues that the ability to "engage racial heterogeneity rather than racial binaries in their study of modern sexuality" would open new ways for scholars to think about constructions of race in the Southwest (177). As resistant to racial binaries, Lucero-White's representation of Dolores and Robert's marriage is significant for its emphasis on the contestation of gender and national identities over racial identity.

Kearny's speech to New Mexicans as he entered the territory promised to protect inhabitants from Indian conflict, to respect Catholic institutions, and to protect their property from even his own troops (Lucero-White "Kearny" 12). The actual, historical Stephen Kearny, with a flair for the dramatic, proclaimed his speeches from rooftops in villages along the way to Santa Fe, yet, "Even as Kearny bragged to his superiors about his bloodless conquest, his speeches revealed his appreciation of a more complicated and potentially dangerous reality" (Gómez 23). He seemed to win over the crowds with his promises, but by leaving the territory under military law, he sent a message that resistance to the conquest would be deadly for the Nuevomexicano elites. Kearny asked elites to imagine themselves already positioned as American citizens. This is problematic because he bestowed territorial citizenship on New Mexicans, requiring an oath of allegiance for civil appointments for the territory, even though as a military commander, he did not have the authority to create a territory (23). Implicit in his speech were the assurances that New Mexicans would be treated as US citizens, a pledge that was quickly contraindicated by delayed statehood, legislative efforts to quash the use of Spanish language, and Jim Crow-like rules regarding voting and office-holding for New Mexican residents. Kearny and the US troops called the conquest of New Mexico "bloodless" to convince themselves that the US invasion was welcomed, but research by Laura Gómez and John-Michael Rivera, among others, tells a story of resistance and violence on the part of the conquered people who were trying to keep their wealth and land holdings intact. Kearny's conquest of New Mexico is both salient factor and background information to Lucero-White's writings.

In fictional representation, all is not lost, though, for the union of West and East, Anglo and Mexican, women and men. In the play, as General Stephen Kearny's army enters New Mexico, Dolores falls in love with the young Lieutenant Robert Kearny and promises to marry him, in a comical ceremony that puts them on equal footing. This union harkens back to what Lucero-White had previously asserted in her defense of the Spanish language: that New Mexico is "the meeting ground [. . . of different races where . . .] a new race will spring from such a union that will far surpass either of its factors in all those traits and characteristics that make man better fitted for high responsibilities" (136). Taken together, these pieces of writing serve to remind Nuevomexicanos and Anglos of their responsibilities in cooperating to create a state where the folk traditions and languages of the inhabitants are respected as rich heritage that adds to the state's appeal. Her goal is for New Mexicans to be seen as, and to imagine themselves as, American citizens regardless of linguistic, cultural, and religious differences from the rest of the US. She recalls Kearny's speech to New Mexicans in order to point out the hypocrisy in laws, and she posits an alternative conquest which resists the denigrated depiction of New Mexican cultural identity.

Resistance is a popular way of conceptualizing recovered Mexican American texts, even when the text in question may participate in deploying ideas of whiteness as an elite, landed, speaking subject separate from the non-elite Mexican or indigenous working class. Tey Diana Rebolledo, in looking at *Nuevamexicana* writers Fabiola Cabeza de Baca Gilbert, Cleofas Jaramillo, and Nina Otero-Warren, claims that women writers of the Modern era employ five narrative strategies of resistance: 1) a consciousness of being colonized and voicing of an ethnic subject; 2) sentimental attachment to the past; 3) blurring of genres to challenge linear Anglo narrative; 4) employing a very feminine voice; and 5) making Hispanos the heroes of the narratives ("Narrative" 135-36). Even though "Kearny Takes Las Vegas" focuses on elite Mexicans, these criteria can be applied to the play to determine how the imagined alternative conquest works as a tool of resistance to Anglo domination and exploitation.

"Kearny Takes Las Vegas" opening scene stars Dolores, on the verge of marriage to Lorenzo, a man her father has chosen for her, and, as the audience will soon discover, noted anti-American coward. Several voices speak to her responsibility to marry as she has been told. Her nurse (duena) Juana comments in an aside to the audience that "She has foreign blood and does not understand it. That comes of these mixed marriages. They never turn out right. Always someone has to pay" (2). Juana disapproves of Dolores's mother and father's Anglo/Mexican marriage, but as a servant in the household, Juana is probably mixed-race herself. As Lucero-White considers in her collection of folklore: "Indians or half-breed servants did all the work and the lady had only to supervise [. . .] servants lived upon the estate [. . .] in a wing of the house set aside for that purpose" (*Literary* 213). As a long-time servant and stand-in maternal figure, Juana has opinions about the family and Dolores's responsibilities. While Juana's hostility may seem mother-blaming or cautionary against involvement with Anglos, the lesson actually seems to be that Dolores represents a mestiza hybridity. Presumably, Dolores is the person paying for her parents' poor judgment in their mixed marriage, in Juana's commentary; however, more likely is a sublimated realization that Juana's own social and racial status was more profoundly affected by the imposition of racial categories after the US-Mexico War than Dolores's was, at least initially. Dolores speaks in the play as someone aware of her duty to her father and herself as an ethnic and gendered subject. However, as she rejects marriage to a man who will defect from his home instead of fight for the future of his people, she experiences a consciousness of colonization with an awareness that she has a responsibility to challenge American dominance.

Dolores wants to marry for love, notwithstanding that she has not fallen in love with anyone yet or that she must marry Lorenzo within days. Despite the fact that her father, Don Juan de Dios, discourages her from marrying for love by telling her the tragic story of his marriage to a woman who "became bored with the life of the rancho and began to long for the life of the capitol—she was from Washington—and because I did not wish to see her suffer I sent her back East" (4), Dolores believes he had made a privileged choice to be with someone he felt passionately about. Soon after returning to the East, the young wife and mother died. Dolores, then, does not look to her mother's story for a sentimental attachment to the past; rather, she prepares for the engagement ceremony with her grandmother in mind. Since she cannot see a way out of this unhappy marriage, she gamely dresses herself for the fiesta: "The mantilla, the peineta, the fan, the slippers, the gown which my grandmother wore, because tonight I must be a true Spaniard" (5). This scene is bizarre because Dolores rejects her American hybridity in favor of a Spanish costume on the eve of her engagement to a man she despises. Willing to participate in the carnivalesque spectacle, Dolores prepares to perform her role in the folk ritual of dance, gifts, and exchange that precede the wedding. Her sentimental attachment to the past nearly causes her to forget herself and her desires, and in this way, Lucero-White departs from the narrative form of communal resistance to give her heroine agency in the scenes to come.

Lucero-White uses a variety of literary genres to counter the peaceful conquest narrative and to assert Nuevomexicanos' rights to their language and culture. The play draws on an extensive knowledge of New Mexican folklore, with the opening commentary about the *prendorio* (engagement) ceremony and the significance of the young woman's solo dance (1). The folkloric elements of the play contrast with the playful way Dolores and Robert banter as they fall in love. She knows the Spanish Mexican customs and follows them in accordance to her father's expectations, but when she meets Robert, her first utterance to him is a sarcastically flirty comment that she cannot live without him. Seamlessly moving between comedic modes and rhetorical devices, Lucero-White demonstrates an adept literary voice. Including a transcript of one of Kearny's speeches as he occupied New Mexico highlights the myth of the "bloodless conquest." When Kearny promised that New Mexico would immediately be considered a US territory, he overstepped his military commission. Secretary of War, William Marcy urged Kearny to exploit "racial and class divisions among the Mexicans that might provide a wedge for American invaders" (Gómez 25). Including Kearny's speech in the play reveals that Lucero-White understood the power of oratory with its ability to sow division or inspire unity. She uses Kearny's speech to highlight an imagined alternative to conquest as Dolores challenges the very moment at which the United States "takes" New Mexico. These multiple genres give voice to the different parties and attitudes at work as the Army of the West invaded New Mexico.

The use of a feminine voice of resistance is evident on the wordplay Lucero-White employs around the word "take." Kearny greets Don Juan de Dios with the news that he expects to "Take this village in the name of the American Government" and requests that Don Juan allow Kearny's nephew to "take my place if you can take him in for the night" (7). The masculine modes of exchange are clear in this conversation. Kearny intends to take (which has sexual connotations) New Mexico by force, but he allows that the Don has a choice of whether to take in the nephew as a member of the family. Predictably, Dolores falls in love with General Kearny's nephew, Robert, and their relationship follows from the "peaceful" conquest, which has resulted in her ex-fiancee's exile in Mexico for refusal to take the oaths of allegiance. Suggested in this plot of taking is a gendered superiority of the United States that supports Laura Gómez's assertion that "the larger war implicated gender roles in American popular culture, with the United States gendered as male and potent and Mexico feminized as weak and vulnerable" (27). Indeed, resistance to this sentiment is apparent at the end of "Kearny Takes Las Vegas" when Dolores and Robert seal their affection. He attempts to assert the conquest by declaring, "You see, the United States has taken New Mexico" as he holds Dolores like a baby in his arms. She jumps down to make her own announcement, "No, New Mexico has taken the United States" (13). This exchange models an alternative conquest, one in which New Mexico is an equal with a choice about what to contribute to the nation.

In reminding New Mexicans of their role in Kearny's taking, Lucero-White is in concert with the hispanistas, who Nieto-Phillips describes as using the Spanish past to "assert racial and civic equality with, yet difference from, the 'Anglo-Saxon' race" (175). While Nieto-Phillips does not group Lucero-White with the hispanistas, her work certainly deploys "hispanidad to denounce the continued social, cultural, political, and economic marginalization of their fellow Nuevomexicanos" (176). Lucero-White goes one step further in "Kearny Takes Las Vegas" to suggest that there is a hybrid vigor to Dolores that compels her to goad her former lover as a "coward" for running away from the American army (9) and to reverse the conquest so that rather than being taken, Dolores is the one who does the taking. In this way, Lucero-White imagines an alternative conquest, in which the title of the play belies the fact that Kearny has not really taken anything that was not freely given.

In the face of martial law in New Mexico, Dolores has imagined an alternative: one in which the Nuevomexicana elite retain their power in congruence with American military presence. In this shift from martial law and the taking of oaths of allegiance, Dolores and Robert have established marital law in which they take each other as partners. Both make an oath to the other which is legally and romantically binding. As the Nuevomexicana power elite, Dolores and her father have chosen to imagine themselves part of the American national body, but only if the American nation will keeps its promises and make space for them to retain the parts of their identity that make them part of the future—the Spanish language, Catholicism, suffrage, and all of the other values the Northern New Mexican population will fight for over the next century. By rooting the play in the past, Lucero-White imagines how the future might have been different for all parties.

Finally, Dolores's actions make her (not her father, not General Kearny, and not Lorenzo) the hero of the Conquest. The imagined alternative conquest allows Lucero-White to revise the narrative surrounding Kearny and the ability Nuevomexicanos had to resist. Meléndez describes the tensions present in the territory. Despite *Neuevomexicanos'* ability to attain some education and political status, Anglo-American power structures "continued to subordinate the regional cultures in the nineteenth century and in doing so they threatened the survival of a Mexicano way of life in the Southwest" (11). Continued assaults on the New Mexican way of life led to veneration of social banditry, like that of Billy the Kid; yet, for most New Mexicans, statehood and acceptance into the nation was essential to political and economic interests. The move toward statehood was a drive to become citizens with full rights, not colonized people, subjects of a far-removed government. Dolores' "taking" of the United States alludes to this not quite peaceful ending. Despite the racism and stacked odds against them, New Mexicans continued to resist exploitation physically and rhetorically.

Most official historical accounts of Kearny's invasion indicate that the acquisition of New Mexico was passive, especially compared to California and Texas. At the same time, Kearny promised New Mexicans respect for their property and religion, his troops and government overreached their influence and mandate in the West. Consequently, Kearny's initially peaceful conquest quickly became bloody through an "elaborate series of secret meetings" that resulted in lynchings and jail for New Mexican conspirators against the military installments left in the territory (Gómez 25). Indeed, Susan Shelby Magoffin's diary details fears American traders experienced. Writing on March 26, 1847, she frets, "we may be seized and murdered in a moment because we are Americans [. . .] a reckless mob is an awful thing" (215). She deplores the behavior of US troops and generals, even to say that the Fourth of July celebration in 1847 should have been postponed since it occurred on a Sunday. She observes, "Gen Kerny I am sure would have deferred it, and by his own example have taught others the propriety of remembering the Sabbath to keep it holy" (236). Magoffin believes Kearny's promises to New Mexicans will make commerce and trade easier for her husband. Ironically, his brother was simultaneously married to a Mexican woman and spied for the US Army. Violence, as enacted by other generals, threatens the peace of Magoffin's home. Despite his reputation, Kearny's legacy in New Mexico was not as bloodless or as peaceful as he claimed.

In another example of resistance to US invasion, Nuevomexicanos planned a 1846 Christmas attack on American officers in New Mexico. Before the rebellion could be carried out, "an unnamed woman notified military officials of the rebellion plan" (Gómez 26). Despite the fact that there was little information about the "female turncoat," accounts speculated about her identity and "motives for cooperating with the Americans" (26). Reports of her traitorous nature turn this unnamed woman into La Malinche of New Mexico. However, her actions probably spared the lives and land of many Northern New Mexican families and allowed later arguments regarding the patriotism of Nuevomexicanos to stand for statehood. While obviously not based on this woman's experience, Lucero-White's play attempts to mitigate misogyny and argue for the unique role women play in the transition to becoming Americans. Dolores refuses to marry a coward who would run from the Americans (9), yet she also refuses to acquiesce to the assumption that she is no longer New Mexican if she becomes a citizen of the United States. Dolores symbolizes women maintaining their identities despite Americanization. She is willing to compromise her national identity for expediency, but she will not compromise her language or her hybridity. While accounts might call this a betrayal of culture (Malinchista), Dolores has seized the tools she needs to make arguments for the future of New Mexico.

In many ways, Lucero-White's play mirrors Jovita González and Eve Raleigh's novel *Caballero*. Written in the 1930s, but set in 1848, the novel uses romance between Anglo soldiers and Mexican daughters to resolve the conflict between the US and Mexico in Texas. John González reads this novel in light of the Texas centennial to show that it "depicts the transformation of tejanas from patriarchal objects of homosocial exchange to autonomous, desiring subjects" (27). The similarity to "Kearny Takes Las Vegas" is striking, and considering these two texts together, even though they were independent projects, adds a persuasive dimension to the ways in which Jovita González and Aurora Lucero-White, primarily folklorists, aimed to use their creative and scholarly talents to affect changes in the way Mexican American perceived themselves as part of the American body politic. Like Lucero-Warren, González was highly educated and made her scholarly investigations the folklore of her community. She was the first Mexican-American woman to receive her MA from University of Texas, Austin. Noting the complexities of writing about South Texas, Leticia Magda Garza-Falcón describes González's affect: "She writes about them from a distanced and sometimes even paternalistic viewpoint influenced by the ethnographic style that prevailed during the late 1920s and by the cultural climate at the University of Texas at Austin" (77). These distances reveal how González negotiates the among and apart aspects of her identity, including the necessity of working with Anglos.

Because *Caballero* conflates events in the 1930s with those following the US Mexico war, critics debate the importance of the historical conditions surrounding the novel. Some conclude that the romance creates "a textual space where the Southwest is transformed into a Mexican-Anglo contact zone that is governed not by the politics of warfare and boundaries but through the formation of an ethics of choice that promotes exchange (Ramirez 38-39) while others declare it an "act of *nepantla* politics" and "a bid to craft a world that was scarcely imaginable amid the racial antagonisms of Texas in the 1930s" (Cotera 169). The reconciliation in the narrative for all the characters, except those inflexible patriarchs, illustrates a historical condition that celebrates hybridity and adaptability. By casting Mexican American women as powerful historical agents, González and Raleigh, along with Lucero-White, reimagine the material conditions of colonialism to relocate the ways in which power circulates and reproduces in the national body.

Ultimately, "Kearny Takes Las Vegas" is a short romance that reminds the audience that they were to be equal partners in a society that has, since 1847, rendered them Other and inferior. The play reasserts the Nuevomexicano right to participation in the national body politic. The gendered bodies in the play symbolically become manifestations of Bakhtin's grotesque body—one "not separated from the rest of the world [. . .] The stress is laid on those parts of the body that are open to the outside world, that is, the parts through with the world enters the body or emerges from it, or through which the body itself goes out to meet the world" (26). Lucero-White's characters see, write, and absorb the world they encounter, making a gendered mark on the space, even as they are marked. Aurora Lucero-White Lea's role as an important folklorist is undisputed today; her position as a creative writer, feminist, and independent scholar should serve to enhance interest in her work and life.

Works Cited

Albuquerque *Morning Journal.* "Miss Aurora Lucero is Wed to Garner D. White," Wednesday, June 25, 1919, p. 5, *Chronicling America*, Library of Congress.

Bakhtin, Mikhail. *Rabelais and His World.* Translated by Helen Iswolsky, Indiana UP, 1968.

Bost, Suzanne. "West Meets East: Nineteenth-Century Southern Dialogues on Mixture, Race, Gender, and Nation." *Mississippi Quarterly*, vol. 56, no. 4, 2003, pp. 647-56.

Cotera, María. "Recovering 'Our' History: *Caballero* and the Gendered Politics of Form." *Aztlán: A Journal of Chicano Studies*, vol. 32, no. 2, 2007, pp. 157-71.

Garza-Falcón, Leticia. *Gente Descente: A Borderlands Response to the Rhetoric of Dominance.* U of Texas P, 1998.

Gómez, Laura. *Manifest Destinies: The Making of the Mexican American Race.* New York UP, 2007.

González, John Morán. *Border Renaissance: The Texas Centennial and the Emergence of Mexican American Literature.* U of Texas P, 2009.

González, Jovita and Eve Raleigh. *Caballero.* Texas A&M P, 1996.

Lucero-White Lea, Aurora. "Kearny Takes Las Vegas." Center for Southwest Research, University of New Mexico Library, 1936.

___. *Literary Folklore of the Hispanic Southwest.* Gathered and Interpreted by Aurora Lucero-White Lea. The Naylor Company, 1953.

___. "Plea for the Spanish Language." *Herencia: The Anthology of Hispanic Literature of the United States.* Edited by Nicolás Kanellos, Oxford UP, 2002, pp. 135-39.

Magoffin, Susan Shelby. *Down the Santa Fe Trail and into Mexico.* Edited by Stella Drumm, U of Nebraska P, 1982.

Meléndez, A. Gabriel. *Spanish-Language Newspapers in New Mexico, 1834-1958.* U of Arizona P, 2005.

Mendoza, Louis Gerard. *Historia: The Literary Making of Chicana and Chicano History.* Texas A&M UP, 2001.

Mitchell, Pablo. *Coyote Nation: Sexuality, Race and Conquest in Modernizing New Mexico, 1880-1920.* U of Chicago P, 2014.

"(Mrs.) Aurora Lucero White (Resume and Lists of Manuscripts). WPA Writer's Project, New Mexico, Miscellaneous Materials, C. 1936-1940, Miscellaneous articles, pp. 017-022. Arte Público Hispanic Historical Collection: Series 2. EBSCOhost.

Nieto-Phillips, John. *The Language of Blood: The Making of Spanish-American Identity in New Mexico, 1880s-1930s.* U of New Mexico P, 2004.

Ramirez, Pablo. "Resignifying Preservation: A Borderlands Response to American Eugenics in Jovita González and Eve Raleigh's *Caballero.*" *Canadian Review of American Studies/ Revue canadienne d'études américaines,* vol. 39, no.1, 2009, pp. 21-39.

Rebolledo, Tey Diana. "Narrative Strategies of Resistance in Hispana Writings." *The Journal of Narrative Technique,* vol. 20, no. 2 1990, pp. 134-46.

___. "Introduction." *Women's Tales from the New Mexico WPA: La Diabla a Pie,* Arte Público P, 2000, pp. xix-liv.

Rivera, John-Michael. *The Emergence of Mexican America: Recovering Stories of Mexican Peoplehood in U.S. Culture.* New York UP, 2006.

US Census Records. "Aurora Lucero." New Mexico, 1900, 1910, 1920, 1940, Ancestry.com. Accessed February 23, 2018.

Western Folklore. "Folklore and Folklorists." Western States Folklore Society, vol. 22, no. 3, 1963, pp. 209-211.

Whaley, Charlotte. *Nina Otero-Warren of Santa Fe.* Sunstone P, 2007.

A Certifiable Past and the Possible Future of a Borderlands Literary and Cultural Episteme

A. GABRIEL MELÉNDEZ
University of New Mexico

As a result of the diligent work undertaken over the last three decades by the literary and cultural critics associated with the Recovering the US Hispanic Literary Program, students and researchers of Chicano literature can no longer overlook the massive archive of writings by Chicanos and Latinos produced in what is today the United States. I say this even as that archive continues to be overlooked and dismissed in many quarters. Written texts produced by the ancestors of present-day Latinos have antecedents that reach back to the Spanish colonial period but are most relevant to us for the way they speak of continuity bridging as they do both the Mexican and the American periods in the US-Mexico Borderlands. Recovery researchers uniformly qualify this archive of writings as one that is broad and variegated (Meyer, 1996; Meléndez, 1997, Kanellos, 2000, Coronado, 2013). As Raul Coronado convincingly argues this archive is better seen as "a broad tapestry of "writing" whose "materiality" emerges out of and is only fully comprehensible by apprehending the dense discursive network that surrounds it (2013).

In this paper I wish to move beyond the identification of the texts (poetry, fiction, drama, etc.) so as to set forth some meta-discursive and conceptual reckoning in the hope of recovering some measure of the intellectual thought that emerged out of a specific civil rights and cultural movement in the Borderlands at the end of the nineteenth century, a movement that had to contend with questions of modernization and modernity at a moment of deep uncertainty and discontinuity, a moment not unlike the one we face today. The first phase of recovery work has been to identify early literary texts themselves and this work alone has been remarkable in uncovering the amazing corpus of literary and cultural texts produced by Latinos. The assumption has been that very few, if any, early texts of literary criticism were written in the same time period that might reference the history or significance of Latino literary writings. This has left us to speculate as what Latinos thought about the work they were engaged in or how they valued the role of their writers and thinkers. The task of contextualizing and interpreting these early texts of literature has fallen to contemporary recovery scholars who have worked without the benefit of even meager amounts of what I am given to call the meta- discursive commentary spoken by those first "critical" consumers of early Latino literature. Concerned as I am with the paucity of a kind of self-reflexive writing, especially of texts given over to discussing what Coronado calls, "the status of the literary," (Coronado 2013), I wish to unearth one such text here with the hope of providing a fuller understanding of how Latinos understood their social, historical and cultural predicament.

In 1896 José Escobar, the editor of a Spanish-language weekly in Denver, published one such text of literary criticism or more properly a tract of literary history he titled, "Progreso literario de Nuevo México –Sus periódicos-historiadores, sus poetas y novelistas" [New Mexico's Literary Progress. Her newspapers, historians, poets and novelists]. My aim is to make the case for "Progreso literario" to be considered as an important piece of Mexican-American self-reflexive thought on the subject of education, literacy and writing. I insist that when read as an early example of literary criticism "Progreso litearío" provides contemporary scholars, a means to estimate the desire of early Mexican-American writers to produce a corpus of self-sustaining cultural knowledge and to set this knowledge upright as a means to further the cultural movement they were party to. The impact of Escobar's text with its exhortations to young people to create works of literature was quite obviously restricted by region and readership. We might rightly ask if any part of his message redounded to subsequent generations and likewise how did it inspire desire in others to participate in this movement by producing works of literature and history? It is certain that the concerns registered in "Progreso literario" remained quite geographically focused, pertaining as they did to Spanish-speaking community of Colorado and New Mexico and yet the content of the Escobar's text transcends place and time. There is evidence to suggest that "Progreso literario" inspired subsequent writers. There is for example the rather anomalous case of five members of one family, the Chacón, who decades later hold steadfast to the ideas Escobar laid out in his essay.

In qualifying "Progreso literario"[1] as an earlier example of Chicano literary criticism I seek to make Escobar's track of intellectual thought manifest and pertinent to our own time. Published in 1896 in the Denver Spanish-language *Las*

Dos Repúblicas, "Progreso literario," is on the one hand an initial survey regarding the development of Borderlands writings among Mexican Americans in one resilient corner of "México de afuera" and on the other, a kind of literary reconnaissance by which to set directions for future generations of writers and journalists.

José Escobar: Devising A Future for Mexican American Letters

José Escobar was a founding member of *La Prensa Asociada Hispano-Americana,* the first Spanish-language press association established by Mexican American journalists in the Southwest. As a member of the association Escobar would make key contributions to the cultural and civil rights agenda that press would come to embrace. A Mexican citizen, Escobar immigrated to New Mexico in the late 1880s and little is known regarding his place of birth, education or formal training as a journalist[2]. Escobar spent some ten years in New Mexico only to leave the area with little more ever being said of him even in the very papers he helped established. The record is sparse concerning José Escobar's activities in Mexico before 1889 and just as perplexing is the abrupt end of any mention of Escobar in New Mexico newspapers after 1898, the year in which he parted company with *El Combate,* a Socorro, New Mexico newspaper he was editing (Meyer 1978).

As the editor of *Las Dos Repúblicas*, Escobar was among the first journalists to offer a substantial amount of reflective commentary on the work of the press and progress of the Neo- Mexicano [New Mexican] community in education and literacy and he wrote the first substantive essay in which he offers a credo for what he saw as an energetic Nuevomexicano cultural movement in letters.

In "Progreso literario" Escobar describes the development of journalism, education and literature among borderlands residents over the course of five decades. Taken together, this catalogue of improvements challenged notions in the eastern press that Spanish-speaking communities were backward and indolent in matters concerning education and learning. Escobar's essay attempts to assess the condition of the culture of print that was growing around him and that was sustained in the main by the founding of newspapers in Mexicano communities across the Southwest.

Escobar opens his essay with bold poetic imagery declaring that he is especially pleased to address the state of letters in the neighboring territory of New Mexico in his weekly column. His stated aim is to "encourage" all those who have invested their life's work in this "sacred literary struggle." His hope is that the small circle of talented writers he sees at work will succeed in their aims and overcome great obstacles, including what he sees as, "the thorn-strewn barriers of envy and ignorance." As he extends his metaphor Escobar equates the birth of this movement to the flight a "condor" rising high above the muck of earth and reaching the blue of the skies, the only space lofty enough to allow the dreams of these cultural workers to soar.

Escobar discusses four features of this regional literary culture: its history and early beginnings, its current status marked by technological and material progress, and, its goal of reversing the persistent mischaracterization of the Mexicano in the American press. Escobar rounds out his assessment by noting the contributions and works of a number of individual journalists and writers whose work he references. As chronicler and eyewitness to a cultural movement taking hold in "nuestro pobre y olvidado Nuevo México" [this poor and forgotten New Mexico of ours,] Escobar gives lie to falsehoods that emerged in the Anglo press that painted Mexicanos as either disinterested or only passive participants of education and intellectual pursuits. By contrast, Escobar extolls the virtues of literacy in Spanish[3] as a means to improve Nuevomexicano social standing, at one point exhorting his readership, "New Mexican youth, the field is yours! Foment your noble ambitions; persevere in your noble struggle" (*Las Dos Repúblicas,* July 11, 1896).

In chronicling the early history of the press in New Mexico, Escobar concludes that the work of the Taos priest Padre José Antonio Martínez (1793-1867), who acquired and established the first press in any language at Santa Fe in 1836, had only a minimal effect on the development of the region. Yet by the very fact that Escobar can draw on historical dates and reference personalities in the Mexicano community suggests he had a prescient understanding of the significance of this first step. Escobar asserts that Martínez's work, albeit hampered by material disadvantages "[gave] impetus to literature and the education of the masses." Escobar concludes that New Mexico, an undeveloped frontier region geographically removed from México D.F. and Washington, D.C, remained a backwater, plagued by poverty, isolation and violence produced by cycles of Indian depredation and settler retaliation.[4] The period as Escobar writes found,

> Las masas del pueblo estaban entonces rodeados de peculiares circunstancias, y , la ignorancia más completa envolvía al nativo, que, separado de los grandes centros [se encontraban] perdido en los inmensos arenales de los desiertos que se extienden de Misuri á las márgenes del Río Bravo del Norte . . . " (The people en masse surrounded by a peculiar set of circumstances and when total ignorance covered the native[5] who remained separated from the great city centers, [were] lost in immense

sandy deserts that extend from the Missouri to the banks of the Rio
Grande . . .)

In the wake of the US-Mexico War unprecedented shifts changed every
aspect of civil life in the borderlands. Andrés Reséndez underscores the magnitude of these shifts by declaring, "Before any other revolutions, Mexico's Far
North experienced the market revolution" (2004, 123). Padre Martínez's efforts
to use the press for the benefit of public letters took effect in the years prior to
the US-Mexico War and just as the mercantile influence of the United States
began to be felt in the Mexico's northern territories. The period already signaled
an economic reorientation toward the material progress available from trade
with the Americans leading to what sociologist, Phillip Gonzales, calls a "new
ethnic materialism" (2016, 74). Reséndez goes further, ascribing this change to
what he calls "market persuasion" (123) a phenomenon induced by the liberal-
ization of trade between Mexico and the United States. Trade of this type
included all manner of manufactured goods including printing presses arriving
in the Borderlands. Reséndez notes that "Frontier residents projected onto these
goods their yearnings and dreams about progress and civilization as well as their
fears of Americanization and dependency" (123). Their fears having been hardened by daily displays of xenophobia, racism and ethnocentrism coupled by a
maniacal repugnance of Mexico's mixed racial heritage displayed by those
Anglo Americans taking possession of the economic, political and judicial
affairs of the region.

Escobar is not blind to the fact that political and economic power of the
United States had become a pre-eminent force in his corner of the Borderlands
but it also appears that Escobar is able to keep important distinctions clear as he
weighs out the pernicious effects of overt subjugation against the possibility of
"fruitful, if difficult liberal integration" (Gonzales 2017,17).

In "Progreso literario," Escobar details the acceleration of social and technological change in the borderlands three decades into the American period and
marked by the arrival of the railroad in New Mexico in 1879. Amid conditions of
subjugation Escobar sees conditions of rapid progress which he subscribes to 1)
the liberal laws of the American government, 2) the establishment of parochial
and secular schools in the territory, and 3) the natural inclination of the populace
to seek enlightenment. Only recently has Latino scholarship on cultural citizenship caught up to Escobar's pronouncements. Phillip Gonzales explains,

> The American takeover altered the relations of culture groups and
> affected local alliances and patterns of production in both cooperative
> and conflict directions, and it is important not to neglect the cooperative

experiences. If particular civic, public, and political development in the United States spoke in terms of universal inclusion, their application varied from region to region and among ethno racial sets. (2017, 17)

Escobar's view on local adaptation is really about local promise and about figuring out how to direct the activities of the present toward the realization of community goals and objectives in regard to literacy and learning. Escobar is clear-minded when recording the acceleration of change that accompanied the proliferation of print culture in a region that previously had been deprived of this technology. In this regard, Raul Coronado reminds us that,

> Historians of print culture no longer take for granted the role of print technology in cultural formations. The narrative had long been established: print technology allowed for democratization of writing and knowledge; it was the medium through which the Enlightenment and republican forms of government arose; and it was the foundation our modernity.

> That is print technology does not merely arrive and set out to transform societies, liberating them from darkness, as if these social worlds were passive objects upon which print technology did its work. Rather, the printed word is incorporated into a culture's already existing systems of symbolic signification. (2016, 269)

Escobar voices the deep cultural episteme of borderlands residents in the clichéd (yet no less accurate) view that a desire for knowledge burned in the heart of New Mexican youth. Escobar senses that here is the mainspring that is powering Nuevomexicano desire for educational attainment. He writes,

> Se vió á nuestra juventud, que hábida de saber, iba desde sus retiradas aldeas á esas instituciones en las que con afán bebía las benditas y dulces aguas de aquellas preciosas fuentes que debían hacer fructificar muy en breve las claras inteligencias de los neo- mexicanos, poseedores en su mayoría de un magnífico talento natural. (It could be seen that our young people were eager for knowledge and that they would leave their remote villages to go to those institutions where they earnestly drank of the blessed and sweet waters of those precious fountains, which, in short time would bear fruit in [the form of] the bright intellect of the New Mexicans; the possessors of magnificent natural talent.)

While the decade of the 1890s would be the zenith of this movement, the same motivating desire Escobar points to had already burned softly for at least a generation. Urbano Chacón (1848-1886) for example, entered the arena of journalism prior to the boom of new presses in the 1890s having published El *Explorador* in Trinidad, Colorado, in the early 1870s and later *El Espejo* in Taos, New Mexico. Urbano's efforts inspired others, catenulating in real ways the members of one generation to those of another. Urbano guided the work of younger journalists, having given Enrique H. Salazar one of the founders of *La Voz del Pueblo* his start in journalism by providing him an apprenticeship at one of his papers. Later while editor of *La Aurora* in Santa Fe, Urbano allowed his son Felipe Maximiliano Chacón (1873 -1949) to publish his first poems in the paper at age fourteen and with these quotidian acts help shape a second generation of readers and writers.

Turning to more recent developments Escobar notes the founding of several successful periodicals which he calls *acreditados órganos* such as *La Revista Católica* (1875, Las Vegas, New Mexico), *La Voz del Pueblo* (1890, Las Vegas, New Mexico), *El Nuevo Mexicano* (1890, Santa Fe, New Mexico), and *El Boletín Popular* (1893, Santa Fe, New Mexico). He notes the improving quality of each of these publications when saying:

> Esa misma prensa, en los últimos años ha mejorado de una manera bien notable, y en sus editoriales y boletines, se observa ya algo más que ese estilo embrionario de la prensa que nace: la argumentacion lógica y justa que combate, ya no por una idea de partido; sino por algo mucho más grande todavía: por el mejoramiento de las masas sin diferencias de creencias religiosas y políticas! (That very press has improved noticeably over the last few years, and in its editorials and bulletins one can observe something more than the embryonic style of a press in its infancy; in its logical and well-conceived commentary that struggles, not for political ideologies, but rather, for something greater yet: for the betterment of the masses irrespective of political or religious belief.)

Escobar points to the existence of literary and debate societies in several New Mexican towns seeing their work as another indication that a movement is underway. He sees these formal and informal gatherings as evidence that a number of individuals are engaged in literary and educational pursuits here-to-fore unknown in the region. Escobar writes:

> Como en la Prensa, en los círculos literarios de aquel simpático suelo, háce [sic] operado un cambio radical, y hoy, lo mismo en las ciudades que en las pequeñas villas, existen sociedades literarias y de debates, en las que la juventud va frecuentemente a ensayar, ya el estro melancólico del bardo; ya el recto juicio del historiador; ó bien la cortante metáfora

de la crítica, ó la difícl concepción de la novela de costumbres y los sentidos romances nacionales. (At present, in the cities as in the small villages, there are literary and debating societies which the young people attend to practice the melancholy inspiration of the poet or the reasoned thought of the historian; or perhaps [to learn] the cutting metaphor of criticism or the intricate design of the slice-of-life novel; or the novel, filled with emotion, of our national literature.)

Escobar was painfully aware of the constant harangue in the English-language press that painted the former Mexican citizens of the territories as hopelessly benighted. This onslaught of caustic and damaging defamatory accusations says Phillip Gonzales amounted to an avalanche of "misrepresentations, calumnies and a 'frenzied animosity' to New Mexico and its people" (2017, 358). Escobar notes that the rash and hasty observations of *los extranjeros* [foreigners], especially those who observe it from the safe space of a passenger train (and they were legion), elide recent efforts by Nuevomexicanos in the spheres of literacy and education:

> Los viajeros que á la fecha recorren en cómodos carros dormitorios las altas serranías, fértiles valles y extensas llanuras de ese territorio, no pueden apreciar en manera alguna el favorable cambio que el genio del progreso ha hecho en ese suelo; pero el que esté familiarizado con la historia de ese heroíco y hospitalario país, no podrá menos que admirar la energía del nativo y del colono extranjero. (Those travelers who at present traverse the high mountains, the fertile valleys and the expansive plains of this territory in comfortable sleeper cars, cannot appreciate the favorable change that the genius of progress has made in this land; but he who is familiar with the history of this heroic and hospitable country, cannot do less than admire the energy of the native and the foreign settler.)

Escobar's Heteroglossia in Gender, Genre and Generation: How to Recover What is Left to Recover?

In the last third of his column Escobar introduces his readers to a coterie of writers whose work he has come to know and value. Escobar provides both biographical detail and a fair amount of critical assessment, employing a descriptive method of analysis that can still provide contemporary students of the period with key insights on the emerging status of letters in the region.

While working in New Mexico and Colorado Escobar would have had ample occasion to become acquainted with three members of the Chacón clan: Rafael, Eusebio and Felipe Maximiliano Chacón. His association with Rafael and Eusebio would have come about when Escobar was in the employ of Eusebio's father-in-law, Casimiro Barela, the owner of *Las Dos Repúblicas* in Denver[6]. We also know that Eusebio and Escobar maintained a tenuous professional relationship over several years. The relationships each cultivated with Casimiro Barela are a likely source of the tension between them since by definition these were a mine-strewn set of associations that pitted Eusebio, a member of the Barela family and a homegrown writer against Escobar, Barela's employee and an outsider. This tangled set of interests all but guaranteed that rivalry would ensue.[7]

"Progreso literario" identifies Eusebio Chacón as the spear point of the intellectual ascendancy of young Nuevomexicano*s* in the 1890s declaring, "The attorney E. Chacón was first, two or three years ago to give the public a small book that consisted of two distinct novellas: the first a work of fantastic writing and the second done in a realist vein."

Escobar's initial identification of Chacón's prominent role as a thinker and writer has been validated by recovery scholars who argue that Eusebio became the most visible defender and spokesman for the Nuevomexicano cause.[8] In this regard, his talent as an orator, more than the elegance of his fiction and poetry, has caught the attention of borderlands scholars. It should be noted that the power of his eloquence did not go unperceived in his own lifetime and the Spanish-language press regularly praised his skill at the lectern.

Escobar credits Eusebio Chacón with laying the groundwork for the development of a Nuevomexicano tradition in the novel and for advancing the cultural agenda of his generation by offering an *ars poetica* which called up his fellow writers to fill the pages of local presses with works of literature and history. Escobar speaks of Chacón as the first among his generation to announce the liberating possibilities of what he termed, *una literatura nacional* (a national literature). Escobar revels in the expectation that Eusebio's call will provide a way for Mexican Americans to become a part of the public imaginary of the United States as a whole. Schooled in the conventions of literary study in Mexico, Escobar points out how Eusebio's incursions in the novel are tied to the Latin American *costumbrista* genre, that is to say to narratives of social custom and tradition. Escobar compares Chacón's *Tras la tormenta la calma* [The Calm After the Storm] and *El hijo de la tempestad* [The Son of the Storm] (1892) to that of the Spanish *costumbrista*, Juan Valera and to the Mexican writer, Padre Coloma:

Se nota desde luego la facilidad de estilo y asombrosa fecundida de la imaginación, del escritor; en tanto que en la segunda, se observa poco después, de la lectura de algunas páginas, la precosidad de un talento superior que desde muy temprano observa y razona. (One immediately notes the ease of style and the amazing force of imagination of the writer, so much so that in this the second [novel, *Tras la tormenta la calma*,] one can observe after reading a few pages the early development of a superior talent that has reasoned and observed from a young age.)

More importantly, Escobar underscores the idea that Eusebio has put forth a literary credo in the preface to his novelettes, declaring, "My writings are the sincere creation of my own imagination and have not been stolen or borrowed from Anglos or foreigners. Upon New Mexican soil, I dare lay the seed of a literature."

Eusebio's disposition as a writer showed a desire to bridge his formal training at Notre Dame[9] and connect it to the kind of homespun literary improvisations that were taking root in his home environment. Prized for thinking on his feet, Eusebio had honed his skills in the impromptu literary-debate forums Escobar mentions in his column.[10] Given the need for mentors in his community, it is safe to say that Chacón's influence spread equally to his peers and to members of his own family leaving with them the challenge to follow his lead in giving back to the community.

Eusebio's oratory took on a deadly seriousness during the fall of 1901, while he was living in Las Vegas, New Mexico when a sizeable group of community residents recruited Chacón to publicly denounce an article penned by Nellie Snider, a Protestant missionary who had been proselytizing in northern New Mexico. An agitated group of some six hundred Nuevomexicanos gathered at the county courthouse for a *junta de indignación*[11] to protest what they perceived as a barrage of derogatory, demeaning attacks on their culture, religion, and way of life appearing the week before in the English-language newspaper, *The Review*. Historian John Nieto Phillips provides a close-range description of Eusebio assuming his role as public intellectual standing with the community:

When Eusebio Chacón stepped before the crowd that fall afternoon in 1901, he did so not as an exercise in class privilege, though certainly his education and social position were not lost on protestors. Rather, he was a defender of the people's honor, selected for that purpose by the *junta pública*. In the context of the moment, Chacón was speaking with the consent of, and in solidarity with his audience. He identified with village traditions, cultural practices and religious beliefs that Nellie Synder had condemned. (2004, 16)

Escobar's Exhortations Concatenating in Time.

Whatever links redound to the present from Escobar's exhortations "¡Paladines de la idea, arriba! ¡Apóstoles de vuestro pueblo, ¡adelante!" [Paladins of ideas, lift yourselves up! Apostles of the people, go forth!] are tenuous, fractured and frayed. They dangle precariously by the bare threads of evidence recovered by scholars of early history of borderlands literary texts. Quite remarkably, I have discovered a peculiar tie back to Escobar's enthusiastic assessment in the work of several members of one particular family which I wish to ponder here. Five members of the Chacón family (Urbano, Rafael, Eusebio, Felipe Maximiliano and Herminia) redound to us today in recovery work through their ties to the literary movement Escobar references in "Progreso literario." At a minimum, each of the five share to one degree or another the aspirational concerns Escobar so energetically extolled over a century ago. To be clear I am not positing a direct line of intergenerational transmission between Escobar's essay and subsequent periods of Mexican American or Chicano literary expression, but I see value in noting this "family of writers" example inasmuch as it indicates that the desire for achievement that Escobar spoke of persisted in time. At the very least the example underscores the notion that Escobar's ideas were known to others and circulated over time with a measure of force and a measure of resolve.

Twenty-six years after "Progreso Literario" was published, Felipe Maximiliano Chacón—Urbano's son and Eusebio's first cousin—assumed the job of editor and general manager of *La Bandera Americana* in Albuquerque. There, he made extensive use of the paper to publish the poems that would become *Obras de FM Chacón: Prosa y Poesía* (1924), a text that appears to be the first published book of poetry by a Mexican American author. The means of publication as much as Felipe's love of poetry shaped the form and style of *Prosa y Poesía* but the fact that *nativos* could point with pride to the book as a textual vessel of Nuevomexicano authorship should not be underestimated.

Felipe's daughter, Herminia, was born to this family of journalists and writers[12]. Her father, Felipe Maximiliano, was a well-known poet and her mother, Otila Cristina Domínguez, hailed from a prominent family in Chihuahua, Mexico. Herminia was educated in parochial schools graduating from Immaculate Conception High School in Las Vegas, New Mexico in 1921. At the time a high school diploma qualified one to teach in the public schools of the state and her first teaching assignment was in Maes, New Mexico, a small, nearly inaccessible ranching community forty miles east of Las Vegas, NM. In 1922, Chacón's father was hired to edit *La Bandera Americana* in Albuquerque and she interrupted her teaching to assist her father in this work.

Herminia was aware that her ancestors had figured in public life of New Mexico and much of her life's work would go to keeping those associations alive. She wrote for publications specializing in regional topics and shared her knowledge and life experience with scholars whenever she was asked. Her grandfather, Urbano Chacón, founded *El Explorador* in Trinidad, CO in the late 1860s and was superintendent of schools in Santa Fe until his sudden death in 1886. Herminia's uncle, Rafaél (1833-1925), reached the rank of major in the US Cavalry and served at the Civil War Battle of Valverde. His memoirs detailing his early education as a military cadet in Mexico and his adjustment to life under American rule were only published in English translation in 1986 by Jacquiline Meketa[13]. Her father's first cousin, Eusebio Chacón (1873-1949), was an accomplished orator, interpreter, poet, historian and novelist considered by some to be the first Nuevomexicano professional writer.

A writer of considerable talent, Herminia contributed short cultural notes to *La Bandera Americana* (Albuquerque) and later to *El Independiente* (Las Vegas). Her columns were brief, varied in subject and most imparted a moral lesson. While years earlier Escobar had pointed out how not only men were producing noteworthy historical and literary work but also women as he explained, "some brilliant talents among the native ladies who employ a pseudonym to give to the press their poetic compositions noted for their purity of spirit." Herminia, however, broke with this convention by signing her work. From this period is Chacón's "La Noche Buena de Samuel" [Samuel's Christmas Eve], a story recovered in *Hispanic American Christmas Stories*. Nicolás Kanellos suggests the story might have appeared in any newspaper in the country. It tells of Samuel, a laborer who is evicted from his boardinghouse. Once on the street, a shop owner employs him to play Santa Claus. Unable to play a convincing Santa to some demanding customers, Samuel is dismissed and heads back to his old haunts, toy sack in hand. Once there he is set upon by the children of the poorer classes who are more than pleased to receive whatever this Santa has for them.

In 1977, at age seventy-four Herminia submitted "The Spies" to "Historical Memories Contest" in the El Paso Historical Society's quarterly *Password*. "The Spies," told in tongue and cheek fashion, describes Herminia's job with the US Censorship Office in El Paso during World War II. On occasion, she crosses the international bridge to Juárez to eat and shop. There she frequents a restaurant run by German immigrants. Spurred on by the climate of those years, "the war was dominating all our lives," Herminia gets it into her mind that the restaurant's clientele are Nazi spies that have found out she works for the US government and wish to do her harm.

Herminia continued to write well into her 90s, and from time to time, submitted historical and cultural notes to *La Herencia del Norte,* a monthly magazine on Hispanic New Mexico published in Santa Fe from 1994 to 2009[14].

In "Progreso literario," Escobar looks forward with a certain measure of optimism, yet all the while sensing a range of possible futures. In one future, borderlands residents take hold of their destiny following their desire to employ letters and education to change their situation. In another, the forces arrayed against them vanquish their desires for peoplehood. In a third, writers like Herminia Chacón and many others continued to be moved by the work of prior generations and press forward despite the odds. From this line of resistance would eventually emerged the renaissance of contemporary Chicano/a and Latino/a writing. In recovering "Progreso Literario" contemporary scholars have the opportunity to reassess the rise and demise of one nacsent cultural movement among borderlands *Mexicanos* and to more accurately gauge a number of attendant concerns all of which covergent on the idea of how self-reflexive texts like "Progreso literario" are crucial to recovering the fullest measure of the Latino thought and writings across a number of historical periods.

Works Cited

The Biography of Casimiro Barela, translated and annotated by A. Gabriel Meléndez, Albuquerque: University of New Mexico Press, 2003.

Brooks, James. *Captives and Cousins: Slavery, Kinship and Community in the Southwest Borderlands,* Chapel Hill: University of North Carolina Press, 2002.

Coronado, Raul. *A World Not to Come: A History of Latino Writing and Print Culture,* Cambridge: Harvard University Press, 2013.

Gonzales, Phillip B. *Política: Nuevomexicano and American Political Incorporation, 1821-1910,* Omaha: University of Nebraska Press, 2016.

___. "La junta de indignación: Hispanic Repertoire of Collective Protest in New Mexico, 1884-1933," *Western Historical Quarterly* 31 (Summer, 2000): 161-186.

Kanellos, Nicolás and Helvetia Martell. *Hispanic Periodicals in New Mexico, Origins to 1960: A Brief History and Comprehensive Bibliography,* Houston: Arte Público, 2000.

___. *Noche Buena: Hispanic American Christmas Stories,* Nicolás Kanellos, editor, Oxford: Oxford University Press, 2000.

Kinnally, Cara. *Forgotten Futures, Colonized Pasts: Transnational Collaboration in Greater Mexico,* Bucknell University Press (forthcoming).

"La Esperanza," El Progreso, Trinidad, Colorado, July 15, 1899.

Lozano, Rosina. *An American Language: The History of Spanish in the United States,* Oakland: University of California Press, 2018.

Meketa, Jacquiline. *Legacy of Honor: The Life of Rafael Chacón, A Nineteenth Century New Mexican,* Albuquerque: University of New Mexico Press, 1986.

Meléndez, A. Gabriel and Francisco Lomelí, *The Writing of Eusebio Chacón,* Albuquerque: University of New Mexico Press, 2012.

Meléndez, A. Gabriel. *So All is Not Lost: The Poetics of Print in Nuevomexicano Communities, 1836-1958,* Albuquerque: University of New Mexico Press, 1997.

___. "José Escobar," author/section entry in *The Greenwood Encyclopedia of Latino Literature,* Nicolás Kanellos, editor, Greenwood Press, 2008: Volume 1: 386-387.

___. "Herminia Chacón," author/section entry in *The Greenwood Encyclopedia of Latino Literature,* Nicolás Kanellos, editor, Greenwood Press, 2008: Volume 1: 220-221.

___. "Preface: Santa Fe Nativa," in *Santa Fe Nativa: A Collection of* Nuevomexicano *Writing,* Rosalie C. Otero, A. Gabriel Meléndez, and Enrique Lamadrid, editors, Albuquerque: University of New Mexico Press, 2009: xv-xix.

___. "Growing Up in the Land of Scarcity and Want," in *With Book in Their Hands: Chicano Readers and Readership Across the Generations,* Manuel Martín-Rodríguez, editor, Albuquerque: University of New Mexico Press, 2014: 131-141.

Meyer, Doris. "The Poetry of José Escobar: Mexican Émigré in New Mexico," *Hispania* 61 (1978): 24-34.

___. *Speaking for Themselves,* Albuquerque: University of New Mexico Press, 1996.

Nieto-Phillips, John. *The Language of Blood: The Making of Spanish-American Identity in New Mexico, 1880s-1930s,* Albuquerque: University of New Mexico Press, 2004.

Recovering the U.S. Hispanic Literary Heritage (Volume I) edited by Ramón Gutiérrez and Genaro Padilla, Houston: Arte Público, 1993.

Reséndez, Andrés. *Changing National Identities at the Frontier: Texas and New Mexico, 1800-1858,* Cambridge: Cambridge University Press, 2004.

Appendix

PROGRESO LITERARIO de NUEVO MEXICO
SUS PERIODICOS—HISTORIADORES SUS
POETAS Y NOVELISTAS.

En nuestro artículo de hoy vamos á ocuparnos de algo que es para nosotros verdaderamente grato: del progreso literario del vecino territorio de Nuevo México, con la mira muy principal de alentar á los que con tanta energía bregan aún en esa santa lucha literaria, y ojalá que como son nuestros deseos, e se pequeño puñado de claros talentos presevere en su buena obra, y pueda, al fin, vencer esos gigantes obstáculos, esas espinosas barreras que la envidia muchas veces, y no pocas, la ignorancia, ponen siempre á la inteligencia, que como simbólico cóndor, se eleva del fango de la tierra para buscar en el azulado manto de los cielos, campo digno donde ensayar su magestuoso vuelo.

Perfectamente estériles, fueron los esfuerzos que el Rev. José A. Martínez, cura párraco de Taos, hizo en el suelo de Nuevo México para dar impulso á las letras y educación popular: **Las masas del pueblo estaban entonces rodeados de peculiares circunstancias, y , la ignorancia más completa envolvía al nativo, que, separado de los grandes centros; perdido en los inmensos arenales de los desiertos que se extienden de Misuri á las márgenes del Río Bravo del Norte,** no tenían más que hacer que luchar dia á dia en defensa de sus vidas y haciendas con las ordas de bárbaros salvajes que á sangre y fuego talaban frecuentemente las nacientes colonias de los criollos civilizados. La instrucción popular estaba por ésto completamente abandonada, y de allí, que los esfuerzos de algunos preclaros ciudadanos á los que de cuando en cuando se unían los esfuerzos del gobierno general y local del territorio, fueran, como dijimos al principio, perfectamente estériles.

Pasaron algunos años. —En ese suelo se verificó repentinamente un cambio completo: y con el arribo del clero francés y bajo las liberales leyes del gobierno americano, nacieron las academias, los institutos y escuelas públicas, y desde entonces, en los establecimientos católicos y las escuelas laícas, **se vió á nuestra juventud, que hábida de saber, iba desde sus retiradas aldeas á esas instituciones en las que con afán bebía las benditas y dulces aguas de aquellas preciosas fuentes que debían hacer fructificar muy en breve las claras inteligencias de los neo-mexicanos, poseedores en su mayoría de un magnífico talento natural.**

Los viajeros que á la fecha recorren en cómodos carros dormitorios las altas serranías, fértiles valles y extensas llanuras de ese territorio, no pueden apreciar en manera alguna el favorable cambio que el genio del

progreso ha hecho en ese suelo; pero el que esté familiarizado con la historia de ese heroíco y hospitalario país, no podrá menos que admirar la energía del nativo y del colono extranjero, que á fuerza de constancia han llegado al fin á hacer de esos antes inclutos arenales, ciudades de tanta importancia como Albuquerque, Las Vegas y Santa Fé.

≈ ≈ ≈

La reaccion en el campo literario, data de muy pocos años a esta parte: En la prensa auméntase día por día las hojas periodísticas; y si muchas veces, éstas desaparecen poco después, siempre a su paso, dejan algo como el reguero de luz del sol poniente; algo como el aroma escapado del incensario y desvanecido en blancas espirales en las altas bóvedas del templo; luz y aroma, que sirven para alumbrar el camino del pueblo, y perfumar los ideales de sus libertades y derechos. Si es verdad que en el campo periodístico del vecino terrritorio ha habido algunas publicaciones efímeras existencia, tambien lo es, que existen **acreditados órganos** que cuentan ya muchos años de vida, y entre los que muy ventajosamente figuran *La Revista Católica, La Voz del Pueblo, El Nuevo Mexicano, El Boletín Popular,* y muchos otros de que no recordamos en este momento y en los cuales pueden verse siempre las tendencias del mejoramiento social. Esa misma prensa, en los últimos años ha mejorado de una manera bien notable, y en sus editoriales y boletines, se observa ya algo más que ese estilo embrionario de la prensa que nace: la argumentacion lógica y justa que combate, ya no por una idea de partido; sino por algo mucho más grande todavía: por el mejoramiento de las masas sin diferencias de creencias religiosas y políticas! Esa es la verdadera misión de la prensa honrada, y por eso, sentimos justo y legítimo orgullo al enviar nuestro cariñoso saludo á los fieles defensores del pueblo neomexicano.

≈ ≈ ≈

Como en la Prensa, en los círculos literarios de aquel simpático suelo, háce [sic] operado un cambio radical, y hoy, lo mismo en las ciudades que en las pequeñas villas, existen sociedades literarias y de debates, en las que la juventud va frecuentemente a ensayar, ya el estro melancólico del bardo; ya el recto juicio del historiador; ó bien la cortante metáfora del la crítica, ó la difícl concepción de la novela de costumbres y los sentidos romances nacionales. Y todo esto, sin plagios, sin oropeles y conceptos robados á otros autores extranjeros; pues que en cualquier género de esa naciente literatura, se encuentra un tinte especial, algo verdaderamente *sui generis,* que como á la poesía sur-americana, le dá un matíz de bellísima originalidad llena de delicadeza y buen gusto.

En los últimos años, escritores tan distinguidos como el muy Ilmo. Arzobispo J.B. Salpointe; el entendido arquélogo, Adolfo Bandelier, y el Sr. Cura J. Defouri, hánse encargado de escribir la historia de la Iglesia Neo-Mexicana; y talentos tan brillantes como los del jóven abogado E. Chacón, han, empeñosamente, comenzado á escribir las primeras disertaciones históricas en español. El simpático Doctor, F.A. Marrón, y el inteligente jurisconsulto, Lic. Octaviano Larrazolo, recientemente, á este respecto, han escrito brillantes piezas oratorias que hemos leído detenidamente con verdadera satisfacción.

≈ ≈ ≈

Si en el campo de la historia se ha hecho ya algunos ensayos, no sucedía lo mismo en el divino arte de la poesía y difícil género de la novela nacional: en el primero han empezado á colaborar, no sólo inteligencias de algunos poetas nativos que como los bardos cubanos, cantan de preferencia las galas de la naturaleza y las epopeyas de su pueblo sentidos romances llenos de sentimiento y no pocas veces de conceptos altamente filosóficos, **sino también algunos brillantes talentos de señoritas nativas que usan el pseudónimo para dar á la prensa sus composiciones poéticas en las que resaltan la pureza de los sentimientos y sus almas,** como resaltan en las flores por ineludible ley, los espléndidos íris de sus colores y las aromadas esencias de sus perfumes.

El Lic. E. Chacón fue el primero que dos ó tres años pásados dió al público un pequeño librito que contenía dos diferentes novelas: la primera del género fantástico, y la segunda de estilo realista. En el primer libro, "El Hijo de la tempestad," se nota desde luego la facilidad de estilo y asombrosa fecundida de la imaginación, del escritor; en tanto que en la segunda, se observa poco después, de la lectura algunas páginas, la precosidad de un talento superior que desde muy temprano observa y razona: hay incidentes en ese volúmen, dignos de las plumas de Valera ó el Padre Coloma; y como en las obras de éstos, se sorprende al talento del jóven literato: unas veces sarcástico y burlesco, y otras, elevado, filosófico y altamente moral. En suma: el librito de Chacón, aunque desconocido de muchos de los nativos, es una verdadera joya en nuestra literatura nacional.

Para terminar, esta breve reseña, diremos algo acerca de la nueva novela histórica que dentro de pocos dias más se dará a luz; novela que se debe al talento de otro hijo del país, á nuestro buen amigo el Lic. Manuel C. de Baca, de Las Vegas. Por una feliz casualidad, y por deferencia de su autor, llegó a nuestras manos ese pequeño libro que lleva el nombre de "Vicente Silva y sus Cuarenta Bandidos.-Sus Crímenes y su Retribución."

Pluma mejor cortada que la nuestra se ocupará de escribir juicio crítico de esa obra, y por eso, nosotros, no haremos otra cosa que hacer pública la impresión que experimentamos al leer ese interesante folleto.

El libro que acaba de escribir el Lic. Baca, es en nuestro juicio, el primero que llena todas las exigencias y reglas de la novela de costumbres, teniendo la peculiaridad de estar escrito en un estilo típicamente nacional. La verdad histórica de los sucesos ha pasado á las páginas de ese libro con toda su pureza, y la trama es de tanto interés, está tan hábilmente tejida por el talento del autor, que una vez leídas las primeras hojas, se sienten vivos deseos de leer,leer y leer, hasta concluir esas páginas en las que además del buen gusto y sencillez de estilo, hay un fondo moral de gran enseñanza para la juventud.

El autor se impuso perfectamente de las circumstancias: trazó con mano magistral las repugnantes escenas de los crímenes que tanto impresionaron á la sociedad veguense, y con pluma verdaderamente maestra, copió los diferentes caractéres de los personajes de esa novela llena de incidentes tan conmovedores como dramáticos, razón por lo que creemos que esa obra tandrá favorable y universal acogida por el pueblo entero de ese territorio en el que Vicente Silva, como el famoso bandido italiano, Luige Vampa, llegó á hacerse tan tristemente célebre por sus nefandos crímenes y temeraria audacia.

Concluyamos: El libro del Sr. Lic. Baca, es una obra que pasará á la posteridad, sirviendo de mucho á los criminalistas y á los que sigan en la ímprova tarea de hace la diseción fisiológica del corazón . . . ! Entre tanto, reciba el Lic. Baca nuestras más calurosas y justas felicitaciones por ese trabajo literario de verdadera utilidad social, y ojalá que su ejemplo estimule á la juventud nativa para que con hechos de ese género, puédamos desvanecer los injustos cargos y torpes calumnias de los *tourisias* que sin conocernos más que *á vuela tren*, nos acusan de falta de cultura y escaséz absoluta de talento.

¡Juventud neo-mexicana, el campo es vuestro! Fomentad vuestras nobles ambiciones de saber; perservad en vuestra noble lucha, y los laureles de la gloria y el triunfo coronarán al fin vuestras altivas frentes. . . ! Paladines de la idea, ¡arriba! . . . ¡Apóstoles de vuestro pueblo, ¡adelante!

LA REDACCION

FR LAS DOS REPUBLICAS, DENVER, COLORADO JULY 11,1896 TOMO 1, NO. 27

Endnotes

[1]The entire text in the original Spanish is included in appendix.

[2]For more see biblio-biographical entry "José Escobar" by A. Gabriel Meléndez, in *The Greenwood Encyclopedia of Latino Literature,* Nicolás Kanellos, editor, Greenwood Press, 2008: Volume 1: 386-387.

[3]For more on language use and policy in the Southwest, see Rosina Lozano's *An American Language: The History of Spanish in the United States,* Oakland: University of California Press, 2018. Lozano's exhaustive unearthing of the politics of the use of Spanish among former Mexican citizens annexed by the United States, a group she identifies as "treaty citizens," Lozano substantiates the prominence of Spanish in terms of Mexican American history, identity and group cohesion. Lozano takes discusses the particular persistence of Spanish in a number of public domains in New Mexico that include areas of education and literacy. In doing so she notes the particularity of this circumstance, indicating, "Of the four states eventually formed from the territories added after the U.S.-Mexican War, New Mexico is exceptional. The territory of New Mexico is the sole example of a Spanish-dominated political and legislative system in the continental United States. Monolingual Spanish-speaking citizens became accustomed to being addressed in their mother tongue in speeches, newspapers, and campaign appeals" (100).

[4]In his definitive study on captivity and exchange between Spanish New Mexicans and indigenous tribes historian James Brooks points out how "borderland cultural and political economies bound indigenous and colonial peoples in a long term relationships of violence, exchange, interdependence, and interdevelopment" (31). Drawing on commentary from the period and the analysis of later historians, Brooks affirms that the intercultural violence between Spanish-Mexicans and native groups is best described as "a chaotic and unceasing predatory war" (35). For a full accounting in exhaustive detail of the internecine violence between Spanish-Mexicans and native tribes see *Captives and Cousins: Slavery, Kinship and Community in the Southwest Borderlands.*

[5]Here Escobar accepts the term *native* as self-ascribed by *Nuevomexicanos* in the 1890s. As I have written elsewhere, "Nuevomexicanos already thought of themselves as native to the region and proceeded to apply the term quite liberally to their experience and condition. It must be understood that when earlier generations of Santa Fe residents took up the term they were not defining themselves against the Native Americans who as first peoples would surely beg to differ with this usage; rather they were defining themselves against Anglo-American wave of immigrants who arrived on the scene in massive numbers in the 1890s. More precisely they were invoking the fuller terms *colono nativo* or

paisano nativo (native settler or countryman) as a shield against the external, extraneous, foreign settler—the *extranjero* or *inmigrante*—those who, while newly arrived, were backed by enough political power and venture capital to call the shots in New Mexico" (Meléndez, et. al., 2009, xvi).

[6]For a more complete look at Casimiro Barela see *The Biography of Casimiro Barela,* translated and annotated by A. Gabriel Meléndez, Albuquerque: University of New Mexico Press, 2003.

[7]For more on professional and interpersonal rivalry between E. Chacón and J. Escobar see my introduction "Eusebio Chacón: Context and Contributions," in *The Writings of Eusebio Chacón.* Albuquerque: University of New Mexico Press, 2012.

[8]See Francisco Lomelí's introduction, "An Illustrious Pioneer of Early Hispanic Letters, Background and Social Context," in *The Writings of Eusebio Chacón: 13-19;* also Nieto Phillips, *The Language of Blood: 13-17* and Kinnally, *Forgotten Futures, Colonized Pasts: 255-267.*

[9]Three of Eusebio's student essays ("The Literature of Mexico, 1, 2 and 3) published in 1889 in *The Notre Dame Scholastic* while he was a student at South Bend leave no doubt regarding his mastery and studied appreciation of Mexican literary works and the corpus of current literary trends in the national literature of neighboring Mexico. See Meléndez and Lomelí (2012).

[10]Trinidad's *El Progreso* for July 15, 1899, reported for example, on a daylong gathering of the Society for Mutual Advancement, the local Hispanic mutual aid association, at the home of Casimiro Barela. The 4 p.m. session gave way to debate and speeches, with Eusebio Chacón, assuming charge as association's honorific president, leading off with a challenge talk, which he improvised on the prompt, "Through the eye of the needle." The article describes how, "He [Eusebio] began his speech on the topic with such eloquent and scientific words, that my pen does not do them justice. I can only say that he moved his talk through 'the eye of the needle' making such sublime comparisons that managed to show that the 'needle' was essential to all industry from the sewing machine to the needle on the governor of the steam engine." This example illustrates the ubiquity of the art of speechmaking in Eusebio's lifetime and shows oratory as both entertainment and a display of intellectual acuity. Clearly, the performance above was a staged event, an improvised demonstration that allowed Eusebio to show off his creative, decision-making skills on a topic chosen to entertain an audience of friends, neighbors, and family members.

[11]Regarding the extent and effectiveness of the *junta de indignación* see Phillp B. Gonzales, "La junta de indignación: Hispanic Repertoire of Collective

Protest in New Mexico, 1884-1933," *Western Historical Quarterly* 31 (Summer, 2000): 161-186.

[12]For more see the biblio-biographical entry "Herminia Chacón" by A.Gabriel Meléndez, in *The Greenwood Encyclopedia of Latino Literature,* Nicolás Kanellos, editor, Greenwood Press, 2008: Volume 1: 220-221.

[13]It is very likely that upon completing his degree at Notre Dame, Eusebio took charge of organizing, editing and preparing typewritten copies of his father's memoirs. See Meketa for more on how one of the surviving copies became the basis of her book, *Legacy of Honor.*

[14]*La Herencia del Norte*, was a quarterly magazine published by Ana Pacheco in Santa Fe for over a decade from 1994 to 2009. *La Herencia del Norte* concerned itself with documenting all aspects of Hispanic borderlands culture. The sixty four issues that constitute the 15-year run of the magazine are interspersed with the work of historians and academics, but significantly in an act resembling the desire of earlier Spanish-language newspapers to incorporate the voice of the people, *La Herencia* regularly published letters and articles by subscribers and everyday people whose recollections of life in the borderlands figure prominently in the magazine.

Literary Detective Work Reclaims Eusebio Chacón From the *Telarañas* of History: Exhuming a Forgotten Generation

Francisco A. Lomelí
University of California, Santa Barbara

I. Detecting, Recovering, Reclaiming

Literary archeology is not exactly a science because it does not involve the study of the material remains of past human life and activities. The artifacts studied here are not bones, stone tools or human-made objects buried in the earth with the intent of unveiling ancient or extinct cultures. The techniques might not be the same but the ultimate objective is comparable or at least inspired by them. Field work is not conducted in ruins or sites requiring diggings, yet excavations occur nonetheless in multiple places: libraries, personal holdings, long-term micro- fiche records, archives and sometimes embedded within other writings (i.e. chronicles, accounts and other historical documents). Whereas traditional archeology concentrates more on the unearthing of physical artifacts, literary archeology focuses on identifying, classifying and analyzing symbolic texts as encoded voices from specific periods of the past. The idea of origins and genealogy have become central to tracing a legacy and consequently connect works as dots that help define a literary history. This kind of endeavor has been instrumental in tracing the origins of Chicana/o literature prior to the Renaissance Period of 1965 when such a literary expression re-emerged with a renewed purpose and vitality. Thanks to the Recovering the US Hispanic Literary Heritage Program at the University of Houston and its mission, the ultimate objective has been to undertake systematic steps working backwards deeper and deeper into time of the lost and forgotten depositories or texts that oftentimes occupied dusty shelves in unknown collections. Literary production by non-European origin ethnic group in the United States has been generally slighted intentionally or unintentionally, and thus excluded from mainstream consideration, as Gerald W. Haslam claims:

> The potential symbolic and intellectual flexibility inherent in a multi-cultural nation is unwittingly obscured in countless classrooms where a course in European-American literature is substituted for one reflecting more accurately the cultural amalgam that is the United States.[1]

This has made the fruits by a cadre of committed Recovery Program scholars even that much more prodigious since 1991, having gathered and documented over 20,000 files, including books, newspapers, weeklies, pamphlets, essays, *coloquios* or short plays, and literary pieces from all genres (i.e. poems, editorials, book reviews), written folklore and other sources.[2] The result is a body of literary expression that qualifies as the most voluminous of any ethnic group in the United States—a fact that my shock many. This essay charts the process of detecting, recovering and reclaiming the work and literary legacy of Eusebio Chacón, which the work and resolve of the Recovery Program makes possible.

Thanks to Luis Leal-the first Chicano Sherlock Holmes in literary history—who in 1973 wrote the seminal article, "Mexican American Literature: A Historical Perspective" (1973),[3] which I took notice of the potential for locating works by Chicanos or their ancestors prior to 1965. Leal provided a periodization scheme to better understand the literature's origins and development, that is, he described the genealogy of its background in order to best capture its context in more contemporary times. Before then, most of the prospective critics of Chicano literature only possessed a nebulous sense of the past. It is not that we undervalued the cultural production of our forbearers, but we were steeped in an urgent situation in which our artistic background had been denied and erased, while not knowing what and how to recover it. I still vividly recall in 1971 when José Antonio Villarreal's *Pocho* (1959) resurfaced from sheer oblivion as an early epic work of the Mexican people in the United States.[4] Its accumulated dust on the shelf was wiped off with a collective gasp. Then we suddenly pondered further possibilities: other early works must assuredly exist somewhere! *Pocho's* unexpected reappearance along with Leal's methodic search for delineating a literary history, first, created hope of finding long-lost works and, secondly, opened the floodgates for uncovering evidence of a potentially tangible Chicano literary heritage. This reached a peak in the early 1990s under the stewdship of Arte Público Press and the Recovery Program, with Nicolás Kanellos as director, which together spurred a comparable second Renaissance by concentrating on seeking out works prior to 1965.

II. Eusebio Chacón: From a Central Cultural Figure to a Missing Link

By retracing the steps of Eusebio Chacón (1869-1848), born in New Mexico but a life- long resident of Trinidad, Colorado, we are able to recover a watershed figure instrumental in uncovering a broad and mixed matrix of writings from 1890-1910, an abundantly literate period. It has been indeed a challenge for Chaconian scholars to create a faithful personal profile on him, requiring years of painstaking efforts to piece together fragmented clues, literary shards in obscure newspaper, notes of interest, isolated published writings and also unpublished samples gathered from relatives, little-known newspapers and other means, as Gabriel Meléndez and I demonstrate in *The Writings of Eusebio Chacón* (2012),[5] which contains every letter, poem, article or essay that could be found relative to this author. Chacón also embodies a strategic person of his era who almost vanished without a trace. Such a circumstance is telling of the degree to which Neo-Mexicano [6] literary history was buried under the weight of Anglo presence.[7] Chacón became a statistic of someone who had played a prominent role among his people but who at the same time was virtually erased from memory after the new East Coast settlers became a strong minority after 1915 and slowly began taking over or coopting Neo- Mexicano institutions. By 1930, his shining reputation became faint and he started to take a back seat to the imported English-dominant aesthetic and literary tastes. However, between 1890 and 1915, he played a key role socially, culturally, discursively and intellectually in the heavily- Hispanic triangle-corridor between Las Vegas and Santa Fe, New Mexico, and Trinidad, Colorado, but after 1930 he can best be described as a puzzling missing link during what was once recognized as an era of vast artistic and literary activity that included literary societies, a proliferation of newspaper outlets, publishing houses, considerable dialogue of the merits of folklore and the written media, and a sophisticated network of contact with writers and intellectuals from Latin America, Spain and other parts of Europe.

Chacón offers a clear glimpse into a complicated past and the many factors that both produced and compromised a Hispanic literary tradition. Before 1975, few of us knew of his existence at all. In a special issue of *De Colores: Journal of Emerging Raza Philosophies* in that same year, co-editors Anselmo Arellano and Julián Vigil reproduced Chacón's famous "Elocuente Discurso" from 1901,[8] a fiery oration consisting of a blistering rebuke against a self- righteous protestant missionary who reviled Neo-Mexicanos for their customs, their Spanish language and their Catholicism. This represented a moment of truth and the tip of an iceberg because Arellano referenced Chacón's notable writings skills without specificity. We later discovered that Chacón formed part of the editorial crew of important Hispanic newspapers *El Progreso* and *Las Dos Repúblicas*, both from Colorado in the 1890s. He was also featured in a portrait in Benjamín M. Reads' and Eleuterio Baca's *Illustrated History of New Mexico* (1912)[9]— praising only his essayistic skills and stature within the community—and mentioned in a quick book review in *Boletín Popular* in 1893 and in another positive review by José Escobar in 1896 who praised Chacón's literary talents. His personal attributes are consistently highlighted for being a model citizen, a man of letters, and a scholar of distinction, thanks in great part to his integrity, honesty, a sense of honor, and wisdom. As a graduate from law school at the University of Notre Dame, he exhibited a classical training with a corresponding broad intellectual background by having mastered most Romance languages along with a reading ability of Aramaic.[10] His fame resides more in his career as a long-time public defender, a notable civil servant, and especially as deputy district attorney in Las Animas County in southern Colorado. In addition, he performed a key role as official translator and interpreter for the United States Court of Private Land Claims or land grants between 1891 and 1904 for the then territories of New Mexico and Arizona.

Despite his many accomplishments, Chacón was generally viewed from two perspectives: Anglos saw him as a uni-dimensional career lawyer whereas Neo-Mexicanos and Hispanic Coloradans appreciated his versatility as both a community leader and a writer. It did not take long before his novelistic prowess was overlooked and faded into the background almost to the point as if he never existed at all. He remained more as a hidden footnote as José Timoteo López, Edgardo Núñez and Roberto Lara Vialpando's 1959 *Breve reseña de la literatura hispana de Nuevo México y Colorado* illustrates. They completely ignored him, even within the references to turn-of-the-century banditry literature. In other words, his contributions to the novelistic genre and his theorizations about how to create a regional literature remained marginalized from 1900 to 1975. Regarding the creation of a regional novel on "New Mexico soil", Chacón states in the Introduction to his two novelettes of 1892, *El hijo de la tempestad y Tras la tormenta la calma; dos novelitas originales*:

> Son creación genuina de mi propia fantasía y no robadas ni prestadas de gabachos ni extranjeros. Sobre el suelo Nuevo Mexicano me atravo á [sic] cimentar la semilla de la literatura recreativa para que si después otros autores de más feliz ingenio que el mío siguen el camino que aquí

trazo, puedan volver hacia el pasado la vista y señalarme como el primero que emprendió tan áspero camino.[11]

As one can easily surmise, he was fully cognizant of his position as a pioneer of the novel genre written in the Spanish language in his region and the United States—a step he considered vital toward achieving some degree of cultural autonomy despite being part of a conquered people that still felt fresh some forty years later. Other editors in Spanish-language newspapers of the time, according to Gabriel Meléndez in *So All Is Not Lost: The Poetics of Print in Nuevomexicano Communities, 1834-1958* (1997), claim that his vision and intent set the foundation for what also came to transcend the regional literary agenda for a "national literature". A fellow editor and friend of Chacón's, José Escobar, reiterated the concept in a 1896 editorial note in the newspaper *Las Dos Repúblicas* from Denver: "Se sorprende al talento del jóven [sic] literato: unas veces sarcástico y burlesco y, otras veces, elevado, filosófico y altamente moral. En suma: el librito de Chacón, aunque desconocido de muchos de los nativos, es una verdadera joya en nuestra literatura nacional."[12]

It appeared that only certain insiders knew of Chacón during his era despite a well- grounded reputation. How did he later fall through the cracks? Why was there little follow-up in terms of his contributions, importance and impact? What other social factors remained in operation that contributed toward obscuring his prominence? While co-authoring with Donaldo W. Urioste in *Chicano Perspectives in Literature: A Critical and Annotated Bibliography* (1976), we fiercely wanted to include every and any work known or unknown published by Chicanos from past and present in order to offer librarians and critics the parameters of the landscape of our literature up to 1976. I ventured into the Special Collections at the University of New Mexico to inquire about early Hispanic writings to test the waters. Out of curiosity, I posed the general question about the existence of any early Hispanic writers and the librarian, thanks in great part to serendipity, said that she vaguely recalled someone recently mentioning a small book by some Neo-Mexicano writer, she thought, whose name began with "Ch". After perusing the old catalogue cards, suddenly, I had in my hands the only remaining and original 1892 landmark copy of Chacón's *El hijo de la tempestad y Tras la tormenta la calma; dos novelitas originales*, published by La Tipografía del *Boletín Popular* in Santa Fe, clearly an outlet for early Neo-Mexicano writers. The book seemed unencumbered, abandoned but in great condition, forgotten by time like some library relic. Precipitously, I grasped the significance of holding in my hand evidence of an artifact of not one early novel but two, admittedly conjecturing this could be the first novel by an author of Mexican descent in the United States.

In fact, Chacón reigned as the "first novelist" in Chicano critical circles for about 16 years between 1976 and 1992, only to later discover that he was preceded by Amparo Ruiz de Burton when her works were recovered and republished in the early 1990s by the aforementioned Recovery Program: *Who Would Have Thought It?* (1872) and *The Squatter and the Don* (1885).[13] Nonetheless, Chacón in the middle l970s stirred unprecedented probabilities. Could a narrative or poetic tradition begin to emerge from this rediscovery? How isolated might these works be? Or is this another tip of the iceberg? Either way, the *telarañas* were being slowly lifted to contemplate antecedents like never before. Encountering Chacón immediately triggered a keen interest among some of us to "rediscover" other older texts that had somehow fallen out of favor, been missing, misplaced, or simply lost and forgotten.

Such a finding reaffirmed my suspicions: there must be other works resting in shelves waiting to be found. How far back should we search? The pressing question was: How can we produce new leads? Where does one look? Shelf by shelf, collection by collection or archive by archive (Inquisition papers, chronicles, accounts)? How should we work backwards? Chacón makes the following case in his Introduction to his two novels: "Sobre el suelo Nuevo Mexicano me atrevo a cimentar la semilla de la literatura recreativa para que si después otros autores de más feliz ingenio que el mío siguen el camino que aquí les trazo, puedan volver hacia el pasado la vista y señalarme como el primero que emprendió tan áspero camino" (2).

Here he was explicitly alluding to the conception and possible creation of an early Neo- Mexicano novel written in Spanish in the region between southern Colorado and northern New Mexico. In tracking dispersed leads and slices of information, I detected a definite profile emerging. A final product came together in 2012 when A. Gabriel Meléndez and I published the definitive compilation of Chacón's works up to now, titled *The Writings of Eusebio Chacón*.

Was he in fact what we might term a missing link of early Chicano literature or simply an illusion, an isolated case, a fortuitous footnote? What other archival materials could be examined to locate and recover new names and their works hidden within unsuspecting sources? For whom were these works produced?

In other words, he led Chaconian scholars from one hidden source to another, including chain of events, unidentified names and conditions regarding a little-known artistic phenomena which had generally been viewed as culturally insular. Such efforts seamlessly fed into the various publications produced by the Recovery Program, but also other notable publications as part of the "Pasó Por Aquí" series, beginning with Erlinda Gonzales-Berry's landmark collection of literary history from 1989, *Pasó Por Aquí: Critical Essays on the New Mex-*

ican Literary Tradition, 1542-1988. Thanks in great part to Luis Leal's historical paradigms and Chacón's emblematic figure, in 1976 Donaldo Urioste and I came across or "rediscovered" the writings of such authors as Felipe Maximiliano Chacón and his *Obras de Felipe Maximiliano Chacón, "el cantor neomexicano": poesía y prosa* (1924),[14] Vicente J. Bernal and his *Las primicias* (1916),)[15] and later perhaps the earliest critical approaches to Hispanic literary production by Timoteo López, Edgardo Núñez and Roberto Lara Vialpando in their pioneering *Breve reseña de la literatura de Nuevo México y Colorado* (1959).[16]

III. A Neo-Mexicano Generation, Movement and Renaissance All in One, 1890-1910

In the early 1980s Anselmo Arellano had already mentioned informally and in his unpublished articles, such as "La poesía nuevomexicana, su desarrollo y transición durante los fines del siglo diez y nueve," that northern New Mexico had been an area ripe for literary productivity and dissemination.[17] Later Meléndez's book *All Is Not Lost* also asserts Chacón's rightful place as a key member of a Neo-Mexicano generation, as part of a "transitional generation,"[18] that was instrumental in the propagation of a literary movement in the 1890s and into the early l900s, but I first proposed Chacón as one of the undeniable leaders of what I called a "modest renaissance" of Neo-Mexicano letters.[19] Largely thanks to these inquiries about Chacón, a watershed of literary voices, creative works and intellectual activities have resurfaced which have contributed toward justifying and unveiling the first ethnic Hispanic renaissance from northern New Mexico and southern Colorado predating the Harlem Renaissance by at least 30 years.[20] Findings from this cultural boom immediately produced major results in the form of a treasure trove of literary happenings, deeds and key personalities who had been completely unrecognized or invisible according to mainstream critical circles, therefore existing as an alternate cultural movement that was in many ways superior to regional Anglo writings at that time because of their more advanced access to print media through newspapers.

Chacón has become an iconic figure from this period for his achievements and moral compass as a public persona, although he was not alone. By examining the broader landscape of figures, newspapers, literary societies and other evidence of literary creativity during those years, we encounter the existence of a substantial cohort of important male figures who together formed both a generation of literati and intelligentsia and an intellectual-literary movement within a Hispanic triangle-corridor from Las Vegas, New Mexico-which served as the epicenter and extended to both Santa Fe and Trinidad from southern Colorado.

While we have yet to identify women writers of the era under study, this generation comprised a Neo-Mexicano pantheon of intellectuals, cultural activists, journalists, poets, orators, fiction writers, novelists, playwrights, essayists, and of course many newspaper editors. These writers operated outside the radar of mainstream Anglo Southwestern letters, truly creating a parallel school of literary production that clearly superseded what Anglos were doing at the time. Because of the language barrier, two literary traditions sometimes co-existed, but oftentimes collided, challenged each other and sometimes participated in not so subtle campaigns of ignoring the other. By 1912 when New Mexico became a state of the Union, the English language gained in prominence and importance, thus partly undermining the gains of the general press and literary production in Spanish up to that point in time. For this reason, the Neo-Mexicano literary movement started to lose some momentum around 1910.

Again, the idea of a missing link haunts us because in pursuing his person and writings a whole backdrop and chain of Neo-Mexicano writings and authors have become known. Many of them resided in or near the city of Las Vegas. The list of authors is indeed extensive, but in large part, thanks to Chacón as a catalyst, we have managed to identify a constellation of numerous illustrious names and cultural pillars of the region, such as Porfirio Gonzales, Casimiro Barela, Manuel C. de Baca, Vicente J. Bernal, José Escobar, José Inés García, Higinio V. Gonzales, Jesús María H. Alarid, José Inés García, Eleuterio Baca, Felipe Maximiliano Chacón, Don Jorge Ramírez, Don Pedro Bautista Pino, Antonio J. Martínez, Ezequiel C. de Baca, Eleuterio Baca, José Manuel Arellano, Antonio Lucero, Camilo Padilla, Severino Trujillo, José Segura, Camilo Padilla, E.H. Salazar, Félix Martínez, Néstor Montoya, and many others.[21] In addition, there are others who started contributing before 1890 but whose writings remained unpublished, such as Manuel M. Salazar with his novel "Aurora y Gervasio, o sea, la historia de un caminante" (1881). The central point here is that literary expression, both oral tradition and written, was flourishing in the late nineteenth century.

Various newspaper columns within the Hispanic triangle-corridor offer observations, assessments and praise for some of the figures cited above, which further underscores the centrality of their contributions to the field of literature. One anonymous editor notes the salient qualities of another local poet named Don Eleuterio Baca as one of the leaders of the city of Las Vegas in these terms:

> Don Eleuterio Baca, fiel y digno discípulo de Calderón y Lope de Vega,
> el primero de los poetas Neo-Mexicanos, estuvo en la ciudad esta semana, de su residencia en Sapelló. [E]s uno de esos genios que la madre

naturaleza dá [sic] pocos al mundo. El arte de hacer versos le viene tan natural a él como le es al [Río] Gallinas su corriente de agua.[22]

It should be clarified that the lists cited above do not adequately reflect nor represent the numerous authors who practiced oral tradition as a lived literature which played a significant and intimate role in the production of literary expression in the region at the same time that the concept of "written literature" significantly expanded between invention and practice. Much of the oral tradition—in the form of poetry, *corridos* and short plays called *coloquios*—has remained undocumented and only efforts by prominent folklorists, such as Aurelio Espinosa, Aurora Lucero White-Lea, Arthur L. Campa, Juan B. Rael, Rubén Cobos[23] and more recently Enrique Lamadrid, Peter García, Tey Diana Rebolledo, and Juan Estevan Arellano, have contributed toward the ample collection of folkloric practices and popular traditions. This is how we came to know nineteenth-century popular poets, troubadours and *cantadores*, for example, El Poeta Negrito, El Viejo Vilmas, Chicoria, Gracia and El Pelón who still populate the imagination of the Neo-Mexicano populace.[24]

There is ample evidence of an endless list of key figures who participated in an ambience of intellectual exchange and literary debates, including the proliferation of alternative artistic institutions such as the plethora of literary societies and mutual aid societies that served as the foundation of an unparalleled Neo-Mexicano cultural renaissance during the 1890s. A 1892 editorial in the newspaper *La Voz del Pueblo* accurately captures the relationship between these *sociedades* and the revitalized cultural activity—in large part, meaning the production and publication of literary pieces—: " . . . cuando en un futuro lejano se haga la historia sobre la vida cultural de Las Vegas [New Mexico], se tendrá que afirmar que 1892 es el año de las sociedades literarias y de ayuda mutua." Not by coincidence, Eusebio Chacón published his two novelettes that same year, which appears to be a watershed landmark.

The boom of this phenomenon was fueled by the explosion of approximately 283 newspapers—mainly in Spanish and bilingual—launched during the period between 1879 and 1900[25] in New Mexico where literacy and readership increased exponentially, gaining greater momentum in the decade of the 1890s. Such a proliferation of newspapers spawned an unprecedented affirmation of a new Neo-Mexicano identity via the printed media while recognizing they were working against all odds in proportion to actual social power. The aforementioned Hispanic triangle-corridor was the principal location of extensive literary activity which radiated throughout New Mexico and into southern Colorado. The city of Las Vegas alone operated as a major hub of the general resurgence with a total of 44 newspapers[26] during the same period which represents an unprecedented number in the American Southwest. Consequently, this explosion generated a widespread interest, impacting virtually every aspect of cultural life in the region. Furthermore, its regional focus might have been its original intent, but it is also characterized by extensive contact and exchange with other international newspapers and writers through unexpected channels and translations. In fact, many newspapers ran weekly literary sections of original writings from regional authors and from other countries, thereby oftentimes highlighting the international scope and interest in such writings.

Numerous literary and mutual aid *sociedades* sprang up in every major town, mainly in northern New Mexico and even in small and obscure villages, including the following partial list:[27] La Sociedad Social, Literaria y de Devates [sic] de Ayuda Mutua de las Vegas (1892), Sociedad Protectora (1895), Club Dramático Hispano-Americana de Las Vegas (1891), Sociedad Filantrópica Latino-Americana (1892), Sociedad Literaria y de Ayuda Mutua de Agua Negra (1898), Sociedad Literaria de Las Vegas (1892), La Estrella Literaria (1893?), Sociedad Dramática Hispano-Americana de Las Vegas (1891), Casino Hispanoamericano (1891), Sociedad Hispano-Americana (1892), El Club Dramático Neo-Mexicano de Las Cruces (1907), and countless other *sociedades* or artistically-oriented groups. By extrapolating information from dispersed archival documents and newspapers, it is estimated that at least 72 *sociedades*, which usually operated in conjunction with mutual aid societies, were founded between 1890 and 1900,[28] thus reinforcing their importance and role as generators and forums of literary thought and also sanctuaries for the pride in the Spanish language. In 1892, a local newspaper reported in an editorial column that six *sociedades literarias* were newly established to complement the other two existing ones, for a total of eight within the city of Las Vegas, New Mexico, within the same year. No other city can boast of such activity with the main purpose of promoting literary production and dissemination in the borderlands.

Chacón was squarely in the middle of this milieu as an important contributor to debates, aesthetic proposals, editorial work in newspapers, social activism as an advocate for Neo- Mexicano issues, professional involvement as a lawyer, and of course his fictional writings. Among some of the titles produced during this period are: *Noches tenebrosas en el condado de San Miguel* (1898) from the newspaper *El Sol de Mayo*, *Historia de Vicente Silva y sus cuarenta bandidos, sus crímenes y retribuciones* (1896) by Manuel C. de Baca in a separate book, *Historia de un cautivo* (1898) by Porfirio Gonzales[29] from the newspaper *La Voz del Pueblo* (1898). As one can surmise, most of these works from the 1890s, including one of Chacón's two novellettes, *El hijo de la* tempestad, deal with bandits, outlawry and some kind of social chaos, directly or indirectly, but his second novelette, *Tras la tormenta la calma*, veers away from this topic, opting instead to present a novel about honor within the tradition of *Las novelas ejem-plares* by Miguel de Cervantes within the Spanish Golden Age. Even the authors of *Breve reseña de la literatura hispana de Nuevo y Colorado* from 1959 con-firms our claim as follows:

> Las novelas aparecidas en Nuevo México a fines del siglo pasado tienen como tema la vida de los bandoleros que se hicieron famosos en toda la 'salvaje frontera'. Al lado de los cuatreros "gueros" eran famosos los hispanos Vicente Silva y Elfego Baca en Nuevo México, Joaquín Mur-rieta en California . . . Las novelas editadas en Nuevo México [están] escritas en español sencillo y casi dialectal lleno de modismos y giros propios del Suroeste. (p. 17)[30]

It must be stated that such works reflected serious concerns for the social instability of the epoch through their metaphoric representations at the same time that other writers contemplated purely aesthetic matters, abstractions, med-itations or romantic reflections in addition to those who practiced artistic criti-cism through essays or editorials. Otherwise, literally, thousands of literary pieces of all genres are located embedded in scattered and oftentimes lost or destroyed newspapers where Neo-Mexicano literary history remained hidden in the form of artifacts waiting to be rediscovered. There is also a long list of news-papers that directly participated in the early Neo-Mexicano Renaissance between 1890 and 1910, including those just mentioned above: *El Boletín Pop-ular* (Santa Fe), *El Nuevo Mexicano* (Santa Fe), *Revista Católica* (Las Vegas), *El Farol: El Unico Periódico Castellano al Sur de Las Vegas y Este del Río Grande* (Las Vegas), *Las Dos Repúblicas* (Denver—which held close ties with Trinidad, Colorado), *El Sol de Mayo* (Las Vegas), *El Estandarte de Springer* (Springer, New Mexico), *El Hispano-Americano* (Las Vegas), *El Progreso* (Trinidad, Colorado), *El Independiente* (Las Vegas), *El Eco del Norte* (Mora, New Mexico), *La Gaceta de Mora* (Mora), *El Mosquito* (Mora), *El Amigo del Pueblo* (Ratón, New Mexico), *El Combate* (Wagon Mound), among many oth-ers.[31] Numerous newspapers from farther south such as *La Bandera Americana* (Albuquerque), *Opinión Pública* (Albuquerque), *El Defensor del Pueblo* (Albu-querque), *Eco del Valle* (Las Cruces) and others supported the general trend of promoting belles lettres in their columns to further support the idea of a general literary rebirth.

An endless number of literary examples could be cited and extracted from the newspapers to provide proof the Neo-Mexicano Renaissance and of course Chacón is still perhaps one of its best representatives, given his contributions, stature and cross-sectional influence in Neo-Mexicano society. What emerges is a broad spectrum of writings, some of which naturally have a close affinity with popular local folklore such as *inditas, cautivos and entriegas*—[32] always favorite genres among Neo-Mexicanos—, but it is also clear that some of the authors were inspired by literary trends from Mexico and Latin America (especially *Modernismo*, Naturalism, Realism and a late Romanticism) and Spain (late Romanticism, Realism and Naturalism), and other writers from France, Germany and Italy via translations (i.e. Homer, Virgil, Shakespeare, Hugo, etc.). What is undeniable is their degree of independence and autonomy in terms of expressing pressing issues or concerns in their respective region, or simply exhibiting a flair for the puns, innuendoes, double entendres or other word plays. The following example from 1899 titled "Décimas curiosas", a popular form of versification from an anonymous author illustrates the poetic dexterity, the discursive elegance and the careful composition in addition to its structural experimentation of being able to read the poem from top to bottom and from bottom to the top in a perfect circular form, while using the preferred octosyllabic verse.

> Te adoro con frenesí
> Y di que miento si digo
> Solamente soy tu amigo
> Cual lo eres tú para mí
> No quiero bromas así
> Con mi ternura y afán,
> El temor del qué dirán
> No pone valla a mi amor
> Si dicen que con ardor Mintiendo mis labios van.[33]

What on the surface appears to be only a romantic poem has as its central objective playfulness and impishness in order to suggest other sentiments. Some ambiguity abounds in its multiply layered message of love, except that the roguish tone dominates the poem.

It is within this context that Eusebio Chacón stands out for his far-reaching versatility, moderate temperament, determined rationality, intellectual prowess, rigorous judgment, professional competence, wide-ranging sensibilities, steadfast social commitment, keen legal mind, deep dedication to Neo-Mexicano society, intense religiosity, a clear sense of historical agency, a dedicated family man, a natural leader, and multiple other talents and attributes. But, most of all, he was devoted to both creating literature as well as to promoting it, thanks to his extensive work as an editor in the newspapers *El Progreso* and *Las Dos Repúblicas* in addition to his many collaborations with other printed media and a failed attempt to create a newspaper that never materialized. He inherited the pioneer spirit from his trailblazing parents and grandparents and translated it into action among his many social and artistic inclinations for the sake of his people's empowerment. He may have become an overlooked figure after 1925, but he clearly exceled in many areas and activities: as a novelist, lawyer, a public orator, district attorney, orator, social activist, translator, statesman, essayist, historian, journalist, editor, poet, a gentleman, and cultural theorist. Together such a background reflects a true renaissance man who left an indelible mark in the cultural and intellectual life in his region for some 50 years. The range of his talents is astonishing in the area of literature in other palpable ways because he provided a means to pursue literary expression as a medium to foster dialogue and accountability within his social-historical milieu. His focus on regional issues occupied much of his time in conjunction with his extensive editorial work with newspapers and the novelettes that served to comment through fiction on his people's strained adjustments to a new political environment.

Aside from his keen interest in the production of literary pieces, he has been one of the central figures in Neo-Mexican literary history by writing a series of at least 9 well-documented essays or treatises on key people and events of in "Descubrimiento y conquista de Nuevo México en 1540 por los españoles: disertaciones de historia patria" between March 14, 1896 and May 23, 1896, which appeared in the Denver newspaper *Las Dos Repúblicas* under the leadership of his father-in-law Don Casimiro Barela. The essays stand out for their foundational nature because he lays out the genealogy of a Hispanic literary tradition found in chronicles and historical accounts. Best known are his well-defined efforts toward consciously founding the novel genre in the Spanish language as a way of manifesting Neo-Mexicano cultural pride. For example, he operated as a principal curator of old documents and manuscripts (a true literary archeologist): chronicles, historical accounts, memoirs, letters and literary works, including an original copy of Gaspar Pérez de Villagrá's *Historia de la Nueva México* of 1610, Don Pedro Bautista's *Noticias históricas y estadísticas de la antigua provincia de Nuevo México presentadas por su diputado a cortes* (1813),[34] and Mexican consul Manuel Alvarez's unpublished "Memorias" (1830s?) where he provided some of the earliest critical reflections and assessments on the kinds of writings by Hispanic peoples during the Colonial (1542-1821) and Mexican (1821-1848) periods.

Chacón was intensely interested as a collector of old manuscripts that have subsequently been instrumental to establish the necessary tenets for the literary history during the Hispanic Period before 1848. He provided the Neo-Mexicano Renaissance greater credence and context while reminding all participants of their historical role as well as cultural importance. For example, he used his unique access to the newspaper *El Progreso* from Trinidad between 1896 and 1897 when he introduced weekly segments of Villagrá's foundational epic poem in special literary columns. This had never been attempted before, thus raising an historical consciousness as well as documented proof of past heroic events that had been eschewed, distorted or simply exoticized. In the process, he reminded the readership that they were descendants of outstanding writers and, consequently, capable of developing sophisticated literary creations, again. In essence, he became a protector and guardian of a tradition and legacy but also a promoter and practitioner of the fine arts. In addition, he set forth a challenge to become procreators of their own creativity while raising the bar for those who might have felt inhibited by a lack of authenticity, consequently kindling a new ethnic and cultural ethos. The implication was that Neo-Mexicanos could in fact craft and re-institute their own literary voices separately, independently and autonomously from mainstream Anglo society at a time when cultural assimilation was being encouraged, particularly during the first decade of the twentieth century when the territory of New Mexico was bidding to become a state of the Union.

IV. Conclusion: A Trailblazer Leads to a Literary

Eusebio Chacón did not voice a separatist political agenda but he did demand respect, validation and legitimacy for his people, subtly suggesting a form of cultural autonomy. How is it, then, that someone can claim that he is still relatively unknown, but most of all, how did it happen that a whole generation has been overlooked and swept off the literary historical pages? Part of it is circumstantial and political. Either way, he is undoubtedly an important cog of the literary scene between 1890 and 1910 who helped establish a revitalized artistic expression in Spanish within the unique triangle-corridor. Chacón was squarely engaged in the epicenter of the Neo-Mexicano Renaissance with his finger in the pulse of the region. As a descendant of a regional environment of hardy people, tough survivors and tenacious strivers, who had witnessed changing identities and nationalities, he came to fully appreciate the historical processes of his forebears from being Spanish subjects to Mexican nationals to American citizens. He developed as a foundational fiction writer and cultural activist within these times of fluctuating allegiances while adhering to a worldview that was multi-faceted, fundamentally tolerant in nature and inspired in the beliefs of social justice and morality. Most of all, he deeply believed in his cultural background and what it could offer the newer generations. Chacón became a new version of a culturally diverse America at the turn of the twentieth century and into the early twentieth century who valued becoming a self-made man for the sake of his people, his two languages and the conviction to positively impact his social environment. Literary detective work has directly contributed to bringing this writer and an early literary boom out of the shadows to prove that all the clues point to an outstanding individual who has played a pivotal role in Chicano letters for the reasons herein discussed. Clearly the *telarañas* are off and Eusebio Chacón stands out as a landmark figure and fixture in the genealogy of early Chicano letters, and thanks to him, we have managed to uncover a whole generation who came together as the first ethnic literary group which we now know as the Neo-Mexicano Renaissance.

Works Cited

Arellano, Anselmo. *Los pobladores nuevomexicanos y su poesía, 1889-1950.* Albuquerque: Pajarito Publications, 1976.

Arellano, Anselmo. "La poesía nuevomexicana, su desarrollo y transición durante los fines del siglo diez y nueve." Original manuscript consulted with his permission. N.d.

Arellano, Anselmo. "The Rise of Mutual Aid Societies Among New Mexico's Spanish-Speaking During the Territorial Period." Original manuscript consulted with his permission. N.d. Arellano, Anselmo and Julián Vigil, eds. Special Issue of *De Colores: Journal of Emerging Philosophies* 2.1 (1975).

Barrio, Ernie, ed. *Bibliografía de Aztlán: An Annotated Chicano Bibliography.* San Diego: San Diego State College. Centro de Estudios Chicanos, 1971.

Bernal, Vicente J. *Las primicias.* Eds. Luis E. Bernal and Robert N. McLean. Dubuque, Iowa: *Dubuque Telegraph-Herald,* 1916.

C. de Baca, Manuel. *Historia de Vicente Silva y sus cuarenta bandidos, sus crímenes y retribuciones.* Las Vegas, NM: NP, 1896.

C. de Baca, Manuel. *Noches tenebrosas en el condado de San Miguel.* Serialized novel in *El Sol de Mayo* (1898).

Campa, Arthur L. *Spanish Folk Poetry in New Mexico.* Albuquerque: University of New Mexico Press, 1946.

Chacón, Eusebio. "Elocuente discurso: pronunciado por el Lic. Eusebo Chacón en la junta de indignación del sábado; caballeroso sí, pero bastante picante." In the Spanish weekly *La Voz del Pueblo,* East Las Vegas, New Mexico, November 2, 1901. Pp. 1, 6-7.

Chacón, Eusebio. *El hijo de la tempestad; Tras la tormenta de la calma; Dos novelitas originales.* Santa Fe: Tipografía de *El Boletín Literario,* 1992.

Chacón, Felipe Maximiliano. *Obras de Felipe Maximiliano Chacón, "el cantor neomexicano": poesía y prosa.* Albuquerque, NM: NP, 1924.

Cobos, Rubén, ed. *Refranes españoles del Suroeste/ Spanish Proverbs of the Southwest.* Cerrillos, NM: San Marcos Press, 1973.

Escobar, José. "Nota sobre Eusebio Chacón." *Las Dos Repúblicas*, July 11, 1896. Np. Espinosa, Aurelio M. *El romancero español, sus orígenes y su historia en la literatura universal.* Madrid: V. Suárez, 1931.

Gonzales, Porfirio. *Historia de un cautivo.* Serialized novel in Spanish weekly *La Voz del Pueblo*, Las Vegas, New Mexico, June 4-September 3, 1898.

Haslam, Gerald W. *Forgotten Pages of American Literature.* Boston: Houghton Mifflin, 1970.

Leal, Luis. "Mexican American Literature: A Historical Approach." *Revista Chicano-Riqueña* 1.1 (1973): 18-32.

Lomelí, Francisco A. and Donaldo W. Urioste. "Eusebio Chacón" in *Chicano Perspectives in Literature: A Critical and Annotated Bibliography.* Albuquerque, N.M: Pajarito Publications, 1976. Pp. 42-43.

López, José Timoteo, Edgardo Núñez and Roberto Lara Vialpando. *Breve reseña de la literatura hispana de Nuevo México y Colorado.* Juárez, Chihuahua: Imprenta Comercial, 1959.

McKeta, Jaqueline Dorgan. *Legacy of Honor: The Life of Rafael Chacón, a Nineteenth Century New Mexico.* Albuquerque: University of New Mexico Press, 1986.

Meléndez, A. Gabriel. *So All Is Not Lost: The Poetics of Print in Nuevomexicano Communities, 1834-1958.* Albuquerque: University of New Mexico, 1997.

Meléndez, A. Gabriel and Francisco A. Lomelí. *The Writings of Eusebio Chacón.* Albuquerque: University of New Mexico Press, 2012.

Rael, Juan B. *Cuentos españoles de Colorado y Nuevo México.* 2 vols. Stanford, CA: The Stanford University Press, 1957.

Read, Benjamín M. *Historia ilustrada de Nuevo México.* Santa Fe, NM: Compañía Impresora del *Nuevo México*, 1911.

Rivera, José A. *La Sociedad: Guardians of Hispanic Culture Along the Río Grande.* Albuquerque: University of New Mexico, 2010.

Ruiz de Burton, María Amparo. *The Squatter and the Don.* Eds. Rosaura Sánchez and Beatrice Pita. Houston, TX: Arte Público Press, 1992.

Ruiz de Burton, María Amparo. *Who Would Have Thought It?* Eds. Rosaura Sánchez and Beatrice Pita. Houston, TX: Arte Público Press, 1995.

Stratton, Porter A. *Territorial Press in New Mexico, 1834-1912.* Albuquerque: University of New Mexico Press, 1969.

Villagrá, Gaspar Pérez de. *Historia de la Nueva México, del Capitán Gaspar de Villagrá.* Alcalá: Luis Martínez Grande, 1610.

Villarreal, José Antonio. *Pocho.* New York: Doubleday & Company, 1959.

White-Lea, Aurora Lucero. *Literary Folklore of the Hispanic Southwest.* San Antonio, TX: Naylor Co., 1953.

Endnotes

[1]See Gerald H. Haslam's *Forgotten Pages of American Literature* (Boston: Houghton Mifflin, 1970), who makes a strong case for pursuing works that have been overlooked.

[2]Nicolás Kanellos has been the key figure in spearheading the effort as director of the Recovery Program, particularly for disseminating the group's findings on frequent panels and conferences nationally and internationally while being in charge of fundraising to maintain the production of a stream of over ten volumes that highlight new findings along with new critical approaches.

[3]See his article published in *Revista Chicano-Riqueña* 1.1 (1973): 18-32.

[4]The exact date can be traced to its omission from the *Bibliografía de Aztlán: An Annotated Chicano Bibliography*, edited by Ernie Barrio (San Diego: San Diego State College, Centro de Estudios Chicanos, 1971), which was already at the publisher's when the novel was "rediscovered".

[5]The work was reintroduced, translated and edited by A. Gabriel Meléndez and Francisco A. Lomelí from the University of New Mexico Press in Albuquerque, 2012.

[6]I deliberately use this term which has the greatest use at the end of the nineteenth and early twentieth centuries.

[7]A common practice among Anglo elite who entered Hispanic towns was to disseminate lists of outstanding civil servants in commemorative collections, usually highlighting and promoting themselves and thus marginalizing or overlooking the more native population.

[8]The speech, also known as "La Junta de Indignación 1901", appeared in the Spanish weekly *La Voz del Pueblo* on November 2, 1901 in Las Vegas, New Mexico.

[9]See this work along with the original in Spanish by Benjamín Read titled *Historia ilustrada de Nuevo México* (Santa Fe, NM: Compañía Impresora del Nuevo México, 1911.

[10]See Jaqueline Dorgan McKeta in *Legacy of Honor: The Life of Rafael Chacón, a Nineteenth Century New Mexico* (Albuquerque: University of New Mexico, 1986), p. 328.

[11]Eusebio Chacón, *El hijo de la tempestad; Tras la tormenta de la calma; Dos novelitas originales* (Santa Fe: Tipografía de *El Boletín Literario*, 1992), p. 2.

[12]This appears in *Las Dos Repúblicas*, July 11, 1896 from Denver, Colorado.

[13]The two novels were reintroduced thanks to the new editions by Rosaura Sánchez and Beatrice Pita, and published by Arte Público Press in Houston, Texas in 1992 and 1995, respectively.

[14]His collection of poetry and narratives (both short stories and a novella) were published in 1924 in Albuquerque, New Mexico but the publisher is not known. His collection contains a novellete titled "Eustacio y Carlota" which evokes Manuel Salazar's "Gervacio y Aurora".

[15]This work represents one of the first attempts at providing a background and context for writings by Hispanics from New Mexico and Colorado. It was published in Juárez, Chihuaua by Imprenta Comercial in 1959.

[16]As a corollary to such archival searches from the late nineteenth and early twentieth centuries, thanks in part to Fray Angélico Chávez's tip about having read something on a "crazy poet" from the colonial period, I was able to locate the eighteenth century poet Miguel de Quintana embedded in the New Mexico Inquisition micro-fiche files in 1982. From such research emerged the book titled *Defying the Inquisition in Colonial New Mexico: Miguel de Quintana's Life and Writings*, co-edited and co-translated by Clark A. Colahan (Albuquerque: University of New Mexico, 2006), in which we pieced together a biographical profile with the few but scattered clues to this colonial writer who wrote some quasi-mystical poems and was engaged in a complex investigation for five years by the Holy Office of the Inquisition from Santa Fe to Durango to Mexico City. Such files only survived, ironically, thanks to the Inquisition's insistence on investigating suspicious activity in the remote frontier that would border on heresy or any other questionable social-religious behavior.

[17]See Anselmo Arellano's unpublished article "La poesía nuevomexicana, su desarrollo y transición durante los fines del siglo diez y nuevo," consulted with his permission. No date.

[18]Gabriel Meléndez in *So All Is Not Lost: The Poetics of Print in Nuevomexicano Communities, 1834-1958* (Albuquerque: University of New Mexico, 1997), p. 40.

[19]See his article titled "Po(l)etics of Reconstructing and/or Appropriating a Literary Past: The Regional Case Model," in *Recovering the U.S. Hispanic Literary Heritage*, edited by Ramón Gutiérrez and Genaro Padilla (Houston: Arte Público Press, 1993), 221-239. Upon pursuing further inquiries, we have come to conclude that this "modest" renaissance has not been as "modest" as first assumed because of its over-arching nature and ceaseless number of works that continue to resurface to strengthen the original argument of a full-fledged ethnic renaissance.

[20]This claim might appear daring on the surface but the magnitude of artistic and literary activity was so widespread for its far-reaching nature into intellectual life principally through the explosion of Spanish-language and bilingual newspapers, weekly publications and literary societies that prevailed between 1890 and 1900. Such a boom influenced daily lives in the Hispanic triangle-corridor

between Santa Fe and Las Vegas, New Mexico and Trinidad, Colorado, creating an unprecedented ambience of sophistication and learned exchanges.

[21]The list of names is a compilation from my own gathering of documents but also gleaned and greatly enriched by what Anselmo Arellano and Gabriel Meléndez have provided in their respective writings. See the former's *Los pobladores nuevomexicanos y su poesía, 1889-1950* (Albuquerque: Pajarito Publications, 1976) and the latter's *So All Is Not Lost: The Poetics of Print in Nuevomexicano Communities, 1834-1958* (Albuquerque: University of New Mexico, 1997).

[22]The note can be located in *La Voz del Pueblo* on February 4, 1893.

[23]These folklore experts dedicated an extensive amount of their careers collecting works: for example, *El romancero español, sus orígenes, y su historia* (1931), *Literary Folklore of the Hispanic Southwest* (1953), *Spanish Folk Poetry in New Mexico* (1946), *Cuentos españoles de Colorado y Nuevo México* (1957), *Refranes españoles del Suroeste/ Spanish Proverbs of the Southwest* (1973), respectively.

[24]Anselmo Arellano's "La poesía nuevomexicana, su desarrollo y transición durante los fines del siglo diez y nuevo," consulted with his permission. No date.

[25]Consult Porter A. Stratton's *Territorial Press in New Mexico, 1834-1912* (Albuquerque: University of New Mexico Press, 1969), p. 24.

[26]Ibid., p. 25.

[27]It should be noted that these *sociedades* also operated as institutions of social assistance, sometimes dispensing protection for community members through a form of financial aid, low-cost insurance or burial funding, fraternal support and fellowship, legal troubles, unemployment other urgent needs. They were instrumental in maintaining the close knit fabric of Neo-Mexicano communities in both urban and rural areas. For more information, consult José A. Rivera's *La Sociedad: Guardians of Hispanic Culture Along the Río Grande* (Albuquerque: University of New Mexico Press, 2010), p.8.

[28]This has been ascertained by carefully examining hundreds of Neo-Mexicano and southern Colorado newspapers through years of research, thus accumulating numerous other names than the ones provided.

[29]Julián Vigil was the first to informally mention the possible existence of this work and I was able to locate it as a serialized novel (June 4-September 3, 1898) in February 1987 in the Spanish weekly *La Voz del Pueblo* from Las Vegas, New Mexico.

[30]It can be noted that perhaps the other works mentioned are written in a simple Spanish filled with idioms, but the novellas by Chacón do not quite fit that assessment.

[31]If such a list is not impressive enough, we can offer further evidence by citing a "Lista de los Ciudadanos que Deberán Componer los Jurados de Imprenta, Formada en el Ayuntamiento de Esta Capital," in which 92 members place their names on this 1834 document from Santa Fe in which they declare to be members in position to uphold and promote the importance of publishing documents in the region. The document helps establish that a tradition for the written word was already strong and entrenched in the region. The list includes many high profile figures from the middle nineteenth century which further supports the long-standing tradition of writing (Mexican Archives, Roll 18, Frame 420).

[32]These constitute folkloric events related to nineteenth-century Native American captivity stories and weddings.

[33]The poem appears in *La Voz del Pueblo* from Las Vegas, New Mexico on July 1, 1899.

[34]The title is also known as *Exposición sucinta y sencilla de la provincia del Nuevo México* (Cádiz: Impresora del Estado-Mayor-General, 1912).

Navigating a Fine Bilingual Line in Early Twentieth-Century New Mexico: *El cantor neomexicano*, Felipe M. Chacón

ANNA M. NOGAR

University of New Mexico

"Espero que mi libro sea acogido con el mismo espiritú en que lo ofrezco; y si el mismo alcanza a server de solaz y recreo, para hacer amenas las horas que se dediquen a su lectura, dentro de sus admitidas limitaciones, quedará ampliamente remunerado el modesto esfuerzo de EL AUTOR." "I hope my book is received in the spirit with which I offer it; and if it serves as a source of solace and amusement, making pleasant the hours dedicated to its reading, within its admitted limitations, then the modest efforts of THE AUTHOR will be more than compensated."

—Felipe M. Chacón, Preface to *Obras de
Felipe M. Chacón, "el cantor neomexicano": poesía y prosa*

"Chacón es un genio, y como todos los genios, no se sabe estimar a sí mismo." "Chacón is a genius, and like all geniuses, he does not know how to value himself."

—Benjamín Read, Introduction to *Obras de
Felipe M. Chacón, "el cantor neomexicano": poesía y prosa*

For New Mexican author Felipe M. Chacón, a public literary figure who edited several Spanish-language newspapers published in New Mexico in the nineteenth and twentieth centuries, there is much to be considered. Chacón was part of a cadre of nuevomexicano intellectuals, writers, and politicians who expressed a resistive positionality carefully couched in nationalistic self-identification. In Chacón's best-known writing, a collection of poetry and stories entitled *Obras de Felipe Maximiliano Chacón, "el cantor neomexicano": poesía y prosa* (1924), the author outwardly conforms to a rhetoric of American nationalist sentiment, while writing against those same objectives both explicitly, in terms of what he includes in the text, and implicitly, in terms of how he intentionally deploys Spanish language. This dynamic is most clearly expressed in Chacón's use of Spanish and English together in his collection, and this essay considers the sociopolitical meaning of that play.

Born in 1873, in Santa Fe, New Mexico, Felipe Maximiliano Chacón came from a family well known on the nuevomexicano political and literary scene. Chacón's biographer Bejanmín Read refers to Felipe M.'s father in the preface of *Poesía y prosa* as "el finado Don Urbano Chacón;" at the time of his death, when Felipe M. was 13, Urbano Chacón was the superintendent of schools in Santa Fe and had founded two newspapers, in one of which, *La aurora*, Felipe M. would later publish. His family's ongoing involvement with New Mexican politics provided Felipe M. Chacón with front-row seat insight into New Mexico's ongoing political condition and situated him sympathetically to nuevomexicanos' most pressing issues.

Felipe M. counted among his published relatives great uncle Rafael Chacón, who wrote about the arrival of American troops to New Mexico and the transition of power from Mexico to the United States; Rafael Chacón's published biography (Meketa) was famously examined by Genaro Padilla in *My History Not Yours: The Formation of Mexican Autobiography* (Padilla). Felipe M. Chacón's cousin Eusebio Chacón, a lawyer and land-rights official in Trinidad, CO, was known for his dignified, yet pointed editorial letters in defense of Hispano history and political participation. Eusebio Chacón's archive was recently re-opened, studied and published by Gabriel Meléndez and Francisco Lomelí, who made his writing accessible and created for it a deep historical context in *The Writings of Eusebio Chacón* (Meléndez and Lomelí). Felipe M. Chacón is the early twentieth-cenutry link in a remarkable family lineage of nuevomexicano authors who wrote with political, cultural and linguistic awareness for their community, concluding most recently with the writing of Felipe M. Chacón's daughter Erminia Chacón.

Though research on Felipe M. Chacón has been relatively quiet for the past two decades, earlier studies brought to light important facets of his biography and historical import. Doris Meyer (1977) considered Chacón a pre-Chicano movement precursor, highlighting his bilingualism and choice of genre in *Poesía y prosa*, and provided analyses of several of his poems. Erlinda Gónazlez-Berry (1989) carefully considered the unique dynamic at play in Chacón's writing, and read his work alongside that of fellow nuevomexicano Vicente Bernal. Gabriel Meléndez, in *So All Is Not Lost* (1997), provides the most detailed and in-depth treatment of Chacón's biography, articulating his role in Spanish-language nuevomexicano newspapers and literary movement of the day, noting how the very publication of *Poesía y prosa* was seen as a triumph and culmination of that movement, substantiating key aspects of Read's role in writing the introduction to *Poesía y prosa*, and analyzing several poems as well as the prose stories in the collection. This scholarship provides a solid basis for the study of Felipe M. Chacón's writing, in particular the vital *Poesía y prosa*, and establishes Chacón among those early nuevomexicano writers most currently in need of literary recovery and critical examination.

The motives for Chacón's writing (and that of his nuevomexicano contemporaries) should come as no surprise to anyone familiar with New Mexico history. The Beveridge Report, a minority report made in 1903 to Congress by Indiana representative Albert Beveridge regarding the incorporation of New Mexico and Arizona into the United States as states, argued that New Mexico was unfit to become as state, and that unfitness was at least partially based on the territory's bilingual and monolingual Spanish inhabitants (Meléndez, 2000). This delayed the admission of the two states by almost a decade, and was part and parcel of a country-wide nativism that ultimately resulted, among other ramifications, in the appointment of state superintendents of education in New Mexico who opposed teaching Spanish in public schools in New Mexico as part of that national appeasement. Even New Mexicans who supported the incorporation of New Mexico as a state (the majority), recognized these allegations for what they were: baseless xenophobia and imposition of hegemonic praxis.

As such, and as Meléndez and Meyers have noted, the type of literary pursuits in which Chacón, Benjamin Read and others participated was no casual affair. Meléndez asserts that historical texts like Read's *Guerra México-Americana* (1910), *Historia ilustrada de Nuevo Mexico* (1910), *Illustrated History of New Mexico* (1912), and *Popular Elementary History of New Mexico* (1915) were sites where nuevomexicanos ensured that they were not written out of the historical record, that their deeds were accurately recorded from their perspective, and that these histories were made accessible to their own community in Spanish. John Nieto Phillips elaborates what Read himself wrote in the introduction to the *Illustrated History of New Mexico*, noting that Read "felt compelled to undertake the writing of New Mexico's past to correct the inaccuracies that plagued Anglo Americans' writing [on the subject]. Knowing little Spanish, he wrote, they often resorted to incorrect translations of Spanish colonial documents. . . . Moreover, histories written in Spanish, he insisted, best preserved the original meaning of Spanish documents" (Nieto Phillips 189).

Chacón and Read seem to have operated on similar (though not identical) principles through their written works. In Read's introduction to Chacón's collection of bilingual poetry and prose there is a tacit acknowledgement of this, a knowing wink built into Read's framing of Chacón's texts. In turn, the acknowledgement of Read on book's the cover page ("Con un prólogo por el honorable Benjamin M. Read, Autor de "Illustrated History of New Mexico," "Sidelights on New Mexico History" etc., etc.") draws attention to Read's significance as a writer on topics related to New Mexican history.

Surprisingly, the book, published in Albuquerque, NM, carries the following copyright information: "Queda hecho el depósito que ordena la ley, para la protección de esta obra en la república de México." It is unusual that an early twentieth-century American writer publishing in the United States would make such a specific declaration regarding Mexican copyright, but perhaps Felipe M. Chacón envisioned a US/Mexico cross-boarder readership such as that which flourished during the nineteenth century. Chacón ensured that from beginning to end the book was in Spanish, for as Read writes at the end of the prologue, he simply approved the text after Chacón had translated Read's original English: "deseo advertir que este Prólogo ha sido vertido al castellano por el Autor mismo de este libro, aprobando yo, implícitamente, su versión de mis conceptos y sentir en el particular" ("I wish to advise that this Prologue has been interpreted into Spanish by the very Author of this book, with myself implicitly approving his version of my ideas and specific sense") (Read 14).

Indeed, Read's introduction positions Chacón's language of choice very precisely, and in a way that recognizes the skill of his Spanish and English writing, while implicitly condemning the elimination of Spanish teaching in public schools and the nativist sentiments that produced the ascendency of English monolingualism; "una prueba de lo bien que nuestro poeta ha sabido aprovechar su tiempo, es la manera en que ha alcanzado aprender y cultivar la lengua castellana, sin ninguna ayuda superior, en un país cuyo idioma es el inglés y donde hay pocas o ningunas oportunidades de aprender el castellano con propiedad" ("an example of how well our poet has taken advantage of his time, is the way he has managed to learn and cultivate the Spanish language, without any help, in a country whose language is English, and where there are few to no opportunities to learn Spanish formally") (Read 7). Read attributes blind monolingual practice to the nation—not to New Mexico—an understated but unmistakable critique of the elimination of instruction in Spanish in New Mexican public schools, as Read, the former superintendent of schools, would have well known. Further, "con propiedad" should not be read as a critique of colloquial spoken Spanish, but rather of the depressing educational outcome of a sociopolitical battle in the process of being lost.

The tension Chacón and other New Mexicans expressed in their writing—walking a fine line between retaining nuevomexicano political agency, self-representation and self-identification, and supporting the ideals of incorporation into the Union—is an ongoing motif, what González-Berry calls the "push-me-pull-me dynamic" of Chacón's writing (González-Berry 195). Chacón wrote for a New Mexican audience that reflected his own experiences as a nuevomexicano enduring a period of social turmoil that involved the erosion of shared culture and language, and which placed their political position at risk. As Meyer notes in her analysis of Chacón's poem "A Nuevo México," he acknowledges in the poem what she accurately identifies as the sense "of many [New Mexican] citizens that recognition [had] been unjustly delayed because of racial prejudice in Washington" (Meyers 117) and that, furthermore, they found themselves "treated like second-class citizens by politicians in the East" (Meyers 117). These questions had to be resolved, as did their relationship to the overarching, outward and inward sign of colonization: the growing predominance of the English language in New Mexico. And yet, as both González-Berry and Meyers note, this tension emerges in Felipe M. Chacón's writing through and amidst the expression of American patriotic sentiment.

A sense for how Chacón expresses this is evident in "A la patria," a poem from *Poesía y prosa* written on July 4, 1918. In it, the rhetoric of the poem spirals upward in strict Romantic verse, praising the new "patria" of the United States: "Mi patrio amor solicito brindarte / Que resistir no puede ni el cinicismo / Las glorias sin igual de tu heroism" ("My patriotic love I seek to offer you / For not even cynicism can resist / The unparalleled glory of your heroism").[1] The poem goes on to laud the nation's founding fathers by name: "Por el suelo rodó la tiranía / al oír de John Adams la elocuencia / Precursora de aquel gloriosa día / En que Jefferson, lleno de preciencia / Tetazó de su inmortal sabiduría / La gran declaración de independencia" ("Tyranny rolled through the land / As the eloquence of John Adams was heard / A precursor of that glorious day / That Jefferson, full of prescience / Drew from his immortal wisdom / The great Declaration of Independence") (Chacón 23). In "A la patria," Chacón doubles down on New Mexico's loyalty to the United States and to the national history in which New Mexico shared.

In "A Nuevo Mexico: En su admission como estado," this patriotic sentiment is first amplified, and then tempered. Chacón opens the poem with ebullience and effortless poetic style: "Por fin habeis logrado, suelo mío / de lauros coronar tu altiva frente, / alcanzando del cielo del estío / Una estrella gloriosa y espendente" ("My homeland, you have finally attained / The crowning of your raised head with laurels / Pulling down from the summer sky / A glorious and brilliant star") (Chacón 43). "¡Que viva Nuevo Mexico, el estado!" ("Long live

New Mexico, the state!") the poem cries (Chacón 45). This dizzying nationalist rhetoric makes Chacón's immediate about face a few stanzas later especially unexpected. He quickly counters the previous patriotic ebullience citing the years and years of xenophobic resistance to New Mexico's statehood: "Luchaste en contra del hado endurecido / Batiendo del Congreso la injusticia / y con ella el insulto proferido / Del prejuicio racial por la malicia" ("You fought against hardened fate / Defeating Congress's injustice / And with it the insults uttered / Of racial prejudice based on malice") (Chacón 43). Chacón's patriotic positioning also perpetuates anti-indigenous tropes, calling out New Mexico's past "luchando con el indio ingoberanable" ("fighting against the ungovernable Indian") (Chacón 43). This is not the only instance of this type of reference to New Mexico's native communities in Chacón's poetry. This regrettable tendency conforms with other hypernationalistic narratives of the period; indeed, Chacón contemporaries María Amparo Ruíz de Burton (California) and Jovita González (Texas) used similar language and tropes in their writing.

The poem also acknowledges and lauds the creation of New Mexican history by its own people—that is, the project Benjamin Read and others accomplished—in the same poem: "quiero ver tus archivos relucientes / De datos limpios que tu nombre ensanchen / A través de los siglos sucedientes" ("I want to see your archives shine / With bright deeds that will bring renown to your name / For centuries to come") (Chacón 44). This overt reproach in a poem celebrating New Mexico's late admission as a state is by no means Chacón's most critical expression in the collection, but it is a concise example of the complexity of his literary game.

"A Nuevo México" lays out for us explicitly Chacón's dual positionality, but this same characteristic is most subtly expressed through Chacón's language choices. While his predecessors in the nuevomexicano intellectual milieu, including José Escobar and Enrique Salazar, shared much of Chacón's political orientation, what they produced was primarily in Spanish and intended for Spanish-dominant readers. Chacón, by comparison, could and did write for several audiences, including a Spanish-English bilingual one, reaching readers who could "palpar la pericia del autor; sus íntimos conocimientos de ambos idiomas" ("appreciate the author's skill; his intimate knowledge of both languages") (Read 9). How and what he writes—in particular how he juxtaposes Spanish and English—is specifically decipherable for these politically-aware bilingual nuevomexicanos.

Read's prologue transmits his own sense for the trepidatious waters of Spanish language perception and reception. Read upholds the New Mexico statehood project, and Felipe M.'s loyal citizenship to the United States "in spite of" his choice of language for *Poesía y prosa*: "En sus 'Cantos Patrios' Chacón ha querido manifestar las alabanzas y loores de los héroes que ha producido el pueblo Americano, al cual él pertenece, no se limitan a nuestro propio idioma, idioma que tanto amamos, el inglés, sino que lo mismo se cantan, con lujo de belleza, en otros idiomas del mundo civilizado" ("In his 'Patriotic Songs' Chacón has sought to express the praises for heroes produced by the American people, to which he pertains, and which is not limited to our own language (the language we love so much-English), but rather which is also sung, bathed in a beautiful glow, in other languages of the civilized world") (Read 6). Read's simultaneous affirmation of Chacón as "un genio netamente Americano" ("a genuinely American genius") (Read 5) and also "el primero que diera lustre a su Patria en el bello idioma de Cervantes" ("the first to make his Patria shine in the beautiful language of Cervantes") (Read 5) squares with how he and Felipe M. Chacón approach these subject in their writing, by composing works that outwardly express patriotic sentiments while laying a steady series of punches from beneath.

This is most evident in the poem "In Mexico" (Read 8-9). Included with two others in the book's prologue, Read explains that the poem is an example (indeed an ironic one) of Chacón's command of English: "Una de las cosas que todos los que le conocemos admiramos, es la facilidad con que escribe lo mismo el castellano que el inglés, lo mismo en poesía que en prosa. Felipe ha escrito muchas poesías en inglés, serias, festivas y de amor, y para dar una idea de su feliz ingenio en el particular, no me parece fuera de lugar el reproducir como muestra de lo mismo, las siguientes tres composiciones" ("One of the things that all those who know him admire is the facility with which he writes in Spanish and in English, in poetry as much as in prose. Felipe has written many poems in English, serious ones, festive ones, and love poems, and to give an idea of his apt wit, it does not seem out of place to me to include the following three compositions as an example of this") (Read 7-8). Yet, I would argue that rather than Chacón's English language ability that stands out, it is his ability to gauge his bilingual audience and deliver a poem that draws on their linguistic abilities as it evokes their political position, which he does with edgy precision.

Perhaps Read could sense this, for he qualifies the poem with the following preemptive explanation: "Estos versos deben tomarse en el espíritu que el autor los intentó: como una ocurrencia de buen humor, y bajo ningún concepto, en sentido ofensivo" ("these verses should be taken in the spirit in which the author intended them: as an instance of good humor, and in no way intended to offend") (Read 9). I see in the poem what Read believed some readers would recognize: a sharp tease in Spanish and English that both pokes fun at English-dominant speakers who claimed to speak Spanish, and which implicitly displays what true symmetrical bilingualism—with a skill for poetic artistry—looked like.

The poem reads as follows:

We met: for me 'twas love at first sight.
She was divine:
I prayed her then my soul delight.
Asked her to make my future bright,
To be but mine,
Said she: "No entiendo!"

I love you more than tongue can tell,
I yield supine:
Without thee life, in sadness' spell,
Is but a winter's barren dell,
Won't you be mine!
Said she: "No sabe."

Unbounded wealth at your command,
Rich, superfine,
All at your feet, belle of this land,
You'll find anon as you demand,
If you'll be mine,
Cried she: "¡Ay Dios!"

Diamonds, gold, all to surprise.
A treasure's thine:
I'll give you, love, a paradise,
A home that queens may long for twice,
Won't you be mine?
Said she: "Oh! Yes me quiere." (Read 8-9)

As Read indicates, Chacón's command of English in this poem is superb. The lexicon impresses not only for the sophisticated words it includes, but also for the inclusion of words that were no longer used in common speech in the early twentieth century, such as "anon" "thine" "'twas" and "thee." Chacón intentionally creates a precise poetic tone, while also showcasing his grasp of the registers and usages of poetic English language. The poem's overall strict conformation to rhyme and rhythm schemes further demonstrate Chacón's creative prowess in English. The first five verses of each strophe follow a strict A-b-A-A-b rhyme scheme, with all of the 4-syllable verses throughout the poem rhyming with each other: "mine" "thine" "supine" superfine" etc. Chacón's execution of the "surprise/paradise/twice" rhyme series demonstrates a particularly subtle grasp of sound combination. In a similar manner, the syllabification is precise and consistent throughout the English portions: a pattern of 8-4-8-8-4 carries throughout, with appropriate contractions ("twas" "won't") and additions ("I'll give you, love, a paradise") to force the verse to fit that rhythmic scheme perfectly. Chacón indicates he can control the handles and levers of English to great poetic effect.

Given the lyricism of the English verse, the four lines of the poem that are partially in Spanish are all the more (purposefully) impactful. In contrast to the high- level vocabulary in English, the Spanish is at best simple (as in "No entiendo") or stereotypical ("¡Ay Dios!"). In the other two cases, it is grammatically incorrect (as in the response to "Will you be mine": "no sabe") and then incomprehensibly mashed between Spanish and English ("¡Oh yes me quiere!" in reply to "Won't you be mine?"). The Spanish, when it is incorrect, it demonstrates a complete lack of appropriate conjugation of Spanish verbs in the first person present tense, usually the first verb form taught in introductory language courses. In addition, the syllabification of the final verses is inconsistent with the precise rhythm scheme set out in the rest of the poem. The Spanish lines are of 5 and 7 syllables, though without any particular pattern, and thus present a strong dissonance with the rest of the poem's tightly wound rhythm.

The Spanish-language verses are jarringly inconsistent and interrupt the fluidity of the rest of the poem. But what exactly is going on here? I believe the answer lies in the structure and premise of the poem, and in the representative politics of language in New Mexico in the late nineteenth and early twentieth centuries. It seems well within reason that the poem could be read as "In New Mexico," especially given the perception of many in the eastern United States that New Mexico was, in fact, Mexico, and the various attempts to change the name of the territory to something other than that which invoked Mexico (Meléndez 2000). Chacón might have chosen "In Mexico" not only as an ironic commentary on this perception, but also perhaps to neutralize his point, to keep it from being too finely or locally critical.

If the setting of the poem is "In Mexico/New Mexico," one can assume the male poetic voice, which is written in English, is, in the context of the poem, actually speaking in Spanish. His poetic language can be read as a translation of what he said in Spanish to the female persona, a monolingual who responds in broken pidgin Spanish. Seen in this way, there is a disparity between the two voices' ability to express themselves in Spanish, with the Mexican or New Mexican voice much superior.

By placing carefully metered and chosen words in the mouth of his nuevomexicano poetic voice, Chacón underscores the historical fact that while nuevomexicanos moved towards Spanish-English bilingualism, the newly-arrived to the state remained mostly monolingual in English. The stock phrases and grammatical train wrecks of the Spanish verses are representations of the poor attempts made by newcomers to the territory to muddle through the nuevomexicanos' "barbarous tongue." In contrast, the speaker who the reader knows to be speaking in Spanish, expresses himself in flawless English—a reflection of the nuevomexicano forced to learn English. This poetic voice displays mastery of the second language, while the English dominant individual says only "Oh yes me quiere!" in pidgin semi-Spanish.

Reading outside the poem as a whole, the bilingual reader would also grasp the great irony of Chacón's ability to so deftly manipulate both languages to such cutting effect, when the message of the poem was an implicit criticism of English monolingualism "In (New) Mexico." Though primarily in English, the poem could not be intended for a monolingual English speaker, who would not be able to decipher the subversive and political meanings embedded in Chacón's use of Spanish. Indeed, in this poem, Felipe Maximiliano Chacón took full advantage to express what he did not often say directly elsewhere; as González-Berry muses, "Perhaps herein lies a clue to Chacón's use of Spanish. He could do, in that language [Spanish], what he dared not do English" (González-Berry 195). By presenting the Spanish-in-English of the primary poetic voice, Chacón addresses a long-standing political inequality in New Mexico that was especially acute for the nuevomexicano bilinguals for whom he wrote. Chacón understood the meaning inherent to who spoke which languages and what that speech signified for nuevomexicano political agency, using his verse as the site for its expression. After nearly seven decades of debate over the question of language in New Mexico; after suggestions that bilingualism on both sides could be desirable (though in practice it did not occur equally across linguistic and ethnic groups); and after the Beveridge Report and accompanying press argued that New Mexico was fundamentally too Spanish-speaking to join the Union (or to govern itself), the poem is remarkably controlled and strategic in its expression of an ongoing and painful dynamic for nuevomexicanos.

But this is by no means the only place in "Poesía y prosa" where Chacón showcases his bilingual skills for a New Mexican reading public. Critical readings of Chacón's writing note that *Poesía y Prosa* includes a number of poems by English-language writers that Chacón translated into lyric Spanish. These seven poems are by Longfellow, Dryden, Byron, Sam Wallis Foss, E. Bulwer Lytton, and an unknown author, and Chacón provides no particular rationale for why he included poetic translations—nor these translations specifically—in the text. I posit that Chacón uses language in this instance to draw attention to his ability as a symmetrically bilingual writer to do poetic translation: in his case, with the exception of one poem that he describes as a free translation, the other translations preserve meter and rhyme scheme in Spanish, reproducing the content as well as the literary sense of the original English- language poems. This is extremely difficult to execute and requires considerable skill, which Chacón exhibits in these translations.

But perhaps the secondary objective of these translated poems is show the lyricism of Spanish as a language, to contest the negativity leveled against the language by critics of New Mexican statehood (and by extension, of nuevomexicanos themselves). It is as if to say that though the poems were masterful in their original language, by translating them into Spanish, not only are they made available to Spanish-language readers, it becomes evident that the Spanish language transmits the same sentiment and with equal artistry. No doubt Chacón himself enjoyed the poems he chose to translate in their original language, but if as Read says in the book's introduction, formal schooling in Spanish in New Mexico was becoming increasingly uncommon, wouldn't plenty of readers have been able to understand the English language original? Chacón may, therefore, have used these translations to resistive or responsive ends, as well as aesthetic ones.

Benjamín Read reveals near the introduction's close his own regard for Felipe M. Chacón's bilingual work, and a reflection on how the author's writing should be seen by both English-speaking Americans and Spanish speakers outside of New Mexico, perhaps assuming bilingual nuevomexicanos would already grasp the importance of his writing: "En mi humilde concepto, el pueblo de los Estados Unidos debe sentirse orgulloso de haber producido uno de sus conciudadanos que diera lustre a su Patria con las producciones de su talento en la lengua de aquellos reyes, los reyes Católicos, que tan señaladamente contribuyeron al descubrimiento de América, el continente que habitamos" ("In my humble view, the people of the United States should feel proud for having produced a fellow citizen who lauds his Patria through works forged from his own talent, written in the language of those kings, the Catholic kings, who so markedly contributed to the discovery of the continent of America, the continent which we now inhabit") (Read 13). He adds, "los pueblos de habla español [. . .] deben dar la más generosa acogida a las obras de Chacón, obras de uno que, desde extranjero suelo, ha sabido hacer honra al dulce idioma de España, lengua de sus propios países, hecho que de suyo reviste méritos acreedores a profundo aprecio" ("Spanish-speaking people [. . .] should receive with generous welcome Chacón's works, works by one who, from a foreign land, has known how to honor Spain's sweet language, the language of its own countries, a fact that in and of itself is a worthy merit deserving deep appreciation") (Read 13). As Read astutely observes, the bilingualism and inherently political message on display in Chacón's writing reveals a New Mexico at a dynamic point of change expressed in the language of change.

Because of this, there is a powerful political and sociolinguistic undercurrent to *Poesía y prosa*, and work remains to be done on Felipe M. Chacón: we read the archive by resurrecting the archive. Research must turn to the archive of Chacón's friends, colleagues, and contemporaries, and to the newspapers that he founded and edited, and where he published much of his writing, including *El faro del Río Grande* in Bernalillo and *La bandera americana*, among others. What might Felipe M. Chacón have said as the editor of *El faro*, as did other major Spanish-language newspaper editors and contributors of his time, such as Enrique Salazar or Eusebio Chacón? Where are the other works of literature that Chacón wrote, of which Read comments "no verán jamás la luz de la publicidad" ("which will never see the light of the public") (Read 14)? How can we better understand Felipe M. Chacón's subject positionality through the bilingual analysis of the works in *Poesía y prosa*, beyond those examined here? Are there other signs of his bi-literacy in Chacón's poetry, such as mestizo prosody, which imposes Spanish prosody on English verse? In seeking out answers to these questions, we may find ideas concretely expressed which are only hinted at through language play in *Obras de Felipe M. Chacón, "el cantor neomexicano": poesía y prosa*.

Works Cited

Chacón, Felipe Maximiliano. *Obras de Felipe Maximiliano Chacón, "el cantor neomexicano": poesía y prosa*. Albuquerque: *La bandera americana,* 1924.

Chacón, Felipe Maximiliano. *Short Stories*. Trans. Julián Josúe Vigil. Las Vegas, NM: Editorial Telaraña, 1980.

Deutsch, Sarah. *No Separate Refuge: Culture, Class and Gender on a Anglo-Hispanic Frontier in the American Southwest, 1880-1940*. New York: Oxford University Press, 1987.

Gonzales, Phillip B. *Política: Nuevomexicanos and American Political Incorporation, 1821-1910*. Lincoln: University of Nebraska Press, 2016.

González Berry, Erlinda. "Vicente Bernal and Felipe M. Chacón: Bridging Two Cultures." In *Pasó por Aquí: Critical Essays on the New Mexican Literary Tradition, 1542-1988*. Ed. Erlinda González-Berry. Albuquerque: University of New Mexico Press, 1989. 185-198.

Meketa, Jacqueline. *Legacy of Honor: The Life of Rafael Chacón, a Nineteenth-Century New Mexican*. Albuquerque: University of New Mexico Press, 1986.

Meléndez, A. Gabriel. "Nuevo México By Any Other Name: Creating a State from an Ancestral Homeland." In: *The Contested Homeland: A Chicano History of New Mexico*. Eds. David Maciel and Erlinda González Berry. Albuquerque: University of New Mexico Press, 2000. 143-168.

___. *So All Is Not Lost: The Poetics of Print in Nuevomexicano Communities, 1834-1958*. Albuquerque: U of New Mexico Press, 1997.

Meléndez, A. Gabriel and Francisco Lomelí. *The Writings of Eusebio Chacón*. Albuquerque: University of New Mexico Press, 2012.

Meyer, Doris. "Felipe Maximiliano Chacón: A Forgotten Mexican-American Author." *The New Scholar* (6) 1977. 111-126.

Nieto-Phillips, John M. *The Language of Blood: The Making of Spanish-American Identity in New Mexico, 1880s-1930s*. Albuquerque: University of New Mexico Press, 2004.

Padilla, Genaro. *My History, Not Yours: The Formation of Mexican American Autobiography*. Madison: University of Wisconsin Press, 1993.

Read, Benjamín. "Introduction." In *Obras de Felipe Maximiliano Chacón, "el cantor neomexicano": poesía y prosa*. Felipe M. Chacón. Albuquerque: *La bandera americana*, 1924. 1-14.

Endnote

[1]Thanks to Monica Mancillas for her contribution to the translation of Felipe M. Chacón's poems.

Of Modern Troubadours and Tricksters: The Upside-Down World of José Inés García

MANUEL M. MARTÍN-RODRÍGUEZ

University of California, Merced

When Chicano/a/x literature first burst (as such) onto the academic scene in the mid-1960s, there was a prevalent sense of newness and a definite feeling of alienation with literary tradition and print culture in general. Chicano/a/x Movement writers (and even most critics) failed to see any significant connection with any previous *writing*, opting instead for relating their works to the oral tradition. Tomás Rivera's comments on writing his 1972 award-winning novel *. . . y no se lo tragó la tierra/ . . . and the Earth Did Not Part* are emblematic in that regard:

> In my work I emphasized the processes of *remembering, discovery and volition.* I will discuss remembering first, I refer to the method of narrating which the people used. That is to say, I recall what they remembered and the manner in which they told it. There was always a way of compressing and exciting the sensibilities with a minimum of words" (366, original emphasis).

Even when Philip D. Ortego y Gasca proposed the term "Chicano Renaissance" to name the flowering of literature and all sorts of cultural activity during the 1960s and 1970s, it was unclear to what "classical" referent, if any, this particular Renaissance might be referring to.[1]

Still, some scholars, as was the case with Stan Steiner, suspected that Chicanos/as/xs had a hidden (or, rather, suppressed) history, whose texts were yet to be located and brought to light. In *La Raza*, Steiner stated: "Upon dusty shelves, frayed and forgotten, the books of this history may still be hidden. By word of mouth, from time to time, there is word of a lost literature, in reminiscences and folk memories" (218).

Three years later, eminent critic Luis Leal issued a challenge to Chicano/a/x literature scholars to hit those dusty shelves and dig up forgotten texts. In the inaugural issue of the influential *Revista Chicano-Riqueña*, Leal suggested: "It is our belief that an effort should be made to trace the historical development of Mexican American literature now that it has been recognized as a subject worthy of serious study" (32). He then exemplified what that literary history might look like by proposing a periodization (largely based on social and political developments), and by beginning to populate it with the listing of works he was familiar with from each of those periods.

Though it took critics some additional years to seriously heed Leal's call for historical research, a number of conferences, individual, and collective retrieval projects began taking shape in the late 1980s to (paraphrasing the name of the most fruitful of those efforts, which this volume celebrates) recover the US Hispanic literary heritage. The success of those projects (which also include the New Mexico-based "Pasó por aquí" series and the Colección Plural Espejo, just launched by the Academia Norteamericana de la Lengua Española) resulted in the first of several paradoxes that I will explore in this paper: the fact that— as I have suggested elsewhere—in the past few decades Chicano/a/x literature has expanded as much toward its past as it has toward its future (*Life in Search of Readers* 5).

This bountiful, newly found past is said to extend all the way back to the 16th century, with such titles as Álvar Núñez Cabeza de Vaca's *Relación* or *Naufragios* [Shipwreck, 1542] and Gaspar de Villagrá's *Historia de la nveva Mexico* [History of the new Mexico, 1610] now considered by many (though not all) to be part of Chicano/a/x letters. As in all similar recovery initiatives, though, the retrieval, reprinting, and analysis of texts and authors has been uneven, with some writers (e.g. María Amparo Ruiz de Burton) immediately becoming part of a newly refurbished Chicano/a/x literary *canon* to which others are unlikely to be admitted on the same terms. Textual recovery, therefore, has produced its own categories and biases which, as of this writing, are still being interrogated.

A second question begging interrogation in the critical assessment of recovery efforts has to do with literary genres and their respective value and usefulness for reconstructing a particular literary history. In the case of Chicano/a/x literature, at least if critical attention and number of recovered works printed could serve us to gauge this particular point, novels and autobiographies have been privileged with respect to poetry (a distant third category) and to the so-called minor genres. In that sense, and with the exception of Jorge Ulica's *Crónicas dia-*

bólicas, published in 1982 (before the major recovery projects took shape) and long out of print since then, virtually none of the Mexican American satirists of the twentieth century have enjoyed new editions or studies of their work.[2] And yet, it could be argued that minor genres are precisely the sites where cultural transformation, social tensions, and political commentary are most easily perceived, and they may be the writings most directly accessible to community (i.e. non professional) readers. Mary Louise Pratt, for example, suggested in 1981 that short stories allow minority and women writers to deal with topics and figures that had remained on the fringes (or entirely outside) of the realm of literature (161). Extending her analysis, as many have done since then, I will argue that humoristic poetry, particularly that which was printed in community newspapers and in other easily accessible printed formats (e.g. leaflets) played an equally important role in developing a popular voice within Chicano/a/x letters, a voice that was distinct not only from mainstream views and values but also from that of the Mexican American middle and upper classes that penned most of the novels and autobiographies in pre-Chicano/a/x Movement times.

My interest in establishing this context stems from the fact that José Inés García is one of those authors whose works remain unrecovered and whose poetics align with the aesthetics of the minor genres in vernacular Spanish. Perhaps as a consequence, García's poetry is virtually unknown to most Chicano/a/x and non Chicano/a/x readers, and he has received almost no critical attention. As far as I can tell, only thirteen of his poems have been printed in "recent" times, in the anthology *Los pobladores nuevomexicanos y su poesía, 1889-1950*, edited by Anselmo F. Arellano in 1976. Still, García was a major cultural figure in the southern Colorado and northern New Mexico area, as we will see in more detail below.[3]

García signed most of his compositions as "El trovador moderno" (The Modern Troubadour), which should explain (in part) my title, as well as the particular juncture he occupies, wedged between a centuries-old oral tradition and the more recent, yet vibrant journalistic industry of the Hispanic US southwest, in which he played a major role. His pen name, therefore, alludes to a second paradox that his contemporary readers, no doubt, appreciated: by calling himself a *troubadour*, García made explicit his connection with the traditional oral poets of the New Mexico/Colorado area; in stressing *modernity* in his pen name, however, he seemed to be suggesting that he could play the role of the ancient bards while adapting to the more recent print culture represented by newspapers.

At the end of this article, I will return to this and other paradoxes that make García and his world a veritable upside-down universe. But first, as with any other lesser-known figure, it may be relevant to give some biographical information to better understand his cultural activities and relevance.

Blindness and Insights: José Inés García as a socially situated cultural leader

José Inés García was born in Chamisal, New Mexico, on January 21, 1871.[4] Two years later, his family moved to Chacón, also in northern New Mexico, where José Inés began his formal education at a Presbyterian school. The extent of his studies is not known, but if the tongue-in-cheek poem "Tengo un burro más vivo que yo" is any indication, it probably was rather limited, as the speaker in the poem says that he never went beyond third grade. More important for my purposes, however, are García's childhood reminiscences in an autobiographical sketch dated 1954. In it, García states the following: "Mi primo Manuel Sandoval, primo hermano de mi mamá, iba de vez en cuando a visitarnos a Chamisal, y cada vez que iba llevaba consigo un libro que decían que se llamaba Biblia. Y en las noches . . . leía porciones a mi papá y a mi mamá de ese libro."[5]

In yet another interesting inversion (at least for his geographic and cultural context), García and his family were Protestants, not Catholics, and García's appreciation for the Bible is evident in many of his serious poems, including "Quiero volver al Rito," where he states: "Ahora expongo y digo: / La Biblia fue mi mejor amigo."[6] What interests me the most from this background is the role that the Bible may have played in shaping not only García's religious beliefs but also part of his aesthetics and approach to print culture as well. Picture young José Inés listening to Manuel Sandoval reading such biblical stories as those of David and Goliath, or the Prodigal Son, or that of Lazarus and the Rich Epulon, and we may have some of the seeds for García's penchant for stories of upside-down worlds and for unexpected twists and turns in plots and in story endings.[7]

Beyond these childhood recollections on reading, we can date García's real entrance into the world of print culture to 1894, when he became the editor of the newspaper *La Crónica* in Mora County. With the new century, García moved to Trinidad, Colorado, then one of the most important commercial and cultural hotspots in the area. In Trinidad, García worked for Casimiro Barela and Salomón García, and he soon became editor of *El Progreso*, a newspaper owned by Barela. García also worked as an interpreter in Trinidad and in Denver, an element to which I will briefly return below.

For reasons that are not entirely clear, García went back to Chacón, New Mexico in 1907. A month after his return, he suffered an accident that left him blind for life, despite numerous efforts to find a cure (for this, García traveled all the way to the Mayo clinic in Minnesota). In García's utmost topsy-turvy world, however, his eyesight problems meant apparently little, because in 1910 he was back in Trinidad as the (blind) editor of *El Progreso*, a paper he left in

1914 to launch his own periodical, *El Faro*. *El Faro* was a 4-page weekly that lasted several decades. Unfortunately, OCLC records no extant issues of this paper, but García's archives contain one issue (from 1937) that may or may not be representative of its entire run.

Upon learning these biographical facts, I was skeptical at first about the extent of García's eyesight problems. Even with such august predecessors as Homer and Jorge Luis Borges, blind authors are not that common, and blind editors and book dealers, to the best of my knowledge, are even rarer. However, while conducting research in New Mexico, I located a political editorial in a Trinidad, CO newspaper that seems to confirm that he was indeed blind. The unsigned article ("Comentos políticos") complains about a new probate judge who had favored some individuals of the opposite political party. Here's the relevant part of that article:

> Se hacen la pregunta nuestros co-partidarios: "¿Qué ha hecho el partido Republicano para Ralston en tanto año que se ha mesclado en política para que él se muestre tan benévolo con nuestros enemigos y los enemigos que han sido de él y de su partido." Se refiere al alguacil e intérprete en Español de su corte que ha nombrado, que son Frank Cescolini y Inez García. Se dice que a éste último ha dicho que lo puso por caridad de ayudarlo que está ciego. Ese ciego hace más dinero en un descuido que el mismo juez Ralston. Pues figuren ustedes: es interprete ante la corte de los dos jueces de paz de la ciudad que día a día lo ocupan a veces hasta dos y más veces; intérprete ante el coronario; intérprete ante el juez de policía y de vez en cuando ante la comición industrial. Tiene dos comercios en la ciudad de Trinidad, uno en la calle primera y otro en la calle principal al oriente y además es aplicante para la nueva compensación de los ciegos del estado. Desde luego cómo no puede uno creer que hace más dinero que el que le dio otra posición por caridad? (2).

The business on First Street was García's printing shop and bookstore (also called *El Faro*). Though a legally blind man, García was the editor and owner of a newspaper, a printing shop, and a bookstore, a veritable topsy-turvy case of the blind man leading . . . his seeing peers. In that latter regard, García's cultural influence in the area was considerable, and I intend to explore in more detail elsewhere such aspects as the books he sold in his store and other elements not directly associated with his own literary production.

As a publisher, García printed an unknown number of books by others (I have located just one, a religious commemorative chapbook)[8] and no fewer than eight of his own works, dated from 1924 to 1945. I should hasten to point out that those dates are taken from the extant copies of each of those nine chapbooks (in all cases, just one known copy per title); this means that there could have been earlier printings of each (or some) of those chapbooks, a fact that I cannot prove at this point, but that I strongly suspect because of this statement García makes in the prologue of *Mi sombrero es pagador*:

> **Querido Lector:** Con la publicación de esta obra titulada "MI SOM-BRERO ES PAGADOR", damos principio a varias otras obras que ya tenemos listas para la prensa. / Hay un campo muy vasto que está demandando más y más libros, y habiendo recibido esa inspiración, nos hemos puesto en esta gran obra de ayudar en suplir esa gran demanda. El amante de las letras, se cansa y se fastidia de un solo libro, luego quiere otro y otro, y quedaremos muy contentos si ayudamos a dar gusto al público. La mayor parte de nuestros trabajos van a ser en poesía. Eso demanda el público, eso le vamos a dar. (n.p.)

The only known copy of *Mi sombrero es pagador* is dated 1945,[9] which would make this title the last one of the nine he published. Not discounting the possibility that he may have printed other chapbooks after 1945, that number must have been minimal, given García's age and the lack of information about any of those later publications. Moreover, García's comments on supply and demand would make little sense at the end of a series of nine publications, but they would be much more meaningful at the beginning of such an undertaking. For these reasons, my analysis of his works will de-emphasize chronology (at least until we have better data) to concentrate instead on the treatment of certain topics and social contexts that may be better indicators of date of composition of his books.

García and the New Mexican folkloric tradition

Most of García's literary output is directly connected with the tone, style, and contents of the New Mexican folk tradition. This includes both serious and humoristic compositions. In the poem, "Me casé sin reflejar" [I Married without Reflecting] for example, we find the traditional personification of virtues and vices so common in the oral tradition (and in some periods of literature as well): "Joven y sin reflejar / Me casé con la Pereza; / Muy mal me fue en la empresa / Y me quiero divorciar". In other poems, García adopts the dialectical tone of folk disputes to explore cultural difference and/or conflict, as in "Un lenguaje extraño" [A Strange Language]:

Hay gentes en este mundo,
Primito, no me ha de creer

Que al hombre le llaman Man
y Woman a la mujer.

No sé dónde aprenderían
Un lenguaje tan extraño,
Pues al mes le llaman Month
Y le llaman Year al año.

The speaker's feigned ignorance about this strange language serves only to emphasize its foreignness and to call attention to its relatively recent arrival to the New Mexico/Colorado area, thus calling subtle but firm attention to questions of political and cultural affirmation and resistance in a land in which the speakers of the *old* language were beginning to be perceived as foreigners in their own land.

Even closer to the folkloric tradition are poems directly intended to serve the traditional needs of the community, such as "Entrega de novios" [The Delivery of the Newlyweds], undistinguishable from the many similar oral compositions (or *trovas*) customarily recited by godparents to present the bride and groom, as a new couple, to the community.[10] Judging from publication records I have been able to document, García must have been quite successful in this regard, since some of his folklore-oriented poems (like "Un indito en su jacal" [A Little Indian in His Hut]) were printed in periodicals throughout the US southwest.

But the one element from the traditional folklore that requires some extended consideration in this paper is the figure of the trickster, to which I will devote the next section.

Of modern troubadours and tricksters

In the Indo-Hispanic traditions of the New Mexico/Colorado area, trickster figures are plentiful, and they have played a significant historical role in the enculturation of younger generations, as well as in their entertainment. Local Native American cultures have told stories about Coyote the trickster from time immemorial, and Spanish-origin folklore brought to the area characters like Pedro de Urdemalas and several other stock figures that, as the true descendants of the Spanish *pícaros* [rogues], soon were equated with marginal life in society, as well as with an uncanny ability to get the best of whatever opponent they might encounter in their continuous traveling and moving around. Some of these tricksters seem to be of New Mexican creation, as the Mano Fashico (a mispronunciation of Hermano Francisco, here referring to a third order Franciscan secular brother) and Don Cacahuate [Mr. Peanut], among others.

Folklorist Enrique R. Lamadrid has suggested a probable reason for the endurance of these characters in New Mexican folklore and fiction. According to Lamadrid, "[t]heir epistemological role in the culture prevents their definite departure. Without them and their literary brethren, Hispanic society has too difficult a time in criticizing itself" (16). They also play an intracultural critical role, as the same critic acknowledges:

> By definition, tricksters and pícaros serve as mythical and social mediators of the contradictions which underlie their cultures. They are culture heroes because they are the only beings fully capable of illuminating or bringing attention to these problems. Their most basic techniques are symbolic inversion and humor. (17)

And yet, in multicultural societies the trickster can also play a role in confronting and in causing intercultural conflict as well, as E. A. Mares has suggested (21).

For a moralist like José Inés García, the trickster's double role of exposing internal cultural flaws while engaging in a consideration of intercultural conflict must have been both apparent and enticing. As we will see below (through the analysis of two of his chapbooks), García leaned rather heavily on the trickster as a figure that was entirely recognizable for his readers, and on the particular narrative structure associated with that character. I will be claiming, nonetheless, that García's use of trickterism ends up surpassing his intended didactic purposes (as exposed in the "Moral" ending section of each of these books), as his stories allow us to see (beyond what García shows us) social anxieties and historical transformations lurking in the background.

Mi sombrero es pagador (or Three Tricksters Tricked)

In a style not unlike those of the Mano Fashico jokes, García's humor is at times peculiar. His comic stories can be hard to get at first because their main premises are somewhat farfetched. *Mi sombrero es pagador* is one of those stories where even the title disconcerts us at first. Above, I proposed a semantically-meaningful translation of this title [My Hat Will Pay] because I have read the book and understand how the story renders the title comprehensible. But before reading the chapbook, one would be hard pressed to guess what the title means (a literal translation would be *My Hat is a Payer*, a hard sentence to understand in either standard or vernacular New Mexican Spanish).

The lack of clarity in the title is reminiscent of the gnomic economy of the oral tradition, and the story begins—indeed—as many folk tales do, in an unidentified land that could be anywhere: "En compañía de la esposa / Vivía el Señor Don Sixto, / Junto al pueblo no sé donde, / En el valle nunca visto" (7). García then gives a somewhat detailed portrait of the family and the landscape, which little by little clarifies that this nowhere land must be in the New Mexico/Colorado area. In this first section of the book, we learn that the family owns a cow, that the drought is ruining the family, and that extreme measures are required to go on living (a story retold in numerous other New Mexican books, such as Fabiola Cabeza de Baca's autobiographical *We Fed Them Cactus* [1954]).

On the recommendation of the wife, they decide to sell the cow, and the husband is entrusted with taking the animal to market the following day. Unbeknownst to the couple, however, a group of good for nothings overheard their conversation and, in true trickster fashion, they decide to deceive Don Sixto. What happens next has a certain Miguel de Cervantes' taste, at least for the reader familiar with *Don Quixote*. Once on the road, Don Sixto meets the first of the troublemakers who wants to know the selling price for Don Sixto's goat. Don Sixto replies that his animal is a cow, and he moves on, rejecting the price the stranger is willing to pay for the (alleged) goat. Down the road, Don Sixto meets a second trickster who, once again, praises his goat while offering the same price to purchase it. After a while, the final hoodlum appears and offers to buy Don Sixto's goat, to which the latter agrees: "Responde don Sisto luego; / 'Dos y medio por la va . . . digo / Por la cabra, sin duda'" (17). Like Don Quixote and Sancho Panza fighting with the barber over Mambrino's helmet, Don Sixto and the three tricksters seem to be testing the limits of perception and representation in this scene, to the point that—as in Cervantes' invention of the word *baciyelmo* to define the highly contested object in *Don Quixote*—García has to refer to the animal as the *vaca-cabra* [cow-goat] on page 21. The tricksters' shameless and somewhat humoristic inversion (by which a cow has become a goat) results in a financial benefit for them, since they buy the cow for the price of a far less expensive goat, and they go on to celebrate in town.

Don Sixto returns home and (still caught in his peculiar Cervantine moment of undecidability) informs his wife that he has successfully sold *the goat*. Mrs. Clemaca (Don Sixto's wife) refuses to play along and announces another twist in the story: "Los que esto te jugaron / Muy caro lo pagarán. / Ahora lo que nos toca, / Es formar bien nuestro plan" (18). Doña Clemaca's strategy (which she spells out for feeble-minded Don Sixto) involves borrowing money to buy a nice hat and then, after discussing the trick with several local business owners, visiting their stores to make substantial purchases; upon completing each transaction, Don Sixto is instructed to say "my hat will pay for it" and walk away.

When the tricksters witness how easy it is for Don Sixto to buy on credit, they realize they need to purchase the hat from him as well. Instructed by Doña Clemaca, Don Sixto plays hardball with the tricksters, refusing to sell the hat until they offer a price he cannot possibly refuse (fifteen thousand, compared to the two and a half he received for the cow—the currency remains unnamed). On page 36, once they realize the hoax, the tricksters concede defeat: "Aquí diremos amigos / Que tenemos una lección / Que el trabajar es honesto / Y el robar es maldición," followed by some additional moral reflection. Apparently not satisfied with their act of contrition, García adds a "Moral" section at the end of the book that consists of seventeen stanzas, most of which repeat and amplify the idea that hard work should be an honest man's occupation and that crime never pays.

The plot structure of this book follows the traditional scheme of the trickster-tricked motif and, as such, it is conducive to the kind of closure that García attempts to give his story with the moral. For the attentive reader, however, some lingering issues remain unresolved and they may be reflective of those social anxieties that I mentioned above. For all authorial attempts to situate his tale in an unnamed land with an undefined currency, the reader has little trouble recognizing this place as New Mexico: the language used by the characters, and the presence of such culturally loaded terms as *resolana* dispel any doubt about the true location of the story.[11] This means that the society depicted in the tale should also be seen as representative of New Mexican reality. As such, *Mi sombrero es pagador* touches upon two elements worth discussing: class and gender. The former plays a lesser role in the story but, in Don Sixto's predicament, an informed reader would easily discern the motif of the loss of class status suffered by many New Mexican landowners who lost their property and way of life when their agricultural and ranch economy was transformed into a capitalist system with the opening of the Santa Fe trail, first, and with the annexation of New Mexico to the United States, later. In that regard, García uses two symbols that a reader interested in pursuing this line of interpretation could easily endow with relevant expressive meaning: first, the unnamed currency situates the village economy in an unsecure, transitional stage in which money has no name, just function; then, the symbol of the hat as guarantor of economic transactions replaces the traditional handshake with which business was settled in pre-1848 New Mexico; the portable, disembodied hat is as fluid a signifier as the nameless currency; while in Spanish and Mexican New Mexico transactions were often settled in kind (sheep, cows, etc.) and certified with the handshake, the new economy operates in much more impersonal and intangible ways.

In that sense, García's economic and social analysis in Mi sombrero es pagador anticipates similar literary treatments of New Mexico/Colorado in post-1965 Chicano/a literature. The following quote from the historical novel Not by the Sword (1982), by New Mexican author Nash Candelaria, is an example among many. Don Francisco, the patriarch of the Rafa family, receives the visit of an Anglo American businessman and his New Mexican interpreter; they come to collect on a promissory note written in English and signed by Don Francisco's son after suffering heavy losses playing cards. The note agrees to transfer ownership of certain lands to Mr. Hammond if Carlos Rafa were to be unable to pay cash within a reasonable time. Don Francisco's reflections upon learning all this, and the ensuing dialogue, go as follows:

> Certain lands? His lands! That one piece that was in Carlos' name, that piece that had been a wedding gift, was still part of the family's proper-ty. It was not to be sold, given away, or lost in a game of cards. . . . /

> "Your son owes me a considerable amount of money," Hammond said stiffly. "I don't want his land. I prefer cash."

> Cash! Always cash. Always a hand out for a loan or for payment of a debt. It was as if some devouring monster was gobbling everything he had. What he had worked a lifetime for. What his father had left him. And his father's father before.

> "Señores. What can I say? I am not responsible for my son's debts. I am not aware of any debts. As I said before, you come to me strangers with a paper in a language I cannot read. I do not see how I can be of help to you." (177)

Candelaria touches upon several issues involving cultural and economic transfor-mation in New Mexico, including the increased role played by cash under the new economy,[12] as well as the motif of the unintelligible note (in an idioma extraño) that replaces traditional business practices, the very same two ideas hint-ed at in García's *Mi sombrero*. In this context, the seemingly incomprehensible acceptance of the cow-goat transformation in Don Sixto's mind begins to make a little more sense, as a symbol of the utter alienation felt by the New Mexican traditional families faced with a new reality they can hardly understand, in which everything has a new name, and practices and procedures have changed as well.

As for gender, the role of Doña Clemaca is also reflective of deep house-hold transformations in the late nineteenth century, as the supreme patriarchal authority of the male head of the family began to be threatened by less submissive sons and daughters and—as in this case—by non-traditional wives whose heightened sense of agency transforms them into the *de facto* decision makers of their household.[13] US Latina/o/x literature from the early twentieth century abounds in examples of the anxiety caused by such non-traditional, transformed gender roles,[14] and it is easy to see that, *sotto voce*, García is also addressing this issue here by placing the brains and strategic thinking in Doña Clemaca, while making Don Sixto a gullible simpleton.

We will see much more clearly how the rise of female agency was perceived as a threat in our discussion of *Sería rata* [Must Have Been a Rat] below.

Of Mice and Women: Gender Anxiety in the Land of (Dis)enchantment

The plot of *Sería rata* is also somewhat peculiar. As the first stanza explains, Don Sebastián, the cheese maker, brings a cheese everyday to Don Juan's household for the daily quesadillas. On a particular day, Don Juan returns home to find no cheese or quesadillas. His wife justifies the lack of food explaining that a mouse ate the cheese. Don Juan contends that it must have been a rat and the couple's argument gets so loud that neighbors become involved. Without exception, every single female neighbor rallies in support of Don Juan's nameless wife, while their male counterparts support Don Juan.

Spanish-language readers will notice right away that this bizarre dispute is partly supported on a grammatical gender difference in that language, in which "ratón" [mouse] is a masculine noun, while "rata" [rat] is feminine. García cleverly anchors gender anxiety (arguably the main theme in this poetry chapbook) in language, anticipating in that way more recent interrogations of linguistic gender bias.

In addition, García also deals with the questions of perception and representation that I discussed in connection with *Mi sombrero es pagador*. Much as that book gave us an image of the cow-goat, *Sería rata* features a drawing of the rat-mouse on page 9. García's awareness of the arbitrary nature of language (or, at least, of the linguistic sign) may have been born out of his experiences as an interpreter. In translating back and forth between the courts and the citizenry, García must have confronted many ambiguous situations in which translation was not easy or even possible. He may have also noticed the way in which a particular individual's speech was affected by her/his own cultural, class, and gender identity (if not bias), as well as by his position of authority (or lack thereof).

In fact, the plot of the story includes a most important visit to the court, where some of the major characters are introduced. When the domestic dispute between Don Juan and his wife escalates to an all-neighborhood free for all, someone suggests visiting the judge. Pages 14-15 of the chapbook reproduce the argument between men and women as it takes place this time inside the court house. After a rather brief inquiry, the judge is about to pronounce sentence when he suddenly notices his own wife among the women. García devotes several stanzas to the ensuing transformation in the judge's previously calm, cool, and collected demeanor:

> El Juez siguió en la tribuna
> En cumplimiento al deber;
> Pero en esto vió a una
> Que parecía a su mujer.
>
> Era su esposa, y razón
> Tuvo el Juez en temblar;
> Iba a dar su decisión,
> Pero no podía hablar.
>
> Unos sudores le ván,
> Otros sudores le vienen.
> Al Juez en tan grande afán
> Sus temores le detienen. (16)

To bide some time, the judge adjourns the court until the following day, and he sends everybody home. New arguments break out in every single household, including his own: the judge's wife taunts him and warns him: "Si crees que fué una rata / Las mujeres estaremos / En contra de tí, mi tata, / Y de tí nos vengaremos" (19). When the confrontation intensifies, the judge's wife becomes a revolutionary figure whose criticism of patriarchy and of the judicial system minces no words: "Lo mismo que tú, así son / Los hombres todos iguales, / Hacen lo que hizo el raton / Y nos echan sebornales" (190; and later: "'¡Justicia! ¡Linda Justicia! / Así la llaman los 'amos' / Dijo ella con malicia, / 'Pero ahora los ahorcamos'" (22).

So that she does not stand out as an outlier whose opinions could be easily dismissed by the reader, García have the other women utter similar criticism:

> A nosotras las mujeres
> Siempre se nos ha tenido,
> Como a cocina y enceres
> O como a un mueble teñido.
>
> Los hombres nos han tratado
> Como caballo de carga;

Más el momento ha llegado,
Que ya todo les amarga. (24)

Having seen the writing on the wall, the judge assesses the deep roots of the problem, and the foreseeable outcomes. Talking about the women's complaints, he says:

Todas reclaman a una
Que libertad no han tenido,
Y que quieren por fortuna
Ser iguales al marido.

Si se hacen estas enmiendas,
De que ellas sean iguales
Luego tomarían las riendas
Como Jueces y Oficiales.

≈ ≈ ≈

Si en caso ellas llegaran,
A servir en los juzgados
Entonces si nos mandarán
Como a niños de mandados. (32-33)

Fully vested in finding a solution that could contain the women's revolt (and professional progress), the judge eventually realizes that neither a rat nor a mouse ate the cheese. Back in court, he cross examines all parties, including the cheese maker, and confirms that no cheese was delivered on that particular day to Don Juan's home, thus explaining its absence. The judge then gives a speech about the need to maintain the peace in every home, which the poet endorses with several stanzas on the same subject, directly addressed to the reader.

Sería rata, therefore, foregrounds the social transformations that were occurring in early twentieth century New Mexico. That fact that García chose to focus on gender issues this time connects him to a literary tradition that ranges from Jorge Ulica's short pieces in the 1910s to José Antonio Villarreal's *Pocho* (1959) and beyond.[15] As I mentioned above, writings of this nature are mostly concerned with the more independent roles that women of Mexican descent found in the United States, and with the consequences that those transformations had on traditional Mexican households in the first half of the twentieth century. In all cases, however (and this is certainly true of García as well), gender transformation is both a direct concern of these writers and a metaphorical or allegorical meditation on the general loss of status of people of Mexican descent since the US annexation of its present-day southwestern states. In García's case, as we saw, that concern is also present in tongue-in-cheek poems like "Un lenguaje extraño," where the foreignness of English is highlighted as clearly as *Sería rata* foregrounds gender changes brought about by the annexation of New Mexico to the United States.

(In)Conclusion

Though I expect to have a more fully developed conclusion at the end of my study of García's poetry, the following remarks summarize my current thinking and assessment of his works.

In the first place, I would like to highlight the original way in which García receives and transforms a diverse cultural inheritance. His poetry, especially the two chapbooks I have discussed in this paper, is molded by Biblical readings, by the New Mexico folk tradition and, quite possibly, by García's (direct or indirect) knowledge of sixteenth- and seventeenth-century Spanish literature. From the latter, García borrows and connects with the figure of the *pícaro* and with the peculiar worldview that Cervantes conveys in *Don Quixote*. Cervantes wrote in a period of deep social transformation in Spain, when old values and economies were being replaced (and rendered obsolete) by modern societal and financial developments; perhaps as a consequence, he placed his characters in a rather fluid medium where things are seldom what they appear to be. Like Cervantes, García plays with undecidability as, perhaps, a metaphor for the confusing state in which the Spanish-speaking population of New Mexico and Colorado found itself during the first half of the twentieth century.

As for the folk tradition, García reproduces with gusto structures and situations that are typical of the oral tales of yore, in particular trickster stories and their penchant for exploring internal cultural flaws and intercultural contact and conflict. This gave García an advantage when connecting with an audience that was familiar with those tales, while allowing him to exploit the modern printed medium to insert variations in the telling of the stories seldom available to the old troubadours (e.g. the drawings that illustrate his stories every 2-3 pages or so).

Finally, from the Bible García derives a strong taste for the moral interpretation of the stories that he tells, rendering them didactic and exemplary.[16] Still, of García's moral endings we could say what Peter Bürger believes to be true of La Fontaine's: that, by inserting the narrator's perspective, his fables can no longer aspire to the character of absolute truth that traditional fables reserved for themselves (794). In García's case, as we saw, this relative value of the moral is further complicated by the social anxieties in the background of his stories that neither the narrator nor the implied author can completely contain.

It is more than likely that life circumstances also informed García's tastes in poetry. Reversals of fortune (like that resulting in his blind condition) and ensuing ironies like that of being the blind owner of a bookstore, a print shop and a newspaper, surely brought home the topsy-turvy essence of the trickster tale and of similar stories in the Bible and in *Don Quixote*. They may have contributed to his keen awareness of the social transformations occurring in New Mexico and Colorado as new economic policies (like the fencing of the plains and the encroachment on communal lands), social changes (including a transformation of the traditional role of women), and political and legal structures eroded the power of the New Mexican Hispanic elites. That he chose to address those transformations through the medium of poetry, and that he chose to avail himself of the printing technology (thus becoming a *trovador moderno*) is clearly to our advantage, as his work has outlived him and is now ready for recovery and reinterpretation.

Works Cited

Bürger, Peter. "Las fábulas de La Fontaine." *Literatura universal: Renacimiento y barroco.* Ed. August Buck. Madrid: Gredos, 1982.

Candelaria, Nash. *Not by the Sword.* Tempe, AZ: Bilingual Press, 1982.

"Comentos políticos." *El Anunciador* (May 31, 1919): 2.

Díaz, José. *P. Galindo: Obras (in)completas de José Díaz.* Ed. Manuel M. Martín-Rodríguez. Houston: Arte Público Press, 2016.

García, José Inés. *Mi sombrero es pagador.* Trinidad, CO: El Faro, n.d.

___. ¡Sería rata! Trinidad, CO: El Faro, 1930.

Kanellos, Nicolás. *Hispanic Immigrant Literature: El Sueño del Retorno.* Austin: University of Texas Press, 2011.

Lamadrid, Enrique R. "The Rogue's Progress: Journeys of the Picaro from Oral Tradition to Contemporary Chicano Literature of New Mexico." *MELUS* 20.2 (1995): 15-34.

Leal, Luis. "Mexican-American Literature: A Historical Perspective." *Revista Chicano-Riqueña* 1.1 (1973): 32-44.

Mares, E. A. "El Coyote: Between Two Cultures." *El Cuaderno (de vez en cuando)* 2.1 (1972): 20-23.

Martín-Rodríguez, Manuel M. *Life in Search of Readers: Reading (in) Chicano/a Literature.* Albuquerque: University of New Mexico Press, 2003

Martínez, Erminio Jesús. "Las poesías de José Inés García, poeta nuevomejicano." M.A. Thesis. New Mexico Highlands University, 1972.

Martínez, Juan Francisco. *Sea la Luz: The Making of Mexican Protestantism in the American Southwest, 1829-1900.* Denton, TX: University of North Texas Press, 2006.

Montiel, Miguel, Tomás Atencio, and E. A. "Tony" Mares. *Resolana: Emerging Chicano Dialogues on Community and Globalization.* Tucson: University of Arizona Press, 2009.

Ortego y Gasca, Philip. "The Chicano Renaissance." *Journal of Social Casework,* May, 1971.

Pratt, Mary Louise. "The Short Story: The Long and the Short of It." *Poetics* 10 (1981): 175-194.

Rivera, Tomás. "Chicano Literature: Fiesta of the Living." 1975. *Tomás Rivera: The Complete Works.* Houston: Arte Público Press, 1992. 338-358.

Steiner, Stan. *La Raza: The Mexican Americans.* New York: Harper, 1970.

"Comentos políticos." *El Anunciador* (May 31, 1919): 2.

Endnotes

[1]Ortego y Gasca, "The Chicano Renaissance," *passim.*

[2]My own edition of the works of P. Galindo (pen name of José Díaz) appeared in 2016.

[3]Given the close cultural ties at the time between both areas, whenever I use "New Mexico" in this paper it should be understoon that I am referring to both New Mexico and Colorado, unless otherwise indicated.

[4]Unless otherwise noted, all biographical details are from Erminio J. Martínez's M.A. thesis. As García's nephew, Martínez was able to share invaluable information on the author.

[5]I quote the manuscript version kept in García's private archive. I have not found a printed version of this essay yet.

[6]As Juan F. Martínez explains, "the Presbyterian church of El Rito (Chacón, New Mexico), was organized after several Protestant families migrated from Chamisal and other communities to a new location to escape Catholic persecution" (128).

[7]I will return to this point below, when I discuss tricksterism.

[8]*Crónica de la Trigésima-Quinta Convención Anual de las Sociedades Hispano Americanas de Esfuerzo Cristiano de los Estados de Colorado y Nuevo México* (1931).

[9]Erminio Martínez dates this book as 1925, but his personal copy, which would substantiate this dating, is presently lost.

[10]This and some of the other poems discussed in this paper can be read in Spanish at http://alternativepublications.ucmerced.edu/?p=248.

[11]*Resolana*, as defined by Miguel Montiel, Tomás Atencio, and E. A. "Tony" Mares is derived from "*resol* (the reflection of the sun) and refers to the sunny side of a building where villagers gather to talk while protected from the elements" (4).

[12]Later in the novel, Don Francisco—still musing about the cash amount demanded by Hammond—does a mental calculation that beautifully illustrates the transformation of the New Mexican economy: "One thousand pesos. That is one thousand sheep" (128).

[13]*Not by the Sword* artfully recreates this moment of transition and uphFFeaval. The following quote summarizes the thoughts of Don Francisco (the protagonist family's patriarch) on the subject: "What was this madness? Don Francisco thought. Where sons talk back to fathers. Where some sons talk rebellion against the government. While other sons rebel again their priests and their church. The world was going mad. Where was tradition? Obedience?" (174).

[14]For an analysis on this trend, see Kanellos, Chapter 5.

[15]For José Díaz, see "Estoy aquello' (64).

[16]The latter in a much more precise sense than the ones Cervantes penned under exactly that title of *Novelas ejemplares* [Exemplary].

Part 3: Of Exile to Immigration: Nationalism, Migrations and Transnationalism

An immigration literature frequently explored racism and ethnic or national identity, conflict, pride in culture of origin, and appealed to justice. It was about adapting and reaching out to the broader society from an existing cultural tradition. An exile literature spoke to forced departures, yearning for the homeland, and seeking balance between new and old places.

—Gerald E. Poyo

[T]o denaturalize notions of nation and national belonging through the concept of the "transnational" . . . would entail contrasting older models of migration that emphasize one-way movement and permanent settlement with newer models that develop the idea of the "transnational subject," emphasizing two-way movements across relatively fluid national borders.

—Yolanda Padilla

Del exilio a la inmigración: *Cosas de los Estados Unidos* de Simón Camacho

CATALINA T. CASTILLÓN
Lamar University

Durante el siglo XIX, hubo un gran número de escritores hispanos que, por razones varias, buscaron asilo político en los Estados Unidos. Este fue el caso de Simón Camacho (1821-1883), un poeta, ensayista, cronista y traductor venezolano que escribió bajo el seudónimo de "Nazareno". Camacho estudió Derecho en Caracas, y ejerció como Secretario de la Cámara de Diputados, pero "cuando el malhadado asunto del 24 de enero de 1848", en el que los conservadores intentaron tomar control del congreso sin éxito, Camacho tuvo que salir de su país por razones políticas (Bruni Celli). Como exiliado, vivió en Puerto Rico, Perú y en Estados Unidos, donde se estableció en Nueva York y trabajó como corresponsal para varios periódicos. Colaboró para el *Diario de la Marina* y la revista *La Lira* de La Habana (DGLV). También actuó como representante político de Venezuela en Washington.

En el exilio, Simón Camacho fue un autor polifacético que realizó traducciones (tradujo a Alejandro Dumas entre otros), y escribió poesía, ensayos críticos y obras de tema histórico- político. Pero lo más destacable de su obra son sus crónicas y artículos escritos desde los Estados Unidos para periódicos cubanos. Muchos de estos artículos fueron compilados y publicados en Nueva York en 1864 en un libro que lleva por título *Cosas de los Estados Unidos*, en los que se refiere a sí mismo con su seudónimo de "Nazareno". También utiliza este seudónimo para firmar sus poesías, algunas de las cuales aparecen salpicadas por entre sus crónicas.

De su producción literaria en los Estados Unidos destacan varias traducciones y obras de tono político e histórico. Estas últimas muestran características típicas de la literatura del exilio, pues su intención principal es influir en el pensamiento político de su patria de origen, y sólo aluden a la patria de acogida con referencia a esto. Por otro lado, sus crónicas y artículos de costumbres en general presentan la creación literaria de un hombre que llegó a los EEUU como exiliado y acaba pensando y expresándose como inmigrante, con preocupaciones tales como el uso del idioma, la condición de la mujer, o el mantenimiento de las tradiciones de la patria de origen, siendo lo que escribe un claro reflejo de las ideologías de los inmigrantes de clase social alta en los EEUU del siglo XIX.

En sus crónicas de *Cosas de los Estados Unidos*, Camacho menciona a su esposa, a quien llama Sofía, y a dos hijos varones de temprana edad. Pero la dedicatoria de su traducción de *La casa en el desierto* (de publicación posterior), es para sus cuatro hijos varones: Leopoldo, Simón Bolívar, Alfredo y Luis Camacho. Otro detalle interesante de su vida se recoge en su obra *Los cuentos de mi abuela* (publicada en Nueva York, 1883), en cuyo capítulo titulado "Póstumo" y escrito por su hijo, Simón Bolívar Camacho, la primera línea dice así: "Mi padre, desde su cama de martirio, me ha dictado lo siguiente:" y pasa a recoger las ideas del padre en cuanto al contenido de este libro histórico, describiendo sus problemas de salud en Washington mientras que llevaba a cabo su labor política. El final de este capítulo da a entender que Camacho muere en Washington representando a Venezuela. En una nota necrológica, *The Nation* le da el título de Ministro de Venezuela en Washington, y comenta que era sobrino del Libertador; parentesco que el propio autor destaca en *Los cuentos de mi abuela*.

Camacho escribe desde la perspectiva del exiliado en obras de carácter histórico tales como *Historia del Perú independiente* o el libro titulado *Los cuentos de mi abuela*. Este último contiene una serie de poemas de arte mayor, normalmente distribuidos en estrofas de ocho versos y rima consonante en ABABABCC. El autor pone en verso los "cuentos" que, supuestamente, le contaba su abuela cuando era niño, y que narran la historia de Bolívar (su tío) en forma épica describiendo batallas, altercados políticos, y hazañas del Libertador. Dentro de, y adjunto a, esta publicación encabezada por *Los cuentos de mi abuela*, se halla una segunda parte. Es otro libro también de tema histórico-político, pero de características diferentes, ya que no es poesía, sino la compilación y comentario de las cartas de Sucre a Bolívar. Lleva por título: *Sucre. Cartas del Gran Mariscal de Ayacucho al Libertador. Extractadas por Simón Camacho*. Una carta escrita por Simón Camacho abre la obra, está fechada el 1 de mayo de 1883 en Nueva York, y dirigida a Simón B. O'Leary en Caracas. Dice así:

> He reimpreso la Autobiografía del Gran Mariscal de Ayacucho, sacada por mí de sus cartas al Libertador, que tú me regalaste.

> Te la envío, pues de derecho te toca, así como el afecto de hermano que te profesa

> SIMON CAMACHO. (sn)[1]

Esta sucinta nota explicativa nos informa que es una reimpresión, y que Camacho la considera "autobiografía" no en el sentido de que va a presentar su propia vida (la de Camacho), sino porque trata de la vida de Sucre de acuerdo a la información que él (Camacho) extrae de las cartas escritas por el propio Sucre con referencia a sí mismo, a sus experiencias personales y a sus pensamientos.

En esta línea (de literatura del exilio) también se encuentra *La vuelta del General J. A. Páez a Venezuela, 1858.* Obra en que Camacho escribe sobre las condiciones políticas en que el General Páez regresa a Venezuela en 1858, deteniéndose expresamente en comentar las fiestas que se dieron en su honor en Nueva York y en Washington, y describiendo con todo lujo de detalles la decoración, los menús, las bebidas y los discursos de brindis, las personalidades asistentes, la moda de las damas, y finalizando con una relación detallada de las galas y el itinerario de las tropas que despidieron al general en el puerto de Nueva York el 27 de noviembre de 1858. El propio Camacho, en una de las fiestas organizadas en honor a Páez, leyó el decreto de la *Convención Nacional de Venezuela* del 5 de octubre de 1858, y lo trascribe por completo en esta obra. Obra que representa características de la literatura del exilio por su contenido político y su intencionalidad para con la patria de origen: Venezuela, pero que también comienza a demostrar algunos rasgos de inmigración en cuanto a sus referencias a los hispanos residentes en Nueva York, las descripciones de las calles y lugares estadounidenses, y de algunas de las costumbres de la patria de acogida. Estos pequeños detalles que sólo asoman ligeramente en este libro, se hacen patentes en muchas de sus crónicas recogidas en *Cosas de los Estados Unidos.*

En cuanto a las traducciones realizadas por Camacho, hemos de destacar dos publicadas en los Estados Unidos. *La casa en el desierto, aventuras de una familia perdida en las soledades de la América del Norte* es una novela juvenil escrita originalmente en inglés por Maine Reid y traducida al castellano por Camacho, que relata las aventuras de una familia en el oeste de los Estados Unidos. Otra de sus traducciones lleva como título principal: *Nuevo tesoro de chistes,* y continúa con el sobre-título de *Máximas, proverbios, reflexiones morales, historias, cuentos, leyendas, extractadas de las Obras de Byron, Walter Scott, Washington Irving, Prescott, Moore, Franklin, Addison, Cooper, Gibbon, Paley, Goldsmith, Hawthorne, Robertson, Story, Marshall, Wyse, Dickens, Bulwer, Hook, Macaulay, Bryant, Pope, Dryden, etc, etc, etc.* Se trata éste, precisamente, de lo que su largo título indica: son chistes, reflexiones, máximas, anécdotas y cuentos de intención didáctica, moralizante, y de entretenimiento, que denotan el gusto de la época por este tipo de publicaciones.

Pero es en *Cosas de los Estados Unidos* donde verdaderamente Camacho sigue el signo de sus tiempos. Este libro, subtitulado "Colección de artículos de costumbres," recopila, como ya se mencionó, varios artículos escritos desde los EEUU. Los artículos de *Cosas de los Estados Unidos* están fechado desde 1856 a 1863, y el libro se publicó en 1864. Son artículos o crónicas escritas para periódicos cubanos y un público predominantemente femenino. Muchas veces en clave de humor, aunque otras de forma más seria, el cronista pasa revista a toda una serie de personajes de diferentes estratos sociales, y comenta la vida y las costumbres en los Estados Unidos. La ópera, el teatro, bodas, mudanzas, supersticiones, viajes, relaciones sociales y la condición de la mujer, así como la política y la guerra civil del norte contra el sur en los Estados Unidos, son algunos de los temas de sus artículos. Sus escritos están llenos de sátira mordaz y de humor, pero sin perder su tono de corresponsalía pues el autor quiere informar y dar cuenta de lo que sucede a su alrededor, aunque sin dejar de entretener. El hecho de que se publicara en Nueva York en el año 1864, indica que era un autor también leído entre los hispanos de los Estados Unidos. Este compendio es una verdadera joya literaria de la literatura hispana en los Estados Unidos, pues presenta la mirada de un escritor en el exilio cuya intención de expresar lo que está pasando a su alrededor hace que su obra pase a ser puente entre la literatura de exilio y la de inmigración. Las características de ambos tipos de literatura, siguiendo la teoría de Nicolás Kanellos[2], son evidentes en la obra[2]. De especial interés son sus descripciones contemporáneas del conflicto bélico y político de la Guerra Civil estadounidense, y sus disquisiciones sutiles sobre el acá y el allá.

En toda su obra, Camacho describe magistralmente el momento que está viviendo, esto es lo más relevante para un lector de nuestros días que quiera conocer la escritura y el pensamiento de entonces de un hispano culto del siglo XIX en los EEUU. Específicamente, en *Cosas de los Estados Unidos*, su alusión a la comunidad hispana en Nueva York es muy interesante, porque menciona a distintos personajes de diversas procedencias pero que mantienen en común la lengua (andaluz, vizcaino, cubanos, puertorriqueños, venezolanos, etc.). No obstante, el autor es consciente de las diferencias entre los grupos hispanos que se hacen patentes incluso en los distintos dialectos del español. Así, por boca del "guía", Camacho escribe:

> No digo nada del túnico que para algunas señoras es vestido esterior [*sic*], como en Lima, y para otras es interior; y el camison que en Venezuela no es una camisa grande sino el túnico del Perú. ¿Qué es manteleta? Pregúnteselo V. á tres señoras y tendrá tres definiciones. (230)

En lo referente al inglés, Camacho es ambivalente. Por un lado lo repudia, pero por otro lo utiliza y hace gala de su labor de traductor, y hace chiste. Como cuando traduce los nombres de los personajes en sus crónicas, un ejemplo lo encontramos donde dice:

> El teniente Leach, del regimiento 3º de Maine, cuyo teniente se llamaria en español el Señor ó el caballero Sanguijuela [..] se ha casado con una linda moza de Lewiston Falls donde las hay tan guapas que el que no cae tropieza, y de ahí el nombre de *Caidas* de Lewiston con que se envanece el lugar. (*Cosas* 251)

O también cuando habla de las costumbres de los anglos como en su descripción de la idea del "go ahead", o las supersticiones del año bisiesto, o la mudanza del primero de mayo. La idea del "go ahead" es un tema que se repite a lo largo de toda la colección de artículos. Con este lema, Camacho hace una crítica del estadounidense y su forma de vida: "Qué vida! qué bureo! qué movimiento continuo! *Go ahead* es el sino del anglo-americano *bound to travel*—obligado á viajar"(*Cosas* 253). Siendo ésta una crítica propia de muchos inmigrantes hispanos en este país.

El propio Nazareno (Camacho) se refiere a sus artículos como "Totilimundi" y "Folletines." Escribe para periódicos de Cuba, y que posiblemente también se leyeran en España y Puerto Rico, así como, de algún modo, en su Venezuela natal. Los primeros artículos se dirigen directamente a un público femenino, y por eso trata de temas que él considera puedan ser de interés para la mujer cubana específicamente. Hace esto, pero sin dejar de tratar temas candentes del momento, usa el viejo tópico del "no te voy a aburrir contándote" para, efectivamente, contar lo que se propone. Este es el caso siguiente:

> Pero ¡voto á cribas! lectora, que habia olvidado lo mas esencial. Te estoy embuchando de política como se embucha de vinagre al pavo gordo en vísperas de gran dia, sin recordar que á tí te gusta la política lo mismo, ni mas ni menos, que el vinagre al pavo. Demos lo dicho por

no dicho y pasemos á algun otro asunto, aunque sea de modas y crino-
lina. (*Cosas* 125)

Camacho escribe esto, pero continúa su crónica con comentarios políticos
en plan burlesco y sin dejar el tema. Así también lo hace en otra crónica con
fecha de 7 de febrero de 1860 y titulada "Tipos Grotescos", en la que trata sobre
la unión y los confederados:

La línea divisoria de la Confederacion del Norte con la del Sur puede
formarse con un lago. El hombre sensato teme hoy que sea de sangre;
pero los cronistas dicen que es de lágrimas.(*Cosas* 135)

En este artículo, Camacho mezcla cuestiones de teatro con política para acabar
diciendo:

Ah! Bobalicones que pensais que nuestros males públicos se originan
en la cuestion de esclavitud y les buscais remedio en el compromiso de
Missouri y en los planes de Críttenden! – Oid la historia verdadera y
sabed la causa única de nuestros males. La cuenta el *Commercial* de
Cincinnati.(*Cosas* 140)

Y pasa a narrar la historia de celos entre Mis Lane (sobrina de Buchanan) y la
esposa del senador Douglas (a quien llama "la castellana"). De este modo,
parece desviar la atención hacia "la historia verdadera" pero no sin dejar de
aludir "la cuestión de la esclavitud."

Es curioso observar su actitud hacia las costumbres y maneras de la mujer
estadounidense o "de América del Norte" como él la llama. Entre sus disquisiciones sobre el comportamiento de la mujer estadounidense y su educación en
contraposición con la mujer hispana, en clave de humor y sátira mordaz, menciona a la mujer soldado, a la mujer en la guerra, y a las mujeres unionistas y
metidas en política como Susan B. Anthony y sus correligionarias. Sus semblanzas de contemporáneos neoyorquinos son excepcionales, también sus descripciones de la ciudad y sus habitantes, y de sus viajes por los EEUU a las cataratas
del Niágara y a Washington. Una descripción de Washington dice:

Washington es una ciudad poblada desde que empezó la guerra, y ocupa
ahora rango de primer órden; ya no se ven las vacas en sus eternas
calles, y los cerdos han huido para no volver desde que visitaron la capital los zuavos de Ellsworth, tan amigos de la caza como del cuartel y
la guarnicion [*sic*]. (*Cosas* 255)

Estos escritos, así como sus comentarios sobre los adelantos técnicos del momento como el ferrocarril, el telégrafo o el daguerrotipo, o sus notas de sociedad, de teatro y de ópera, nos permiten apreciar cómo era el ambiente de la farándula y de la calle en aquel tiempo.

Nazareno nos presenta un ambiente, una ciudad, una región y un país en un momento histórico crítico para los EEUU y para el mundo. Aunque él diga a sus lectores que la política de los EEUU no le interesa y no le importa nada, sus artículos representan vivamente la situación del momento. El primer artículo de la colección lleva por título "La capital de los Estados Unidos" y comenta su viaje a la ciudad de Washington y su visita a las cámaras de gobierno. El tercer artículo se titula "La inauguración de un presidente en los Estados Unidos" y describe su participación en los eventos que tuvieron lugar durante la inauguración de Buchanan. Es en este artículo en el que describe el embarcadero del ferrocarril en Washington como "torre de Babel" (25) . Luego, va comentando la guerra civil de los EEUU, y presenta la visión de un extranjero.

Camacho es consciente de ser un extranjero que vive en NY, de sí mismo dice: "Mi cara retostada y la cadena de oro que asomaba por debajo del chaleco, me delataban como *indiano*" (*Cosas* 213). Es de clase social educada, sus escritos incluyen alusiones a otros escritores y circunstancias históricas y políticas que así lo hacen ver. Comenta que no le interesa lo que sucede en su país de acogida, pero, al menos en este libro-compendio, nunca se dirige directamente a su patria Venezuela para arengar o intentar el cambio político. En un artículo en que habla de que vuelve a Venezuela, termina con firma de Nueva York, y el lector queda pensando que todo ha sido simplemente un deseo o una ensoñación. Sin embargo, a veces habla de los EEUU como de su patria, con la celebración del 4 de julio y otras costumbres. Comenta anécdotas y episodios junto a costumbres del lugar, como la celebración de la Navidad con Santa Claus:

> Con la Noche-Buena debia llegar Santa Claus, segun la tradicion inglesa. Santa Claus es santo y no santa, pues donde quiera que lo pinta la historia, le regala unas barbas mas completas que las del mejor lechuguino. Pero santo ó santa (que no hemos de reñir por diferencia de mas ó de menos) quiere la tradición que se cuele por la chimenea y ponga á las doce en punto de la noche del 24 del frio mes de diciembre cuantos dulces y juguetes desea el querubin de la casa, ó apetecen los querubines, ó querubinas con que alguna otra santa se haya dignado favorecer á la familia. (*Cosas* 210)

En otra ocasión dice que no le importa el porvenir de la patria sino el de su familia cuando escribe: "Pensé con tristeza por primera vez en el porvenir de la familia, ya que el de la patria no me incumbe, y toda la comedia del suelto se me convirtió en tragedia" (*Cosas* 270). Y critica a los Estados Unidos de la siguiente manera:

> Nadie puede negar que en materia de progreso este pais iba á la vanguardia en todo y por todo. Entonces ¿cómo pretender que en materia de guerra civil (desde que perdió el seso para empezarla) hubiese de quedar rezagado? (*Cosas* 271)

Aunque luego haga comentarios en que se proclame de su parte: "¿Qué premio mayor que el de servir á la patria natural ó adoptiva?" (279), y se mofa de los extranjeros nacionalizados en los EEUU que no quieren participar en la guerra civil cuando escribe: "Ya dije que los nacionalizados se quieren desnacionalizar . . . *y el que me los descontantinopolizare, buen descontantinopolizador será*" (275).

Aún cuando la mayor parte de sus artículos mantienen la clave de humor, de vez en cuando surge su perfil filosófico y serio, otras veces trata temas que le llevan a la ensoñación y la nostalgia. Como cuando escribe:

> Cuando arrancó el tren conté 22 carros, fuera de las máquinas y del de los equipajes. Donde quiera que parásemos, éramos bastantes para fundar una colonia. Instintivamente pensé en los paises de la América del Sur, y en una breve pero ardiente oracion mental pedí al cielo que el ferrocarril estendiese [*sic*] sus rieles hasta el Cabo de Hornos. (21)

Cierto es que Simón Camacho es un exiliado, y muchos de sus escritos presentan estas características, pero su pluma va más allá. Podríamos decir que se trata de un escritor a caballo entre la escritura de exilio y la del inmigrante. En su obra, un ejemplo de los muchos que podríamos citar es el siguiente:

> la mayoria de los paseantes en corte que emplean el guia, vienen con el ánimo hecho de que en esta bendita tierra todo está por el suelo, [..] Ahí [*sic*] de los apuros del que sirve de eslabon entre la sociedad de allá y la de acá. El choque de las ideas viejas y de las ideas nuevas lo sufre sin remedio el eslabon como una descarga eléctrica que le sacude hasta la médula de los huesos.(*Cosas* 227)

Posiblemente que él se consideraba de exilio, pero sus escritos revelan un interés por lo que sucede a su alrededor, aunque sea un interés debido a su profesión. Su situación social le permite ver otras cosas, pero también esto le hace ser un individuo entre dos realidades, pues necesita escribir y trabajar para comer, y esto lo asemeja a un inmigrante.

Esta idea de considerarse a sí mismo como trabajador extranjero en los EEUU, queda plasmada sobre todo en su artículo titulado "Soy corresponsal", en el cual Simón Camacho se presenta a sí mismo como corresponsal, y al hacerlo no sólo habla de él, sino que también de sus circunstancias, y se dirige a sus lectoras para informarles de las diferencias del acá y el allá en los modos y las costumbres de la mujer del momento. En este artículo comenta también sus peripecias para hacer llegar sus escritos a tiempo antes de que el vapor parta del puerto, al hacerlo relata su ambiente, el momento histórico, sus ideologías respecto a la mujer hispana y a la estadounidense, etc. Todo refiriéndose a una lectora de las islas, pero, al publicarse este libro, también lo va a leer la mujer hispana de Nueva York, con lo cual está ayudando a construir el acá, el "mundo o país hispano de afuera" ya que siempre incluye a personas de cultura hispana de procedencia diversa.

"Soy corresponsal" presenta muchos de los rasgos distintivos de las crónicas de Simón Camacho compiladas en *Cosas de los Estados Unidos* como son sus descripciones y semblanzas, sus alusiones a los avances tecnológicos del momento, la clave de humor, su crítica de la sociedad estadounidense, su percepción del idioma inglés o su conciencia de extranjería. También encontramos detalles de tipo técnico o tipográfico, como el hecho de la ortografía utilizada, que aunque en ocasiones no es sino muestra de la ortografía de la época, en otras son crasos errores que se deben a su publicación en Estados Unidos con maquinaría tipográfica que no se adaptaba al alfabeto castellano.

Camacho critica los avances técnicos cuando dice que

> el alambre del telégrafo no sabe las noticias que trasmite, la máquina neumática, la cámara oscura y el embudo no conservan la impresion del efecto que producen. Son instrumentos inertes que el hombre usa para su propio beneficio y que arroja ó abandona sin volver á recordarlos, hasta que la necesidad de una nueva obra los hace indispensables. Así tambien con el corresponsal. (43)

De esta manera, Camacho hace una analogía entre las máquinas y su oficio de corresponsal. Todo es símbolo de los tiempos y el lugar en que está viviendo, todo es de usar y olvidar. No sólo esto, sino que él es extranjero y no es lo mismo ver o imaginar las cosas desde lejos que apreciarlas de cerca:

> La desventaja mayor del que para el extranjero escribe, consiste en que las impresiones ultramarinas, adquiridas en el rincon de una alcoba, son casi siempre distintas, generalmente opuestas á las que se forman con el

tráfico *de visu et tacto* de la cosa misma. Desde los palcos se ve un cuadro esplendente, donde los árboles se menean al contacto de la brisa y el rio corre espumoso por sobre las peñas cubiertas de musgo. Entre bastidores los árboles son de papel pintado y se mueven por medio de una cuerda atada a un brazo, y el rio es un trapo medio sucio, y el musgo y las piedras cartones embarrados de ocre y almagra. (44-45)

Camacho indica aquí el viejo tema de "no es oro todo lo que reluce" tan prodigado entre los escritores hispanos de la literatura de inmigración en los Estados Unidos. Este pensamiento es constante en sus crónicas, como también lo es la crítica y comparación entre el acá y el allá:

Y héteme aquí en un pantano! Rodeado de un mundo enteramente estraño [sic], con ideas enteramente diversas y costumbres que pudieran llamarse opuestas á las costumbres é ideas del mundo para el cual me tocó en lote escribir, ¿qué le diré á los que "llaman el pan pan y el vino vino," sin llevarme de encuentro la verdad ni herir preocupaciones, ó si se quiere, pensamientos profundamente arraigados en un carril tan distinto?

En la medida de mis lectores todas las cosas de por acá vienen anchas como necesaria é imperiosamente habrá de suceder, atendidos los diversos orígenes de dos nacionalidades que no fueron creadas para andar juntas sin que el roce destruya á la una ó á la otra.(45-46)

Trata esta temática para dedicarse de pleno a enjuiciar a la mujer. Y comenta que:

Allá es pecado, ¿qué digo? delito lo que en nuestras ciudades se ve repetido diariamente sin hacer novedad. Llevando el análisis al campo de la mujer, objeto principal, diosa á quien mi pluma ha sacrificado siempre en holocausto sus inocentes habladurías, [. . .]

El "escándalo" de semejante conducta haria poner los gritos en el cielo á la sociedad indignada contra la que osó ultrajar sus convenciones erijidas [sic] en leyes. Tanto valiera á la hija del profeta levantarse el velo en presencia de un estrangero [sic]. El moro usaria inmediatamente de su alfange [sic] para cercenar del tronco una cabeza impura con la profanacion. La sociedad latina usaria su alfange [sic], diré, su puñal de anatema y desprecio que no mata del golpe, mas deja que la herida se desangre y se gangrene lentamente hasta dar la muerte. (46)

De esta forma, Camacho comenta en "broma" pero trata en serio las diferencias culturales respecto a la mujer en ambas culturas. El estudioso del siglo XXI puede preguntarse hasta qué punto el autor repudia las formas estadounidenses, ya que más adelante dice que:

> Ni horror ni calumnia hay, sin embargo, en la narracion de lo ocurrido ayer, de lo que ocurre hoy, de lo que mañana ocurrirá bajo un código de leyes que ha dicho á la muger [*sic*] : "Eres libre, gobiérnate. Eres bella, cautiva. Te hago poderosa porque te doy constantemente la razon, defiéndete." No horror, porque la armonia social, el bien público, la felicidad doméstica, el fervor conyugal no se han debilitado con esas preeminencias que allende son demasías. No calumnia, porque es un hecho. Cruzad el mar y donde piseis tierra allí lo vereis al saltar el muelle.(47)

Camacho aquí está defendiendo lo que él escribe, diciendo que todo lo que presenta es la realidad, pero también dice que no es horror, pues, aunque sea diferente, ciertas cosas de importancia como "la armonía social, el bien público, la felicidad doméstica, el fervor conyugal" aún no se han debilitado. Es más, a pesar de su crítica, pide a sus lectores que no juzguen duramente ya que:

> Desde que se echa en olvido que los teatros son distintos y que los actores obran no en el proscénio propio sino en el ajeno; desde que pretendemos asimilarnos una sociedad que no es la nuestra, unas costumbres con las cuales no congeniamos, una civilizacion que no viene de nuestra misma fuente, ni va donde va la nuestra, ni marcha por nuestros carriles, la imaginacion se ofusca, pierde su aplomo, y el raciocinio cimentado en falsas premisas arranca (no deduce) conclusiones falsas, aunque sinceras, contra hechos y hombres que no deben ser juzgados ni comprendidos en límites y cotos para ellos no calculados.(47)

Vemos entonces que Camacho, a pesar de su crítica mordaz al comportamiento de la mujer estadounidense y la sociedad que lo fomenta, intenta comprender y hacer comprender, o al menos procura evitar juicios. Esto parece una contradicción, ya que en sus propias críticas está juzgando. Es obvio que si no le molestara el comportamiento de la mujer en los Estados Unidos, no habría escrito crónicas como ésta; también es obvio en otros escritos su actitud general hacia la mujer. Así, por ejemplo, en otro artículo escribe:

Yo no he visto jamas a Cuba, pero me ha tocado en lote consagrarle todos mis pensamientos; adoro sus cigarros, sus mugeres [*sic*] y sus danzas- ¿No está eso en órden?(80)

Camacho coloca a la mujer en segundo lugar, detrás del tabaco, siendo éste un símbolo de la masculinidad y, según dice en otro de sus artículos, de lo mejor de Hispanoamérica. Representa el pensar típico de su época, y nos indica que aunque no quisiera juzgar directamente a la mujer estadounidense, en realidad desaprueba su conducta; y cuando pide a sus lectoras que no juzguen, en realidad lo que pide es que no le juzguen a él por escribir crónicas que relatan este comportamiento escandaloso en el mundo hispano.

Es interesante también su descripción de lo que le rodea, como cuando comenta que:

En la calle 50 ó 60 donde fué escrita hay un ómnibus, *guagua* montada sobre rieles que va con la velocidad del relámpago, de un estremo [*sic*] de la ciudad hasta el otro, soltando hombres, mugeres [*sic*] y niños por todas partes, como el caballo de Troya. En la *guagua* hay un asiento para todo el que posea seis centavos y tenga una epidérmis ecsenta [*sic*] de tintes.(48)

Pues al leer este párrafo aprendemos detalles interesantes, como el precio de la guagua, la técnica de rieles, quién usaba este medio de transporte, y las imposiciones del racismo imperante.

Otro detalle a destacar sería el del uso del inglés en este artículo ("Soy corresponsal"), como por ejemplo en el siguiente párrafo:

En medio de mi afan por llegar á tiempo y cuando voy sobre una carreta varada entre dos coches con pasageros [*sic*], me asalta media docena de mugeres[*sic*] mas viejas y feas que el pecado, vendiéndome naranjas de la Habana:

—*Oranges, sweet oranges from Havana. Three for a shilling.*
—Libros! grita un muchacho, y me mete por los ojos unos cuadernos impresos,
—Periódicos! *Herald, Tribune, Times and Weekly papers,* un número del *Harper's Journal of Civilizacion* me cierra el paso con la fealdad de un retrato de alguna . . . (49)

Aquí, no sólo se incluye el uso del inglés para producir una descripción más realista del momento, sino que el autor contrapone la venta de las naranjas que vienen de la Habana, con la de los libros y los periódicos. Esto hace pensar al lector en "la carta" a que se refiere el corresponsal, y cuyo destino es Cuba para allí ser publicada. Las naranjas vienen de Cuba para ser vendidas en Nueva York, mientras que lo escrito por Camacho va en la dirección contraria, y es también mercancía.

"Soy corresponsal" es un artículo que podría seleccionarse como representante de todos los otros que se compilan en *Cosas de los Estados Unidos,* pues presenta características típicas de la literatura de inmigración aludiendo a una evolución dentro de la obra de Camacho. Algunas de estas características son la comparación entre el allá y el acá, así como la preocupación por el comportamiento de la mujer en los EEUU y la influencia de las formas sociales estadounidenses en la mujer hispana. Esta preocupación es patente en gran parte del artículo. También lo es el que el autor no esté seguro de que crean lo que él escribe desde los Estados Unidos en los lugares a donde van destinadas sus cartas. Por otra parte, no podemos ignorar que, como libro publicado en Nueva York, este compendio de crónicas posiblemente tuviera lectores hispanos en los EEUU. Para ellos este escrito sirve de aviso, y contribuye a su creación de un acá que se asemeje al mundo de allá, al mismo tiempo que alerta para que no permitan que el acá se mancille, y lo mantengan intacto y lo más parecido al allá que sea posible.

El artículo refleja la visión de un hombre de clase media alta que escribe para vivir; pero que, como intelectual, intenta influir en el pensamiento de sus lectores. Encontramos aquí semejanzas con lo que también estaba pasando en otras comunidades hispanas de los EEUU en el siglo XIX (en Texas, Nuevo México, California, Florida, etc), en las cuales se intentaba imponer una forma de pensar desde las clases sociales altas hacia abajo en lo que respecta al mantenimiento y creación de un acá que conservara las características culturales del allá. Esto, junto a las descripciones de sus experiencias como corresponsal, de la ciudad de Nueva York, y de sus lectores y otros personajes, también hacen de este artículo un ejemplo interesante y muy a propósito para mostrar una corriente de pensamiento y literaria que surge entre los hispanos de los EEUU en el siglo XIX.

En general, la obra de Camacho presenta diversas características, no sólo por su variedad temática y de género, sino también por el tono y su conceptualización. Siendo Camacho un exilado, escribe algunas obras cuya preocupación principal es la patria, su historia y su política. En estas obras el entorno estadounidense sólo se menciona o cobra importancia en cuanto a su relación con la patria de origen (Venezuela) y cómo ésta pueda verse afectada. Por otro lado, en sus crónicas o artículos de costumbres, nos encontramos con el Camacho periodista, cuyo trabajo consiste en escribir, y que vive de sus escritos. Es un profesional, un corresponsal. Para él la literatura es mercancía. Hace crónicas y relata su entorno a cambio de un salario. Vive de este trabajo en los EEUU; y al describir lo que le rodea, describe también su forma de vida como hispano en Nueva York. Sus percepciones, conceptos y enjuiciamientos muestran la forma de pensar de muchos inmigrantes del momento. Es entonces cuando su obra toma características distintas de las obras de exilio. *Cosas de los Estados Unidos* presenta muchísimas reminiscencias de Hispanoamérica, pero ahora le preocupa más la vida en los EEUU, y comenta las peripecias de los hispanos en este país. Personajes típicos de la literatura de inmigración como "el verde" o "la agringada" aparecen en sus líneas. Las comparaciones entre el acá y el allá son constantes, con su crítica del aquí y su añoranza del allá.

Aún cuando las obras de Camacho escritas en el extranjero y las publicadas en los EEUU de características de exilio también merecen un estudio detallado, *Cosas de los Estados Unidos* trata temas de gran interés, ya que ofrece un amplio espectro del Nueva York de los años 1856 a 1863. En estas páginas, el lector del siglo XXI puede hacerse una idea de cómo era la vida en aquella época, y observarlo todo a través de la mirada de un hispano en Nueva York.

La mujer, las clases sociales, la vida urbana, los viajes al interior, los adelantos técnicos del momento, la religión, la política, la guerra, los comercios, los conflictos internos e internacionales, y un largo etcétera de temas y personajes pasan por la pluma de Simón Camacho, y muestran su visión del exiliado convertido en inmigrante de Nueva York.

Obras citadas

Bruni Celli, Blas. "Simón Camacho." *Venezuela en 5 siglos de imprenta*. 1998. http://www.fpolar.org.ve/veroes/5000/cl/1148.htm

Camacho, Simón. *Los cuentos de mi abuela*. Imprenta al vapor de C. Espinal, 1883.

___. *La vuelta del general J. A. Páez á Venezuela, 1858*. Impr. De J. F. Trow, 1858.

Camacho, Simón, y James Durand. *Cosas de los Estados Unidos*. Imprenta de "El Porvenir", 1864.

DGLV—Diccionario General de la Literatura Venezolana (autores). Centro de Investigaciones Literarias. U. de los Andes, 1974.

Kanellos, Nicolás. *En otra voz*. Arte Público, 2002.

The Nation. 11 Oct. 1883: 305.

Paz Soldán, Mariano Felipe, y Simón Camacho. *Historia del Perú independiente.* Impr. Del Courrier de La Plata, 1888.

Reid, Maine, Simón Camacho y Antonio Hernández. *La casa en el desierto,
aventuras de una familia perdida en las soledades de la América del Norte.*
D. Appleton y compañía, 1869. (1877)(1885) (1899) (1913)(1923)

Roemer, Jean, y Simón Camacho. *Nuevo tesoro de chistes, máximas, proverbios, reflexiones morales, historias, cuentos, leyendas, extractadas de las
obras de Byron, Walter Scott, Washington Irving . . .* D. Appleton y compañía,
1855.

Notas

[1]Todas las citas directas de la obra de Camacho se reproducen en este ensayo tal
y como aparecen en el texto original. Por lo tanto, de manera *verbatim*, se
reproducen las faltas de ortografía, los errores de acentuación y tildes, así como
el uso de puntos y comas. En ocasiones, para subrayar errores crasos, se hará
uso de la notificación [*sic*]. Es de destacar que, en la época en que se publican
estos textos, algunos de estos errores tipográficos posiblemente se debieran a la
imprenta y no al autor.

[2]Para un estudio detallado de las características de exilio e inmigración en la literatura hispana de los EEUU, se recomienda la obra de Nicolás Kanellos *En
otra voz.* Arte Público, 2002.

Recovering Forgotten Voices:
Cuban Newspapers in Florida, 1870-1895

GERALD E. POYO

St. Mary's University

The Cuban press in the United States began publishing in New York and New Orleans during the 1820s-1850s when exiles first led separatist movements against Spanish rule. Many more newspapers appeared after the US Civil War and the outbreak of the Cuban Ten Years War (1868-1878). They continued publishing through the end of the century, mostly in New York and Florida. Beginning in the early 1990s, a Recovering the US Hispanic Literary Heritage Program identified and made available for research numerous Cuban newspapers, mostly published in New York, that had reached the safety of libraries and archives in the United States (Kanellos, 285-286). The same was not true for most of Florida's Cuban newspapers of this period. Few survived in the United States, but exiles returning home after Spain's defeat in 1898 donated important collections to Cuban research depositories (Batista Villarreal, 203-204). Unfortunately, these collections have not fared well in Cuba's resource poor libraries and archives. Due to their delicate state, they are generally not available for research anymore and their slow deterioration has reached critical proportions. Without restoration and digitalization, they may soon be gone.

Fortunately, nineteenth century Cuban newspapers published in United States, including many from Key West, also found their way to Spain. As part of Spain's intelligence gathering strategies in the United States during most of the nineteenth century, consular officials kept a close watch on Cubans in Key West, Tampa and Jacksonville. In their extensive correspondence with Spain's Embassy in Washington and the Spanish Foreign Ministry in Madrid, consuls

387

often included copies of the newspapers, which eventually made it to the Archivo Histórico Nacional (Madrid) and Archivo General de Administración (Alcala de Henares).

Now part of the Recovery collection, these newspapers provide a portal into the historical communities of Key West and Tampa during the 1880s and early 1890s. Most Cubans in Florida worked in cigar factories stripping tobacco leaf, rolling cigars, or sorting and packing *puros* into boxes for shipment, but they also owned factories, ran a diversity of businesses typical of any community, attended to religious matters, founded baseball leagues, and enjoyed music and theatre, among other things.

The newspapers reveal much evidence of that daily life, but they also documented and interpreted the ideological imperatives of the day, the complexities of politics, the often harsh and divisive social realities, and unique cultural expressions that defined identity. The press provoked community discussion, produced dissension, and sometimes even instigated violence. Except for Key West's *El Yara,* which published for twenty years, the individual newspapers in Florida did not enjoy much longevity, but collectively they remind readers of the nationalist passions that motivated Revolutionaries intent on destroying Spanish colonialism in Cuba. The newspapers reveal the centrality of nationalism in Florida communities, along with the great interest Cubans had in American politics and labor activism. The three themes filled the columns of the typically four page editions published weekly or, at times, daily formats for five and ten cents an issue, and are the focus of this essay. Besides providing an example of the rich materials Recovery research makes available to the public, the essay is also a reminder of the importance of preserving these important collections of newspapers and bringing to light the many long forgotten voices within their pages.

Nationalism

Juan María "Nito" Reyes fled Havana to Key West early in 1869 to avoid persecution in the aftermath of the outbreak of revolution in Cuba the previous October. A relatively well-known journalist who wrote for Havana's reformist newspaper *El Siglo* and worker-oriented *La Aurora*, Reyes first found a job as lector at the Samuel Wolff cigar factory in Key West. He then recognized the need for a revolutionary newspaper in this rapidly growing and highly politicized working class community and took the lead in founding *El Republicano*.

José D. Poyo, who worked as a lector in the Vicente Martínez Ybor factory joined Reyes in his journalistic endeavor. Before departing for Key West, thirty-four year old Poyo had worked as a proof-reader at *La Gaceta de Habana*, a semi-official, privately owned newspaper that earned its keep publishing government-related announcements and information. The two men did not forge an economically viable enterprise, which was usually the case with these small newspapers, but they helped maintain the Cuban insurrection in the forefront of community consciousness (Poyo, 22-23; Castellanos, 221). As newspaper publishers and *lectores* they both became influential figures in this emerging revolutionary center.

El Republicano provided some community news, but primarily disseminated anti-colonial propaganda. The newspaper expressed itself in militant and partisan tones, and with demands that Cubans defeat Spaniards on the battlefield, even burning the sugar cane fields if necessary. In late 1869, *El Republicano* engaged in polemical debates with Havana's *La Voz de Cuba*, a pro-Spanish newspaper in Havana that had incited *voluntario* violence against those suspected of sympathizing with the insurgency earlier in the year. A series of mutually insulting articles in January 1870 provoked the Spanish newspaper's editor Gonzalo Castañon to travel to Key West and challenge Reyes to a duel. At their first meeting, the younger Castañon insulted and struck Reyes enraging a nationalist activist who later shot the Spanish editor dead at his hotel. (El Republicano, 1869-1870). Key West gained a reputation in Havana as a hotbed of criminality and revolutionary sentiment.

In January, even before Castañon arrived in Key West, Reyes had turned over the editorship of the newspaper to Poyo. Reyes became active in Republican Party politics until his tragic death in a shipwreck returning from a trip to Tampa in 1877 (El Republicano, February 16, 1870). Poyo remained editor until a political dispute in 1873 resulted in his ouster from the newspaper. He also was expelled from the *Asociación del Sur*, the newspaper's sponsoring organization the he helped found. The new editor, Federico de Armas, edited *El Republicano* until its demise in 1876. Later that year, Poyo and Armas founded *La Igualdad* and *La Libertad* respectively, but neither newspaper survived more than a few months. Poyo tried again with *El Patriota* in April 1878 and finally later that year founded his enduring journalistic enterprise, *El Yara* (Batista Villarreal, 155, 180; Castellanos, 221). It saw light on October 12 to coincide (though two days late) with the decade anniversary of the *Grito de Yara* that had inspired the first independence war. Poyo described *El Yara* as a radical voice committed to freeing Cuba from Spanish rule. It advocated a democratic republic committed to racial and class equality for all its citizens. *El Yara* published in Key West until 1898 and according to New York's *Patria*, its doctrinal or ideological character, longevity, and revolutionary posture cemented its reputation as "the dean of the Cuban press abroad" (Castellanos, 222).

El Yara endorsed Cuba's brief revolt known as The Little War (1878-1880) and remained the only newspaper in exile promoting independence and revolution until April 1883 when twenty-three-year-old Manuel P. Delgado established *La Voz de Hatuey,* possibly with the financial help of recently arrived Ten Years War veteran Fernando Figueredo (Stebbins, 172). Born in Havana, eight-year-old Delgado arrived in Key West with his parents in September 1869 where he studied in the public school and then made his living as a cigar maker (Castellanos, 302). He became a citizen and spoke English fluently, but always remained committed to his Cuban identity and independence. When a *New York Herald-Tribune* reporter asked Delgado in 1891why he did not "stand up for the United States" and support Cuba's annexation to the United States, he replied that while he recognized and fully embraced his duties as an American citizen, his heart remained with his native land to which he would eventually return. Cuba was perfectly capable of self-government, he further remarked, and treaties and other agreements would govern Cuban relations with the United States (Florida). Delgado honored Hatuey in the title of his newspaper because of the legendary Taíno rebel chieftain's refusal to convert to Catholicism even when faced with execution. Hatuey reasoned that this would spare him spending eternity with Spaniards. *La Voz de Hatuey's* rejection of Spanish colonialism mirrored *El Yara's* revolutionary fervor and support for activities in Key West and New York to reignite the anti-colonial struggle in Cuba.

A third newspaper, *El Ubiquitario*, appeared in Key West later that year as the voice of the *Cuban Nihilist Club of Key West,* which backed the same initiatives (Stebbins, 129-143). Cuban nihilist clubs formed in various cities of the United States during 1883 inspired by Irish-American clubs working against English rule in Ireland. In the 1870s, Fenians in New York used dynamite, Alfred Nobel's 1866 invention, to enhance their struggle, and in 1881 detonated explosions in Liverpool and London with bombs manufactured in the United States. The next year they had a "dynamite school" operating in the Greenpoint area of Brooklyn (Whelehan).

The three Key West newspapers took up support for this controversial strategy, which they referred to as "scientifc warfare." *El Ubiquitario's* anonymous editor demanded "the abandonment of the territory of Cuba by the Spanish government within a year." This included surrendering all public properties without any claim to indemnification, the release of all political prisoners, and Spain's recognition of Cuba's national sovereignty. The Key West Nihilist Club further announced the existence of affiliated clubs in Cuba waiting for a signal to unleash the work of destruction because "we are ready to succumb under the ruins of Cuba before consenting that she continue as the richest jewel in the

Castilian crown." Furthermore, *El Ubiquitario* urged nationalists to destroy their Spanish enemies using dynamite,

> in their entrenchments, in their camps, in their stores, in their houses, in their palaces; while dining, sleeping, working, during leisurely walks, resting; basically, wherever they can be attacked, in the same way they annihilate our compatriots, who unfortunately have not wanted to adopt the advice that it is better to die fighting than be surprised and assassinated, preferring to believe the enemy that during certain periods feign softening their ferocious instincts"("A Ciudadado." See also, "Oportunidad," "NuestrasVentajas,").

La Voz de Hatuey published about a year before Delgado joined *El Yara's* staff and married Celia, Poyo's eldest daughter. *El Ubiquitario* lasted even less time, but *El Yara* continued the radical discourse.

In mid-January 1884, José Rafael Estrada, veteran Lt. Colonel in the Ten Years' War founded another newspaper, *La Propaganda*. A mulatto originally from Sancti-Spiritus, Estrada fought with the liberation army almost from the insurrection's inception in 1868 until shortly before the Zanjón Pact ended the war in 1878 when he broke his leg in battle and was captured ("Estrada"). Estrada escáped Spanish custody and in 1880 made his way to Key West where he joined a large number of veteran fighters who had relocated there with their families. *La Propaganda* also followed the community's intransigent revolutionary line and regularly engaged in polemical debates with the pro-Spanish press in Cuba.

Unlike *El Yara*, which at the time focused mainly on doctrinal and Cuba matters, *La Propaganda* published as a community newspaper much engaged with local political issues. Estrada had an aggressive and combative style in defense of nationalist goals and took the offensive whenever Cubans questioned the community's militant posture or the English-language press maligned Cubans (La Propaganda, 1886-1888). Estrada may have also edited a humorous but sharp and pointedly acid newspaper called *El Jejen* (*The Gnat*). Estrada's aggressive temperament led to an untimely demise. On March 7, 1888, another Cuban shot him in the head during an argument in a local café. He died ten days later and his newspaper ceased publishing shortly thereafter ("Suceso lamentable," "Estrada").

Not all Cuban newspapers in Florida promoted a revolutionary nationalist editorial line. At least two nationalist newspapers considered militant action a fanatical and even immoral stance. On November 25, 1883 J. Enrique Soler Enríquez published the first issue of *La Opinión Pública*, which primarily concerned itself with community news and rejected what it considered the rabid nationalism of newspapers like *El Ubiquitario*, *La Voz de Hatuey* and *El Yara*. A resident of Key West since 1869, Soler announced his intention to conduct his publication with "tranquil reasoning and cultured moderation" in order to "conquer the esteem of strangers" ("Prospecto"). He particularly objected to the nihilists and criticized *El Yara* for repeating the radical propositions of what he considered patently foolish newspapers ("periódicos jocosos,") like *El Ubiquitario* ("Comentos"). After just three months, on February 26, 1884, *La Opinión Pública* announced that with the arrival on the scene of *La Propaganda* it could no longer afford to compete financially. Its economic misfortunes may have resulted from its less than militant nationalism in a community, at that moment, fully dedicated to launching another revolutionary effort against Spain ("Al público").

Later, another nationalist newspaper, *El Cubano*, also criticized the militant line. Its editor, Pedro N. Pequeño, arrived in Key West and established the newspaper in 1886. An unlikely editor for a newspaper in Key West's multiracial community, Pequeño had enjoyed a career writing for popular "bufo" theatre in Havana, an art form that included the use of blackface. In 1868, Pequeño co-authored one play of a trilogy called *Negros catedráticos*, which was the signature play of the famed troupe *Bufos Habaneros*. In 1882, he authored another called *La Africana*. He also published *El Moscón*, (*Periódico Político, Zumbón, Jocoseria y Agridulce con Caricaturas*) or *The Botfly* (*Political Newspaper, Buzzing, Comico-Serious, Bittersweet with Caricatures*) (Lane, 111). A popular entertainment form, bufo often criticized and challenged Spanish colonialism. Blackface characters reflected a national mestizo sensibility popular among criollos which often made Spaniards the target of their jokes. But this theatre also revealed racial tensions in Cuban society. Performances of whites painted black pointed to insensitive and racist assumptions of the writers and actors, as well as their audiences (Lane, 60-102; Thomas, 84-85).

It is not surprising, then, that Pequeño took a moderate tone when it came to political strategies for achieving Cuban independence. Rather than mirroring militant discourses disseminated in *El Yara* and *La Propaganda*, Pequeño followed the less aggressive sensibilities that dominated middle class Cubans in New York. Enrique Trujillo's newspaper, *El Avisador Cubano*, best expressed these sensibilities and regularly criticized exile activities aimed at launching expeditions against Cuba as unproductive and even immoral. *El Cubano* too condemned the frequent expeditionary efforts in Key West and rejected the collaboration of local revolutionary leaders with bandits in Cuba who were adept at kidnapping and ransoming sugar planters to raise funds for the cause. *El Cubano* argued for extra-legal deportations from Key West of known bandits, regardless of their value to the local nationalist movement ("Los farsantes en camisa"). Pequeño published the newspaper until the end of 1889 when he returned to Cuba denouncing the tactics of the "separatist party" and announcing his conversion to autonomist ideas (Stebbins, 182-183; "Nuestra política;" "Limpiemos;" "Ratificamos").

While not unanimous about strategies for freeing Cuba from Spanish colonialism, these newspapers played a critical role in promoting nationalism and keeping the nationalist cause in the consciousness of Florida's overwhelmingly working class community.

American Politics

Participation in local politics also attracted the attention of Cuban journalists in Key West who quickly understood the importance for Cubans of garnering influence in the broader community to advance their socioeconomic interests and nationalist aspirations. Cubans arriving in Key West in the early 1870s found a town deeply divided by post-Civil War Reconstruction politics. At the war's end, northern troops occupied the southern states, Republicans took charge of reorganizing government, and white southerners were politically sidelined. Courting former slaves and carpetbaggers, black immigrants from the Bahamas, and white and black Cubans, Republicans in Key West fashioned electoral majorities. Committed to slave abolition at home, Cuban exiles felt more ideologically compatible with what they referred to as the "the party of Lincoln" than with pro-slavery white southerners who controlled the Democratic Party. Immigrants took advantage of Florida laws that gave them the vote after six months residence if they filed an intention to seek citizenship, which federal law allowed them to acquire after five years.

Republican Party leaders cemented their coalition with Cubans through carefully calculated patronage appointments as country judges, justices of the peace, and customs house officials and inspectors. These appointments were particularly important for an insurrectionary community involved in smuggling arms and munitions to Cuba on vessels departing Key West. Republicans also led the way in nominating Cubans for electoral office. Among the first, Carlos Manuel de Céspedes y Céspedes, the son of Cuba's first insurgent president, won the mayoral election in 1875. In November 1880 and 1882, Republicans Manuel Escassi and Fernando Figueredo respectively stood for Monroe County representatives to the Florida Assembly, though the latter stood as a member of a Republican splinter Independent Party. While both lost their elections, they furthered the influence of Cubans in local politics. Eventually, Republicans Fernando Figueredo (1884), Manuel Moreno (1889), and José Pómpez (1890) won elections in Monroe County to the Florida House of Representatives in Tallahassee (Poyo, 168-178; Stebbins, 167-171; *Weekly Floridian*).

The Cuban press promoted this activism in local politics. In 1880, twenty-four-year-old Ramon Rivero y Rivero, who arrived in Key West during the Ten Years War, established *La Fraternidad* in support of Republican candidates (The Semi-Weekly Floridian, September 18, 1880). A tobacco worker and leader of the cigar classer's union, Rivero supported Republicans who stood for working class interests against the cigar manufacturers. Other newspapers supported Republican candidates including *El Eco* and *La Opinión Pública* edited respectively by Miguel Thimon and Soler Enríquez, mentioned earlier ("Nada adelantan;" "El desaire").

Both reported on local political and economic matters and, on at least one occasion *La Opinión Pública* rejected an editorial in *El Yara* arguing that Cubans not let American politics distract them from their primary obligation to nationalist politics. "We are not in any way in agreement with those who say that Cubans naturalized in this country should not participate in American politics," the newspaper declared. Always welcomed in the United States, it argued, immigrants had an obligation to participate in the political system and help improve the country. Moreover, this provided Cubans with experience in civic governance which served them well for when they returned to build their own republic. Soler also took the opportunity to make a partisan pitch for the Republican Party, which would ensure Cubans maximum influence in their adopted community ("Hagamos política").

A minority of Cubans also supported the Democratic Party. In the mid-1870s, some Cubans, disgusted with Ulysses S. Grant Administration's failure to help the Cuban insurgency, set out to make the Republican Party pay a political price, at least locally. During the electoral campaign in 1876, several formed a Cuban Democratic Club that attracted two or three hundred followers (Browne, 69). José Rafael Estrada, before he founded *La Propaganda*, with a few others established *El Localista* to support Democratic Party candidates in 1880 and helped the Democratic Party to victory in the October municipal election and in the November election for state and federal offices (*Semi-Weekly Floridian*, September 17, October 8, 12, 15, November 23, 1880; February 7, 1882).

The economic interests of some Cubans better aligned with the Democratic Party, especially businessmen who did not like the local Republican Party's heavy reliance on cigar workers. Militant nationalist journalists like Estrada linked to the Democrats probably did so because they thought pro-labor Cuban Republicans distracted workers from nationalist activism. This included *El Yara's* reporter and sometimes Editor Manuel P. Delgado, Poyo's son-in-law, elected as a Democrat from Monroe County to the Florida legislature in 1889.

El Yara itself, however, remained mostly uninvolved in local political affairs unless they directly affected the nationalist movement.

Whether siding with Republicans or Democrats, local Cuban newspapers and journalists maintained a close watch on local political affairs always with an eye toward advancing local and nationalist interests. Some nationalists felt that involvement in local political affairs distracted the community from its primary goal of launching revolution in Cuba, but most saw merit in local political activism and engaged it with enthusiasm.

Labor

During the second half of the 1880s, the complexion of the Cuban press in Florida became more complicated as labor issues competed with nationalism and local politics for the attention of readers. After the Ten Years War and the Little War, some tobacco workers in Key West became skeptical of the possibility of inciting another war in Cuba but most remained generally supportive of revolutionary efforts especially when charismatic veteran generals Máximo Gómez and Antonio Maceo joined organizing activities in 1884. After valiant efforts, the generals finally admitted failure in 1886 and called off further activity leaving Key West's workers disappointed and angry that their labor-management compromises and considerable financial contributions had been for naught.

Discontent among labor leaders regarding the primacy of nationalist over labor concerns first appeared during the 1870s. Local nationalists had in principle supported worker demands and strike actions, but had also counseled compromise with manufacturers to avoid derailing fundraising in the factories for the war in Cuba. In 1874, socialist activist Federico de Armas, editor of *El Republicano*, and a group of workers publishing *Boletín de la Huelga*, called for worker solidarity in the face of what they considered capitalist manipulation of the nationalist theme for their own advantage, illustrating the challenge of trying to balance political and labor issues.

In the 1880s new labor voices entered the fray. After his newspaper *La Fraternidad* closed, Ramón Rivero y Rivero turned to publishing labor newspapers, including *La Unión* (1881), *La Opinión* (1884) and *El Ecuador* (1886). Martín Morúa Delgado joined him with *El Pueblo* in 1886. Born in Matanzas during 1856 of a Basque immigrant and a black *criollo* mother, Morúa Delgado worked as a cooper (barrel maker) in his youth, and organized a union in Cuba during the 1870s. At the end of the Ten Years War he established a newspaper in Matanzas, which supported Cuban autonomy within the Spanish empire but more importantly advocated for the abolition of slavery and black rights. The newspaper declared itself "organo official de la raza de color." Morúa's criticism of Spanish policies led to imprisonment after which he left Cuba to join the revolutionary nationalists in Key West.

He arrived in January 1881 and immediately published articles in *La Fraternidad* and *El Localista* declaring his solidarity with the nationalist cause. Morúa then went to New York and joined journalist Ramón Rubiera de Armas in editing two nationalist newspapers *El Separatista* and then *La República* during 1883-1885. Although a staunch supporter of reinitiating a revolutionary war in Cuba, he lost confidence in the viability of revolution in the short-term after Maceo and Gómez failed to land an expedition in Cuba.

Rivero and Morúa Delgado both took seriously the tensions first laid bare between labor and nationalism in the mid-1870s. In December 1880, with the urging of *El Yara*, a nationalist oriented labor union, *Unión de Tabaqueros,* closed its doors to Spanish and Chinese workers, arguing that local jobs in Key West be limited to Cubans ("La Sinrazón de 'La Razón"). This strategy was to ensure that Key West remained a community militantly dedicated to nationalism and not populated by workers uninterested in the Cuban independence cause. Although Rivero was a nationalist, his newspaper, *La Unión,* rejected the idea of discriminating against non-Cuban workers, including Spaniards. He called for worker solidarity regardless of ethnicity or nationality. The Cuban union newspaper *El Obrero* criticized him bitterly (*El Yara*).

Rivero's *La Opinión* in 1884 remained committed to the need for worker solidarity and he found support among unexpected allies the next year when the Knights of Labor began organizing among Key West's Hispanic community ("Union"). The Knights of Labor organized around the ideas of worker unity regardless of trade or ethnic-national origin and formed its assemblies along territorial lines, which appealed to Rivero and other Cuban labor organizers interested in promoting worker interests. Seeing the appeal among Hispanics, a local Knights leader, Charles B. Pendleton, invited Rivero to edit a Spanish language section of his newspaper, *The Equator*. The insert, *El Ecuador*, promoted the Knights of Labor to the Hispanic community and numerous Cuban labor activists contributed, including Carlos Baliño, Francisco Segura, Guillermo Sorondo, and Margarito Gutiérrez who shared Rivero's views on the primacy of labor solidarity (El Ecuador).

Morúa's *El Pueblo,* like *El Ecuador*, promoted labor activism and support for the Knights of Labor (Pérez Landa, 29, 39-121). The two newspapers explained to Cuban workers the latest in United States labor thought and challenged the community's one-dimensional focus on revolutionary nationalism. They demanded that political and social matters be treated separately and of equal importance. They urged that labor issues be handled in the factories and unions, and that nationalist issues be managed in the political clubs. Furthermore, they rejected *El Yara's* and *La Propaganda's* continuing concern that increasing Spanish immigration to Florida threatened to dilute the intensity of nationalism and they reaffirmed opposition to maintaining unions exclusively Cuban. Rivero and Morúa did not believe that Spanish tobacco workers posed a threat to Cuban nationalism and encouraged Cuban workers to accept them in the factories without fear (El Pueblo; El Ecuador).

Matters changed again in the late 1880s when the Knights of Labor lost support across the United States including in Florida and especially among Cubans who increasingly looked for inspiration to a growing anarchist movement in Havana. The anarchists mirrored the Knight's commitment to worker solidarity but the similarities ended there. Anarchists endorsed class struggle and the elimination of capitalism, which contradicted the Knight's ideology of class harmony and cooperation. In 1887, a new anarchist newspaper *El Productor*, published in Havana, circulated in Key West and Tampa and called on Cuban workers to supplant revolutionary nationalism with revolutionary socialism. *El Productor's* editor, Enrique Roig de San Martín, included in the newspaper regular reports from Key West that expressed grievances and outlined worker demands. Though few Cuban labor leaders in Florida rejected the nationalist project wholesale, they urged workers to privilege socialist and anarchist activism until a viable independence struggle appeared in Cuba (Casanovas, 147-177). In the meantime, the Knights of Labor lost its local champions. Rivero closed *El Ecuador* in 1888 and moved to Ybor City. The next year, Morúa Delgado shuttered *El Pubelo*, but started another paper called *La Nueva Era*. It is not clear what prompted Morúa to change the title of his newspaper, but, whatever the case, he was ultimately dismayed with the revolutionary politics of Florida's nationalists. With the protection of a general amnesty, Morúa returned to Havana and continued publishing *La Nueva Era*, but as an autonomist newspaper.

During 1888 and 1889, three newspapers tried to fill the journalistic vacuum privileging labor issues, including Carlos Baliño's *La Tribuna del Trabajo*, Enrique Creci's *El Buñuelo*, and Federico Corbett's, *La Justicia* (El Productor). Born in Guanajay, Pinar del Rio, Carlos Baliño left Cuba in 1869 shortly after his father's arrest for insurgent activity and deported to the Spanish penal colony on Fernando Poo (off the African coast). Although university educated, Baliño worked in a cigar box factory in New Orleans and then became a cigar selector. He moved to Key West in 1880 and became a leader in the cigar selector's union, which openly supported the nationalist movement (Instituto de Historia, 9-11). In 1886, he followed Rivero, Morúa and others in prioritizing labor organizing over nationalist activism and was elected president of the District Assembly of the Knights of Labor in Key West. During the next couple of years, *El Productor* and anarchism influenced Baliño who began to preach a revolutionary anarchist line *La Tribuna del Trabajo*. The role of agitators he argued was to show workers the injustice of the current industrial order, which would be overthrown of its own accord. However, a vanguard of men of good will ("filas de avance") were needed to promote emancipatory propaganda and reach the common ideal ("Agitación").

Like Baliño, Enrique Creci also developed a much more radical perspective than Rivero and Morúa Delgado, but, unlike Baliño's ideological development which took place in Key West, Creci formed his ideas in Havana's socialist labor movement. Little is known of his origins, but in 1883 Creci worked as a typographer on the autonomist newspaper *La Discusión* in Havana before joining the staff of *El Obrero* (1883-1884) with Roig de San Martín. Among the earliest newspapers in Cuba advocating revolutionary socialism, *El Obrero* was a precursor of *El Productor* for which Cerci later wrote. Creci arrived in Key West in 1889 to help organize workers and established *El Buñuelo*. The newspaper also supported a grand anarchist strike in Key West in late 1889 that closed down the industry for four months and advocated social, not political, solutions to Cuba's problems (Cabrera, 121-130). Of Corbett's, *La Justicia*, little is known except of its support for anarchist doctrines during this same time.

In Ybor City, Ramón Rivero also underwent an ideological transition and opened *La Revista de Florida*. This was the first Spanish language newspaper in Tampa since *El Yara*, which published there for five months. A portion of the tobacco industry moved to Tampa after a devastating fire burned down a third of Key West on March 30, 1886, including dozens of cigar factories. *El Yara* made the move along with thousands of cigar workers to ensure that a strong nationalist voice existed in this new Cuban community. However, Poyo returned to Key West in March 1887 after a local confrontation between Cuban nationalist and labor activists resulted in the expelling of seventy nationalists including him. *La Revista de Florida* focused primarily on labor issues though Rivero now supported anarchists, no longer the Knights of Labor. On the curious occasion of All Souls Day in 1889, Rivero asked the community to remember Cuba's nationalist martyrs but also recalled Roig de San Martín who had passed away the previous September. Roig, he wrote, "lit the bright torch that revealed the path toward our anxious aspiration and goal to improve the condition of workers through dignifying labor" ("El dia de difuntos").

When a Key West general strike in late 1889 closed down the entire tobacco industry, strike leaders established a *Boletín de al Huelga* and *Boletin Del Embarque* to coordinate worker activities. The Key West anarchist newspapers supported this strike unconditionally, while *El Yara*, the only surviving nationalist newspaper, predictably urged compromise for the sake of continued nationalist revolutionary action. Rivero also expressed absolute support for the Key West strike and its strategy of encouraging workers to leave the city even if it meant destroying the cigar industry. *El Yara* considered such a strategy unpatriotic and warned that it would kill efforts to launch rebellion in Cuba and undermine the most important nationalist community in exile. *La Revista de Florida* replied that it understood abandoning Key West would undermine twenty years of hard work, "but what are we to do?" Labor could no longer allow the bourgeoisie to lord over them and called on workers to reject the idea that leaving Key West would be unpatriotic. The days when nationalists told the workers what to do were gone, and labor acted for its own interests ("Cuidado con la sorpresa"). Rivero encouraged a fund raising campaign to purchase steamer tickets for workers wanting to leave for Tampa ("Ahora o núnca").

Workers in Florida celebrated a complete victory when Key West manufacturers gave into their demands in January 1890, but despite their victory anarchist labor leaders failed to convince workers of the long-term irrelevance of revolutionary nationalism. *El Yara* quickly regained traction with workers in light of a couple of developments. First, in 1889, General Antonio Maceo accepted an amnesty from the Spanish governor to return to Cuba if he gave up his revolutionary aspirations. Not serious about making peace with Spain, he immediately began organizing another insurrection. Maceo contacted the nationalist leaders in Key West for support and the community responded with enthusiasm, showing that despite their labor interests Cuban workers were willing to place nationalism as a first priority whenever they saw revolution as a viable possibility (Poyo, 131-133). Also that year, the Spanish governor initiated repression against the increasingly popular anarchists in Havana. This convinced many Cuban anarchist leaders in Florida that little opportunity existed in Cuba to promote worker interests as long as Spain controlled the island (Casanovas, 202-214).

Among the last hold-outs, Creci remained steadfast in his anarchist activism. Even after nationalist threats forced him to leave for Tampa, he wrote for *La Revista de Florida* and criticized those Key West workers who returned to the nationalist fold. They had ceased to be socialists and had become politicians, he argued, but ironically Creci would be the only one of these exile journalists to eventually die on Cuba's battlefields (Cabrera, 121-130). Even in Ybor City, the tide turned toward nationalism in 1890. Ramón Rivero ceased publishing *Revista de Florida* and replaced it with *Crítico de Ybor*. *El Patriota* also appeared edited by Emilio Planas, a Cuban of color, born in Key West in 1868 (Casasús, 461-462). Both newspapers advanced nationalist agendas and marked a transition from primarily labor to mostly nationalist politics in Tampa.

Anarchist activism in Florida certainly did not disappear, but the movement made its peace with the nationalists illustrated in the career of Luis Barcia Quilabert. A Spanish-born anarchist originally from a small town near Bilbao, Barcia arrived in New York in 1890 from Tampa, and Havana before that, where he had learned the tobacco and printing trades. He lived in Brooklyn among Spaniards and Cubans dedicated to anarchist ideals and they formed a newspaper called El Despertar. Barcia served as one of two inaugural editors along with José Campos, a long-time anarchist activist in New York. The newspaper maintained the traditional anarchist line against nationalist movements and ignored the growing Cuban independence activism led by José Martí. In 1893, Barcia established another anarchist publication, El Ideal, but the next year returned to Tampa and started El Esclavo. Barcia came to the same conclusions as had other Florida anarchists or he simply recognized the sentiment of the overwhelming majority of cigar workers including many Spaniards. Without abandoning anarchism, El Esclavo fully supported Cubans independence struggle (Castañeda, 79-83, 88).

Conclusion

Even though Antonio Maceo's initiative floundered when he was arrested in Havana and deported in late 1890, *El Yara* continued its nationalist propaganda hoping to convince workers to continue providing resources for revolutionary activity. This gained dramatic traction in November 1891 when *El Yara* covered a high profile visit to Ybor City of New York's charismatic nationalist leader José Martí. The newspaper supported Martí's visit to Key West in December, where representatives of the Key West and Ybor City communities approved Martí's idea for the Cuban Revolutionary Party (PRC). *El Yara* became the *de facto* official voice of the Key West PRC chapter and in January 1893 Rivero founded *Cuba,* which became the PRC's official newspaper in Tampa. *Cuba's* first issue affirmed its political purpose of supporting the PRC and Cuban independence and announced that it was not in its mission to take up divisive socioeconomic issues as long as Cubans remained subjected to Spanish rule ("Nuestro programa,"). These two newspapers and José Martí's *Patria* established in April 1892 in New York became the three most important newspapers promoting the Cuban independence war that began in February 1895.

Works Cited

"A Ciudadano General Castillo," *El Ubiquitario*, November 12, 1883.
"Ahora, o núnca," *La Revista de Florida*, November 2, 1889.

"Al público," *La Opinión Pública*, February 26, 1884.

Alvarez Estévez, Rolando. *La emigración cubana en Estados Unidos, 1868-1878.* Havana: Editorial de Ciencias Sociales, 1986.

Batista Villarreal, Teresita, Josefina García Carranza, and Miguelina Ponte. *Catálogo de publicaciones periódicas cubanas de los siglos XVIII y XIX.* Havana: Biblioteca Nacional José Martí, 1965.

Boletín del Embarque, October 28, 1889.

Boletín de la Huelga, November 2, 21, 1889.

Browne, Jefferson B. *Key West. The Old and the New.* Gainesville: University of Florida Press, 1973.

Cabrera, Olga. "Enrique Creci: un patriota obrero," *Santiago.* 36 (December 1979), 121-150.

Casanovas, Joan. *Bread, or Bullets! Urban Labor and Spanish Colonialism in Cuba, 1850-1898.* Pittsburgh: University of Pittsburgh Press, 1998.

Casasús, Juan J. E. *La emigración cubana y la independencia de la patria.* Havana: Editorial Lex, 1953.

Castañeda, Christopher J. "Times of Propaganda and Struggle: *El Despertar* and Brooklyn's Spanish Anarchists, 1890-1905. *Radical Gotham: Anarchism in New York City, 1870-2011.* Ed. Tom Goyens. Urbana: University of Illinois Press, 2017.

Castellanos García, Gerardo. *Motivos de Cayo Hueso.* Havana: UCAR, Gracia, y Cia, 1935.

"Comentos," *La Opinión Pública*, January 19, 1884.

"Cuidado con la sorpresa," *La Revista de Florida,* November 2, 1889.

"El desaire," *La Opinión Pública,* January 24, 1884.

"Despedida," *Patria*, August 25, 1897.

"El día de difuntos," *Revista de Florida*, November 2, 1889.

El Ecuador, 1886-1887.

"Estrada," *El Yara*, March 17, 1888.

"Los farsantes en camisa," *El Cubano*, February 18, 1889.

"Florida: A Cuban City in the United States," *New York Herald-Tribune*, May 15, 1891.

González Mendoza, José to Hilario Cisneros, July 20, 1875, described in Aleida Plasencia, *Bibliografía de la Guerra de los Diez Años*, 191.

"Hagamos política," *La Opinión Pública*, February 9, 1884.

Instituto de Historia. *Carlos Baliño. Documentos y artículos.* Havana: Partido Comunista de Cuba, 1976.

El Jejen, May 31, 1884.

Kanellos, Nicolás and Helvetia Martell. *Hispanic Periodicals in the United States. Origins to 1960. A Brief History and Comprehensive.* Bibliography. Houston: Arte Público Press, 2000.

Lane, Jill. *Blackface Cuba, 1840-1895.* Philadelphia: University of Pennsylvania Press, 2005).

"Limpiemos," *El Cubano*, June 11, 1888.

"Nada adelantan," *El Eco*, September 22, 1883.

"Nuestra política," *El Cubano*, January 11, 1888.

"Nuestras ventajas," *El Yara*, February 28, 1884.

"Oportunidad," *La Voz de Hatuey*, May 5, 1883.

Pérez Landa, Rufino. *Vida Pública de Martín Morúa Delgado.* Havana: Imprenta Carlos Romero, 1957.

Plasencia, Aleida. *Bibliografía de la Guerra de los Diez Años.* Havana: Instituto del Libro, 1968.

Poyo, Gerald E. *Exile and Revolution: José D. Poyo, Key West, and Cuban Independence.* Gainesville: University Press of Florida, 2014.

El Productor (Havana), 1888-1889.

La Propaganda, 1884-1888.

"Prospecto," *La Opinión Pública,* November 25, 1883.

El Pueblo, 1886-1887.

"Ratificamos," *El Cubano,* June 13, 1888.

El Republicano, 1869-1870.

El Republicano, February 16, 1870.

Reyes, Juan Maria to Hilario Cisneros, August 19, 1875, described in Aleida Plasencia, *Bibliografía de la Guerra de los Diez Años,* 191.

The Semi-Weekly Floridian (Tallahassee), September 17, October 8, 12, 15, November 23, 1880; February 7, 1882.

El Siglo, 1868.

"La Sinrazón de 'La Razón," *El Yara*, December 11, 1880.

Stebbins, Consuelo E. *City of Intrigue, Nest of Revolution. A Documentary History of Key West in the Nineteenth Century.* Gainesville: University Press of Florida, 2007.

"Suceso lamentable," *El Cubano*, March 7, 1888.

Thomas, Susan. *Cuban Zarzuela.* Urbana: University of Illinois, 2009.

"To the Americans of Key West," *El Republicano*, July 13, 1875.

Weekly Floridian (Tallahassee), November 21, 1882; January 23, April 12, 1883

Whelehan, Niall. "'Scientific warfare or the quickest way to liberate Ireland': The Brooklyn Dynamite School," *History Ireland* 16:6 (Nov/Dec 2008).

"Unión," *La Opinión*, March 29, 1884.

El Yara, September 3, 17, 1881.

Before Exile: Unearthing the "Golden Age" of Cuban Theater in Tampa

KENYA C. DWORKIN Y MÉNDEZ
Carnegie Mellon University

Introduction

After more than two decades of searching for primary sources on early Cuban theater in Tampa, and examining over 55 unpublished but recovered theatrical works from the 1920s to 1960, it is finally possible to trace the presence of a Cuban immigrant and subsequently native genre, and its creators and presenters, in Tampa, Florida from 1886 and beyond. The overall project of which this focus on early theater written in Cuba and presented to Cubans in Tampa is only one part, island Cuban theater as well as plays written and produced by local Cubans and others was presented over a period of approximately eigthty years, from 1887 to the 1960s.

The plays I recovered and comment upon in this essay are part of a larger project dedicated to recovering the history and importance of Cuban theater and its derivations in Tampa. The Recovering the US Hispanic Literary Heritage Program at the University of Houston, founded and directed by Dr. Nicolás Kanellos, is dedicated to the recovery of the presence of Hispanic letters in what eventually became the United States, from the sixteenth century to 1960 (now 1980).[1]

Unequivocally, though, the 1920s were the 'golden age' of the more island Cuban variant of this theater. This corpus, while surely incomplete, also facilitates the analysis of certain recurring topics for the community that witnessed and also performed in these plays, e.g., ideology, race, gender, inter-ethnic relations, and identity, subjects clearly important to this pre-1959 and even pre-1898 group of Cuban émigrés to Florida, who established the cigar manufacturing business there.[2] The term "Before Exile" in this essay's title is a reference to a period of Cuban residence in the US prior to the Cuban migratory phenomenon popularly known as 'Cuban exile' associated with the post-1962 out-migration after the triumph, on January 1, 1959 of the Fidel Castro-led Cuban revolution. However, there are multiple earlier episodes of different Cuban out-migrations staying in the United States (and elsewhere) in exile, dating back to the early nineteenth century. For example, a significant number of Cubans had already migrated to New York City, Philadelphia, and New Orleans by 1820. Their numbers increased dramatically after the failed independence wars of 1868-78, 1879-80, and 1895-98, many of them going to Key West and Tampa.[3]

Tampa Cuban theater between 1887 and 1960—the texts themselves—can be divided and subdivided into five categories, very much along the lines the University of Houston's Recovery Program, and its publishing concern, Arte Público Press, employed when preparing two, unique, comprehensive anthologies of largely unknown US Hispanic literature in the United States (a history that starts in the 1500s)—*Herencia* (Oxford 2001) and *En otra voz* (Arte Público Press 2002). The categories I designed to catalogue and examine Tampa's Cuban theater works with respect to origin and context are (1) origins (1886-1910s); (2) Cuban (the 1920s, the "golden age" of theater from the island performed in Tampa; 3) Cuban-Tampan (1930s-early 1940s); 4) Cuban-"American" (from 1942 to 1959); 5) nostalgic and exile (post-1960).

Likewise, given that those who wrote and presented the plays were caught up in constantly moving back and forth, and residing in either Cuba or Tampa, or were born on the island and raised in Tampa, this identity group-the people who wrote and/or performed the plays—can also be divided into five categories, to acknowledge authorship and/or presenters: (1) Spaniards; (2) Cubans (often of Spanish origin); (3) Cubans (either or Spanish or Tampa Cuban origin); (4) Tampa Cubans (who had other immigrant or US roots, e.g., Spanish, Italian, Anglo-American, or other roots); and, (5) Cuban Tampans (Cuban and Tampans arrived from Cuba after 1959).

An exploration of some of these recovered texts, particularly those from the late 1920s, allow one to document and analyze a specific perspective regarding the feelings, triumphs, and failings of this Martí-inspired vanguard in Tampa, and that of their countrymen on the island. To be Cuban in Tampa described not only the past or present: it projected a future iteration of that identity in a city that essentially became Cuban in culture much before Miami was transformed by the exiles and émigrés of the 1960s and beyond.[4] The arrival of an infinite number of Cuban cigar workers and cigar factory owners who crossed the Florida Straits—the watery border between Cuba and the United States—by overnight ferry, occurred after the failed Ten Years War (1868-1878), a war free-dom-loving Cubans fought to be independent of Spain, and threatened to spark twice again before the definitive one that began in 1891. This number once again increased during and after the war known here as the Spanish-American War (another Cuban war for independence from Spain, but in which the United States intervened, in 1895). This, geographic, economic, socio-cultural, and political proximity, initiated what would be many decades of to and fro move-ment by Cubans between the two countries. Yet, even before the promulgation of the 1924 Johnson-Reed Act that officially and significantly limited 'legal' immigration to the United States, these immigrants had already left their stamp on the architecture, labor practices, and culture of Tampa within its factory towns—primarily Ybor City and West Tampa (and a few other, small ones) in areas segregated from the white, Anglo-Saxon population. The fact this reality continued into the 1920s, 1930, and beyond made it so these communities became and remained borderless spaces between Tampa and Cuba.

Transnational families and homes were commonplace in Tampa, as were its industry, mutual aid societies, newspapers, unions, and theatrical materials. Cuban transnationalism in Tampa—real or imagined—revealed the "connec-tions and flows" representative of human action—or lack of thereof—present in this constant political and economic coming and going of people, attitudes, and products (Concannon, Lomelí & Priewe 2008: 5, 29). Even so, this group of Cubans, members and descendants of *la vanguardia de Martí* [Martí's van-guard], used to refer to Cuban supporters of Cuban independence living in the United States as these "new pines," contributed to and nourished their own per-spective about how things were going on the island after more than twenty years of multifaceted American intervention and influence. They considered the new migratory obstacles on what had till then been unrestricted back and forth move-ment to and from Tampa and from Cuba; articulated and read opinions about the island's corrupt and increasingly dictatorial government under Gerardo Macha-do, thanks to newspapers and cigar factory readers;[5] constantly cycling, Cuban migrants and, in the Círculo Cubano and La Unión Martí-Maceo, mutual aid societies for white or light-skinned, Cubans who could pass, or black or dark-skinned Cubans, and who had their own theaters.[6]

The earliest spawning ground for Cuban popular theater in the United States. Southeast developed in 1887, in Tampa, immediately after a rapid debut in Key West, in 1886. The first Spanish-language play staged in South Florida was Ventura de la Vega's nineteenth-century play *Amor de Madre,* presented by Cuban cigar maker-actors brought from Cuba, when the island still belonged to Spain. What began as a logical continuation of Spanish theater quickly evolved into distinctly Cuban theater and then Tampa-Cuban theater. For decades after, it reflected the lasting ties migrant Cuban and Tampa-Cuban cigar makers had to Cuba, despite their residence in the United States.

The very first thing Cuban cigar workers arriving in Key West and Tampa did beyond securing a place to live was establish their patriotic clubs and, eventually, mutual aid societies, each one of them with their own theater and acting group.[7] Regarding Cuban cigar worker ideology as seen through the lens of the island Cuban and Tampa Cuban popular theater that was presented in the Latin enclave, one can appreciate a very marked sense of its impact, a great deal of *criollo,* pro-independence, and nationalist sentiment. Yet, one can also discover certain ambiguities that resulted from this site of production being a segregated city in the racist South with a culture and customs totally foreign to the immigrant workers. This ambiguity could be due to Tampa continuing to receive new émigrés and simultaneously experiencing the coming and going of Cuban cigar workers in search of better work or contact with family for specific periods of time. Another reason could be that Tampa's Cuban residents closely followed the political and economic situation of their island, even after the obstructed independence of 1902.

When combined with the complex demographics that emerged in Tampa's foremost, Cuban areas, Ybor City and West Tampa, which were inhabited primarily by Cubans, but also by Spaniards, Sicilians, German and Romanian Jews, African- Americans, Chinese, and some Anglos, these factors might have significantly affected not only the slowly evolving, local theater's characters and settings, but also the subjects covered. Without a doubt, this all left its stamp on the essential conceptualization of what it meant to be Cuban in Tampa and, in fact, produced a quintessential Tampa Latin identity indisputably linked to Cuban identity. Yet, the Cuban troupes and plays that came from the island and were presented equally with native, Tampa Latin theater, also impacted the underpinnings of that Tampa Cuban identity. This identity, sometimes plural, was sometimes open and quite influenced by island, United States, and even global events. Its precepts were progressive, pro-labor, internationalist, and always very much in keeping with José Martí's ideals.

However, for our purposes here, we focus on plays written in Cuba and presented on both the island and in the Círculo Cubano during the 1920s. Many of these are works that allow us to document and analyze a particular view of the feelings, triumphs, and shortcomings or weaknesses not only of island Cubans but also of Martí's vanguard and its descendants. Through them, it becomes obvious that to be Cuban in Tampa was not only about the past and present: it was also very much about projecting the future of that identity in a city that became truly Cuban in culture many decades prior to the arrival in South Florida of Cuban exiles in the 1960s and later. The arrival of innumerable Cuban cigar workers and factory owners, who crossed the Florida Straits between the two countries via an overnight ferry to make new lives for themselves in Key West and Tampa, forever changed their host societies. This resulted from the failed Ten Years War (1868-1878) and the equally mitigated independence of Cuba after 1902, with the burden of the Platt Amendment in their newly written Constitution. Before and even after the promulgation of the 1924, Johnson-Reed Immigration Act, which formerly and significantly limited "official" immigration to the United States, these immigrants left their stamp on Tampa's architecture and labor practices from within racially and ethnically delimited spaces, as well as on the spaces and cultural practices of the white Southern population. This reality, which lasted throughout the 1920s, 1930s, and beyond, into the eighties and nineties, transformed these spaces, making these communities places without borders between themselves and Cuba, due to their nearly identical industries, mutual aid societies, unions, newspapers, architecture, foods, language, and theatrical materials and productions. Real or perceived, Cuban transnationalism in Tampa unequivocally revealed the "connections and flows" represented in the behavior, or lack thereof, present in the constant political and economic to and fro of people, attitudes, and products (*Imagined Transnationalism* 5, 29).[8]

Fat or Skinny[9] Cows & the Roaring Twenties: American Influence & Intervention

Given the intent of this article is to briefly document what can now be unmistakably defined as the 'golden age' of island Cuban theater in Tampa, a small but revealing corpus discloses both island and Tampa Cuban preoccupations with an identifiable set of issues, including: the impact of Cuban government corruption, divided feeling regarding President Machado, continued social class differences on the island, American influences—cultural, linguistic, and economic, on 'authentic,' Cuban identity. These preoccupations, and the factors that caused them, also shape the Tampa Cuban imaginary and its theater regarding this community's identity and position vis-à-vis forces both internal and external.

Specifically, I focus on two, recovered plays from the late 1920s, presented at the *Círculo Cubano* in Tampa, that allow us to see how the Tampa Cuban community saw the ambiguous nature of Cuban sovereignty and identity, as well as the role that US English, the media, and capitalism, and its effect on island and émigré Cuban members of the working and middle class. *Los espejuelos de Machado* [Machado's Spectacles],[10] a 1927 work by Antonio H. Ramos and Roberto "Bolito" Gutiérrez" (one of Cuba's best known blackface characters) is a perfect example of a play written and presented transnationally: its authors were Cuban; the cast, Cuban and Tampa Cuban. It would have been staged in both Cuba and Tampa to a Cuban and mixed public.[11]

In this work, Mr. Fotoplay, a photographic correspondent for *Photoplay*,[12] a US film fan magazine, travels to Cuba during the time of Prohibition (1920-1933),[13] an era that in great measure overlaps with President Gerardo Machado's first term.[14]

Photoplay was one of the first magazines enthusiasts of the silver screen and the lifestyles of its rich and famous actors, an image energetically promoted in Cuba and internationally (for a time, there were Spanish-language spinoffs of *Photoplay* produced in Los Angeles for some parts of Latin America). Yet, the twenties and early thirties were also a period of economic instability in Cuba, given the constant ups and downs of the tenuous sugar market, Machado's construction of many public works, which made him famous, and the early years of the Great Depression. Mr. Fotoplay is charged with photographing the marvels accomplished by this president in this US tourist paradise and playground. Notwithstanding, the wealth generated by the president's projects was somewhat "unevenly distributed, " and did more to serve the interests of Cuban investors and American stakeholders.[15] This soon brought about a dramatic increase in protests by workers, trade unionists, and students, activities that were brutally repressed by Machado's forces.[16] The Yankee photographer, who was not expecting any of this, had accidentally stumbled on a reality in Cuba different from the one he had been commissioned to document. It is a reality that his eventual guide and other ordinary Cubans, try to explain to him as he ambles along.

Wealthy Cuban protagonist Don Jaime is who has invited Mr. Fotoplay to gather visual evidence of his version of Machado's "new and wonderful" Cuba, which reflects more about his own success and that of others like him, than anything else. At breakfast, he comments to his wife Doña Sinforosa, whose name conjures up sweetness and delicacy, but in reality is kind of a harpy with him, about the wonders achieved by Machado. She, who is reading the newspaper at the table, retorts: "Déjate de guatequerías y lee" [Stop your silly flattering and read] (Ramos & Bolito 2). Her husband derives his opinions about the president and his attainments based upon the leader's commitment to economic development on the island, the unification of the island by the great Central Highway, his desire to repeal the Platt Amendment in the country's constitution, and to renegotiate or change the Reciprocity Act with the United States, which affects sugar production and its price on the world market. However, Sinforosa orders him to read the news so he can see how wrong he is about how well things are going for and in Cuba. We can assume that she is referring to newspaper articles in the Cuban press about the darker side of all this prosperity and the president, himself, his dictatorial aspirations, his violence against communists, trade unionists, workers, and students, reorganization of the military, and his generally brutal tactics.[17]

When Mr. Fotoplay arrives in Cuba, Don Jaime orders his black servant, Tintorero, to accompany his guest and take him for a walk around Havana, so he can "see the sights." The photographer, whose attitude is a bit arrogant, whose Spanish- speaking skills are limited, and who insists on "seeing" only certain things—and in only a particular way—follows Tintorero around and encounters an unexpected reality. It is here that the playwrights create a heteroglossic experience between the American, whose lens is trained or preadjusted to see only what interests the US public and pro-Machado Cubans want to see, and what a population whose diversity of voices and opinions about their reality completely belies Don Jaime's and Gerardo Machado's version of Cuba. Each one of Mr. Fotoplay's interlocutors, some serving as personified, inanimate allegories, offers a rhymed,[18] musical criticism or compliment about Cuba under what some of them see as its "shortsighted," bespectacled president.[19] *Calles* [Streets], for example, extols the architectural marvels of the capital:[20] the *Gallego* [Galician] praises "Gerardito" because as an immigrant, he had been sent by his nearly destitute family in northwestern Spain, to which he was now able to send considerable remittances thanks to the business he was able to build up, 'Fernández García and Company.[21] *La Prensa* [the Press], quickly tells us he provides intense, documented information about what was good and bad in Cuba; *El Político* [the Politician] doesn't want Tintorero—Mr. Fotoplay's guide—to allow the visitor to say anything negative, alluding to the fact that at least some portion of the island's press is not free. *Cuba Libre* [Free Cuba], a drunken woman, explains that she has to drink to forget her sorrows, adding that she had been anxious for freedom when the island fought for its independence. She had lost one of her sons but felt proud, because redemption had come later for her sovereign compatriots. Yet, she explains bitterly that this had brought with it the American flag that waved above Morro Castle. She shouts "Long Live Free Cuba!"[22] *Liborio* [an adjective for Cuban, and here a personification] explains that he is from Camagüey and owns a large farm called "Cuba" at which he grows potatoes, *yuca* [cassava root], beans, and tobacco. Now, instead of planting sugar cane, he grows other things, so he can be more independent of the sugar market; he wants to cultivate *plátanos manzanos* [Apple bananas], a small scale, native crop; *Plátano manzano* [Apple banana] extols the virtues and superiority this Cuban fruit, calling it the best and most independent crop grown in Cuba;[23] *El Tabaco* [Tobacco], for his part, announces that Liborio has sown tobacco and that there is no better tobacco in the whole world than Cuban tobacco; that it tastes heavenly;[24] *El Borracho* [the Drunkard] defends Bolshevism, shouting that Capital should die; he wants a social revolution; down with those above, up with those below; he proclaims there is more hunger than justice in Cuba;[25] that the Constitution allows him to go speak to the president and that he has a message for Gerardo Machado; *Tío Sam* [Uncle Sam] congratulates Liborio for having been able to survive and support himself after the collapse of the sugar market; he reminds Liborio that he is his friend, and that he has demonstrated this; Liborio expresses gratitude and acknowledges Uncle Sam's "greatness," but adds that he puts his faith in God; he tells Uncle Sam that he does not need his help. Then a female Spain expresses her fraternal love for Cubans: *"Los españoles que aquí hay, así lo demuestran. Nunca olvidaré vuestras bondades y cuente con nuestro agradecimiento"* [We Spaniards from here and from there are one with you" [I will never forget your kindness to us; count on us and our gratitude] (Ramos & Bolito 9). A female Cuba enters Spain's *bohío* [shack] and is welcomed; she begins to explain that she regrets having planted so much sugar cane;[26] Liborio asks her to make him some coffee using beans collected during his last harvest, emphasizing his desire for economic independence. At the end, Liborio shows Uncle Sam something very "pretty," the new, commercial agreement between Cuba and Spain, thanks to president Machado, which allowed Cuba to sidetrack the United States. Liborio no longer has to consult the United to conduct his business. Mister Fotoplay responds courteously but cynically, asking "Quien ese Cubano ser / mi quiere estrechar su mano" (sic) [who is this Cuban / I want to shake his hand while] (11). Liborio assures him: "Enseguida lo ha de ver. / El presidente Cubano / el que lleno de optimismo / y con entusiasmo y fe / salvó a Cuba . . . " (sic) [You will meet him right away / the Cuban president / who filled with enthusiasm and faith/saved Cuba] (12). Of course, he is referring to Gerardo Machado. It is now the play's end, the curtain goes down, and we hear *La Bayamesa,* the Cuban National Anthem.

Throughout the play, the voices Mr. Fotoplay encounters present myriad direct and indirect reasons for why Cubans loved or hated their current reality on the island, and its president. All the commentaries possess a broad spectrum of very specific and personal perspectives regarding Cuba vis-à-vis the United States or Cuba, political and/or economic independence, and the trappings of monoculture and corruption. Yet, only some of these situations directly or indirectly implicate Machado, and Liborio seems to be pragmatic. He is more adamant about not allowing more monoculture and US intervention, than any other negative issue the other voices mentioned. Thus, he defends Machado as a true patriot because he is the only president in Cuba's brief history that has challenged the United States and garnered some economic independence for Cuba in the world market. It is not that he disregards the worries expressed to the Yankee journalist by his compatriots; he just undervalues them. Neverthe-less, the presence of this diversity of voices substantiates the complexity of Cuban feelings and dialogues after 1902, during a decade known as the time of the *vacas gordas* [fat cows], due to the economic benefits enjoyed by those with capital to invest in Machado's projects, which, of course, the majority of folks did not have.

Another recovered play from 1927 presented and witnessed by audiences in both Cuba and Tampa, was *Yo quiero ser senador* [I Want to be a Senator], by Felipe Rivera Matheu (an author about whom I have not yet been able to find any information). In this play we find a bourgeois, conceited Cuban who thinks he deserves a seat in the Cuban Senate. His pretentiousness leads him to speak to his Cuban family in Peninsular Spanish, using, for example, the "vosotros" pronoun instead of "ustedes," which could be an indirect allusion to his prefer-ence for things Spanish, and not Cuban, since after 1920 Spanish merchants on the island did extremely well, and ended up in a much better economic position than Cuban veterans of the War of Independence. Yet, he has also decided that English should replace Spanish in his home, and for his future, because it is the language of power and progress. It may even guarantee him a seat in the Senate. He even admits that this is not due to any altruism on his part, but instead because he wants to gain an advantage and new position: "Oh. Cada vez estoy más seguro de salir electo por voto popular de las masas ignoras" [Oh. I am ever more convinced that I will be elected by the ignorant masses popular vote] (Rivera Matheu 10). It is not to improve Cuba, only for him to garner the priv-ileges of the Cuban oligarchy. He is even willing to "sell" his daughter to a sup-posed, Yankee banker from Chicago.

Little does he know that his daughter and her true love Raul, who is, among other things, an actor, have other plans. They have not been able to get Don Ser-afín to give them permission to marry because, as Blanca explains it: "[Y] ahora que le ha dado la mania por ser senador, y por aprender Ingles, esta insor-portable" (sic) [And now that he has gone on a toot, and his new obsession is to become a senator and learn English, he is unbearable" (2). In a scene during which the father explains to his daughter and wife his opposition to Raul—he is a poet, musician, and playwright—Don Serafín uses English to take leave of them and also highlight his ambitions: "Gud nay . . . Ya sabéis que mi deseo es desterrar por completo el castellano de esta casa. Aquí pronto no se hablará más que inglés, la lengua gloriosa del inmortal de Shakspeare" (sic)" [Good night . . . You all know that only English will be spoken here from now on, the glorious language of the immortal Skakspear [sic] (3). When his daughter cor-rects his pronunciation, the stubborn old man answers: "Da lo mismo chispir que chispar. Esta lengua me ha de encumbrarme a una poltrona del senado. Yo seré senador y vosotras seréis lo más chip de la capital. Under-stand?" [Chispear or chispar; it doesn't matter. I shall be a Senator and you both will be the chiquest ones in the capital. Understand?] (3). Upon answer *jes* [yes], Serafín responds:

"Güel . . . Ol ray . . . Muy bien. Ahora hija, retírate que tengo que hablar a solas con your mother para decirle que esta mañana en el Casino me encontré con Mister Roberts, el americano ese (sic) que llegó para las fiestas de cuatro de julio . . . " [Well . . . alright . . . Very good. Now, daughter, take your leave because I have to speak to your mother, alone, to tell her that I ran into Mister Roberts at the casino this morning, that American who arrived in time for the July 4th celebrations . . .] (4). When his wife contradicts him, Serafín insists: "Blanca se casará con Mister Roberts, tan seguro, como que hay God in the escay" [Blanca will marry Mister Roberts as surely as there is a God in the sky] (4)

Meanwhile, Esteban, the house's black servant, is going around babbling as he practices his English:

"*Di cat*, el gato. *Di rat*, el ratón [mouse]. *Di chis* el queso [cheese]. *Di teivol*, la mesa [table]. *Di pipol*, el pueblo [people]. Bueno, de pueblo a *pipol*, van como diez quintales . . . Ahora sí que me salvé yo; yo, que no sé hablar bien en castellano, ahora tengo que aprender la lengua . . . ésta, porque a *míster* Serafín le ha dado la manía por ahí . . . " [Well, it's a long way between *pueblo* and people . . . Now I'm really in a spot; I, who don't even speak Castilian well, have to now learn this language . . . because Mister Serafín is hell bent on doing the same . . .] (5)

The aspiring Senator begins to practice English, enumerating in his "powerful" English all the benefits of being elected by an ignorant mass: "Jau greyt. Jau puri. Jau excelent. Jau biuriful. Jau . . . jau . . . jau . . . " [How great. How pretty. How excellent. How beautiful. How . . . how . . . how], which causes his servant to comment that it sounds like there's a loose dog around there somewhere] (9).

Concomitantly, the beleaguered Raul, has decided to take advantage of his potentially future father-in-law's ambitions and his own talents as an actor, all this so he can win Blanca's hand in marriage. He will do so by playing the role of a rich American, and although he does it brilliantly, the English he employs is terrible. However, in his desire to be solicitous, Don Serafín, who does not recognize him, begins to praise him, in equally bad English, about the Yankee's Spanish, which is also fractured:

Serafín: *"Oh, mister. Gud nait . . . O mister . . . Ah. Jau ar yuar famil-ia?"* [Oh, mister. Good night. Ah. How are your family?]

Raúl: Oh, mocho bueno; *zenqui*. Yo llamarse *Mr.* Johnson . . . Ahora, yo decir la motiva de mi venir a este casa. Yo ver en un periodica . . . periodico, una retrete . . . " [Oh, much good. Thank you. I am called Mr. Johnson . . . Now, I tell the reason for me come to this house. I see in a periodical . . . newspaper, a toilet . . .]

Serafín: "Pero, dígame, *mister,* ¿cómo usted siendo americano habla tan bien el castellano"? [But, tell me, mister. How do you being American speak so well the Spanish?]

Raúl: "Oh, mocho poquita. Solo dos mesas en Puerta Rico [sic]" [Oh, very little. Only two months in Puerta Rico (sic)

Serafín: Pues, lo habla usted como un nativo del país" [Well, you speak it like a native of the country]

Raúl: "Pues, como yo le decir antes, yo enamorar de muchacho bonito en retrete y quererme casar enseguida . . . Yo ser banquero de Chicago y yo querer casar . . . "[Well, as I say to you before, I fall in love with beautiful boy in toilet and want myself marry right away]

Serafín—en un aparte [in an aside]—: "Caramba, banquero y americano . . .

No me parece mala proporción . . . " [Darn, a banker and American . . . Doesn't seem to me be a bad deal . . .] (14)

The wedding takes place immediately and only after Raul's trick is revealed. Simultaneously, a letter arrives for Serafín from the Nominating Committee informing him that he has not been selected as a candidate. On the spot, Serafín takes stock of everything, that his intense faith in English as the language of the Americans, and the possible influence he might have had by speaking it and imitating the customs he saw in the successful country to the north, have all been in vain. The whole plot has backfired on him. Upon this realization, he quickly rescinds his position on English: "Ahora quiero advertiros una cosa. Desde hoy, no quiero volver a oír aquí, en esta casa, ni una sola palabra en inglés" [Now hear this! From today forward I don't want to hear a single word of English in this house ever again] (17).

Aside from its obvious humor and criticism, *Yo quiero ser senador* is very revealing if we consider the cultural and sociolinguistic reality of the play's audiences both in Tampa and, especially, in Cuba. Its bilingual wordplay required this audience to be at least sufficiently linguistically competent to recognize and understand its malapropisms and ungrammatical statements, and its horrible English and Spanish pronunciations. It would be logical to assume, perhaps, that the Tampa Latin community was incipiently bilingual, however the supposition regarding Cuba is significant. Historian Louis A. Pérez has documented the increase and notoriety of English and learning English among middle-class Cubans after 1902, and it was promoted among those who aspired to the professional class, as well. But, both in Tampa and Cuba, knowledge of English among cigar makers (most of the audience in Tampa) was less common during those same, early decades in the Latin enclave or in Havana. However, many of those who had already gone back and forth to Tampa, and resided there between 1887 and the early decades of the 1920s, might very well have known (some) English. This explains why it is likely that the Tampa Latin audience of the twenties was indeed somewhat bilingual, even if English did not serve as the community's *lingua franca* till after World War II.

In conclusion, the 1920s, a decade from which we have identified 17, heretofore, unrecovered play scripts, mark the dynamic transition of Spanish-language theater in Cuba from a Spanish or Cuban genre (bufo, a natural derivative of mid nineteenth-century, anticolonial theater), to a specifically Cuban one of interest to audiences in both Cuba and Tampa. Just as on the island, Cuban theater from the 1860s and beyond employed racist blackface so that white actors could openly talk about nationalist sentiments and the emergence of an anticolonial position. Cuban theater in Cuba and Tampa during the 1920s revealed the transnational character of its political, economic, and anti(neo)imperial attitudes of Cubans on both sides of the Florida Straits. At the very least, this theater was bi-national in its creation and presentation, just like the cigar making industry itself, and worked to undermine the national and political borders that separated Cubans on both sides from the culture. It was quintessentially Cuban theater, by definition, even in Tampa, precisely because it had one foot in the island and a dramatic, sustaining foot in Florida that allows these Cubans to belong to and experience certain realities that not even geography, language, or politics can divide.

Works Cited

Benjamin, Jules R. 1975. "The Machadato and Cuban Nationalism, 1928-1932." *The Hispanic American Historical Review*, 55: 1, 66-91.

Concannon, Kevin, Francisco A. Lomelí and Marc Priewe. 2008. *Imagined Translationalism: U.S. Latino/a Literature, Culture, and Identity*. N.Y.: Palgrave, 1-13, 29-46.

Duany, Jorge. 2017. "Cuban Migration: A Postrevolution Exodus Ebbs and Flows," https://www.migrationpolicy.org/article/cuban-migration-postrevolution-exodus-ebbs- and-flows. Accessed July 8 2017.

Dworkin y Méndez, Kenya C. 2005. "La patria que nace de lejos: Cuba, lo 'nacional,' y la tradición cultural de los tabaqueros cubanos en Tampa." *Cuban Studies*, 36; Pittsburgh: University of Pittsburgh Press, 1-22.

___. 2000. "From Factory to Footlights: Original Spanish-language Cigar Workers' Theatre in Ybor City and West Tampa, Florida." *Recovering the U.S. Hispanic Literary Heritage* III. Houston: Arte Público Press, 332-350.

___. 1995. "The Tradition of Hispanic Theater & the WPA Federal Theatre Project in Tampa-Ybor City, Florida." *Recovering the U.S. Hispanic Literary Heritage Project* II. Houston: Arte Público Press, 279-294.

González Suárez, Dominga. 2005. "Los españoles en Cuba: conflictos y estereotipos". *Cuba in Transition* 15, 205-220.

Greenbaum, Susan. 2002. *More than Black: Afro-Cubans in Tampa*. Gainesville: University Press of Florida.

Kirk, John M. 1983. *José Martí, Mentor of the Cuban Nation*. Tampa: University Presses of Florida.

López, Alfred J. 2006. *José Martí and the Future of Cuban Nationalisms*. Gainesville: University Press of Florida.

Macías Martín, Francisco Javier. *La diplomacia española ante el 'Machadato' y la crisis cubana de 1933*. ftp://tesis.bbtk.ull.es/ccssyhum/cs50.pdf.

McCullom, Justin. 2011. "A Brief Historiography of U.S. Hegemony in the Cuban Sugar Industry." *The Forum: Journal of History*, 3, 1. http://digitalcommons.calpoly.edu/forum/vol3/iss1/8/.

Mormino, Gary R. and George E. Pozzetta. 1993. "The Reader Lights the Candle: Cuban and Florida Cigar Workers' Oral Tradition." *Labor's Heritage*, 4-27.

Pérez, Jr., Louis A. 1990. *Cuba and the United States: Singular Ties of Intimacy*. Athens, GA: University of Georgia Press, 82-148.

Pozzetta, George E. (ed.), *Immigrant Institutions: The Organization of Immigrant Life* (New York: Garland, 1991): 187-190.

Pozzetta, George E. and Gary R. Mormino. 1998. "The Reader and the Worker: 'Los Lectores' and the Culture of Cigarmaking in Cuba and Florida." *International Labor and Working-Class History*, 54. New York: Columbia University Press, 1-18.

Segre, Roberto. 2004."El sistema monumental en la Ciudad de La Habana: 1900-1930". http://www.habanaelegante.com/Fall2004/Ronda.html.

Tinajero, Araceli. 2010. *El Lector: A History of the Cigar Factory Reader.* Austin, TX: University of Texas Press.

Endnotes

[1]This material includes from chronicles of exploration in territories such as La Florida and the Southwest, dating from the establishment of Spanish America, to the Hispanic and other civil rights movement of the 1960s. For more information about the Recovery Program, visit: https://artepublicopress.com/recovery-project/.

[2]For a summary of the founding of Tampa and Ybor City see Gary Mormino & George Pozzetta, *The Immigrant World of Ybor City: Italians and Their Latin Neighbors in Tampa*, 1885-1985 (Champaign, IL: University of Illinois Press, 1986), 43-62; Durward Long, "The Making of Modern Tampa: A City of the New South, 1885-1911, *The Florida Historical Quarterly*, vol. 49, No. 4 (Apr., 1971), 333-45; José Rivero Muñiz, *Los Cubanos en Tampa*, La Habana, [n.p.], 1954), 9-29; Wenceslao Galvez, *Tampa: Impresiones de emigrado* (La Habana: Establecimiento Tipográfico de Cuba, 1897), 1-16; and, Del Río, Emilio, *Yo fui uno de los fundadores de Ybor City* (Tampa, FL: [n.p.], 1950), 2-10. For a description of the founding of West Tampa see Armando Méndez, *Ciudad de Cigars: West Tampa* (Cocoa, FL: Florida Historical Society, 1994), 1-4.

[3]For information about historical and more recent Cuban immigration to the United States, see: https://www.migrationpolicy.org/article/cuban-migration-postrevolution-exodus-ebbs-and-flows.

[4]For information about and analysis of the theater of the Cuban exile community in Miami, see Yael Prizant, "Ninety Miles Away: Exile and Identity in Recent Cuban-American Theatre," *Performance, Exile and 'America'* (N.Y.: Palgrave, 2009): 47-65.

[5]For a thorough overview of the cigar factory reader tradition, see Araceli Tinajero, *El Lector: A History of the Cigar Factory Reader* (Austin, TX: University of Texas Press, 2010). For more specific look at *lectores* in Tampa, see Louis A. Pérez, Jr., "Reminiscences of a Lector: Cuban Cigar Workers in Tampa," *Florida Historical Quarterly*, 53 (April 1975): 445.

[6]According to Tampa historian George E. Pozzetta, State and local authorities pressured Tampa's 'white' Cubans to segregate the Círculo Cubano club (the custom among Anglo Floridians and Tampans, and the Federal law after 1896). See George E. Pozzetta (ed.), *Immigrant Institutions: The Organization of Immigrant Life* (New York: Garland, 1991): 187-190.

[7]The vast majority of the major clubs had their own theaters, which also served as movie houses at different times, although almost all the film fare was American, the live performances (comedies, dramas, musical revues, zarzuela, and opera) were Cuban, Spanish, or Italian. For a description of the mutual aid societies see Durward Long, "An Immigrant Cooperative Medicine Program in the South, 1887-1963," *Journal of Southern History*, XXXI (1965), 417-34; Mormino & Pozzetta, 175-209.

[8]For a discussion of transnational character, see Kevin Concannon, Francisco Lomelí, and Marc Priewe, "Introduction" and Nicolás Kanellos, "A Schematic Approach to Understanding Latin Transnational Literary Texts," *Imagined Translationalism: U.S. Latino/a Literature, Culture, and Identity* (N.Y.: Palgrave, 2008): 1-13; 29-46, respectively.

[9]For an overview of these two time periods in Cuba named for well-fed and starving cows, and their importance to and impact on the country's economic and social life, see "De las Vacas Gordas y las Vacas Flacas," *Trabajadores: Órganos Central de los Trabajadores Cubano* (agosto 26, 2014): 1. Retrieved 17 May 2017. http://www.trabajadores.cu/20140826/de-las-vacas-gordas-las-vacas-flacas/

[10]This and all translations are mine.

[11]By a 'mixed' public in an immigrant enclave audience, I mean a mean a mixture of Cuban, Spaniards and, possibly, Sicilians/Italians, all of who formed a more cohesive group identity after living and working together during the first decades of the twentieth century. This more cohesive identity came to be known as the Tampa Latin identity. Tampa Latins' are the historical and contemporary descendants of Cubans, Spaniards and Sicilians/Italians in Tampa. The name was simultaneously applied to them by the city's mainstream, Southern, white population, and adopted by the 'Latins' themselves, given 'Latin' was English for *latino*. Its eventual use by the immigrant community reflected a more collective view of the group identity that began to emerge in the late 1930s as a result of prolonged cohabitation, common agendas, and external assimilatory pressures. 'Latin' in Tampa includes not just Spanish speakers from Cuba and Spain, but also Sicilians and Italians. We submit that the reason the community was willing to adapt the English; identifying appellation was because they saw it as a translation of *latino,* originally an adjective describing anyone who spoke a language derived from Latin. In the United

States, the Spanish word *latino* was later transformed into the English 'Latino' to describe people of Spanish-speaking ancestry. The English term 'Latin' in the Tampa context predates the twentieth-century US use of 'Latino' for referring to Spanish-speakers and their descendants in this country.

[12]*Photoplay* was one of the earliest film magazines, started in 1911, in Chicago. It started out publishing movie plot summaries, but was documenting the lives of Hollywood screen legends by the 1920s, following their exploits and travels . . .

[13]In 1919, a group of American temperance fanatics and Protestants lobbied for and got the US government to ratify the Volstead Act, the 18th Amendment to the nation's Constitution, which made the production and sale of alcoholic beverages illegal. The laws were largely disregarded and underground production and consumption stoked the fires of gangsterism and criminal activity. See S.J. Mennell's "Prohibition: A Sociological View," in *Journal of American Studies* 3:2 (Dec. 1969): 159-175.

[14]For a concise chronological examination of the rise and fall of Gerardo Machado, see Gregorio Selser, *Cronología de las intervenciones extranjeras en América Latina: 1899-1945* (Mexico City, MX: UNAM, 1994), 432-598.

[15]For an excellent, detailed, and well-documented analysis of Cuba's social, cultural, and economic development and stagnation after its 1902 independence, see Francisco Javier Macías Martín, *La diplomacia española ante el 'Machadato' y la crisis cubana de 1933*. Thesis. Spain, 1998. For a thorough study of the different forms of Cuban nationalism that emerged during the Republic's first thirty years and, specifically, the rise and later fall of Gerardo Machado, the socio-political impact of his presidency, and his response to groups that opposed him, see Jules R. Benjamin, "The Machadato and Cuban Nationalism, 1928-1932," *The Hispanic American Historical Review*, 55, 1, 1975, pp. 66-91, ftp://tesis.bbtk.ull.es/ccssyhum/cs50.pdf

[16]There is hardly any more passionate or better written description of Cuba under Machado and his brutal tactics that Alejo Carpentier's, when he published "Retrato de un Dictador: Gerardo Machado," in 1933 (published in Spain, but written in Cuba while imprisoned by this president), *Octubre*; Madrid (septiembre-octubre), 1933. It was republished in *La Jiribilla: Revista de Cultura Cubana* (enero 2010). *http://epoca2.lajiribilla.cu/2010/n453_01/453_04.html* . Accessed 27 July 2017.

[17]See Raúl Roa García, "Cesarismo y Revolución," Transcript of radio program Universidad del Aire (23 de marzo de 1952) published in *Areito Digital* (primavera 2008). http://www.areitodigital.net/PRIM-VER.07/RAUL.ROA.SOBRE.MACHADO.PRIM-VER.07.htm.

[18]Importantly, the style of verse utilized in the responses of all those Mister Fotoplay and/or Tintorero encounter are written entirely in *romancero*-style octosyllables, not unlike those composed centuries earlier.

[19]The glasses, for which Gerardo Machado, whose countenance is unmistakable in Cuba portraiture and photography, was known, were distinctive. The playwright's use of these spectacles to stand in almost as a synecdoque for the brutal president himself and his fierce control in Cuba is very clever. Machado is all seeing and all knowing, despite the reality he knows very well other Cubans see. This is quite reminiscent of the F. Scott Fitzgerald's use of the T.J. Eckleburg sign above the spectacle store. The eyes in those glasses also see everything, all the decay that Gatsby, himself, and his social cohort do not want to see.

[20]For a summary of President Gerardo Machado's public works projects, the Forestier Plan, and their financing, see Roberto Segre, "El sistema monumental en la Ciudad de La Habana: 1900-1930," 2004. http://www.habanaelegante.com/Fall2004/Ronda.html

[21]For a long and ample discussion of the tensions between Spaniards and Cubans before, during, and after the establishment of the Republic of Cuba, in 1902, see Dominga González Suárez, "Los españoles en Cuba: conflictos y estereotipos," *Cuba in Transition* 15 (2005): 205-220.

[22]By the time the United States wanted to intervene in the Spanish-Cuban conflict of 1891-1895, and sought a mechanism by which to garner support from the American public for said intervention, the island of Cuba began to be portrayed as a beleaguered damsel in distress (Spain, being the villain) in need of assisstance Thus it is not unusual that the playwright chose to represent *Cuba libre,* the foil, as just this sort of woman. Later on, when the foil represents the masculine, agriculturally industrious island, he uses *Liborio,* a name that stands in as an adjective for Cuban man. For a detailed examination of the insertion and impact of the Platt Amendment into the first Cuban Constitution after the United States bestowed independence on Cuba, in 1902, see Louis A. Pérez, Jr., *Cuba and the United States: Singular Ties of Intimacy* (Athens, GA: University of Georgia Press, 1990): 82-148.

[23]For information about American influence and money in Cuban agriculture, particularly with sugar, see Jules Robert Benjamin, *The United States and Cuba: Hegemony and Dependent Development, 1880–1934* (Pittsburgh, PA: University of Pittsburgh, 1977).

[24]For a Cuban audience at this time, on either side of the Florida Straits, but especially in Tampa, the reference to tobacco cuts to the quick, as it was the primary source of the employment. S*enate Documents* vol. 5, Part III (Washington, D.C.: Government Printing Office, 1922): 2515, concretely discusses

for the official record the importance of the cigar manufacturing business between in and to Tampa, Florida.

[25]For a review and analysis of early, twentieth-century political and social movements, particularly the establishment of the first Cuban Communist Party, trade unionism, and anarchism, see Kirwin R. Shaffer, *Anarchism and countercultural politics in early twentieth-century Cuba* (*Gainesville, FL:* University Press of Florida, 2005).

[26]This is another direct reference to monocultural agricultural activity in Cuba. See José Álvarez, "Cuban Agriculture Before 1959: The Political and Economic Situations," EDIS document FE479, a publication of the Department of Food and Resource Economics, UF/IFAS Extension, Gainesville, FL,2004: 2, 4. https://edis.ifas.ufl.edu/pdffiles/FE/FE47900.pdf.

In Their Own Words: Recovering the History of the Spanish Immigrant Experience in the United States Through Immigrants' Writing

ANA VARELA-LAGO

Northern Arizona University

Between1880 and 1930, over three million Spaniards joined the mass migration of Europeans to the Americas. Most of them travelled to Spanish-speaking America, particularly Cuba (a colony until 1898) and Argentina, but a significant number settled in the United States. While the Spanish immigrant presence in the country was never large, the number of Spaniards registered by the U.S Census increased exponentially in the first decades of the twentieth century, growing from 7,050 in 1900 to 22,108 in 1910 to 49,535 in 1920 (Rueda 282-283). This upward trend would have probably continued had it not been for the anti-immigrant legislation of the 1920s, which reduced the arrivals from Spain to a trickle.[1]

The study of this migration, once confined to a handful of pioneering works (Gómez 1962; Rueda 1993), has seen an upsurge, particularly in the past two decades. Recent scholarship has contributed significantly to our knowledge of regional patterns of migration. Bieito Alonso (2006), Nancy Pérez Rey (2008), and Ana Varela-Lago (2008) have researched the migration of Galicians to New York, Florida, and Louisiana. Luis Argeo (*AsturianUS*; 2009), Suronda González (1999), and Thomas Hidalgo (2001) have documented the migration of Asturians to West Virginia, and Carlos Tarazona Grasa (*Borregueros*; 2017) that of Aragonese shepherds to the American West. María José García Hernandorena (2013), Teresa Morell Moll (2012), and Enric Morrió (2014) have studied the migration of Valencians to New York.[2] In the United States, the Center

421

for Basque studies at the University of Nevada, Reno has become the point of reference for scholarship on the Basque immigrant experience throughout the Americas.[3] The past two decades have also seen an increase in the number of memoirs and family histories published by descendants of Spanish immigrants across the United States.[4] Social media has contributed to the recovery and dissemination of the Spanish immigrant experience, as projects such as the "Asturian-American Migration Forum" and "Traces of Spain in the United States" illustrate.[5] Beyond the study of these complex transnational networks, scholars on both sides of the Atlantic have enriched our understanding of the multilayered Spanish immigrant experience by examining its social, cultural, and political dimensions, ranging from the development of an immigrant ethnic identity (Bunk 2016; Varela-Lago 2018), to participation in the international anarchist movement (Castañeda 2017; Sueiro Seoane 2017) and activism in support of the Republic during the Spanish Civil War and, later, against the dictatorship of General Francisco Franco (Feu-López 2016, Varela-Lago 2015).[6]

My current research exploits a relatively rare primary source—immigrants' personal notebooks—to analyze the Spanish immigrant experience in the United States. The set of three pocket-size notebooks I discuss in this essay belonged to José González, a Spaniard who migrated to Tampa in 1905. They are now housed in the Special Collections Department of the University of South Florida in Tampa.[7] Florida was one of the states that received a substantial influx of Spanish immigrants at the turn of the twentieth century. They came to work in the Clear Havana Cigar factories built primarily in Key West and Tampa as a result of the colonial wars in Cuba in the late nineteenth century. In Tampa, once considered the "cigar capital of the world," Spaniards joined Cubans and Italians to forge what Anglo-Americans dubbed the "Latin" enclaves of Ybor City and West Tampa. There, a thriving immigrant community supported by labor unions and mutual aid societies developed a rich cultural life manifested in an array of literary productions, including newspapers, theater plays, novels, and memoirs. (Dworkin y Méndez 2002; Mormino and Pozzetta 1987).

Tampa Latins have produced a number of immigrant narratives going back to 1897 when Cuban expatriate Wenceslao Galvez wrote his *Tampa: Impresiones de un emigrado.* In 1965, Angelo Massari, an immigrant from Sicily, authored his autobiography extending from the 1890s to the 1920s. Two years later José Yglesias published *The Good-Bye Land,* a moving autobiographical account of his return to Galicia, the land of his immigrant father who had died there in the 1920s when José was only a child. The tradition has continued with more recent publications by Ferdie Pacheco (1994), Jack Espinosa (2007), or Frank Urso (2005), among others. Many more memoirs probably lie unpublished in private family archives.

Immigrant narratives are a vital complement to equally useful but more impersonal sources (like census records or ship manifests) generated by the state or by companies the migrants may have dealt with in their journey. The lives of many immigrants do not make it into the pages of American newspapers or, for that matter, the immigrant press; another valuable source for historians of migration. But, as Xosé M. Núñez Seixas and Ruy Farias (2011) have indicated, immigrant biographies and memoirs, often written many years later, with the inevitable reframing –in some cases reinvention—of events, must be used with care.

Though personal notebooks offer no guarantee of historical accuracy, they do present a greater degree of immediacy than memoirs, for they were usually written near the time of the events they record. While they may be reflective, they tend to be less processed, and, to some degree, more authentic, in the sense that the authors may be less concerned with presenting themselves in a positive light, or pleasing a potential audience. These qualities make them particularly valuable as a source to study immigrants' lives. Jose González's notebooks served various purposes. They functioned as logbooks of earnings and expenses, including the sums he sent to his family in Spain. They also worked as address books, illuminating transnational networks that connected locations in Spain, Cuba, and the United States. In their pages, José jotted down notes, committed an errant thought to writing, or wrote a love poem to an unidentified young lady. The very diversity of these personal annotations offers a window into aspects of the immigrant experience seldom accessible through other sources.

The first challenge for the historian reading these notebooks is to determine the dates that frame them. Although the initial year marked in the text is 1905, the first entry summarizes events that took place over six years (from 1905, the year José left Spain, to 1911, when, due to a long strike in the Tampa cigar industry, he had relocated to Key West). Similarly, there are almost no entries for the years 1921 and 1922, and the few that exist seem to have been added later. Thus, most of the entries date from 1912 to 1920.

While the notebooks served as a combination of journal, account book, and address book, the journal occupies the most space. There are 630 entries from 1912 to 1920. With an average of six entries per month, yearly totals ranged from a minimum of 25 in 1913 to a maximum of 131 in 1917. The majority of the text is written in Spanish, but some sections are written in English. A few words and expressions appear in Italian (José was an opera buff) and others in Bable, the language spoken in the Spanish region of Asturias, where he hailed from. At this stage, one can only speculate as to what prompted José to start keeping a journal or what moved him to use different linguistic codes.

My research involves "recovering" this singular and little known source and studying it to broaden and deepen our understanding of the Spanish immigrant experience in the United States at the turn of the twentieth century. While this is part of a larger project, in the following pages I will briefly illustrate how the information in the notebooks in some cases complements what we know from other sources, but can also complicate and problematize a simple narrative of migration that is often reduced to dichotomies (push versus pull factors; rural versus urban environments; the immigrant "huddled masses" versus American middle-class comfort). In the interest of space, I will use excerpts from the notebooks to explore four aspects of José's experience: 1) the departure, 2) labor conditions in the United States, 3) community life, and 4) family and identity.

1) The departure

The very first entry in the notebook provides an account of José's journey from his native Asturias to Tampa. It reads:

> 1905. Salí de Luarca, mi pueblo natal, en Asturias, el 15 de N[oviem]bre de 1905, llegué a Coruña después de pasarme día y medio en la Caridad, la noche del 17 de No[viem]bre.
>
> Salí de la Coruña en el vapor Frankfort, hacia el 20 de No[viem]bre y llegamos a la Habana el 4 o el 5 de D[iciem]bre. Estuve en Triscornia 2 días y creo q[ue] el 8 salimos para New York en el Monterrey, no fuimos directos a Tampa a causa de la cuarentena que existía entre los dos puertos . . . Creo a los dos días llegamos a New York, aposentándonos en el Hotel América y al otro tomamos el tren para Tampa a la cual llegamos el 15 de D[iciem]bre de 1905.
>
> Me costó el viaje 853.30 pts o sea $170.66. Entré en la fabrica de José Lovera para aprender a rezagador, por mediación de mi primo Atilano con el cual vine de España, mas vista la poca remuneración que se hacía a mi trabajo . . . salí de allí y entré en Elinger, la cual se terminó como a los dos años y fui a terminar mi aprendizaje en La Rosa Española taller perteneciente, como Elinger, a la Havana American C°.

Elsewhere in the journal José wrote that he had been born in April 1891. Thus, he was fourteen and a half years old when he left his hometown to go to Tampa with his cousin.

This and other entries illustrate the conditions that encouraged, and the infrastructure that made possible, the migration of Spaniards (chiefly young single males) to the Americas at the time. They also show the relative ease with which these workers moved between Spain, Cuba, and the United States as part of a global labor market.

José made the trip from Luarca to the town of La Caridad, where his cousin lived. They then traveled to Coruña, in the neighboring region of Galicia, to board a German steamship that took them to Havana. Foreign shipping companies were prominent in the transportation of Spanish emigrants, particularly at the turn of the century, as Spain's navy and merchant marine were still hurting from the colonial disaster in Cuba and the Spanish-American war of 1898.

Despite the loss of Cuba, the Spanish migratory networks of the twentieth century were built upon the colonial geography that linked the peninsula to her former colonies. The Clear Havana Cigar industry in the United States is a prime example of the survival of these transnational colonial networks in the postcolonial world. Thus, even though they arrived at American shores, most Spanish immigrants were employed by firms either owned or managed by fellow Spaniards. In fact, in Florida, the establishment of the cigar factories in the late nineteenth century marked the beginning of the industrialization of an overwhelmingly rural and unpopulated state. When Spaniards Vicente Martínez Ybor and Ignacio Haya first visited the area in 1885, Tampa had fewer than a thousand residents, its population declining steadily since the Civil War. With the establishment of the cigar industry there the population boomed. By 1900, it had risen to 15,839 residents, a third of them foreign born. Of these, 16% had been born in Spain. By 1910, when José was already living in Tampa, Spaniards represented close to 27% of the foreign-born population in the city (Mormino and Pozzetta 43-62).

Why were emigrants leaving so young? They did so in part because of the opportunities that America offered, but also to avoid the military draft. Military service at that time lasted from three to seven years. Families could bail out their sons for a fee or pay a substitute to go in their stead. Both options required money that most working families lacked. It was cheaper to pay for the passage to America and hope that the expense would be offset by remittances sent by the emigrant as soon as he was able to earn a living. (Shubert 43-46, 174-176). It is interesting to note that José's father, a retired army officer, signed the consent affidavit granting him permission to emigrate.

José's journey, accompanied by his cousin; his entrance in the Lovera cigar factory a few days later as an apprentice; the remittances sent to Spain and carefully recorded in the account book, all illustrate the process of chain migration that contributed to building long-lasting transnational networks. Indeed, as was a common practice among immigrants elsewhere, a few years after his arrival, having secured some savings, José helped pay for the trip of two younger siblings: a sister in 1913 and a brother in 1916. In both cases, he provided emotional and financial support during his siblings' apprenticeship in the cigar factories, until they started working and became financially independent.

José's trip (whose cost was also recorded in the journal) illustrates another important aspect of the immigrant experience that has sometimes been misunderstood. Many of those leaving Europe to "make America" were not landless peasants or people on the lower rungs of the social scale. In fact, as migration historians have indicated, they "occupied positions somewhere in the middle and lower-middle levels of their social structures" (Bodnar 13). The truly needy, for the most part, stayed put or were involved in local migration in the homeland. As a Madrid newspaper remarked in 1900 on the massive emigration of Asturians to the Americas, whose jobs were taken up by Castilian peasants: "[los castellanos] se contentan con ganarse la vida, [los asturianos] quieren hacer un capital," which translates roughly as "Castilians are happy just making a living, Asturians want to get rich" ("Emigración").

Like other immigrants who arrived in Tampa at the turn of the twentieth century, José began working right away. The city itself was booming. As José started out on his trip from Luarca on November 15, 1905, Tampa was host to the first state fair in Florida. As the headline of the *Tampa Morning Tribune* announced, the festivities were meant to highlight the "state's era of prosperity." It is interesting to note that the program of events gave a prominent place to the immigrant community. The fair opened with a luncheon for the Governor and a number of city and state officials at the Gran Oriente, a restaurant owned by a Spanish immigrant, Manuel García. This was followed by a great parade that began in Ybor City and ended at the Courthouse where Governor Broward delivered his address. The banner on top of the masthead encouraged readers "Don't Fail to Visit Ybor City, the Havana of America. Largest Cigar Factories in the World; Dine in the Spanish Restaurants—See Life in the Cafes and Theaters" ("First").

José missed the state fair, but he arrived in Tampa right on time for the 50th anniversary of the city the following month, as the *Tampa Morning Tribune* called on the people of Tampa "to keep moving and move together." "Let every citizen get busy and keep busy" ("Semi-Centennial"). Although José probably could not read English at that time, he was ready for the message. This leads us to a second aspect of the immigrant experience covered by his notebooks.

2) Labor conditions in the United States

In the previous section we touched briefly on labor conditions in the cigar industry in Tampa at the turn of the twentieth century. A number of the cigar factories where immigrants went to work were either owned or managed by Spaniards. Labor was often secured through personal networks. José's cousin, Atilano, provided the connection that allowed José to immigrate to the United

States and start working as an apprentice in the factory of José Lovera, just a few days after his arrival. In the following paragraphs we get one more glimpse of how the industry worked:

> Estuve de aprendiz 3 años, tiempo estipulado por el gremio de reza-gadores para aprender dicho oficio. Fui operario en Julio 1º de 1909.
>
> Con motivo de un movimiento existente en pro de la organización de los obreros del ramo del tabaco, las fábricas arrojaron operarios a la calle para poner trabas por medio del hambre, al impulso de la organi-zación, a mi me tocó el embate el 25 de Junio de 1918 (Sic).
>
> Hubo una huelga enorme en la cual se paralizaron unos 10,000 obre-ros, durando 7 meses desde el 25 de Junio 1910 al 25 de Febrero de 1911.
>
> Cuando se terminó la huelga entré a trabajar en el taller de Regens-burg donde estuve desde últimos de Febrero hasta últimos de Junio de 1911. Salí de allí porque aflojó mucho la cosa y como es natural me des-pidieron.
>
> El jueves 21 de S[e]p[tiem]bre, salí para la Habana, donde arribé el sábado . . . estuve allí 3 días y luego volví a Key West, donde me encuentro, el martes 26 . . . viajé de Tampa a la Habana y de esta a Key West . . .
>
> . . . El miércoles 22 Nov[iem]bre salí del Cayo para Tampa . . . con trabajo para Monticello, Fla en unas escogidas de tabaco en rama (Sumatra).

The cigar industry had a rigorous system of apprenticeship monitored by the union, which in the case of the *rezagadores*, as José stated, lasted three years. The process of cigar making involved several steps once the tobacco reached the factory. High quality tobacco leaves would be used as wrappers, while leaves of lesser quality would be the fillers inside the cigar. *Mojadores* moistened the tobacco leaves to prepare them for the *despalilladoras*, women whose job was to remove the stem from the leaf. The wrapper leaves were then sent to the *rezagadores*, who sorted them according to size, shape, quality, and color, into the different grades of cigars manufactured in a given factory. The selected wrappers were then sent to the cigarmakers who rolled the cigar (Ingalls and Pérez 61-67).

The *rezagadores* were the highest skilled and best paid cigar workers in the factory, but completing the long apprenticeship did not guarantee employment. Following his three years of apprenticeship, José became an *operario* in July 1909. A year later, though, "una huelga enorme" left him unemployed. Strikes had defined immigrant life in Tampa since the beginning of the cigar industry. In the 1880s and 1890s some of these strikes were connected with the political disputes that fueled the colonial wars in Cuba. The very first strike in Ybor City happened shortly after its foundation, when Cuban cigarworkers protested Martinez Ybor's appointment of a *peninsular* bookkeeper in his factory (Mormino and Pozzetta 66).

The American occupation of Cuba consolidated a trend towards the monopolization of the tobacco industry. In 1899, cigar manufacturers centralized production under a new trust: the Havana-American Company. The subsequent increase in the manufacture of clear Havana cigars in the United States led to the rise of immigration to Florida, but it also had an impact on labor relations in the industry (Varela-Lago, "Conquerors" 138-144). After 1898, strikes in Tampa were no longer caused by colonial politics. Instead, they were a response to the perceived erosion of the cigarworkers' control over their craft as the new trust and the cigar manufacturers tried to transform the industry through "efficiency" methods of standardization and mechanization. José mentions a seven-month strike in 1910-1911. An even longer strike, lasting ten months, would take place in 1920.

The unusual length of the first journal entry (five pages) and its content (a record of events spanning six years) indicate that it was not actually written in 1905, but more likely towards the end of 1911, in Key West, where José had gone in the aftermath of the strike in Tampa. One wonders whether it was this displacement, and his impending move again from Key West to Monticello, in northern Florida, that prompted him to start writing an account of his life in the United States.

José did not write about what he did during those months of forced unemployment. But we know that when the strike ended he returned to the factory. This was short lived, though. Three months later, in June 1911, with no job prospect in Tampa, he began the peripatetic life of the members of what Patricia Ann Cooper dubbed "the travelling fraternity" (75). From Tampa, José left for a short trip to Havana, returning to Florida to settle in Key West where, unable to find work as a *rezagador*, he learned to roll cigars. In mid-November he received his first wages as a cigarmaker. After a few months in Key West, on Thanksgiving of 1911, he left for Monticello, on the other side of the state. There, on February 22, 1912, Washington's birthday, as he noted in his journal, he opened up a small cigar factory with other associates. He remained in Monticello for a few months and returned to Tampa on June 30, where his cousin found him a job as *rezagador*. On July 13, he wrote: "Hoy cobré sobre de rezagador, después de 12 meses de ausencia en el oficio."

Jotted notes in one of the notebooks indicate that José had joined the Cig-armakers International Union soon after he became *operario* in 1909, and he had been active in Local 493, which represented the *rezagadores*. The Local had disappeared in 1912 as a result of the 1910 strike. In 1913, José again became involved in the union, as secretary and treasurer of the *Unión de Rezagadores* and remained an active member of the union through the years covered by the journal. He was also involved in the Centro Asturiano, one of the five major mutual aid societies in Tampa.[8] In 1913, he was named "Vicepresidente de la Sección de Recreo y Adorno," and, in 1917, "presidente de la Sección de Instrucción."

3) Community life

Interspersed with the accounts of José's work life are also remarks about his social life. During his stay in Key West in 1911, for example, he wrote:

> Estuve el 21 de Octubre en el baile que dió la delegación de este Cayo (Centro Asturiano), donde me presentaron algunas jóvenes agra-dables entre otras Rosalía Harris, las Carrasco, Caridad, Adelina Dele-nay y otras.
>
> . . . El miércoles 22 Nov[iem]bre salí del Cayo para Tampa . . . con trabajo para Monticello, Fla en unas escogidas de tabaco en rama (Sumatra).
>
> Encontré a Rosalía [Harris] en Tampa y le hice una visita a su familia de la cual me despedí el sábado 25 Nov para tomar el tren del Seaboard Air Line con dirección a Monticello.

As a young single man, José spent much of his social life with fellow Span-ish-speaking immigrants, including young ladies. "La delegación" he refers to in this entry is the Key West branch of the powerful *Centro Asturiano de la Habana*. Asturian residents had founded this mutual aid society in Cuba in 1886. By 1902 a delegation had been established in Tampa. These transnational associations offered immigrants cradle-to-grave coverage with an array of ser-vices: libraries and night schools, dances and theatre performances, health care in their hospitals, and burial in their cemeteries (Mormino and Pozetta 175-205).

While José was a member of the Centro Asturiano, paying his monthly dues religiously as he moved from town to town in search of work, he also participat-ed in events organized by other mutual aid societies in Tampa. He was particu-larly fond of Italian Opera. On March 8, 1913, for example, he attended a performance of *Il Trovatore* represented by an Italian company in the theater of the *Centro Español*. The following day he returned to see *La Traviata*. As in Havana or Buenos Aires, immigrants in Tampa enjoyed a vibrant social and cultural life, nurtured not only by the major mutual aid societies but also by a mixture of smaller clubs and associations, including unions, lodges, and political, often anarchist, groups, as well as a thriving immigrant press that reported on local and international events.

While many immigrants had not enjoyed the benefit of schooling, they were well educated and informed about world events. This was in part a product of these clubs and associations, but it was also due to the benefits of the *lectura*, an institution that had been a staple of the Cuban cigar industry since the 1860s. Many Tampa factories had readers (*lectores*) who were paid by the workers to read to them while they sat at their table rolling cigars. The *lectura* was usually divided in four sections, each dedicated to a specific type of reading: national news, international politics, the labor press, and literature. The latter included classic novels by authors such as Emile Zola or Benito Pérez Galdós. (Mormino and Pozzetta 102; Tinajero 2007).

High rates of literacy contributed to this lively literary culture. They also made it possible for migrants to maintain frequent epistolary contact with family and friends overseas during the long years abroad. José recorded in several of his journal entries: "Escribí a España" or "Recibí carta de España." Despite the distance, it was not unusual for immigrants to return to Spain. José's journal is peppered with references to people travelling back and forth across the Ocean. I have selected just a few examples that illustrate some of the reasons for these trips.

Unemployment: "a causa de haber sido rebajado en Nov. 30 [Pelaez] se va para España (December 11, 1913).

Sickness of a close relative: "Piloña marchó para España a causa del cable en que le decían su padre estaba grave" (December 17, 1914).

Weddings: "Salió Anita Colado para España a casarse" (June 7, 1915).

These journeys to Spain usually lasted several months. José's own trip in 1917 would last close to a year. One might argue that some of the most illuminating sections in José's journal are his observations during his visit to the homeland after an absence of twelve years. The degree to which his stay in the United States had shaped his worldview became evident when a man of twenty-six now returned to the land he had left as a fourteen-year-old lad. In fact, this section offers one of the few instances in which José seems to be openly questioning his identity.

4) Family and identity

José began his trip on September 16, 1917 travelling from Tampa to New York, where he boarded a steamship to the Andalusian port of Cádiz. One of the first things that surprised him, when he arrived in Spain a couple of weeks later, was the preeminent role of the Catholic church. Of Cádiz, José wrote: "es una ciudad entregada al culto." And as he travelled north by train he remarked of the town of Marmolejo in Córdoba: "muchos curas."

After a short visit to his family in Asturias, José headed south to visit his paternal family in a village of Segovia, north of Madrid, for three weeks in the fall of 1917. The impression that rural Castile made on him can be seen at a glance by the increased length of his journal entries and his comments on the influence that the clergy held in the region. In one of the longest entries of the journal he details all the money priests received from the villagers for their services. José thought that the priests charged too much (and for too many things) to the peasants whose life was very difficult. He wrote:

> Las misas que se ofrecen por los q. están enfermos cuestan 4 pts más un real q. se da por cantar el Resurcesim Lazarus.
>
> Los entierros con misa y dos oficios cuestan 82 reales, más los responsos q. improvisa el Cura q. le dan cerca de una peseta cada uno. Aquí dice tres en el sepelio y dos de vuelta en la iglesia y luego los que dice en la misa, en fin una mina y los labradores sudando para ganar una perra. (November 10, 1917)

But José was also critical of the people for allowing this to happen. When he found out that a young woman he had met could not read or write, he commented: "Aquí se presta más atención a los curas que al maestro." (November 14, 1917) He also decried the hypocrisy of a culture where Catholic morality coexisted with premarital sex and pregnancy. As he wrote: "se reza con desusada frecuencia" and yet "son muchas las jóvenes que llevan en el vientre el fruto materno cuando se van a casar." (November 7, 1917).

The oppressive environment of rural Castile seemed to have provoked a sort of identity crisis in José who, despite being surrounded by relatives whose company he appeared to enjoy, felt increasingly alienated. Two weeks into his stay, for the first time in the years he kept his journal, he switched from Spanish to English. While this may have been a simple precaution to hide his comments from potential prying eyes, the rhetorical tone he employed indicates that this was not just a mere change of linguistic register. Written with a sense of empathy and yet the detachment more akin to a cultural anthropologist, the entry gives us a sense of the depth of this cultural distance:

> There is a familiar phrase among this people: 'Qué hacer' whose meaning is in some cases: 'certainly,' 'of course.'
>
> They don't care about wash[ing] their hands and face as they get up from bed, neither after work nor when they go to eat.
>
> They are healthy people and they live many years. What they eat it is composed generally of vegetables and corn. The wine they made from the grapes they harvested is a fine one and very nutritive.
>
> Queste dulce far niente non me piache (sic). I'm getting very tired of it. The bath over here is unknown at home. (November 14, 1917).

A week later José left Segovia and returned to Asturias. If we are right in considering José's use of English to be a way of coming to terms with the culture he lived in and belonged to –and a way of understanding it and dealing with his own sense of inadequacy—it is interesting to note that this period of adaptation took yet another month. He went back to writing in Spanish in January of 1918. By then he had decided to remain in Spain (in part because of the difficulties of travelling to the United States while the Great War was still raging in Europe) and he had enrolled in one of the best-known commercial schools in Oviedo, the Academia Ojanguren. The prestigious school was a magnet for many prospective emigrants to Cuba, where they were sought-after as recruits in industries and commercial enterprises in the island. In fact, some of the students José met at the Ojanguren academy in 1918 ended up in Tampa in 1921, when the Banco Internacional de Cuba in Havana, where they had found employment, went bankrupt. So, ironically, almost in a reprise of his first emigration, José was getting an education in Spain in order to further his opportunities in America.

While Oviedo presented a more dynamic urban environment than either rural Segovia or the small towns of Asturias, it left much to be desired for a person who had lived in Havana, Key West, or Tampa. On March 11, 1918 José wrote a lengthy entry where he expressed some of his views on the provincial capital. He thought that the city's customs, as well as its buildings and monuments, looked to the past. He saw few signs of progress. He described this graphically talking about city transportation (or the lack thereof): "Existe un solo tranvía tirado por tres caducas mulas que parece van a fenecer de un momento a otro." In his view, women in churches and men in cafes wasted too many "horas que pudieran diariamente rendir beneficios provechosos a la vida, aplicadas a las industrias y artes."

The army, clergy, and bureaucracy, he wrote, "tiende (sic) a enrarecer este ambiente y a formar más ineptos y odiadores de la actividad y el trabajo." With little industry to speak of, Oviedo became "esencialmente, un pueblo de desocupados y despreocupados." José was also disappointed by Spanish politics, ruled by a corrupt system of political bossism known as *caciquismo*, and what it meant in terms of lack of civic engagement. "Se adula y regala al votante en época de elecciones, y después de encumbrado, se desprecia y se hace mofa del que fué la causa del encumbramiento," he wrote. But he also remarked that: "un pueblo que vende su voto, no merece otro representante." He conceded that the social structure, not the people, were to blame, as these very same individuals, when transplanted to America "u otro pais, se abren camino y llevan a cabo obras que glorifican su nombre y son orgullo de la humanidad." (March 11, 1918).

With this outlook on conditions in Spain, it must have been difficult for José to consider staying in Asturias longer than he had originally planned. Indeed, five months after he entered the Ojanguren school, he was offered a job, but he declined, as he had decided to return to Tampa. At the beginning of the summer recess, in June 1918, José headed for Gijón, and in an interesting linguistic turn, as he had shifted to English when he was struggling with his identity in rural Castile, now that he prepared his trip to the United States, he wrote several short entries in English and one in Bable, the regional language of Asturias. José also enjoyed listening to family histories and he compiled a list of some of the peculiar expressions used by his grandfather and other relatives. As the date of his departure drew near José visited his maternal family in Luarca and joined in the festivities honoring the town's patron saint, San Timoteo, in August. He then returned to Oviedo for the feast of the Virgin of Covadonga at the beginning of September. When this cycle of ritual festivities was over he was ready to leave, his trip only delayed by the influenza pandemic that forced the suspension of sea travel for several weeks.

On October 22, 1918, José left Spain, and two weeks later he celebrated the end of World War I in Havana. On December 10, 1918 he returned to his work as *rezagador* in the factory of Sanchez and Haya. In the following months, the full entries that had run for several pages in Spain thinned as he reported briefly on his activities in the cigarmakers' union and in the Centro Asturiano during 1919 and 1920. In 1921 and 1922, the entries slowed to a trickle, with the last reference in the journal being in May of that year, a few months before his wedding.

This has been a short introduction to a remarkable primary source that deserves further study and analysis. Historians would need to look at other sources to recreate the full story of José González's life, but his years of faithful annotations and observations in his notebooks open a unique window into the experience of a migrant's journey as well as the broader transnational community of which he was a part. In some cases, these annotations reinforce what is already known from other sources, for example, about the importance of chain migration or the conditions migrants found in the host societies. In other cases, such as José's visit to Spain, they uncover the complex reality facing migrants returning to the homeland as they struggled with their identity and reexamined relations with relatives and friends. As José Gonzalez's notebooks illustrate, the intersection of social, economic, political, and cultural factors that shaped the experiences of migrants also affected those who "stayed behind." The recovery and study of personal documents such as these notebooks will help us complete the picture of this global movement that left few people untouched.

Works Cited

Alonso, Bieito. *Obreiros alén mar. Mariñeiros, fogoneiros e anarquistas galegos en New York*. A Nosa Terra, 2006.

Argeo, Luis. "Asturian West Virginia." *Goldenseal*, vol. 35, no. 3, Fall 2009, pp. 14-18.

AsturianUS. Directed by Luis Argeo. Neutral Density Films, 2006.

Bodnar, John. *The Transplanted. A History of Immigrants in Urban America*. Indiana University Press, 1985.

Borregueros: Aragoneses en el Oeste Americano. Directed by Carlos Tarazona Grasa, Bartolo Edizions, 2008.

Bunk, Brian. "Boxer in New York: Spaniards, Puerto Ricans, and Attempts to Construct a Hispano Race." *Journal of American Ethnic History*, vol. 35, no. 4, 2016, pp. 32-58.

Castañeda, Christopher J. "Times of Propaganda and Struggle. *El Despertar* and Brooklyn's Spanish Anarchists (1890-1905)." *Radical Gotham. Anarchism in New York City from Schwab's Saloon to Occupy Wall Street*, edited by Tom Goyens, University of Illinois Press, 2017, pp. 77-99.

Cooper, Patricia A. *Once a Cigarmaker. Men, Women, and Work Culture in American Factories, 1900-1919*. University of Illinois Press, 1987.

Dworkin y Méndez, Kenya C. "Cuban Theater, American Stage: Before Exile." *The State of Latino Theater in the United States*, edited by Luis A. Ramos-García, Routledge, 2002, pp. 103-130.

"Emigración." *El Imparcial*, 6 October 1900, p. 1.

Espinosa, Jack. *Cuban Bread Crumbs*. Xlibris, 2007.

Fernández, James D., and Luis Argeo. *Invisible Immigrants. Spaniards in the US (1868-1945)*. White Stone Ridge, 2014.

Feu-López, María Montserrat. "'Transatlantic Trenches' in Spanish Civil War Journalism. Félix Martí Ibáñez and the Exile Newspaper *España Libre* (Free Spain, New York City 1939-1977)." *Journal for the Study of Radicalism*, vol. 10, no. 2, Fall 2016, pp. 53-77.

"First Annual State Fair Opens Today; Tampa Gives Glad Welcome to Guests." *Tampa Morning Tribune*. 15 November 1905, p. 1.

Galvez, Wenceslao. *Tampa. Impresiones de un emigrado*. "Cuba," 1897.

García Hernandorena, María José. "Una aventura americana. Carletins als Estats Units d'Amèrica." *Carletins*, vol. 1, 2013, pp. 50-55.

Gómez, R. A. "Spanish Immigration to the United States." *The Americas*, vol. 19, July 1962, pp. 59-78.

González, Gavín W. *Pinnick Kinnick Hill. An American Story*. West Virginia University Press, 2003.

González, Suronda. "Forging Their Place in Appalachia: Spanish Immigrants in Spelter, West Virginia." *Journal of Appalachian Studies*, vol. 5, no. 2, 1999, pp. 197-206.

Hidalgo, Thomas. "En las Montañas. Spaniards in Southern West Virginia." *Goldenseal*, vol. 27, no. 4, Winter 2001, pp. 52-59.

Ingalls, Robert P., and Louis A. Pérez, Jr. *Tampa Cigar Workers*. University Press of Florida, 2003.

López, Gloria. *An American Paella*. Autry Lopez, 2007.

Martinelli, Phylis Cancilla, and Ana Varela-Lago, editors, *Hidden Out in the Open: Spanish Migration to the United States (1875-1930)*. University Press of Colorado, 2018.

Massari, Angelo. *The Wonderful Life of Angelo Massari*. Exposition Press, 1965.

Mormino, Gary R., and George E. Pozzetta. *The Immigrant World of Ybor City. Italians and Their Latin Neighbors in Tampa, 1885-1985*. University of Illinois Press, 1987.

Morell Moll, Teresa. *Valencians a Nova York. El cas de la marina Alta (1912-1920)*, Edicions 96, 2012.

Morrió, Enric. "Binillobers als Estats Units d'Amèrica." *Alberri*, vol. 24, 2014, pp. 213-261.

Nishimuta, Juli Ann. *The Nishimutas: An Oral History of a Japanese and Spanish Family*. iUniverse, 2006.

Núñez Seixas, Xosé M., and Ruy Farias. "Las autobiografías de los inmigrantes gallegos en la Argentina (1860-2000): testimonios, ficción y experiencia." *Migraciones y Exilios*, vol. 11, 2011, pp. 57-80.

Oural, José R. *Oural: The name, the family, and the story as I remember*, 2002.

Pacheco, Ferdie. *Ybor City Chronicles. A Memoir.* University Press of Florida, 1994.

Pérez Rey, Nancy. "Unha achega á emigración galega a Nova York." *Estudos Migratorios*, vol. 1, no. 2, 2008, pp. 31-61.

Rueda, Germán. *La emigración contemporánea de españoles a Estados Unidos. De "dons" a "misters."* Mapfre, 1993.

"Semi-Centennial of the City of Tampa; 50 Years Old Today." *Tampa Morning Tribune.* 15 December 1905, p. 1.

Shubert, Adrian. *A Social History of Modern Spain.* Unwin Hyman, 1990.

Steele, Patricia Ruiz. *The Girl Immigrant.* Plumería, 2013.

___. *Silván Leaves*, Plumería, 2014.

Sueiro Seoane, Susana. "Anarquistas españoles en Estados Unidos: Pedro Esteve y el periódico *El Despertar* de Nueva York (1891-1902). *North America and Spain: Transversal Perspectives (Norteamérica y España: Perspectivas Transversales*), edited by Julio Cañero, Escribana Books, 2017, pp. 76-86.

Tarazona Grasa, Carlos. *Borregueros: Desde Aragón al Oeste Americano.* Barbastro, 2017.

Tinajero, Araceli. *El lector de tabaquería: Historia de una tradición cubana.* Verbum, 2007.

Urso, Frank. *A Stranger in the Barrio. Memoir of a Tampa Sicilian.* iUniverse, 2005.

Varela-Lago, Ana M. "Conquerors, Immigrants, Exiles: The Spanish Diaspora in the United States (1848-1948)." Dissertation, University of California San Diego, 2008.

___. "A emigración galega aos Estados Unidos: Galegos en Louisiana, Florida e Nova York (1870-1940)." *Estudos Migratorios,* vol. 1, no. 2, 2008, pp. 63-84.

___. "From Migrants to Exiles: The Spanish Civil War and the Spanish Immigrant Communities in the United States." *Camino Real. Estudios de las Hispanidades Norteamericanas*, vol. 7, no. 10, 2015, pp. 111-128.

___. "Working in America and Living in Spain: The Making of Transnational Communities among Spanish Immigrants in the United States." *Hidden Out in the Open. Spanish Migration to the United States (1875-1930),* edited by Phylis Cancilla Martinelli and Ana Varela-Lago, University Press of Colorado, 2018, pp. 21-65.

Yglesias, José. *The Good-Bye Land.* Pantheon, 1967.

Endnotes

[1]The Immigration Act of 1921 set the annual national quotas for immigrants of the Eastern Hemisphere at 3 percent of the foreign-born population of each nationality residing in the United States in 1910. The Immigration Act of 1924 set the quotas at 2 percent of each nationality residing in the country in 1890. The Spanish quota went from 912 in 1921 to 131 in 1924.

[2]Juli Esteve has also produced several documentaries on this migration in a series entitled *Del Montgó a Manhattan. Valencians a Nova York.*

[3]A complete catalogue of the Center's publications is available at https://www.unr.edu/basque-studies/cbs-press

[4]This is a small selection, in chronological order, of works published in the past two decades: Oural 2002, González 2003, Nishimuta 2006, López 2007, and Steele 2013, 2014.

[5]Asturian-American Migration Forum (www.asturianus.org); Traces of Spain in the United States (tracesofspainintheus.org). The latter project has also led to the publication of a book (Fenández and Argeo 2014).

[6]See also the chapters in Martinelli and Varela-Lago 2018.

[7]I thank the USF Library Special Collections for facilitating my research on this collection.

[8]Besides the Spanish clubs—Centro Español and Centro Asturiano—Tampa also housed the Círculo Cubano, La Unión Martí-Maceo (the Afro-Cuban mutual aid society), and L'Unione Italiana.

Part 4: Jorge Ainslie Writes Immigraton: Methodologic and Analytic Approaches to Literary and Periodical Representation

The more recent publication of a good number of other late nineteenth- or early twentieth-century texts will no doubt also continue to generate critical assessments and reassessments within the fields of Chicano/a – Latino/a history and literature. The Recovery Program has fomented, nurtured and made possible this critical dialogue . . .

—Rosaura Sánchez

Critical Translation: The Politics and Writings of Jorge Ainslie

JOSÉ F. ARANDA, JR.
Rice University

After 1848, the Spanish-language press of what became the Southwest and West of the United States forged an unusual role of social advocacy for its readership. Fully aware of the complicated terrain it navigated, it spoke for a readership that was at once desired by its editors, writers, printers, and hawkers, as well as simultaneously disparaged, disregarded, and ignored by the larger body politic of the United States. To be sure, the imagined community of the Spanish- language press was fragile, fleeting, and located narrowly in specific places. And yet, from San Antonio to San Francisco from Brownsville to Chicago, the press thrived in spite of spaces of contradictory possibility. One of the most pressing challenges for any of these presses was to chronicle and protest the political, economic and discriminatory practices that targeted their readership, while also advocating for a life of culture, philosophy, and the arts for its readers.

This essay argues for the critical importance of early twentieth century writer Jorge Ainslie and his writings by tracing his life from his activities during the Mexican Revolution, to his transformation as an exiled immigrant in Los Angeles, and finally to his emergence as a major literary voice for "el México de afuera."[1] Following the seminal work of Nicolás Kanellos on the Spanish- language press of the United States, I argue that the print presence of Hispanic writers, especially during moments of national and hemispheric crisis, offers unique opportunities to analyze how newspapers effected social and political culture well beyond reporting the "news."[2] Jorge Ainslie is a prime example of a writer totally immersed in the political unconscious of his generation, and as a such, his writings underscore an underappreciated feature of the Spanish-language press in the United States: its role as translator and its varied acts of translation. Because of its peculiar relationship to the nation-state, the Spanish-language press of the United States acquired an institutional-like responsibility to interpret and communicate the social, cultural, political, and economic realities that conditioned the communities of readers they were attempting simultaneously to forge, represent and serve. For Laura Lomas, acts of translation "emerge. . . specifically to counteract the silencing, erasure, ignorance, or animosity that often increases friction and violence at the boundaries of colonial languages (152)."[3] Though clearly not always anti-colonial and not always performing classic notions of translation, the Spanish-language press of the United States, I would argue, invested itself, locally and regionally, with a similar "sustained critical interpretation of the dominant culture" (152) Lomas has come to identify with José Martí and his anti-colonial work through translation.

Indeed, the Spanish-language press, after 1848, was arguably the only institution remaining in the previous northern territories of Mexico that could offer any kind of report, commentary, analysis, critique, or outright opposition to the ongoing implementation of "Manifest Destiny" in government, the courts, politics, culture, and language. Ironically, the Spanish-language press could do so because it was better protected under the First Amendment of the US Constitution than former Mexican citizens under the Treaty of Guadalupe Hidalgo. In this context, the Spanish-language press became the only viable center of knowledge production for former Mexican citizens and future Mexican immigrants alike (see Kanellos).

Much of that knowledge production, I will emphasize, became invariably tied to translation. By translation, I mean the process through which the Spanish- language press strove to make legible to its readership the nature of the new epistemological and ontological world order. The Anglo American seizure of territories and the subsequent introduction of a new settler colonial logic disrupted a Spanish coloniality that had begun in earnest almost three centuries before. At first, the Spanish-language press produced acts of translation that chronicled the abrupt post-1848 political, economic, and cultural regime change. But as the changed circumstances of social life became the new norm, the press reported and assessed the different and contradictory phases of laws and policy that would effect people of Mexican descent, whether they were long settled or recently immigrated. Later still, this same press would be equal parts challenged but invigorated by the Mexican Revolution, making the case for the revolution as it evolved, as well as the case for the idea and potency of "el Mexico de afuera." Reinvigorated by revolution, the press would come to name and promote the idea of a true nation in exile. It saw itself as able to counter the excesses and confusions caused by civil war. And eventually from those exiled in the United States, Mexico's modern renewal would come at the hands of those who returned.

Along the way of this critical moment, however, the Spanish-language press forged a readership that would not return. Instead, its readership stayed and joined other readerships from older Spanish-Native-Mexican communities that experienced first-hand the border change in 1848. Because of the historic need to represent these diverse but linked communities, the Spanish-language press, we can now observe more clearly in retrospect, acted in the capacity of what I call an "institutional" translator for its readers. For better and worse, the press was the only institutional center that recognized the value of individuals and communities of Mexican descent. Significantly, the press would become an institution whose own continuity created legitimacy among communities of Mexican descent rarely found elsewhere.

I have two goals in this essay. First, I make the case why Mexican national and immigrant to the United States, Jorge Ainslie, deserves the critical focus placed on early Mexican American writers like María Amparo Ruiz de Burton, María Cristina Mena, Jovita González, and Daniel Venegas. Second, I make the case that the acts of translation after 1848 in the United States offers a glimpse into a much larger theoretical argument about the production of knowledge and the arts by communities whose members exhibit very uneven relationships to settler coloniality and nation state ideologies. After 1848, people of Mexican origin would come to understand themselves along a spectrum of settler identities: colonizer, colonized, and everything in-between. Such a range of subjectivities required what I see as "translation" to account for a new and evolving set of literacies that accompanied Anglo American modernity/coloniality. Walter Mignolo uses the concept of "conflict of literacies" (309) to characterize the creole and hybrid communities that emerged in the years immediately after Spanish European contact with indigenous societies in specific geographic locations and through print culture. I argue that an analogue of those earlier "confict of literacies" can be found in the wake of the Mexican American War and in the evolving collisions between competing colonialisms in the former territories of Mexico. These post-1848 conflicts of literacies, I argue, have had a tremendous influence in the print cultures that have developed since then.

Jorge Ainslie's writings quite clearly takes up latter day examples of "conflicts of literacies" common to Mexican immigrants of the 1930s. Nationality, national loyalty, citizenship, gender politics, language, and labor issues all come to a crisis for a generation of Mexican immigrants dissatisfied and alarmed with what they see in "Mexican" children born and raised in the United States. By writing toward this crisis, and calling attention to the need to interpret the character of "Mexican" children born in the United States, Ainslie consolidates into a literary work a "conflicts of literacies" that is geographically, ideologically, and discursively pervasive along the borderlands of the United States and Mexico, and points further south. In what follows, I unpack the significance of Ainslie's writing on the figure of the "pocho," as well as argue that the institutional role the Spanish- language press as translator constitutes a specific field of intervention I identify as critical translation.

Part I

Long before becoming a popular writer for *La Prensa,* Jorge Ainslie fled/immigrated to the United States during the Mexican Revolution. Like many of his class and education, immigrant life in the United States made unexpected demands, forcing him to make a living in a variety of ways, from laborer to restaurant owner to real estate agent to publishing and editing a magazine and finally fiction writer for the Lozano newspapers.[4] Immigration records establish that he was born in Hermosillo, Sonora, Mexico on July 12, 1888.[5] He was the son of Alejandro D. Ainslie and Manuela Andalsol de Ainslie who immigrated to San Francisco around 1918. There in San Francisco, the father Alejandro D. Ainslie becomes "Director" of a weekly newspaper, *Hispano America,* which he edited until his death two years later.[6] Alejandro Ainslie had also been an editor and writer in Sonora prior to immigrating.[7] Some time after his death, his son, Leopoldo Ainslie, appears working at the Los Angeles newspaper, *El Heraldo de Mexico,* where eventually both his sister, Lily, appears in notices, as does Jorge Ainslie. One notice directly links him to other *El Heraldo de Mexico* writers, like Luis Alvear V and Rafael Ybarra; another links him to Leo P. Hubert, the husband of Lily Ainslie, as they both travel to San Francisco for business interests and to visit family. In all, Jorge Ainslie in one way or another is connected to two Spanish-language newspapers well before appearing in the pages *La Prensa* of San Antonio, Texas, as a fiction writer.[8] In fact, *Hispano America* publishes a notice of his entry to the United States on June 23, 1918, in the company of "su esposa señora Adelaida Taboada de Ainslie y el señor Leopoldo Ainslie" (p. 5). Though a common practice enough to publish these kind of notices at the time, such notices set up biographically not only Jorge Ainslie's familial relationship to the Spanish-language press, but also the social and cultural landscape that the press provided for its readers. It will be the Spanish-language press that also publishes, for the last time, another notice, this one of Ainslie's untimely death on October 24, 1938.[9]

Although *La Prensa* identifies Jorge Ainslie as a long time editor of the Lozano newspapers (2-27-1938, p. 8), he becomes best known to its readers in a span of just over three years, between April 1934 and January 1938. In this period, he publishes three novels, one novella, over twenty short stories, and three memoirs, each fictionalized to different degrees.[10] Altogether, his writings cover a range of issues, events, and topics, from the Mexican Revolution and immigrant life in the United States, to more common melodramatic love stories, to tales of mystery and the unknown. Perhaps because of his growing popularity in the press, Ainslie also appears as a major source in someone else's article. In "El Herrero Con Asador De Palo: Como Vivien Los Mexicanos De Simons, Calif," by Rafael Ybarra and Carlos Amezcua, Ainslie appears as an informant to an exposé of the brick factory town in Simons, California, where he once owned a restaurant, catering to the Mexican immigrant labor force that toiled under the oppressive control of the factory owners (11-29-36, p. 25). Interestingly, the history of this brick factory and the Mexican barrio that grew around the factory will become the basis of the well-known 1988 Chicano novel, *The Brick People,* by Alejandro Morales. The only other time Ainslie appears in *La Prensa* is in 1946, when one last short story is attributed to him.

Like his better-known contemporary in Mexican literary circles, Teodoro Torres Jr., Ainslie was similarly invested in exposing the real life travails of Mexican life in the United States, as well as in promoting the voluntary repatriation of Mexican nationals to Mexico. The years 1934 and 1935 represent a heightened awareness in the pages of *La Prensa* on the topic of repatriation. The forced, xenophobic expulsion of Mexican and Mexican Americans from the United States were routinely covered. It also reported on the Mexican government's attempts to colonize its northern territories by offering Mexican immigrants in the United States land they could farm.[11] It is in this volatile social and political context that Ainslie makes a name for himself in *La Prensa.* Like Torres' 1935 *La Patria Perdida,* Ainslie's serialized novels, *Los Pochos* (1934) and its sequel *Los Repatriados* (1935), capture the concerns, fears, and hopes for the Mexican immigrant community in the United States that were commonplace on either side of the border during the Great Depression.[12] But unlike Torres' novel that was initially published in Mexico and only much later serialized in *La Prensa* in 1942, Ainslie seems to have found an immediate, if complex, audience among the readers of *La Prensa* (and one suspects the other Lozano publication, *La Opinion,* in Los Angeles as well).

In both novels, *Los Pochos* and *Los Repatriados,* Ainslie clearly aims to narrate in a literary manner; he employs plots and sub-plots; his characters show psychological depth, and his narrators contribute to the overall gestalt of the novels. And because he draws from his own personal experience of the Mexican Revolution and his travails as an Mexican immigrant in the United States, his representations of immigrant life are filtered through a complex prism of competing Mexican and US modernities. All the same, through the medium of *La Prensa,* he theorizes immigrant life in the US as a mode of critical translation. The lives and experiences of Mexican immigrants become an analytic lens by which to make sense of their historic moment and the ideologies that shape their communities. In taking up that analysis and communicating it, Ainslie's writing behaves more like a translation than a straightforward literary text. Ainslie's concern with translation represents an important aspect of the cultural work of literature in the Spanish-language press.

In my view, translation of a fraught social reality becomes, for Ainslie, a transactional, writerly method. This method invites "lectores," readers, into a mode of critical reading that is sensitive to the dynamic exchanges of local and regional historical contests, whose origins are traceable to the intersection of modernity with coloniality. Ainslie is not writing social realism for simple consumption; his readers are his characters, and vice versa. Fiction and non-fiction writing intertwine here precisely for the sake of training readers in analyses, critiques, and arguments. For this reason, issues and tropes of translation, including a range of didactic strategies, are constantly forwarded in attempts to highlight the unique nature of immigrant life, its painful limits, but also its epistemological and ontological possibilities. In the narrative social landscape that Ainslie and *La Prensa* construct, one finds examples of what Walter Mignolo calls "colonial difference," a space where local histories with global designs become visible.[13] In the context of the Spanish-language press, when such a space becomes visible, a critical field of translation over conflicted literacies emerges actively vying for the attention of the newspaper reader.

The Spanish-language press in this period, and perhaps for much of its existence in the United States, exhibits the kind of conflict over semiotic systems that Mignolo identifies for the colonial period:

> Writing and recorded knowledge in colonial America, at least in areas with strong written traditions, became a battlefield, a complex system of interactions and transformations both of writing systems and of sign carriers. The complexities of the history of writing in the colonial period impinged not only on the writing systems themselves, but on the materiality of reading and writing cultures as well (308-309).[14]

Without calling it such, Mignolo's above assessment, like much of the work in the same collection where his essay appears, describes a transactional phenomenon typically associated with translation. When Mignolo refers to the ample evidence that indigenous writing systems did not simply disappear with the appearance of the administrative language of the conquering Spaniards in the 1500s, nor did this administrative Spanish remain pure, free from the influence of indigenous writing systems and sign carriers, he is in fact describing the effects and after lives of translation.

The intensity of colonial conflict as measured through "writing systems and sign carriers" is also on display in André Lefevere's *Translating Literature: Practice and Theory in a Comparative Literature Context* (1992). Renewed contemporary attention to translation studies, he argues, comes at a historic moment when global processes are bringing cultures and literatures in ever increasing proximity to one another. Here, Lefevere argues that "translation is acculturation" (12), that is "a process of negotiation between two cultures" (11). For Lefevere, translation is more accurately described as rewriting, one byproduct of negotiation between two cultures: "Rewriting therefore exerts enormous influence not only on the image one literature is given of another but also on the image members of a culture are given of their own and other literatures. It is the hidden motor behind literary evolutions and the creation of canons and paradigms" (14). For Lefevere, translation as rewriting plays a role in the canonicity of any literary work: " If a work of literature is not rewritten in one way or another, it is not likely to survive its date of publication by many years or even many months" (14). Survival of a literary work is both local and global, and thus translation, we can extrapolate, is one of those processes of modernity that also contributes to a world system.

Lefevere's equation of translation with acculturation, and canonicity as an evolving legacy of negotiations between cultures, brings us intriguingly close to what Cuban anthropologist, Fernando Ortiz, argued as "transculturation," a transactional phenomenon between cultures but one underwritten heavily by colonialism.[15] For Lefevere, the stakes for translation are high in the current global moment:

> If translation is acculturation, the phenomenon can be approached from two angles that can be complementary but do not have to be. Translation can teach us about the wider problem of acculturation, the relation among different cultures that is becoming increasingly important for the survival of our planet, and former attempts at acculturation-translation can teach us about translation. Studies in literary translation focus of necessity on literature and on the evolution and interpretation of literatures as part of the wider area of acculturation. (12)

Laura Lomas points to such a "wider area of acculturation" when she argues for the translational turn in cultural studies that Oritz's theory of transculturation and literary and cultural productions of the Caribbean in general have contributed over the decades. Lomas writes:

> As we pursue the implications of cultural and linguistic interaction in contact zones or in borderlands of empire such as the Caribbean, I propose we attend to innovative translators, poets, and theorists of the hispanophone Caribbean diaspora who articulate in- between subjectivity, bilingual poetic forms, and the constant work of cultural translation that characterizes Hispanic Caribbean New York. (148)

By carefully tracing how Oritz's work influenced Mary Louise Pratt's concept of the "contact zone," which in turn influenced Emily Apter's "translation zone," coupled with a Caribbean critical tradition focused on the "postcolonial 'talking back' to empire" (149), Lomas treats translation as a critical field where the languages of empire seek to "subjugate the languages of subject populations, but these minoritized languages do not disappear" (151). Instead, they resist, and precisely because of their diversity, these languages form a bulwark against empire (151). Most importantly, Lomas insists: "hybrid Caribbean forms [of language challenge] translation studies to grapple with and tentatively express languages in a constant process of 'becoming' rather than assuming that translation might express a fixed state of 'Being' (151)."

Taken holistically, retrospectively, and in view of Annibal Quijano and Immanuel Wallerstein writing on the first world-system made possible by modernity, coloniality, and the rise of capitalism, one can see how Lomas's tension between "becoming" and "being" also illuminates the emergence of the press in the Américas.[16] It was precisely set up to continue the processes of empire that began in the colonial period, and as well as processes Ortiz calls acculturation, and Lefevere calls acculturation and rewriting. Altogether these processes were set up to install, mirror, and maintain the coloniality of power of the first world-system. They also invariably installed the possibility of local subversion, radical thought, and acts of colonial difference through the pages of the press and in the reception of its pedagogies. The symbolic, societal, and material manifestations of translation in settler colonial geographies are not only expressions of what Quijano calls coloniality of power. [17] They illustrate the ongoing "conflict of literacies" in the Américas, and elsewhere. I would argue that a critical field of translation emerges precisely out of the very same nation-building processes that made use of and transformed the vestiges of indigenous writings systems and sign carriers. Mignolo writes: "While writing in colonial situations staged a conflict of literacies, writing in neocolonial situations became the decisive victory of Western literacy and of the languages of the colonizers as the languages of the new and emergent national-building processes" (309). For Mignolo, these processes culminated in a precise moment:

> [A]ncient writing systems became the treasure trove of and a commodity for travelers and businessmen for whom the economic expansion of their countries allowed a transformation of cultural legacies into exotic commodities. As a consequence, writing in colonial and postcolonial situations requires, more than a grammatology, theories of materiality of reading and writing cultures and their relevance to understanding colonial expansion and ideologies of expansion.

Critical translation is offered here as an instance of "theories of materiality of reading and writing cultures." Critical translation has underwritten and sustained the logic of the Spanish-language press in the Américas in general, especially after the American and Haitian revolutions, but in particular the Spanish-language press that has evolved in what became in the United States since the nineteenth century.

However, one major caveat needs to be recognized. If Benedict Anderson's thesis for the role of the press in nation-building processes generally holds true for Western nations, it falters for sure in settler colonial situations, but significantly, it nearly collapses entirely in the context of Spanish-language press in the United States, where it and its readers have existed outside of the realm of the nation-state for most of its history.[18] For people of US Mexican descent, it is the Civil Rights Movement, and the Chicana/o Movement in particular, that inaugurates a national discourse on their historical presence as a community. Up to then, since 1848, writing by Mexican Americans was largely written, published, and received in local and regional contexts. Although this writing was hardly parochial—national and international subjects were often entertained—its production and reception was never nationally recognized as meaningful for the nation state. Despite a coherent national identity, people wrote nonetheless, producing a complex and enduring print culture.

All the same, precisely because of its contradictory allegiance to discursive and material forms that are Eurocentric in origin (European languages, print technologies, and circuits of information) but also dependent on creating, maintaining, and developing readers from local or trans-local settler colonial situations, the Spanish-language press in the United States was uniquely and historically situated. It was obliged by local needs to enact a critical field of translation in order to legitimize its very existence. Hence, one can observe in the evolution of its print cultures a discursive space where it modulates between expressions of imperial difference and colonial difference. Imperial difference treats Eurocentric epistemologies and ontologies as redeemable through critique. Colonial difference does not: it questions the universality of Eurocentric epistemologies and ontologies and seeks from local histories more than critique. It seeks de- colonial strategies to undo the darker, more oppressive effects of modernity and coloniality.[19] The history of the Spanish-language press and the presence of its archives reveal themselves as an evolving critical site. Critical translation enacts what Mignolo has identified as a contest over literacies in the colonial period, "a battlefield, a complex system of interactions and transformations both of writing systems and of sign carriers." At times of severe crisis, the press becomes a site for de-colonial knowledge production, even with its Eurocentric affinities and settler colonial attributes.

Part II

No where is this discursive battlefield more in play as in the years of the Mexican Revolution when the whole idea of Mexico as a nation is suspended not only between warring factions but also with those "Mexicans" who fled/immigrated to the United States. Once across the border, they were hailed as part of "el Mexico de afuera" by a Spanish-language press newly installed by members of that very same displaced peoples. In his writings, Ainslie produces his own version of this "battlefield." In *Los Pochos* for example, Ainslie vividly portrays the departure of his protagonists, taking time to detail his characters own fears and horrors of the realities of war, hunger, and displacement. Fleeing the ravages of war is clearly the precursor to his characters' crossing over, but importantly and symbolically, it is the birth of their children in the United States that anchors the meaning and social construction of the term, pocho.[20] Though primarily used to identify pejoratively anyone of Mexican descent born in the

United States, it is used to identify someone who is less than "Mexican," some-one who is Americanized, someone who speaks an Anglicized version of Span-ish, and someone who has little or no appreciation for Mexican culture, tradi-tions, and history. In short, the idea of, as well as the actual word, pocho, becomes the active site of translation for the novel as a whole.

By 1934, Jorge Ainslie had joined many other writers to chronicle and rep-resent the trials and tribulations of Mexican immigration to the United States. Like Daniel Venegas' novel, *Las Aventuras de Don Chipote, O Cuando Los Peri-cos Mamen* (1928), before, Ainslie's *Los Pochos* was clearly written to be under-stood as an anti-immigration novel. Like the *La Prensa* in general, Ainslie par-ticipated in the concept of a viable exiled and/or expatriate Mexican community in the United States—"el Mexico de afuera," "la patria chica"—in order to exhort paisanos, fellow countrymen, to return to Mexico. Thus, Mexico appears in *Los Pochos* in two basic ways: as the broken economic, cultural, political, and social landscape of a country at war with itself; and from the perspective of the dissat-isfied first-generation immigrant, as the memory and repository of what it means to be Mexican, including all its gendered, class, and racial hierarchies. In this context and from the vantage point of its promotion as "novela Mexicana," *Los Pochos* supports and/or celebrates the idea that a "Mexico" exists south of the US border. What Ainslie critically unpacks and translates from a wealth of personal and communal anecdotal evidence in his anti-immigration novel, and in concert with the editorial aims of the press, is the actual experiences of immigrants for whom Mexicanness devolves disgracefully, and especially shamefully in second-generation children, hence the title of the novel.

This perspective is more or less the cultural and political context that news-papers, like *La Prensa,* drew from in shaping the pejorative discourse on the fig-ure of the "pocho" in the United States and Mexico. It is this discourse that is in fact present, but in English, in José Villarreal's ground-breaking novel, *Pocho* (1959). Though this text is roundly regarded in Chicana/o literary studies as the first "Chicano" novel, it is decidedly not the first novelistic attempt to portray "el pocho." That distinction, for the moment, belongs to Mexican writer, Jorge Ainslie, who wrote *Los Pochos,* a serialized novel, with illustrations by Enrique de la Peña, for the Lozano family newspapers in the United States, and which first appeared in *La Prensa,* San Antonio, Texas on April 22, 1934. Like Villar-real's novel, Ainslie writes a story that begins in Mexico during the revolution, focused on a male protagonist that must flee to the United States in order to secure a better life. But unlike the Villista revolutionary, Juan Manuel Rubio, Ainslie's Féderico Godínez, aspires to a middle class life as a government bureaucrat or manager of some business, and in fact his departure to the US is hastened by the imminent arrival of Villa's troops in the town of Santa Rosalia, Chihuahua. Like Rubio though, Godínez commits a crime that also hastens his departure. Afraid that he will lose everything once the Villistas take control of the town, he steals the timber company's cashbox where he works. Once he crosses into El Paso, he's not alone like Rubio, who gunned down someone who disrespected him, but in fact Godínez travels with his pregnant wife, María, and it is in El Paso that she gives birth to a daughter.

Though *Los Pochos* is in actuality about many things affecting the lives of Mexican nationals living in the United States in the 1930s, making the case repeatedly about the need for the Godínez family to return to Mexico, it is the birth of the children in the United States, Virginia, and later her brother, José, that anchors this novel as an anti-US immigration text. The novel firmly espouses the idea that US-born children of Mexican parents have no better recourse than to be repatriated to Mexico. As an anti-immigration text, *Los Pochos* has much in common with Daniel Venegas' *Las Aventuras de Don Chipote.* As in *Las Aventuras de Don Chipote,* Godínez's first memorable experiences of "el otra lado" are in El Paso. But unlike Don Chipote who is motivated by his extreme poverty and his family's hunger, Ainslie spends no time detailing the rigors of the actual border crossing. Whereas the reader witnesses the humiliation Don Chipote is forced to suffer when his body and clothes were disinfected by US border agents, because Godínez has stolen money, over thirty-two thousand pesos we come to learn, he is able to purchase train tickets, food, and comfort in order to cross the border. While *Las Aventuras de Don Chipote* is a parodic text, comically portraying Don Chipote as a latter-day, bumbling Don Quixote, with a stray dog as his Sancho Panza, written for a middle-class readership, *Los Pochos* is also clearly written toward the middle-class readership of *La Prensa* of the early 1930s, but its more dramatic 'novel of manners' style allows for a more complex and ultimately uneven reckoning of ethical and moral accountability. Whereas the reader is meant to excuse Don Chipote's greenhorn tribulations because of his country bumpkin ways and lack of education, Godínez's education and penchant for rationalizing his mistakes, especially when as a greenhorn in the United States he is duped out of his money after one failed business venture after another, the reader is nonetheless encouraged to have a sentimental regard for an otherwise foolish character.

In this regard, Don Chipote and Godínez are the same foolish character, but from very different class background, with different economic goals. Don Chipote has heard that the streets of the United States are paved with bricks of gold; he wants to live the life of leisure of the elite. Godínez feels he must flee the political uncertainty of Mexico in order to continue to aspire to a middle class life of the well-educated intelligensia. There is leisure in Godínez's aspirations, but it has to do more with social status and long life security from violence. In this respect, Godínez has much in common with Américo Paredes' Gumercindo Gómez in *George Washington Gómez (1930s, 1990),* who also flees from the violence of the revolution, if only to fall victim to the violence of the Texas Rangers. Nonetheless, although held to a promise he made to a dying Gumercindo, Feliciano, the brother-in-law, believes him to be a foolish man, unschooled in the ways of the border. While Villarreal's Juan Rubio is decidedly written not to appear foolish like Godínez or Don Chipote—here he has much in common with Feliciano—he nonetheless becomes foolish the longer he remains in the United States as a reluctant immigrant. The more his patriarchal authority is questioned and undermined, the more Rubio becomes rigid, author-itarian, and violent, not unlike Jovita Gonzalez's and Eve Raleigh's Don Santi-ago in *Caballero* (1939, 1996). Like Rubio, who is pushed out by his family well before the end of the novel, Godínez and his wife María, reluctant immi-grants as well, are also unable to assert their combined patriarchal and matriar-chal authorities over their children as Mexican parents. Once they become of age and earn money, the children do not push out or abandon their parents, but neither are they ruled by them. In this power struggle over filial values, national belonging, and gender norms, the title of the novel promises to represent and analyze it all.

Like Venegas before him and Villarreal in the future, Ainslie's narration also captures the social and economic conditions of those thousands of Mexican nationals who left for the United States, marking along the way how these immigrants consciously attempt to retain their ties to Mexico and Mexican her-itage while simultaneously isolated, if not reviled, by mainstream American society:

> Conociéndose despreciados por los hijos del país, que han creído siem-pre superiores, se aislaron voluntariamente formando para vivir, un bar-rio aparte, donde por su afinidad de ideas y costumbres hacían la misma vida que llevaran [*sic*]en su tierra natal.

> Sin excepción, los habitantes de aquel barrio eran descendientes de la clase más humilde de su país. Habían emigrado en busca de trabajo para mejorar su situación, siempre con la idea de regresar más tarde a la patria, cargados de oro. Poco a poco, sin sentirlo, olvidaron sus propósi-tos y se establecieron para siempre en un país donde encontraban más fácil y cómoda la vida; restándole con esto a la patria, un contingente muy numeroso de brazos fuertes y hombres útiles, tan necesario para el engrandecimiento de un pueblo. (05-06-1934, Capítulo IV, 22)

While admitting to, and seemingly sympathetic of, the vast majority of Mexican immigrants who are humble and of the lower classes, Ainslie's narrator also vaguely charges them for abandoning the rebuilding of Mexico, presumably in the wake of the Revolution, and lending their skilled hands instead to a life of ease and comfort in the United States. This life of ease and comfort is under-stood within the class terms of the working poor all the same:

> El barrio a que nos referimos, situado a espaldas de la Mísión, estaba formado por un hacinamiento de casas y jacales de Madera y pobrísi-

mos, que pregonaban la idiosincrasia de nuestro pueblo por todo lo que
era progreso y adelante. (05-06-1934, Capítulo IV, 22)

Again, seemingly sympathetic to these immigrants' humble life, the narrator
nevertheless calls attention to the ramshackle and discolored condition of their
homes, only to project embarrassedly how they are read by Anglo Americans as
indicative of the idiosyncratic, anti-modern, anti-progressive whole of Mexico.
Despite this embarrassment, Ainslie carefully represents the migrant farm labor
that anchors such a barrio. He betrays an intimate understanding of the political
economy that defines an immigrant bachelor society: one that works from Mon-
day to Friday for cash pay, earnings that go to paying off debts made during the
week and drinking on the weekends; a cycles that starts all over again on Mon-
day. It is here in this kind of barrio that the Godínez family, accompanied by his
wife's long time trust servant, Julián Gutiérrez, former mayordomo of María's
sister's rancho, come to visit Raymundo Godínez, Féderico's brother who himself left to make his fortune years before.

   Given his middle-class aspirations, and in his mind the sacrifice he made to
leave Mexico, Ainslie sets up the reader to witness Godínez's clash with the
lower class culture of Mexican immigrants in the United States. Within minutes
of their arrival in the barrio of San Fernando, California, Féderico and María are
scheming for the quickest escape possible from Raymundo's offer of hospitality.
Godínez cannot believe how far his brother had fallen:

> Cuando recibió su carta en El Paso, se lo imaginó buenazo y sencilloso,
> pero nunca supuso que hubiera descendido hasta el grado de adquirir
> los modales y el lenguaje de la gente más humilde. Sus padres fueron
> pobres, y él también se habia criado bajo un ambiente de miseria. Pero
> lo que les faltaba en recursos, lo tenían en educación y maneras. (05-06-
> 1934, Capítulo IV, 32)

Although he could understand how Raymundo might live in poverty, after all
they grew up miserably poor with their own parents, what he could not countenance was his adoption of his humble neighbors' speech and ill manners. Raymundo should know better given his education. By speech, Ainslie means not
just the lower class inflected language that Godínez is accustomed to hear in
Mexico, but also linguistic elements and social cues that reflect a reshuffling of
values that made sense of race, class, gender, and nationalism in one national
context but not another. Even when Raymundo reveals his actual wealth—he
runs a successful general store in the barrio—Féderico cannot overcome his
own class prejudices, nor his fascination with the appearance of class markers
of wealth, power, and security.

   In this same chapter, "Capitulo IV," where Ainslie stages the meeting of
brothers within this barrio, he introduces the word and concept of "el pocho."
First, he does so in the rough and tumble language of Doña Librada García,

owner of la fonda, the local restaurant where she feeds the migrant labor community and acts as their unofficial banker. Around eighty years old, Doña Librada is so beloved by all that she's affectionately referred to as the barrio's "Abuelita." Full of generosity, Abuelita also knows how to pilfer profits on the sly here and there and to talk to men of all ages. She's also a renowned storyteller. When asked to tell one of her stories, she replies in a teasing manner:

—A todos ustedes les he visto nacer", "Pochos" arrastrados —les decía bromeando—. Y a tu padre y a tu madre también, —les decía a dos o tres señalándolos con el dedo.

—Cuántas desveladas y sustos me han dado ustedes malditos. . . y luego pá que ni me lo agradezcan siquiera! (05-06-1934, Capitulo IV, 22)

By way of playing the reluctant storytelling, Abuelita indirectly reifies her importance in the barrio. She has in truth, she claims, helped birth many in her audience as a local midwife. She calls them wretched "Pochos," because for her a "pocho" is someone of Mexican parents born in the United States. Of course, their shared wretchedness is also tied to living in the United States. It is with this definition in mind that Abuelita greets Féderico's and María's newborn, Virginia:

. . .¡Pero qué requetebonita! —prosiguió destapándole la carita—. Se parece a usté. ¿Dónde nació? . . . ¿en México?
—No, —contestó Godínez—, en El Paso.
¡Ah! . . . Entonces es pochita.
—¿Pochita? ¿Y qué es eso?
—Pos les decimous "pochos" a los muchachos mexicanos que nacen gringos. Río el matrimonio de la fraselogia que usaba la anciana y del apodo con que llamaba a su hija. (05-06-1934, Capítulo IV, 34)

Although the parents laugh at the strange phrasing used by Abuelita and her term "pochita" for Virginia, Federico and María do not understand how contradictory terms of identification, to be Mexican and gringo at the same time, can be nonetheless true. This term, pocho, will come to dominate how they make sense of their children's lives in the United States, and theirs by extension. Unable to return to Mexico for fear of being arrested for the stolen company money, Godínez proceeds to Los Angeles with all his misconceptions intact. Overtime because of his business dealings, he becomes poorer than his brother Raymundo. The hope of returning to Mexico fades with each passing year. He becomes a member of a community he condemned and ran away from in San Fernando.

Unlike the bildungsroman structure found in *George Washington Gómez* and *Pocho,* Ainslie's *Los Pochos* finds a resolution of its characters' conflicts through a marriage plot. The importance of this marriage plot is similar to those found in *Who Would Have Thought It* and *The Squatter and The Don (Ruiz de Burton, 1872, 1885),* as well as *Caballero.* But in this marriage plot, the groom-to-be is Mexican, not Anglo American, and the bride-to-be is Virginia, la pochita, and not the coherent Californiana or Mexican daughter in those other novels. Before any marriage can be consummated, the narrative obliges the Godínez family to come to terms with their "pocho" way of life. The appearance of Rafael, the son of María's sister, the ranch owner, precipitates a series of events that culminate in the eventual departure of the Godínez family. Tall, dark, handsome, and loaded with money, Rafael, without any preconceived notion of what this trip would entail for him except to meet his extended family who had not seen him in seventeen years, and to be a tourist in Los Angeles, comes to symbolize the healthy and robust recovery of Mexico from the ruins of the Revolution. Within hours of his arrival, the family's future is penned on his broad Mexican shoulders, starting with Virginia.

As usual in such anti-immigrant texts, Virginia's and Jose's adoption of American customs is the site of much confusion, and subsequent criticism, for the ways that Anglo values disrupt gender and filial norms in traditional Mexican culture. Right before Rafael's arrival, the narration makes it clear that while the children's ability to earn a living relieves economic hardship, it comes with a price:

A los pocos meses de empezar a trabajar y dar dinero para el gasto de la casa, se volvieron libertinos y malcriados, exigiendo de la madre servicios de criada y contestando con groserías los reproches del padre.

En una ocasión que José llegó borracho a la casa. Godínez quiso castigarlo con la mano.

—Si me pegas me largo de la casa. Aqui no estamos en México donde los hijos son esclavos de la casa.

Doña María quiso intervenir, pero Virginia se opuso:

—No te metas en lo que no te importa. José tiene razón. Pues no faltaba mas que no pudiéramos hacer lo que nos dé la gana, cuando nosotros pagamos por la comida.

La pobre madre se contentó con retirarse a su cuarto llorando.

Godínez acabó por acostumbrarse a las groserías de sus hijos y optó por hacerse el desentendido. (05-20-1934, Capítulo V, 22)

Although a common enough scene we would now identify as teenage rebellion in any immigrant family, Ainslie paints a picture of troubled domestic life that anticipates not only the teenage angst and rebellion found in *Pocho* but also later in much of Chicana/o literature, from Tomás Rivera's . . . *y no se lo tragó la tier-ra* (1971) to Sandra Cisnero's *House on Mango Street* (1984). Speaking on behalf of the parents, the narrator labels Virginia and José as libertines and ill-mannered in their speech and disrespectful in behavior toward their elders. By contrast, José evidences his frustration of being held to Mexican values that con-done a child's servitude to a parent's wishes, rational or not. He threatens to leave home for good if Godínez attempts to discipline him through physical force. While Godínez refrains from hitting his son, María leaves for her room crying, having been rebuffed by her daughter who defended José. Virginia argues that since they pay for their food, they can now do what they want. Having grown accustomed to their boorish behavior, Godínez decides to look the other way.

This stalemate of filial rupture and parental disempowerment explains Godínez to María is all his fault for having raised the children in the United States: "Es inútil tartar de corregirlos. Yo tengo la culpa para haberlos criado en este ambiente. Pero tan luego como volvamos a México, ya verás como cam-bian. Los malos ejemplos los ha pervertido" (05-20-1934, Capítulo V, 22). It's useless to try to correct their behavior, for behavior in Godínez's reckoning is related to national belonging. Since they do not belong in Los Angeles, all the children have is bad examples to follow. It is these bad examples that have cor-rupted their children and spoiled their family life. In the face of such disappoint-ment, when and how to return to Mexico becomes Federico's and María's mid-life crisis:

—¿Y cuándo volveremos?

—Ahora sí que muy pronto. Nos vamos con Rafael. En un tren de repa-triados o como se pueda; pero nos vamos. ¡Eso sí te lo aseguro yo!

—Cuántas familias han sufrido como nosotros los rigors del destierro sin embargo, no se van, ni quieren volverse,—dijo doña María, suspi-rando.

—Ya volverán. . . cuando se convenzan de que es más sabrosa una tor-tilla comida entre amigos, que una tajada de jamón entre enemigos . . . o cuando los echen, como han estado haciendo con otros! (05-20-1934, Capítulo V, 32)

In response to María's desperate desire to leave for Mexico, Federico insists that they will get to leave with Rafael, even if by one of those trains used by the gov-ernment repatriating Mexican citizens during the Great Depression. Such is Maria's frustration with her family's wellbeing that she cannot help but wonder out loud about the many families that share their misery of living in exile. Fed-erico predicts that families will leave when they come to realize that it is better to eat a tortilla among friends than have a slice of ham among enemies, or when they get kicked out forcibly on these repatriation trains.

From there the novel quickens to an end. Even José softens his exterior bravado and agrees to return with the family. Packed and in the car, all that remains declares María is to pay their respect to Julián Gutiérrez, the faithful charro friend of the family who served them until he died from exhaustion and a broken heart, unable to return to Mexico. With everyone in tears at the thought of his poor old bones in a country that did not want him nor he it, first Federico and then Rafael promise to repatriate Julián's remains to Mexico in the near future. And with that promise to leave no one behind to suffer any further the poverty and indignities of living in the United States, Federico offers María one final consolation:

—No llores,—le dijo atrayéndola hacia sí—. Es cierto que dejamos enterrado a nuestro mejor amigo, pero en cambio, nos vamos de la tierra donde desperdiciamos lo major de nuestra vida, bastante afortunados somos con llevarnos a nuestros hijos! (06-03-1934, Capítulo VII, 35)

Urging her not to cry any further for Julián, he asks her to appreciate that even though they have wasted their lives by leaving Mexico, nonetheless as parents they can feel fortunate in returning their children to their "tierra," land of their birthrights. So ends in Federico's mind the pocho lives of their children.

There is no doubt that Ainslie's ending is a romantic fantasy of sorts. Beyond thriftiness and their penny-pinching ways, Rafael does not really explain how his parents have built the wealth of their ranch since the end of the revolution. Further, none of the characters actually question how the family preserved their wealth during or after the revolution. Ainslie just simply projects an inevitable aura of well-being around Rafael and his coherent masculine identity, which includes being wealthy. In this regard, Ainslie's novel plays into the political cracks and fissures of a global economic crisis, with wide spread unemployment, hunger, and massive displacement of families whether in the United States, Mexico, or elsewhere in the world. His fantasy narrative was certainly one of many to be found in 1934.

Conclusion

Given the celebratory conclusion of *Los Pochos,* the Godínez family is literally in route to Mexico as the novel concludes, one might assume that the sequel, *Los Repatriados,* would be a triumphalist narration of the regeneration of the reluctant but nonetheless prodigal Mexican immigrant, a re-linking of the immigrant to the national time of Mexico after the revolution. Instead, there is plenty of evidence that Ainslie becomes fascinated, if not also conflicted, how his writing might trouble the text's presumed legitimacy as a Mexican novel. Nonetheless, what makes this fantasy of the return to patria possible is Ainslie's initial narrative insistence that the family is returning to a Mexico that they will recognize and desire. To Ainslie's credit, when he takes up of the topic of repatriation and representing the trials and tribulations of returning Mexican nationals, who have been thoroughly influenced, if not transformed, by their immigrant experience in the United States, he represents a Mexico that has not remained static since the end of the Mexican Revolution, nor any less complicated in its national politics. The period, 1934-1935, are the early years of the presidency of Lázaro Cardenas, that includes the nationalizing of the oil industry, and more importantly for the plot of *Los Repatriados,* agrarian reform in the northern states of Mexico.[21]

In his sequel, *Los Repatriados,* Ainslie concludes his two novel arc by imagining the uplift of Mexico from the wake of the revolution on the shoulders of two "pochos"—Joe and Cuca—who marry and leave to honeymoon in Mexico City. Unlike other characters who become re-Mexicanized through repatriation, Ainslie allows for the possibility of "pochos" as the necessary and much needed agents of change for Mexico during the Great Depression. And yet, he simultaneously keeps investing in the perspective of the parents of the "pochos," who see in "el retorno" a means to un-do an Americanization that has sullied and scarred everyone forever, making the "pochos" particularly unfit to be patriotic "Mexicanos," much less nationalists. All the same, between the columns of *Los Pochos* and *Los Repatriados*, Ainslie hints that there is in fact a difference between "amor por patria," "amor por tierra," "amor por familia," and being a nationalist. Threading a line between an ontological sense of being Mexican and an epistemological rendering of a nationalist citizenship as Mexican, Ainslie sends his "pocho" couple to Mexico City. Given how he appears in the pages of the Spanish-language press of the United States as a revolutionary agent, laborer, restaurant owner, magazine publisher, and real estate agent, Ainslie's literary presence in *La Prensa* offers us much to think on the transnational role of pochos, in the United States and Mexico, but also on how the concept of pochos might shed light on other topics.

Over time, a major focus in any discussion of *Los Pochos* and *Los Repatriados* will revolve, I suspect, around a premise that *La Prensa* often makes about the novels it serializes: novela Mexicana. This identification and categorization at first glance looks solid, but instead of grounding itself in a stable reality it actually deconstructs and questions its own proposition of being Mexican. How can *Los Pochos,* for example, count or be treated like a Mexican novel, given its site of publication and the content of its story? In terms of modernity and the role of the enlightenment in producing the concept of the nation-state, and especially secularizing sovereignty around the protection of property and the accumulation of wealth through capitalism, any nationalist claim outside the borders of the state is instantly vulnerable to attack, if not outright dismissed on the grounds that its production lies outside the nationalist time of the state as demanded by modernity. If so, *La Prensa*'s insistence on "novela Mexicana," is simply an argument, a rhetorical gesture seeking inclusion in the progressive historical narrative of Mexico. Or, like much of *La Prensa*'s role in the United States on behalf of its readers, "novela Mexicana" might signal another instance of the press's ongoing translation of immigrant life in the United States, including the semiotics of nationalist recognition as "paisanos," but one that nonetheless defends against that other operative term for immigrants, pocho.

So in this context, *La Prensa*'s insistence of many of its serialized novels, as "novela Mexicana," literally takes on a different aspect of critical translation, much more in the realm of the national politics and social issues of Mexico. And yet, we have to remind ourselves that even if we observe and grant the discursive power of "el México de afuera," that the pages of *La Prensa* promoted, practically from the very beginning of its establishment, the site of publication for *Los Repatriados* is San Antonio, Texas, and perhaps Los Angeles, California too. These sites of publication should disturb any easy assumption that this is indeed a Mexican novel. The readerly reception of these novels, and the growing prestige of Ainslie as a writer, is fundamentally north of the border. The contradictory and slippery foundations of "la novela Mexicana" in the Spanish language press of the United States—pointing southward but existing northward—reveal this much larger question: the radical nature of translation, and the roles of individual writers within an institution like *La Prensa*. Because of its origins as an immigrant newspaper, *La Prensa* is always caught in the unconscious act of translating, even to the point of translating Mexico to its readers of Mexican origin, especially when it exhorts its readership to return to Mexico, even if it means ironically setting up "pochos" as the basis for a political and cultural future. If this is the case, then we must begin to think of translation not just as a textual practice, nor just as a social transaction, but more broadly as part of the ongoing unpacking, critique, and theorizing of the burdens of modernity and coloniality. The Spanish-language press of the United States is not just the chronicler of the lived experience of US Latinas and Latinos, nor just an advocate of civil rights for its readers, but also the repository of competing literacies and pedagogies that sought to offer a better translation of "local histories with global designs" whoever its reader might be. Reading in the Spanish-language press, especially rereading in the case of us who wander the digital database of Hispanic American Newspapers, is akin to Lefevere's rewriting as translation.

Thus, the material act of reading "Los Pochos," and "Los Repatriados," whether during the fragile, fleeting moment of actual publication, or rereading decades later as part of scholarly interventions, are both equally infused with multiple but different iterations of translational possibility. As in *Los Pochos, Los Repatriados* reiterates the argument that the experience of immigrating to the United States has forever threatened the ability to ever live again under the sign of "Mexico" or "Mexican." How can we understand this dilemma but as the consequence of some deep transformation, or rather deep translation as I have argued here. For Joe and Cuca, theirs is a double translation of their status as "pochos," once in the United States and now in Mexico. Ainslie imagines their future to be determined with Mexico City on the horizon, provocatively suggesting that to be "pocho" is to always be in the mode of translation. Much like the culture of newspapers in general, today's headlines must give way to tomorrow's news and then the tomorrow after that. What will become of this pocho couple after Mexico City? Who knows? Joe's and Cuca's ongoing translation waits for a rewriting and/or a rereading not too far into the future. This is no doubt an important legacy of the Recovery Program: to stage this question of the future of US Hispanic literature through its past, and in staging it usher in the next generation of translators.

Works Cited

Ainslie, Alejandro. *Business Spanish and Commercial Vocabulary*. San Franscisco, 1916.

___. *El "Delirium Tremens" Democratico de 1909*. Mexico City, 1910.

___. *French for the Army and Navy*. San Francisco, 1917.

___. *Paginas Locas*. Hermosillo, 1903.

___. "Pecadora." *La Estrella* [Las Cruces, New Mexico], 7 August 1915.

___. *Versos*. Hermosillo, 1903.

Ainslie, Jorge. "Camino a la Gloria," Cuento. *La Prensa* [San Antonio, TX], 11 April 1937 and 18 April 1937. Readex, *Hispanic American Newspapers, 1808 1980*, https://infoweb-newsbank. Accessed on 30 August 2018.

___. "El Bobo," Cuento. *La Prensa* [San Antonio, TX], 16 May 1937 and 23 May 1937. Readex, *Hispanic American Newspapers, 1808-1980*, https://infoweb-newsbank. Accessed on 30 August 2018.

___. "El Crimen del Carro Especial." *La Prensa* [San Antonio, TX], 14 November and 21 November 1937. Readex, *Hispanic American Newspapers, 1808-1980*, https://infoweb-newsbank. Accessed on 30 August 2018.

___. "El Fantasma, Cuento. *La Prensa* [San Antonio, TX], 17 October 1937 and 24 October 1937. Readex, *Hispanic American Newspapers, 1808-1980*, https://infoweb-newsbank. Accessed on 30 August 2018.

___. *El Hijo del Diablo*, a mi fino amigo Dr. Efrén Valdés, Novela Corta. *La Prensa* [San Antonio, TX], 19 April 1936 and 26 April 1936. Readex, *Hispanic American Newspapers, 1808-1980*, https://infoweb-newsbank. Accessed on 30 August 2018.

___."El Jugador," a la señorita Jeanne Berry, Cuento. *La Prensa* [San Antonio, TX], 7 March 1937. Readex, *Hispanic American Newspapers, 1808-1980*, https://infoweb-newsbank. Accessed on 30 August 2018.

___. "El Lullaby," Cuento. *La Prensa* [San Antonio, TX], 10 October 1937. Readex, *Hispanic American Newspapers, 1808-1980*, https://infoweb-newsbank. Accessed on 30 August 2018.

___. "El Secreto," Cuento. *La Prensa* [San Antonio, TX], 5 December 1937. Readex, *Hispanic American Newspapers, 1808-1980*, https://infoweb-newsbank. Accessed on 30 August 2018.

___. "El Sistema," Cuento. *La Prensa* [San Antonio, TX], 4 April 1937. Readex, *Hispanic American Newspapers, 1808-1980*, https://infoweb-newsbank. Accessed on 30 August 2018.

___. "El Sombrero," Cuento. *La Prensa* [San Antonio, TX], 17 January 1937. Readex, *Hispanic American Newspapers, 1808-1980*, https://infoweb- newsbank. Accessed on 30 August 2018.

___. "El Tonto y El Licenciado," Cuento. *La Prensa* [San Antonio, TX], 24 January 1937. Readex, *Hispanic American Newspapers, 1808-1980*, https://infoweb-newsbank. Accessed on 30 August 2018.

___. "Fuera de la Ley," Cuento. *La Prensa* [San Antonio, TX], 28 June 1936. Readex, *Hispanic American Newspapers, 1808-1980*, https://infoweb-newsbank. Accessed on 30 August 2018.

___. "La Calavera de Pancho Villa," Cuento. *La Prensa* [San Antonio, TX], 28 March 1937. Readex, *Hispanic American Newspapers, 1808-1980*, https://infoweb-newsbank. Accessed on 30 August 2018.

___. *La Ciudad Perdida, Novela Inédita. La Prensa* [San Antonio, TX], 6 January 1935-24 February 1935. Readex, *Hispanic American Newspapers, 1808-1980*, https://infoweb-newsbank. Accessed on 30 August 2018.

___. "La Leva," a mi fino amigo el Gral. Ramón B. Arnáiz. *La Prensa* [San Antonio, TX], 3 January 1937. Readex, *Hispanic American Newspapers, 1808-1980*, https://infoweb-newsbank. Accessed on 30 August 2018.

___. "La Libertad," Un Nuevo Cuento. *La Prensa* [San Antonio, TX], 23 June 1935. Readex, *Hispanic American Newspapers, 1808-1980*, https://infoweb-newsbank. Accessed on 30 August 2018.

___. "Los Escapularios," Cuento. *La Prensa* [San Antonio, TX], 1 March 1936. Readex, *Hispanic American Newspapers, 1808-1980*, https://infoweb-newsbank. Accessed on 30 August 2018.

___. "La Estrella y El Lord," Para mi estimado amigo Rafaél Ybarra. *La Prensa* [San Antonio, TX], 15 March 1936. Readex, *Hispanic American Newspapers, 1808-1980*, https://infoweb-newsbank. Accessed on 30 August 2018.

___. "La Sublevacion en Colima, El Autor en Viaje de Sorpresas." *La Prensa* [San Antonio, TX], 30 March 1937, 6 June 1937, and 13 June 1937. Readex, *Hispanic American Newspapers, 1808-1980*, https://infoweb-newsbank. Accessed on 30 August 2018.

___. *Los Pochos, Novela.* Los Angeles, Latin Publishing Company, 1934.

___. *Los Pochos, Novela Mexicana. La Prensa* [San Antonio, TX], 15 April 1934-3 June 1934. Readex, *Hispanic American Newspapers, 1808-1980*, https://infoweb-newsbank. Accessed on 30 August 2018.

___. *Los Repatriados, Novela Mexicana. La Prensa* [San Antonio, TX], 22 September 1935-17 November 1935. Readex, *Hispanic American Newspapers, 1808-1980*, https://infoweb-newsbank. Accessed on 30 August 2018.

___. "Mi Anecdotario Mímino." *La Prensa* [San Antonio, TX], 19 December 1937, 26 December 1937, and 9 January 1938. Readex, *Hispanic American Newspapers, 1808-1980*, https://infoweb-newsbank. Accessed on 30 August 2018.

___. "Mi Novia," a mi fino amigo Gabriel Navarro, Cuento. *La Prensa* [San Antonio, TX], 12 December 1937. Readex, *Hispanic American Newspapers, 1808-1980*, https://infoweb-newsbank. Accessed on 30 August 2018.

___. "Mis Andanzas en la Revolucion Escobarista." *La Prensa* [San Antonio, TX], 18 April 1937. Readex, *Hispanic American Newspapers, 1808-1980*, https://infoweb-newsbank. Accessed on 30 August 2018.

___. "Se Mareó Cupido," Un Cuento. *La Prensa* [San Antonio, TX], 23 March 1937. Readex, *Hispanic American Newspapers, 1808-1980*, https://infoweb-newsbank. Accessed on 30 August 2018.

___. "Tenía Buen Corazón." *La Prensa* [San Antonio, TX], 9 June 1935. Readex, *Hispanic American Newspapers, 1808-1980*, https://infowebnewsbank. Accessed on 30 August 2018.

___. "Un Buen Consejo." *La Prensa* [San Antonio, TX], 4 August 1946. Readex, *Hispanic American Newspapers, 1808-1980*, https://infoweb-newsbank. Accessed on 30 August 2018.

___. "Un Enfermo Como Hay Muchos," Cuento. *La Prensa* [San Antonio, TX], 2 February 1936. Readex, *Hispanic American Newspapers, 1808-1980*, https://infoweb-newsbank. Accessed on 30 August 2018.

Andrés, Jr., Benny J. "Invisible Borders: Repatriation and Colonization of Mexican Migrant Workers along the California Borderlands during the 1930s." *California History*, vol. 88, no. 4, 2011, pp. 5-65.

"Ayer regresaron. . .de Mont Lowe." *El Heraldo de México* [Los Angeles, CA], 17 March 1925, p. 7. Readex, *Hispanic American Newspapers, 1808-1980*, https://infoweb-newsbank. Accessed on 30 August 2018.

Balderrama, Francisco E., and Raymond Rodriguez. *Decade of Betrayal: Mexican Repatriation in the 1930s*. Albuquerque, University of New Mexico Press, 1995.

Brammer, Ethriam Cash. "La Patria Perdida o Imaginada: Translating Teodoro Torres in 'El México de Afuera'." Dissertation, Wayne State University, 2011.

Cabrera, Jorge Palafox. "Letras asesinas: Historia de la literatura policial mexicana, (1930-1960*)*." Tésis, El Colegio de San Luis, A.C., San Luis Potosí, S.L.P., March 2014.

"El Sr. Ainslie Mejorado," *El Heraldo de México*, [Los Angeles, CA], 10 August 1927, p. 6. Readex, *Hispanic American Newspapers, 1808-1980*, https://infoweb-newsbank. Accessed on 30 August 2018.

"Falleció el novelista Jorge Ainslie." *La Prensa* [San Antonio, TX], 25 October 1938, p. 2. Readex, *Hispanic American Newspapers, 1808-1980*, https://infoweb-newsbank. Accessed on 30 August 2018.

Hernández, Guillermo E. "Las Carateristicas Comicas Del Pocho Y Del Pachuco." *Nuevo Texto Crítico*, vol. 2, no. 3, 1989, pp. 171-181. Itzigsohn, José, and Matthias vom Hau. "Unfinished imagined communities: States, social movements, and nationalism in Latin America." *Theory & Society*, vol. 35, no. 2, 2006, pp. 193-212.

Kanellos, Nicolás and Helvetia Martell, editors. *Hispanic Periodicals in the United States, Origins to 1960: A Brief History and Comprehensive Bibliography*. Houston, Arte Público Press, 2000.

Lawhn, Juanita Luna. "María Luisa Garza: Novelists of El México de Afuera." *Double Crossings/EntreCruzamientos*, edited by Mario Martín Flores and Carlos von Son. New Jersey, Ediciones Nuevo Espacio, Academia, 2001, pp. 83-96.

Lomas, Laura. "Translation and Transculturation in the New York-Hispanic Caribbean Borderlands." *Small Axe*, vol. 20, no. 3, Nov. 2016, pp. 147-162.

Mignolo, Walter D. Afterword. "Writing and Recorded Knowledge in Colonial and Postcolonial Situations." *Writing Without Words: Alternative Literacies in Mesoamerica and the Andes*, edited by Elizabeth Hill Boone and Walter D. Mignolo, Durham, Duke University Press, pp. 292-312.

___. *Local Histories/Global Designs: Coloniality, Subaltern Knowledges, and Border Thinking*. Princeton, Princeton University Press, 2000.

___. "The Geopolitic of Knowledge and the Colonial Difference." *The South Atlantic Quarterly*, vol. 101, no. 1, 2002, pp. 57-96.

"Notas de Sociedad, 'Muere Un Periodista Mexicano'." *Hispano America*, [San Francisco, CA], 9 October 1920, pp. 4. Readex, *Hispanic American Newspapers, 1808-1980*, https://infoweb-newsbank. Accessed on 30 August 2018.

Ortiz, Fernando. *Contrapunteo cubano del tobaco y el azúcar (Advertencia de sus contrastes agrarios, económicos, históri- cos y sociales, su etnografía y su transculturación)*, with introduction by Bronislaw Malinowski (1940 [1937?]; repr., Havana: Dirección de publicaciones, Universidad Central de las Villas, 1965); translated by Harriet de Onís as *Cuban Counterpoint: Tobacco and Sugar*, with new introduction by Fernando Coronil. Durham, Duke University Press, 1995.

"Para la ciudad de San Francisco," *El Heraldo de México* [Los Angeles, CA], 19 July 1927, p. 6. Readex, *Hispanic American Newspapers, 1808-1980*, https://infoweb-newsbank. Accessed on 30 August 2018.

"Para San Francisco." *El Heraldo de México* [Los Angeles, CA], 1 January 1928, p. 5. Readex, *Hispanic American Newspapers, 1808-1980*, https://infowebnewsbank. Accessed on 30 August 2018.

Quijano, Anibal, and Immanuel Wallerstein, "Americanity as a concept; or, The Américas in the modern world-system." *International Social Science Journal*, vol. 64, no. 4, 1992, pp. 549-557.

___. "Coloniality of Power, Eurocentrism, and Latin America." *Nepantla: Views from South*, vol. 1, no. 3, 2000, pp. 533-580.

Sonora, Mexico, Civil Registration Births, 1866-1930. *Ancestry.com Operations, Inc. 2015.* Provo, UT, https://www.ancestry.com/. Accessed on 30 August 2018.

Rodriguez, Maggie Rivas. "Ignacio E. Lozano: The Mexican Exiled Publisher Who Conquered San Antonio and Los Angeles." *American Journalism*, vol. 21, no. 1, 2004, pp. 75-89.

Rosales, F. Arturo. *Dictionary of Latino Civil Rights History*. Houston, Arte Público Press, 2006, pp. 429-30.

Salas, Miguel Tinker. *In the Shadows of the Eagles: Sonora and the Transformation of the Border During the Porfirato*. Berkeley, CA, University of California Press, pp. 204.

Torres, Teodoro. *La Patria Perdida*. Mexico City, Ediciones Botas, 1935.

"Viajeros," De Nuestra Sociedad. *El Heraldo de México*, [Los Angeles, CA], 29 April 1925, p. 9. Readex, *Hispanic American Newspapers, 1808-1980*, https://infoweb-newsbank. Accessed on 30 August 2018.

Walsh, Casey. "Demobilizing the Revolution: Migration, Repatriation, and Colonization in Mexico, 1911-1940." *Working Paper 26*. The Center for Comparative Immigration Studies, University of California, San Diego, November 2000, pp. 1-26.

Endnotes

[1]For more, see entry on Rodolfo Uranga, who is credited with coining the term in *Dictionary of Latino Civil Rights History*, F. Arturo Rosales (Houston: Arte Público Press, 2006, p. 429-30; see also for more background, "María Luisa Garza: Novelists of El México de Afuera," Juanita Luna Lawhn in *Double Crossings/EntreCruzamientos*, eds. Mario Martín Flores, Carlos von Son (New Jersey: Ediciones Nuevo Espacio, Academia, 2001, p. 83-96)

[2]For more, see *Hispanic Periodicals in the United States, Origins to 1960: A Brief History and Comprehensive Bibliography*, eds. Nicolás Kanellos with Helvetia Martell (Houston: Arte Público Press, 2000).

[3]See Laura Lomas, "Translation and Transculturation in the New York-Hispanic Caribbean Borderlands," *Small Axe*, 20.3 (November 2016): 147-162.

[4]For more on Lozano newspapers, see "Ignacio E. Lozano: The Mexican Exiled Publisher Who Conquered San Antonio and Los Angeles," Maggie Rivas Rodriguez, *American Journalism*, 21.1 (2004): 75-89.

[5]Source: Ancestry.com. Sonora, Mexico, Civil Registration Births, 1866-1930 [database on-line], Provo, UT, USA. Ancestry.com Operations, Inc. 2015.

[6]See "Notas de Sociedad, 'Muere Un Periodista Mexicano'," *Hispano America*, 10-09-1920 (San Francisco, CA), p. 4 (online database, *Hispanic American Newspapers, 1808-1980*, Readex).

[7]Before arriving in San Francisco, Alejandro D. Ainslie had been the editor of the state newspaper of Sonora(See Miguel Tinker Salas, *In the Shadows of the Eagles: Sonora and the Transformation of the Border During the Porfirato*, Berkeley, CA: University of California Press) 204), as well as the author of volumes of poetry, a political treatise, and books of language instruction in Spanish and French published in San Francisco: *Versos* (Hermosillo, 1903); *Paginas Locas* (Hermosillo, 1903); *El "Delirium Tremens" Democratico de 1909* (Mexico City, 1910); *Business Spanish and Commercial Vocabulary* (San Franscisco, 1916); *French for the Army and Navy* (San Francisco, 1917). There is also a record of a poem, "Pecadora," published in the newspaper, *La Estrella*, Las Cruces, New Mexico (8-7-1915).

[8]See following notices: "Ayer regresaron. . .de Mont Lowe," *El Heraldo de México* (Los Angeles, CA), 03-17-25, p. 7; "Viajeros," De Nuestra Sociedad, *El Heraldo de México* (Los Angeles, CA) 04-29-25, p. 9; "El Sr. Ainslie Mejorado," *El Heraldo de México* (Los Angeles, CA) 08-10-27, p. 6; "Para la ciudad de San Francisco," *El Heraldo de México*, (Los Angeles, CA) 07-19-27, p. 6; "Para San Francisco," *El Heraldo de México* (Los Angeles, CA) 01-01-28, p. 5 (online database, Hispanic American Newspapers, 1808-1980, Readex).

[9]See "Falleció el novelista Jorge Ainslie," *La Prensa* (San Antonio, TX), 10-25-38, p. 2 (online database, Hispanic American Newspapers, 1808-1980, Readex).

[10]The following only lists Jorge Ainslie's literary publications in Ignacio Lozano's newspaper *La Prensa* of San Antonio. Lozano's other newspaper, *La Opinion* of Los Angeles, is another place to look for publications since Ainslie lived in Los Angeles. But at the moment, the archives of *La Opinión* are not digitized; therefore only an on site review of library holdings at UCLA or UC Berkeley will reveal what publication record Ainslie has there. What follows is list of Ainslie's publications from the online database, Hispanic American Newspapers, 1808-1980, Readex: *Los Pochos, Novela Mexicana* (4-15-1934, 4-22-1934, 4-29-1934, 5-6-1934, 5-13-1934, 5-20-1934, 5-27-1934, 6-3-1934); A related version, *Los Pochos, Novela*, was published by the Latin Publishing Company in book form that same year. Intriguingly, the title page records the date of publication as "Enero 6 a Febrero de 1934," whereas the copyright page records the date of publication as a"1934." The former date corresponds generally to the length of time it might have taken to publish the

novel by installments, presumably in *La Opinión*. Other publications found in *La Prensa* include: *La Ciudad Perdida, Novela Inédita* (1-6-1935, 1-13-1935, 1-20-1935, 1-27-1935, 2-3-1935, 2-10-1935, 2-17-1935, 2-24-1935); "Tenía Buen Corazón" (6-9-1935); "La Libertad," Un Nuevo Cuento (6-23-1935); *Los Repatriados, Novela Mexicana* (9-22-1935, 9-29-1935, 10-6-1935, 10-13-1935, 10-20-1935, 10-27-1935, 11-3-1935, 11-10-1935, 11-17-1935); "Un Enfermo Como Hay Muchos," Cuento (2-2-1936); "Los Escapularios," Cuento (3-1-1936); "La Estrella y El Lord," Para mi estimado amigo Rafaél Ybarra (3-15-1936); *El Hijo del Diablo*, a mi fino amigo Dr. Efrén Valdés, Novela Corta (4-19-1936, 4-26-1936); "Fuera de la Ley," Cuento (6-28-1936); "La Leva," a mi fino amigo el Gral. Ramón B. Arnáiz (1-3-1937); "El Sombrero," Cuento (1-17-1937); this short story also appears in the Mexican literary magazine, *Misterio*. According to Jorge Palafox Cabrera, "Jorge Ainslie con su narración titulada 'El sombrero' que tras ser en apariencia un texto fantástico en que un hombre adquiere un sombrero y siempre se le desaparece cuando lo lleva puesto y reaparece sin motivo en su casa, no era más que un truco publicitario" (p. 83). Cabrera also mentions: "Rodolfo Chávez, que en el número dos publica el relato de aventuras "Sobre el continente africano" y en el número 38 la novela fantástica titulada "La ciudad perdida" (p. 81). It's curious to see the same title as Ainslie's in 1935. A comparison is in order. See Jorge Palafox Cabrera, "Letras asesinas: Historia de la literatura policial mexicana, (1930-1960)." Tésis, El Colegio de San Luis, A.C., San Luis Potosí, S.L.P., March 2014. "El Tonto y El Licenciado," Cuento (1-24-1937); "El Jugador," a la señorita Jeanne Berry, Cuento (3-7-1937); "La Calavera de Pancho Villa," Cuento (3-28-1937); "El Sistema," Cuento (4-4-1937); "Camino a la Gloria," Cuento (4-11-1937, 4-18-1937); "Mis Andanzas en la Revolucion Escobarista" (4-18-1937); "El Bobo," Cuento (5-16-1937 & 5-23-1937); "Se Mareó Cupido," Un Cuento (5-23-1937); "La Sublevacion en Colima, El Autor en Viaje de Sorpresas (5-30- 1937, 6-6-1937, 6-13-1937, fictional narrative based on fact); "El Lullaby," Cuento (10-10-1937); "El Fantasma, Cuento (10-17-1937, 10-24-1937); "El Crimen del Carro Especial" (11-14-1937, 11-21-1937); "El Secreto," Cuento (12-5-1937); "Mi Novia," a mi fino amigo Gabriel Navarro, Cuento (12-12-1937); "Mi Anecdotario Mímino" (12-19-1937, 12-26-1937, 1-9-1938, memoir); "Un Buen Consejo" (8-4-1946).

[11]For more on repatriation, see: Francisco E. Balderrama and Raymond Rodriguez, *Decade of Betrayal: Mexican Repatriation in the 1930s* (Albuquerque: University of New Mexico Press, 1995); Benny J. Andrés, Jr., "Invisible Borders: Repatriation and Colonization of Mexican Migrant Workers along the California Borderlands during the 1930s," *California History*, 88.4 (2011): 5-65.

[12]For more on Teodoro Torres, *La Patria Perdida*, and "El México de Afuera, see Ethriam Cash Brammer, "La Patria Perdida o Imaginada: Translating Teodoro Torres in 'El México de Afuera'," dissertation, Wayne State University, 2011.

[13]For more on colonial difference within a local/global context, see: Walter D. Mignolo, *Local Histories/Global Designs: Coloniality, Subaltern Knowledges, and Border Thinking* (Princeton, NJ: Princeton University Press, 2000); "The Geopolitic of Knowledge and the Colonial Difference," *The South Atlantic Quarterly*, 101.1 (2002), 57-96.

[14]See Walter D. Mignolo, "Afterword: Writing and Recorded Knowledge in Colonial and Postcolonial Situations," in *Writing Without Words: Alternative Literacies in Mesoamerica and the Andes*, Eds. *Elizabeth Hill Boone, Walter D. Mignolo* (Durham, N.C.: Duke University Press, 1994): 292-312.

[15]See Fernando Ortiz, *Contrapunteo cubano del tobaco y el azúcar (Advertencia de sus contrastes agrarios, económicos, histori- cos y sociales, su etnografía y su transculturación)*, with introduction by Bronislaw Malinowski (1940 [1937?]; repr., Havana: Dirección de publicaciones, Universidad Central de las Villas, 1965); translated by Harriet de Onís as *Cuban Counterpoint: Tobacco and Sugar*, with new introduction by Fernando Coronil (Durham, NC: Duke University Press), 1995.

[16]See Anibal Quijano and Immanuel Wallerstein, "Americanity as a concept; or, The Américas in the modern world-system," *International Social Science Journal*, 64.4 (1992): 549-557.

[17]See Anibal Quijano, "Coloniality of Power, Eurocentrism, and Latin America," *Nepantla: Views from South*, 1.3 (2000): 533-580.

[18]For this critique within the context of Latin America proper, see José Itzigsohn, Matthias vom Hau, "Unfinished imagined communities: States, social movements, and nationalism in Latin America," *Theory & Society*, 35.2 (2006): 193-212.

[19]See Walter D. Mignolo, "The Geopolitic of Knowledge and the Colonial Difference," *The South Atlantic Quarterly*, 101.1 (2002), 57-96.

[20]For more on the figure of the "pocho" in society and literature, see Guillermo E. Hernández, "Las Características Cómicas Del Pocho Y Del Pachuco," *Nuevo Texto Crítico*, 2.3 (1989): 171-181.

[21]For more on agrarian reform and repatriation, see Casey Walsh, "Demobilizing the Revolution: Migration, Repatriation, and Colonization in Mexico, 1911-1940," *Working Paper 26*, The Center for Comparative Immigration Studies, University of California, San Diego (November 2000), 1-26.

Sintiendo vergüenza: Intersections of Class, Race, Gender and Colonial Affect-Culture in Jorge Ainslie's *Los Repatriados* (1935)

LORENA GAUTHEREAU

University of Houston

During the Great Depression (1929-1939), approximately one million people of Mexican descent living in the United States repatriated to Mexico, either voluntarily or forcibly through local government raids, as they were scapegoated during the period of economic downturn (Balderrama and Rodríguez 151). The most infamous immigration raid of the 1930s occurred in Los Angeles Plaza (affectionately known as "La Placita") on February 26, 1931. Walter E. Carr, local superintendent of the US Immigration Service, recruited agents from nearby cities to aid in this massive raid (73). At three o'clock in the afternoon, the tranquility of the Mexican square was broken by the abrupt and unexpected appearance of immigration agents. Police officers physically blocked the entrances. Chaos ensued as four hundred Mexicans enjoying the Placita that day suddenly found themselves forced to line up and prove their legality by showing "their passports or other evidence of legal entry and residency. . . . What was or was not acceptable proof of legal entry or residency was entirely up to the whim of the interrogating officers" (73). Upon hearing news of the raid, Mexican Vice Consuls Ricardo Hill and Joel Quiñones immediately made their way to the Placita in order to aid the immigrants. They too "were accorded rude and discourteous treatment until their diplomatic identity was established" (74). Raids such as these occurred across the Southwest as well as major US cities. Like the xenophobic attacks launched on people of Mexican descent in 1910-1920 by the Texas Rangers,[1] these raids targeted any person whom the immigration officials deemed to "look Mexican." And, as Francisco E. Balderrama and Raymond Rodríguez (2006) point out, "[a]ll Mexicans, whether legal or illegal, looked alike to immigration officials" (70). After the raids, the chaos was punctuated by "women crying in the streets when not finding their husbands" (70).

Several emotionally charged descriptions of Mexican Repatriation (1930-1940), such as the one above, were published in newspaper articles and Mexican American novels, offering insight into the lived experience of people of Mexican descent living in the United States at the time. One example is Jorge Ainslie's *Los Repatriados* (1935), a novel serialized in San Antonio's Spanish-language newspaper, *La Prensa*. This novel follows the García family—the matriarch and business owner Doña Refugio, her husband Don Filemón, and their daughter, Cuca—as they voluntarily repatriate from Los Angeles, CA to Santa Rosalía, Chihuahua, Mexico. Doña Refugio García, a maid turned owner of several very successful *tortillerías*, two nixtamal mills, and two rental properties, decides to sell everything and move her family back to Mexico in hopes of achieving social ascension. What she does not foresee, however, is having to cede her role as head of household to her husband (the unemployed professor) in order to navigate Mexican society. Class, labor, and gender become sites of shame, or *vergüenza*, for the repatriating characters in the novel as they cross the US-Mexico border. In my analysis of this novel, I focus on *vergüenza* to demonstrate how Mexican Repatriation inflicted feelings (or affects) of *vergüenza*, but more specifically, how this *vergüenza* is the materialization of racialized labor and gender. That is, people of Mexican descent didn't just feel ashamed at the act of repatriating; rather, they were made to feel ashamed by a US sociopolitical culture that devalued them and their labor. The racialization of labor and class is internalized or felt in and on their bodies as *vergüenza*. This devaluation, in turn, is a product of what Anibal Qujano (2000) calls the "coloniality of power" that organized race, gender, and labor in hierarchies.

Departing from Quijano's (2000) "coloniality of power" theory—which argues that the legacy of coloniality continues to replicate colonial hierarchies in the modern world—I develop a mode of analysis that takes into account the ways in which colonialism created an affect-culture that justified class hierarchies based on racial difference. Rosemary Hennessy (2013) defines affect-culture as "the transmission of sensation and cognitive emotion through cultural practices . . . the materiality of affect-culture is inflected by the social relations through which needs are met" (50). Furthermore, as Hennessy elaborates, "[o]ne of the ways this inflection takes place is in the circulation of cultural narratives that are themselves sites of struggle as they encode mythologies that reproduce dominant power relations and alternative narratives that question or reinvent them" (50). I argue that the affective component of cultural forms helped produce embodied *consent* to the *power* of coloniality. Rather than merely dictate the hierarchies, the role of affect in a colonial cultural value system fueled the lived belief that "global cultural order" revolved around "European or Western hegemony" (Quijano 540) and the feelings of superiority based on relations to capital became codified in race and gender relations and justified the devaluation of all non-Western epistemologies and ontologies. I introduce "colonial" in the theorization of Hennessy's "affect-culture" to account for the ways that coloniality structures the cultural practices and social relations that materialize in the policies, wages, and violence that discriminate against people of color.

Relying on Hennessy's definition of affect-culture, I propose that colonial affect-culture transmits the "sensation and cognitive emotion" of racial hierarchies that structured life during the colonial period. To pivot off of her abovementioned definition, the "materiality" of colonial affect-culture is "inflected" by the "cultural narratives" of hegemonic power (immigration policies, official rhetoric surrounding immigrants and racialized bodies, etc.) that "reproduce dominant power relations." It is through an analysis of the circulation of affects, or emotive registers such as *vergüenza*, that we can begin to create and understand "alternative narratives" that can "question" or contest the hegemonic narratives that fuel the coloniality of power.[2] Most important for my reading of *Los Repatriados* is the way that *vergüenza* is inflected by a larger sociopolitical history and climate: the Great Depression and its scapegoating of people of Mexican descent that led to Repatriation. For Mexican repatriates of the 1930s, including Ainslie's characters, negative feelings or affects (such as resentment directed at people of Mexican descent) had a very real effect on their lived experience. Physically shunted, shoved, tackled, and corralled—the bodies of Mexicans in the United States experienced the material consequences of resentment, which was received and interpreted as pain, discomfort, and above all, *vergüenza*.

While *Los Repatriados* does not present the reader with an interaction between Mexicans and Anglo Americans, reading for moments of *vergüenza* through colonial affect-culture demonstrates how coloniality (and its hierarchies) are experienced in daily life. Once in Mexico, for example, Doña Refugio comments on the Anglo perception of Mexican immigrants.

Speaking to her friend, Doña María Godínez, Doña Refugio remarks: "Siquiera aquí le entienden a uno y le tratan a uno como la gente. . . . No que allá qué somos?" (Ainslie 13 Oct. 1935).[3] There is dark silence in Doña Refugio's words as she trails off. The gap, marked by ellipses in the original text, notes something unspeakable. She searches for words, but only comes up with a question: "qué somos?"[4] This something is the colonial affect-culture that gives a negative inflection to the lived experience of Mexicans in the United

States. While the characters can name some *vergüenzas* experienced in the United States, it is their debasement that she cannot name. After her silence, she asks, *what (qué)* are we in the United States—not *who (quién)* are we. Her comment suggests that people of Mexican descent are not treated as people, much less equals. The claim that the Anglo Americans do not treat the Mexican immigrants with respect suggests that outside of the Mexican barrio, Anglo Americans perceive Doña Refugio to be of a lower class because she is Mexican, despite the fact that she is a business owner.

Yet, because it is a consequence of coloniality, the colonial affect-culture of *vergüenza* is not limited to US spaces. Instead, it extends to Mexico and draws upon gendered caste hierarchies. My critique of *Los Repatriados* highlights how women of Mexican descent figure prominently in this imaginary and as such are in danger of being subsumed by colonial gendered hierarchies, as we shall see in the example of Doña Refugio. Colonial affect-culture, like coloniality and capitalism, is a transnational phenomenon that devalues the Mexican American community and its labor. The Mexican American lived experience, too, is discounted as it is filtered through colonial hierarchies and perceptions of racialized class and gender. In other words, the devaluation of the Mexican American lived experience is occurring north and south of the border. Reading representations of the lived experience of Mexican Americans requires an analysis that acknowledges and accounts for the intersections of race, class, gender and coloniality in their confrontation with and expression through affect. Mexican repatriates like the Garcías soon realized they had to negotiate their lived class experiences in the US within a colonial history that organized class and gender along colonial hierarchies within Mexico. The act of repatriating to Mexico, thus, allows a retroactive recognition for the characters of the *vergüenza* that they experienced in the US, while simultaneously highlighting the *vergüenza* experienced in Mexico. Repatriation demonstrates how historical conditions and colonial histories intersect not only with race, gender, and class, but also with affect. Furthermore, reading for colonial affect-culture allows us to gain a more complete picture of the ways people of Mexican descent experience the materiality of gendered and racialized labor.

The racialization of labor plays a significant role in the perception of a racialized class hierarchy and attaches social prestige to only certain types of work. I argue that a colonial affect- culture is attached to these constructions of class, as historical colonial caste systems continue to dictate the definition of social prestige. Colonial affect-culture skews the relationship between labor and lived class experience by imagining distance between the type of work performed and the epistemology of class experience. Under a racialized class system, in other words, class differs from a *lived* economic reality. For the characters in *Los Repatriados*, this means that while the protagonist Doña Refugio can experience class mobility as she works her way up from domestic laborer to entrepreneur, this mobility—and its acceptance as such—is limited to the space of the US Mexican barrio. Colonial affect-culture dictates the social prestige attached to different types of labor and prestige shifts based on the social and cultural space, be it a US Mexican barrio, the US (outside of the barrio), or Mexico. As a result, when the characters repatriate to Mexico, Doña Refugio finds herself subjected to a colonial affect-culture that values her husband's socially-acceptable intellectual labor as a professor more than her labor as the owner of various *tortillerías* and nixtamal mills. Once in Mexico, her husband, Don Filemón, continuously attempts to regulate her behavior by shaming her. By pointing out her incorrect Spanish and telling her she should feel *vergüenza*, he demonstrates *vergüenza* represents the devaluing of her racialized and gendered class. *Vergüenza*, however, is not only reserved for repatriated women, but also represents the devaluation that occurred through deportation.

Repatriation was coded in and justified through official US discourse surrounding immigration legislation and Great Depression economic concerns that marked people of Mexican descent as racialized scapegoats. This official US discourse, of course, resounds with contemporary politics as crime, drug abuse, and unemployment are continuously attributed to undocumented immigrants by policymakers, news anchors, and then-presidential candidate, Donald Trump in his infamous reference to Mexican nationals as criminals. While the Great Depression-era English-language press celebrated the mass deportations of people of Mexican descent by touting the number of rail departures (of train cars overfilled with Mexican immigrants) (Kropp 35), US Spanish-language newspapers, such as *La Prensa,* denounced the racism behind the immigration raids and kept readers informed of both forced and voluntary repatriation.[5] Ainslie's novel, published in *La Prensa*, came as a response to immigrant narratives, such as Daniel Venegas' *Las aventuras de Don Chipote, o cuando los pericos mamen* (1928),[6] which, as Nicolás Kanellos (2000) asserts, attempted to convey to readers "why Mexicans should not come to the United States, that they should stay in Mexico and continue being Mexicans—even while in the United States" ("Introduction" 7).[7] Indeed, Ainslie, an immigrant himself, was concerned with reporting the life of people of Mexican descent during Repatriation. José F. Aranda (work-in-progress) notes that Ainslie was:

> invested in both exposing the real life travails of Mexican life in the US, as well as promoting the voluntary repatriation of Mexican nationals to Mexico. The years 1934 and 1935 represent a heightened awareness in the pages of *La Prensa* on the topic of repatriation, from the forced,

xenophobic expulsion of Mexican and Mexican Americans from the US to the Mexican government's attempts to "colonize" the northern territories by offering Mexican immigrants in the US land they could farm. It is in this social and political context that Ainslie makes a name for himself in *La Prensa*. (6)

In light of the immigration raids and the Mexican nationalistic discourse, *La Prensa* demonstrates how voluntary repatriation and the rhetoric surrounding it, attempted to circumvent the *vergüenza* of deportation and to recode the experience as a Mexican nationalistic endeavor. However, Ainslie's novel reveals that voluntary repatriation did not completely circumvent *vergüenza* for Mexican repatriates.

Voluntary repatriation attempted to avoid *vergüenza* inflicted as the result of forced repatriation or deportation; therefore, reading for affect in *Los Repatriados* reveals that Mexico, like the US, reiterates colonial hierarchies of labor and gender, so that the characters must re- learn how to negotiate Mexican society. Instead of the shame of deportation, Doña Refugio is made to feel shame about her gender and her racialized business (her chain of *tortillerías*). *Los Repatriados* also highlights the differences between lived class experience in the US Mexico barrios and the Mexican nation-state. Reading for *vergüenza* in this novel underscores the racialization of class and labor. Although people of Mexican descent could achieve some economic success in the US, their ability to achieve social approval and respect is limited to the Mexican *barrio*. As the character Doña Refugio quickly learns, the US Mexican *barrio* functioned as a unique transcultural space where she was seen as a community leader, entrepreneur, and autonomous woman. Yet, outside of that space, her business and labor are racialized and she is groomed to become a submissive Mexican wife and abide by colonial racialized and gendered hierarchies.

Los Repatriados opens as *Licenciado* Anselmo Mendoza attempts to deceive a group of Mexican immigrants living in the US to exchange their hard-earned businesses and property for over-priced land in Mexico. Doña Refugio is easily seduced by his description of the high society life that inevitably awaits her in Mexico. While listening to his shady business proposition, she is carried away by her desires for social class ascension:

> . . . Doña Refugio sentía que un suave cosquilleo de placer le recorría todo el cuerpo, al pensar en la oportunidad que le deparaba la suerte en la persona del licenciado, que iba a sacarla de su humilde posición y convertirla mediante unos cuantos miles de dólares en una señora hacendada, respetada y tratada por igual por todos los terratenientes de

la comarca. Ya se veía sentada cómodamente en un equipal en los portales de la casa de la Hacienda, dando órdenes al mayordomo, regañando a los peones o tomando chocolate con los vecinos. (Ainslie 22 Sept 1935)[8]

Doña Refugio's working-class background and social aspirations are key. Back in Mexico, she worked as a maid for a Porfirista family who later escaped to the US during the onset of the Mexican Revolution. Unfortunately, when the family returned to Mexico, they left her behind in a country where she did not know the language. After finding a hospital cleaning job, Doña Refugio slowly managed to save enough money after years of hard work to open a *tortillería* and sell tortillas to the Mexican restaurants in the barrio. She ascended from working class to business owner—or, to frame it in Marxist terms, from proletarian to petite bourgeoisie. While the petite bourgeoisie are subject to economic trends and precarity (and therefore share more with the working class than with "big capitalists," who own the means of production), Doña Refugio does distinguish herself as a business owner with no debt, as she always insists on paying in cash in order to avoid loan traps (22 Sept. 1935). By the beginning of the novel, her business has expanded to include several *tortillerías*, two nixtamal mills, and various rental properties (22 Sept. 1935). She employs others to carry out the day-to-day labor of the businesses (such as making and distributing the tortillas), leaving her to look after her businesses from the comfort of a cozy chair (22 Sept. 1935).

As a business owner, Doña Refugio no longer lives off the physical labor she once suffered as a maid. And among her compatriots in the Mexican barrio, she is a respected member of the Mexican immigrant community. In the meeting with Licenciado Mendoza, the group turns to Doña Refugio for her thoughts on the proposition because of her status in the barrio and her business acumen. Like Doña Refugio, many "independent businessmen, merchants, shopkeepers, farmers, and property owners" who "catered to the special needs and interests of the colonia" had to "liquidate their properties" and return to Mexico (Balderrama and Rodríguez 136). The meeting described at the start of *Los Repatriados* reflects the active efforts by the Mexican government to colonize the lands it had reclaimed after the Mexican Revolution. Yet, because the United States was suffering from the economic downturn of the Great Depression, Mexican repatriates found that:

> Possessions and property that had taken a lifetime of hard work to acquire now had to be disposed of for a few cents on the dollar—if one were lucky enough to find a buyer. . . . As a last resort, attempts were

made to exchange commercial real estate for property of equal value in Mexico. A major problem in effecting an equitable trade was the scarcity of good farmland south of the border. (137-8)

Despite Doña Refugio's ownership of her businesses and properties, the economic downturn of the Great Depression, and (more significantly in this novel) Mexican Repatriation, reveal the precarity of small business owners. With the increasing threats of forced deportation, people of Mexican descent were forced to "dispose" of their hard-earned possessions and property "for a few cents on the dollar."

The promotion of voluntary repatriation, however, attempted to protect people of Mexican descent from the *vergüenza* produced by US resentment. Consul General Eduardo Hernández Cházaro expressed this nationalism in his discussion of repatriation. Repatriation, he claimed, "presented an opportunity for bringing back Mexico's prodigal sons and daughters. Successful repatriation, he believed, would preclude any future exit of compatriots to the United States" (171).[9] On September 27, 1931, Hernández Cházaro made a heartfelt, nationalistic appeal to Mexicans living in Texas to support the 800 families who, having depleted their financial resources, planned on making the 150-mile trip to the border on foot. Through *La Prensa*, Hernández Cházaro expressed a "caluroso llamamiento a todos los mexicanos"[10] to contribute in some way to this "obra humanitaria de repatriación"[11] ("800 Familias Mexicanas" 2). Hernández Cházaro characterized aid as nationalistic, calling it an "obra de caridad a favor de los nuestros,"[12] which resulted not only from generosity, but, perhaps more importantly, from the community's shared *Mexicanness*: " . . . yo espero fundadamente de su altruismo, de su mexicanismo y de sus sentimientos géneros, que sabrán acudir en ayuda de nuestros compatriotas de la región de Karnes en el trance tan aflictivo en que se encuentran" (2).[13] Hernández Cházaro went on to warn Mexican immigrants not to wait until the last minute to repatriate otherwise their return would be "muy difícil y lleno de penalidades" (2).[14] Hernández Cházaro's appeal suggests, as Balderrama and Rodríguez (2006) note, that he was "determined to avoid the 'shameful spectacle' of twenty-seven hundred men, women, and children, many of them suffering from malnutrition, hiking over 250 miles to Nuevo Laredo, Mexico" (170-1).

Hernández Cházaro's plea was not only couched in nationalist discourse; instead, it also iterated a desire fueled by camaraderie that aimed to avoid *vergüenza*. He sought to protect the US Mexican community from having to suffer the introjection of resentment. Negative affects associated with immigration and deportation, such as *vergüenza* and fear, are detailed in Chicana/o and Mexican literature dealing with the theme of immigration. These affects appear in

Chicana/o and Mexican fiction and non-fiction texts such as: Alicia Alarcón's collection of *testimonios* (testimonies) *La Migra Me Hizo Los Mandados* (*The Border Patrol Ate My Dust,* 2002), Gloria E. Anzaldúa's *Borderlands/La Frontera* (1987), Carlos Fuentes' *La frontera de cristal* (*The Crystal Frontier,* 1995), Graciela Limón's *The River Flows North* (2009), Rubén Martínez's *Crossing Over* (2002), ire'ne lara silva's *flesh to bone* (2013), and Luis Alberto Urrea's *The Devil's Highway* (2005). *Vergüenza,* however, is not only reserved for repatriated Mexicans, but also represents the devaluation that occurred within the US as Anglo American resentment and rancor (other negative affects) evoked shame in people of Mexican descent as they were scapegoated and deported during the Great Depression era. This resentment and rancor identified people of Mexican descent as other, not belonging, illegitimate, and the cause of their misery during the Great Depression.

Faced with the potential to be *avergonzados,* ashamed or made to bear shame, repatriation seemed to offer an alternative, especially when coupled with Mexico's ongoing colonization projects. Mexico's Secretaría de Agricultura y Fomento[15] seemingly anticipated the mass repatriation in August of 1929 when it began surveying land that could be used for a colonization project (Balderrama and Rodríguez 197). After the Mexican Revolution, lands from haciendas and other landed estates were seized for redistribution. In light of the Great Depression in the United States, colonization, for repatriating Mexicans,

> presented an opportunity to escape the worst travails of the depression and to put their agricultural skills to personal use. The dream of owning their own small farms seemed within their grasp, at last. Rather than enriching the gringos, they would be working for themselves. . . . Imbued with the hope and expectation of potential success, unemployed Nationals flocked to apply for acceptance as colonizers. (Balderrama and Rodríguez 198-9)

Let down by the dream of achieving economic success in the United States,[16] many people of Mexican descent decided to take their chances in their homeland. They brought with them the dream of ownership, which was inflected with elements of the American dream.

Due to the relationship between affect, coloniality, and capital, people of color are *perceived* as belonging to a lower class even today. Affect plays a role as the projection of negative qualities onto raced bodies enforces social hierarchies, which in turn reproduces colonial structures of subordination, the "coloniality of power." Rather than merely dictate hierarchies, the role of affect in a colonial culture value system fueled the lived belief that "global cultural order" revolves around "European or Western hegemony" (Quijano 540) and animates feelings of superiority based on capital-codified race relations. The "coloniality of power" replicates colonial power structures even in the modern world with the disintegration of colonialism and slavery.

As Doña Refugio soon learns, the types of labor one engages in and the types of businesses one can own are categorized according to a culturally-assigned value system. Don Federico Godínez warns the Garcías:

> Por ningún motivo vayan a decir que ustedes tenían tortillerías en Los Angeles, no porque sea una vergüenza . . . sino, que para la gente que se llama aquí de sociedad, hay ciertos trabajos que ellos conceptúan humillantes, y prefieren entramparse y vivir de préstamos, a ponerse a trabajar en cualquier oficio honrado, que les dejara lo suficiente para vivir. . . . Que [digan que] don Filemón era Profesor de español en una Universidad, y que usted tenía dos o tres Boticas.[17] (Ainslie 13 Oct. 1935)

The conceptualization of class and social status through this value system is connected to the Marxist claim that modern capitalism has skewed our perception of class. Growing access to credit cards, payment plans, pay advances, and loans helps to obfuscate our continued relationships to capital, labor, production, and commodities. It is no coincidence that the issues of *La Prensa* containing the installments of Ainslie's novel boast several advertisements for products such as clothing and furniture that can be purchased through installment plans or by opening store credit card accounts (29 Sept. 1935, 3-4). This imaginary access to instant capital allows us to own property associated with markers of a higher class, such as cars and homes. Consequently, we tend to think of class in terms of our relationship to property, rather than our relationship to the means of production. Thus, the *perception* of class experience is predicated upon our imagined relation to property (what we own) and not the question of whether or not we have to sell our labor in order to possess said property. Tied into our perceptions of class is also the lingering colonial affect-culture that culturally assigned value to different raced bodies and the type of labor performed by these bodies.

Negative affects (such as resentment) directed at persons of color helped maintain social order during the colonial period, and continue to influence cultural perceptions of class. Within this imaginary, the relationship to the means of production was—and is—forgotten. What becomes more important is distancing oneself from the bottom in order to participate in a different social class *experience*. Whereas Doña Refugio and her family undoubtedly experienced much better quality of life than their working class compatriots (or even a much better quality of life as compared to her previous working life as a maid), their social class *experience* in the US, because of their ethnicity and immigrant status, are undoubtedly distinct from the class *experience* of Anglo Americans in similar economic brackets. This is precisely why Doña Refugio decides to return to Mexico. Despite having achieved economic success in the US, she recognizes the impossibility of reaching *social* ascension there. She hopes that owning land in Mexico will grant her the social status of *hacendada* that will allow her to rub elbows with Mexico's elite.

Unlike Doña Refugio, her husband, Don Filemón held a higher social position back in Mexico prior to the Mexican Revolution as "Profesor de Instrucción Primaria" (Professor of Primary Instruction). Once in the US, however, he finds himself living in squalor. Unwilling to deign to perform physical labor, he lives off the pity of his acquaintances, and decides to propose to Doña Refugio as a way out of his miserable poverty. Ainslie depicts Don Filemón as bearing a gendered *vergüenza* in the US. As a Mexican immigrant, his body is racialized and the class and privilege once afforded to him in Mexico is revoked north of the border. His elite status as an intellectual is not recognized. Despite gendered hierarchies in the US, Ainslie portrays Don Filemón as having no agency and no male privilege. He is powerless in his marriage and completely submissive to his wife, Doña Refugio. Moreover, Ainslie describes Don Filemón as the emasculated husband of a "bossy" entrepreneurial wife and in his demotion from *Profesor* to *repartidor de tortillas*[18]: "Cuando me casé con Refugio, y empecé a repartir tortillas, sentía vergüenza en desempeñar tan humilde oficio, después de haberme quemado tantos años las pestañas, estudiando para catedrático" (27 Oct. 1935).[19] He silently accepts his fate and doesn't complain until he has the opportunity to re-instate his class and male privilege. While in the US, Doña Refugio acts as the head of the household and makes all the monetary decisions, including the one to sell her businesses and purchase Mexican lands. Don Filemón, on the other hand, makes no business decisions and silently obeys her (13 Oct. 1935). Yet, upon crossing the US- Mexico border, Doña Refugio immediately loses her status as head of household and decision- maker. After 20 years of marriage, Don Filemón decides to rebel:

Aquí ya no estamos en Estados Unidos donde la mujeres le pegan a los maridos; nos encontramos en México, y aquí dejo de ser el repartidor de tortillas y me convierto de nuevo en el Profesor García; y te voy a advertir otra cosa . . . si quieres que yo te presente con mis amigos como mi mujer, debes de ir aprendiendo a hablar español como la gente y

dejarte de *trajites, vinites, juites* y tantas otras barbaridades que dicen.[20]
(6 Oct. 1935)

Rather than acknowledging the shared patriarchal hierarchies of the US and Mexico, Ainslie portrays the US as a space where the privilege of gendered hierarchies does not exist for Mexican men. Instead, *Los Repatriados* employs stereotypes of American women as controlling and "overly" independent to "warn" Mexican men of the consequences of immigration and assimilation. In the US, Don Filemón claims in his angry outburst, women can beat their husbands. Such stereotypes emphasize Ainslie's promotion of voluntary repatriation and represent the return to Mexico as a return to order, specifically for Mexican men. It is significant that his rebellion comes precisely as they cross into Mexico. Social order and social status take precedent over economic class in Mexico, according to Ainslie's depiction. Indeed, Doña Refugio was aware of her husband's Mexican social status when she married him. Whereas Don Filemón proposed to Doña Refugio to rescue himself from poverty, Doña Refugio accepted *because* of his higher social lineage.

Just as the distinction between immigrant and nonimmigrant bodies matters in the US, so does the distinction between male and female bodies as they cross the border. The novel suggests that women are permitted to succeed and own businesses in the US, whereas in Mexico this position of economic power is reserved for elite men. In the US, Doña Refugio refused to let her husband participate in any business decisions; and he was happy to oblige. Once in Mexico, however, Don Filemón takes it upon himself to assume all monetary responsibility and to become the sole decision-maker. He has no agricultural experience, but actively begins his blind attempt at cultivating the Mexican land his wife purchased. The gender politics at work here, like the politics surrounding race, class, and labor mentioned earlier, is also tied to coloniality. According to María Lugones (2007), heterosexism functions "as a key part of how gender fuses with race in the operations of colonial power" (186). Colonial/modern Eurocentered capitalism imposed changes to indigenous social systems through "slow, discontinuous, and heterogenous processes that violently inferiorized colonial women" (201). What is most relevant to my analysis of this novel is Lugones' interest in the intersections of race, class, and gender which underscores the indifference men and men of color, specifically, "exhibit to the systematic violences inflicted upon women of color" (188). Once in Mexico, Don Filemón immediately takes advantage of the superiority assigned to him by colonial legacy—a superiority of class and gender that Ainslie describes as denied to Mexican men in the US. He wastes no time in reclaiming the social prestige assigned to him by lineage and gender. Knowing or perhaps sensing his wife's desire for social mobility, he threatens her access to it by saying he will not introduce her to his friends as his wife if she continues to display non-conformity to Mexican gender and class-sector norms. Moreover, the couple attempts to fit in colonial social structures by creating a socially-acceptable past. They lie about who earned the money, how they earned it, how much money they have, and how they lived.

For both Doña Refugio and Don Filemón, the operative affect is *vergüenza*. A haunting legacy of colonial hierarchies that racialized labor produces a colonial affect-culture of *vergüenza* in Mexican immigrants and Mexican Americans. Doña Refugio is instructed to feel *avergonzada* of her business under both Mexican and US colonial cultures. Affect-culture works to racialize the *tortillería* and devalue it as a commercial enterprise. Only within the US Mexican barrio can Doña Refugio enjoy economic and social ascension. Outside of the barrio, however, Doña Refugio's labor infused with *vergüenza* because of the race she bears on her body. There is a significant relationship of body and mind to *vergüenza*, as Gilles Deleuze (1993) writes of shame: "The mind depends on the body; shame would be nothing without this dependency...the mind is ashamed *of* the body in a very special manner; in fact, it is ashamed *for* the body. It is as if it were saying to the body: You make me ashamed, You ought to be ashamed" (123). In Mexico, Don Filemón emphasizes gender and social hierarchies that code her gender as subordinate. He points out that her speech betrays her lack of education and if she refuses to speak as an educated woman, he will block her access to high society in Mexico. Colonial hierarchies, thus, code her body through race, gender, and tongue and teach her (and her husband) to assign *vergüenza* to her racialized, gendered, uneducated mind and body. "Shame," writes Elspeth Probyn (2010) "is subjective in the strong sense of bringing into being an entity of an idea through the specific explosion of mind, body, place, and history. Shame is the product of many forces" (81). Here, shame, or *vergüenza*, is the explosion of mind, female/Mexican body, the movement from US Mexican barrio to Mexico, and Mexico's own history of colonialism.

While moving from the United States to Mexico seems to offer Doña Refugio the opportunity to ascend in class status as an *hacendada*,[21] it comes at the expense of her autonomy. Unlike other novels of immigration, *Los Repatriados* offers an immigration story from north to south. It provides the opportunity to think about how the repatriated characters bring back their experience of US colonial affect-culture to Mexico. As mentioned above, Doña Refugio once enjoyed the respect of her fellow compatriots as a leader of the Mexican immigrant community. She not only makes the decisions for her family, but also influences the decisions of others, as occurs in the opening scene. After *Licenciado* Mendoza pitches the Mexican land parcels to the group of Mexican immigrants, they all look to Doña Refugio for her reaction, turning to her, one of them says, "a ver qué dice doña Refugio, que es la que tiene más propiedades, y la que está más entusiasmada" (22 Sept. 1935).[22] She, of course, decides to repatriate. The long car ride to Mexico accentuates the transnational coloniality the pervades the US-Mexico borderlands. Like repatriates in real life, the García family joins a caravan of twelve other cars and while Cuca reads a magazine of love stories, Don Filemón is invested in recounting the colonial history of California and the US Southwest (20 Oct. 1935). He takes joy in retracing the steps of the conquistadores who "se atrevieron a cruzar por aquí en busca de aventuras . . . Eso sí que eran hombres!" (20 Oct. 1935)[23] Don Filemón collapses colonial conquest into masculinity here, and foregrounds his own investment in a colonial hierarchy that privileges men. While Filemón imagines the conquest, Doña Refugio just complains. Although Doña Refugio originally decided to repatriate in order to gain social prestige as part of a higher class, what she loses in the move is the ability to voice her complaints. As the novel progresses, she complains less and less as the Mexican colonial affect-culture begins to sink in and she is groomed, in essence, to be a submissive Mexican wife. "En boca cerrada," says the old Mexican adage, "no entran moscas."[24] At this point, it is still open to question whether or not Ainslie was aware of the way he constructed the US Mexican barrio as a space where Mexican women can achieve autonomy. Nevertheless, his use of negative stereotypes in describing Doña Refugio as a dominant, headstrong, and opinionated woman who becomes quieter and more submissive upon returning to Mexico suggests some sort of cultural shift experienced by the characters.

Ainslie's novel ends on the high note of the *pochos* (assimilated Mexican Americans) Cuca and Joe getting married and departing for Mexico City. The term *pocho*, is a widely-used term among Mexicans to describe Americanized Mexicans who speak Spanish with an accent or who speak Spanglish. It is sometimes used affectionately and sometimes used as a critique of assimilation.[25] The novel's concluding scene signals that these *pochos* can and should play a significant and nationalistic role in rebuilding post-Revolutionary Mexico. Yet, repatriation for *pochos* was not always such an easy transition. Already accustomed to the language and culture of the US, first-generation Mexican Americans (such as the *pochos* in *Los Repatriados*, the two García daughers, Cristi and Cuca, and Cuca's love interest and fellow repatriate, Joe) found it difficult to accept their parents' decision to repatriate to Mexico. As Balderrama and Rodríguez (2006) note:

> . . . bitter arguments erupted as older children tried to talk their parents into letting them remain behind. When parents refused, desperate last-

minute solutions or alternatives ensued. Young boys ran away from home or hid, teenage girls got married, older children opted to stay with friends or relatives. . . . The prospect of living in Mexico created tension, anxiety, and consternation among young Mexican Americans. (130-1)

During the Repatriation years, families suffered divisions because of deportation, but they also suffered divisions when voluntarily repatriating. Here, too, do people of Mexican descent feel the effects of Anglo American resentment and rancor, as Mexican parents experienced bitterness directed at them not just from outside the community, but also from inside their own families.

This suffering is interpreted as bitterness, sorrow, anger, and *vergüenza,* as parents feel the weight of the impossibility of keeping their family together. In the novel, Doña Refugio and Don Filemón are forced to deal with their eldest daughter, Cristi's resistance. When asked by her *comadre* (godmother of her daughter) where Cristi is, Doña Refugio responds by communicating *vergüenza*:

> — . . . pos nomás de acordarme me pongo furiosa. . . . ! la muy sinvergüenza!. . . . Pos nomás afigúrese que el día que le dije que nos íbanos, se puso como una fiera y me dijo que'lla no s'iba, porque no quería irse a limpiar con periódicos ni comer frijoles tatemados. Pos cuando oyí aquello, se me pusieron los ojos colorados y vide amarillo, nomás al verla tan despatriota y mal hija; y me le juí encima pa' darle unas guantadas...... pero la muy chivata se me escapó de las manos y agarró rumbo a la puerta;.... Allí se paró, y cuando me l'iba yo a echar encima otra vez pa' matarla . . . Sabe usté' lo que hizo? Pos me sacó la lengua.... Y no jué eso lo pior, sino que me hizo un ruido muy feo con la boca.... la muy arrastrada agarró por la cocina y luego se jué por el porche.... agarró pa' la calle y se trepó en el automóvil dese baquetón del Samaniego, que dizque es su novio.[26] (20 Oct. 1935)

The reader does not get a first-hand account of the event. Nor does the novel include Cristi's perspective at all. The only account the reader gets is Doña Refugio's memory of the event. In fact, Cristi does not appear in *Los Repatriados,* except as a reference in the above dialogue.

Doña Refugio's recounting of her eldest daughter's defiance reveals a rollercoaster of affects and emotions. Doña Refugio expresses anger, bitterness, resentment, and rage ("before I could get at her again to kill her"). She accuses Cristi of being *sinvergüenza,*[27] reading her refusal to repatriate as a lack of Mexican patriotism. According to Mexican cultural vernacular, then, Cristi is read as a *vendida,* a sellout to her cultural roots. Quite simply, Doña Refugio interprets her daughter's defiance as the sign of being a "bad" Mexican. Through her disobedience, she simultaneously breaks with the conservative, Mexican Catholic model of the heteronormative family while also breaking up her own family. Doña Refugio even goes as far as insulting her daughter, calling her an "*arrastrada*"²⁸ when she chooses to run off with Samaniego. The insult conveys Doña Refugio's critique of Cristi's sexuality, which does not comply with older Mexican customs of courtship—Cristi is enacting an elopement with a "*baquetón*"²⁹ of whom her parents do not approve. The two elope, of course, in order to remain in the United States. The couple refuses to bear the *vergüenza* that the Mexican immigrant community has dictated as the "appropriate" response to American culture. Instead, the repatriating Mexican family must bear the weight of this other *vergüenza*—children who they read as betraying their (Mexican) cultural roots in favor of the country who didn't want them in the first place.

Ironically, however, Doña Refugio herself doesn't fit the mold of the traditional "good" Mexican wife, either. Both Cristi and Doña Refugio challenge the patriarchal hierarchy of the conservative Mexican tradition. Doña Refugio assumes that repatriating to Mexico will help her gain more prestige and allow her class mobility, but she doesn't realize that class ascension within a colonial hierarchy will be at the cost of her gendered independence. While Cristi is most likely not completely aware of the degree to which repatriation would change her life, she does recognize that the move to Mexico would inevitably stifle her growing autonomy. Similarly, early Chicana feminists recognized the limiting nature of traditional Mexican customs and vocalized the oppression of traditional Mexican gendered hierarchies as their movement began to gain more visibility during the Chicana/o movement of the late 1960s.³⁰

While Cristi and Samaniego represent the shameless *pochos* seduced by American culture, Cuca and Joe represent the hope for a bright Mexican future. The very last line of the novel, spoken by Cuca's father, Don Filemón, voices this desire: "Me siento feliz porque hemos conseguido que se vayan rumbo al Sur; hacia el rumbo que deban seguir todos los mexicanos que se encuentran allá en los Estados Unidos; al Sur; hacia la patria" (17 Nov. 1935).³¹ Parenting for Mexican immigrants, then, is imbued with patriotic goals. Ainslie's novel also emphasizes the role parents should play in encouraging their children to remain loyal to their Mexican roots. *Los Repatriados* slowly builds to the climax of Joe and Cuca's wedding, yet it also conveys some of the difficulties that the couple experiences in navigating a different set of social norms. Joe and Cuca express their difficulty adapting to life in Mexico and their desire to move back to Los Angeles as soon as they are married. At the beginning of their courtship, when Cuca is newly- arrived in Mexico, Joe asks her to take a stroll with him, but warns her, "no me hables en inglés, porque van otra vez a empezar a decir que soy un agringado" (13 Oct. 1935).[32] His warning suggests that he resents this label, though he wants to return to Los Angeles (13 Oct. 1935). Unlike the "shameless" Cristi, who firmly asserts and enacts her connection to the US through bodily expressions of rebellion (sticking her tongue out, making an "ugly" noise at her mother, and running away), Joe still associates *vergüenza* with assimilation. He finds himself in a double bind that threatens to cast *vergüenza* on him: that of being called *agringado* and that of wanting to return to the United States, abandoning what the novel's concluding lines suggests is a duty to "the homeland."

The narrative's slow buildup to the wedding ceremony seems to hint at a sudden change of heart in the *pocho* couple, as if the Mexican ritual itself (and the honeymoon in Mexico City) has the power to re-baptize them as "true" Mexicans. I read this as a slippage on the part of the author, since no explanation is offered as to why Joe and Cuca would choose to remain in Mexico after they spend so much time complaining about Mexico. At the beginning of their courtship, Joe suggests to Cuca that he doesn't like Mexico's customs; he claims that there is something unspeakably absent: "A mí no me gustan estas costumbres de que no salgan con uno [a] solas...además, yo quiero volverme a Los Angeles. . . . A tí tampoco te va a gustar. Ya lo verás. Aquí la gente es muy buena pero falta algo . . . no sé qué" (13 Oct. 1935).[33] While raids and deportations sought to control Mexican bodies in the US space, Joe observes that Mexican conservative traditions control the body's sexuality and autonomy, especially with regard to young people. And as his previous warning related to language suggests, the national culture also regulates their tongues. Refusal to obey these cultural norms can result in being shamed. Since appearances matter in Mexico's colonial class hierarchy (as Don Filemón tells Doña Refugio in the car), *vergüenza* can affect social perception of class belonging. Yet, Joe and Cuca subtly resist Mexico's colonial affect-culture as they begin to fall in love. When Cuca recounts to Joe that she told Doña Refugio that they were going to get married and return to Los Angeles, the couple inadvertently slips back into English: "E instintivamente empezaron a hablar en inglés. Volvían a usar el idioma de su niñez, que les facilitaba más expresar lo que sentían ambos" (3 Nov. 1935).[34] Although the *pochos* are fluent in Spanish, they find it hard to express their love for each other in Spanish. Instead, they revert to "the language of their childhood," the language in which they think and, more importantly, *feel* (or use to process their affects and emotions).

Thus, Ainslie's novel never resolves the bicultural and bilingual heritage of Mexican Americans who find themselves labeled as outsiders by the colonial affect-cultures of both the US and Mexico. Instead, *Los Repatriados* highlights how navigating Mexican colonial affect- culture was much more daunting for young Mexican Americans. Reading for colonial affect- culture in this novel also reveals the extent to which repatriated Mexican Nationals also encountered difficulties in navigating differences between the gendered and class hierarchies that existed on either side of the border. Throughout the novel, the characters find themselves having to abide by a new set of social rules once in Mexico, but they also find themselves lying about their class and social experience in the US in order to fit into Mexico's societal expectations. The lies expose the role of affect in the construction of this hierarchy since affects code all the forms of coloniality in the novel. As a result, Doña Refugio ends up trading her voice and autonomy for dubious class ascension in Mexico that continuously reminds her to feel *avergonzada* of her lower-class upbringing. None of the characters, not even the young *pochos,* Cuca and Joe, are exempt from colonial affect-culture. This persistence across generations, as demonstrated by the novel, is what makes coloniality especially damaging.

The perceptions and assumptions made around the loci of race, class, gender, and coloniality are dictated by a colonial affect-culture that continues to exert power even in today's world. One needs only to turn to news reports or social media to witness the violence colonial affect-culture wages on people of Mexican descent. Such examples include: the rhetoric that labels people of Mexican descent as troublemakers, drug dealers, rapists, and criminals; the desire (indeed, the political platform) to build a wall between Mexico and the US; families ripped apart by Immigration and Customs Enforcement (ICE) raids; the Department of Homeland Security's June 2017 announcement to repeal the Deferred Action for Childhood Arrivals (DACA) immigration policy; and many more. The circulation of affects–specifically feelings of superiority, resentment, and rancor–continue to fuel and justify policies and legislation that uphold colonial hierarchies and impose feelings of fear and *vergüenza* on people of Mexican descent.

Works cited

"800 familias mexicanas se disponen a emprender a pie su vieje de regreso a la patria." *La Prensa*, 27 Sept. 1931, pp. 1-2. Advertisements, various. *La Prensa* 29 Sept. 1935, 3-4.

Ainslie, Jorge. *Los Repatridos.* San Antonio: *La Prensa,* 1935. (22 Sept. 1935, 29 Sept. 1935, 6 Oct.1935, 13 Oct. 1935, 20 Oct.1935, 27 Oct. 1935, 3 Nov. 1935, 10 Nov. 1935, 17 Nov. 1935).

___. *The Repatriates.* Trans. Taller Americano de Traducción. Ed. José F. Aranda, Lorena Gauthereau, and Elena Valdez. Work-in-progress. Rice University, Houston.

Aranda, José F. "Critical Translation: The Politics and Writings of Jorge Ainslie." Work-in- Progress. Rice University, Houston.

Balderrama, Francisco E. and Raymond Rodríguez. *Decade of Betrayal: Mexican Repatriation in the 1930s.* Albuquerque: University of New Mexico Press, 2006.

Deleuze, Gilles. "The Shame and the Glory: TE Lawrence." *Essays Critical and Clinical.* Trans. Daniel W. Smith and Michael A. Gresco. Minneapolis: University of Minnesota, 1997, pp. 115-125.

Gauthereau, Lorena. *Manos de Obra: Race, Class, Gender, and Colonial Affect-Culture in Mexican American Literature.* Dissertation, Rice University, 2017.

Hennessy, Rosemary. *Fires on the Border: The Passionate Politics of Labor Organizing on the Mexican* Frontera. Minneapolis: University of Minnesota Press, 2013.

Kanellos, Nicolás. "A Brief History of Hispanic Periodicals in the United States." *Hispanic Periodicals in the United States, Origins to 1960: A Brief History and Comprehensive Guide.* Houston: Arte Público Press, 2000, pp. 3-136.

___. "Introduction." *The Adventures of Don Chipote, or When Parrots Breast-feed*, by Daniel Venegas, Trans. Ethriam Cash Brammer. Houston: Arte Público Press, 2000, pp. 17.

Kropp, Phoebe S. "Citizens of the Past? Olvera Street and the Construction of Race and Memory in 1930s Los Angeles." *Radical History Review*, no. 81, 2001, pp. 35-60.

Lugones, María. "Heterosexualism and the Colonial/Modern Gender System." Hypatia, vol. 22, no. 1, 2007, pp. 186-209. Online. www.jstor.org/stable/4640051. Accessed 16 Feb. 2017.

McKay, Reynolds M. "The Federal Deportation Campaign in Texas: Mexican Deportation from the Lower Rio Grande Valley during the Great Depression." *The Borderlands Journal*, vol. 5, no. 1, 1981, p. 97.

Probyn, Elspeth. "Writing Shame." *The Affect Theory Reader.* Eds. Melissa Gregg and Greogry J. Seigworth. Durham: Duke University Press, 2010, pp. 71-90.

Quijano, Anibal. "Coloniality of Power, Eurocentrism, and Latin America." trans. Michael Ennis. *Nepantla: Views from the South.* Vol. 1, no. 3, 2000, pp. 533-580.

Endnotes

[1] For more on the Texas Rangers, see Charles H. Harris and Louis R. Sadler, *The Texas Rangers and the Mexican Revolution: The Bloodiest Decade, 1910-1920.* Albuquerque: University of New Mexico Press, 2007. For a literary representation, see Américo Paredes, *George Washington Gómez: A Mexicotexan Novel.* Houston: Arte Público Press, 1990.

[2] For more on my theorization of colonial affect-culture, see Lorena Gauthereau, *Manos de Obra: Race, Class, Gender, and Colonial Affect-Culture in Mexican American Literature.* Dissertation, Rice University, 2017.

[3] All translations of *Los Repatriados* are from *The Repatriates,* Taller Americano de Traducción, Rice University (Work-in-progress): "At least here they understand us and treat us like people . . . over there, what are we?"

[4] "what are we?"

[5] For more on Repatriation and newspapers see Francisco E. Balderrama and Raymond Rodríguez, *Decade of Betrayal: Mexican Repatriation in the 1930s.* Albuquerque: University of New Mexico Press, 2006 and Lorena Gauthereau, "Sólo un miraje: The Spanish-language Press, Mexican Repatriation, and Lived Class Experience of Rancor and *Verngüenza* in Jorge Ainslie's *Los Repatriados* (1935)," *Manos de Obra: Race, Class, Gender, and Colonial Affect-Culture in Mexican American Literature.* Dissertation, Rice University, 2017.

[6] During this time period, the Spanish-language press published various *crónicas* (chronicles)—short, weekly literary publications that "humorously and satirically commented on current topics and social habits in the local community," especially in light of the way that the "very existence [of the Mexican community] was seen as threatened by the dominant Anglo-Saxon culture" ("A Brief History" 44-45). Although Jorge Ainslie's novel, *Los Repatriados* (1935) is longer in length than the typical *crónica*, his writing style employs the genre's use of humor to discuss the way that current events and social topics had an effect on the local community. Daniel Venegas' *Don Chipote* also employs humor, albeit more burlesque in tone, to engage with topics of immigration, labor, and racism. While Venegas writes to dispel the myth of the American dream and "streets paved in gold," through the figure of a poor laborer, Ainslie acknowledges that, while economic ascension is possible for Mexican nationals, the social atmosphere makes life there undesirable. And Ainslie, unlike Venegas, portrays the return to Mexico as a triumphant national endeavor.

[7] Other examples of novels that portray Latino immigration to the United States as undesirable include: Alirio Díaz Guerra's *Lucas Guevera* (1914) and Conrado Espinoza's *El Sol de Texas* (1927).

[8]"Doña Refugio felt a soft tingle of pleasure run through her body. She thought about the opportunity apparent in the person of the licenciado, which would extract her from her humble social position and make her, through just a few thousand dollars, into a *hacendada*, respected and treated equally by all landowners in the region. She could already see herself seated comfortably in a nice wicker chair on the veranda of the house of the *Hacienda*, giving orders to the foreman, reprimanding the peons or drinking chocolate with the neighbors."

[9]There appears to be an error in the Balderrama and Rodríguez citation. This article is cited as *La Prensa*, 4 September 1930 (qtd. in Balderrama and Rodríguez 171), but I could not find this article in *La Prensa*. This article may have come from *La Opinón* instead; however, the archives of *La Opinion* have not been digitized yet and I was unable to access them.

[10]My translation: "a warm plea to all Mexicans."

[11]My translation: "humanitarian work of repatriation."

[12]My translation: "work of charity in favor of our own [people]."

[13]My translation: " . . . I hope, based on your altruism, your mexicanness, and your generosity, that you will know to come to the aid of our compatriots in Karnes, who find themselves in such an afflictive crisis."

[14]My translation: "very difficult and full of hardship."

[15]Department of Agriculture and Planning

[16]American cultural critics, such as Sacvan Bercovitch, argue that the American space has been envisioned as the location of economic fulfilment since the colonial period. Even before the term "the American dream" was coined, as Bercovitch notes (1978, 2012), Puritan colonists imagined the mission in America as offering "unparalleled opportunities for economic advancement" (xiii). As mentioned in note 6, *Don Chipote* references the ability to sweep gold off the streets in the United States (21, 23, 126). Yet, many writers saw through the fiction of such economic success and wrote about their disillusion with the US; examples include: F. Scott Fitzgerald's *The Great Gatsby* (1925), Ole Edvart Rolvaag's *Giants in the Earth* (1927), Upton Sinclair's *The Jungle* (1906), Anzia Yezierska's *Bread Givers* (1925), and Daniel Venegas' *Don Chipote* (1928). Specifically in reference to Chicana/o literature, literary critic Raymund A. Paredes (1981) has argued that the concept of the American dream was (and is) steeped in the exploitation and racialization of the lower classes. Paredes identifies that, for writers of Mexican descent, the American dream has "held little attraction, seeming at turns an essentially harmless illusion and a cruel and insidious hoax" (71). For more, see: Raymundo A. Paredes, "Mexican American Authors and the American Dream." *The Ethnic American Dream*, special issue of *MELUS*, vol. 8, no.4, 1981, pp. 71-80.

www.jstor.org/stable/467390. Accessed 21 June 2017 and Sacvan Bercovitch, *The American Jeremiad.* Madison: The University of Wisconsin Press, 2012.

[17]"And I am going to suggest another thing to you all. Under no circumstances should you say that you owned tortillerías in Los Angeles, not because it is a shame . . . but because, for the people called society here, there are certain jobs that they perceive as humiliating, and they would rather get tangled up and live by loans, than to work in any honest trade that provides them with enough to live by . . . [Say] [t]hat Don Filemón was a Spanish professor at a university, and that you had two or three drugstores."

[18]Tortilla deliveryman

[19]"When I married Refugio and began to distribute tortillas, I felt ashamed to perform such a horrible job after having burned the midnight oil for so many years studying to be a professor . . . "

[20]"And I'm going to tell you something. We are not in the United States any-more, where the women abuse their husbands; we are in México, and here I stop being the tortilla deliveryman and once again become *el Profesor García*; and I'll tell you another thing—he continued with arrogance—if you want me to introduce you to my friends as my wife, you must learn to speak Spanish like civilized people do and stop with the *trajites, vinites, juites* and all the other atrocities that 'they' all say."

[21]Land owner.

[22]"Let's see what Doña Refugio says, since she owns the most property and she is the most enthusiastic."

[23]"dared to cross through here in search of adventures . . . Those were truly men!"

[24]My translation: "Flies do not enter open mouths."

[25]Ainslie also published a novel titled *Los Pochos* in *La Prensa* in 1934. It is the precursor to *Los Repatriados* and employs many of the same characters. It was serialized in the following issues of *La Prensa*: 15 April 1934, 22 April 1934, 29 April 1934, 6 May 1934, 13 May 1934, 20 May 1934, 27 May 1934, 3 June 1934.

[26]"Don't speak to me of that Cristi, *comadre*...don't talk to me of that tart because it makes me want to vomit . . . just thinking about it makes me furious. . . . ! That shameless girl! Don't ya know what she did to me? Well just imag-ine that the day I told her we were leaving, she turned into a wild animal and told me that she ain't leaving, because she didn't want to go clean with news-papers or eat stewed *frijoles*. . . . Once I heard that, my eyes turned bright red and I started seeing yellow, just seeing her so unpatriotic and such a bad daughter. I went at her to give her a few slaps, but the little *chivata* [squealer] got away from my hands and beat a path toward the door. She stopped there

and before I could get at her again to kill her, do you know what she did to me? . . . Well, she stuck her tongue out at me, and that's not the worst of it, because she made an ugly sound at me with her mouth . . . the little tart headed toward the kitchen and then toward the porch . . . she headed toward the street and got into the car of that good-for-nothing Samaniego, who she says is her boyfriend."

[27]Shameless.

[28]Tart.

[29]Good-for-nothing.

[30]See Alma M. García (ed.), *Chicana Feminist Thought: The Basic Historical Writings.* New York: Routledge, 1997.

[31]"I feel happy because we have succeeded in getting them to go Southward; toward the path that all Mexicans living over there in the United States have a duty to follow; to the South; toward the homeland."

[32]" . . . don't speak to me in English, because they'll start saying I'm *agringado* [Americanized] again.."

[33]"I don't like these customs that do not allow you to be alone with one another. Besides, I want to return to Los Angeles. . . . You won't like it either. You'll see. Here the people are good but something is missing, I just don't know what."

[34]"And instinctively they began to speak in English. They returned to using the language of their childhood that aided them in expressing what they both felt."

Recovering the Memory of Revolutionary Activity in the Texas Periodical *La Prensa:* Jorge Ainslie's "Mis andanzas en la Revolución Escobarista"

DONNA M. KABALEN DE BICHARA

Tecnológico de Monterrey

Hispanic print culture produced in various regions of the United States, and particularly the literary production of Spanish-language newspapers, provides us with information that points to various types of issues concerned with identity, culture, and history. Of interest in the development of the US Hispanic Press was the possibility of presenting the uncensored views of those who emigrated from Mexico and were often forced to live in exile. *La Prensa* of San Antonio, Texas, established by Ignacio Lozano in 1913, is an example of a periodical that focused on the readership of the Spanish-speaking Mexican community and provided a forum for the political and cultural views of various groups, including México de Afuera, a México outside its territorial limits. The history of this type of print culture is possible through the work of scholars who have participated in the Recovering the US Hispanic Literary Heritage Program which has focused its efforts on the collection, critical study, and dissemination of literary material that would remain lost to others interested in Hispanic history, culture and literature from the Colonial period through 1960. It is through a recovery effort that focuses on Spanish- language periodicals like *La Prensa*, that it is possible to bring readers into contact with political, religious, social and identity issues that are addressed in editorials, serialized novels, short stories, and various types of special-interest columns. Recovery and study of the writings of dissidents such as Victoriano Salado Álvarez, José Juan Tablada,

José Ascensión Reyes, Teodoro Torres, Nemesio García Naranjo, Martín Luis Guzmán, José Vasconcelos and Juan Sánchez Azcona provide readers with information and critical viewpoints related to the sentiments of México de Afuera. Through their writing they made the claim that the ideology they espoused represented a more pure vision of governmental practices and certain cultural traditions that circulated in what Luis Leal defines as "México de Adentro (Mexico as a territorial unit)" (242).

As a means of framing the discussion of exiled writers who contributed to *La Prensa*, it is relevant to mention Kanellos' discussion of the characteristics of US Hispanic literature, especially in terms of exile literature. Although the list of characteristics comparing exile literature to immigrant and native literature is extensive, the following types of references mark the texts of exile literature: "[r]eturn to the homeland;" "[p]rotest politics in the homeland;" "[p]olitical/revolutionary nation building;" and "revolutionaries and counterrevolutionaries" (23). These characteristics are useful in recovery research that contributes to the process of unlocking the meaning of those texts created by exiled Mexicans who took up residence in the United States and who published their writing in Spanish-language newspapers.

One of the writers who contributed to periodicals such as *La Prensa* was Jorge Ainslie who left Mexico and then made his home in Los Angeles, California. A prolific writer, Ainslie contributed twenty-one short stories, three novels, a short novella, anecdotes, and narrative texts that chronicle journeys to and from the United States and throughout various spaces in Mexico. A major element of Ainslie's texts concerns historical references. For example, two of Ainslie's novels, *Los Pochos* (1934) and *Los Repatriados* (1935), are based on historical events that have to do with the situation of Mexican exiles, their journey to the United States, and their return to Mexico.

The novel, *Los Pochos*, presents the reader with views of the Mexican working class and the dilemmas of their economic situation in Mexico prior to the Mexican Revolution. In the first chapter of the novel Ainslie presents literary referents regarding the lack of opportunity for families in Mexico in the years leading up to the Revolution of 1910. The chapter sets the literary stage for the development of different types of social formations involving positions of poverty as well as power: "La pobreza en que habían vivido siempre: aquella miseria; la había heredado él, como si un hada maléfica lo hubiera maldecido para toda su vida" ("The poverty in which they had always lived: that misery; he had inherited it, as if a wicked fairy had cursed him for his whole life") (*LP* 15 April 1934, 2).[1] Godínez was finally able to secure a government administrative position as "Recaudador de Rentas del Estado ("State Rent Collector") (2). Once news of the Revolution broke out, and after the assassination of Madero and the beginning of Carranza's revolution, he stole thirty-two thousand pesos and gold coins that allowed him to live comfortably after leaving his home in Santa Rosalía and escaping with his wife. His journey by train took him first to Torreón, then to El Paso, Texas and finally to Los Angeles, California.

Los Repatriados deals with a different period in history, and it is a novel that involves national and transnational references intended to transmit cultural memory that emphasizes the effects of exile and deterritorialization. This novel focuses on a different type of journey that can be understood in the context of the repatriation of Mexican nationals and American citizens of Mexican descent who had lived and worked in the United States. Many of those who repatriated left voluntarily, but many were coerced into leaving during the 1930s to resettle in Mexico. An important number of issues of *La Prensa* include articles on the theme of the repatriation of Mexicans during the 1930s; yet this same issue is also addressed in 1917 when thousands chose to return to Mexico rather than be drafted to serve in World War I. The causes for repatriation in the 1930s include factors mentioned by Balderama and Rodríguez who note that,

> Americans, reeling from the economic disorientation of the depression, sought a convenient scapegoat. They found it in the Mexican community. In a frenzy of anti- Mexican hysteria, wholesale punitive measures were proposed and undertaken by government officials at the federal, state, and local levels . . . Contributing to the brutalizing experience were the mass deportation roundups and repatriation drives" (1).

Based on the conditions encountered by a community of people who lived through the process of voluntary repatriation to the homeland during the 1930s, *Los repatriados* opens with a reference to a store owned by Raymundo Godínez, Federico Godínez's brother. Tellingly, the first lines of the novel refer to the sign on Raymundo's store: "Los Recuerdos de México" ("The Memories of Mexico") (*LP* 29 Sept. 1939, 3). *Los repatriados* highlights the way Mexican immigrants living in the US are duped into giving up their businesses and property in exchange for property sold at inflated prices in Mexico. However, it is the name of Raymundo's store that points to an underlying memory and connection to the home country. Raymundo refuses to listen to the offer to give up his store in return for land in Mexico, yet his brother Federíco, along with other Mexicans and their families, returns in search of a dream of economic success and social recognition.

In keeping with the historical emphasis evident in Ainslie's writing, this essay examines four narrative installments, published in *La Prensa* between April 18 and May 9, 1937, that chronicle a rebellion initiated by the Sonoran, José Gonzalo Escobar. Another major intention of this study is to explore the discursive elements of Ainslie's four texts on his "andanzas" ("adventures") in the Rebelión Escobarista, and the way they demonstrate the writer's intention to appeal to an exiled reading public interested in reconstructing the narrative of historical events surrounding the rebellion.

In the four installments the writer narrates journeys to Sonora and alludes to the possibility that the journeys he made between Los Angeles and Nogales, Sonora involved his participation in Escobar's rebellion. A close reading of a series of texts created by Ainslie's, "Mis andanzas en la Revolución Escobarista" ("My Adventures in the Escobar Rebellion"), raises questions concerning the author's identity and personal history in Mexico prior to and during his life as an exile in the United States. The reader begins to question whether the episodes of the narratives concerning his journeys are in fact based on the author's actual life experiences, or whether they were purely fictional. Although it is impossible to determine an answer to these questions, literary studies demonstrate that life experiences function as the creative stimulus of an author's writing. Thus, it can be assumed that Ainslie's narratives function as a window into his own memories and life. Of further interest for the present discussion, however, are the historical references that serve as a context for Ainslie's writing.

To preface the four installments published in *La Prensa*, it is important to mention an article entitled, "Se Desconfía en Washington de la Victoria de las Tropas del Gobierno: Obregán será apoyado hasta lo ultimo," ("Washington Distrusts the Victory of Government Troops: Obregón Will be Supported to the End") which was published in *La Prensa* on January 10, 1924:

> La capital americana espera con interés y con mucha curiosidad la lle-gada aquí, mañana, de una delegación de representantes de los rebeldes mexicanos. Al presentarse los revolucionarios en el departamento de Estado, no se les tratará con más cortesía que la que puedan recibir cualesquiera otros visitantes . . . El personal de la delegación delahuertista está formado por Antonio Manero, secretario particular del **jefe rebelde Jorge Ainslie**,[2] Rafael Montenegro, Miguel Flores Villar, Jorge Bas y Basilio Camino. (1)

> The American capital awaits with interest and much curiosity the arrival here tomorrow, of a delegation of representatives of Mexican rebels. When the revolutionaries arrive at the Department of State, they will not be extended any courtesy beyond that of other visitors . . . The personnel of the De la Huerta delegation includes Antonio Manero, personal secre-tary of the head rebel Jorge Ainslie, Rafael Montenegro, Miguel Flores Villar, Jorge Bas and Basilio Camino.

This is the only article in *La Prensa* that connects Jorge Ainslie with the Rebellion led by Adolfo de la Huerta that took place in 1923, just 6 years prior to the rebellion headed by Escobar.

The historical background of the 1923 rebellion involves Adolfo de la Huerta, Plutarco Elias Calles, and Álvaro Obregón—all of whom played key political roles in Sonora. Due to discontent over Carranza's ideological position as president (1917-1920), De la Huerta and Calles, "issued the Plan de Agua Prieta, calling for the nation to rise up and overthrow Carranza" (Gonzales 179- 80). Ultimately Carranza was assassinated and Adolfo de la Huerta, "revolutionary commander and governor of the state," (184) assumed the position of interim president thus paving the way for the first four-year period of Álvaro Obregón's presidency. Obregón, whose presidency was supported by the United States, served as president of Mexico from 1920-1924. However, at this moment in history, because presidential terms in Mexico were for a four-year period, and because reelection was impossible, he chose Calles as his successor with the intention of returning as president after Calles' presidential period (Meyer 146). However, Obregón's Treasury Minister, Adolfo de la Huerta, who had served as the interim president in 1920 before Obregón became president, had his own ambitions to become president. De la Huerta ultimately organized a rebellion against Obregón in 1923. A good number of Villistas, including a number of generals, supported De la Huerta's armed revolt,[3] but the rebellion was ultimately crushed given the support Obregón received from the CROM labor movement (Meyer, 231)[4] Adolfo de la Huerta eventually fled Mexico to Los Angeles (Gonsalez 201);[5] however, De la Huerta, like other exiles, would continue to meddle in Mexico's political affairs. With this history as background, one is left to ponder Ainslie's life as a "jefe rebelde" who also left Mexico and went into exile in Los Angeles.

Regarding Ainslie's text and his description of his "andanzas" with the generals involved in the Rebelión Escobarista, historian Tzvi Medin's study focuses on Mexico's history during the period between 1928 and 1935.[6] From his point of view the drama facing the country after Carranza's death concerned a reality involving "[l]a autoridad del caudillo, la fuerza militar, la necesidad de legalidad constitucional, el legado revolucionario, [y] las fuerzas populares desatadas durante la revolución" ("[t]he authority of the leader of a political faction, the military forces, the need for constitutional legality, [and] a revolutionary legacy, popular forces detonated during the revolution") (13). He further suggests that the "Caudillos: Carranza, Obregón, Calles [y] las fuerzas militares: Serrano, Amaro, Escobar, Almazán" ("Politically-backed leaders: Carranza, Obregón, Calles [and] military forces") (13), were part of an effort to find a final political solution to Mexico's post-revolutionary state. Despite these efforts, numerous revolts based on regional interests continued. According to Georgette Valenzuela, the Rebelión Escobarista lasted from March through May 1, 1929 (24), and it is one among numerous rebellions following Obregon's reelection and later assassination in 1928.

Ainslie's chronicles provide historical elements concerning political and revolutionary activity in Sonora that may or may not be true. Indeed, as suggested by Hayden White, the historical novel provides both "real" and "imagined" elements (89). Ainslie's obvious intention is to enter into dialogue with his reader and offer his own view of historical events; however, he also uses the installments to highlight the intrigue surrounding the members of what Alan Knight has termed, the "Sonoran regime of the 1920s" (vol. 2, 100) which was led by Álvaro Obregón.

Obregón's desire to serve a second term as president of Mexico and his subsequent assassination in 1928,[7] provide the historical context for "Mis andanzas en la Revolución Escobarista." The four installments refer to the rebellion led by General José Gonzalo Escobar as "Jefe Supremo" ("Supreme Head") of a movement whose aims were published in Sonora, México in the Plan de Hermosillo in 1929. The document declared non-recognition of Emilio Portes Gil as the provisional president of Mexico after the assassination of President Álvaro Obregón. Ainslie's texts are heavily accented with historical references to various rebelling factions in Mexico. Furthermore, they also present specific references to the narrative "I" which leads to questions about the author's own life experiences in relation to the rebellion led by Escobar.

To explore those questions related to Ainslie and his possible participation in the Escobar rebellion, Derrida's notion of "differénce" provides a lens through which to examine the four literary installments. The concept of "differénce" sets the tone for questioning language, thought, and meaning which are not fixed, and Derrida asserts instead that there are multiple layers of meaning at work in language; thus, language is constantly shifting. Derrida also questions the concept of consciousness, and the idea of whether we are truly present to ourselves. In this direction he notes that "The center is not the center," but rather "a point of departure" where we find "repetitions, substitutions, transformations, and permutations [that] are always taken from a history of meaning [sens]" ("Structure, Sign and Play in the Discourse of the Human Sciences" 279). Because of this sense of a shifting center, because "we cannot grasp or show the thing, state the present, the being-present, when the present cannot be presented, we signify, we go through the detour of the sign. We take or give signs. We signal. The sign, in this sense, is deferred presence" ("Differánce" 3-27). From this perspective then, Ainslie's references to self, the repetition of "I", can be understood as signs that signify his own "history of meaning." However, the reader senses the writer's determination to detour the reader's attention and blur those signs within the chronicles. As such, this theoretical explanation regarding self-presence as fiction, does not completely satisfy the reader's curiosity as to whether the "I" in Ainslie's narratives represent true personal history of his journeys to Nogales where he supposedly met up with revolutionary groups. A possible explanation of these textual detours has to do with the history of the De la Huerta rebels, many of whom were sent to El Paso, San Antonio, Los Ángeles, and Cuba to acquire needed arms for the rebellion (Placencia de la Parra 108). However, while living in the United States, figures such as generals Enrique Estrada, Aureliano Sepúlveda and Ramón Arnáiz were arrested on counts of violating US laws that prohibited foreigners from raising funds for foreign wars while in US territory (123). After the failure of the rebellion, most of the major figures went into exile in the US. De la Huerta himself fled to Los Angeles where he and other exiles were under careful scrutiny by the US government. This history, therefore, is most probably the reason that Ainslie will humorously mask details about his "andanzas" in the Escobar rebellion.

In the first installment, "El autor hace penoso viaje hasta Nogales" ("The Author Makes a Painful Trip to Nogales") , a return to the homeland, and a tone of continued revolutionary fervor mark the text: "Cuando llegó a Los Angeles la noticia del asesinato de Obregón, todos los refugiados políticos abrigamos la esperanza de que muy pronto reventaría en México otra revolución, que nos daría la oportunidad para regresar a nuestra patria, ya fuera pacíficamente o con las armas en la mano" ("When news of Obregon's assassination reached Los Angeles, all the political refugees [we] harbored the hope that another revolution would soon explode in Mexico, [one] that would offer the opportunity to return to our country, either peacefully or with arms in hand") (*LP* 1 Apr. 1937, 31). A key point in this fragment is Ainslie's use of the third person plural, "abrigamos." Through this linguistic construction the writer clearly meant to include himself as one of the political refugees mentioned here.

By referring to the trip undertaken by "el autor," or the author, Ainslie signals his presence as one of those who made up the group of political refugees. If indeed he was among the exiles mentioned here, and also a rebel leader in the De la Huerta Rebellion, he and other rebels most probably believed that further revolutionary activity was necessary, especially after Mexico's congress determined that Portes Gil should step in as interim president after Obregon's assassination. In his study Medin describes the beginning of the rebellion as follows: "El 3 de marzo de 1929 se publican en Sonora el Plan de Hermosillo, en el que se desconocía al presidente Portes Gil la investidura de presidente provisional, reconociéndose en cambio al general José Gonzalo Escobar como 'Jefe Supremo' de este movimiento y del ejército renovador" ("March 3, 1929 the Sonora Plan of Hermosillo was published, in which Portes Gil's inauguaration as provisional president was not recognized, [and] instead recognizing General José Gonzalo Escobar as the 'Supreme Chief' of this movement and the army of renewal") (50). This installment points to news that arrived in Los Angeles on March 2, 1929 about what the writer calls another revolution. Initially, the narrator insists that he is comfortable in Los Angeles where he publishes a magazine and he expresses wariness about the possibility of becoming involved "en un campo de personas desconocidas para mí, y con quienes no me ligaba ni amistad ni afinidad de ideas" ("in a group of unknown people, with which I had no friendship or affinity of ideas") (*LP* 1 Apr. 1937, 31). Despite this expression of having little in common with the group, he ultimately decides that his participation is necessary so as to "apoyar el derrocamiento de los que se habían entronizado en México, y teniendo la firme convicción de cualquier cambio político podría beneficiar a mi patria" ("to support the overthrow of those who had been enthroned in Mexico, and having the firm conviction that any political change would benefit my country") (31). In keeping with Derrida's notion of "history of meaning," the discursive sign "mi patria," or "my country" signals the writer's determination to imbue the text with meaning about his own sense of connection with the home country. His desire to continue to participate actively in the affairs of Mexico is the basis for his adherence to the spirit of the rebellion led by Escobar.

The text immediately establishes the relation between the narrator and generals such as Ramón B. Arnáiz and Federico Silva:[8]

Al día siguiente, 3 de marzo, me apersoné con los generales Ramón B. Arnáiz y Federico Silva, buenos amigos míos: revolucionarios honrados, que habían como yo militado en las filas delahuertistas. Después de discutir por algunos minutos la forma que nos transladaríamos (sic) a Nogales, Sonora, puerto fronterizo en poder de las fuerzas escobaristas y el más próximo a Los Ángeles, decidimos hacer el viaje en el automóvil del capitán Ignacio de la Torre y llevarnos a otro general, Nicolás Barajas, revolucionario tapatío. (*LP* 18 Apr. 1937, 31)

The next day, March 3, I met with Generals Ramón B. Arnáiz and Federico Silva, good friends of mine, who like me had fought in De la Huerta's ranks. After a discussion of a few minutes about how we would travel to Nogales, Sonora, a border town under the domination of Escobar's troops and the closest to Los Angeles, we decided to travel in Captain Ignacio de la Torre's automobile and to take with us another general, Nicolás Barajas, a revolutionary from Guadalajara.

This fragment presents a narrative "I" that identifies the narrator as someone who, like Arnáiz and Silva, had participated in the rebellion led by De la

Huerta and who was now intent on discovering information about the Escobar rebellion. Interestingly, however, the figures that illustrate the first page of the installment, picture five men warming themselves by a fire. Four of them are dressed in trench coats one has knee-high boots on, and another is wearing a sport coat. All of them are wearing fedora hats of the period. This sign, or text-image, constructs an imaginary related to men who leave a comfortable lifestyle to tread once more upon the possibility of becoming involved in revolutionary activities. Yet, when their car runs out of gas, and they are faced with pushing the car the four-mile distance to their destination in Nogales, the narrator refuses to cooperate and he describes himself as well-dressed, a "catrín banquetero," ("a party-going dandy") unwilling to act as an "acémila" or mule.

Rather than functioning as clues to the identity of the narrator, the textual asides signal the writer's intention to provoke laughter rather than simply explains his association with men interested in becoming involved in rebel activities in Mexico. The narrator's sense of being dapper and far-removed from the demands of revolutionary activity provide a humorous tone to the text that continues as he describes how the other four men pushed the car because, "al cabo como militares han de estar acostumbrados a empujar cañones" ("after all they are soldiers and must be used to pushing cannons") (31). This portion of the text demonstrates the writer's sense of humor, but it also stands in contrast to his original statements about the possibility of joining up with former generals to aid the politics of "la patria." This shift in tone functions as a departure from a serious objective to the seeming comic situation of having to push a car to the group's final destination. The writer's use of humor is deliberate. Ainslie is laughing at himself and his companions for their lack of preparedness in the face of a possible revolution. By provoking laughter, Ainslie is attempting to mask his own history of actual participation in the Escobar Rebellion which, like the De la Huerta rebellion, was a failure. Because the writer is reconstructing a painful past, his laughter can be interpreted as a mask for the bitter sense of failure he and his compatriots experienced after both rebellions—rebellions that resulted in unwanted exile for them.

The rebel group continues its journey and finally arrives in Nogales, Sonora, and the band of men is described as "Llenos de contento . . . [para] prepararnos para pasar la frontera y presentarnos en el Cuartel General de las fuerzas revolucionarias, que se encontraban a cargo del general Francisco Bórquez . . . Al llegar al hotel se formaron dos grupos; uno formado por Silva, Barajas y de la Torre y otro por Arnáiz y el que esto escribe" ("Content . . . [about] preparing to cross the border and present ourselves at the General Headquarters of the revolutionary forces, that were under the charge of general Francisco Bórquez . . . Upon arriving at the hotel two groups were formed; one formed by Silva Barajas and de la Torre and another by Arnáiz and he who writes this [narrative]") (*LP* 18 Apr. 1937, 31). Here the text presents another change in the writer's positionality from a well-dressed observer to someone who is aligned with men involved in rebel activity. Once the travelers cross by foot into Nogales, Sonora the text presents an imaginary that focuses on the homeland and a moment of nostalgia when Arnáiz says, "Oiga, Don Jorge, aquí todos los letreros están en español—Pues si ya estamos en México, le contesté" ("Listen, Don Jorge, here all the signs are in Spanish—Of course we are now in Mexico, I answered") (14).

The second installment of Ainslie's chronicle, entitled "En el campo rebelde de Nogales, Son.," ("In the Rebel Camp of Nogales, Sonora") focuses once more on the identity of the five travelers from Los Angeles as well as a number of "Viejo[s] conocido[s]" or old acquaintances (*LP* 25 Apr. 1937, 32). The first page of the installment includes a text-image of well-dressed men gathered in a bar, and it includes the following caption: ". . . a una cantina a tomar el aperitivo, y allí encontré con la mayoría de los bebedores habían sido condiscípulos míos y amigos" (". . . to a bar to have a cocktail, and there I found that the majority of the drinkers had been fellow classmates and friends of mine") (3). The image communicates a space of ease, one that is distant from the imaginary of the rebel camp announced in the title of the text. We find that two of the travelers, Arnáiz and the writer leave their hotel in search of the general headquarters, but they are greeted instead by two armed men who threaten to arrest them. The narrator's response centers on the identity of the five travelers from Los Angeles: "Al principio sentí cierto desasosiego, dado como habíamos sido delahuertistas, y por lo tanto enemigos de los que ahora íbamos a buscar, no tenía la seguridad si seríamos recibidos con los brazos abiertos o bien nos mandarían al paredón" ("At first I felt a certain unease, given that we had been [followers of] De la Huerta, and therefore enemies of those for whom we were now searching, I was not sure if we would be received with open arms or if they would instead send us to a firing squad") (3). This portion of the text signals the identity of Ainslie as a collaborator of De la Huerta during the 1923 rebellion; most importantly, however, the fragment emphasizes the enmity between various political camps involved in continuing revolutionary activity. The narrator then shares his thoughts with the reader: "vaya una forma en que este par de léperos reciben a dos patriotas que vienen a ofrender sus vidas en aras de la libertad de pensamiento, la no reelección, la no imposición y el deseo de volver a su patria" ("indeed what a way for this pair of rude [men] to receive two patriots who come to offer their lives in the name of freedom of thought, non- reelection, non-imposition and the desire to return to their country") (32). The discursive usage of phrases such as "la libertad de pensamiento, la no reelección, la no imposición"[9] draws on ideological views that formed the basis for the militant activities of De la Huerta and his followers as well as those of Escobar; that is, the question of the imposition of Calles as president and Álvaro Obregón's reelection are implicit in the discourse of this fragment of the text that signals political allegiance. Moreover, this fragment makes discursive reference that highlight the lofty ideals that marked the Mexican Revolution as well as later rebellions led by De la Huerta and Escobar. Furthermore, Ainslie's text repeatedly gives voice to the exile, who hopes to return to a homeland that has achieved its revolutionary ideals.

The text once more emphasizes a history of meaning that focuses on the "I" as the narrator introduces himself and the general who accompanies him: "—El señor es el general Arnáiz y yo soy Jorge Ainslie" (—The gentleman is general Arnáiz and I am Jorge Ainslie") (13). Once the two soldiers discover Arnáiz's identity, they eagerly take both men to the General Headquarters where they meet with General Francisco Bórquez.[10] Both generals great each other effusively, but Ainslie is totally ignored by them; he is later told that because he is a civilian, he will have to wait for the arrival of General Topete. The text then moves from the space of the headquarters to a nearby cantina where Ainslie arrives with "el Diputado Dr. Uruchurto" ("Congressman Dr. Uruchurto") who was from Ainslie's hometown:

> y al contemplar aquel grupo de amigos de la niñez a quienes no veía desde hace 20 años, cuando mi padre me llevó a la capital de la República y me dejó de interno en el Colegio Inglés, empezaron a agolpar me a mi mente los recuerdos de mi primera edad . . . Todos éramos ya hombres, y si en nuestra juventud nos unió la amistad, allí estábamos de nuevo reunidos peleando por una misma causa; unos por ideales, los menos, y otros por conveniencia. (*LP* 25 Apr. 1937, 32)

> and to contemplate that group of childhood friends that I had not seen for 20 years, when my father took me to the capital of the Republic and he left me as an intern at the Colegio Inglés, memories of my early age began to hit my mind . . . All of us were now men, and if friendship bound us during our youth, there we were again reunited [and] fighting for the same cause; some because of ideals, the lesser number, and others out of convenience.

This childhood memory, and the repetition of textual signs regarding what is familiar, once more hint at the writer's personal history and his relation to those he meets and their common cause. Essentially, this encounter functions as a reference to the multiple identities that the text projects concerning Ainslie as an

exile comfortably settled in Los Angeles, his identity as a young boy from Sonora, and ultimately his revolutionary identity. The fragment which nostalgically
recalls memories from his past stands in stark contrast to his identity as a member of revolutionary groups. It is the latter identity that prevents him from
returning to his homeland.

The remainder of this installment points to news regarding the rebellion
that "caminaba de triunfo en triunfo en Nuevo León, Coahuila y Chihuahua"
("progressed from triumph to triumph in Nuevo León, Coahuila and Chihuahua") (34). The historical focus of the text includes mention of General
Fausto Topete, also born in Sonora, and who had originally collaborated with
Obregón in the Mexican Revolution. [11] The text signals Ainslie and Topete as
acquaintances: who had met previously in Los Angeles. Topete greets Ainslie
warmly and gives orders to assign Ainslie to the position of "agente propagan-
dista de la revolución en California" ("agent of propaganda for the revolution in
California") (LP 25 Apr. 1937, 32), and as a member of the commission to
appear before the government in Washington (33). Ainslie's revelation of his
self- presence as an exile who is still active in the political conflicts in Mexico
clearly underlies the meaning of the text.

The final portion of the installment once again emphasizes the splintering
factions that are part of the history of the Escobar rebellion. For example,
Ainslie points out that, rather than remaining at general headquarters, General
Arnáíz decides to join forces with General Topete and both would fight in the
southern part of Mexico. Ainslie further complicates the final portion of the
installment by mentioning the arrival of Gilberto Valenzuela who was the presidential candidate favored by the leaders of the Escobar rebellion.[12] Here the
writer mentions that he already knew Valenzuela when he was Assistant Secretary of the Interior. He then adds information about his own government role
during that same period when he held the postion of was "Delegado de Con-
traloría, comisionado en esa Secretaría y el Gobierno del disto" ("Delegate of
the Office of the Comptroller commissioned in that Ministry and in the District
Government") (33).[13] Through repetitive references to participants in the Escobar rebellion and allusion to the author's personal history in relation to Valenzuela, the text contributes to a "web of social meaning" (Tyson 291). As such
Ainslie's narratives provide a historical chronicle that emphasizes alternative
governing groups in conflict.

The third and fourth installments of Ainslie s chronicle, continue to narrate
the conflicting positions of various military actors involved in the rebellion led
by Escobar. The third installment, "La dudosa actitud del General Manzo"[14]
("The Doubtful Attitude of General Manzo"), finds Ainslie waiting for news
about progress of the rebellion. The text is illustrated with an image of two men

dressed in suits, and both wearing fedora hats. A third bearded man, professor Manrique, seems to be the center of attention. The text image contributes to the meaning of the text that begins by focusing on Manrique and his intention to meet up with Escobar who is expecting attacks by federal troops. Another shift in the text points to ex- followers of De la Huerta who express interest in participating in the Escobar rebellion, and they request funds to do so. This type of information is used by the writer as a commentary on the frustrating lack of cohesion among the generals fighting in various camps.

The narrative shifts once more toward the self-presence of the author and his disillusion with the rebellion which he describes as being in disarray. He explains that he expected to participate as part of the commission organized by General Fausto Topete: "Como mi estancia en Nogales no tenía objeto, y aún no se decidía la fecha de la salida de la Comisión que Topete pensaba enviar a Washington y de la cual formaba yo parte, decidí regresar al día siguiente a ésta, donde creí poder hacer algo de propaganda y algunas declaraciones, las cuales fueron publicadas en LA OPINIÖN y el Evening Herald" ("Since there was no reason to remain in Nogales, and since the date when the Topete Commission was to be sent to Washington had not been decided, of which I formed part, I decided to go back the next day to where I thought I could work on some propaganda and some declarations, which were [then] published in LA OPINIÓN and the Evening Herald") (24). Interestingly, the illustrations of the final installments continue to demonstrate participants in the rebellion dressed in trench coats and fedoras, thus leading the reader to question, once more, the author's actual participation in the rebellion. As mentioned above Ainslie's role seems to be limited to promoting propaganda for a possible future trip to Washington.

In keeping with the focus of exile literature and its emphasis on revolutionary activity that was intended to contribute to nation building, Ainslie's desire to promote the cause he was associated with is emphasized in the final installment of his chronicle: "El autor estuvo en peligro de ser fusilado" ("The author was in danger of being shot"). The title is clearly meant to appeal to the reader's eagerness to discover more information about the uprising. Ainslie explains that after having spent three weeks in Los Angeles trying to discover further news about the Escobar rebellion, he decides to journey back to the border region of Sonora where he finds a changed atmosphere. He then notes: "La ciudad presentaba un aspecto muy diferente [sic] a como lo había dejado yo. El ir y venir de los militares y civiles revolucionarios había desaparecido, y en la cara de los pocos que aún quedaban se retrataba la desilusión y la tristeza. Escobar había sido derrotado en Reforma y Manzo se estrellaba ante la resistencia que hacían los Federales en Mazatlan" ("The city appeared very different compared to the way I had left it. The coming and going of revolutionary soldiers and civilians had disappeared, and the faces of the few who remained portrayed disillusion and sadness. Escobar had been defeated in Reforma, and Manzo against the resistance of the Federal army in Mazatlan") (*LP* 5 May 1937, 24). After hearing of the failure of the rebellion, Ainslie then describes his return to headquarters and his search for Bórquez. This moment is illustrated with another image on the first page of the text where a man in his trench coat and fedora seems to be talking to a soldier who is holding his rifle. The text that accompanies the image, "Frente a la casa solo había un centinela y dos muchachos 'jugando al caballo' sobre el barandilla del porch" ("There was only one guard in front of the house and two boys playing at [riding] a horse on the handrail of the porch") (24). Observing that only one man is standing guard, Ainslie expresses his perception that "Escobar había sido aniquilado completamente" ("Escobar had been completely annihilated") (24). It becomes clear by the end of the installment that, although Ainslie's "andanzas" in the rebellion minimal, or non-existent, he is intent on writing his presence into the history of two rebellions that form part of the complex post-revolutionary history of Mexico.

Of particular interest in the final installment of the chronicles however, is an emphasis on the effects of the political unrest caused by the failure of yet another rebellion which resulted in further migration north. The writer appeals to his reading audience by describing the reality of post-revolutionary Mexico and the "[g]ran cantidad de familias procedentes del interior del Estado [que] llegaron al puerto fronterizo cargadas con lo que de más valor poseían y pasaban inmediatamente la frontera buscando refugio en los Estados Unidos" "([l]arge number of families who were from the center of the State [of Sonora] and who arrived at the border loaded down with their most valued possessions and immediately crossed the border to find refuge in the United States") (24). This literary moment once again emphasizes the historical intertwining of the history of Mexico and its effect on the world space of the border region of the United States as Mexican citizens seek refuge to escape the turmoil prevalent after yet another uprising during a period of tumultuous events. The narrative continues and Ainslie describes another journey to Sonora where he finds that a number of his "amigos ex-delahuertistas" ("ex-delahuertista friends) had decided to head south and continue fighting. Ainslie describes his own disillusionment about information he receives from Topete explaining that the trip to Washington had been cancelled. After returning to Los Angeles once more, he continues to promote the revolutionary cause, but he tells the reader that after attempting to promote propaganda at several radio stations: "me convencí de que era inútil querer hacer propaganda en favor de la revolución ya que no solo los periódicos, sino el público estaba a favor del gobierno de Portes Gil y empezaban a llamarnos bandidos" ("I was convinced it was useless to want to promote propaganda in favor of the revolution now that not only the newspapers but the public was in favor of the government of Portes Gil and they started calling us bandits") (*LP* 9 May 1937, 24). Indeed, as suggested by Jean Meyer, "[e]l poder del Estado reposa sobre el ejército y los sindicatos en el interior, sobre la ayuda americana en el exterior" ("[t]he power of the State rests on the army and the unions within the country, on American support outside [the country] (158). The writer ultimately realizes that propaganda was not enough without the backing of the US; this was true for the uprising led by De la Huerta, and equally true for Escobar's short-lived rebellion. After deciding to return to Los Angeles Ainslie assures the reader he intends to forget the rebellion: "Me anoto en mi Carrera revolucionaria otro fracaso y me dedico a mis negocios" ("I will note another failure in my revolutionary career and dedicate [my efforts] to my businesses") (24).

The results of the failed rebellion are emphasized in the final installment as Ainslie explains that after fifteen days, exiles began their return. One of the first exiles was Doctor Uruchurta and Ainslie then meets another "desterrado" ("exile") who tells him: —De la que te salvaste—me dijo después de saludarme—Si has vuelto a Nogales te fusilan" "("—What you escaped from—he told me after greeting me—If you had returned to Nogales you would have been shot") (25). The writer then explains that because one of the generals believed Ainslie to be a spy for Calles, he had given orders to have Ainslie killed. In terms of the truth or fiction of the chronicle of events, in the final installment, the author simply states that:

Después de ocho años es muy difícil recordar detalles y fechas, cuando no se ha tenido la curiosidad de llevar un diario, pero como este no es un relato histórico sino una simple narración, creo que ciertos detalles y fechas carecen en absoluto de importancia; pero de lo único que estoy seguro de que lo que digo aquí, fue lo que vi o me relataron. Los Angeles California, 1937. (*LP* 9 May. 1937, 26)

After eight years it is very difficult to remember details and dates, when [one] has not been curious enough to keep a diary, but because this is not a historical account but only a simple narration, I believe certain details and dates lack absolute importance; but the only thing I am sure of is that what I say here, was what I saw or what I was told. Los Angeles California, 1937.

The text is marked with a sense of loss and disillusion on the part of the writer and his compatriots in their attempt to affect political change in the homeland. Yet the change they fought for, what Meyer describes as "el nuevo México

en gestación que buscaba penosamente su camino" ("the new Mexico in gesta-
tion that searched painfully for its path") (133), was not to be. As Medin asserts,
the development of Mexico during this historical period rested on the fact that
"los protagonistas principales intentaron dar diferentes respuestas en función de
la realidad Mexicana" ("the major protagonists attempted to find different
answers in relation to the Mexican reality") (13). Ainslie's chronicle is a reference to one of those responses and demonstrates how the historical narrative,
despite questions regarding the supposed real or imagined truth of the text and
the identity of its author, performs the function of producing further knowledge
about the Mexican political and military upheaval that lasted from 1910-1930.
Most importantly, however, the chronicle involving Ainslie's supposed participation in the Escobar Rebellion appeals to readers, many of whom were exiles
and perhaps among those who sought asylum in the United States after the
rebellion.[15] By referring to activities concerning the "rebelión delahuertista" and
the "rebelión Escobarista," the writer draws his readers into an imaginary that is
constructed on a historical reality that marked the lives of the many exiles who
took up residence in cities such as San Antonio and Los Angeles and beyond.
Thus, Ainslie's texts demonstrate use of a discursive method of bricolage, a literary practice that allows him to borrow "concepts from the text of a heritage
which is more or less coherent or ruined" (Derrida, "Structure, Sign and Play",
400). In the case of political exiles like Ainslie, the text plays on questions of
history and an artistic appropriation and manipulation of events that only hint at
the author's own participation in rebellious activities. Truth is hidden within the
art form of the text, and the reader can only guess at where the "jefe rebelde
Jorge Ainslie" fits into Mexico's history. Ainslie's four chronicles represent a
"point of departure," where the history of those who were expelled from Mexico's ruling center, and their efforts at revolutionary nation-building, are narrated. Ultimately, however, it is through continuing archival work in the area of
periodical print culture, that these "other" histories can be recovered and thus
contribute to the effort of broadening the transnational history of the United
States and Mexico.

Works Cited

Ainslie, Jorge. *Los Pochos. La Prensa 15, 22, 29 Apr. 1934,* 6, 13, 20, 27 May,
    y 3 June, 1934. *Periódicos hispánicos de los Estados Unidos. Readex, His-
    panic American Newspapers, 1807-1980.* Biblioteca digital, Tecnológico de
    Monterrey. Accessed 15 Jan. 2015.
___. Los repatriados. *Readex, Hispanic American Newspapers, 1807-1980. La
    Prensa 13, 27 19 Sept. 6, 13, 20 Oct. y 3, 10, 17 Nov. 1935. Periódicos his-*

pánicos de los Estados Unidos. Biblioteca digital, Tecnológico de Monterrey. Accessed 10 Feb. 2015.

___. "Mis andanzas en la Revolución Escobarista: el autor hace penoso viaje hasta Nogales" *La Prensa* 18 Apr. 1937, pp. 31-32. *Periódicos hispánicos de los Estados Unidos*. *Readex, Hispanic American Newspapers, 1807-1980*. Biblioteca digital, Tecnológico de Monterrey. Accessed 20 Jan. 2015.

___. "Mis andanzas en la Revolución Escobarista: en el campo rebelde de Nogales, Sonora." *La Prensa* 25 Apr. 1937, pp. 32-34. *Periódicos hispánicos de los Estados Unidos*. *Readex, Hispanic American Newspapers, 1807-1980*. Biblioteca digital, Tecnológico de Monterrey. Accessed 22 Jan. 2015.

___. "Mis andanzas en la Revolución Escobarista: la dudosa actitud del Gral. Manzo." *La Prensa* 2 May 1937, pp. 24-26. *Periódicos hispánicos de los Estados Unidos*. *Readex, Hispanic American Newspapers, 1807-1980*. Biblioteca digital, Tecnológico de Monterrey. Accessed 15 Jan. 2015.

___. "Mis andanzas en la Revolución Escobarista: el autor estuvo en peligro de ser fusilado." *La Prensa*, 9 May 1937, pp. 24-26. *Periódicos hispánicos de los Estados Unidos*. *Readex, Hispanic American Newspapers, 1807-1980*. Biblioteca digital, Tecnológico de Monterrey. Accessed 15 Jan. 2015.

Balderama, Francisco and Raymond Rodriguez. *Decade of Betrayal: Mexican Repatriation in the 1930s*. U of New Mexico, P, 2006.

Diccionario de Generales de la Revolución Mexicana A-L Tomo I. Instituto Nacional De Estudios Históricos de las Revoluciones de México, 2014. www.inehrm.gob.mx/work/models/inehrm/Resource/305/1/images/dic_grales_r ev_t1.pdf Accessed Dec. 2016

Diccionario de Generales de la Revolución Mexicana M-Z Tomo II. Instituto Nacional De Estudios Históricos de las Revoluciones de México, 2014. http://www.inehrm.gob.mx/work/models/inehrm/Resource/305/1/images/dic_gr ales_rev_t 2.pdf Accessed Jan. 2017.

Derrida, Jacques. "Différance." *Margins of Philosophy*, translated by Alan Bass, U of Chicago P, 1982.

___. "Structure, Sign, and Play in the Discourse of the Human Sciences." *Literary Theories in Praxis*, edited by Shirley F. Staton, U of Pennsylvania P, 1987.

Gonzales, Michael J. *The Mexican RevolutIon 1910-1940*. U of New Mexico P, 2002.

Kanellos, Nicolás. *Hispanic Immigrant Literature: El sueño del retorno*. U of Texas P, 2011.

Kanellos, Nicolás and Helvetia Martell. "A Brief History of Hispanic Periodicals in the United States." *Recovering the U.S. Hispanic Literary Heritage*

Series: Hispanic Periodicals in the United States, Origins to 1960. A Brief History and Comprehensive Bibliography. Arte Público P, 2000.

Knight, Alan. *The Mexican Revolution, Volume 1: Porfirians, Rebels, and Peasants.* U of Nebraska P, 1990.

___. *The Mexican Revolution, Volume 2: Counter-Revolution and Reconstruction.* U of Nebraska P, 1990.

Leal, Luis. *A Luis Leal Reader.* Northwestern UP, 2007.

Meyer, Jean. *La Revolución Mexicana.* Translated by Hector Pérez-Rincón-G., Tusquets Editores, 2004.

___ "Revolution and Reconstruction in the 1920's." *Mexico since Independence,* edited by Leslie Bethell, Cambridge UP, 1991, pp. 201-240.

___. *La Cristiada. La guerra de los cristeros.* Siglo XXI, 1973.

Medin, Tzvi. *El minimato presidencial: historia política del Maximato,* 1928-1935. Ediciones Era, 1990.

Placencia de la Parra, Enrique. "El exilio delahuertista." *Estudios de Historia Moderna y Contemporánea,* No. 43, 2012, pp. 105-134. http://www.revistas.unam.mx/index.php/ehm/article/view/32068/29537Accessed 12 Nov. 2017

Pozas, Ricardo. "El Maximato: El Partido del Hombre Fuerte, 1929-1934)." *Estudios de Historia Moderna Contemporánea,* No. 9, 1983, pp. 251-79. http://www.historicas.unam.mx/moderna/ehmc/ehmc09/114.html Accessed 3 Jan. 2018.

"Se Desconfia en Washington de la Victoria de las Tropas del Gobierno: Obregán será apoyado hasta lo último." *La Prensa,* 28 Dec. 1919, p. 10. *Readex, Hispanic American Newspapers, 1808–1980.* Electronic Database Biblioteca Tecnológico de Monterrey.

Topete, Fausto. *Diccionario de generales de la Revolución Mexicana Tomo II.* Instituto Nacional de Estudios Históricos de las Revoluciones en México, 2014, pp. 1004-1005. http://www.inehrm.gob.mx/work/models/inehrm/Resource/305/1/images/dic_grales_rev_t 1.pdf Accessed 10 Dec. 2016

Tyson, Lois. *Critical Theory Today: A User Friendly Guide.* Routledge, 2015.

Valenzuela, Georgette José. "Introducción, selección y notas."

Memorias del General Antonio I. Villarreal sobre su participación en la Rebelión Escobarista de marzo de 1920 y otros documentos. Instituto Nacional de Estudios Históricos de las Revoluciones de México, 2006.

White, Hayden. "The Historical Text as Literary Artifact." *Narrative Dynamics: Essays on Time, Plot, Closure, and* Frames, edited by Brian Richardson. Ohio State UP, 2002. 191-210.

Endnotes

[1]All translations are mine, unless otherwise stated.

[2]The highlighting of words in bold is mine.

[3]As noted by Michael J. Gonsalez, Pancho Villa had "suffered his greatest defeats at the hands of Obregón and Calles (200) and both Obregón and Calles were fearful of a possible alliance between Villa and De la Huerta. See *The Mexican Revolution: 1910-1940.*

[4]The De la Huerta Rebellion took place between December of 1923 and March of 1924.

[5]For a more detailed account of the rebellion led by De la Huerta, see Michael J. Gonzales's *The Mexican Revolution: 1910-1940.*

[6]According to Ricardo Pozas, this period is marked by three presidencies that lasted only two years—Emilio Portes Gil (1928-30); Pacual Ortiz Rubio (1930-32); and Abelardo L. Rodríguez (1932-34). Lázaro Cáredenas would finally serve a full six-year term (1934-40). During this period the National Revolutionary Party (PNR) consolidated power and general Calles became the "Jefe Máximo" of the revolutionary forces. See "El Máximato: El Partido del Hombre Fuerte, 1929-1934."

[7]Mexico's Constitution of 1917 declares "sufragio efectivo no reelección" or effective vote and non-reelection. However, Plutarco Elías Calles was at the forefront of an attempt to amend the Constitution so as to allow re-election.

[8]Ramón B. Arnáiz participated in the Escobarista Rebellion. For a more detailed account of the Escobar's army and its intention to join the Cristero forces under the command of General Gorostieta, see Jean Meyer's *La cristiada: la Guerra de los Cristeros*. Federico Silva Villegas fought in the Mexican Revolution against Diaz's government in the forces led by General Pablo González. He also fought with González against Pancho Villa and the government of the Convención de Aguascalientes". For further description of Silva's military activities, see *Diccionario de Generales de la Revolución Mexicana Tomo I & II* http://biblio.upmx.mx/textos/148499.pdf.

[9]Francisco Madero's slogan was "sufragio efectivo y no reelección" 'effective suffrage and non-reelection." The Plan de Chihuahua of 1912 mentions "libertad de pensamiento" ("freedom of thought").

[10]Francisco Bórquez was a member of the revolutionary army and served in the Sonora Batallion under General Álvaro Obregón. See http://www.antorcha.net/biblioteca_virtual/historia/autobiografia/5_4.html and Obregón's political memoir, *8,000 kilómetros en campaña.* http://www.antorcha.net/biblioteca_virtual/historia/obregon/1.html.

[11]Fausto Topete Almada had been one of Álvaro Obregón's most loyal followers and defendants, supporting the Plan de Agua Prieta. He fought against the De la Huerta Rebellion. In 1927 he was elected governor of Sonora and in 1929 he became affiliated with General Gonzalo Escobar, leader of the rebellion against Emilio Portes Gil. After the Escobar rebellion failed, Topete went into exile in Mexicali, B.C. See *Diccionario de generals de la Revolución Mexicana* http://www.inehrm.gob.mx/work/models/inehrm/Resource/305/1/images/dic_grales_rev_t2.pdf.

[12]After Obregón's death Emilio Portes Gil was designated by congress as the interim president from 1928 to 1930, and he was expected to make a formal call for a presidential election.

[13]Gilberto Valenzuela, was ex-Secretary of the Interior under Calles, and was one of a group of men who declared their discontent with the imposition of Calles by Obregón as a means of assuring Obregon's reelection in 1928. According to Lorenzo Meyer, Gilberto Valenzuela, "[p]ara febrero de 1929 era ya candidato independiente a la Presidencia y su retórica anticallista coloreó el ambiente" ("[b]y February of 1929 he was an independent candidate for the presidency and his anti-Calles rhetoric colored the atmosphere") (86). Valenzuela went into voluntary exile in El Paso, Texas. See John W. Sherman's *The Mexican Right: The End of Revolutionary Reform, 1929-1940.*

[14]General Manzo was one of the leaders of the Escobar rebellion, and was commander of the army that fought in Mexico's northern states. He went into exile after the failure of the rebellion. See *Diccionario de Generales de la Revolución Mexicana M-Z Tomo II.*

[15]Of particular importance in Ainslie's four narratives are those memories regarding a failed rebellion that is echoed in Antonio Villarreal's own memoirs that are intended to stand as a historical document: "Todo estaba perdido. La rebelión definitivamente aplastada . . . El éxodo de los generales y jefes hacia el destierro lacerante, cerraba quizás un ciclo de esfuerzos fallidos que quisieron impedir el afianzamiento de una dictadura sin programa ni luces, primitiva, confusa, vesánica" ("All was lost. The rebellion had been crushed definitively . . . The exodus of the generals and chiefs into a painful exile closed a cycle of failed efforts that were intended to prevent the entrenchment of a dictatorship without a program or beacons, primitive, confusing, and insane") (40).

Appendices

The appendices that close this commemorative volume reveal the process of recovering and reclaiming the Latina/o/x literary heritage of the United States and its multiple transnational nexuses. They attest to the scholarship that the Recovery Program has made possible across a quarter of a century through professional conferences, funding, and other resources indispensable to the intellectual and academic project of recovering literary works from the oblivion into which a hegemonic history relegated them. The Recovery Program has created a vital institutional base and essential research funding through grants-in-aid, archival, publishing and other resources, which have authorized the transformative scholarship that is shaping new literary worlds and epistemologies.

Books Relating to Recovery Research

Recovering the US Hispanic Literary Heritage has generated original research in the form of literally hundreds of papers at scholarly conventions, articles in academic journals and conference presentations of all types throughout the nation and abroad. Since the program's inception, academic presses from coast to coast have published more than one hundred monographs, book-length studies and anthologies, at times with Recovery grant-in-aid support. The following is a partial list of Recovery-related books.

Albro, Ward S. *To Die on Your Feet: The Life, Times, and Writing of Práxedis G. Guerrero.* Ft. Worth, TX: Texas Christian Press, 1996.

Ameal-Pérez, Alberto. *En Babia de José Isaac de Diego Padró: Una novela total.* NY: Peter Lang, 2013.

Aranda, José, *When We Arrive: A New Literary History of Mexican America.* Tucson: University of Arizona Press, 2002.

Baeza Ventura, Gabriela. *La imagen de la mujer en la crónica del "México de Fuera."* Juárez, Mexico: Universidad Autónoma de Ciudad Juárez, 2005.

Balestra, Alejandra, Glenn Martínez and Irene Moya, eds. *Recovering the U.S. Hispanic Linguistic Heritage: Sociohistorical Approaches to Spanish in the United States.* Houston: Arte Público Press, 2008.

Barton, Paul. *Hispanic Methodists, Presbyterians and Baptists in Texas.* Austin: University of Texas Press, 2006.

Beebe, Rose Marie, and Robert M. Senkewicz. *Junípero Serra: California, Indians, and the Transformation of a Missionary.* Norman, OK: University of Oklahoma Press, 2015.

___. *Lands of Promise and Despair: Chronicles of Early California, 1535–1846.* Norman, OK: University of Oklahoma Press, 2015.

___. *Testimonios: Early California through the Eyes of Women, 1815–1848.* Norman: University of Oklahoma Press, 2015.

Ben-Ur, Aviva. *Sephardic Jews in America.* NY: New York University Press, 2009.

Calderón, Roberto R. *Mexican Coal Mining Labor in Texas and Coahuila, 1880-1930.* College Station, TX: Texas A & M University Press, 2000.

Castañeda, Antonia, Patricia Hart, Karen Weathermon and Susan H. Armitage, Eds. *Gender on the Borderlands: The Frontiers Reader.* Lincoln, NB: University of Nebraska Press, 2007.

Castañeda, Antonia. *Three Decades of Engendering History: Selected Works of Antonia I. Castañeda.* Ed. Linda Heidenreich. Denton, TX: University of North Texas Press, 2014.

Candelaria, Cordelia, ed. *Multiethnic Literature of the United States. Critical Introductions and Classroom Resources.* Boulder: University of Colorado at Boulder, 1989.

Chávez, Angélico. *The Short Stories of Fray Angélico Chávez.* Ed. Genaro Padilla. Albuquerque: University of New Mexico Press, 2003.

Concannon, Kevin, Francisco A. Lomelí and Marc Priewe. *Imagined Transnationalism: U. S. Latino/a Literature, Culture, and Identity.* NY: Palgrave Macmillan, 2009.

Coronado, Raúl. *A World Not to Come: A History of Latino Writing and Print Culture.* Cambridge, MA: Harvard University Press, 2013.

Cotera, María Eugenia. *Native Speakers: Ella Deloria, Zora Neale Hurston, Jovita González, and the Poetics of Culture.* Austin: University of Texas Press, 2010.

Cutler, John Alba. *Ends of Assimilation: The Formation of Chicano Literature.* NY: Oxford University Press, 2015.

Gil Maroño, Adriana, and María Luisa González Maroño. *La invasión de Veracruz en la mirada de Luz Nava.* Mexico City: Instituto Nacional de Antopología e Historia, 2014.

González, John Morán. *Border Renaissance the Texas Centennial and the Emergence of Mexican American Literature.* Austin: University of Texas Press, 2009.

___, ed. *The Cambridge Companion to Latina/o American Literature.* NY: Cambridge University Press, 2016.

___, and Laura Lomas, eds. *The Cambridge History of Latina/o American Literature.* NY: Cambridge University Press, 2018.

González, Jovita, and Eve Raleigh. *Caballero: A Historical Novel.* Ed. José Limón. College Station: Texas A & M University Press, 1996.

González Lara, Gerardo Salvador. *El obispo migrante.* Monterrey, Mexico: Universidad Autónoma de Coahuila, 2014.

González Malo, Jesús. *Correspondencia personal y política de un anarcosindicalista exiliado (1943-1965).* Santander, Spain: Universidad de Cantabria, 2016.

Herrera-Sobek, María, and Francisco Lomelí and Juan Antonio Perles Rochel. *Perspectivas transatlánticas en la literatura chicana. Ensayos y creatividad.* Málaga, Spain: Universidad de Málaga, 2004. 235-242.

Hinojosa, Gilberto M. *A Borderlands Town in Transition: Laredo, 1755-1870.* College Park, TX: Texas A & M University Press, 2000.

Kabalen de Bichara, Donna M. *The Construction of Latina/o Literary Imaginaries.* London: Cambridge Scholars Press, 2018.

____. *Telling Border Life Stories: Four Mexican American Women Writers.* College Station, TX: Texas A & M Unviersity Press, 2013.

Kanellos, Nicolás, ed. *Greenwood Encylcopedia of Latino Literature.* 3 Vols. Westport, CN: Greenwood Press, 2008.

____et al. *Herencia: The Anthology of Hispanic Literature of the United States.* New York: Oxford University Press, 2002.

____. *Hispanic First: 500 Years of Extraordinary Achievement.* Detroit: Gale Inc., 1997.

____. *Hispanic Literature in the United States: A Comprehensive Reference.* Westport, CN: Greenwood Press, 2005.

____. with Helvetia Martell. *Hispanic Periodicals in the United States, Origins to 1960: A Brief History and Comprehensive Bibliography.* Houston: Arte Público Press, 2000.

____. *Thirty Million Strong: Reclaiming the Hispanic Image in American Culture.* Golden, CO: Fulcrum Publishing, 1998.

Lazo, Rodrigo, and Jesse Alemán, eds. *The Latino Nineteenth Century.* New York: New York University Press, 2016.

____. *Writing to Cuba: Filibustering and Cuban Exiles in the United States.* Raleigh-Durham, NC: University of North Carolina Press, 2005.

Lomas, Laura. *Translating Empire: José Martí, Migrant Latino Subjects, and American Modernities.* Raleigh-Durham, NC: Duke University Press, 2009.

Lomelí, Francisco. *The Chican@ literary Imagination: A Collection of Critical Studies by Francisco A. Lomelí.* Alcalá de Henares, Spain: Universidad de Alcalá de Henares, 2012.

____, and Donaldo W. Urioste, eds. *Historical Dictionary of U.S. Latino Literature.* NY: Rowman & Littlefield Publishers, 2016.

____, and Denise A. Segura. *Routledge Handbook of Chicana/o Studies.* NY: Routledge, 2018.

____, and Clark Colahan. *Defying the Inquisition in Colonial New Mexico: Miguel de Quintana's Life and Writings.* Albuquerque: University of New Mexico Press, 2006.

____, Genaro Padilla and Victor A. Sorell. *Nuevomexicano Cultural Legacy: Forms, Agencies, and Discourse.* Albuquerque: University of New Mexico Press, 2002.

López de Mariscal, Blanca, Donna M. Kabalen de Bichara and Paoloma Vargas Montes. *Print Culture through the Ages.* London: Cambridge Scholars Press, 2016.

Martín-Rodríguez, Manuel M. *Life in Search of Readers: Reading (in) Chicano/a Literature.* Albuquerque: University of New Mexico Press, 2003.

___. *Cantas a Marte y das batalla a Apolo: Cinco estudios sobre Gaspar de Villagrá*. Washington, DC: Academia Norteamericana de la Lengua Española, 2014.

___. *Gaspar de Villagrá: Legista, Soldado y Poeta*. León, Spain: Universidad de León, 2009.

___. *With a Book in Their Hands: Chicano/a Readers and Readerships across the Centuries*. Albuquerque: University of New Mexico Press, 2014.

Meléndez, Gabriel. *So All Is Not Lost: The Poetics of Print in Nuevo Mexicano Communities*. Albuquerque: University of New Mexico Press, 1997.

___. *Spanish-Language Newspapers in New Mexico, 1834-1958*. Tucson: University of Arizona Press, 2005.

___. *The Book of Archives and Other Stories from the Mora Valley, New Mexico*. Norman, OK: University of Oklahoma Press, 2017.

___. *The Writings of Eusebio Chacón*. Eds. and trans. A Gabriel Meléndez and Francisco Lomelí. Albuquerque: University of New Mexico Press, 2012.

Meyer, Doris. *Speaking for Themselves: Neo-Mexicano Cultural Identity and the Spanish-Language Press, 1880-1920*. Albuquerque: U of New Mexico Press, 1996.

Montes, Amelia María de la Luz, and Anne Elizabeth Goldman. *María Amparo Ruiz de Burton: Critical and Pedagogical Perspectives*. Lincoln, NB: University of Nebraska Press, 2004.

Niggli, Josefina. *Mexican Village*. Ed. María Herrera-Sobek. Albuquerque: University of New Mexico Press, 1994.

___. *The Plays of Josefina Niggli: Recovered Landmarks of Latino Literature*. Ed. William Orchard. Madison: University of Wisconsin Press, 2007.

Olivas, Michael, ed. *In Defense of My People: Alonso S. Perales and the Development of Mexican-American Public Intellectuals*. Houston: Arte Público Press, 2013.

Orchard, William, and Yolanda Padilla, eds. *Bridges, Borders, and Breaks: History, Narrative, and Nation in Twenty-First-Century Chicana/o Literary Criticism*. Pittsburgh: University of Pittsburgh Press, 2016.

Osio, Antonio María. *The History of Alta California: A Memoir of Mexican California*. Eds. and trans. Rose Marie Beebe and Robert M. Senkewicz. Madison: University of Wisconsin Press, 1996.

Otero, Rosalie C., A. Gabriel Melández and Enrique R. Lamadrid, *Santa Fe Nativa: A Collection of Nuevomexicano Writing*. Albuquerque: University of New Mexico Press, 2009.

Padilla, Genaro. *The Daring Flight of My Pen: Cultural Politics and Gaspar Pérez de Villagrá's Historia de la Nueva México, 1610*. Albuquerque: University of New Mexico Press, 2010.

Perales, Mónica, and Raúl A. Ramos, eds. *Recovering the Hispanic History of Texas*. Houston: Arte Público Press, 2010.

Pérez, Emma. *The Decolonial Imaginary: Writing Chicanas into History*. Bloomington: Indiana University Press, 1999.

Pérez de Villagrá, Gaspar. *Historia de la Nueva México*. Ed. Manuel Martín-Rodríguez. Alcalá de Henares, Spain: Universidad de Alcalá de Henares, 2010.

Pérez Rosario, Vanessa. *Becoming Julia de Burgos: The Making of a Puerto Rican Icon*. Urbana, IL: University of Illinois Press, 2014.

____, ed. *Hispanic Caribbean Literature of Migration: Narratives of Displacement*. NY: Palgrave Macmillan, 2010.

Poyo, Gerald E. *Exile and Revolution: José D. Poyo, Key West, and Cuban Independence*. Gainesville, FL: University Press of Florida, 2014.

Puglia, Santiago Felipe. *El desengaño del hombre*. Ed. Antonio Saborit. Mexico City: Fondo de Cultura Económica, 2014.

Ramos, Raúl. *Beyond the Alamo: Forging Mexican Ethnicity in San Antonio, 1821-1861*. Chapel Hill, NC: University of North Carolina Press, 2010.

Reyes, Bárbara O. *Beyond the Alamo: Forging Mexican Ethnicity in San Antonio, 1821-1861*. Austin: University of Texas Press, 2010.

Ruiz, Vicky L., and Virginia Sánchez Korrol, eds. *Latinas in the United States: A Historical Encyclopedia*. 3 Vols. Bloomignton, IN: Indiana University Press, 2006.

Saborit, Antonio. *Una visita a Marius de Zayas*. Veracruz, Mexico: Universidad Veracruzana, 2009.

Sánchez Korrol, Virginia. *Feminist and Abolitionist: The Story of Emilia Casanova*. Houston: Arte Públcio Press, 2013.

____. *Pioneros II: Puerto Ricans in New York City 1948-1998*. NY: Arcadia Publishing, 2010.

____. *The Season of Rebels and Roses*. Houston: Arte Público Press, 2018.

____, and Marysa Navarro, eds. *Women in Latin America and the Caribbean: Restoring Women to History*. Bloomignton, IN: Indiana University Press, 1999.

Sánchez, Rosaura. *Telling Identities: The Californio Testimonios*. Minneapolis: University of Minnesota Press, 1995.

Silva-Gruesz, Kirsten. *Ambassadors of Culture: The Transamerican Origins of Latino Writing*. Princeton: Princeton University Press, 2001.

Suárez Díaz, Ana. *Escape de Cuba: El exilio neoyorquino de Pablo de la Torriente-Brau (marzo, 1935-agosto, 1936)*. Havana: Centro de Investgación y Desarrollo de la Cultura Cubana Juan Marinello, 2008.

Tatum, Charles. *Chicano and Chicana Literature: Otra voz del pueblo.* Tucson: University of Arizona Press, 2006.

___, ed. *Encyclopedia of Latino Culture: From Calaveras to Quinceañeras.* Westport, CN: Greenwood Publishing Group, 2013.

Torres-Padilla, José L., and Carmen Haydée Rivera, eds. *Writing off the Hyphen: New Critical Perspectives on the Literature of the Puerto Rican Diaspora.* Seattle: University of Washington Press, 2008.

Torres-Saillant, Silvio. *An Intellectual History of the Caribbean.* NY: Palgrave Macmillan, 2006.

___. *El retorno de las yolas. Ensayos sobre diáspora, democracia y dominicanidad.* Santo Domingo: Ediciones Librería Trinitaria y Editora Manatí, 1999.

Velásquez, Loreta Janeta. *The Woman in Battle: The Civil War Narrative of Loreta Janeta Velazquez, Cuban Woman and Confederate Soldier.* Ed. Jesse Alemán. University of Wisconsin Press, 2003.

Vera-Rojas, María Teresa. *"Se conoce que es usted es 'Moderna'". Lecturas de la mujer moderna en la colonia hispana de Nueva York (1920-1940).* Iberoamericana Vervuert, 2018.

Young, Elliot. *Catarino Garza's Revolution on the Texas-Mexico Border.* Durham, NC: Duke University Press, 2004.

Zamora, Emilio. *Claiming Rights and Righting Wrongs in Texas: Mexican Workers and Job Politics during World War II.* College Station, TX: Texas A & M University, 2008.

___, Cynthia Orozco and Rodolfo Rocha, eds. *Mexican Americans in Texas History, Selected Essays.* College Station, TX: Texas A & M University Press, 2000.

___, ed. *The World War I Diary of José de la Luz Sáenz.* College Station, TX: Texas A & M University Press, 2014.

Zamora O'Shea, Elena. *El Mesquite.* Eds. Andrés Tijerina and Leticiia M. Garza-Falcón. College Station: Texas A & M, 2000.

Zayas, Marius de. *Crónicas y ensayos.* Ed. Antonio Saborit. Mexico City; Universidad Nacional Autónoma de México, 2008.

Zeller, Neici M. *Discursos y espacios femeninos en República Dominicana, 1880-1961.* Santo Domingo, Dominican Republic: Letra Gráfica, 1202.

Special Issues of Journals Dedicated to Recovery

"Special Issue: *El Clamor Público.*" *California History* 84.2 (Winter 2006-2007).

"Literatura puertorriqueña del continente recuperada/Puerto Rican Literature of the Continent Recovered." *Centro de Estudios Puertorriqueños* Ed. Nicolás Kanellos. 26.1 (Spring 2014).

Editions of Recovered Works Published by Arte Público Press

Belpré, Pura. *Firefly Summer.* (1996).

Capetillo, Luisa. *A Nation of Women: An Early Feminist Speaks Out / Mi opinión sobre las libertades, derechos y deberes de la mujer.* Ed. Félix V. Matos Rodríguez. (2004).

___. *Absolute Equality: An Early Feminist Perspective / Influencias de las ideas modernas.* Ed. Lara Walker. (2008).

Chávez, Angélico. *Cantares: Canticles and Poems of Youth.* Ed. Nasario García. (2000).

Colón, Jesús. *Lo que el pueblo me dice.* Ed. Edwin Karli Padilla Aponte. (2001).

___. *The Way It Was and Other Writings.* Eds. Edna Acosta-Belén and Virginia Sánchez Korrol. (1993).

Colón, Joaquín. *Pioneros puertorriqueños en Nueva York 1917-1947.* Ed. Edwin Karli Padilla Aponte. (2001).

De Reygados, Fermín. *Astucias por heredar un sobrino a un tío.* Ed. Pedro García-Caro (2015 ebook).

Díaz, José. *P. Galindo: Obras (in)completas de José Díaz.* Ed. Manuel Martín-Rodríguez. (2016).

Díaz Guerra, Alirio. *Lucas Guevara.* Eds. Nicolás Kanellos and Imara Liz Hernández. (2001).

___. *Lucas Guevara.* Eds. Nicolás Kanellos and Imara Liz Hernández. Ethriam Brammer. (2003).

Espino del Castillo, Moisés. *The "Calaveras" of Don Moisés Espino del Castillo.* Ed. Ellen Rojas Clark. (2015 ebook).

Espinosa, Conrado. *El sol de Texas / Under the Texas Sun.* Ed. And trans. John Pluecker. (2007).

González, Jovita. *Dew on the Thorn.* Ed. José Limón. (1997).

___. *The Woman Who Lost Her Soul and Other Stories: Collected Tales and Short Stories.* Ed. Sergio Reyna. (2000).

Grillo, Evelio. *Black Cuban, Black American: A Memoir.* Ed. Kenya Dworkin y Méndez. (2000).

Paredes, Américo. *Cantos de adolescencia: Songs of Youth (1932-1937).* Eds. and trans. Omar Vásquez Barbosa and B. V. Olguín. (2007).

Kanellos, Nicolás, Kenya Dworkin y Mendez, José Fernandez, Erlinda Gonzales-Berry, Agnes Lugo-Ortiz and Charles Tatum. *En otra voz: Antología de literatura hispana de los Estados Unidos.* (2002).

El laúd del desterrado. Ed. Matías Montes Huidobro. (1995).

Martí, José. *Versos sencillas/Simple Verses.* Ed. And trans. Manuel A. Tellechea. (1997).

Mena, María Cristina. *The Collected Stories of María Cristina Mena.* Ed. Amy Doherty. (1997).

Núñez Cabeza de Vaca, Alvar. *The Account: Álvar Núñez Cabeza de Vaca's Relación.* Eds. And trans. José Fernández and Martín Favata. (1993).

Otero, Jr., Miguel Antonio. *The Real Billy the Kid.* Ed. John-Michael Rivera. (1998).

Paz, Ireneo. *Life and Adventures of the Celebrated Bandit Joaquín Murrieta.* Ed. Luis Leal. Trans. Francis P. Belle. (1999).

___. *Vida y aventuras del más célebre bandido sonorense Joaquín Murrieta: Sus grandes proezas en California.* Ed. Luis Leal. (1999).

Pérez, Louis. *El Coyote, the Rebel: A Nonfiction Novel.* Ed. Lauro Flores. (2000).

Rebolledo, Tey Diana, and María Teresa Márquez, eds. *Women's Tales from the New Mexico WPA: La Diabla a Pie.* (2000).

Ruiz de Burton, María Amparo. *Conflicts of Interest: The Letters of María Amparo Ruiz de Burton.* Eds. Rosaura Sánchez and Beatriz Pita. (2001).

___. *The Squatter and the Don.* Eds, Rosaura Sánchez and Beatriz Pita. (1997).

___. *Who Would Have Thought It?* Eds, Rosaura Sánchez and Beatriz Pita. (1995).

Selva, Salomón de la. *Tropical Town and Other Poems.* Ed. Silvio Sirias. (1998).

Tafolla, Santiago*A Life Crossing Borders: Memoir of a Mexican-American Civil War Soldier/ las memorias de un soldado méxico-americano en la Guerra Civil Americana.* Eds. Carmen and Laura Tafolla. (2009).

Varela, Félix. *Jicoténcal.* Eds. Luis Leal and Rodolfo Cortina. (1995).

Venegas, Daniel. *Las aventuras de Don Chipote, O, Cuando los pericos mamen.* Ed. Nicolás Kanellos. (1998).

___. *The Adventures of Don Chipote, or, When Parrots Breast-Feed.* Ed. Nicolás Kanellos. Trans. Ethriam Brammer. (2000).

Villegas de Magnón. Leonor. *La rebelde.* Ed. Clara Lomas. (2004).

___. *The Rebel.* Ed. Clara Lomas. (1994).

Zavala, Adina de. *History and Legends of the Alamo and Other Missions in and around San Antonio.* Ed. Richard Flores. (1996).

Zavala, Lorenzo de. *Journey to the United States of America / Viaje a los Estados Unidos del Norte de América.* Ed. John-Michael Rivera. (2005).

List of Grants-in-Aid Awarded

From 1994 to 2010, the Board of Advisors awarded grants-in-aid to as many as five projects per year to conduct research on Recovery-related topics, search to discover lost documents and prepare scholarly editions of recovered material. The following is a list of the funded projects that were brought to completion.

List of Grants-in-Aid Awarded (continued)

PROJECT NAME	NAME	INSTITUTION
The Eugenio María de Hostos Recovery Project	Tellechea, Manuel A.	
Hispanic Short Fiction in the United States	Torres-Padilla, José	Colegio Universitario de Cayey
Recovering Hispanic Womens' Voices: Central American Women who became Citizens of the United States from the Colonial period to 1960.	Toruño, Rhina M.	University of Texas of the Permian Basin
Un Afro-Hispano en Estados Unidos: Vida y Obra Literaria de Martín Morúa Delgado	Benemelis, Juan F.	
Viajeros Cubanos a los Estados Unidos (Siglo XIX)	Campuzano Sentí, Luisa	
Luchar y Morir en Nueva York. El Patrimonio Literario y Político de Emilia Casanova	Curnow, Ena de los Angeles	
Daughters of Camila/ Hijas de Camila: Recovering a Legacy	de Filippis, Daisy Cocco	York College - Jamaica
	Gillespie, Jeanne L.	Southeastern Louisiana University
Poesía del Pueblo. The Popular Political, Cultural and Social Poetry of Nuevo Mexicanos, 1888-1935	Gonzáles, Felipe	University of New Mexico
Carpa, Teatro, and the Mexican American Public Sphere in San Antonio, Texas	Haney, Peter Clair	University of Texas - Austin
Gaspar de Villagrá	Jaramillo, Phil	Adams State College
Ynformes of Old Mission San Juan Bautista	Mendoza, Rubén	CSU Monterey Bay
	Myers, David R.	New Mexico State University Library

Title	Author	Institution
New Mexico 1581-1583: A Bilingual Edition of the Narratives of the Rodríguez-Chamuscado and Espejo Expeditions	Ahern, Maureen	Ohio State University
CUENTOS Y MÁS: Traditional Literature of the Borderlands—A Survey of the traditional stories and storytellers of the US Mexico Borderlands community including selected stories and pláticas with the Storytellers	Cantú, Norma E.	Texas A&M International University
Documents of the 1680 Pueblo Revolt: Spanish Editions and a Catalogue of Manuscripts	DeMarco, Barbara	University of California - Berkeley
Continuation of the Initial Documentary Relations of the Southwest Survey	Fossa, Lydia	University of Arizona
Sources of Spanish Colonial, Mexican, and Mexican-American Music in the United States: A Bibliography, Inventory, and Discography	Koegel, John	University of Missouri -Columbia
Identification, Location and Recovery of the Correspondence of Jaime de Angulo and Franz Boas	Lomelí, Lligany	Instituto Politécnico Naciónal
Francisco. El Ingenio ó las Delicias del Campo. Edición Crítica de Humberto J. López Cruz	López Cruz, Humberto J.	University of Central Florida
The Role of María Luisa Garza in La Cruz Azul Mexicana	Luna-Lawhn, Juanita	San Antonio College
Pedro Menéndez de Aviles and Florida - Select Letters to Phillip II - Annotated Edition	Mercado, Juan C.	University of Pennsylvania - East Stroudsburg
Tracing Theatre Performances - Mexican Popular Entertainments in Los Angeles, 1920-1934	Nielson, Lara Bargellini	New York University

List of Grants-in-Aid Awarded (continued)

PROJECT NAME	NAME	INSTITUTION
Recovering, transcribing, compiling, translation, editing and writing an introduction to the Civil War letters of Captains Joseph De La Garza and Manuel Yturri	Thompson, Jerry	Texas A&M International University
Towards a Genealogy of Mexican American Masculinity: An Archival Study	Varón, Alberto	University of Texas at Austin
Cristero Exile's Publications in the United States: An Annotated Bibliography	Baeza Ventura, Gabriela	University of Houston
Cataloging of the Henry V. Besso Library	Belinfante, Randall C.	American Sephardi Federation with Sephardic House Library
Nuevomejicanas Bequeath: The Prayers and Supplications of Eighteenth and Nineteenth Century Women	Deena J. González	Loyola Marymount University
The manuscript of Pablo Tac: A grammar, dictionary, and story about the conversion of luisenos that reveals Luiseno Religious Thought, Practice, and Translations of Christianity	Haas, Lisbeth M.	University of California
Back to the Future: A Colonial Mexican Re-Inscription of Vieira's Historia do Futuro	Kallendorf, Hilaire & Gregory L. Cuellar	Texas A&M University, College Station
Gathering, Indexing and Cataloging Religious Documents, Phase I	Mouton, Norma	University of Houston
Highlighting and Preserving the West Texas Religious Ethos (1920-1960): Selected Documents from the Cleofas Calleros Papers	Tinajero, Robert J.	University of Texas at El Paso

Title	Author	Institution
Literary, Intellectual, and Spiritual Resources for Nineteenth- and Early Twentieth-Century Spanish-speaking Protestant Ministers Along the US-Mexico Borderlands: A Review of the Maximo Villarreal Collection	Barton, Dr. Paul T.	Espiscopal Theological Seminary of the Southwest
Texas Tides: A Project to Locate, Preserve and Provide Access to Nacogdoches' Spanish Catholic Archives	Galan, Rachel B.	Stephen F. Austin State University
The Basilian Fathers and the Mexican Missions of South East Texas	Hernádez, Dr. Marie-Theresa	University of Houston
The Vernacular Religious and Paraliturgical Poetic Legacy of the Spanish-Speaking Sephardim	Salama, Dr. Messod	Memorial University of Newfoundland
Feminist Thought Through Religious Action: The Work of Clotilde Betances Jaeger	Vera-Rojas, Maria Teresa	University of Houston
The Prayer Life: Women's Spiritualities in Native California	Castañeda, Antonia	St. Mary's University
The Impact of Hispanic Religious Thought in the Formation of Hispanic Identity	De Los Reyes-Heredia, José Guillermo	University of Pennsylvania
Pentecostés en Puerto Rico, O La Vida de un Misionero	Espinosa, Gastón E.	University of California
The Life and Times of Padre Martínez	Espinosa, Paul	Espinosa Productions
The Presence of Afro-Cuban Religion in the United States during the Nineteenth-Century Cuban Insurrectionary Movements	López Cruz, Humberto J.	University of Central Florida
Of Heretic and Interlopers: The Hispano Protestants of New Mexico	Madrid, Arturo	Trinity University
Las Almas y las Letras: Fray Angélico Chávez's Religious Poetry	Martin-Rodríguez, Manuel M.	Texas A&M University

List of Grants-in-Aid Awarded (continued)

PROJECT NAME	NAME	INSTITUTION
Ghosts of "Old California": Myth and Mimicry in the Lives of Leo Carrillo	Pérez, Vincent	University of Nevada - Las Vegas
Cuban Catholics in the United States, 1960-1980: Exile, National Identity and Integration	Poyo, Gerald	St. Mary's University
Don Felix Varela Morales, Exilio y Obra Religiosa (Nueva York 1823-1847): Integración y Síntesis	Suárez, Ana M.	Centro de Investigación y Desarollo de la Cultura Cubana "Juan Marinello"
Desde Washington: Pedro Henríquez Ureña's E.P. Garduño reports to El Heraldo in Cuba 1914-1915	de Filippis, Daisy Cocco	York College, CUNY
Recovering the Works of Conrado Espinosa in the United States and Mexico	Dupré, Sonia	University of Houston
Con Sus Calzones al Revés/With His Underpants on Inside Out: Cultural Economy and Patriarchy in Pablo de la Guerra's Letters to Josefa Moreno de la Guerra, 1851-1872	Gutiérrez, Gabriel	California State University - Northridge
A Critical Introduction and the Reprinting of the Son of Two Nations and Mary Smith by Pedro Labarthe	Irizarry, José M.	University of Puerto Rico - Mayaguez
Revision of Dissertation "The Passage of Crisis: Threshold Time in Chicano Literature" for book publication	Johannessen, Lene M.	University of Bergen
A Texas Revolutionary of 1915	Johnson, Benjamín H.	University of Texas - San Antonio
Milagros y Portentos: Foundational Legends in Colonial and Post-Colonial New Mexico	Lamadrid, Enrique R.	University of New Mexico

Title	Author	Institution
Sources for the Recovery of Latino Labor History in New York City, 1880-1960	Lauria-Santiago, Aldo Antonio	College of the Holy Cross
En Busca de Josefina Niggli	McFarlane, Veronica M.	North Carolina A&T State University
Translation of Recovered Primary Documents: "La Vida Que No Viví. Novela Historico-Liberal de la Revolución Mexicana"	Medina, Lara	California State University - Northridge
Recovering the US Hispanic Literary Heritage in the Midwest: The Calumet Regional Archives	Mendieta, Eva	Indiana University - Northwest
Rediscovering a Literary Legacy: A Cuban Writer in Texas (1929-31)	Morton, Carlos	University of California - Riverside
Towards a New Genealogy of Mexican American Poetry: The Legacy of Américo Parades' "Cantos de Adolescencia"	Olguín, Ben V.	University of Texas - San Antonio
A Personal Narrative Recounting Childhood Experiences from the 1940s to 1960	Perez, Mary Helen	Lee College
Chicana Leadership in the Chicano Movement: A Case Study of Houston	Quintanilla, Linda J.	University of Houston
Adrian Ramírez (1909-1988), Storyteller: An Intersection of Oral History, Autobiography, and Oral Literary Expression	Ramírez, Arthur	Sonoma State University
A Search for the Cultural Poetics of a "Dia de los Muertos" Literature in San Antonio, Texas: "Calaveras"	Riojas-Clark, Ellen	University of Texas - San Antonio
La Crónica en el Exilio y Sus Representaciónes Sociales. El Caso de Revista Mexicana y el Cronista Silverio	Santibáñez, Christian M.	University of Houston
Archival Research on Elena Torres and the Organization she founded, the Mexican Feminist Council	Tinnemeyer, Andrea J.	Utah State University

List of Grants-in-Aid Awarded (continued)

PROJECT NAME	NAME	INSTITUTION
Angelina Elizondo de García Naranjo y Ana Caridad de León Garza. Escritoras en San Antonio en los 1900	Villarroiel, Carolina A.	University of Houston
Índice Onomástico de las Memorias de Nemesio García Naranjo	Villarroel, Carolina A.	University of Houston
Translation of Lucas Guevara's (Chapter 13-43)	Brammer, Ethriam	
Se Llamaba Elena. Antología de Textos de Elena Arizmendi, Nueva York, c. 1920-1940	Cano, Gabriela	Universidad Autónoma Metropolitana
Antología de Emilia Casanova	Curnow, Ena de los Angeles	
La Obra de Carlo Mario Fraticelli	Días, Austin	University of Hawaii – Manoa
An Inventory of Hispanic-Related Texts at the American Antiquarian Society (Worcester, MA)	Lauría-Santiago, Aldo Antonio	College of the Holy Cross
Translating Luisa Capetillo's Mi Opinión [1911], the First Puerto Rican Feminist Treatise	Matos Rodríguez, Félix	Centro de Estudios Puertorriqueños
Immigration by Proxy: The Letters of Luz Moreno, 1950-1953	Orozco, José	Whittier College
An Edition of the Out-of-Print and Unpublished Poetry, Plays, and Fiction of Josephina Niggli (1910-1983)	Padilla, Amparo Yolanda; Orchard, William E.	University of Chicago

Title	Author	Institution
Máximo Soto-Hall's The Shadow of the White House (1927): Dollar Diplomacy and Early Central American Immigration to the United States	Rodríguez, Ana P.	University of Maryland, College Park
Segunda Etapa del Projecto de Edición Ampliada del Panorama de la Literatura Norteamericana (1600-1935) Escrita y Publicada en Español por el Intelectual Cubano José A. Ramos	Suárez, Ana M.	Centro de Investigación y Desarollo de la Cultura Cubana Juan Marinella
Archive of José Rodriguez Located at the Library of Congress Manuscript Division in Washington, DC	Ubieta Gómez, Enrique	Biblioteca Nacional "José Martí"
A Puerto Rican Poet on the Sugar Plantations of Hawaii	Dias, Austin	University of Hawaii – Manoa
Uniendo Orillas. La Dimensión Universal del Pensamiento de Victoria Kent	Holgado, Isabel	
From Puerto Rico to Pasadena: The Memoirs of Mario Del Monte, 1920s-1950s.	Nieto-Phillips, John M.	New Mexico State University
Sangre Mexicana/Corazón Americano: Ideology, Ambiguity, and Critique in Chicana/o and Latina/o War Narratives, Art, and Film	Olguín, Ben V.	University of Texas - San Antonio
Chicana Voices in the Wind: Mexican American Cultural Poetics from the Kansas Plains	Platt, Kamala J.	University of Texas - San Antonio
The Recovery and Preservation of Miguel Antonio Otero	Rivera, John-Michael	University of Texas - Austin
Blas Lorenzo Aldarete Poetry Recovery Project	Rodriguez, Guillermo; Sisneros, Samuel	
Proyecto de Edición. Ampliada del "Panorama de la Literatura Norteamericana (1600-1935)", Escrita y Publicada en Español, por el Intelectual Cubano José Antonio Ramos (1935)	Suárez, Ana M.	Centro de Investigación y Desarollo de la Cultura Cubana "Juan Marinello"

List of Grants-in-Aid Awarded (continued)

PROJECT NAME	NAME	INSTITUTION
The Eugenio María de Hostos Recovery Project	Tellechea, Manuel A.	
Hispanic Short Fiction in the United States	Torres-Padilla, José	Colegio Universitario de Cayey
Recovering Hispanic Womens' Voices: Central American Women who became Citizens of the United States from the Colonial period to 1960.	Toruño, Rhina M.	University of Texas of the Permian Basin
Un Afro-Hispano en Estados Unidos: Vida y Obra Literaria de Martín Morúa Delgado	Benemelis, Juan F.	
Viajeros Cubanos a los Estados Unidos (Siglo XIX)	Campuzano Sentí, Luisa	
Luchar y Morir en Nueva York. El Patrimonio Literario y Político de Emilia Casanova	Curnow, Ena de los Angeles	
Daughters of Camila/ Hijas de Camila: Recovering a Legacy	de Filippis, Daisy Cocco	York College - Jamaica
	Gillespie, Jeanne L.	Southeastern Louisiana University
Poesía del Pueblo. The Popular Political, Cultural and Social Poetry of Nuevo Mexicanos, 1888-1935	Gonzáles, Felipe	University of New Mexico
Carpa, Teatro, and the Mexican American Public Sphere in San Antonio, Texas	Haney, Peter Clair	University of Texas - Austin
Gaspar de Villagrá	Jaramillo, Phil	Adams State College
Ynformes of Old Mission San Juan Bautista	Mendoza, Rubén	CSU Monterey Bay
	Myers, David R.	New Mexico State University Library

Title	Author	Institution
New Mexico 1581-1583: A Bilingual Edition of the Narratives of the Rodríguez-Chamuscado and Espejo Expeditions	Ahern, Maureen	Ohio State University
CUENTOS Y MÁS: Traditional Literature of the Borderlands—A Survey of the traditional stories and storytellers of the US Mexico Borderlands community including selected stories and pláticas with the Storytellers	Cantú, Norma E.	Texas A&M International University
Documents of the 1680 Pueblo Revolt: Spanish Editions and a Catalogue of Manuscripts	DeMarco, Barbara	University of California - Berkeley
Continuation of the Initial Documentary Relations of the Southwest Survey	Fossa, Lydia	University of Arizona
Sources of Spanish Colonial, Mexican, and Mexican-American Music in the United States: A Bibliography, Inventory, and Discography	Koegel, John	University of Missouri -Columbia
Identification, Location and Recovery of the Correspondence of Jaime de Angulo and Franz Boas	Lomelí, Lligany	Instituto Politécnico Naciónal
Francisco. El Ingenio ó las Delicias del Campo. Edición Crítica de Humberto J. López Cruz	López Cruz, Humberto J.	University of Central Florida
The Role of María Luisa Garza in La Cruz Azul Mexicana	Luna-Lawhn, Juanita	San Antonio College
Pedro Menéndez de Aviles and Florida - Select Letters to Phillip II - Annotated Edition	Mercado, Juan C.	University of Pennsylvania - East Stroudsburg
Tracing Theatre Performances - Mexican Popular Entertainments in Los Angeles, 1920-1934	Nielson, Lara Bargellini	New York University

List of Grants-in-Aid Awarded (continued)

PROJECT NAME	NAME	INSTITUTION
"La Diabla a Pie.' The Women's Cuentos of the WPA"	Rebolledo, Tey Diana	University of New Mexico
The Recovery of Salomón de la Selva's Tropical Town and Other Poems	Sirias, Silvio	Appalachian State University
Libby Life: Experiences of a Prisoner of War in Richmond, Virginia, 1863-64 by Federico Fernández Cavada	Sirias, Silvio	Appalachian State University
José de la Luz Saenz and los Mexicanos y La Gran Guerra; A Research and Editing Project	Zamora, Emilio	University of Houston
The Papers of Ricardo Flores Magón: A Binational Project to Locate, Identify, Collect, and Prepare for Publication all the Writings of Ricardo Flores Magón	Albro, Ward	Texas A&M University - Kingsville
Compilación de las Obras Completas de Ricardo Flores Magón	Barrera Bassols, Jacinto	Dirección de Estudios Históricos (INAH)
Women on the Margins of Empire: Primary Documents from Spanish-Mexican California	Bouvier, Virginia	University of Maryland
Catholic Women's Activism in Mexico During the 1930s and its Impact on the Church-State Conflict: Clandestine Communities, Bribes and Border Crossings in Guanajuato, Mexico and the United States of America	Boylan, Kristina A.	University of Oxford, U.K.
The Oral Folk Tradition of Tampa, Florida/ The Tampa *Romancero*	Cohen, Henry D.; Rodríguez, Rodney T.	Kalamazoo College

Title	Author	Institution
Cuban to the Core: Immigration, Identify and Cultural Continuity through Tampa Latin Theatre	Dworkin y Mendez, Kenya C.	Carnegie Mellon University
Initial Documentary Relations of the Southwest Survey	Fossa, Lydia	University of Arizona
Which Language Will Our Children Speak: One-Hundred Years of Spanish-language Native Rights Struggle in New Mexico	Gonzales-Berry Erlinda; Gonzales Velásquez, María Dolores	University of New Mexico
Recovering Life Histories from the Mexican American Farándula	Haney, Peter Clair	University of Texas - Austin
The Secular Folk Plays of New Mexico: Texts and Contexts	Lamadrid, Enrique R.	University of New Mexico
Palabra y Acción: Spanish-language Newspapers in the United States and The Cuban Question, 1848-1851	Lazo, Rodrigo	University of Maryland
Recovering the Minorcan Heritage	Lyon, Eugene	Flagler College
US Latino Literature in Translation	Manzo, Jude Thomas	Jamestown College
Performing Public Cultures of Difference: Spanish-Language Theatre and Citizenship, Los Ángeles 1920-1934	Neilson, Lara	New York University
Lydia Mendoza/Songstress of the Tradition of the Corrido. The Story of the rise of Lydia Mendoza from a singer in her family to the 1st Female 12 string Guitarist of the Southwest	Oropeza, Luis	Latin American Theatre Artists
Reconstructing the Cultural History of Boston's Latino Communities	Pacini Hernández, Deborah	University of Connecticut Harvard University
The Vaquero/Cowboy Connection: Masculinity and Miscegenation in the "Blood-and-Thunder" West	Packard, Christopher F.	Parsons School of Design

List of Grants-in-Aid Awarded (continued)

PROJECT NAME	NAME	INSTITUTION
Recovering History: Mujeres Empujando the Constraints of Land	Ramírez, Amelia M.	University of Denver
La Pastorela: Los Diez Mandamientos	Rodríguez, Cirenio A.	California State University - Sacramento
"Lesbian, Bisexual, Transgender and Gay Latino Communities of San Francisco, California: Identifying the Sources for Historical Research"	Roque, Horacio N.	University of California - Berkeley
Recovery of Early Narratives: Boturini and Ramírez Codices	Tinnemeyer, Andrea J.	Rice University
Making the Ancient Hispanic Religious and Secular Folkplays of New Mexico Accessible to Students of Foreign Languages and Drama in the Public School Systems for Presentation and Production	Torres, Larry T.	Golden Apple Foundation Taos High School
Fray Francisco de Ayeta and the 1680 Pueblo Revolt: Spanish Documents of the Period	DeMarco, Barbara	University of California - Berkeley
The Latino Reader: Writings in an American Tradition	Fernández Olmos, Margarite	Brooklyn College, CUNY
Spanish-American Identity and Folk Literature and Music in New Mexico. Production of Meaning and Social History through Literature	García, Peter J.	University of Texas - Austin
The Judice Letter Book Project - Translation of Spanish governor's and commandant's letters	Girouard, Julia C.	University of Southwestern Louisiana

Title	Author	Institution
Chicanas Bequeath: Nineteenth-Century New Mexico Willmakers	González, Deena J.	Pomona College
Recovering Early Puerto Rican Narrative: Luisa Capetillo	Sánchez González, Lisa	University of Texas - Austin
"Indexing and Publicizing the Historical Literary Sources of Mexicanos and Mexicanas in Nineteenth-Century Los Angeles "	Fireman, Janet R.	Natural History Museum of LA County
The Magonistas in South Texas 1904-1919	Larralde, Carlos M.	
"Pueblos Hispanos and the Journalistic Production of Julia de Burgos"	López, Ivette	Universidad de Puerto Rico
"Cuarenta Años de Legislador: Recovering Neo-Mexicano Biography"	Meléndez, Gabriel	University of New Mexico
The Memoirs of the First Mexicans of San José, CA	Mora-Torres, Gregorio	San Jose State University
The 1861 Diary of a Californiano Collegian: Jesús María Estudillo	Mora-Torres, Gregorio	San Jose State University
Latin American Oral Histories in Cleveland	Ruiz, Jacqueline	Western Reserve Historical Society
A Critical, Annotated Edition of the "Autos Tocantes a la Sublevación de los Indios de Nuevo México"	Sempere-Martínez, Juan A.	San Jose State University
"Recovering Nineteenth-Century Historical and Literary Sources from the South Texas Border/Region"	Valerio-Jiménez, Omar S.	University of California Los Angeles
Texts in Context: The Nogales Dispute, 1791-92. An Episode in Spanish-Indian Relations in the Lower Mississippi Valley	Weeks, Charles A.	St. Andrew's Episcopal School
Adina de Zavala and the Politics of Restoration	Flores, Richard R.	University of Wisconsin - Madison

List of Grants-in-Aid Awarded (continued)

PROJECT NAME	NAME	INSTITUTION
Miguel de Quintana: Poetry, Prose and Propositions Before the Inquisition	Lomelí, Francisco A.	University of California - Santa Barbara
Toward a Spanish-Language Literary History of Seventeenth Century *La Florida*	Shields, Jr., E. Thomson	East Carolina University
To Die on Your Feet: The Life and Writings of Práxedis G. Guerrero	Albro, Ward	Texas A&M University - Kingsville
Culture and Identity: Periodical Literature in Puerto Rican Archives	Aponte Alsina, María	
Obras Inéditas de Manuel M. Salazar, Prosa y Poesía	Arellano, Anselmo	
Identification and Recovery of the Colonial Hispanic Documents at the Gilcrease Museum: An Annotated Bibliography	Chase, Cida S.	Oklahoma State University
Antonio Bañuelos Project	De la Isla, José	
	Escalane, Virginia	
Information on Cassette Tapes in Archive Boxes	García, Nasario	New Mexico Highlands University
A Resource Catalog of Spanish Political Exiles in the United States (1824-1833): A Listing of Miscellaneous Spanish Literary Works Published in America	Martin, Greogio C.	Duquesne University
The New Mexico WPA Writers' Project	Márquez, María Teresa	University of New Mexico
Recovery Grant in aid Project	Meléndez, Gabriel A.	University of New Mexico

Caballero: The Recovery of a Historical Novel of the United States-Mexico Border	Limón, José	University of Texas - Austin
Dew on the Thorn	Limón, José	University of Texas - Austin
Literary Output by Californianos and Mexicano Immigrants/ Californianos and Mexican American Writers	Rosales, Arturo F.	
A Comprehensive Bibliography of the Judeo-Spanish Romancero in the United States	Salama, Messod	St. John's—Newfoundland
Publication of the First Epic Poem on the United States "La Florida" by Escobedo	Sununu, Alexandra	
Catarino Garza: A Late 19th-Century Texas Mexican Intellectual	Young, Elliott